For the Good of the Program:

A Century of

Middle Tennessee Scouting

at Boxwell, 1921-2021

Grady Eades

Middle Tennessee Council Boy Scouts of America

For the Good of the Program: A Century of Middle Tennessee Scouting at Boxwell, 1921-2021

Published by Clovercroft Publishing, Franklin, Tennessee in association with Larry Carpenter of Christian Book Services, LLC.

Written by Grady Eades

Cover and Interior Design by Grady Eades and Ian Romaine.

Front cover photo by Roman Reese, ca. 1999
Back cover photo by Michael Seay, 1975

Second edition, paperback, March 2022.

Printed in the United States of America

978-1-7340850-5-1

For everyone who has served on a
Boxwell Staff

CONTENTS

Author's Note to the Reader

...On History

This work is a formal history. It will not attempt to tell every single thing that ever happened at Boxwell. It cannot tell every story. It cannot dig into every experience. What it will do is endeavor to make some big picture observations and then provide evidence from sources to demonstrate that those observations are true. While not all of the details may fit with your personal experience, hopefully the big picture observations will be consistent with your time at Boxwell, regardless of what role—Scout, leader, or staff--you enjoyed.

A proper, formal history of a topic begins with an argument. The author lays out the general premise of the work and then provides ample evidence to support to that argument. The introduction, which the casual, general reader skips over, is generally a summation of that argument, giving a brief synopsis of what is to come in the pages to follow. A formal history endeavors to promote a sense of objectivity, giving the author distance from the work that is being presented.

Thus, the central argument for this work is that the summer camp program at Boxwell has transformed as time has passed to support the larger agendas of the Middle Tennessee Council, Boy Scouting, and the nation. As the nation has changed, so too has Scouting and the Council, and therefore how the Boy Scouting program is implemented at Boxwell. Specifically, *For the Good of the Program* will outline how the early Boxwells at Linton and the Narrows of the Harpeth built their programs on citizenship training, while the Rock Island Boxwell began a transition to a family centered program. The Old Hickory Boxwell began with a family centered program, but transformed as the years went by to reflect a more individualistic, conservative program, and finally embraced an approach more centered on entertainment and uniqueness.

Historians make choices about the stories they want to tell. There are other stories to be told about Boxwell. But this is the story I felt needed to be told and presented the fullest portrait of a powerful experience.

...On Sources

Sources are critical to any work of history. These may be incredibly diverse in nature and may include photographs, letters, committee minutes, newspaper articles, movies, architecture, and of course personal interviews. This work has made its best effort to include as many different sources as possible.

If you are not familiar with a formal history, you will note that most paragraphs in this book end with a small, superscript number. This is an endnote. You may flip to the back of the book to find the note and read the citation. I chose endnotes instead of footnotes so as not to disrupt the flow of the narrative.

These notations are incredibly important for two reasons. First, the endnotes include the citations for that particular paragraph. Whatever the source material for that particular paragraph was, it is in the endnote. Virtually everything can be verified against these citations. Second, while most endnotes are citations, several include comments. These comments are extra detail that do not belong in the main text, but are still worth recording. In some cases it may be a list of names at a dedication, while in others it may be a legend or further needed context. In some places, earlier works are corrected when they presented incorrect information. Regardless, the endnotes are valuable in their own right. I encourage you to explore them.

Finally, a wealth of information has been collected in the process of creating this work. Now that *For the Good of the Program* is complete, the new work can begin: processing all of this information for preservation. My current plan is to turn over most of this material to the Tennessee State Library and Archives. My hope is that should others wish to perform research on Scouting in middle Tennessee or even specifically on Boxwell Reservation that the resources be available to do that work. In short, I want to pass on what I have learned.

...On Sensitive Content

Typically, histories are written about issues that, while often relevant and potentially instructive to the modern day, were resolved in the past in some way. Many of the people involved are long dead and gone and their decisions and actions become the material of academic debate. The history which follows here is somewhat unique in this regard. *For the Good of the Program* brings the reader directly into the modern day and therefore touches on a variety of issues that are not only current, but still unresolved and sometimes very sensitive and painful.

Therefore, it must be noted that the material expressed herein does not represent or reflect the views of the Middle Tennessee Council. The material herein is simply a history of events and the individuals discussed important components in that history.

...On Acknowledgements

No work of this size could be accomplished without the assistance of many people and institutions. I am forever indebted to all of those who contributed in some ways to make this a full and rich production. I cannot hope to thank everyone individually as I know I will miss someone. To all of those who have answered an e-mail, donated a picture, provided some context, contributed in some way to the old *Boxwell News* newsletter and then later to the various social media accounts under the Virtual Boxwell umbrella, thank you. This would not have been possible without your help.

There are some though who deserve direct acknowledgement. Candace Boyce designed the line art that opens each chapter. The Nashville Public Library staff, specifically those in connection with the *Nashville Banner* room, was always extremely helpful. The Cheatham County Clerk, Patrick Smith, was critical in tracking down the actual deed to the Narrows of the Harpeth property. The Friends of the Harpeth River State Park was the first group to really spur this project on by trying to uncover the history of Boxwell at the Narrows themselves. Accompanied by members of the Association and the Rangers at the Narrows, I roamed the property and we put together a pretty solid working map of where the camp was and how it was laid out. Chuck Neese, my contact with the Association, was particular invaluable, asking questions of local residents to learn what people in the area still remembered. And a special thanks to Larry Carpenter of Clovercroft Publishing, who volunteered to help publish this work and whose assistance and patience have been invaluable.

Since 1996, interviews have been conducted with Scouts and staff, volunteers and professionals, going all the way back to the Narrows of the Harpeth. These interviews have mostly been conducted by myself, but there were several early, invaluable interviews conducted by Kerry Parker and Russ Parham that have been part of this research. The list of those interviewed is long, but each of these individuals gave of their time in a deliberate and significant way. As completing this work has taken so long, some who were interviewed have since passed away. To that end, I will note below if the interviewee has passed on. The stories and insights from each of these individuals breathe life into the history that follows and I am deeply indebted to each person. A heartfelt thanks to: Carl Adkins, James Akers (deceased), Ward C. Akers (deceased), Michael Allen, Bob Alley, Dominick and Jonathan Azzara, Matthew Bailey, Ron Bailey, Jerry Barnett, Jim Barr, Candace Boyce, Lisa Boyce, O. E. Brandon (deceased), Jason Bradford, Mike Brown, Perry Bruce, Christy Willhite Bryan, John Bryant, Carrie Buck, Betty Claud, Willie Claud (deceased), Eric Cole, Ken Connelly, Vivian Connelly, Megan Barnett Cook, Archie Crain (deceased), Audrey Creighton, Emmie Donaldson, David Dotson, John Estes, Steve Eubank, Troy & Elaine Feltner, Emily Fish, Jason Flannery, Wes Frye, Howard Gentry, Larry Green, Lee Hagan, John Hickman, Leann Human Hillard, Kathy Howard, Cindy Human, Jimmy Joe Jackson (deceased), Beverly Landstreet (deceased), Chester LaFever (deceased), Meredith MaGuirk, Claus "Dutch" Mann (deceased), Ed Mason, Lisa Human McCormack, David McWilliams, Tom Neal, JJ Norman, Ron Oakes (deceased), John Parish, Sr., Russ Parham, Rachel Paris, Kerry Parker, Aaron Patten, Floyd "Q-ball" Pearce (deceased), Robert Ponder, John and Pearl Schleicher (deceased), Michael Seay, E. D. Thompson, Tim Ratliff, Tom Roussin, Charlie Ray Smith, Greg Tucker, Ron Turpin, Lance Ussery, Andy Verble, Billy Walker (deceased), John Walker, Danny Waltman, Rob Ward, Web Webster, Andy Whitt, Tom Willhite (deceased), and Steve Wright.

The interviews were the backbone to this work from Rock Island forward. In order for these interviews to be useable they had to be transcribed. While a very worth effort was made by Jimmy Hargrove at Volunteer State Community College for her efforts to help transcribe this material during her time as a secretary for the Social Science and Education Division, the amount of material was just overwhelming. I launched a GoFundMe campaign in 2018 to raise enough money to have the interviews transcribed through a transcription service. Here modern day technology proved absolutely invaluable. Social Media allowed me to campaign for funds and GoFundMe allowed me to raise several thousand dollars to complete this project. Let there be no question, there would be no book without the transcripts. As a result, I am forever indebted to both the anonymous individuals who contributed and those listed here who helped make this dream possible: James Akers, John Baldwin, Steve Belew, Keith Bell, Chris Bilbro, April & Joseph Boyd, Irene Bradford, Jason Bradford, Mike Brown, James Bumpus, Mary Anne Byrnes, (family of) Tyler Christman, Jennifer Ciarleglio, Michael Danielson, Chris Davis, Adam Dozier, Celeste & Justin Duke, Randy Dunnavant, Ken and Kathy Eades, Michael Eades, Mike and Susan Eades, Steve Eubank, Wes Frye, Bob Fyke, Cameron, Grady Roger Gray, Lee Hagan, Alan Hamlin, Kathleen Hardy, (family of) Ed Human, Loney John Hutchins, Evan King, Ed Mason, Jordan McConnell, Bill Murphy, John Neal, Laura Black and Eric Hall for Justin and James Northrup, Russ Parham, John Parish, Sr., Aaron Patten, Brad Perling, Stella Pierce, Matt Robinson, Ted Rodgers, Richard Rouch, Michael Salazar, Michael Seay, Jason Shumaker, Livy Simpson, David Smith, Sarah Smith, Kathryn Stewart, Jed Sundwall, Andy Verble, Danny Waltman, Web Webster, David Wells, Ben Whitehouse, Jonathan Wright, and Cory Younts,

Unending gratitude must also be given to Christy Willhite Bryan, Steve Eubank, Russ Parham and Jason Shumaker, who read drafts of the chapters and provided both historical and grammatical insight. Waves of adulation must descend upon Patricia Baines who read nearly every chapter—even ones that were cut from the final draft—and had insightful and creative suggestions. Any points of brilliance of hers; any faults are my own. The final product is only stronger because of these readers' efforts.

To simply say "thank you" to Dr. Ian Romaine is insufficient. Dr. Romaine has been responsible for facilitating this entire process. Having the Middle Tennessee Council publish this work was his suggestion. He secured the approval from Middle Tennessee Council Executive Larry Brown. He worked with the printer. He laid out the chapters. Whatever heavy lifting was required in terms of the process once the writing was complete was all thanks to Ian Romaine.

Finally, I have two families to thank. First, is my Scouting family. This includes not just all of those listed above, but in particular a small group of men who have been so integral to this project it would be completely appropriate to give them co-credit. Much of the early part of this project was their work, which I built upon as time progressed. These men are not only inseparable from own camp staff experience, but aside from my actual kin, they have been a greater influence and presence in my life than any other individuals. To Michael Seay, Russ Parham, Charlie Ray Smith, and Kerry Parker... I simply do not have the words to describe all you have done. Thank you.

And, of course, the other family is my actual family. Since beginning this project, I have married and had a child, who is now a Cub Scout. To Renee' and Emerson, thank you for putting up with and living with this insane project that often took on a life of its own. Your patience and tolerance are appreciated. I hope the final product does you both proud. Thank you for your love and support.

Opening Campfire

Opening campfires are wrapped in mystery. Scouts arrive at camp full of anticipation and anxiety. But the afternoon of the first day is often anticlimactic. A tour of the camp, a swim check if it is needed, and preparing one's tent for the week is not the stuff from which great stories are made. By dinner time, camp begins to improve. At the first assembly at the flagpole, the staff marches in, singing, setting an impressive tone of uniformity and professionalism. That first dinner in the dining hall shows that camp is not going to be like school and that's exciting. But then for Scouts it is back to the tent while the Scoutmaster has a start-of-week meeting with the camp leadership.

But that first campfire... that first campfire is something special. The first day's activities are mostly mundane, but a campfire is different. It begins when Scouts and their troops assemble again at the flagpole as the sun concludes its slow descent into the horizon. Dressed in Class A uniforms, the assembly has an air of mystery as the flag has already been retired for the evening. No staff march in or assemble at the flagpole for this second congregation. When the guide finally arrives, the Scout Sign—three fingers raised on the right hand—is given and Scouts enter a prolonged period of silence.

For the uninitiated, the Scout sign is a foundational symbol in Scouting. It is made by holding the three middle fingers erect, while the pinkie and thumb fold across the palm. This sign could be used as a salute, but it could also be a unique focal tool. When held upright at the top of ninety-degree angle made by the upper arm and forearm, the Scout sign means "Be Quiet and

Pay Attention." Thus, when Scout signs are "in effect," no one speaks.

Appropriately silenced, Scouts leave the assembly area and being the journey to the campfire area. However long it may seem, the journey is in fact not long at all, only exaggerated by the requirement to stay silent. Every footfall is amplified by the enforced silence. Gravel crunches. Leaves crackle. Even on pavement, there is a sound of rubber shoe soles landing, gripping, and releasing. In the quiet, every step takes on its own importance, has its own gravitas, and adds to its own mystery.

When Scouts finally enter the campfire area, they are greeted by a small sea of railroad crossties, each crosstie acting as bench seating. Around camp, many of these are known as "sleeper ties," which are somewhat different that normal crossties. A normal railroad crosstie, the kind used for home landscaping, is about a foot across and six to eight feet long. A sleeper tie is larger. These railroad ties are a solid twelve feet long and about a foot and a half across. The other ties are standard crossties, eight feet long and perhaps a foot across. These are more like kinds of crossties used in landscaping, but work well here too. both kinds of ties are found all over the property, useful for bridges over small gullies and for seating at campfires areas at Boy Scout camps. They may ooze black, tarry creosote, but they are ideal for creating the appropriate setting. Nothing says "camp" like the smell and texture of cross tie seating.

Scouts enter the area and file down to the end of the first row of crossties, Scouts signs still in effect. Once this row is full, the long, single file line of Scouts move to the second row, sometimes separating troops and friends. This continues through several rows of ties, each row arched in a large semicircle around a stone fire altar. An unlit stack of logs and tinder sit upon the orderly pile of stone in the middle of the woods. In short, a bonfire awaited.

Lighting the fire may take various forms. Over the years, a multitude of methods have been employed. The spirt of Native Americans have been

2

invoked, who call on the gods of nature to light the fire. Sometimes the fire then explodes, or perhaps a fire ball flies through the forest. At other points, a rifle wielding marksman shoots a match, which lights the fire. Even a single torch has been used. There are many ways that the fire can be lit and break the silence imposed by the Scout sign.

Once the fire is lit, the scene changes. In the early minutes of the opening campfire, this bonfire burns with an incredible intensity. Even on the back two rows of crossties, one can feel the heat from that fire. With the campfire roaring in the foreground, faces are lit by the flickering, changing light of that same campfire. A light bubble envelopes the whole area, illuminating one side of the surrounding trees—the cedars, the oaks, the maples— while the other side is cloaked into shadow. This is a warm light, not the cold white light found indoors. Here, the whole area is bathed in a warm orange and yellow glow. The fire itself constantly pops and crackles, drowning out the growing nighttime sounds of crickets and whippoorwills. Hot orange cinders shoot into the air in crazy, random directions, slowing circling down and vanishing as their heat dissipates. The fire itself is powerful program. It is elemental. It is raw.

It is in the space between the fire and the seating where the campfire program exists. Performed are songs, skits, and cheers. There are running gags and one-time only skits. Cheers and songs break up the evening, encouraging—*requiring*—audience participation and engagement. Through sweltering summer heat and Southern humidity, accentuated by the inferno nearby, the campfire program unfolds. To a young Scout though, it is great theater.

The opening campfire concludes with what is called a Scoutmaster's Minute in Scouting circles. A Scoutmaster's Minute can take several forms. It can be a reflection on the day's events, an attempt to add meaning to the occasion. It can be an attempt to pass on knowledge or lessons that are worth learning. It can also be used to pass on history to add context to a moment. In essence, it is a sermon in Scouting. For the Sunday night campfire, an adult member of the staff, either the program director or the camp director, saunters up before the campfire and speaks his mind for a few minutes. It is a tradition dating back decades.

The Scoutmaster's Minute can take a variety of forms. At Boxwell, the opening campfire is on Sunday night and the Minute given here is often a history of the camp. The story told is simple. This Boxwell, Boxwell Reservaton on Old Hickory Lake, is the fourth Boxwell, but there have been others. The first Boxwell was in Linton, TN. The second was at the Narrows of the Harpeth in Cheatham County, while the third was at Rock Island, near McMinnville, Tennessee. And just like that, the history of the first three Camp Boxwells is over. The remaining few minutes are devoted to the history of the current Boxwell. The other Boxwells are never spoken of again.

And yet, the other Boxwells existed and each has a story. Each story reflects the changing world in which those Boxwells existed. The program offered at Boxwell over the preceding century reflects the changes in Scouting and society. Virtually every change at Boxwell from its opening to the present day has been in service of a program to promote these shifting values. These pages tell that story.

Larry Jackson prepares Scouts for a cheer at an opening campfire at Camp Parnell, Boxwell Reservation, 1970. Photo by Chris "Kit" Eckert.

Scouts and leaders sit on crossties enjoying an opening campfire at Camp Parnell, Boxwell Reservation, 1970. Photo by Chris "Kit" Eckert.

Camp Boxwell in Linton, Tennessee, in the 1920s. Personal Collection of Harry "Beany" Elam.

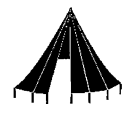

Chapter I

Citizens in Training:

Camp Boxwell at Linton

1921-1929

Leslie G. Boxwell had a problem. Recently elected chairman of camping for the fledgling Nashville Area Council of the Boy Scouts of America, Boxwell was charged with preparing a summer camp. When the Council formed in March of 1920, it had promised "a good camp" as a benefit of creating a local organization. The Council hired a paid executive in June and though he missed the 1920 summer camp season, he was "making plans for a big Scout camp" the following year. Even as early as January 1921, months before summer camp would even begin, one of Nashville's two leading newspapers, *The Nashville Tennessean*, implored boys—Scouts and non-Scouts—to "begin saving a camp fund now" in order to take advantage of the opportunity to attend the camp.[1]

Boxwell had been working hard to get a summer camp ready. In March of 1921, the bespectacled Nashville industrialist had solicited suggestions from Nashville citizens about where a good location for a summer camp might be held, asking only that the camp be "within thirty miles of the city and provided with good water, drainage and other camping facilities." In April of 1921, he bought tables and benches for a dining area from the Nashville Industrial Corporation. In May, the Council authorized Boxwell to purchase the materials needs for a "complete camp outfit." In June, Boxwell hired two critical players: a camp director, C. W. Abele, formerly of the Nashville Young Men's Christian Association, or Y.M.C.A., and a camp cook, Walter Whittaker of Kissam Hall at Vanderbilt University. Camp Director Abele was considered a significant win. He had "wide experience in conducting boys' camps and is thoroughly familiar with scout work and the conduct of scout camps." Abele had the experience the new Boy Scout council needed.[2]

Boxwell and a committee of Council volunteers also explored several sites as possible locations for a Scout summer camp. Some were simply not acceptable. Other locations were strong possibilities, but just did not work out. For example, in April 1921, Boxwell and members of the camping committee inspected a potential camp at Fernvale Springs. Fernvale Springs was near Fairview, Tennessee in Williamson County, southwest of Nashville. Offered to the Council free of charge, the specific location under consideration was 3,500 acres and connected to the springs themselves. For reasons that have not survived, the Fernvale Springs site was not chosen.[3]

Boxwell and the camping committee also considered camping at Sycamore Creek, near Ashland City. Northwest of Nashville, the Sycamore Creek site already had a history of Scout camping. Though the Nashville Area Council formed in 1920, Scouting existed on an informal basis for almost a decade before this date. Those Scouts in the 1910s needed a place to camp; this place was Sycamore Creek. Owned by A. P. Jackson, farmer-politician of the area, the site was on a tributary of the Cumberland River, which "had been dammed to supply water for a powder mill that once operated on the site." Nashville Scouts had been having some sort of summer camp program here since 1913 and thus this was a logical place to continue a more formal program. Indeed, Jackson's "generosity and friendly attitude toward the Boy Scouts [was] a decided argument in favor" of the location. Nevertheless, Sycamore Creek was not chosen either. Boxwell and his camping committee were looking for something else, something different than Sycamore Creek.[4]

Boxwell's efforts finally paid off. On June 20, 1921, *The Nashville Tennessean* announced that the chairman had finally settled on a location. The Nashville Council's first summer camp was to be "17 miles from Nashville, on the Memphis-to-Bristol highway, two miles beyond Newsom Station, near the Harpeth River" with access to the railroad. The site was "on a tableland high and dry, and very near an everlasting spring of pure, cold water with an athletic field very convenient. Nearby [was] an extensive swimming hole, considered as safe as an indoor pool, where all the fun of swimming may be had with the least possible risk." The new council physician, Dr. R. C. Derivaux, still needed to complete a routine check on the drinking water, but this was the place. Indeed, one scoutmaster immediately made reservations for the first ten days of camp at this new location.[5]

Then the water check came back. Instead of "an everlasting spring of pure, cold war," "[s]amples of the drinking water at the proposed site for a summer camp of the Boy Scouts of Nashville...have been pronounced unfit for consumption." The Newsom Station site was out. The Council had no summer camp; Boxwell had to find a new location.[6]

The pressure grew. The failed Newsom Station water sample test was reported on Friday, June 24th. Summer camp was scheduled to begin on Tuesday, July 5, 1921. Boxwell scrambled over the weekend to find alternate sites. By Monday the 27th, with only a week remaining before summer camp was scheduled to begin, he had three different locations under inspection. All three potential locales were within eighteen miles of Nashville, but no specifics were given to the newspapers. Boxwell had learned his lesson; he would wait for Dr. Derivaux to complete his check on the water before he made any announcements this time.[7]

The Nashville Tennessean only added to the pressure on Boxwell's work. Declaring the camping chairman "the busiest man in town" as he sought to secure a site, the paper made grandiose promises about the camp that was to be. "The council camp will be a camp with a purpose," the paper proclaimed, "and aims to send every boy away from camp a better boy socially, a better mixer and with a better personality... The camp aims to build every boy physically and send him home in the best of physical fitness, to teach alertness, appreciation of the out-of-doors and independence—the ability to do things for himself." The Nashville Council's summer camp was apparently going to be quite transformative![8]

Derivaux's announcement of "absolutely pure" water came on Wednesday the 29th of June—less than a week before the camp was to open. The selected site was a small, four acre section of farmland. The property was part of a larger holding known as the Allison-Morton farm, or sometimes the S. S. Morton farm. The site had spring water for drinking and had direct access to the South Harpeth River. Accessible by traveling the winding Harding Road, it was approximately seventeen miles outside of the city, just beyond Bellevue, in a little community known as Linton. With the site settled, work could begin. Camp Director C. W. Abele traveled to the camp over the weekend, taking workmen and tents with him to prepare the location.[9]

Leslie G. Boxwell could finally breathe a sigh of relief. He had accomplished his task. On Saturday, July 2, the Nashville Area Council's Executive Board—the governing body of the Boy Scout Council—recognized the efforts of "the man who has worked untiringly to make the camp a success in every way." The Executive Board unanimously agreed to name the site "Camp L. G. Boxwell."[10]

The Need for Scouting

In the early twentieth century, the United States experienced rapid and profound industrialization and urbanization. As historian Eric Foner explained, this transformation was "one of the most profound economic revolutions any country has ever experienced... By the early twentieth century, American manufacturing production had surpassed the combined total of Great Britain, Germany, and France. Railroad mileage tripled between 1860 and 1880, and tripled again by 1920, opening vast new areas to commercial farming, creating a national market for manufactured goods, and inspiring a boom in coal mining and steel production." Cities filled with young men looking for jobs and were joined by millions of immigrants. Industrial work beckoned to all. Companies which had previously employed twenty or thirty people, now employed hundreds. Industrialization also made farming more mechanized, meaning fewer people were needed on the farms. By 1920, for the first time in American history, the majority of Americans lived in or near cities. This transformation took place over a single generation.[11]

The rise of these corporations and the new industrial world raised questions about the nature of independence and citizenship, values and character. Many feared that the move to the city presented children, boys especially, to an unconscionable array of vices, challenging the moral health of the boy. School attendance was not yet compulsory in many states, so many boys had an abundance of potentially unsupervised time. In addition to potentially working to help make ends meet, young boys might fall in with older boys of poor values. The fear of gangs was palpable and real. Equally unsettling was the fear that the natural environment, "the great outdoors" so many considered wholesome and critical to American character, was being lost as well. Industrial development and the closing of the frontier led to both conservationist and preservationist movements to better utilize and to better protect natural resources. To all of this was added the changing world of business. Large corporations meant bureaucracies and working and managing others in ways that had not been necessary in previous generations. Industrialization changed the way businesses operated and the kinds of opportunities available. Parents worried about how to best raise a boy in this new world.[12]

The Boy Scouts of America provided an answer. Officially incorporated by newspaper magnate William Dickinson Boyce on February 8, 1910, the Boy Scouts of America was largely based off the work of the British Boy

11

Scouts, founded by Lord Robert Baden-Powell. As the legend goes, Boyce was on a business trip in London when he got lost in a heavy fog. An unknown Boy Scout directed him to the correct destination. When Boyce offered the unknown Scout a tip, he refused, wanting nothing in return. It was his responsibility to do a good turn. Boyce was impressed. Here was a boy of good values and character in an urban and industrial environment. Boyce found the local Scout office, took some literature on the movement, and brought the idea back to the United States.[13]

As with all great ideas, programs for boys existed before Boyce incorporated the Boy Scouts in 1910. Anyone familiar with the history of the program would have at least a passing acquaintance with the Sons of Daniel Boone and the Boy Pioneers, the two boy-centric programs of Daniel Carter Beard. Both of the organizations focused on the outdoors through the prism of the pioneer life. Another program with a similar focus, but with a Native American emphasis was Ernest Thompson Seton's Woodcraft Indians. Beard and Seton were eventually brought into the Boy Scouts of America fold and considered founders of the movement along with Boyce, but they were just the tip of the iceberg. There were many youth-centered organizations at the time. Indeed, even before incorporation, there was evidence of Boy Scout troops existing in the United States, independent startups that used Baden-Powell's *Scouting for Boys* handbook as their guide. Clearly, there was unease amongst Americans about the future of their boys and Scouting, in whatever form, seemed to provide an answer.[14]

What the Boy Scouts of America offered was a program to build boys into men. Clearly, boys would grow into men without any guidance, but the Boy Scouts were interested in creating a certain type of man. As the Preface to the first official Boy Scout handbook explained, "The BOY SCOUTS OF AMERICA is a corporation formed by a group of men who are anxious that the boys of America should come under the influence of this movement and be built up in all that goes to make character and good citizenship." This one sentence says a great deal. Older men, anxious about how the next generation was turning out, were creating a movement to teach values and citizenship. The first chapter went even further, stating, "The aim of the Boy Scouts is to supplement the various existing educational agencies, and to promote the ability in boys to do things for themselves and others... This is accomplished in games and team play, and is pleasure, not work, for the boy. All that is needed is the out-of-doors, a group of boys, and a competent leader."[15]

Scouting was thus the confluence of two different approaches to manhood. One approach stressed the outdoor life. The programs and work of Beard and Seton drove this aspect of the program. Being able to "do for yourself" was a throwback to the ideas of "rugged individualism" that made Americans strong and vibrant. But if one pauses to think about this for a moment, this world was quickly disappearing. The Boy Scout program was supposed to help the boys who were not exposed to this world. Thus, the second approach to manhood stressed preparedness for a corporate world. This was the approach stressed by the national organization, by men like Chief Scout Executive James E. West. The goal of Scouting was to tie these two approaches together to create a man who could not simply survive and navigate the new modern world, but succeed in it.[16]

To accomplish this goal, Scouting emerged as a fairly simply two level program. The first level was advancement. The first ranks—Tenderfoot, Second Class, First Class—were basically skills oriented. Complete a list of specific outdoor skills, such as first aid, compass work, basic knot tying, and advance. These skills were not only fundamental for further advancement, but a good starting point for how Scouting built up boys into men. As the first Scout Handbook declared, "A tenderfoot...is superior to the ordinary boy because of his training." There were no time requirements. Once a Scout completed the rank's requirements, he could begin work on the next rank. Thus, a First Class Scout represented a fair amount of work. Upon completion of this rank, a Scout could begin working on merit badges. Merit badges exposed the

13

Scout to more occupation-specific or interest-specific material. To advance to the ranks of Star, Life, or Eagle specific merit badges, both in number and topic, had to be completed. Service work to the troop and community had to be completed as well.[17]

Advancement was only part of the equation. A Scout had to show leadership as well. To this end, Scouts were organized into patrols and troops. While an individual Scout worked on his advancement, he worked on his leadership skills within the group. He needed to serve his immediate peers in his patrol, a group of eight to twelve boys, and his troop, a group made up of patrols with no limits on size. He could serve in any number of leadership roles from patrol leader and senior patrol leader to quartermaster for the troop or scribe. Every leadership position was to train him not simply to grow personally, but to grow in service and leadership to others. In short, personal outdoor experiences were married to interpersonal management training.

If everything these anxious men in the early twentieth century assumed about youth was true, then summer camp was critical to implementing the Scouting program. A local Scout council and the smaller Scout troop were both wonderful organizational tools, but both would most likely be in the very urban environment that Scouting was trying to address. A summer camp though provided the necessary component to make Scouting work, to navigate the two approaches to manhood. A summer camp provided an outdoor experience, while simultaneously providing opportunities for leadership and templates of "good men." Promoting not only the interests of the National movement, but the interests and needs of the local council as well, a summer camp existed for the good of the Scouting program.

Creating the Nashville Council

Scouting came to middle Tennessee almost a full decade before the Nashville Council formed. Curtis B. Haley of Nashville, prompted by an article about Scouting found by his two nephews Lawrence and James Hirsig, wrote to the national office "applying for a commission as a Scoutmaster" on July 4, 1910. Haley's request was granted in September of that year as Commission No. 337. He thus became the first Scoutmaster in middle Tennessee, a position he retained until 1935 when he retired from active Scouting. Troop 1 was his troop, centered around Montrose Avenue and Waverly Place. Haley was appointed Scout Commissioner in September 1912, leading to the creation of an informal council, which was little more than a loose organization of area troop Scoutmasters. For the most part, individual troops and Scoutmasters were on their own.[18]

The same situation was true for summer camp. Without a local council, troops created their own summer camps. In fact, to bestow the title "summer camp" on these encampments was generous. As Creighton and Johnson point out in their 1983 history of the Nashville (later Middle Tennessee) Council *Boys Will Be Men*, with no local state highways or interstates yet, having a centralized camp for troops was virtually impossible. As a result, most troops simply camped on their own. The first attempt at a group summer camp was the Sycamore Creek camp of A. Perry Jackson in Ashland City, mentioned above. This first camp operated for a single ten-day stretch and was run by four Scoutmasters—and their wives. The wives stayed in an on-site cabin, while the men and boys stayed in tents. Approximately thirty boys attended the camp, including one of Curtis Haley's nephews who helped start it all, James Hirsig. The Sycamore Creek camp continued to serve as a summer encampment until the United States entered the First World War in 1917. After a brief hiatus, the camp resumed after the war.[19]

This situation could have continued for some time, but external and internal pressures led to the creation of the formal Nashville Council in 1920. Externally, Stanley A. Harris, southeastern director of the National Boy Scouts, was working to increase the number of councils through the southeastern United States. He visited the Nashville area multiple times after 1917, encouraging the local Rotary Club to sponsor the organization. The National

Boy Scouts of America organization wanted to see the movement grow.[20]

These pleas would likely have fallen on deaf ears if the internal pressures had not grown so strong. The Nashville area had been experiencing strong population growth. From 1900 to 1930, the population of Nashville almost doubled. For the same period, the mid-state cities of Springfield, Murfreesboro, Dickson, and Lebanon more than doubled. More people meant more troops, which naturally meant more organization. But this growth also meant that Nashville was starting to experience the same issues other areas had been dealing with, namely the fear that more boys in the cities meant boys getting into trouble. "Trouble" here meant not only the urban gangs of the previous decade, but now the fear that lazy or idle boys would fall prey to bolshevism (communism), part of the Red Scare that swept the country after the First World War. More boys tempted by trouble also meant more boys who needed what Scouting offered. The crisis that had started the Boy Scouts of America and scouting-like movements across the nation had come to middle Tennessee by 1920.[21]

Based on the suggestion by Stanley Harris, the Nashville Rotary Club estimated that $7500 a year for two years would make it possible to serve 2,000 Scout age boys. With a goal set, the Nashville Rotary Club launched a campaign to raise the funds for a formal Boy Scout council. The campaign claimed Scouting would teach boys "to be useful," would establish "habits of thrift and trustworthiness, the greatest enemies of Bolshevism," and would reduce "crime by giving the boy an outlet for his energy." Most importantly, Scouting was "not play, but a plan to make real men out of real boys by a real program that works." The funds raised would be used to pay for "at least one full-time executive," to help troops already formed and create new ones, and "to equip and develop a Scout camp." On March 10, 1920, the Rotary Club conducted the single day campaign and exceeded the $15,000 goal.[22]

Having completed "the quickest campaign ever conducted in the history of Nashville, and the only really successful one since the [Great] war," Rotary Club President Edgar M. Foster next held an election of officers for the new Nashville Council, B.S.A. As would be the trend for decades to come, the Executive Board brought together prominent men from all over the service area. Foster himself, business manager of the *Nashville Banner,* was elected President. James G. Stahlman, soon to take over the role of publisher of the *Banner* from his father Major E. B. Stahlman, also served on the board. Curtis Haley, who founded middle Tennessee Scouting, also served on the board along with several other Nashville businessmen and established Scouters. Two other names of note were Dan McGugin, Vanderbilt University's football coach and local lawyer, and William J. Anderson, Vanderbilt's track coach. McGugin served as the Council's Scout Commissioner—essentially a volunteer liaison between the Council and the troops—while Anderson was elected head of camping.[23]

With a council formed, the next step was to hire a Council Executive, someone to handle the day to day operations of the Council. While the Executive Board was made of volunteers who made the decisions of the Council, the Executive was a paid professional who executed the decisions of the Board. In addition to a secretary, these two individuals would be the only paid employees of the Nashville Council. After considering "many men," William Anderson, native of Robertson County, was offered the position. Anderson did not want the job, but one of the men who offered him the position gave him a Scoutmaster's Handbook and asked the track coach to read it. As Anderson explained years later, "I took it home that night and read it for one hour. At the end of that hour, it dawned on me that I could do not better serv [ice] to mankind than by entering this work." On June 19, 1920, "Coach" Anderson became Nashville's first paid professional Scouter and Nashville's first Scout Executive.[24]

At thirty-six years old, Anderson was still early in his career. After completing his undergraduate studies, he graduated from Vanderbilt's law school in 1906. However, his real fame came in athletics. Anderson had been a member of the Vanderbilt track team for the five years he attended the university. High jump and hurdles were his events and he set records in both. When chosen to lead the Nashville Council, Anderson already had a full-time job: he was Vanderbilt's track coach, a position he held since 1907. And he was good at this post. He coached unbeaten teams from 1910 to 1932. Deeply conservative and religious, Anderson was also a Mason, a Presbyterian, and, obviously, a Rotarian. The new Council Executive was tall and thin with waves of jet-black hair swept back over his head, though this nest was often hidden under either a straw hat or a fedora. When coaching, he always had an umbrella by his side. Anderson's promotion to Scout Executive opened the door for Leslie G. Boxwell to lead the Camping Committee.[25]

Only a year older than the Vanderbilt coach, Boxwell had already made a name for himself by 1920. Not graced with the tall, athletic build of Anderson, Boxwell left his native state of Ohio and put his engineering degree from Ohio State University to work at the 1904 St. Louis World's Fair, where he helped build the Cascades exhibit. From St. Louis, he moved to Memphis where he worked as a salesman, finally landing in Nashville in 1908. By 1912, he was working for the Tennessee Metal Culvert Company, had started his own small side company, and married a local woman, Nettie Stacey. Known as "Box" to his friends, Boxwell joined the Tennessee Good Roads Association to promote road-building in the very rural Tennessee and joined the Nashville Board of Trade, the predecessor to the Chamber of Commerce. During the First World War, Boxwell served as a Four Minute Man, giving four minute speeches to raise money for war bonds to finance the war. He also founded Nashville's "Fit-to-Fight League," where local businessmen promised to stay physically fit into "order to serve the country efficiently at the home base in [those] abnormal times." Boxwell even managed a four-wheel drive truck company, Duplex. By the 1920s, he was secretary and general manager of the Tennessee Metal Culvert Company and he served on a variety of civic and social

William J. Anderson and Leslie G. Boxwell in their later years in Scouting. Anderson photo from personal collection of Beverly Landstreet. Boxwell photo from Middle Tennessee Council

organizations. Leslie G. Boxwell was a mover and shaker in turn-of-the-century Nashville.[26]

At the time of Anderson's appointment and Boxwell's move to the Camping Committee, Nashville Scouting was in need of vigorous leadership. While there had been troops in the area over the previous decade, few lasted any significant length of time. "I spent a whole month trying to find one troop," Anderson recalled years later. "They told me there were several troops in the county, but at the end of that thirty days, I had found only four that were active. These I used as a nucleus around which to build." Anderson's guiding philosophy was "One More Boy," always trying to capture one more Scout and bring him into the program. The philosophy paid off. After opening a Council office in September 1920, by the end of the Council's first year, there were nineteen troops and 294 Scouts. The Nashville Council was growing and those boys were going to need a summer camp.[27]

Camp Boxwell at Linton

And so it came to pass that on Tuesday, July 5, the first Camp Boxwell opened to Scouts. Open flat-bed trucks from Boxwell's culvert company met local Nashville Scouts where Harding Road intersected with the terminus of the Belle Meade street car line. The trucks arrived just before 10am and again at 4:30 p.m. and would transport the Scouts and their extensive equipment[28] free of charge out to the newly established camp. Harding Road was a winding, twisting route, which meant the seventeen miles from Nashville to Linton was not exactly a quick jaunt![29]

Once they arrived, Scouts beheld a very simple camp. Though Camp Director Abele had prepared the site with assistance from Boxwell's culvert company, it was fair to say that the camp was rustic. The beech tree covered site was a mere four acres, located along the South Harpeth River, just south of the Harding Road bridge, which had been put in place in 1917. *The Nashville Banner* described the site this way:

> The scout camp is sanitary and healthful in every respect. The camp has a splendid pure water supply. It is located in a beautiful grove of beech trees on the banks of the Harpeth, with a large open stretch of ground immediately in front of the tents, giving plenty of sunlight and space for all kinds of games and drills… The old swimmin' hole, which is one of the main features at the camp, is a fine stretch of water, ranging in depth, with gravel beach, and two real, springy diving boards that the boys enjoy as much as they do the actual swimming.

Military surplus tents from the Great War served as lodging for the camp. The large, white tents, supported with a center pole, resembled single point circus tents. Once erected, they were mostly roof, but the lower side flaps could be rolled up for ventilation. Each tent covered a floor space of approximately 16 X 16 feet and held eight scouts. With sixty Scouts attending each week, there were eight tents that first summer. However, there were no campsites; the tents were grouped together in a line with a flagpole erected out front and volleyball net nearby. The kitchen and dining hall was the only semi-permanent building on site, consisting of wooden walls, but needing to be covered and screened.[30]

The daily schedule was straight-forward this first year. Scouts were awakened at 6:30am by the dulcet tones of a bugle sounding reveille. Before breakfast, the boys engaged in exercises, a quick swim, and flag ceremonies. The exercises may have been jumping jacks, a quick run around the camp, or a variety of physical engagements. Breakfast began at 7:30am, cooked by Walter Whittaker, and announcements were made at the end of the meal. Scouts returned to their tents to clean up themselves, the tent itself, and the surrounding area for inspection. After inspection, morning advancement work in the requirements for Tenderfoot and Second class began at 9am. More advancement sessions continued at 10am and demonstrations in Scout skills, such as cooking, first aid, axe work, and orienteering were held at 11am. There was a brief swim time before lunch; after lunch, there was a period for resting and tutoring anyone who was behind in their skills. In the afternoon, there was a large block from 1:30 p.m. to 3:30 p.m. for more Scout skill activities, such as hiking, athletics, and animal tracking. A mid-afternoon swim followed with end of the day flag ceremonies just before 6 p.m. With the flag lowered, dinner followed and then time was set aside for writing home, games, and more tutoring. As the sun sank into the horizon, there was an evening campfire for singing and story-telling. This period was also used for studying the stars, both for recreation and advancement. Scouts were to begin getting ready for bed around 9 p.m. and taps was blown at 9:30 p.m.[31]

Still, real life was more interesting than this schedule. A guiding principle of the Linton Boxwell was that "all share alike." If a parent sent food to a son at camp that week, said food had to be equally divided; no one got more than anyone else. Boys were often sent gifts of ice cream, melons, and marshmallows from their parents and it was all shared with the group. Wilbur F.

Creighton, Jr., co-author of *Boys Will Be Men*, was a Scout at the Linton Boxwell in 1921 and 1922. His material on the camp was as much a personal memoir as it was an actual history, providing first hand insight into the camp. As Creighton explained,

> ... After planning camp throughout the spring and counting the days until it began, scouts rattled in streetcars out to the juncture of Harding Road and Bellemeade Boulevard in West Nashville, where they met John Holmes [a Leslie Boxwell employee] with a truckload of weary campers and their paraphernalia headed home. The returning group crawled down from the truck and the new group clambered up, then waited. Coach Anderson always rode in the truck and his secretary met him so he could take care of the previous week's mail and paperwork. That task took minutes which seemed like hours to the eager boys waiting in the truck.

> After the scouts arrived at Linton, the daily routine began. Early each morning the troops were rousted out to stand inspection by their tents. The physician looked at each scout and Anderson or the camp director inspected the tents. Scout school occupied about two hours each morning, during which time the scouts worked toward merit badges and rank advancement, followed by a swim before lunch.

> Each scout brought with him a tin plate and cup and flat silverware with his initials scratched on each piece. At the end of meals they washed their own plates in a tub of hot water, using a small mop, then rinsed under running water. "The food itself," said one scout, remembering from the perspective of sixty years, "seemed to me the most delectable and appetizing I have ever had." Walter Whittaker was so superb a cook that veteran scouts commonly played a practical joke on novices during the first weekend at camp. Whittaker left each Saturday evening for home, and the older boys told the new recruits that he had gotten angry at Coach Anderson and would not be returning. That lie was a terrific shock to the novices, who thought the greatest cook in the world was abandoning them, and the sighs of relief were almost audible when Whittaker

A full page of photos from the Linton Boxwell's first summer. Note the truck to bring Scouts to camp and the morning exercise. "Nashville's Boy Scouts in Camp at Linton," Nashville Banner, August 28, 1921.

returned on Sunday afternoons.

Scouts who needed between-meal snacks earned them by killing flies. Though the dining room was screened, flies still were
a pest, and Coach Anderson gave a candy bar as reward to
boys who swatted fifty flies. Being scouts and on their honor,
they merely told Anderson they had killed fifty flies and received the candy bar without question, a trust that startled
them.

Creighton left out that Boxwell himself provided magazines for the boys to
read during their rest time and the Scouts were encouraged to write home then
as well. Evenings meant campfires, which involved telling stories, singing
songs, guest speakers, and showcasing the talents of the Scouts. Visitors to the
camp were surprised as how efficiently the camp was run. R. Lee Thomas of
Columbia, TN, was one such visitor. In a letter to Anderson, he was very direct, "[W]ithin the last few years it has been my privilege to visit quite a number of Boy Scout summer camps in different parts of the country, and I desire
to say unqualifiedly that yours was the best I ever seen."[32]

Still, the camp was not a modern Scout camp by any stretch of the
imagination. There was virtually no paid staff for the summer. Aside from
Camp Director Able, Dr. Deveriaux, "waterfront" director Lallie Richter, and
cook Walter Whittaker, everyone else was a volunteer. Scouts came to camp
as individual boys, not as troops. When Scoutmasters did come to camp, they
often came up for the week to serve as instructors. Visitors had a specific day
to visit—Thursday afternoon—and were encouraged to stay away other days.
The camp had no phone. Nearby Linton—a popular hiking destination—had
only four stores and between them only one telephone line to Nashville. Mothers were thanked for observing the regulation regarding visitors day and
"comparatively few have insisted upon being called over the phone for a daily
report."[33]

Another way the first Camp Boxwell differed from a modern Scout
camp was the Council did not own this camp. It was a loaner. The entire

property, including the renovations and improvements made by Abele and Boxwell before camp started, still belonged to S. S. Morton. Of course, given that the camp was filled to capacity all three weeks and that members of the Executive Council who toured the camp were deeply impressed, efforts were made to purchase the camp at the end of the first summer. Anderson suggested that a permanent camp would cost approximately $10,000, excluding the land itself. The Linton location was discussed as a possible site. In order to be a first class Council, the Nashville Council needed to own the camp. Whether a deal was offered has not survived. All that is known is that Camp Boxwell stayed at the Morton property for the next several years and the Council never owned the property—the only Camp Boxwell for which this was true.[34]

The above gives a wonderful picture of daily life at Camp Boxwell for the three weeks it was open in 1921; none of this however addressed the critical issue of how the camp was supposed to fulfill the promise of Scouting to Nashville Scouts. The truth was those details had not been worked out. While big promises were made, the first summers at Camp Boxwell were experiments in camp program. What exactly should a camp program do? How should it support Scouting? What were the most important ideals of Scouting that a Scout camp should be demonstrating?

As the 1922 camp season approached, the values and goals were more clearly defined. *The Nashville Banner* laid out these ideals in the ten days before Camp Boxwell opened that year.

> Scouting would not be Scouting without camping. In fact, camping may be considered the very foundation and backbone of the whole Scouting plan. But one might ask, "[H]ow about the laws and the oath and the moral standards and principles that Scouts are support to be taught?" These are implanted in the heart of the boy and made a part of his life not by preaching or teaching theoretically.
>
> Camping life, with all of its great diversity of action and attraction, is not only the primal inspiration for living the moral

code, but is its greatest single test. The boy learns that it is through his work and play and study and all activities that the laws must be lived up to. It is the boy who "wears well" that is developing the strongest character. There is no greater test of "wearing" than camping.

The very fundamental principles of citizenship training are the very ones that are at the bottom of successful camping, namely: unselfish service, or in the motto of the Three Musketeers, 'One for all—all for one.'

Then comes the real deepest permeating influence of camp life—the love of nature. It is the getting away from the deteriorating influences of our modern over-civilization, from the material things and routine living out into the open to become acquainted with the real, the true, the beautiful, that works its own quiet automatic influence on the life of any response human being.

In short, the very values of Scouting—the morals, the character building, the citizenship training—are all accomplished through camping and life in the outdoors. The importance of a summer camp program could not be understated.[35]

The 1921 Camp Director C. W. Abele had been brought in because of his experience with summer camps, but that experience was primarily with YMCA camps. Indeed, so tightly associated was the Linton Boxwell with the Nashville Y that when the Boy Scout camp ended on Tuesday, July 26, the YMCA took over the camp on Thursday the 28th. Abele was not brought back in 1922; the camp director that year was Hugh Nixon, captain of Anderson's track team at Vanderbilt. Whether Nixon wanted the job or was hired by Anderson at the last minute is unknown. Three days before camp started, L. G. Boxwell, still chair of the camping committee, said that Nixon was "gifted with an unusual understanding of the boy." While decidedly cryptic, there is little indication here that Nixon brought anything to the mix beyond what Abele had introduced the year before.[36]

Indeed, 1922 looked very similar to 1921 with a few changes. A truck brought the boys to camp. Scouts worked on advancement in the morning and had lots of time to swim. They built a slide at the waterfront. Walter Whittaker still knew "how to sling hash and sing along with the best of them." "Prominent citizens" still came out to speak to the boys. A new campfire area had been chosen for 1922 and "Indian ceremonials" were mentioned for the first time in the history of the camp. Also mentioned for the first time was "a special non-sectarian service for all, where songs, stories and talks" will close Sunday evening. The camp ran for four weeks instead of three and each week held eighty Scouts instead of sixty. To that end, "nine new army tents and thirty cots" went to the camp to accommodate the increased size.[37]

The camp also tested two ideas this summer, both a hint of what was to come. The first was a "camp scribe," a Scout who wrote back to "Scout HQ" in Nashville about happenings at the camp. These "reports" often ended up as articles in the local newspapers. The scribe would change every week, and some were more prolific than others. Wilbur F. Creighton, Jr., at Boxwell for his second summer, took to this job like a fish to water. He wrote a letter virtually every day, recounting the mundane and the exciting: Seven boys got their heads shaved. Camp Director Nixon bested another adult in a boxing match. The boys in one tent raided the boys in another.[38]

And at least once, Creighton touched on the other new experiment for 1922: a tenters' council of Scouts, which Creighton called a "jury." Creighton explained it this way in his letter to Scout Commissioner Dan McGugin,

> My Dear McGugin: A troop of new Scouts came to camp Monday and were told the rules and regulations of camp and cautioned not to talk after taps or before reveille. That night they got a little obstreperous, and three times Mr. W. J. Anderson called them down. When they continued to break rules it seemed the best thing to send them home, but the question was put up to a jury of twelve Scouts, consisting of tent leaders and other Scouts. The case was heard and it was

> decided to give them another trial, and that further infraction
> of the rule would bring dismissal from camp for the ones
> guilty. The next night one boy talked and disturbed the camp,
> and he was sent home without further trial.

In short, Scouts decided the fate of other Scouts through a jury of peers. Rules were made and announced, but if those rules were broken, this assemblage of representatives from each tent administered the punishment. This one incident was the only time this jury was mentioned all summer, so it was entirely possible this group did not operate all four weeks. Nevertheless, it was a harbinger of things to come.[39]

A Program of Self-Governance

1923 was the year everything changed. As explained by *Nashville Tennessean* reporter Helen Dahnke in "Scouts Rule Own Kingdom on the Harpeth,"

> Four years ago this summer [1927], W. J. Anderson woke up
> at Camp Boxwell one morning with 80 boys on his hands and
> with none of the young men whom he had employed to assist
> him in the camp's direction and discipline present. He called
> the boys together and explained that they were their own rulers
> and that it might be well to work out a government of their
> own choice. The system that those boys decided on is in prac-
> tice now and so far as is known Camp Boxwell is the most
> completely self-governed boys' camp in the world.

This may have been an overstatement, but the point was correct. Anderson had been "general management" in 1922, hiring someone else as Camp Director. In 1923, Anderson took on the post himself and from the very first week, it was clear camp was going to be different. There was still virtually no hired staff and most instruction was still done by visiting Scoutmasters. However, governance of the camp—who made and enforced the rules—was no longer set by the adults. The Scouts ran the camp.[40]

Once established, Anderson's system of self-governance was implemented almost immediately after Scouts arrived at camp. After the first camp-fire on the first night of camp, a series of elections ensued. The first elections were for positions that benefitted the entire camp and were voted on by a camp-wide constituency. These "elected officials" could be from any tent, but they served the interests of the whole camp. The second elections were held in the tents. Each tent was treated essentially as its own district or ward and accordingly, each tent elected its own representative for the camp council, or tenters' council. It was this council that was the heart and soul of Boxwell's self-governance as the council had legislative, executive, and judicial functions. This was all re-enforced with awards and the day time program.[41]

There were four camp-wide positions in the first round of elections and all were focused on day-to-day operations of the camp. A Scout could be elected to scribe, dining hall director, lost-and-found man, or postman. Occasionally, there were be an assistant scribe, a morning officer or an inspection director, but these four positions always remained. They were the heart of camp-wide operations.[42]

The scribe was first tested in 1922 with letters to the Nashville office, though they often were published in the newspaper. Under the new system, this pretense of "writing to the home office" was dropped: scribes wrote directly to the *Banner* or the *Tennessean*. Often the official scribe wrote to one paper and the assistant scribe the other. It was these articles that provided the greatest insight into life at camp. The scribes covered the elections, the games and tournaments played and who won, the visitors and the speakers who came to camp. They covered daily happenings, like a hike taken to Lost River Cave, treats such as ice cream or fresh peaches sent to the boys and enjoyed by the camp, and even the occasional (and literal) big fish story.[43]

The other positions were less flashy, but equally as important. The postman was exactly what it sounded like: he delivered the mail that arrived in camp and took care of the mail that was going out. He was the link to the outside world. The lost-and-found man, also known as the equipment man, was closely linked to the camp's athletic activities. Afternoons were not for advancement, but for games, such as horseshoes, baseball, tennis, and volleyball. Someone had to keep track of all the equipment used for the games and track down any components that vanished during use, like a baseball knocked out into the middle of nowhere. This was the job of the lost-and-found man. The dining hall director did not actually run the dining hall operations. Camp Cook Walter Whittaker handled those responsibilities. The dining hall director might better be labeled a "table caller." At each meal, he was the one who determined who got to eat first. When Whittaker's rolls, pancakes, or barbequed pork were on the menu, then who was allowed to eat first mattered. The above four positions were chosen at the first campfire from the entire group of Scouts attending Boxwell that particular week. A Scout who stayed two weeks, which happened fairly frequently, was eligible with each new week.[44]

The second set of elections was for a tent representative. Each representative could only be elected from his particular tent. As explained above, each tent held eight Scouts, so these were small elections. For a week of eighty Scouts, this would mean ten representatives to the tenters' council. Election to a camp-wide post did not guarantee election as a tent representative, but neither did it prevent holding a second office. Once elected, a tent representative had two responsibilities. The first was to manage the tent and prepare for inspections. The "tent leader" had to make sure his tent mates arrived on time to "Scout school" in the morning and meals during the day. He also had to insure that both the tent and the Scouts themselves were clean and orderly for the post-breakfast inspection, usually conducted by the adult leadership, often the camp medic and camp director.[45]

The second responsibility was to serve on the tenters' council, which was where the real power in this position was invested. The tenters' council held legislative, executive, and judicial power. In other words, it made the rules, it enforced the rules, and it judged violations of the rules. As the *Banner*

Scouts prepare for the morning tent inspection. Inspection included not only the tent and the area around the tent, but the boys themselves, all the way down to their fingernails. A Scout is Clean. Personal Collection of Harry "Beany" Elam.

explained in 1926,

> The camp is governed entirely by Boy Scouts, and not by the adult leaders. Each tent elects a councilman, and these twelve councilmen are the lawmaking body of the camp. They are possessed of full legislative, executive and judicial power, and from their decisions there is no appeal. Scoutmasters and those men who visit the camp are virtually one in the feeling that self-government at Camp Boxwell is more effective, more satisfactory and yet stricter than any possible government imposed by adult leaders.

The rules of the camp were laid out the beginning of the week to all the Scouts. From that point forward, the council met every morning after breakfast to review violations of said rules. The "council chamber" was beneath the shade of five "big beech trees" and doubled as "the guardhouse," essentially a jailhouse or penalty box for violating the rules after the council's decisions were made. Anderson, who attended these meetings "as chairman and advisor, had to interpose to keep the penalties from being too severe."[46]

As the above implies, the rules and the punishment for violation were not always commiserate, but both reflected the priorities of the camp. Some rules seemed trifling. "[N]o boy shall touch and play with the ropes on the flagpole." "It was decided that there would be a Sunday afternoon inspection and that twenty cents should be the limit spent for candy at the store in Linton." Other rules were more serious. In 1928, three Scouts were punished because "they had laughed and talked before reveille," a rule every summer. In 1924, the "thrice-weekly trips to the store were abolished" because two freezers of ice cream had arrived. Of less severity, but equal importance was a 1928 rule that changed the daily schedule, moving the inspection to before breakfast, and thereby providing the Waterfront Director Lallie Richter a longer period to work with beginning swimmers. And of course, some rules were not to be broken under circumstances. For instance, no one—Scout, leader, or visitor—was to swim without the permission and supervision of either the waterfront director or his staff. Further, no scout could attend camp without a health certificate "certifying that he carries no communicable disease."[47]

When violations occurred, punishment was meted out. Every morning after breakfast, the tenters' council reviewed the infractions of the previous day and decided on what actions to take. Generally, the principle punishment was spending time in the "guardhouse." Known as being "campused," the philosophy here was that making boys sit and watch the others have fun, unable to participate, unable to leave the guardhouse, was tortuous to those boys. The time here varied; it could be a half-day or a whole day. Suggestions for harsher punishment were sometimes discussed in council, but the guardhouse tended to be the primary solution. The primary exceptions were the sacrosanct rules. If a Scout had no health certificate, he could not step foot on the property. If a Scout violated the swimming rule, he was sent home. Fortunately, the existing record suggests that most infractions were small. It was common for a new boy unfamiliar with the process to test the boundaries of the rules, particularly the no talking after taps rule, the first night. Thus, the guardhouse was often full the early in the week, but it was decidedly less so as the week progressed.[48]

Good behavior was recognized as well. Anderson encouraged this personally with small rewards, such as the candy bars for killing fifty flies. However, as self-governance was critical here, rewards were necessary to reinforce the desired behavior. A tent that won the inspection for the day was awarded the honor flag, a literal representation of their success for all to see. The flag created a sense of rivalry. One tent wanted to keep the flag; all the others wanted to take it. Cleaner quarters and better personal hygiene from all resulted. Upon winning inspection for the week, the tent received an reward, perhaps ice cream or chocolate bars.[49]

There were also individual awards. Each week at the closing campfire, the Scouts held their final election. This time they chose the best of their peers. A scout could win one of several superlatives, which changed over the years, but all superlatives carried some sort of remembrance with it, such as a Scout knife. Possible categories included Best Scout of the Week, best spirit of brotherhood and service, best advancement performance, or even best story or stunt at campfire. As the years went by, the list stabilized. Best Scout of the Week, most popular and a most-runner up, and most advancement all became regular weekly achievements. Other awards came and went, but by 1926, these four were constants.[50]

Anderson's program of self-governance fulfilled the promises made about summer camp. In a letter sent out to parents before camp began in 1924, the Council Executive wrote that the summer camp had been so successful, "Nashville Council voted unanimously to make it a permanent feature as a contribution to the betterment of the boyhood of this city." Indeed, the very way Anderson spoke about camp changed. "Camp Boxwell is really a training school where scout tests are passed and scout ideals instilled by volunteer scout leaders of our city—those men who are giving freely of their time and talent to develop your boy into a strong and manly man. All of the hiking, the games and swimming are wholesome, healthful recreation. All this, however, is but a means to the end of character and development."[51]

And it was developing character—developing responsible citizens and men—that was at the heart of this "training school" program. Clearly, the elections modeled a citizen's responsibility to vote and to serve. The eight man tents with an elected leader was the patrol system, the foundation of a Scout troop. The rules and punishments created and acted upon by the tenters' council used the twelve-points of the Scout Law as an unwritten constitution. The awards given at the end of the week highlighted and rewarded exemplary behavior, the kind of behavior the adults wanted Scouts to emulate.

But there was even more here. Anderson only had advancement—"Scout school"—in the morning hours. There were no merit badges or Scouting education in the afternoon. This time was exclusively for recreation. In this sense, Anderson was also focusing on the core concerns that led to Scouting's creation, namely how to prepare boys for a new world. Outdoor Scout skills were taught, but these skills were less about the outdoors and more about self-motivation and independence. The skills taught a boy how to rely on himself. The afternoon recreation taught him the complementary lesson: how to work with others. It should be no surprise that most of the afternoon activities were team sports. In a modern world, not only did a man have to have confidence in his own abilities, but he had to be able to work with others. Modern bureaucracies required it.

Perhaps the most fundamental lesson here was that self-governance at Boxwell had both an overt and a covert agenda. The overt agenda was the government of the camp. The elections, the tenters' council, the rules and punishments were all outward expressions of the Scouts' abilities to govern each other. The covert agenda was that these same arrangements taught the boy to govern himself. If he wanted to avoid the punishment of the tenters' council, he had to exercise self-control. He had to govern his passions to do whatever he wanted. Self-government had a double meaning.

When Council President Edgar M. Foster died suddenly in 1926, Leslie G. Boxwell gave up his chairmanship of the Camping Committee. He became the Council's new President, a position he would hold for the next twenty-seven years. By this point though, Camp Boxwell had already changed. The camp may have been named for Leslie G. Boxwell, but the program of the camp—the training school—belonged to William J. Anderson.[52]

Linton's Heyday

As Anderson found his way with his program of self-government, his approach to camp changed too. Anderson wanted to make sure the camp experience was available to as many Scouts as possible. So, in 1923, the first year of self-government, the cost of camp dropped. Originally $5.25 per week, the cost of a week at Camp Boxwell dropped by more than a dollar to $4.20. Even more critical here was the fact that the cost dropped because the Council subsidized the cost. As Boxwell himself reported to *The Tennessean,* "The actual outlay is more than twice the amount paid in. The object of the camp is to build character and the opportunity is offered to parents and scouts to co-operate in making the final manhood. No Scout can afford to be denied this privilege." To make sure no Scout was denied the privilege of attending camp, the cost was made more reasonable.[53]

Attendance was further encouraged by the camp's registration process. Anderson tied camp's duration to registration. Instead of setting aside four weeks or six weeks, he continued to offer summer camp as long as he could get enough boys to fill a week. Remember that Scouts came as individuals, not with troops. Thus, an individual Scout stayed one week or two or, possibly, even three. Registration was simply to prevent overcrowding. However, preference was given to two groups. The first were Scouts who had not attended camp yet. Thus, a Scout could attend as many weeks as he desired, but if his return prevented a new Scout from attending, he was denied. The other preference was given to those Scouts who had to attend summer school. These Scouts received first week preference so they could complete their educations.[54]

Anderson's faith in the benefits of Scouting and his own program at Camp Boxwell led him to open the camp to those who most needed it most: reform school boys. The summer camp was available to the orphan boys of the Tennessee Industrial School (TIS), but by the late 1920s, Anderson also made the opportunity available to Scouts at the Tennessee State Agricultural and Training School at Jordonia, the state reform school. These Scouts often came the last week of camp, but they intermingled with non-reform school boys at camp. They participate in all the same activities and were given the same opportunities, rewards, and punishments as the other boys. Anderson would continue to make Camp Boxwell available to these Scouts for years to come, even as parents began to voice concerns. Reform school boys needed Boy Scout summer camp too.[55]

Once at camp, the options available to Scouts—reform or otherwise—for advancement seemed limitless. During the two hour block of time in the mornings dedicated to advancement or "instruction in scout work," specific merit badges were not identified or scheduled. The skills for the ranks of Tenderfoot, Second Class, and First Class were regularly offered, but the merit badge offerings shifted depending on what that particular set of boys needed on a given week. While having an adult leader available who was an expert in the field was definitely preferable, the idea of "certified instructors" was nonexistent here. Thus, the merit badges offerings were wide and varied. At the Linton Boxwell as Scout could take Athletics, Bird Study, Camping, Carpentry, Cement Work, Cooking, Electricity, Firemanship, First Aid, First Aid to Animals, Life Saving, Personal Health, Public Health, Safety, Swimming, Wood Carving, and Woodwork. And even this list was not exhaustive. If a need

Scouts on the waterfront at the Linton Boxwell. Over the years, Scouts added two diving boards and a slide. Personal collection of Harry "Beany" Elam.

arose, almost any merit badge could be taken.[56]

The most popular—and the most important—area of activity for Scouts was undeniably the waterfront. From 1922 forward, every summer the "swimming pool" on the South Harpeth River at Linton was overseen by Lallie Richter. Lallie's brother, Boos Richter, often assisted and the two men were accompanied by at least two other adults. According to Creighton, this group could "teach any one to swim." Like many of the adult staff at Camp Boxwell, the Richters had a Vanderbilt athletic connection, both playing basketball at the university and for the local Nashville team, the Terrors. A Hume-Fogg graduate, Lallie was considered one of the best basketball players ever produced in Nashville. He was apparently quite the swimming instructor as well. Scribes often reported that every Scout at camp that week learned to swim under his direction. And remember, the tenters' council voted to change the camp schedule to move morning inspection, allowing Richter more time to work with non-swimmers. His abilities were deeply trusted.[57]

The Richter waterfront had two interesting practices associated with it. The earliest was "the gauntlet." To mark the completion of swim time, a member of the waterfront staff yelled "All out!" He then counted to ten, by which time every Scout was to be out of the water. But if a Scout didn't get out fast enough, he had to endure "the spanking machine." This meant running up two lines of Scouts—a gauntlet—while get slapped on the buttocks by every boy who was already out. This practice was to let Scouts know that when the count of ten was reached, everyone had to be out.[58]

The second practice was less a local tradition and more a change in Scouting. In 1928, Lallie Richter introduced the "buddy system" to Camp Boxwell. The system was fairly simple. As both the *Tennessean* and the *Banner* explained at the time, "In this system scouts enter the pool in pairs and in consecutive numbers. Upon a given signal by the bugle at any moment the united hands of each pair are raised for inspection. A scout is charged with keeping ever in touch with his buddy. They are checked out together at the conclusion of the swim." Implemented nationwide that summer, the buddy system would be used at all iterations of Boxwell from that point forward.[59]

The nightly campfires also served an important function at camp. Quintessential parts of the camp experience, campfires were used for awards and elections. Campfires also served as a tool for Scouts to have fun. They could tell stories, sing songs, and show skills at these nightly events. Indeed, scouts sometimes boxed at campfires! These "special skills" campfires were called "stunts" and the "stunt night" campfires, which included skits as well, were quite popular with the boys.[60]

Campfires could also serve Anderson's program goals. With great regularity, prominent local citizens came to Camp Boxwell to give talks. Some of the speakers were athletes, some were Scouters, some were businessmen, some were world travelers; all were men. These men discussed places they had traveled. They discussed hunting and fishing. They discussed sporting tricks of the trade. Veterans discussed war and their experiences in the field. All of these presentations were quite literally "man-speak." Here was a very literal example of men talking to boys about being men and the kinds of things men did. In a world that feared boys becoming "soft" or unprepared for the bureaucratic world of industrialization, the campfire speakers provided very real templates on how to live and "be men" in this new world.[61]

It should be noted that while all of these program ideas certainly satisfied the adults, the Scouts themselves enjoyed Boxwell as well. The scribe submissions were filled with stories about adventures at camp. They took pride in the results of the elections and inspections. The reports spoke with admiration of the campfire speakers. Scouts also enjoyed the physical activities, including boxing matches, hiking, and exploring a local cave. There were pranks too. One tent would raid another tent, turning over beds. The attacked tent would retaliate. And of course, what Boy Scout camping experience would be complete without the time-honored tradition of snipe-hunting?[62]

The Tragedies of the Linton Boxwell

The first Camp Boxwell had many powerful aspects, but there were failings there as well. The self-government program did a superb job of training Scouts in the values necessary for navigating adult life, but there were two areas the program was of little value. The first area was the protection against nature; the second area was racism. Both of these failings of the program were tragedies, though for different reasons, and deserve attention.

By July of 1925, the attention of most Tennesseans and quite a few Americans was focused on the state, but not because of Camp Boxwell. In Dayton, Tennessee, local leaders had hatched a plan to drum up publicity for the town. To do so, they encouraged a local teacher, a man by the name of John Scopes, to break a new Tennessee law, known as the Butler Act, which prohibited the teaching of evolution. The media circus that erupted over the so-called "Monkey Trial" dominated newspaper and radio reports, bringing Dayton the notoriety it had desired, but perhaps not quite in the way it had intended. Since the end of June 1925, there had been little room in the headlines for anything other than the drama unfolding in Dayton.[63]

Thus, it was especially unsettling when an article showed up above the fold on the July 14th *Tennessean* titled, "Boy Scout Killed, Another Injured in Camp Boxwell." This was the first time Camp Boxwell had made the front page of the *Tennessean*. Unfortunately, the situation could not have been avoided. A strong storm came through the area on the first day of camp for week four. A new set of boys had arrived recently, specifically a group of sixteen from Gallatin, who were planning to stay two weeks. The storm downed trees in Linton and crippled phone service. At least one report said the storm was actually a tornado.[64]

Following the safety practices of the camp, Scouts sought shelter in the tents. The tents were not placed under any trees, but in a location to get the best shade from the trees. Regardless, the winds were strong enough to break off several branches. Many Scouts received cuts and bruises, even within the tents.[65]

Two Scouts from Gallatin were not so lucky. Thompson Brown and Samuel Lackey sheltered with six other boys when a strong wind carried a limb a short distance and through the roof of the tent. The impact from the limb was severe. Brown suffered two broken legs and a skull fracture. Lackey was knocked unconscious, suffering a fracture at the base of his skull and intestinal injuries. The injury occurred at approximately 4:30 in the afternoon. An ambulance rushed the boys to St. Thomas Hospital. Brown died on the operating table at 5:30 p.m. Meanwhile, Lackey was moved to an infirmary where he remained unconscious. While there was "some hope for his recovery," Lackey succumbed to his injuries and died the next day at 6:15 p.m. Both boys were fifteen years old.[66]

The flag at Camp Boxwell was flown at half-mast for the boys. Condolences and sympathy were extended. And program continued; elections were held. Nothing could have been done to avoid the deaths and reasonable precautions were taken. And while unavoidable, nothing changed the fact that Brown and Lackey became the first deaths at Camp Boxwell and the only ones at the Linton location.[67]

As tragic as these deaths were, they were out of the control of Anderson, his staff, and any adults on site. The other tragedy of the Linton Boxwell was wholly different. This was a tragedy of understanding, a betrayal of Scouting's ideals. So ingrained in the thinking of the camp and Scouting at the time, the blatant racism was scarcely even acknowledged as an issue.

As progressive as camp program was in many aspects, it was also decidedly backward in regard to race. Camp Boxwell was a segregated camp. There were no African-American troops that participated in camp life or attended the first Boxwell. In fact, the Nashville Council did not even officially organize any black troops *at all* until the 1930s. And even then, those troops were organized under a segregated division. None of this should be surprising. The period from 1890-1920 was called the "nadir of American race relations" by historian Rayford Logan because of the spread of segregation, disfranchisement, and lynching. Specifically, these years surrounding World War I were the same years when the Ku Klux Klan re-emerged and most Confederate monuments were built around the United States.[68]

Unfortunately, the national Scouting organization allowed this segregation. Officially, African American boys had been allowed to join Scouting since the very beginning. The reality, however, proved a bit more complicated in the South. As Chuck Wills explained in *Boy Scouts of America: A Centennial History,* "In the South, where the majority of African Americans lived at this time, Scouting was almost completely segregated... In some Southern communities, Scouts weren't even permitted to wear the uniform." Local councils were allowed "home rule" in much the same way education was handled. As historian Benjamin Rene' Jordan explains, "Local Councils could decide whether or how to admit African American boys and Scoutmasters, and... the national office would not charter African American troops governed by a Local Council." In the rural South, where many areas were not governed by a local council, very few African American troops existed or were ever recruited. This was clearly the case in middle Tennessee, where most of the area outside of Nashville was "unorganized" territory.[69]

At Camp Boxwell, there were no black Scouts or black troops, but there was Walter Whittaker, the lone black man. Whittaker, as mentioned above, was the head cook at Kissam Hall at Vanderbilt when he was recruited for summer work by L. G. Boxwell in 1921. His meals were the epitome of Southern cooking. While it was his rolls that became legendary, he prepared so much more. Pancakes, syrup, and cocoa were common. Dinner included cream peas, "old-style Southern stew (hash)," barbeque pork, lima beans, apple sauce, blackberry pie, and lemonade, though not usually all at one sitting. Scouts might help Whittaker with kitchen duties, such as cleaning pots and pans, but it was his kitchen and he was in charge there.[70]

Whittaker's influence extended beyond cooking; he was an integral part of camp life. At both campfires and the Sunday morning services, Whittaker sang songs. Usually "negro folk songs," Whittaker covered tunes such as "Hallelujah, Little David," "Swing Low, Sweet Chariot," and "Steal Away." But he also contributed in other ways. Whittaker participated in some of the camp games, most notably the horseshoe tournaments. He was unquestionably a visible camp personality.[71]

And yet, Whittaker was also clearly an "other." With few exceptions, Whittaker was almost always referred to simply as "Walter." While other men are given respect by listing either their full names or by giving the appropriate salutation, such as "Mr. Anderson," Whittaker did not receive this same consideration. And while Whittaker was often identified as "negro," this often was implied. By simply identifying him as "Walter, the cook" the message of his race was sent. Even Helen Dahnke's full page feature on Camp Boxwell and its program from 1927 failed to identify Whittaker's last name, but provided the full names of the white minors. Indeed, in at least one case, Whittaker's name was completely incorrect. He was identified as "the negro cook, Buford"! The camp scribes picked up on this convention as well as they too referred to Whittaker simply as "Walter," demonstrating that the practice was passed down to the next generation.[72]

And lest the mis-naming of Whittaker not seem enough to prove the inferiority of race in the eyes of the leaders and boys, one final anecdote demonstrates the ingrained belief. On June 23, 1928, camp scribe Edwin Bowden briefly reported on the events of the previous few days. One event was the Friday night campfire, which was a stunt night, a campfire where Scouts showcased their skills or participated in skits. This particular week third prize went to a tent that performed a "black-faced comedy stunt." Acting out racial stereotypes was not only part of accepted play around the campfire, it could also be rewarded.[73]

"Character Building and Citizenship Training"

The achievements of the Nashville Council in its first decade were impressive. Local leaders had formally created a council with a fund drive that exceeded its stated total. The new council had then hired a full time paid executive in William J. Anderson, the Vanderbilt track coach. Camping Committee Chairman L. G. Boxwell established the first council summer camp. So pleased was the Executive Committee of the Council with his work, the camp was named after Boxwell. But more importantly than all this, within a few years of the first summer, a program had been established as Camp Boxwell that promoted citizenship and prepared the Scouts to be men. There were

43

some issues, but the camp thrived. Camp Boxwell grew from the sixty Scouts a week for three weeks in 1921 to eighty Scouts a week for seven weeks in 1929.[74]

The final article on the 1929 summer at Linton sums up the first Boxwell's success well. There was not a single indication that this was to be the last summer at the Linton camp. So, barring some extreme circumstance, it seemed clear Camp Boxwell would return to Linton in 1930. No by-line was given, but the language suggested the author was Anderson himself:

> Completing one of the most successful camp seasons of the Nashville council, the scouts of Camp Boxwell broke camp Monday afternoon and returned to their respective homes and institutions.
>
> Character building and citizenship training are the prime objects of scouting and were especially to the forefront during every hour of the encampment.
>
> The high ideals of the scout obligation and of the twelve scout laws were kept before the scouts at all times and were in evidence at all times as the result of the position taken especially by the Boy Scout council at camp which is composed of twelve scouts who were selected by the fellows at the beginning of each period.
>
> In physical development the camp made a good record in teaching eighty-six to swim. These boys could not swim at all and left camp able to swim across the river and return.
>
> Other scouts developed their respective swimming abilities and were taught in rescue work and life saving so that they may be ready at all times to help anyone who may be in distress in the water.

Character building, citizenship, preparedness. Though not challenging the social values of the day concerning race, the summer camp program at Camp Boxwell at Linton fulfilled the promises of Scouting the new Nashville Council had promoted at its inception.[75]

A flag lowering at the Linton Boxwell, 1922. Published in the Nashville Banner, *July 30, 1922, page 4.*

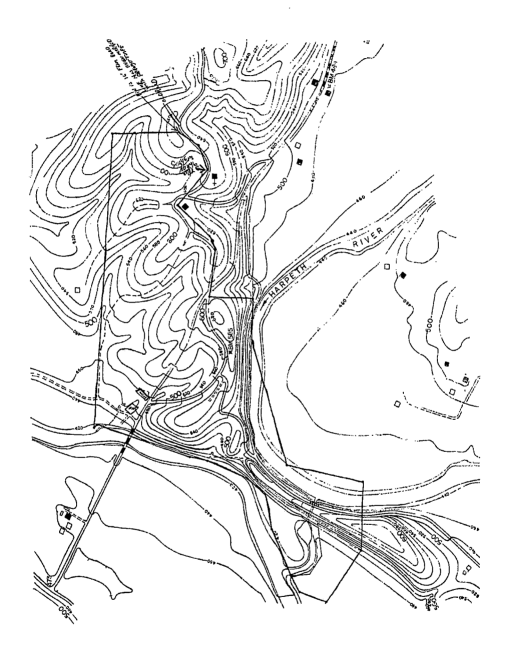

Narrows of the Harpeth Map, ca. 1942. Personal Collection of the author.

Chapter 2

Anderson's Boxwell:

Camp Boxwell at the Narrows of the Harpeth

1930-1948

On Wednesday evening, June 4, 1930, "Coach" William J. Anderson made a rather surprising announcement. After a successful run of almost a decade at Linton, Camp Boxwell would "be located at the Harpeth Narrows this summer." To ease any concern, Waterfront Director Lallie Richter was on hand to point out that the swimming facilities at the new location were "the best afforded in a radius of 35 miles of Nashville." Well known for the Montgomery Bell tunnel and the long loop for which the Narrows earned its name, the new site was provided to the Nashville council at no rental charge by John W. Blair, W. L. Lucas, and Justin "Jet" Potter. Construction would begin the following week so camp would be ready to begin on Monday, June 23. Camp Boxwell had a new home.[1]

To someone who had not been following the news very closely, Camp Boxwell's move may have seemed abrupt. After all, when the Boy Scout camp at Linton closed in July of 1929, it was declared "one of the most successful camp seasons of the Nashville council." However, between July 1929 and June 1930, quite a bit had happened. Linton was no longer the location to best serve Nashville's Scout population.[2]

47

The Roaring Twenties and the Great Depression

The Nashville Council's early years coincided with some favorable statewide circumstances. Austin Peay of Clarksville was elected governor in 1922 and brought with him important changes to education, transportation, and taxation. Peay's 1925 education reform funded an eight month academic year for public schools, "supplemented teacher salaries, [and] standardized teacher certification." Peay also championed a gasoline tax to fund road-building. There was a contentious battle for passage with opponents, such as Leslie G. Boxwell's Tennessee Good Roads Association, favoring a bond to fund construction. Peay's "pay-as-you-go" approach with the gasoline tax ultimately became law and allowed the creation of the state highway system. The decade began with a mere five hundred miles of paved roads statewide; by 1930, Tennessee had over six thousand miles of paved roads. Leslie G. Boxwell's culvert company was just one of many companies to benefit from this road-building boom.[3]

While the education reforms and the highway construction boom led to economic growth, other developments of modern life challenged Tennesseans' traditionalist social values. The state's urban population continued to grow as people from the country-side moved to the cities. This was true of African-Americans as well. While many moved north in a movement known as "The Great Migration" in the years following World War I, escaping racial violence and looking for new opportunities, many others remained. Local black leaders, such as James C. Napier in Nashville, emerged, largely due to their ability to mobilize voters. The passage of the Nineteenth Amendment in 1920 and the (failed) push for the first Equal Rights Amendment brought challenges to gender norms in the state. The most famous example though was the wide-spread support of both the Butler Act and William Jennings Bryan's prosecution of John Scopes. As mentioned previously, the Scopes Trial dominated headlines for weeks. Bryan became something of a Tennessee celebrity.

He had a regular column in the *Nashville Banner*, essentially sermon in print. When he died suddenly on July 26, 1925, virtually every article on the front pages of both the *Banner* and the *Nashville Tennessean* was devoted to covering his life or funeral.[4]

Perhaps one of the most interesting examples of the confluence of modernity and traditionalism in Tennessee was the rise of radio and country music. National Life and Accident Insurance operated in Tennessee and twenty other states. Edwin W. Craig, son of Cornelius Craig, co-founder of the company, saw radio as an "advantageous force" to promote the company. Inspired by a radio built for him by Jack DeWitt, Craig was determined to build a radio station. The fifth floor of the National Life Building in downtown Nashville on Seventh Avenue became the home to the new station, whose call letters were "WSM," which stood for a catchy insurance advertisement: "We Shield Millions." At the time, "radio broadcast signals were unlimited, and WSM transmitted to both coasts." Realizing the potential here, WSM tested a fiddle music broadcast in November 1925. The response was so strong the station began a regular "old time music program every Saturday night." The Grand Ole Opry, a Tennessee institution, was born. Of course, it should be noted that the Opry were designed "to increase life insurance sales to rural customers," a task at which it succeeded. Craig's combination of business and country music clearly spoke to Tennessee's traditionalism.[5]

All these developments benefitted mid-state Scouting. The education reforms provided a solid and consistent three month period in which a summer camp could operate. The creation of the state highway system also made it easier for Scouts outside of Nashville to attend summer camp. The traditional values of Tennesseans helped the overall program in the state grow, which meant more Scouts to camp. By 1925, Scouting in Nashville had "grown more rapidly than in any other city in of the South." When Anderson started as Council Executive in 1920, he had trouble finding a single whole troop. In fact, "only about 60 Scouts existed in his area at that time." Five years later,

49

the Nashville Council had grown to more 1,400 Scouts. The program was considered successful. Juvenile Court judge Barton Brown reported in 1925 that "there has not been a Boy Scout before the juvenile court this year." Indeed, Judge Brown went on, in the five years he had "served as judge of the juvenile court the Boy Scouts have been conspicuous by their absence."[6]

The success was not limited to Nashville. In June of 1927, a new Council formed. Composed of troops in Murfreesboro, Tullahoma, Winchester, Shelbyville, McMinnville and the areas in between, the Davy Crockett Council would serve five counties. Later that same year, in December of 1927, the first Middle Tennessee Council formed. This council served the towns of Clarksville, Columbia, Dickson, and Lebanon. Middle Tennessee was completely organized by the end of the decade. Scouting was growing.[7]

And then, three months after the Scouts left Camp Boxwell in 1929, the Great Stock Market Crash shook financial markets. The equivalent of $30 billion was lost as the markets bottomed out. Historian Eric Foner summarized the financial impact: "By 1932, the gross national product had fallen by one-third, prices by nearly half, and over 15 million Americans—25 percent of the labor force—could not find work. For those who retained their jobs, wages fell precipitously; not until 1940 would they regain the level of 1929." Historian Lawrence Levine focused on the equally powerful psychological shock, writing, "Probably no people is ever really prepared for major economic crisis. But it would be difficult to find a nation as unprepared as the United States was in 1929." From Hoover-villes and Hoover blankets to Dorthea Lange's "Migrant Mother," the stories of loss and hardship in this period are legion. But while the nation-wide calamity is fairly well known, both Scouting and Tennessee had their own unique problems.[8]

For Tennessee, the Great Depression accelerated some changes that were already underway. The need for jobs brought even more white people from rural areas to industrial centers and urban areas; the black population actually declined as more African Americans looked for work in the North or West. In 1932 alone, 578 businesses in the state failed. Some teachers were paid in scrip, not currency, while "[i]n the countryside, people dug ginseng or sold walnuts to make a little extra income." For a predominately agricultural state, owning land—not tenant farming—was the key to survival.[9]

Tennessee was particularly hurt by the collapse of the Caldwell and Company banks in 1930. The failure of these banks "liquidated the saving of thousands of depositors and $7 million in state funds." Caldwell banks had floated bonds to the state to continue funding road construction after Governor Henry Horton moved from taxes to bonds to finance this project development. When the Caldwell banks collapsed and the deposits of the state were lost, there was a movement to impeach Governor Horton on the idea that he had conspired with Rogers Caldwell and his associates to defraud the state. The movement ultimately failed, but the damage to the state was done. For those involved in road-building contracts with the state, recovery would take years.[10]

For the Boy Scouts of America (BSA) itself, the Depression created hardships for both local councils and the national organization. Locally, the financial situation made it difficult for Scouts to buy uniforms or pay dues or even go to summer camp. The costs were just too high. Nationwide, "many professional Scouters in local councils couldn't get paid at all as banks failed across the nation. According to some accounts, professional Scouters in urban areas took to selling apples, pencils, or matches on the street to survive." Professional Scouters at the national organization took a 15% pay cut. Still, the organization put its best face forward. In the BSA's 22nd Annual Report to Congress in 1931, Chief Scout Executive James West wrote, "In certain sections of the country there have been reductions in budgets and personnel, but generally speaking, there is evidence of determination on the part of the community to maintain the standards of scouting in the face of all obstacles."[11]

The Great Depression affected the Nashville Council as well. Funding for the council through the Community Chest (today's United Way) fell by half. Some Nashville Scouts could not afford a handbook or registration fees as their fathers were unemployed. Anderson fell back on his track coach salary to support himself and his family. Leslie Boxwell had difficulties as well. As Anderson recalled years later, Boxwell's "business was facing the rocks and darkness lay only two months ahead, [however] his means and service to Scouting did not falter." Boxwell likely found himself in dire straits after the failure of the Caldwell and Company banks. While the Tennessee Metal Culvert Company would recover by securing contracts from the Tennessee Valley Authority (TVA) in 1935, these were lean years. One story even suggests that Boxwell and E. E. Murrey, Council treasurer, took out personal loans to guarantee summer camp opened during these years. Given the low enrollments—only four weeks of scouts—in 1932 and 1933, this story is likely rooted in truth.[12]

Camp Boxwell at Linton was affected by all of these developments as well. The road building boom of the Twenties led to the straightening of Harding Road, now known as Highway 100. This new road required a new bridge. Completed in 1929, the Highway 100 bridge over the South Harpeth River moved down river approximately 200 hundred yards or more and into the four acres used by Boxwell. The site likely could still be used or slightly moved, but the new bridge surely created a problem.[13]

The more critical event occurred just days before Anderson's announcement on June 4. A little over one week earlier on Tuesday, May 27, 1930, Anderson met with representatives of the Middle Tennessee and Davy Crockett Councils. The point of the meeting was "to consolidate or devise means whereby the Davy Crockett council and the Middle Tennessee area councils could be brought under the supervision of the Nashville Council B. S. A." While the ensuing negotiations lasted several months, an agreement with these collapsed councils was finalized in November. The Nashville Council would absorb the councils and its new service area would now include thirty-five counties, making it one of the largest Scout councils in the nation.[14]

Absorbing new councils though would mean that the little four acre loaner camp on the South Harpeth River wasn't going to be enough anymore. Indeed, given the increased service area, even a single camp might not be enough. Those councils and Scouts to the West of Nashville had used Camp Lupton in Dickson, near Ruskin Cave. The Scouts could fairly easily move to a Nashville camp, if it was centrally located. For Scouts to the east of Nashville, especially as far east as McMinnville, Camp Boxwell at Linton was simply too far away, even with the state's improved roads. The Davy Crockett Council had maintained a camp in Manchester on the Duck River called Camp Fisher, which generally ran for two weeks. After the merger, the Nashville Council maintained Camp Fisher for these Scouts in 1931 and 1932. But should there be any question, the Executive Committee recognized the "other approved scouts camps in the territory," but Camp Boxwell was the "central camp." By 1933, Fisher was closed and only the "new" Camp Boxwell at the Narrows of the Harpeth remained.[15]

Camp Boxwell at the Narrows of the Harpeth

The "new" Boxwell came courtesy of Justin Potter. Potter was, in many ways, the poster child for Scouting values. Known by his nickname "Jet," Potter started his career working for his father as a bank clerk for $45 a month. At the time of his death, he was a "a multimillionaire Nashville insurance executive, industrialist and financier… one of the wealthiest men in the South." Known for speaking his mind and his sense of humor, he was also described as "the epitome of rugged individualism," both in terms of personality and "physical type." He was conservative and frugal, both in politics and personal living. He stayed in inexpensive hotels when he traveled and opposed high executive salaries, stock options, and unions. Potter attended Hume-Fogg and then Vanderbilt and served in the First World War as a second lieutenant in the Air Corps. He started the Nashville Coal Company in 1920 and retired for the first time in 1938, at 40, already a millionaire. He sought his second fortune by diving back into coal in 1938 and took great pride none of his mines ever organized into a union. It is unclear how Potter came into possession of the Narrows property, but he offered the site to the Council free of charge in June of 1930. He would eventually sell the property to the Nashville Council in 1944, allowing the Council to actually own their summer camp outright.[16]

Located in Cheatham County in the Kingston Springs area, the Narrows of the Harpeth were not far from the Linton location, but the two sites were quite different. Whereas the Linton Boxwell had covered only four acres, the Narrows Boxwell covered 105, encompassing impressive sites for Scouts to utilize. The most striking of these were the Harpeth Narrows themselves—an approximately five-mile bend in the Harpeth River where the river winds back so that it is only separated from itself by a few hundred feet. So close is the narrowest point that in 1818 the property's original owner, a slave owner named Montgomery Bell, had his slaves dig out a 288 foot tunnel. The tunnel not only connected the two sides of the river, but the waterfall from the tunnel powered an iron foundry. The foundry was long gone by 1930, but the tunnel remained and Scouts and visitors alike regularly climbed all over it and had their photos taken on it. The hilltop Montgomery Bell mansion remained as well, in ruins after a fire in 1929, but it was still there. It was a regular hiking destination as well the site of the campfire circle.[17]

While the bluffs made by the Narrows themselves were the most impressive part of the property, most of the camp was actually located to the north and east of the oxbow and the tunnel. Approximately 2oo yards down the river from the Montgomery Bell tunnel a Scout would find the waterfront. Steep banks dropped into the river. The Waterfront itself was easily identifiable by two small docks, both anchored to logs underneath. Here a Scout would learn swimming and lifesaving merit badges as well as canoeing. Recreational

The Montgomery Bell Tunnel at the Narrows of the Harpeth was just one of the many features that made this camp exciting for the Scouts. Personal collection of Harry "Beany" Elam.

swim was frequent and wildly popular.[18]

Once the Scout crawled out of the river onto the wooden docks, he climbed the wooden stairs up the embankment onto a plain above the river. Directly before him was a small hill with a plateau about mid-way up to the ridge. To his left, a dirt road circled the hill and disappeared. As he began his slow ascent, on the first small plateau he would find a volleyball court and the dining hall, a mostly permanent building. Creighton's *Boys Will Be Men* described the dining hall as having "a sawdust floor and a roof of canvas stretched over the rafters." Olpha E. ("O.E.") Brandon, Jr., a Scout at camp in 1937 and a staff member from 1938 through 1940, gave a detailed description of this first dining hall, now covered by wooden shingles:

> The dining hall was about 40 feet by 80 feet with a first
> floor covered with saw dust, but was strongly constructed
> from rough-sawed lumber. The kitchen was built on to the
> dining hall, and I believe also had a dirt floor. In the por-
> tion of the building used as a kitchen there was a large stor-

age closet and a large walk-in ice box. The stove was mainly heated by coal... The outside of the dining hall was covered with boards flat on one side and back on the other up
to about five feet from the ground. The area above the
wood was screen, but could not be closed.

This dining hall would be replaced in 1940 with a newer building further up
the hill on the ridge, but this structure would remain, becoming a craft shop
for summer 1941.[19]

On the other side of the hill was a clearing, which served as the heart
of the camp. There was the flag pole, of course, and the accompanying parade
grounds. Flag ceremonies—complete with a de-limbed tree as a flagpole--were
held here as well as the morning calisthenics. The baseball field was located
here as well as and camp tents, which peppered the area in a variety of configu-
rations. Along the backside of the clearing was the dirt road, "Boy Scout
Road," which ran up a second, much longer, steeper hill to the entrance of the
camp. Frequently the tents would be placed in the parade ground area encircling the flagpole. However, some summers found the tents placed in pairs or
occasionally even split into two large groups: one group of tents up the second
hill opposite the dining halls while the other was in the valley around the flagpole. Regardless of placement, gone were the white single upright World War
I surplus tents, for by 1930 the camp had moved to large green walled tents,
each still housing eight Scouts.[20]

Gallatin, Tennessee resident Tom Neal attended the Narrows Boxwell
in 1945. He was thirteen years old that summer, attending the same week that
the United States dropped the atomic bomb on Hiroshima to end the Second
World War. He recounted the basics of Camp Boxwell this way:

[W]e lived in tents, like an eight man army tent. I don't
know if that was a surplus they got somewhere, but most
all of us were in eight man tents. There was no wooden
floors in them like they do nowadays when they have tents
that have floors; it was just the dirt. And unfortunately,

where our tent was we didn't know how to properly pitch
the tent and we had a heck of a rain one night and it about
washed all of us away. We just had regular army cots and
army blankets; that's all we had. We didn't have sleeping
bags. That was something unheard of back then.

According to Neal, it rained a lot during his week that summer, giving he and
his tent mates plenty of practice in pitching the tent to withstand "a heck of a
rain.[21]

The Narrows Boxwell had more to offer than just what was encompassed by the 105 acres boundary line. There were caves about four miles
from the camp. Even closer, about two miles away, was a Native American
Mound site, Mound Bottoms, which dated back to the Mississippian period as
well as a small graveyard, dating back to the late 19th century. All made excellent hiking destinations. One final spot of great interest to Scouts was a
swinging bridge. Located near the tunnel, upriver from the waterfront, the
bridge was essentially a monkey bridge made of wire with wooden planks to
walk upon and wooden steps leading to it. E. D. Thompson, a Scout at the
Narrows in 1937, recounted crossing the bridge as both terrifying and as a
badge of honor. Even at 93 years old, Thompson's tale of the bridge and his
sister still stuck with him.

And so whenever anyone went to camp, they had to try
that swinging bridge. I mean, you were an idiot if you did-
n't at least try it, you know? And I did it. But that son of
a... it swang. I mean, you'd better hang on. All you got is
a wire over there. You better hang on for dear life. And
it's scary. And every step you take that thing swings, you
know. And so, my sister decided she would try to go
across it and so she did, screaming all the way, from the
one side of the river to the other. And she made it somehow by the hardest [effort]... Oh Lord. But when it came
time to go back across the bridge, she said, "No, I'm not
going on that thing again." And so, [staff member] Ed
Fitzwater, who they called "Doc Fitzwater"-- he was the

dentist in UT and working on his dental degree. And so, he told her... that's when he met her... he says, "I'll go down and get a canoe and come across and get you." That's where my sister and Ed Fitzwater met and they married about a year later! He became my brother-in-law! But he got the canoe and came back and got her and took [her] back over. She wasn't going to cross again. But everybody had to try the swinging bridge and I did too.[22]

Setting aside the differences in the physical layout and facilities, much about the Narrows Boxwell was the same as the Linton Boxwell. Scouts in Nashville still congregated at the intersection of Belle Meade and Harding Road to be picked up by one of L. G. Boxwell's trucks and then taken to camp. The boys sometimes played mumbledy-peg, a knife throwing game, while they waited. L. G. Boxwell often drove the truck himself and Anderson often came along to take care of paperwork. If a Scout did not live in Nashville, he took whatever means were available to get to camp. Billy Walker of Franklin attended Camp Boxwell in 1942 and 1943; he went to camp in the back of a milk truck! Upon arriving at the new camp, there was "a mad rush for tents." Scouts changed clothes and immediately made their way to the river for swimming. Had a Scout attended Linton in 1929 and the Narrows in 1930, he would have found a great many remarkable similarities.[23]

Indeed, in terms of program, this was still very much William Anderson's Boxwell. The program of self-government that developed at Linton was simple transplanted to the new location. Self-government still meant governing the group and governing the individual. For Anderson, boys needed habits. From birth, a boy was "a rank individualist," caring about none but himself. But engaging in good habits and surrounding him with good people, would teach the child to be a good man. Traditional formal education was not enough to accomplish this goal; home, church, and Scouting provided the extra elements needed. Raise a good citizen and a good man by keeping the boy engaged and filling his life with good habits and positive examples. The program at Linton served these goals and therefore the program at the Narrows did the same.[24]

It was at the Narrows that Anderson's approach stabilized and ma-tured. The elected positions—dining hall director, postmaster, lost-and-found man, scribe, tent leader, and councilmen—were all here. The council chamber came along too, and though clearly it could no longer be situated in the grove of beech trees, it remained "in a shady part of the campus." The tenters' council still made the rules that governed the camp. The advancement portion of the camp, now called "Scout School" by the boys, still only lasted the morning hours, while afternoons were still dominated by sports and evenings by campfires. The last night of camp was an awards campfire, which included elections Most Popular, Most Popular Scout runner up (now known as the "Camp Wit"), and Best All-Around Scout. And all of this continued to be offered to Scouts for the very reasonable cost of $4.50 a week. A small price to pay to save boys from a life of crime and juvenile delinquency![25]

Two aspects of Anderson's Boxwell program deserve further attention here. Advancement was important part of Scouting and so Scout school was first thing in the morning every morning. But as mentioned above, Anderson believed there was more to learning than a formal education: good habits mattered. In fact, habits "influence us materially in accepting the code of honor prevailing in our country and the mandates of our moral order. Habit is that complement to our learning that makes us what we are." So, while Scout school mattered, there were other habits Anderson needed his camp program to model: the Sunday service and the group athletic activities.[26]

Often held under "the big sycamore tree," Boxwell's religious services were simple events. A staple of these services was sentence prayers, short simple statements expressing faith, making a request, or giving praise. One such prayer in 1940 had Scouts expressing "their gratitude for the privilege of living in a country free from the murder, plunder, and ravages or war." These prayers were often led by a Scout, as was a Scripture reading. Occasionally, twelve different Scouts would each recite and explain one of the twelve points of the Scout Law, not just the 12th Point, "A Scout is Reverent." Walter Whittaker, the African American camp cook, sang a song or two. There might be a doxology or some informal preaching. The conclusion of the hour usually brought a sermon from Anderson himself. For just about every year that Anderson operated Camp Boxwell, a week of camp always extended through a Sunday. There would be years when the summer schedule would change, but Scouts were <u>always</u> at camp on Sunday morning. So important were the Sunday services to this program of character building that it was the only event for which Scout School was suspended.[27]

The Council Executive saw Scouting and Christianity as tightly interwoven. God had given man "the knowledge of right and wrong, of helpfulness, unselfishness and brotherhood." In fact, "[t]he principles of the Boy Scout plan were announced by the Great Scoutmaster in the Sermon on the Mount and brought down to the boy's understanding and acceptance in the Scout oath and law." Therefore, when a Scout recited the Scout Oath, he proclaimed to "help other people at all times"—a modern interpretation of "the greatest commandment [which] calls for love of my neighbor, proven in service." And it was only through service—a "sacred assignment"—that a person could be great. And these boys could be great. Reflecting on the evils the world had witnessed, Anderson wrote, "In all of my intimate contacts of Jews, Catholics and Protestants, mingling in the same church basement or Scout troop cabin, or at Camp Boxwell, I have never yet seen or heard of the slightest act or thought of intolerance or of the minutest feeling directed toward a Scout or any other person of different faith. Jesus followed this way of life, not yet traveled fully by grown-ups, but definitely traversed by Boy Scouts." As above, youth, properly educated with good habits, would secure the future. Thus, when Anderson wrote in 1940 that the effectiveness of the hour long religious service at Camp Boxwell was "probably not surpassed in any other [hour] throughout the year," he meant it.[28]

Equally critical for the development of men was athletic competition. "[W]e believe that an abundance of wholesome fun is one of the divine prerogatives of boyhood," Anderson wrote in 1941. "All the physical activities at Camp Boxwell and in scouting are merely the means toward the attainment of ideals and the development of character." In other words, keeping a boy busy through physical activity should not be misinterpreted as simply playing games; this was training too. Anderson continued, "Men of scouting are convinced that the only successful way to keep evil out of lives is by filling them full of those things which are pure and wholesome." It was during the hours of leisure—those periods of unstructured time outside school and the home—when a boy would get into trouble and begin down the wrong path.[29]

And so, the afternoons were packed full of wholesome activities. Some activities were advancement related. There were hikes to caves, to the Narrows and the Montgomery Bell Tunnel, to the Mounds, and just out and about to do bird study. There was also boating and swimming in the afternoon occasionally. Advancement activities were important, but for the most part afternoons were filled with competitive sports.[30]

There were a number of games played at Camp Boxwell and they were organized in a number of different ways. Scouts at camp participated in baseball, volleyball, horseshoes, "kitten ball" (softball), and track events (perhaps not surprising given Anderson's other day job). The games were important events as the camp was generally divided into teams. Sometimes it was the "Hilltoppers" versus the "Valley"—how the tents were arranged—and sometimes it was the Scouts against the adult staff. Sometimes the camp played local community teams. There were a myriad of combinations. Generally though, the games were team related and/or multi-game tournaments. Perhaps one of the most important aspects to these games to remember was that the adults were very much involved. Anderson pitched at baseball games and at horseshoes. He sometimes led one team against another team led by another staff member. Camp Cook Walter Whittaker was also often involved in the horseshoe tournaments.[31]

The best combination of competition and Scout skills came on the last day of camp at the water carnival. The water carnival was quite an event, involving a number of different boating and swimming events. There were the expected swimming races, such as the fifty yard backstroke and fifty yard "dash." The canoe races were a highlight though. The Scouts would race canoes in a variety of combinations. There was a quarter mile small canoe race, a 220 yard one man canoe race, a canoe race without paddle, and a "tail race," where a Scout in the bow of the boat paddled backward with the tail of the canoe upstream. Perhaps the most exciting races though involved the "war canoes." The camp owned at least two of these large canoes. The canoes held one man in the bow and one in the stern, but four pairs in between. War Canoe races—all of the races—from the Waterfront were crowd pleasers. Area locals and parents often came to observe the water carnival, with the boys showcasing their skills and teamwork. As one scribe observed, on race day, the air was filled with "[t]he exciting scream of the visiting mothers" who were cheering on their sons.[32]

The waterfront was extremely popular with Scouts. For starters, Swimming, Life-saving, and Canoeing were all taught at the waterfront. But the importance of safety was not lost here. One of the long standing rules by the tenters' council was that a Scout—or anyone—could not swim without supervision of the waterfront staff, attesting to how much Scouts wanted to be in the water. The waterfront also used the Buddy System, a requirement of the National Boy Scouts since the 1920s. A Scout had to enter the water with a "buddy," and the two were to stay together at all times. When a signal was given, the buddies had to demonstrate they were together by holding up their united hands. Billy Walker learned to swim at the Narrows Boxwell and remembered "they had supervision from the canoes… as well as right with you in the water." Here was playtime, coupled with team-building and advancement.[33]

Scribes and attendees of the camp constantly mentioned the waterfront, especially Lifesaving merit badge. Frank Sutton, who would portray the character "Sergeant Carter" in the television series *Gomer Pyle, U.S.M.C.*, was a member of Troop 34 from Clarksville, and a camp scribe. He earned his Lifesaving Merit Badge at the Narrows in 1937. E. D. Thompson was a Scout who attended Camp Boxwell the same summer as Sutton, so their experiences were likely similar. As Thompson recalls,

> To work on the lifesaving merit badge, [Waterfront Director Talmadge Miller would] have us swim the width of the river and it's not too narrow right there if you remember. But we'd have to swim the width of the river and then we'd bring somebody... he'd teach us how to carry 'em and get 'em back to shore and all that. But the final day, on the exam day or graduation day, whatever, it was kind of funny, because then you had to jump in the water with your clothes on and your shoes. And then underwater, you'd take your clothes off and your shoes. I'm the one who got the shoes in a knot, but I stayed with it until I got the shoes off. And then we only had to swim HALF way out in the Harpeth and bring somebody back. And we told everybody, Oh, that's a piece of cake! We've been swimming the width of the river all summer. Now all we have to do is go halfway and bring somebody in. So that's no problem. I was surprised to get that lifesaving badge.

Tom Neal's experience was a bit more harrowing. Because of all the rain his week, the river was up and running swiftly. Still, he took Lifesaving Merit Badge at camp.

> And one of the exercises for lifesaving was, your partner had to approach you from the back and grab you, so you couldn't get loose and you have to figure how to get loose from 'em. Well, went down to the bottom of the river that guy grabbed me, wasn't going to turn loose. I thought I was going to drown down there. I like to never gotten loose from that guy. I finally, finally got loose and came back up.

*Like Linton, the waterfront at the Narrow was extremely popular. In the top photo,
Scouts take a morning swim. The bottom photo show the original waterfront docks.
Top Photo from Nashville Tennessean, July 22, 1934; Bottom Photo from The
Bugle, the Nashville Council Newsletter, Vol. I, No. I, October, 1938.*

I told him that you're taking this too seriously! You almost drowned me! But I did, I did get the merit badge for that. And I remember that the water was really, really cold.[34]

Of course, the waterfront was not the only area with exciting elements to it. Apparently, snakes were also wildly popular with Scouts and the Narrows Boxwell was covered in the reptiles. A regular adult instructor was the Reverend Alonzo C. Adamz of Tracy City. Known as "the Apostle of the Mountain," Reptile Study was the reverend's specialty. In fact, back home he had a huge personal museum with 100,000 specimens of snakes, crocodiles, turtles, and more. Scouts were fascinated by the man and his "unholy fascination" for snakes. He often caught rattlesnakes bare-handed and conducted regular "snake hikes" while at camp. Junior Staff member O. E. Brandon had some vivid memories of Adamz, writing,

> He came frequently to our camp to collect specimens and to collect snake venom to be sold for making antivenom shots. He would notify loggers cutting timber in the vicinity of the camp when he came for a stay. When the logging crews ran across a poisonous snake in the woods they would send a man in a truck to notify Father Adamz while the other loggers using sticks kept the snake from getting away. The Father would jump in his car, usually taking one of us with him, and follow the truck driver to where the snake was. By the time he got there a crowd would have gathered to see "that crazy priest" handle the poisonous snake. Father Adamz would put on a good show, catching and milking the snake. He would bring the snake alive and the little vial of venom back to the camp. He put the venom vial in a box in the camp ice box, being careful that Walter Whittaker, the black camp head cook, did not know what was in the box. Walter was deathly afraid of snakes, and as a result was the object of many jokes.

Unfortunately for Whittaker, snake dinners were an advertised part of the Boxwell experience! James Gribble, Camp Director in 1938, promised "scouts will have several snake dinners at Camp Boxwell this summer as a result of the

Rev. Adamz's hunting trips." Indeed, according to E. D. Thompson, Gribble was fascinated with snakes himself. Upon finding a ten foot rattlesnake on a hike, Gribble "put us all in a circle out there, around this rattle snake, out in the middle of us. And he was explaining to us about poisonous and non-poisonous; poisonous snake has fangs; non-poisonous has the... little half-circle of teeth." Gribble killed the snake and gave it to Whittaker to cook. Anyone who wanted a bite could try it. Wholesome fun and adventure, indeed![35]

To deliver all this "wholesome fun" required a staff and, as with Linton, Anderson staffed Camp Boxwell at the Narrows with men of character, exemplars of the values he was trying to teach. And, as with Linton, the Narrows had a fairly stable set of individuals who returned every summer to assist with the camp program. While a few men were paid to work all summer, most of these individuals were volunteers, Scoutmasters who came up for a week or more to help deliver instruction, like Rev. Adamz. Not all volunteers were Scoutmasters though. John Caldwell of the State Department of Conservation came out and taught conservation. Therefore, there was a variety of instruction and options throughout the summer.[36]

Another noteworthy and regular volunteer was Harry "Beany" Elam of Springfield, TN, Scoutmaster of Troop 144. He was the secretary-treasurer of the Springfield woolen mill during his professional life, but it would be hard to call this his passion. From at least 1937 forward, Elam was a fixture at Camp Boxwell. And he would have been hard to miss. A tall, lanky bespectacled man, Elam had a powerful sense of humor and sense of dedication to his Scouts. Indeed, his nickname "Beany" was a grade school sobriquet; he was known as "Bean Pole," which was shortened to "Beany," a name Elam enjoyed and kept. A friend of his once said, "He's the funniest fellow you ever saw, but he's terribly serious too. He'd sit up all night to play a joke on somebody. *And he'd do the same thing to encourage a wayward boy to return* to school or a backslider to go back to church." When he heard that some Scouts at camp needed blankets, Elam sent a box of blankets. Additionally, the man was an exceptional artist. He was constantly sketching, often caricatures, but always something uplifting and personal. This artistic and positive approach was an aspect of adulthood a Scout could enjoy that was not replicated anywhere else. "Manhood" could take many different shapes.[37]

Most of the paid staff made up the camp leadership. Many of these individuals came from Anderson's Vanderbilt connections. It was not uncommon to have an athletic or activities director who was a member of Anderson's track team. The camp medic also often came from Vanderbilt connections, usually a medical student, often also with a track connection. Occasionally, one of the paid staff would not be directly connected to Vanderbilt. Ed Fitzwater, who had been a camper at Linton, was one such individual. As mentioned in Thompson's anecdote above, Fitzwater was working on his dental degree at the University of Tennessee when he returned to Camp Boxwell in 1935. He stayed on through 1937, when he met Thompson's sister. The rest, as they say, is history.[38]

Aside from Whittaker, the longest serving paid staff member at the Narrows was Talmadge Miller. A teacher and later principal in the Davidson County school system, Miller became the long-standing Waterfront Director, following in the tradition of Lallie Richter. Richter had worked the first summer at the Narrows, but either because of the move or because he married earlier in the year, he did not return after 1930. Talmadge Miller was a Scoutmaster of Troop 18 and Red Cross certified in lifesaving and first aid. He served most summers as Waterfront Director or Camp Director from 1932 until 1947. In 1943, Miller became Assistant Scout Executive, providing Anderson with some needed help managing the growing council.[39]

Miller provided additional character for the camp. First and foremost, he was a teacher, and apparently a good one. One article described Miller this way: "He is sympathetic, has a rare understanding of youth and is service minded." Often seen around camp in his uniform of a white tank top, shorts with a belt, and low rise socks and shoes, Miller brought a competitive spirit to Boxwell. He often pitched horseshoes with and against Anderson and did the same with baseball. Scribe Scobey Rogers expressed great surprise in 1933 when, for the first time in Boxwell's history, the team of Anderson and Miller won a horseshoe tournament. "This winning team," the scribe wrote, "was a surprise to the entire camp because it is evident that the executive [Anderson] and camp director [Miller] cannot pitch horseshoes. The adult leaders and 80 scouts felt that an unusual line of luck brought the combination out on top. The pitchers alone call it science." As frequent waterfront director, Miller often made sure Scouts who completed Red Cross lifesaving and swimming requirements were added to the honors list at the final awards campfire. And, for reasons that are never explained, Miller often raised chickens at camp. Miller appeared the embodiment of the wholesome fun approach to Scouting.[40]

Improvements and Challenges at the Narrows

Self-government and "wholesome fun" were Anderson's guiding principles for his summer camp program and clearly these ideas carried over from Linton. However, there were significant ways that Camp Boxwell at the Narrows differed from the Linton Boxwell while still using the same basic program. The water carnival was one example of using the same principles, but applying them to the unique surroundings and circumstances of the Narrows of the Harpeth. Some differences though had very little—if anything—to do with the natural environment and were in fact just program differences that changed with time.

Campfires were an excellent example of these program changes. As at Linton, campfires at the Narrows were a nightly event with a center piece being the adult male speaker, modelling "a man's life" with stories and wisdom. These male guest speakers were fairly common in 1930 and 1931, but after 1932, the mention of speakers in the scribe reports was few and far between. While there were still some speakers, they were no longer a regular feature after

1931. Also, as apparently part of a "new and attractive campfire program" instituted in 1934, every night the campfire revolved around a different theme. There was of course the election campfire at the start of the week and the awards campfire at the end, but in between were some rather eclectic themes. There were two campfires for story telling as well one for wrestling or boxing matches. One campfire was for the "Indian pow-wow," which was essentially a Native American themed campfire with Native American dancing and legends. As the Order of the Arrow (OA) grew, these nights became more elaborate (see below). There was finally a campfire called "stunt night," where Scouts showcased their talents, or "stunts."[41]

Some changes were less advertised, but arguably still mission critical. For instance, tents were no longer simply referred to by a number. Previously, when a tent had won an inspection, the tent was referred to as "Tent no. 8" or "Tent 3." Clear, but hardly personal. Starting around 1932, the Scouts began naming their tents. Not surprisingly, the names varied wildly from "Cooties" to "Eagle Lodge." While at first blush this might not seem significant, it was actually an important organizational change. By no longer thinking of the tents as simply groups of boys who stayed together for a week, naming the tents was actually naming the patrol. The tent leader then became the patrol leader. A simple shift in approach not only added another level of self-government, but brought the program even more clearly in line with Scouting principles and organization. It also made the experience more personal and fun for the Scouts.[42]

The most significant changes to the program were to the self-government dimensions of Camp Boxwell. The basic approach of the tenters' council—now arguably a Patrol Leaders' Council—was the same as before. The Scouts made the rules and there were punishments when those rules were violated. Infractions of the rules at Linton had resulted in time served in the "guardhouse"; at the Narrows, this practice quickly fell away. Time served was replaced with another idea that was far more in keeping with Scouting principles: service. For instance, on July 6, 1931, a scribe reported that there had been many violations of camp rules, resulting in "141 hours duty" for the coming week. Another scribe reported that the hours to be completed by violators would be "work helpful to the campers." Examples included "toting rocks, building fires, [and] peeling potatoes."[43]

This change to service was accompanied by another democratic necessity that had previously been missing: an appeals process. Beginning the same summer as the shift to service, the tenters' council added a secretary and a committee on appeals. However, the work of the three man appeal committee is almost entirely absent from the record. Conversely, there is also no record that a sentence was ever overturned on appeal. In fact, there is some evidence that the tenters' council adapted to this change by assigning some punishments with a caveat: no clemency.[44]

While these changes began as modifications that were more democratic and therefore stronger examples of self-government, they had long term practical impact. After the years of 1932 and 1933, summer camp numbers rebounded. In fact, the numbers not only rebounded, they increased. By 1938, camp was booked solid for weeks in advance. Part of the reason for this was a development unique to the Narrows Boxwell: Scouts routinely stayed for two weeks, even though "camp" was a week-long phenomenon. The two-week camper reality had been going on since at least 1931, but when overall numbers were low, Scouts staying two weeks was not an issue. As enrollments grew, so too did the stress on the camp's capacity. Thus, in 1939, a new rule was instituted by the tenters' council: "All Scouts in camp who wish to return a second week, are required to be in the first 80 per cent in service, advancement and behavior." In other words, if a Scout constantly broke the rules, he could not return a second week, leaving his spot available for another Scout. Clemency or no clemency, appeal or no appeal could clearly affect this situation. And, in 1945 when the Scout quota was increased from 80 to 100 Scouts a week, that ability to stay a second week became even more critical. Space was an issue as the Council was growing.[45]

Improving the program at the Narrows Boxwell was sometimes the result of addressing specific challenges. Addressing these challenges led to innovations, though some were not as successful as others. For example, Anderson and his staff tinkered with a simple idea: open camp for two week periods, which would fit with what boys were already doing. Thus, there were years when camp opened for two week stretch, then closed for a few days, and then opened for another run of two weeks, usually making up four periods total. Prior to this, camp ran weeks of operation back to back. At the same time that Scouts were picked up at Belle Meade and Harding, Scouts from the preceding week were dropped off. Breaks did not exist. Thus, the stated rationale was, not surprisingly, better program:

> To contribute to a more efficient summer service the camp
> period is broken with a three or four-day rest after each
> period of two weeks. It was found that the leaders who
> assumed the responsibility for 24 hours in the day and sev-
> en days in the week grow a bit stale and inert with no brief
> period of rest from their duties… In the past, individual
> leaders who have left camp for a short spell have returned
> with vigor and with eagerness to resume the work.

1939 was the first summer to try this new method, and it may have been continued in 1940. After this, Boxwell appeared to return to the single week sessions, back to back all summer. Why the idea was abandoned remains unclear, but for whatever reason, it did not continue.[46]

Another significant challenge that led to program improvement was an issue as old as Scouting itself: how to handle the "older boy problem." From its inception, Scouting struggled to keep boys engaged in the program after a certain point, usually some time in their mid-teens. Other interests developed and if there was nothing to keep the Scout engaged in the program, he moved on. Camp Boxwell addressed this issue with two solutions: one local and one national.

The local solution was the introduction of Junior Leaders to the staff. Junior leaders were boys with more experience, not just in Scouting, but with Camp Boxwell specifically. The first summer to officially employ junior leaders was 1932. A cadre of eight Eagle Scouts was recruited for the positions and all had previously attended the camp as campers. Each junior leader was placed in a Scout tent and would "counsel and instruct Scouts in every test from tenderfoot through the various merit badges." In some ways, they were redundant; Junior Leaders were performing a function similar to the tent leader. This reality was not lost on the scouts themselves, who periodically elected Junior Leaders as the tent representative to the tenters' council. For example, one week in June 1933, four of the eight Councilmen were Junior Leaders, who also served as the Council's secretary and the three man appeals committee. There is no evidence that this particular idiosyncrasy existed past 1933, suggesting the Junior Leaders idea also evolved as time passed. Generally, Junior Leaders helped with all kinds of instruction, both on the waterfront and elsewhere in camp. Some years they were also responsible for campfires and recreational activities. Other years, Junior Leaders opened and closed the religious services with the sentence prayers.[47]

The introduction of a youth staff presented its own set of challenges. Older teenage boys running around in the woods for weeks at a time *sometimes* got into things they should not. Olpha E. "O.E." Brandon was a Junior staff member from 1938 to 1940. His tenure coincided with the experiment of two week sessions with a few days off in between. Junior staff apparently made good use of this down time:

> Every two weeks at camp most of the last Friday, and
> [then] Saturday and Sunday were weekends when there
> were no campers in camp so that supplies could be replen-
> ished, new latrines dug, and needed repairs made. The Jr.
> Leaders did these chores, usually with [camp physician]
> Hartwell Weaver, the nearest person to being an adult, in
> charge. The first thing we did when the last adult disap-

peared down the road was take the camp canoes on a canoe trip around the bend of the Narrows of the Harpeth. The Harpeth River made a little over a five-mile bend in the shape of a horseshoe. By paddling the canoes upstream about half of a mile, then carrying the canoes about 150 yards across a gap in a ridge (the Narrows), we could then put the canoes in the water and float downstream around the horseshoe bend back to camp. There were several whitewater rapids in the river along the bend, and since the canoes were moulded wood covered with canvas, it was strictly taboo to go around the bend because of the likely-hood of damaging the canoes. We immediately recovered and painted over any damaged canvas on the canoes as soon as we got back to camp.

While this was clearly an example of youth staff breaking the rules, there were other times when youth staff did what was necessary for the good of the camp. Brandon also related this tale about a national inspection:

The scout camp was scheduled for an inspection by repre-sentatives of the national council on a Monday following one of cleanup weekends. We Jr. Leaders were told very emphatically that we must do a good job with cleanup and the digging and properly preparing a new pit latrine. Just before James Gribble, the Camp Director, left camp we discovered that there was not enough lime to spread over the new latrine. Lime is a white caustic powder that helped keep down bacteria and odor in an open pit latrine and was a must for good sanitation. Gribble assured us that he would be back Sunday afternoon with the lime so that it could be put out for the Monday morning national council inspection. We dug the new latrine and went about the other cleanup and restocking chores. Groceries, ice, and other needed supplies were delivered and stored on Satur-day as scheduled. Sunday night was approaching and no James Gribble with the lime. We had no way of knowing that his old car had broken down, and there were no tele-phones within miles for him to call us. All we knew that there had to be lime on the latrines for Monday morning. What we did have was plenty of baking flour that looked just like lime. We rationalized that this was an emergency and that we would not be violating the first Scout Law, "A Scout is Trustworthy" if we spread lime over the flour when we got some, so we spread a generous coating of baking flour over the latrine Sunday night. The National Council inspectors were complimentary over the good sanitary appearance of the latrine.[48]

Junior Leaders were part of Anderson's Boxwell until the Scout Executive's retirement. Not only did these Scouts provide needed assistance in running the camp, they also served to inspire younger Scouts. With enough experience (and usually the rank of Eagle), any Scout could join the Boxwell staff. Junior Leaders were a wonderful tool to showcase how well Anderson's program of citizen-building worked. A Scout who came to camp, worked hard, and advanced could be rewarded with a Junior Leader position. He had benefitted from the program and could now give back "to the next generation." Indeed, the Junior Leaders idea was another dimension to citizen-building as it clearly demonstrated a responsibility to give back to the community that had fostered one's development, growth, and success.

James Gribble was the poster-child of this approach. Attending Camp Boxwell as a Scout in 1930 and 1931, Gribble was an active participant in camp program from the start. He was elected the representative from his tent both summers. When the first slate of Junior Leaders was announced prior to the start of camp in 1932, Gribble's name was on the list as one of the eight Eagle Scouts with previous Boxwell experience. Here was an individual who understood both Scouting and the system at Boxwell. Indeed, Gribble excelled in this position. In addition to assisting with first aid during this summer, he was so popular as a Junior Leader that he won the election for most Popular Scout one week and Best All Around Scout the next![49]

All of this would have been plenty to showcase how a Scout could ex-

Junior Leaders at Boxwell in 1939. From left to right are O. E. Brandon, George Stone, Roy Shaub, and Gerald Greene. Kneeling is Joe Gilliam. Personal Collection of O. E. Brandon.

cel under Anderson's system of self-government and prove to older boys they had a reason to return to camp. But it was not enough for Gribble. He returned as a Junior Leader from 1933 through 1936. Over these years, he taught Pioneering merit badge, was in charge of campfires and recreational activities, acted as the "Sunday School Superintendent," conducted the election of officers, assisted Anderson in running the camp, and worked on the Waterfront with Miller. If it seemed like Gribble was running the camp, he was. Anderson thought so too. In 1936, Anderson made Gribble Camp Director.[50]

And then came the big leap. Effective January 1, 1938, Gribble joined the Nashville Council as Assistant Scout Executive. In other words, Gribble's performance was so outstanding that Anderson created a position for the former Junior Leader just below himself in the Council. Gribble was now a full time employee of the Nashville Council. Part of his responsibility was to serve as Camp Director at Boxwell, which he continued until the Second World War interrupted his service. After Pearl Harbor, he joined the Navy as a recruiter, but returned as Assistant Executive in 1946. Gribble would continue on in this role at least until Anderson's retirement in August 1947. Here was the exemplar of what the program could do: raised under Anderson's citizen program from the beginning of his formative years, Gribble assumed increasing levels of responsibility, continuously giving back to his community. He eventually "lived the dream" by having Scout work become his life. His time was interrupted only by greater service—the call to serve his nation in wartime. Gribble showed how Camp Boxwell's citizenship program and its Junior Leader program could benefit boys; specifically Gribble's example demonstrated that the Junior Leader program could help solve "the older boy" problem by providing an avenue for older Scouts to remain involved in the program.[51,52]

The national solution to the older boy problem was the introduction of the Order of the Arrow (the OA), a honor camper society. The OA traced its beginnings to the Philadelphia Council, when, during summer camp in 1915, the camp director and assistant camp director founded an honor society for older boys. The idea was to give these older boys a reason to return to camp. The national Boy Scouts of America accepted the program as experimental in 1922 and then made it officially part of the Boy Scout program in 1948. Thus, by the time Anderson secured a chapter charter for the Nashville Council on April 21, 1938, the OA had been around for some time.[53]

Named Wa-Hi-Nasa, Lodge #111, the Nashville Lodge inducted its first members at a ceremony on May 21, 1938. Five youth—Roy Shaub, Hilary Osborn, O. E. Brandon, Jr., Lynn Farrar, and Forest Glascow—were inducted at this event. All were older boys themselves, each having attended Camp Boxwell for several years by 1938. At least three had already earned their Eagle Scout Award. Anderson and Gribble were both inducted at this first OA ceremony as was another adult leader, Tillman Newsum, who was the Assistant Scoutmaster of Brandon's troop, Troop 3. Over the course of the summer, thirty-two more boys were inducted. This was a significant number. The Lodge's charter "allows only one Scout in 20 to be elected." Thus, as the elections were made at camp, thirty-two inductees meant 640 Scouts were served that summer.[54]

The OA fit in nicely with Anderson's approach to Scouting and building citizens. Once a Scout was eligible because of his rank and his service record, his was nominated by his peers. The nominations were then voted upon by peers. This approach was completely in fitting with the responsibilities Anderson saw for future citizens. Further, the OA embraced Native American culture and rituals, such as dress, dance, and traditions. The name "Wa-Hi-Nasa" was chosen by the charter members because it was Cherokee for "Eagle Lodge." While it might be debatable how accurate these rituals were at this time, the fact remained Native American culture was central to the OA. Nevertheless, this emphasis fit well with Boxwell's program, where a weekly campfire dedicated to a "pow-wow" was ready made for the OA. The inclusion of the OA was a natural complement to Anderson's Boxwell.[55]

As Camp Director in 1938, Gribble took the opportunity provided by the OA's mythos and ran with it. The Pow-Wow campfires continued, but now with Gribble as the centerpiece. He dressed in a leather suit with a headdress of 100 feathers. He was accompanied by Hartwell Weaver, who wore just a breech clout. The campfire was held at the ruins of the Montgomery Bell house each week, which provided an impressive vista over the whole property. The Scouts arrived dressed in breech clouts and their faces were "painted with mercurochrome and other coloring in the weird designs which ornamented the warriors of various tribes." They were stopped on their way up the hill by other staff members dressed as guards or runners, questioning whether they should enter. Each tent (patrol) had been given an ordeal to complete during the day, which was usually pretty simple. A tent could present a live snake, a geode, or arrowheads. Alternately, they could build a fire or catch a fish. Regardless, it was an impressive, engaging event, which including smoking a peace pipe, beating a drum, and war dancing. Having set the stage of the mystery and intrigue of this world, OA elections were held at the campfire the following night.[56]

The Wa-Hi-Nasa Lodge and Camp Boxwell quickly developed a sym-

77

biotic relationship. The camp promoted the OA through campfires and ceremonies, and the Order promoted summer camp in return at troop meetings
across the council. Perhaps the best example of this was James Kilgore's film *A
Day at Camp Boxwell*, the first Boxwell promotional film. Kilgore was not
only a Scout in Troop 26, but one of the early Arrowmen in the OA. To secure his membership at the Brotherhood level of the OA—the next level beyond Arrowman—Kilgore shot the film during the summer of 1939. It was
only 15 minutes long and silent, but it was an excellent representation of the
Camp Boxwell experience. The Nashville Council's newsletter *The Bugle* explained the film well in March 1940,

> The motion picture, "A Day at Camp Boxwell," produced
> by the Order of the Arrow at camp in 1939, is now availa-
> ble to all troops within the city of Nashville. This film
> shows the Scouts' activities in camp from the time of First
> Call until To the Colors is blown and the flag is lowered at
> the end of the day. Showing scenes of handicraft, inspec-
> tion, swimming, hiking, recreation, canoeing, and [Walter]
> Whit[taker] pitching horseshoes, "A Day at Camp
> Boxwell" will recall many good times to the minds of old
> Scouts and increase the younger boys' enthusiasm for going
> to camp this summer.

The Bugle went on to point out that the film "can be easily fitted into the regular troop meeting. It is also an effective medium for bringing Scouting before
the mothers and fathers of the Scouts and is recommended for use at parent
night celebrations." Film, projector, and operator would all be provided without cost. This was but the first step in a long partnership.[57]

Camp Boxwell also faced more mundane challenges. As a summer
camp operating for almost twenty years, it had physical facility issues. In
1938, a new road was built in the area, leading to a new bridge across the Harpeth, just downriver from the Waterfront. The road—New Cedar Hill
Road—did much the same at the Narrows that Highway 100 had done at
Linton: the new road brought a straighter path through the area, bisecting the

existing winding road in several places. *The Bugle* noted there were "difficulties caused by the new road to the camp," though those problems were not specified.[58]

Not long after this, the Council embarked on its first capital improvements project. Extensive renovations began in 1939, but were not completed until after summer camp in 1940. The original dining hall was replaced by a larger building, "completely screened and equipped with kitchen apparatus to take care of any number of hungry scouts." The "kitchen apparatus" in question included a new stove, ice-box, sinks, and other kitchen equipment. The new building cost $2000, not a small sum of money at the time, and was built up on a ridge above the previous dining hall.[59]

By itself, the dining hall alone would have been a significant improvement, but there were other improvements as well. The camp could now boast a new "health house," a modest three room building dedicated to sick Scouts. The old dining hall was converted to a craft shop and a new boat dock was added to the waterfront. But the "delight of the Executive's heart is the new shower room where Scouts can wash their little necks and ears. Wash basins and toilets have been installed, and a [rechargeable generator] Delco lighting system."[60] In order for all of this running water to work, the camp also installed a new filtration plant that provided water "at various points on the campus." No longer would Scouts have to swim in the river to bathe or purify their water to have something to drink during the day. Camp Boxwell had finally moved from a glorified camping area to an actual Scout Camp.[61]

The renovations were enjoyed by Scouts in the summer of 1941, but then the Second World War came to the United States. The attack on Pearl Harbor on December 7, 1941 caused ripples across the nation. Thirty-one million Americans registered with Selective Service; more than fifteen million Americans—men and women—served in the war. The demand for industrial goods to execute the war led to enormous social changes at home. More women entered the industrial workforce; over a fifth of the population at large moved to find new jobs and explore new opportunities. The war effectively ended the Great Depression.[62]

The war affected the Nashville Council Boy Scouts as well. Scout Billy Walker remembered walking the streets of Franklin with his fellow Scouts asking for someone to serve as their Scoutmaster as their leader had left for the war. Anderson called on the local community to provide trucks and drivers to help collect scrap metal "too heavy for boys to carry." Gribble joined the Navy as a recruiter. With Gribble gone, Anderson hired Miller as Assistant Scout Executive. And yet, amazingly, the Council continued to grow. Since 1938, the Nashville Council had increased membership every year. This translated into the increased quota at Boxwell in 1945. When the war ended and Gribble returned, Anderson's Boxwell quickly achieved its peak years in 1946 and 1947.[63]

"The Distinction of Race"

Despite all the improvements and challenges Camp Boxwell at the Narrows had encountered and conquered, Anderson's program still suffered from a glaring failure. Like the Linton Boxwell before, the Narrows Boxwell was a segregated camp. The only African Americans on the property at all were camp cook Walter "Whit" Whittaker and his assistants.

This is not to imply that Whittaker and his assistants were not appreciated. While very little is known about the assistant cooks, Whittaker remained a camp fixture. He sang at the church services, he taught cooking to the Scouts, and he regularly played horseshoes with Anderson. Not a summer passed that one of the scribes did not mention Whittaker by name, often in conjunction with his cooking of course. And the praise was high. "We have good eats and the best cook in the state," one scribe wrote. Boys went back regularly for seconds and thirds for the meals. To this day, Jere Towe still holds the Boxwell "long distance eating record." While no one else could go

Left: The original dining hall before it was converted to the craft house. Personal Collection of James Flatt. Right: Walter Whittaker, camp cook. Personal Collection of Harry "Beany" Elam.

back for more than fourths, Towe went back twice for fifths and once for a seventh—each day. This was the power of Whittaker's cooking acumen. Indeed, perhaps the greatest example of the adoration for Whittaker came in 1947, when he was made an honorary member of the OA by a unanimous vote. Anderson noted, "It's a case of brotherhood, cheerfulness and service, the three things for which the Order of the Arrows stands, transcending the distinction of race."[64]

And yet, there was a distinction of race at Camp Boxwell at the Narrows. This distinction was clear in the scribes' reports. The most ever written about Whittaker's assistants was this sentence from 1935: "For Walter Whittaker, expert negro cook who has been in charge of the camp kitchen since the annual encampment was inaugurated, an assistant has been obtained this year and is lending Walter every aid in the preparation of the tons of hot cakes and other delicacies served to the scouts." When Whittaker himself was written about, he was given praise as above, but then was always referred to as either "Walter" or "Whit." Not a single publication from the period ever refers to any of the white leadership simply by their first name alone. Whittaker may have been "a prince of a fellow" and had a "magnetic personality," but he was still seen as different.[65]

This reality was compounded by a key difference between the Linton Boxwell and the Narrows Boxwell. Throughout the entire run of Camp Boxwell at Linton, there were no official black Boy Scout troops in the Nashville Council. They existed, but they were independent and ran their own shop. This did not remain the case though. Though there was fear black Boy Scouts might "become a burden to the movement," the Nashville Council officially extended Scouting to African American boys in 1933. By 1936, the Council appointed a dedicated Commissioner to recruit scouts and build troops. There was also a dedicated division, the J. C. Napier Division, within the council. In other words, there was a fully functional council, complete with committees and offices in a separate building, for African American Scouts under the supervision of the Nashville Council. Scoutmaster trainings for black leaders were held as well. By 1938, there were eight African American troops, totaling 156 Scouts and sixteen leaders. The Council was actively courting African American scouts for its in-house, segregated council.[66]

In fact, black Scouting grew during the war years. Anderson hired a full-time professional, not simply a volunteer like a Commissioner, to oversee the Napier Division in 1943. The Napier Division held a summer camp for African American Scouts in 1943 and 1944 at Greenwood Park, five miles outside of downtown Nashville on Lebanon Road. In 1945, the camp was again held for three weeks, just like the previous summers, but at a new location, on a farm three miles outside of Murfreesboro on Nashville Pike. This was Camp Davis. The following year, the Council bought fifty-five acres on

Couchville Pike near the intersection of Bryant's Creek and Stones River. When camp opened July I, this became the first Camp Burton. In 1947, the Napier Division even conducted a capital campaign to build three buildings at Burton, at least one of which—a dining hall with kitchen and pantry—was built in 1948.[67]

These details raise several critical questions. If Anderson's program was to make men from boys and both Scouting and Camp Boxwell were so ideally suited for this task, why segregate African American Scouts? If African American Scouts were not going to be allowed to utilize Camp Boxwell, why actively recruit these Scouts and build a separate camp for them? And perhaps most importantly for this work, how was having a segregated Camp Boxwell for the good of the program?

There are not good answers—certainly not morally satisfying answers—to some of these questions. Nevertheless, the place to begin was at the national level. Here a plan was developing by the mid-1920s "to recruit southern African American boys for a simplified and segregated version of Scouting, which would train them to be dutiful laborers and loyal to the nation rather than economic and political leaders like regular Scouts." The idea stemmed from the practices of the Louisville, Kentucky council. Known as the "Louisville Plan," this approach promoted African American Scouting as long as it was done "voluntarily, slowly, and with no publicity." Councils would bring these Scouts into segregated troops, which would ease white fears about public safety, social order, and racial purity.[68]

The National Executive Board created the Inter-Racial Service (IRS) in 1927 to implement this recruitment plan. African Americans boys would be recruited in segregated troops with African American leaders. Institutional sponsors, like churches, would be critical and a supervisor of black Scouting for the council would report to a white Council Executive. The boys' training would not focus on the responsibilities of citizenship, but instead African

American Scouting would emphasize creating industrious laborers. To achieve this, African American Scoutmasters had to undergo extensive training (by white men) before taking up their responsibilities as leaders. Once formed, the separate division often named itself after African American heroes, either national or local names. And while never really the plan, the troops that made up these divisions often faced discrimination, by being denied access to local pools, Scouts camps, and in some cases even uniforms. Clearly, denial of the summer camp program was particularly problematic, as advancement was incredibly difficult without the resources in manpower and equipment a summer program offered. Despite the clear issues, the Nashville Council followed this outline as if it were a roadmap.[69]

Thus, the fact that Camp Boxwell was a segregated camp was in fact part of the program. This approach also explained why Whittaker could be so warmly embraced, but African American Scouts not allowed. In the world of Southern segregation, African Americans could be seen as kind-hearted and warm people, but just not capable of handling the same responsibilities as whites. Once recruited, of course, African Americans got a separate camp; they were not being trained to be responsible citizens and future businessmen, who need to work with others and develop leadership skills. They were being trained to be trustworthy and reliable laborers. Whittaker therefore could be praised and even loved; he exemplified "the good Negro" that Scouting was trying to mold.

The End of the Narrows Boxwell

When Anderson announced his retirement on July 31, 1947, he had built a legacy of which he could be proud. When he took on the position in March of 1920, there were only about sixty Scouts in the Nashville Council and the territory wasn't too much larger than the city itself. His guiding principle had always been "One More Boy" and with that idea, the Council grew. By the end of his tenure, the Council covered "36 and a half Middle Tennessee counties, registered 8,200 members during the run of the year, including 2,000 adult workers." The Council also owned and operated three Scout Camps: Camp Boxwell and Camp Burton, both discussed above, and the new Camp Arrowhead, added in 1946 near Sparta to once again service Scouts in the eastern part of the Council.[70]

His professional staff had grown too. The initial campaign by the Rotary Club in 1920 had raised enough money to fund a single full-time professional—Anderson—and a secretary. For many years, that secretary was Bernice Rives, who met Anderson at the truck drop-off with paperwork to be signed during the camp season, but was otherwise left alone during the summer as Anderson was at Boxwell. By the time of his retirement on September 15, 1947, the Council continued to employee Rives, but also Gribble and Miller as Assistant Executives, Tillman Newsum as a field executive in Tullahoma, and Charles W. Cooper as the head of the J. C. Napier Division. The Council had even won an Acorn Award, a national recognition for membership achievement, every year since 1937 for its growth. Still, Anderson remained humble in reviewing his time as Council Executive:

> In round numbers there are some 40,000 boys for cub age
> of 9 through scouts age of 16 who need this program.
> They are definitely my responsibility and yours. No fewer
> than 25,000 boys each year are longing to become Boy
> Scouts and a waiting line is virtually begging for the pro-
> gram. They grow into their majority disappointed and
> denied this great advantage which we have failed to offer.
> I cannot gloat over the progress of the Nashville Area
> Council when the picture of our failure is so vividly paint-
> ed before our eyes.

That noted, none of the newspaper articles covering Anderson's retirement saw his work as a failure. Indeed, James G. Stahlman wrote an editorial in his paper the *Nashville Banner*, praising Anderson's work, writing,

Middle Tennessee owes much to "Bill" Anderson, who has

been the example, the inspiration and the driving force for
programs addressed to young manhood's finest culture.
For 27 years he has occupied a place of leadership in this
work. He had given it his time and his unsparing effort, a
service whose fruitage is the thousands of lives benefitted
by that service.

That Scouting has expanded so notably during these 27
years is its own testimonial to his success in a labor that
was his foremost.

Hardly the sort of admonition one gives for failure.[71]

Regardless, Anderson was not retiring because he had not reached
enough boys. His stated reason was that his retirement was dictated by national policy, "which establishes the retirement age for its officials." Thus, while
Anderson's retirement was effective on his birthday on June 28, he continued
to serve until a replacement was found. Still, there were clearly other wheels
turning here. With Gribble back, Anderson could rest easy that Camp Boxwell
would be in good hands under his protégé and Talmadge Miller. And it is entirely possible Anderson and Boxwell himself may have coordinated a joint exit
following Boxwell's wife's death in May of 1947. After Anderson announced
his retirement in August, Leslie G. Boxwell stepped down as Council President
at the next Executive Board meeting in January 1948. Both men had been with
the Council since its inception; both clearly realized it was time to move on.[72]

Ward E. Akers of Jonesboro, Arkansas took over the Nashville Council on September 15, 1947, welcomed by Anderson (now "Executive Emeritus"), Gribble, Miller, Council treasurer E. E. Murrey, and Scout commissioner
Will R. Manier. A new man in charge meant new ideas and new ideas meant
changes. Whatever the internal conversations were, a few facts are evident.
James Gribble was out before the year was over. The Council office was
moved. Unsatisfied with the progress of Scouting under Anderson in terms of
both recruitment and funding, Akers also set about reorganizing the council,
breaking the thirty seven counties into eight districts, each with its own com-

missioner and professional. This was just the start of a massive reorganization, a reorganization which would affect summer camp as well.[73]

As the 1948 season began, the new man began implementing his new ideas. Camp Burton opened with its new dining hall on June 28. The camp was slated to run for two weeks. In 1947, Burton had operated for five weeks. Camp Arrowhead on the Caney Fork in Sparta opened on July 27, though there is no indication of how long it operated that summer. There is no further mention of Camp Arrowhead in the newspapers. 1948 appears to have been its last summer.[74]

Camp Boxwell at the Narrows of the Harpeth opened on June 20, 1948. Immediately the changes were evident here as well. Unlike Anderson who would continue to keep the camp running as long as there were boys who signed up, Akers defined a set period. Camp Boxwell would be open one month, period. One month was the shortest camping season Boxwell had run since the summers of 1932 and 1933, when the Depression was at its lowest point. And while the camp was open to the 100 Scouts quota established a few years prior, the first week only had sixty boys, which was again, a low point. The staff was different too. Pictured in the *Banner*, the Boxwell staff for 1948 was seventeen people besides Akers. It is unclear who was paid and who was not, but a staff of this size for the whole summer was a significant change from years past. Fortunately, Walter Whittaker was still on board.[75]

Something else was different here. Neither the *Banner* nor the *Tennessean* were filled with articles about life at camp. It appeared that the scribe system—likely the entire democratic system of citizenship building set up by Anderson—had been jettisoned. The three articles on Camp Boxwell that do appear in both papers for summer 1948 do not paint a flattering picture. The *Banner* reported, "The camp, according to Ward Akers, scout executive, is in keeping with the progress of scouting. The boys will receive instruction in shooting, boating, swimming, and archery." A June 17 article in the *Tennesse-*

an said essentially the same thing, but a June 27 article added this detail: "The first group of 60 Scouts spent last week clearing the edge of the river at the swimming beach and removing brush from the archery range." This was camp at Boxwell in 1948.[76]

1948 was also the last summer for Camp Boxwell at the Narrows of the Harpeth. Wilbur F. Creighton, Jr. rationalized leaving the Narrows Boxwell in *Boys Will Be Men* this way, "lacking money for capital improvements, the council camp at the Narrows of the Harpeth had deteriorated beyond repair alone; moreover, Akers thought the site at the Narrows entirely unsuitable for the scope of the scouting program he hoped to develop." Later, Creighton offered further explanation, writing, "Ward Akers was not pleased with [the Narrows of the Harpeth] site for several reasons: improvements had long been neglected, major capital investments were needed for new facilities, and at best it could serve no more than a hundred scouts a week. The Council executive board tended to agree with him and seized an opportunity in 1949 to relocate the camp to a third site."[77]

Whether Creighton was unfamiliar with the history of the Narrows Boxwell or was just an avid defender of Akers remains a mystery. What is clear is that most of Creighton's explanations are not supported by the existing evidence. Clearly the Council had money for capital improvements as a dining hall at both Burton and Arrowhead had just been built in the period prior to the 1948 season. To say that the Narrows Boxwell had "deteriorated beyond repair" stretches credulity. The Narrows Boxwell had just completed a campaign that built a dining hall, a washhouse with showers, a new kitchen, a new filtration plant with water access across the camp, and a lighting system. All of these were had been used for the first time in the 1941 camping season, only seven years earlier. That these facilities had "deteriorated beyond repair" in such a short time is unfathomable.

Creighton was correct about two points though. First, the Narrows

Boxwell would comfortably serve about 100 Scouts per week. It had been doing this for several years by 1948, so this was unquestionably true. Second, Akers "was not pleased with the site." Of this, there can be no doubt. Akers clearly had a different vision for the Council and for Scouting in middle Tennessee. As a result, the Narrows Boxwell was not going to support that vision. Thus, a new Boxwell was needed and it would open in Walling, Tennessee in June of 1949.

As for the Narrows property itself, the Council bought the land from "Jet" Potter in 1944. Thus, just because Boxwell moved did not mean the property was going away. The site continued to be used for a few years for weekend camping and canoeing, but was largely abandoned. In one of the great ironic twists that sometimes happens in history, the Narrows site saw a second life, briefly, as a Scout camp starting around 1957. Camp Burton, after several location shifts in the mid-1950s, finally landed at the Narrows of the Harpeth, where it stayed for the next several years. The site that had been segregated to African American Scouts became the last location for the Council's segregated Scout camp. When Boxwell Reservation on Old Hickory Lake integrated in 1965, the Narrows went back to weekend camping and canoeing. The site was mostly derelict when the Council sold the property to the state of Tennessee in 1978. It is today part of the Harpeth River State Park.[78]

Leaving the Narrows

"No person can rise higher than his ideals, and it is imperative that the life of a boy be dominated by worthy ambitions," Anderson wrote in 1941. "There are no negatives in the ideals of scouts nor in the system at Camp Boxwell. Everything is positive, inspiring and compelling, for the finest personality and deepest character is developed, not be continually telling a person to refrain from evil, but by attracting him to that which is good." Anderson believed in Scouting and he believed in what Boxwell did for Scouting. His faith was not unfounded. Troops with boys who attended Boxwell did not fold.

Scouts who attended Boxwell were more likely to advance; of the 125 Eagle Scouts in Nashville in 1939, 117 had attended Boxwell. And the program of citizenship at Boxwell was "so well impressed upon the scouts who attended [Boxwell] that the knowledge and information is carried back to the troops and helps form the bases for troop procedure and troop government." Inspired by the program and their experiences there, Scouts "at Camp Boxwell are led to strive for the best."[79]

Of course, this inspiration was largely because of the personal touch of "Coach" William Anderson. He gave "peppery lectures on morals and philosophy" to Scouts at breakfast. For first timers at the camp, Anderson personally gave little tours, pointing significant sights and locations to Scouts. As noted above, he routinely engaged in the afternoon activities with the boys, such as softball, baseball, or horseshoes. He was easily identifiable at these games by his "big straw hat." He was not above letting his scribes take him down a notch. One scribe—Scobey Rogers—was shocked when Anderson and camp director Talmadge Miller won the horseshoe tournament "for the first time in the history of Camp Boxwell" in 1933. "This winning team," the scribe wrote, "was a surprise to the entire camp because it is evident that the executive [Anderson] and camp director [Miller] cannot pitch horseshoes." Over a decade later, another unnamed scribe noted that Anderson pitched and umpired for both sides during a baseball game "to make sure his side wins." Scribe Edwin Hughes noted in 1933 that "we are glad to report the progress made by our scout executive in making coffee. He has advanced to the point where muddy water is no longer required to give it that certain color, and some of the more hardy leaders are actually drinking it." There would never again be a Council Executive who built this kind of relationship with the Scouts themselves.[80]

And yet, despite his efforts, despite this program of service and citizenship, there is no marker to William Anderson today. Not a single building, campsite, or body of water anywhere in the thirty-eight counties of the Middle

William J. Anderson gives a personal tour to a new group of Scouts who have just arrived at the Narrows of the Harpeth Boxwell. Nashville Tennessean, *July 14, 1935.*

Tennessee Council honors Anderson. A camp bearing Leslie Boxwell's name continues to exist and thrive, but nowhere on that property is any recognition to the man who made the camp survive and excel. Anderson has vanished from the landscape he helped to create.

But perhaps Anderson received his tribute in 1940. In writing an article on the camp that summer, *Tennessean* reporter Emily Towe asked "a freckled-faced" twelve year old boy what was the best way to describe Camp Boxwell. The boy smiled and with a seriousness to his voice answered, "The best way to describe Camp Boxwell is to call it a Boy Scout's heaven on earth..."[81]

Anderson would have agreed.

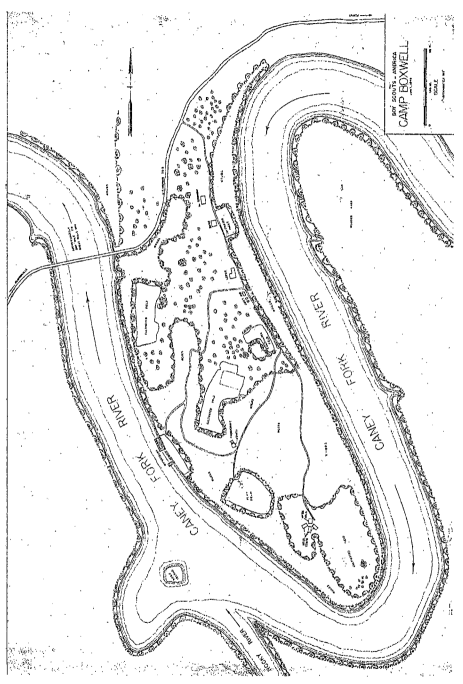

Map of the Rock Island Boxwell its first year, 1949. Personal Collection of author.

Chapter 3

The Temporary Camp:
Boxwell at Rock Island

1949-1959

Ward Akers had been very busy. Since starting as Council Executive in September 1947, Akers had divided the Council's thirty-five county service area into twelve districts. Davidson County alone was divided into four districts, while the areas outside Nashville made up another eight. Of the counties making up this service area, twenty-five had no Scouting program present. To bring Scouting to all of the mid-state area, five new professionals were added to the council's payroll. By January 28, 1949, the Nashville Council was no more. With an expanded and growing professional staff, the Nashville Council was reorganized and reborn as the Middle Tennessee Council.[1]

Camp Boxwell was not immune to this reorganization. Unhappy with the Narrows of the Harpeth location, Akers abandoned the site after one summer. On April 11, 1949 the Council's Executive Committee voted to move the camp to a new location in Walling, TN. "Camp Boxwell III" would be located "at the reservoir developed by the Great Falls Dam at Rock Insland [sp], and faces U. S. 70 Highway, about fifteen miles from McMinnville." The site was the summer retreat of deceased University of Michigan football coach Fielding H. Yost, but had been sold to the Council by Yost's descendants. The site encompassed "[s]ome 200 sleepy acres of pine forest" and would serve as the summer home for approximately a hundred Scouts a week. Camp would open on June 26 and run to August 13, a full seven weeks of Scout camping.[2]

The new site was hardly ideal. Whereas the Linton Boxwell and the Narrows Boxwell (now called "Camp Boxwell II") had both been within twenty miles of Nashville, "Boxwell III" was just short of a hundred miles. While the state highway system was much improved from years before, such a trip from Nashville would still take over an hour and a half down Highway 70. Further, the camp was located at the confluence of the Rocky River and the Caney Fork River. While this made a great location for boating, the river's depth complicated swimming. A giant "crib"—an enclosure with a bottom surrounded by a floating dock—was built to keep non-swimmers and beginners from drowning. There were also no permanent facilities. The "dining hall" was really just three large military tents placed together. The kitchen was a wooden shack. Nevertheless, at two hundred acres it was larger than the Narrows and thus could grow.[3]

Of course, none of these shortcomings was much of an issue and for good reason. "Set up on a temporary basis, the camp will not necessarily be considered for future operations beyond the 1949 season." The Rock Island Boxwell was a temporary camp and was always intended to be. Clearly Akers was looking for something else, something more grandiose. Until he found this undiscovered location, the Rock Island Boxwell was a chance to work out some ideas and establish a program to serve the Scouts of middle Tennessee living in a new post-war environment.[4]

Bombs, Babies, and Boy Scouts

To say that the United States—and even the world—was a changed place after the Second World War would be an understatement. Just as industrialization had dramatically changed virtually every aspect of American life, World War II had a similar effect. The war brought dramatic changes in technology, including not just atomic weapons, but the first computers. The United States traded its traditional isolation for international commitments and leadership. This was prompted in large part by the rivalry that developed with one of the nation's wartime allies, the new global antagonist, the Soviet Union. A new conflict developed, a "cold war," where two opposing ideologies—one championing democracy, one championing communism—sought to exercise their influence on nations around the world. There could be no sharing; one side had to win, one side had to lose. The development of stronger weapons and delivery of those weapons led to both an arms race and a space race. Americans were also terrified that communists were infiltrating every aspect of their lives: their businesses, their schools, their government, and even their social organizations, including the Boy Scouts. Some of this was rampant paranoia; some of it was not.[5]

The new political environment was accompanied by two unprecedented surges in growth. One surge was an economic boom, an uninterrupted period of economic growth from 1946 to 1973. The second boom was a baby boom. "Between 1946 and 1964 American women bore more than seventy-five million infants, compared with barely fifty million in the preceding nineteen years. At its peak, the birthrate averaged 3.6 babies per woman, nearly double the rate in the 1930s." The two were mutually reinforcing. The nation's economic power came in part from the United States rebuilding Europe and other devastated areas after the war. But the growth was also driven by the rise of a new consumer economy, which was fed by the baby boom. Pent-up demand—both for consumer goods and families--during the Depression and the wars years was unfettered. More children meant a move to the suburbs and a bigger home. A bigger home and more children meant more furniture and appliances and even television sets (50 million by 1960), which meant more jobs to fill all these desires. The move to the suburbs necessitated a car to get to work and the store, both of which had been walking distance in the city. "By 1960, suburban residents of single-family homes outnumbered both urban and rural dwellers and the detached home had become the physical embodiment of hopes for a better life." The arrival of businesses like McDonald's and Wal-Mart kept Americans focused on spending. A consumer America was born.[6]

The two booms—baby and economic—created "a historical aberration, out of line with long-term historical trends." In other words, the post-war period's idealized vision of women staying home to tend to just the children and the home was an anomaly. High wages and low divorce rates were part of this reality, but this "domestic bliss" was equally a "reaction against Depression hardships, wartime upheavals, and Cold War insecurities." A perfect storm of circumstances temporarily setback the longer trends toward smaller families, more frequent divorce, and more economic and political opportunities for women. Many Americans believed this aberration was the way life was supposed to be and embraced that view enthusiastically.[7]

Challenging the idea of the 1950s as a complacent and calm period were the changes involving race and segregation in this period. African Americans had been winning legal victories that were chipping away at the foundation of segregation, but *Brown v. the Board of Education of Topeka, Kansas* in 1954 was the game changer. The U.S. Supreme Court ruled in *Brown* that, "in the field of public education, the doctrine of "separate but equal" has no place. Separate educational facilities are inherently unequal." While the *Brown* verdict was focused specifically on public schools, it signaled the end of segregation as it had existed for the last sixty years. And while not always clearly understood, this decision was rooted in the larger realities of the Cold War. The United States could not present a strong case for democracy over communism to the countries of Africa and Asia if that democracy allowed segregation of colored peoples by whites. Nevertheless, the ramifications of *Brown* would reverberate for years to come, and often very painful, especially in the South.[8]

Closer to home, Tennessee was affected by post-war changes as well. By 1960, the population of the state was, for the first time, mostly found in the cities, leaving fewer and fewer farms. In 1945, there were 235,000 farms in

Tennessee; by the end of the 1960s, there were nearly 122,000. Agriculturally, the state moved from cotton production to tobacco, soybeans, and cattle. Politically, the post-war period saw a state-wide cleansing of political corruption, including several new election laws. In 1947, the state passed its first sales tax with public school teacher salaries as the primary beneficiaries. Racial integration had enormous impact too as Tennessee was ground zero for several important events, discussed more fully below. The Tennessee Valley Authority was critical here as well. Created in 1933, the TVA built twenty hydroelectric dams between 1933 and 1951 in the Tennessee River watershed at various points. With the dams in place, flooding could be controlled, water depth for navigation could be stabilized, and cheap hydroelectric power could lift the entire region out of poverty. The cheap, stable, and federally controlled electric power of the TVA was a motivating factor in the location of atomic bomb production at Oak Ridge (1942) and the location of the Arnold Engineering Development Center in Tullahoma (1949). Whether military or civilian in nature, the TVA projects not only led to job creation through dam construction and operation, but also attracted a range of businesses and industries because of the cheap electricity.[9]

The Boy Scouts of America (BSA) benefitted greatly from this new world that was taking shape. In fact, the post-war years were probably the high water mark for the program. Membership surged as the baby boomers entered the ranks of Cub Scouts and then Boy Scouts. In 1955, the overall membership of the BSA was 4 million youth, double what it had been in 1940. Parents in the post-war period had more money, more leisure time, and, most importantly, more cars. This allowed more adults to be involved in the program and made taking a weekend camping trip away from home much easier. Indeed, adult enrollment surged as well, from 34,000 before the war to 1.3 million by 1960.[10]

Summer camps in particular enjoyed significant benefits in this post-war world. Because the BSA qualified as a "non-profit entitled to buy surplus [government] property at wholesale prices with special priority," the institution became a major recipient of military materials. This meant that councils—and their summer camps—could buy tents, cots, sleeping bags, jeeps, and trucks at discounted prices. New technology led to the creation of powdered drinks, known as "bug juice" at camps across the nation. Post-war summer camps also saw the rise of troop camping. "After studying the matter, the BSA recommended a switch to whole troops going to camp together and staying in their own campsites." This was a profound change in approach because having troop leadership available allowed camp staffs to focus more on running program and teaching in their "program areas," such as the waterfront or craft area.[11]

To be fair, Scouting's growth and success was due to more than simply a good program. After all, the Scouting program in the post-war period was not substantially different than the program before the war. However, what *had* changed were ideas about childhood, how to raise children, and what was expected of men in the post-war world. The same confluence of events that allowed for stay-at-home moms and single income families led to the flourishing of the Scout program. Understanding post-war child-rearing is the key here. As historian Steven Mintz explains, how one raised one's child was "the key to producing not simply a healthy, happy child, but also psychologically well-adjusted adults and a harmonious democratic society." A "good child" then was one who could work well in a group, was interested in consensus, was adaptable, and well-behaved. Indeed, the watchword so often associated with the 1950s—"conformity"—applied well here. Parents did not want exceptional children; they "wanted their children to be normal and average.... [to] be like others rather than conspicuous."[12]

Child-raising practices in the 1950s also emphasized gender norms as well as the family. There were expectations about how boys were to behave. "Sissiness" was to be stamped out in boys for fear that a "sissy" boy might be impotent or gay as an adult. Chores and activities therefore were encouraged by parents to reinforce these gender roles. While these ideas about gender clearly encouraged parents to become involved in Scouting—mothers with Cub Scouts, fathers with Boy Scouts—they also demonstrated a shift in thinking about expectations. Boys were not being trained to be good businessmen or citizens anymore; they were being trained to be good husbands and fathers.[13]

Scouting had a role in this development. Scouting served as a way to promote the desired gender roles for boys. Further, the program provided a space wholly separate from the family for boys. This space was shared by peers and thus encouraged by the family to insure children "grew up well adjusted and sociable." Indeed, membership in Scouting was seen as "a way to promote social skills and to defuse the intensity of the highly privatized, inward-turning middle class family." Schools and churches performed these functions as well, but in a mixed gender context; Scouting did so in a gender-specific way. It should not be surprising then that single-gender summer camp attendance surged. It was these ideas about how childhood and childrearing in the post-war period, coupled with the sheer number of children brought by the baby boom, which accounted for Scouting's phenomenal growth in this period. Scouting provided a "respectable" group for youth to be a part of as well as place to learn consensus building.[14]

And this was the growth—and the anxiety—Ward Akers wanted to capitalize on as Scout Executive of the middle Tennessee area. A native of Roanoke, Virginia, Akers did not start his professional life in Scouting. After attending "Roanoke College in Salem, Va., where he was a member of Kappa Alpha fraternity and lettered in football, track and boxing," Akers worked briefly in banking. He took this strong background in finance into professional Scouting, where he served in Baton Rouge, LA as an assistant Scout Executive. His work there led him to cross paths with the owner of the Baton Rouge Metal Culvert Company, a man by the name of Leslie G. Boxwell. In 1941, he became Council Scout Executive of the East Arkansas Area Council. As Council Executive in Jonesboro, he spent a great deal of time with their council

Ward Akers and adult staff test the new water filtration system at Rock Island, 1949. Left to right: Floyd "Q-ball" Pearce, Talmadge Miller, Everett Hertenstein, Floyd Laney, Craig Ayers, Ward Akers, and Wayman Hillis. Photo by Gordon H. Turner, Nashville Tennessean, June 28, 1949.

camp, Cedar Valley. It was in Arkansas that Akers developed a reputation as a powerful money man, a professional who was adept at raising funds, getting gifts in kind, and stretching a dollar. A long-time friend of Akers', Floyd "Q-ball" Pearce, told a story of how Akers pulled the council out of debt during his years there by "wander[ing] all over them hills and he'd buy eggs and milk and stuff like that" to feed Scouts at camp on the cheap. His son Ward C. Akers related another story from Cedar Valley, when Akers would get Scouts to fill up on saltine crackers and water before the meal so they would eat smaller portions. A council in debt during the Second World War clearly led to some creative solutions. Still a young man with a bit of baby face beneath his black hair, Akers was hired by L. G. Boxwell to head up the Nashville Council at a salary of $4800 a year. When he arrived in Nashville, Akers had the look of a charming man, blessed with a photogenic and trusting face.[15]

Thus, when Akers reorganized the Nashville Council into the Middle Tennessee Council in 1948, these larger social and economic trends were already becoming apparent. Membership in the Council was down slightly—

5,500 boys—but the pool available of Scout aged boys available was well known (65,000) and it was growing. To recruit the most Scouts and raise the most funds, Akers put his experience from banking and previous councils to work. The Nashville Council had to be reorganized into small districts. District Executives would give more personal contact to the families of these service areas; this attention in turn would lead to larger and sustained membership. Camp Boxwell had to move. All indications were that the Narrows location was, in Akers' vision, too small for the growth that was coming.[16]

Moving Boxwell meant more than simply changing locations. It meant time. The Rock Island location gave Akers and his professional team time to figure out what program would best suit this new world. Anderson's emphasis on citizenship was out-of-step in this new post-war world. A different type of summer camp program would be needed to fulfill the new understandings of what Scouting was supposed to do for boys. Expanding the Council meant bringing the program to more boys, but it was summer camp at the Rock Island Boxwell where the real experiment occurred: a family-centric program to help boys become husbands and fathers of good character.

Camp Boxwell at Rock Island

The third Boxwell was a peninsula, jutting out into the Caney Fork River. In fact, the site was in a truly unique location, situated at the exact confluence of the Rocky River and the Caney Fork River. Off the point of the peninsula, where the Rocky River joined the Caney Fork, was the actual rock island for which the whole area took its name. The community of Rock Island, just a few miles to the east of Boxwell, was a small resort town with visitors vacationing all summer long. By the time Camp Boxwell moved to the area in 1949, the Great Falls Dam, just a mile upriver, had been in operation for over thirty years, since 1917.[17]

The property that became "Boxwell III" was originally the summer home of Fielding H. Yost, the famous University of Michigan football coach.

Yost died in 1946 and his family leased the site to the Middle Tennessee Council. Creighton and Johnson told the story this way:

> When the council in 1920 had considered a site for its first camp, Commissioner Dan McGugin had favored a site at Rock Island, in a bend of the Caney Fork River where he and Coach Fielding Yost [...] had summer homes, but Coach Anderson had objected because of the distance from Nashville and the condition of the roads at that time. In 1949, Fielding Yost, Jr., having no interest in the property, planned to sell it on the open market, but after a discussion with L. G. Boxwell, Kendrick Hardcastle, and Dan McGugin, Jr., he offered it to the Middle Tennessee Council at a very low price for use as a scout camp. Boxwell, Will Manier, Jr., and E. B Stahlman, Jr., immediately leased the property in the name of the council and took an option to buy the 120 acres for $12,000, rushing the deal in order that the 1949 summer camp could be held at the site.

The *Nashville Banner*—of which Stahlman was Executive Vice-President and co-publisher—reported the site as much larger at 195 acres and under lease in the summer of 1949. Final purchase was reported as completed in October 1949. Regardless of these details, the major outline of this sequence of events as told by Creighton and Johnson is most likely accurate.[18]

By most measures, the Rock Island Boxwell was more rustic than the Narrows of the Harpeth Boxwell. There were only two permanent buildings on the site, the Yost Lodge and a fishing lodge. Both were at the top of the peninsula, near the entrance off of Highway 70. For 1949, the Lodge served as staff quarters and the fishing house (also referred to as a guest house) performed double duty as a hospital and office. Neither were especially large buildings. The Fishing Lodge had a stone foundation and appeared to have a small basement or storage area under the house. The ranch-style building had a front with two doors into the building on either end of the roofed porch. Wood shingles and shakes adorned the walls and roof. The building was under a thousand square feet.[19]

The Yost Lodge, the summer home, was double the size of the fishing lodge. The Lodge was essentially three parts. In the middle was a ranch-style center, complete with a small roofed porch. Screened front doors opened to the house here. To the right was a small wing with a chimney and to the left a larger addition, running perpendicular to the center. The Lodge also had wooden shingles and shakes, though these were not consistent types all around the house. James "Jim" Akers, one of Ward's sons, had fond memories of the Lodge:

> The Yost home was a beautiful old lodge with a large front porch at the highest point on Boxwell, that Yost used as a summer football camp for his University of Michigan football players. It was a mystical lodge with stone fire places and wood paneled walls and large bay windows. It had three bedrooms, huge living room and a primitive kitchen that had been added in the rear. The kitchen had a wood burning stove and a[n] ancient refrigerator. Best of all, the lodge had electricity and a flushing toilet.

Additionally, Yost's muzzle loaded gun sat mounted on the mantle. The Lodge did not remain as staff quarters and instead became the temporary summer home for Ward Akers' family. The staff would stay elsewhere.[20]

For a Scout walking the property, a right hand turn past the Yost Lodge would take one to the western side of the peninsula and straight down to the waterfront. The Caney Fork was much wider than either the South Harpeth or the Harpeth Rivers had been at the previous Boxwells and the location of the Great Falls Dam a mile up river guaranteed minimal heavy water traffic. The Rock Island—the actual half acre island—was clearly in sight about a half mile away, right at the point where the Caney Fork and Rocky River came together. Every summer when Scouts engaged in the mile swim, they would swim out from the waterfront past the island, around it, and then back to the waterfront.[21]

While the island made for a fascinating focal point, the waterfront also had a truly unique innovation, something not seen at any of the other Boxwells. The river was not only bounded by steep banks and the water was very deep, perhaps twenty to thirty feet. There was no "zero entry" area into the water or even a shallow portion in which to teach non-swimmers (those who couldn't swim at all) and beginners (those who could swim some) how to swim. Thus, to solve this problem the Rock Island Boxwell employed swimming cribs. These "cribs" were docks that enclosed an open space. The open space was a swimming area, but it had an underwater floor to ensure a Scout could not get away from the watchful eyes of the waterfront staff. As staff member Bob Alley described it, a crib "was a floating tank like a huge lobster trap that had a depth of about 3 feet for non-swimmers, about 4 feet for beginners and around six for advanced beginners." There was one crib when the camp opened in 1949; a second was added in 1951.[22]

If a Scout could swim, he could enjoy the other activities at the waterfront. A swimmer was not bound to the cribs and so could swim in the swimmer's area, where there was no false bottom. There was a rubber raft in the middle of this area and Scouts would climb on and jump off. There were no diving boards here, but there was a boat dock in addition to the cribs. The dock had dories (rowboats) were moored to the docks, while the canvas covered, wood canoes were stored on racks on the banks. All the docks were floating on fifty-five gallon steel drums, were custom built on site, and were left in the water throughout the year. When the water levels dropped from "summer level," the docks could simply rest upon the drums.[23]

While the cribs and the docks were unique dimensions to the Rock Island waterfront, other items were common to other camps and other Boxwells. The waterfront used the buddy system, just as every Boxwell had back to 1928. At Rock Island though, this led to an innovation not seen previously as this Boxwell used campsites. Each site, sometimes referred to as a "village," had a place on a "buddy board"—a painted square board with hooks to hold buddy tags. Each Scout had a buddy tag on the hook under his village's name. The tag not only reflected the Scout's swimming skill level, but because the board had an "in" and "out" section, waterfront staff could tell instantly how many

Rock Island's waterfront, complete with two "cribs." The swimmers' area, along with an inflatable raft, sits in between. Dories were tied to the dock and canoes were stored on rocks on the backs to the left. The actual "Rock Island" is in the background. Personal collection of John Cooper & Ernie Ragsdale.

were in the water and how many were not. This provided an additional safety check on the river. In this regard, the Rock Island waterfront would seem very similar to a modern summer camp waterfront.[24]

Should the Scout traveler not turn right at the Yost Lodge and instead choose to follow the main trunk of the road straight ahead, he would quickly find himself deeply immersed in he property. During the walk, the scout would have quickly been overcome by a central truth of the Rock Island Boxwell: pine was everywhere. Posts were made of pine. Any structures the staff built on site were made of pine. Campfires burned pine logs. The forest of pine was itself so thick there was very little undergrowth. And of course pine smell permeated everywhere. A Scout could not walk the property without being overcome by the aroma.[25]

The road down to the end of the peninsula had one other artery that branched off to the right. This was a long loop road that eventually tied back to the main trunk road. The branch that ran down to the waterfront curved back to this loop as well. Like all the roads at Rock Island, the road was dirt; dusty when the weather was dry, muddy when the rains came. But this main loop road was important because it ran through the true heart of the Rock Island Boxwell: the Activities area.

Aside from the waterfront, the Activities Area held most of the instructional locations for the camp. Here the pine forest opened up into a large clearing, a large grassy field. The Assembly area was here. A flagpole—made of pine—rose from near the center of the field. Some years, the pole was pioneering wonder: it would actually "float" above the ground, sitting atop several crossing ropes connected to three-foot tall (pine) stakes. Stakes and the pole were anchored in a small web of roped tension to keep everything upright. This area was where Scouts would circle up for flag ceremonies, recite the Pledge of Allegiance, and salute the flag while it was raised and lowered.[26]

If our wanderer stood on the road and looked directly at the flagpole, he would quickly see some tents hiding in the line of pine trees on the opposite side of the field. These were not camper tents, but the camp's program areas. New to the post-war era of Scout camp, a program area was a specialized teaching area where similar merit badges were taught together. Obviously, water related merit badges were taught at the waterfront, so a similar approach was taken with three instructional areas here: the Activities Yard, the Conservation Yard, and the Handicraft. The Activities Yard taught the skills for the early ranks of Tenderfoot, Second Class, and First Class as well as several merit badges, namely Camping, Cooking, and Pioneering. The Activities Yard had a knot bar to demonstrate knots and would often build pioneering projects, such as monkey bridges or the "floating" flagpole, at other areas in the camp. The Conservation Yard was next. Here was taught Nature, Soil and Water Conservation, and Forestry. In addition to the principle tent here, one would find

The Rock Island Dining Hall consisted of three large tents. Every summer the staff built the cedar frames. The floors were sawdust. A more permanent kitchen and water filtration system sat behind these tents. Personal collection of the author.

a leaf board and an axe yard. And finally along this line of teaching areas, almost where the road completed its loop, was the large Handicraft tent. Here our wanderer would find Basketry, Leatherwork, and Art. There was a lot going on in a small space.[27]

As the loop completed its circuit, the Scout traveler would find that just up a short, but steep hill was the dining hall. Using the term "dining hall" or even "mess hall" was overly generous. The "mess hall" was actually not a single building at all. There was a wooden building for a kitchen and three large military tents served as dining rooms. From above, the arrangement appeared as a hand with three splayed fingers. The floor was sawdust. Food was cooked over wood burning stoves and the kitchen was the only building other than the

107

Rock Island's Trading Post, complete with bottles of cola. Personal collection of the author.

Yost Lodge to have electricity and running water. There was also a water tank here, where the camp's filtered water was kept. As a result, the only shower facilities in camp were here as well and these were only for staff showers. As James Akers explained, "there was a little wood burning stove next to the shower and if it was fired off you could get warm water showers, but that was reserved for the senior staff." The shower was not a closed building however. It was open, just boarded around the sides.[28]

The dining hall was the terminus for the main road and the loop road. But while the dining hall was literally "the end of the road," it was not the end of the camp. There was a trail that left the mess hall for the bottom portion of the peninsula. Leaving the mess hall, a Scout would find the cooks' tents not far away. A little further on the opposite side of the trail was the tent for rifle range instructor, a Fort Campbell Sergeant on-loan for the summer. Just past this tent was the baseball field. And finally, after a little walk, was a good sized sinkhole. The walls of the sink hole making a good natural berm, this was the rifle range. There was nothing else at the point of the peninsula. All one could do now was walk back.[29]

Upon beginning the trek back to the Yost Lodge up the main trunk, a Scout would encounter two other locales of importance. One was the first aid tent. While the old fishing lodge may have been identified as a "hospital" in the papers, both the Rock Island Boxwell map from 1949 and the surviving staff members who have discussed it remember a first aid tent on the main road back up toward the house. The second structure was a wooden shack on the right hand side of the road. This wooden shack was a completely new innovation for Boxwell. It was a commissary. Here Scouts could buy candy, cookies, peanuts, and sodas. A Scoutmaster could buy cigars. The treats were virtually all recreational. Over the course of different correspondence, James Akers described the Commissary this way:

> We sold food only. All the handicraft stuff was still sold at the Handicraft tent... We sold candy, Lance products like peanut butter cookies, peanuts, etc. and sodas. My favorite. Dr. Peppers and Baby Ruths. We pretty much were there 24-7 because we lived in the back. We were open right after break[fast] and we closed before taps....
>
> I worked in the Commissary that was almost NEVER closed. I was in there 7 days a week. It was the only place to get something to eat that was "fun" and bad for you. It was there that I got addicted to Dr. Pepper. I still drink it. (Diet now, of course.)

While James Akers swore the Commissary did not sell instructional materials, the *Banner* reported the commissary sold "everything from handicraft articles to flashlight batteries," much like a modern day Trading Post. Regardless, the mere existence of a place on site where money was spent on consumables was a new dimension to Boxwell. The desire to spend—and the desire to get a captive population to spend—had come to middle Tennessee Scouting.[30]

In addition to facilities with which to deliver the program, legends accompanied the property, providing an added mystique. There was a large gulley that ran through the heart of the camp. The Activity Yard often built monkey bridges across it. One legend claimed the gulley was actually an old road, the Old Kentucky Trail. This was said to be the same trail by "which Daniel Boone, Davy Crockett and Lewis and Clark traveled on their way to history-making adventures." For the less famous, the road allowed pioneers to travel north and south through the region. In another legend, the Yost Lodge was said to sit on the site of what was either an old travel lodge or stage coach stop. Much like the ubiquitous "George Washington slept here" markers, it was rumored that "Andrew Jackson used to spend the night after a day of traveling" at the site. Still a third legend held that "the last Indian battle in Tennessee was fought" on the grounds. Here men from Sumner County "defeated Cherokees and captured their chief." There was even a story of buried Confederate treasure somewhere on the grounds, though it has never been found. Finally, there was a large tree near the handicraft tent that was said to be an old "hanging tree." Regardless of their veracity, the legends made the Rock Island Boxwell a more exciting place for the boys and connected them with a large American mythos of rugged individuality.[31]

A Citizenry of Gentlemen

The Rock Island Boxwell was marred its very first summer by a personal tragedy. On Saturday, July 16, 1949, about halfway through the summer, staff member Henry Fitts was riding a motorcycle home for the weekend break before a new session began. "Around 2:45 p.m. as Fitts swung his vehicle around a soft drink truck," he pulled right into the path of an oncoming car. He survived the initial wreck badly injured, but died from the collision on Monday the 18th. Fitts had been a Boxwell staple for years. He had attended the camp at the Narrows as a Scout and been inducted into the OA there. He served as Junior Staff under Anderson at least one summer. Fitts was also an honor graduate of Montgomery Bell Academy as well as an Eagle Scout. At eighteen years old, he clearly had a promising future and according to his parents, much of that future was going to be devoted to Scouting. Thus, Fitts' parents asked that instead of flowers, contributions be made to Camp Boxwell. Because of his connection with the OA, the Wa-Hi-Nasa Lodge announced they would use the funds "toward construction of a lodge building whenever a permanent camp side [site] is obtained by the Middle Tennessee Council." Fitts' death hung like a shroud over the camp the remainder of that first summer.[32]

Of course, that first summer was all there was supposed to be. The original announcement by the Council Executive Committee on moving to the site said quite clearly "the camp will not necessarily be considered for future operations beyond the 1949 season." Rock Island was supposed to be a temporary stop, not a permanent camp. The tragedy of the first summer certainly did not increase any interest in remaining at the site. Unfortunately, no other options appeared. A reappraisal began. The facilities and the legends at Rock Island provided a solid foundation for building a new program to fit the new post-war world.[33]

By spring 1951, having spent two summers at the "temporary" location, a decision was made that for the time being, this was where Boxwell would stay. To that end, Akers and the Council launched a capital campaign to improve the Rock Island Boxwell. The campaign kicked off in May 1951 and was spearheaded by chairman of the Council's Camping Committee, Vanderbilt's Dr. Rudolph Light. A contour map of the camp was developed by the Vanderbilt School of Engineering and published in the *Banner* and used for promotion. The plan was for "extensive development," including construction of a central office, an equipment storage area, a central lodge, a parking area, and thirteen troop lodges. These were all important developments, but as Akers himself noted, the "first project on the building agenda of the camp committee will be a new mess hall, to be constructed as soon as funds were available." The total campaign called for $102,000, of which $25,000 would be needed just for the dining hall.[34]

The development campaign was designed in part to solve a growing problem: how to get more Scoutmasters and troop committeemen to stay at Boxwell. Scouts were now encouraged to attend camp as troops, not as individuals. Still, the day to day handling of the Scouts was handled by the staff once the boys arrived. Scoutmasters were encouraged to come to camp, but they were not really needed. Further, with growing young families at home because of the baby boom (well under way and expanding by 1951), a father taking a week to come to camp leaving the rest of the family at home was less than desirable. So, the campaign was going to solve that problem by allowing "each Scouter to bring his family with him to camp next summer. Special quarters for families will be constructed."[35]

The campaign was something of a qualified failure. It was not adequately promoted. There were a few articles in the *Nashville Banner*, but the *Tennessean* did not carry a single word about it. By this point in time, the *Banner* and the Stahlman family were clearly avid supporters of the Council and the camp, but not a single article in the *Tennessean* suggests the word was not spread very widely. Further, no surviving staff member from the period had any recollection that such a campaign was ever launched. The fact that Rudolph Light saw himself as out of his element as Camping Committee chair likely contributed to the campaign's lackluster achievements as well. Of all the promised items of "extensive development," none were built. The only new facility that emerged at Rock Island was the family campsite. While this was an important development as well as the cheapest option, it was hardly enough to declare a victory for the campaign.[36]

The campaign marked an important turning point though. It demonstrated a clear and marked shift toward embracing a more family-centric version of summer camp. The family campsite would well support other aspects of the program that were taking shape. The campaign also pointed toward a resignation on behalf of Akers to find another location. Unless something changed, there was no reason to go elsewhere. By 1951, the Rock Island site was clearly no longer temporary and investments—in time and program, if not money—needed to be made. A strong camp program, coupled with a way for families to stay at camp, would strengthen Akers' hand in the future should an opportunity to move arise. Finally, the campaign demonstrated that Akers was trying to get people to "think big" about summer camp. The goals for the campaign may have been modest, but there was subtle, but critical change here in the way people talked about Camp Boxwell in 1951. Beginning with the first announcement of the campaign in May, all official publications about Boxwell began referring to the site not as "Camp Boxwell," but "Boxwell Reservation." There was no plan of any kind to build additional camps, which would have been required for the site to actually be a reservation. Simply the change in language suggested a new, bigger way to start thinking about the summer camp program. It was not a "camp"; it was a *reservation!*

It took time for the Rock Island Boxwell to find a clear path to a new program. Akers did not want to follow the program of citizen building that Anderson had built. The paucity of records demonstrates that the scribes and tenters' councils were retired the first summer that Akers was in Nashville. The Rock Island program that finally emerged had covert and overt elements, just like Linton and the Narrows did, but now family life, fatherhood, and even leadership were emphasized in ways that would not have mattered before World War II.

The changes were evident in the most basic decisions. A week of summer camp at the Rock Island Boxwell began on Sunday afternoon and continued until Saturday morning. Part of this decision was practical; Rock Island's distance made bringing troops from the Nashville area on a Monday prohibitive. To do so would have meant a day off of work. But there were ideological reasons as well. For Anderson's Boxwell, Sunday morning service had been a critical component of character building. For Akers' Boxwell, Sunday morning services should be spent in your religious institution with your family. Scout camp was not going to compete with the critical one-two combination of family *and* church. In a Cold War world where the United States government added "In God We Trust" to the currency and "under God" to the Pledge of Allegiance to emphasize how Americans were different from the atheistic communists, this shift in a summer camp week was not surprising.

Arriving and residing at camp were also approached differently. Previously, Scouts had arrived at camp independently. A group may have traveled together, but generally Scouts came and stayed as individuals. Troops were now encouraged to come to camp as a troop. In fact, each of the new districts had their own weeks, meaning that troops from the same district would all attend together. This schedule allowed for the family to plan their summer around the summer camp visit as well as allowed the District Executive (a council professional) to come up to Boxwell for a specific week and tend to his flock of Scouts and Scouters.[37]

Unlike at Linton or the Narrows, where Scouts rushed to claim beds in the handful of tents available upon arrival, Rock Island provided a wholly different and far more organized experience. Staff members met the Scouts and ushered them to assigned campsites. From there, "swimming tests are required of each camper, and finally, each and every boy, desiring to take part in Boxwell's activities, must undergo a medical examination." The organized chaos of a Sunday arrival continued from here:

> The campers are checked from foot to head each week by doctors, who give their time to help make Boxwell a safe place to visit. Physicians from all over Middle Tennessee take turns in spending Sunday afternoons examining Boy Scouts.
>
> Another activity which takes place at the Reservation on the first of each week is the "Round Robin." This is a set up whereby each camper may see the various sections of the camp. The boys are divided into groups, and are guided around the camp by staff members.
>
> One of the places the Scouts visit is the Activities Field. Under the direction of experienced staff members, a number of camping skills such as axemanship, knot tying, compass work, and stalking are prac-

ticed there.

The campers also visit the waterfront, where they are given a thorough swimming test to determine their swimming abilities.

A bright camp fire marks the closing of the first day of a promising week at Boxwell Reservation.

Sunday afternoon was a dizzying array of activity. Sleep came easily the first night![38]

Moving the day camp began and the starting activities was only one way Rock Island was charting a new path. Scouts stayed "bivouac style in American and Canadian army tents spotted through the dense pine thickets." In other words, Scouts did not stay in large eight man tents. They were in two man and four man tents, complete with a cot and mattress, scattered around the property. The "bivouac style" suggests that there was some grouping of tents around the camp, but that these sites were not permanent... at first. With no plans to stay at Rock Island beyond 1949, there was no need to create anything more permanent. As the residency at Rock Island became more settled and entrenched, so too did the campsite locations. In fact, the sites became more than just a place to sleep; they were a critical program component.[39]

Initially, there were six campsites with two more were added by the time the camp closed in 1959. Sites all followed the same basic design. Fifteen to twenty two man tents for the Scouts were often arranged in a semicircular or half-moon shape in the site. The tents were directly on the ground, but each tent had military cots and cotton mattresses inside. The site also contained fire buckets—large cans filled with water—as well as a water fire extinguisher, a metal drum that served as a trash can, and a picnic table. A fire ring in the site was for campsite campfires and each site also had its own two-hole pit latrine. As James Akers explained, "When one filled up to a certain level, then the staff dug a new one and moved the outhouse, filling in the old one with the dirt from the new location. The old location was marked so a new outhouse wasn't placed there again." In keeping with the Native American traditions associated with the site, each campsite was given a Native American name, or at least a name that *sounded* Native American. Camp tradition said the names were those of actual Cherokee chiefs—Sleeping Rabbit, Black Fox, Bushy, Head, Wanuke, Thee-nah-teehee—and some staff even called the sites "villages" as a result. Other names, such as With a La Coochie, were clearly made up.[40]

Staff members lived in the sites with the Scouts. The staff stayed in either large four man tents or in two two-man tents placed together. The staff tent stood at the center of the site, often at the center of the half-moon arrangement. At least one of the staff members was the site leader; he may have had an assistant. The site leader was also program staff. He worked in the Activities Yard or the Conservation Area as an instructor. The other staff members who were not site leaders had jobs elsewhere. The Waterfront staff and kitchen staff for instance, stayed in campsites, but generally were not site leaders.[41]

The site leader was responsible for every one of the thirty to forty Scouts in his site. Generally an older high school or college aged staff member, the site leader introduced his Scouts to the camp and to the site. He provided a legend or unique history of the site, led site campfires and planned out the day for the Scouts in his charge. At the flag lowering ceremony every day in the Activities field, Scouts lined up by site. The site leader would report to the camp director as to the status of his charges. Further, every morning the site leader made sure the Scouts prepared the site for the daily inspection (after all, winning the inspections for the week meant a watermelon for the site!). The site leader also was responsible for insuring his site had a skit ready for the mid-week skit campfire. He was responsible for getting the site set up at the start of the summer and tearing it down at the end of the summer.[42]

The role of the site leader was critical to the new system developing at Rock Island. As Scouts were arriving and attending as troops, they needed leadership. And as seen above, particularly in the early years, getting Scoutmasters to come to camp and stay a week was difficult. Even when adult Scoutmasters came, they often stayed in the family site. Site leaders filled the void. And while the camp's leadership did not want to step on any toes, the expectation was that the camp staff would run their program. The 1955 *Bulletin for Unit Leaders* provided a good example of this thinly veiled expectation:

> Your week at Boxwell Reservation should be the camping highlight of the entire year. Your whole Troop should attend and know in advance of your coming, what you want to do. We have a central staff of fine young men who will operate our part in the program. This staff should in no way take the place of your Troop leader. They are there for specialized jobs such as Waterfront Activities, Archery Range, Handicraft, etc.
>
> Therefore, our part in the camp program becomes a series of schedules... that your Troop may or may not use. Keeping in mind that you can operate your own program with your own leadership if it is the desire of your Troop.

In other words, a troop could run its own program, but there was no need to do that. The staff had it covered.[43]

Nevertheless, despite these pleasantries, the staff was well aware that they were stand-ins for the adult leadership of the troop. They understood and accepted that responsibility. Bob Alley, who became a site leader in 1955, said it most succinctly: "[T]he Old Boxwell was a model of a scout troop. [The staff was] just kids, you know, they may have been in college or older high school, but they were just kids, like patrol leaders or junior assistants to the scout master, or whatever." The idea of Boxwell as a model for a troop worked. The Camp Director was the Scoutmaster and the site leaders were the patrol leaders. Looking at the camp experience through this lens provided Scouts with some valuable leadership insight.[44]

Another critical foundational decision involved the dining hall. "As part of the Scout program," read the section on "Dining Tent" in the *Bulletin for Unit Leaders*, "we are interested in raising a citizenry that are gentlemen… This is especially so in the dining hall." Meals at Rock Island were delivered using what was known as the monitor-host system. Scouts no longer had to bring their own tin plates and silverware; utensils, plates, platters, bowls, and cups were all provided by the camp. Each table sat eight people. One of those eight was designated "host" and another as a monitor. The monitor would go to the dining hall before the meal when a bugle call notified them it was time. Upon arrival, the monitors took enough plates and flatware for everyone at his table. The kitchen staff divided the food out into platters and bowls; again, enough for the eight people at each table. When the other Scouts in the group came to the dining hall, the monitor had the food on the table ready for them. After a prayer over the meal, the meal could begin. If more food or drink was needed during the meal, the monitor (sometimes called "the steward") would get it. The table's host served all the food on to the plates, which were passed around the table. An assistant host sat to the host's right; to his left, the monitor. The table rotated so everyone there shared the responsibility.[45]

During the meal, a member of the staff was likely to sit at the table with the Scouts. In this way, an adult—or at least an adult figure—was always there to supervise the meal. Still, it was the Scouts at the table who were responsible for the critical functions of the meal. After the meal, the entire table contributed to making life a little easier for the monitor. Uneaten food was pushed onto one plate (not a serving bowl or platter!). Utensils were handled in a similar fashion. From here, everyone else could leave the dining hall while the monitor cleared and cleaned the table. Scoutmasters were asked to "help in this matter by counseling with your Scouts in the proper table manners." As hungry Scouts often by-passed the host and served themselves, "counseling… in the proper table manners" was a necessity.[46]

There was efficiency to this style of service. "Everything was put in

Scouts in the dining hall at mealtime. The meal has ended and the monitor is already collecting the platters and plates. This is family style in action. Personal collection of author.

the middle," Alley explained, "and you had cups of Kool-Aid in the middle of the day, and milk at the end of the day, and everything else was just whatever was on the menu for that day. The food ... I thought the food was good. You know, I was just a kid, but I had no complaints about the food." Further, the clean-up was very organized. "[T]hey'd call for the cups, and then they'd call for the silverware and the plates... [I]t was highly organized and it was very well run. I mean, I still [laughing], I still wash things in that order!"[47]

It is difficult to overstate the importance of the mealtime service to the covert agenda of the camp program. The mealtime service clearly promoted family values and gave Scouts the opportunity to practice their future fatherly roles as head of the table. Each Scout was given a chance to serve as host and thus a chance to be "father." The others had to ask for seconds and the "host" served them at his leisure. Thus, the meal not only supported the call for courtesy—table manners—but gave practical experience in leading the patriarchal family meal. The fact the meal was in a tent and the floor was sawdust took some of the edge off of this dress rehearsal. Nevertheless, this was the epitome of the post-war domestic vision Americans embraced. It is perhaps not surprising that this serving system was often called "family style."

The creation of the family campsite in 1952 buttressed this new family/father emphasis. The site was located on the main road, close to the dining hall and even closer to the Commissary. Still, it was just off the beaten track in terms of where most Scout activities would take place. Designed for Scoutmasters and their wives and children, the adult leadership of the camp, including the camp director and medic, stayed here as well. The site was slightly more comfortable than the Scouts' sites. The tents were large four man tents on wooden platforms rather than on the ground. Each tent also had electricity. There was no specific program for these individuals, but simply having the site was important. It not only provided an incentive for Scoutmasters to attend camp for the week, but it reinforced the family values and fatherly responsibility messaging of the period. Family was so important, it came with you when you took vacation time. Father's vacation was spent in service to the family. The family campsite allowed Scouts to see that commitment and sacrifice.[48]

While program aspects like family style feeding or the troop model approach with the campsites and site leaders were clearly promoting an unstated (covert) agenda, this was not the case with advancement. Advancement in Scouting has always been a very clear and overt priority for the program. Advancement exposed boys to the outdoor environment deemed so important to masculinity. Advancement through the specialized topics provided by merit badges exposed boys to the training they would need as adults, perhaps even in the field they wished to enter. And, most simply, advancement provided the positive feedback to keep Scouts in Scouting. Still, Rock Island approached advancement quite differently than Linton or the Narrows. There was a block of time in the morning, starting around 9 a.m. and running until 11 a.m. After lunch, the "rest time" remained, but then the afternoon (2 p.m. – 4 p.m.) was spent with more advancement time instead of organized play as had been the case at the previous Boxwells. There was even a brief instructional time in the evening, simply defined as "after supper." While there was a baseball field and some camp-wide games, the idea of the afternoon wholly dedicated to group sports was no more.[49]

Indeed the very set up of the camp demonstrated that advancement was more critical than it had been. Specific "program areas" as described above were dedicated to instruction on certain merit badges or skills. By extension, the staff who worked in those areas had been hired for those areas. Thus, they did not teach to a pell-mell menu of options, they taught specific "courses" all summer, making them resident experts on the topic. This system allowed for higher quality instruction, but severely limited the offerings available. Rock Island offered a regular slate of merit badges as well as instruction in the skills required for the early ranks of Tenderfoot, Second Class, and First Class. As *Banner* reporter Louis Hine explained,

> Staff members offer merit badges each week to the campers. A merit badge is given upon completion of work in a subject of special interest to Boy Scouts. After the first class rank, boys must advance in scouting by means of merit badges. Merit badges for such subjects as swimming, forestry and stalking are offered each week. In all, a total of 29 merit badges are taught each week by staff members and specialized counselors, who take time off from their regular jobs to help make scouting the activity it is.

Specialized instructors teaching specialized content was a change from the idea that just about anyone could teach a merit badge.[50]

The new approach at Boxwell was upfront about the role advancement was to play. Indeed, one of the first things Scouts did at the beginning of every week was participating in what was called "the county fair method." As a troop, Scouts would visit the different program areas and watch demonstrations of instruction in that area. This would best help leaders and Scouts understand where they needed to focus their attention instead of making blind, uninformed decisions. Again, Louis Hine of the *Nashville Banner* laid out the principles at play here,

> With emphasis being placed on scout advancement, staff members are especially trained to fulfill the objectives of the reservation, 'to see that every boy has an opportunity to participate in a full program and to be treated with courtesy and respect, so that he will enjoy and find the five objectives for the individual: that is, fun, health, skills, adventure, and friends.' When a scout finds these things in camp, his scout troop had been strengthened....
>
> "Advance another rank at Boxwell" is a second scout slogan at the reservation, and the majority of the campers follow that slogan.

Advancement was not treated as a check-box. In the Activities Yard, it was not uncommon to hike to nearby Bone Cave and explore the caverns within. A Scout could complete a requirement and have fun doing it. With cook-outs, hikes, and overnight canoe trips to add some small sense of adventure to it, the emphasis was still clearly rooted in completing the merit badge or the skill in a way it had never been at Linton or the Narrows. A Scout was not to return home from summer camp empty-handed.[51]

This is not to say that there were not activities that were primarily for entertainment. There were. There were camp-wide activities every week that were meant to keep camp entertaining to Scouts. Perhaps the single best example of this was the Friday afternoon water carnival. The waterfront was already popular with Scouts, but the carnival was widely remembered as the highlight of the week. The event was a series of competitions between sites, involving swimming and boating and other water events. Indeed, it was one of the few aspects of the Rock Island Boxwell that was not *that* different from the previous camps. James Akers remembered how as a rather portly Scout, he won the floating contest every week. He had to be barred from participating so other

Scouts could win. The carnival usually ended with a greased watermelon competition. A watermelon was greased with lard, thrown into the water, and Scouts tried to retrieve it. It was a powerful way to end the week's activities.[52]

Campfires also served an entertainment function. As mentioned above, there were site campfires, which were mostly informal events and could happen just about any night the site leader chose to hold one. There was often one on Wednesday night, but the program was not set. One site might tell ghost stories and sing songs, another might have a devotional, and a third might elaborate on the site's history. It was the site leader's discretion on what and when to have this site campfire.

Camp-wide campfires were bigger, more formal events, held in a dedicated campfire area. Scouts sat on logs arranged in a semi-circle in front of a crude stage, which was nothing more than modified tent platforms. There was a totem pole here as well. The actual campfire was usually lit with subterfuge of some kind. Whether it be an "Native American" calling out to the four corners of the world, an archer's flaming arrow, a staff member with a bullwhip striking a match, or something equally mind-boggling, the campfire really was lit by starting a chemical fire at the appropriate moment. There was an introductory campfire on Sunday night, which was primarily put on by the staff. It included songs and story-telling, all done by the staff. Several years even had a Rock Island band, the Poison Ivy Leaguers, made up of staff, singing early rock 'n' roll covers, changing lyrics of existing songs to match camp life, and even a few originals. Friday night had a second camp-wide campfire, a closing campfire. Here Scouts performed their own skits, but the staff also gave out various awards, such as accolades from water carnival or a watermelon from site inspections. Native American traditions and dancing, or at least approximations thereof, were common elements as well.[53]

There were camp-wide games, too. In addition to the occasional softball games or volleyball matches, there was a Rock Island specific game called

"The Indian Village." Not surprisingly, this involved the sites (and their site leaders) competing against each other. The game was a variation of Capture the Flag where the scouts in each site had a piece of cloth on their belts, held on by a rubber band. These "scalps" were to be removed by Scouts from other "villages." Once all the "scalps" were removed, that village was out. The site which maintained their "scalps" was the winner.[54]

Of course all of this was organized via bugle calls. Camp life moved as the bugle calls dictated; each event, each meal, each assembly was signaled by the bugler. The bugler was a camp staff member who could play the bugle (or who could play a trumpet and just adapted). There was reveille in the morning and taps at bedtime. There was a call for monitors and a call for meals. Free swim at the waterfront also had its own bugle call. Assembly was called for the evening flag lowering ceremonies (there was no assembly for flag raising) as well as for campfires. At the evening assembly, Scouts and staff arrived in formal "dress" uniform. Site leaders gave their report to the camp director, the pledge of allegiance was recited, and the flag was lowered.[55]

Making all of this program happen was the camp staff. As has already been intimated, the Rock Island camp staff was significantly larger than either Linton or the Narrows staffs had been. At his largest, Coach Anderson had a staff that included himself, Gribble as Camp Director, Talmadge Miller on the waterfront, eight Junior Staff, a medic, and two to three cooks. Volunteers helped out, but as far as the camp staff, it was a small group. Anderson's Boxwell was a camp of volunteers by volunteers for volunteers. Akers' Boxwell was a camp by professionals for volunteers.

In 1949, Ward Akers and his staff of thirty-four arrived a solid two weeks before Scouts arrived to set up camp. As the *Banner* reported,

> More than 12 loads of supplies, equipment and provisions
> have been trucked into the isolated area, which now has the
> appearance of Second Army maneuver area at the height of the
> war games. Supply tents, bivouac tents, vehicles, canoes, a PX,

the large mess hall, a water tank and portable refrigeration
equipment and more than a half mile of cable strung for lighting present the appearance of a small, busy army field headquarters.

Akers was onsite during setup and served as camp director during the camp's
nine week run. Over one thousand boys were expected during the summer that
would establish the precedent for most summers to come. Staff would arrive
two weeks before the camping season began to put together the camp. This
meant not only setting up the sites again every year, but cutting fresh pine trees
to build the frames for the mess tents. It was an involved process every year.[56]

Akers served as Camp Director again in 1950, but never again. In
1951, economist Clarence R. Jung, Jr. was hired as Camp Director. Jung began teaching economics at Ohio State University after camp, but returned in
1952. He was not highly regarded by the camp staff and perhaps because of
this Akers went a different direction from 1953 forward: he used his own professional staff. From 1953 through 1958, Richard Parker either served as
Camp Director by himself or in conjunction with another professional. Gene
Tolley, James Johnson, and Don Starkin all served as co-directors with Parker
and all were council professional staff. It was only the last year of the camp,
when Parker, now as Camping and Activities Director for the whole Council,
was needed on the Capital Campaign for the new Old Hickory site did he step
aside as Camp Director. In that year, 1959, long time conservation director
Chester LaFever took up the mantle.[57]

Parker had an exceptionally strong relationship with the staff, far more
so than Akers did. Twenty-five years old when he began, the Greenbrier native
was just thirty-two years old at the end of Rock Island's time as Camp
Boxwell. It was not simply his age though. Parker worked closely with his
staff on a personal level, while also allowing them professional space they needed to do their jobs. This was a man who could both engage in a two hour
wrestling match with two teenagers—Johnny Parish and Bob Alley—but also

125

could say with a straight face to a *Banner* reporter, "Discipline is no problem here." The thirty-seven counsellors that made up the camp staff were "as good as money can hire." And as much as Parker was proud of his staff, they were proud of him. "Everyone thought [he] hung the Sun," explained James Akers, the younger son of Ward Akers. Parker was a man who was loved by his staff and as a result, they worked hard for him.[58]

There were other adults who were not professional Scouters. As mentioned above, Chester LaFever was Camp Director in 1959, but he had been on Rock Island Staff since at least 1956. He was the Conservation Area director and given training by the State Game and Fish Commission. An assistant principal at Donelson High School and later principal of McGavock High School, LaFever brought that educational background with him to camp. Steve Eubank was a Scout at Rock Island in 1959 when he and some fellow first time Scouts got caught swearing. As Eubank recounted years later,

> All the rest of us were sent to the Camp Director, Chester La-Fever. Mr. LaFever was a baldish, very dark-haired gentlemen, kind of refined in a lot of ways. And I remember Mr. LaFever sitting at the end of this desk at the end of a two-man tent, and there was one bench on each side. So, we all lined up and went inside... And he asked every one of us what we had said. Each one of us started down the line on the bench, and told what was said or what we thought was said. Then we all started crying because we were scared to death. After Mr. La-Fever had listened to our "profane words," he said, "Well boys, I have two options. I'm going to probably take you down to McMinnville, put you on a Greyhound and send you back [home] to Pulaski. We're going to throw you out of Boxwell, put you out of camp." Well, that really caused a lot of crying; we were really upset. And then Mr. LaFever said, "Okay boys, you're going to stay here for the rest of the week, but I'll be checking on you." Mr. LaFever was on every trail that could be found on Rock Island. Every time that I'd go down a trail, I'd hear Mr. LaFever say, "Eubank, how's it going?" I'd say, "Oh, it's doing fine, Mr. LaFever. Having a

good time!" Needless to say, Mr. LaFever didn't hear of any-more profanity from our troop![59]

There were other men whom boys remembered decades later for their influence. There was Floyd "Q-ball" Pearce, a folksy master craftsman, whom Akers brought with him from Arkansas. Pearce would work at either the Trading Post or the Handicraft and then return home to Arkansas after camp every summer. Luke Gaffin also served in the handicraft. The Handicraft tent was by the legendary hanging tree and Gaffin would tell tales "about a horse thief that was hanged there." Gaffin clearly had a sense of humor as he made sure there was "still" a rope tied to that limb every year. And, of course, there was Doc Hayes, sometimes referred to as "Band-Aid" Hayes. An older man responsible for the camp's first aid needs, Hayes wasn't a real doctor. In fact, not a single article or interview even revealed his first name. He was just one of those adult characters you could find at Boxwell in these years.[60]

Innovations

Clearly, Boxwell at Rock Island represented a departure from its predecessors at Linton and Narrows of the Harpeth. The goals of the program were different and methods used to achieve those goals were different. Indeed, in many ways, the Rock Island Boxwell was an experiment. Much like Linton was a work-in-progress before the more robust and functional Narrows of the Harpeth Boxwell, Rock Island was a work-in-progress as well. Akers knew he was going to move at some point; he just did not know when. Thus, Rock Island served as a location to test and implement ideas.

Some of the innovations new to Boxwell have been discussed above. The Family Camp Site, the Trading Post, and even the 1951 Capital Development Campaign were all significant developments. Indeed, given the post-war period, the addition of a family camp site and a trading post seemed completely appropriate. They easily reflected both the family values and consumerism of the period. They demonstrated that a changing society meant a changing

Scout program and summer camp program.

The 1951 Capital Development Campaign is a bit more difficult to categorize. In terms of Rock Island itself, the campaign was clearly an innovation. The changes suggested by the campaign--a central office, an equipment storage area, a central lodge, a parking area, and thirteen troop lodges--were all obvious improvements to a camp that was, in most respects, more rustic than its predecessor. But in terms of the longer arch of Akers' history and Boxwell's history, such a campaign was not a surprise. Camp Boxwell had a capital development campaign in 1940 for the improvements made at the Narrows. Akers had "been active in building three other camps," which suggests a capital campaign was not new for him either. But while this innovation was not particularly successful, it was an excellent lesson. If another campaign was to be attempted, a different approach would be required.[61]

Other innovations were really adaptations and improvements of existing programs. The most obvious example here was the Order of the Arrow. While the OA originated at the Narrows, it continued and grew with Rock Island. "With" is an important word here because by the post-war period, the Wa-Hi-Nasa Lodge was growing and was independent of the summer camp program. By 1954, the Lodge boasted 850 members. The OA had a special, separate campfire area at Boxwell. This location was used for ceremonies and kept secret from the uninitiated. The rock island itself was also used as a ceremonies ground. Scouts were carried there from the waterfront in the camp's "war canoes" and deposited on the shore of the island, where the ceremonies were held. OA Ordeals themselves—the secret initiation weekends—were held at the Rock Island Boxwell as well. Staff member John Parish remembered that all of his friends were active in the OA and the lodge even had an active dance team that performed at Boxwell.[62]

The death of Henry Fitts in 1949 demonstrated the growing resonance and impact that the OA was having on camp life. Clearly the Lodge was growing, but the contributions to the Fitts memorial showed that bigger dreams were in the works. Lodge members wanted a physical Lodge, an actual building in which to conduct their business. James Akers' suggested that the Yost Lodge was itself used as an OA Lodge in later years at Rock Island. However, the Fitts family was quite clear that this was not sufficient. When a *permanent* Boxwell was found, a lodge should be built dedicated to Henry Fitts' memory. The OA was growing in influence on camp life.[63]

There were two innovations however that were completely new. Both dealt with training. The first was the introduction of the adult training program known as Wood Badge. As another program idea taken from England's Scouting program, Wood Badge had been slow to take root in the United States. The first attempt had been in 1936, but failed. In 1948, a second attempt to implement the program took hold. The course was the first one held in the South. Akers and Billy Jim Vaughn of Troop 1 in Brentwood had participated in the course in 1950. They were impressed with the offering and brought Wood Badge to Boxwell at Rock Island. A national version of the course (No. 34) was held at the camp in 1952. Middle Tennessee Council's first Wood Badge course—known as MT-1 and run by Springfield Troop 144's Scoutmaster, Harry "Beany" Elam—was in 1954.[64]

Wood Badge was not for the faint of heart. An eight day course at the time, it was a hands on crash course on Scouting leadership and outdoor skills. This meant both "class work" and also practical, in-the-field training. Jack Bond, a feature writer for the *Nashville Banner*, participated in the program in 1959 in the fifth Wood Badge course offered by Middle Tennessee Council, MT-5. As Bond reported, the group was greeted by Elam with these humbling words: "Every time I stand in the presence of a group of men such as you, I feel extremely humble – for you would not be here if you didn't want to help someone. It is great and wonderful to love your son; but it is even greater to love your neighbor's son, for this is the true spirit of Scouting." From there, "Formal instruction and demonstrations are conducted throughout the day with candidates taking notes and participating. Upon completion of the eight-day practical phase of the course, each candidate must pass an intensive written examination. This comprehensive part of the program can take as long as three years." Bond also pointed out that the program "covers every phase of the patrol method employed by the Boy Scouts of America. It applies only to adult Scouters who have demonstrated outstanding ability in their volunteer work. Enrollment is by invitation from the Middle Tennessee Council and is limited since this council is one of only 18 in America authorized to conduct the intense course."[65]

Bond also poked fun at himself... and perhaps other adults tackling the realities of Scouting on the ground. "The next time I undertake to report something like this Wood Badge training course," Bond complained, "please let me scrimmage a few weeks first with the Vanderbilt football squad, so I can be ready." The course was "a souped-up version of basic training, OCS, and a college-level civics class combined. It's most interesting and wouldn't be quite as frustrating if a sadistic group of grown-ups in short pants—known as staff instructors—didn't keep telling us: 'Have Fun.'" Indeed, Bond's "unofficial" reports to his editor dripped with a sarcastic truth about his experience:

> Everywhere we go around here we sing songs. At first, most of the Wood Badge candidates (who have voices that croak like mine) were sheepishly self-conscious about this: but now it sounds pretty good—maybe I've been here too long already.
>
> Food here is excellent. Until it's cooked, that is. We're doing our own cooking. However, when you get as much exercise as we do, it still tastes good...
>
> Then there is a special little ceremony which is carried on between patrols. The 'program patrol' must take a kudu horn with them everywhere they go. This is a very rare object, since there just aren't any kudus left in the world...
>
> Under Wood Badge rules, the keeper of the kudu horn must never let it touch the ground (or let the other patrols appro-

Middle Tennessee Council's first Wood Badge Troop, MT-I held at Rock Island in 1954. Harry "Beany" Elam, back row, far left, served as Scoutmaster. Personal collection of James "Jimmy" Stevens & Harry "Beany" Elam.

priate it). The antler-like object is about four feet long and shaped like a cork-screw. Believe me, Bob [Bond's editor], you have never lived until you've spent 24 hours acting as a guardian to a kudu horn—especially in a sleeping bag.

However, Bond also gave respect where respect was due. And respect was due to program Scoutmaster "Beany" Elam.

Life here has an inspiring side, too, in spite of the physical strain and not having enough time in the day. When "Beanie" Elam conducts campfire lectures, you begin to feel the greatness of Scouting and realize that it is the best hope this world has for future generations of boys.

While gathered around a fire beneath the starts on our first night here, I sensed a completeness that I haven't known in a long time. The night was filled with the sound of crickets and katydids and tree frogs trilling their mixed paean—and far off on a ridge, an excited hound voiced his plaintive note to an unheeding world.

Somewhere an owl screeched and the fire made sputtering

sounds, sending showers of sparks streaming heavenward to
join the stars. The resonant voice of Scoutmaster Elam rolled
like a benediction in the flickering light, and I knew then why
so many men sacrifice many of their personal pleasures in order to work with Boy Scouts.

Elam expressed it this way: 'The very earth on which we stand
beats the tom-tom of your heart, pounding the rhythms of
that which you believe.' He believes that training tomorrow's
citizens is an important mission. I'm inclined to agree with
him.

Covered with chigger bites by the end of the eight days, Bond was clearly hum-
bled by the experience.[66]

It was important to the Council that the Wood Badge program succeeded. Indeed, staff member John Parish recalled that the Rock Island staff
was used for training purposes before the council started offering the program.
This training by the youth staff was undoubtedly the germ for the Long Rifle
program. "Operation Long Rifle" was a leadership program for youth that ran
at Rock Island before camp started. The program was patterned after Wood
Badge and was designed to train Explorer Scouts—older youth—to be junior
leaders. Half the participants were to be camp staff members. The only evidence of this program was an article in the *Banner* in 1952, so it is unclear how
long the program ran. However, the fact that the first Wood Badge course the
Council ever hosted was at Rock Island Boxwell in 1952, it seems likely that
"Operation Long Rifle" was in reality the Wood Badge training program that
to which Parish referred.[67]

The final innovation pioneered at Rock Island was another idea that did
not quite stick at the time. In 1951, the same year of the abortive capital development campaign, Boxwell had two women as part of the "Senior," or
adult, staff. Mrs. Jean Murdock and Mrs. Tom Pedigo worked in the kitchen.
According to the *Banner*, "Mrs. Jean Murdock and Mrs. Tom Pedigo work
with planning the campers' meals, and Mrs. Murdock is the leading dietitian."

The idea of two women (wives whose full names were never provided no less) working to provide food for boys would be very consistent with the family roles presented in this era. How successful this idea was or even who Mrs. Jean Murdock and Mrs. Tom Pedigo were are lost to history. None of these characters appear in the record again. Nevertheless, the two wives were the first women to serve on Boxwell staff.[68]

Innovations though were a double edged sword. For every good innovation, there was fear of what change might cost. In July of 1958, David Dunbar, the assistant national director of camping, declared that "Camping has got soft in the last 20 to 30 years... We have made it an entertainment for people, instead of group living in the out-of-doors, so that a boy now arrives at camp and says, 'Here I am. Entertain me.'" Dunbar blamed Scout leaders who were "babying" their Scouts at camp with modern conveniences and luxuries, such as "dish washing machines, potato peelers, hot showers, deep freezes, air mattresses, heated cabins and even vacuum cleaners." While admitting such improvements were partly the result of Scout camping's ten-fold increase over the previous thirty years, Dunbar believed older Scouts should be interested "in more rugged camping." Almost fifty years into the program and national leadership was still wringing its hands over "weak" boys.[69]

Scouts and staff at Camp Boxwell—by now Boxwell Reservation—dismissed this notion. One Scout quipped, "We don't even have television," acknowledging how prevalent the invention had become. Another Scout was more direct. "You ought to try sleeping on one of those mattresses," the boy declared. "They're harder than rock." Chester LaFever owned up to having some of the conveniences Dunbar mentioned. He had a potato peeler "but that was all."[70]

Indeed, for Middle Tennessee Council, the Rock Island Boxwell may have been the last truly rough summer camp the Council ever operated, if Dunbar's comments can be used as a measure. *The Tennessean* made it a point to demonstrate how the local camp was not a "sissy camp" and the boys were getting a proper outdoor experience.

> Tucked in among the tall pines are eight cleanly kept groups of tents. The tents have only earth for a floor, but they are equipped with cots and mattresses...
>
> Besides the mattresses, there are few other remnants of 'sissy city life' at the camp except for a carefully concealed comic book or two.
>
> The campers do get a first-hand encounter with nature, mostly in the way of chiggers and poison ivy...
>
> If they are not roughing it, the boys with their muddy knees at least look like they are. Most of them are too wary of the camp's one shower—cold water only—to bother removing the signs or smells of the backwoods...
>
> Each day camp life starts at 7 a. m. with a bugle call. Breakfast and a rigorous camp cleaning follow before the Scouts are allowed to begin the day's full program of hikes, swimming, boating, and merit badge work.
>
> Richard Parker, director of the camp, carts in three quarters of a ton of food every three days in order to keep the boys fit for their introduction to outdoor life.
>
> "When taps sounds at 9:30 every night, I'm just worn out," said Ronnie Florence, 12, son of Dr. and Mrs. T. H. Florence, 956 E. Clayton Ave., Nashville.

The paper left no doubt that the Middle Tennessee Council's summer camp was growing men, just as a good summer camp program should. Indeed, from the 875 Scouts the camp served in 1949, by the time of these articles, camp attendance had risen to 2300. Summer camp was building *a lot* of men.

And Dunbar's idea that Scouts arrived at camp and said, "Here I am, entertain me"? Not at Boxwell. As staff member Luke Gaffin explained, "Here it is more like they come and say, 'Here I am. Show me how to do it'."[71]

134

Down the Cumberland: The Rock Island Staff

It should not be much of a surprise, but the staff of the Rock Island Boxwell was a very tight knit group. Either because of the brevity of the camp's existence, the way the living quarters were arranged, the strength of the leadership, or just the right combination of folks, these staffs got along well. And not just on site at Boxwell, but after camp as well. Sit down with any Rock Island staff member and he will immediately regale you with a list of friends and what they went on to do. Then, he will tell you about their exploits together. There was a pride in this group, not just in the job they did and the program they provided, but in each other.

John Parish was an excellent example of this. In discussing his time on Rock Island staff, as soon as the door opened to discuss the people he worked with, he started rolling off names. Bill McWhorter was in his tent. Payne Hardison was a waterfront guy. Harold Sparks ran the mess hall. Bob Alley was part of the Activity Yard. What did all these names have in common for Parish? "We all became really good friends going forward. In fact, they were all in our wedding. That's how close we were." And after a moment to catch his breath, Parish continued, "And Jack Bouchard... Jack was in our wedding also." And Parish was in Bouchard's wedding.

Parish, himself the son of Council President Charles E. Parish, relished in explaining the accomplishments of the men he worked with and their family connections. Tony Gotto, waterfront staff, "became the guy that did the research and development of the lipid drugs for cholesterol." Payne Hardison became an oral surgeon. John Omohudro became a Nashville eye doctor and would travel with Parish to Minnesota and Canada. Cliff Briley was the son of Metro's first mayor, Beverly Briley. (Beverly Briley was himself a product of the Linton Boxwell). John Bouchard was the namesake, and later ran, the family company, John Bouchard & Sons, a well-known construction infrastructure company over a hundred years old. The two became incredibly close, hiking on the Appalachian Trail three separate times and taking their wives to Canada. The time lines were never clear; the friendships were so fresh the time did not seem to matter.

And then came the stories. Campbell Smoot, son of the local doctor who helped the camp medic when the injuries became more serious, worked on the waterfront. Smoot "was a wild man, absolutely a wild man. He was uninhibited." He carried a machete and a gun and chased rednecks when they gave him trouble. Of course, there were stories with best friend Bouchard. The two were pouring trash into the camp dump, a sinkhole, and horsing around. Bouchard threw a tin can to Parish with a call to "Catch this pass Parish!" Parish missed it and... "You see this wrinkle right across here? It laid my head open right here. So [Doctor Smoot] sews that up without any painkillers."[72]

All the surviving Rock Island staff members had similar reactions and stories. Bob Alley recalled, "Staff life was fun. All were accepted, even the nerds and geeks. A lot of time in off hours was spent in deep conversation about the meaning of life, God, good and evil, etc." He also recalled once when "one of the staff members presented assistant cook Lovey with a snake. Lovey didn't like snakes and so, Lovey left. And so the Camp Director, whose name was Richard Parker, met Lovey out on the highway with his suitcase and brought him back." And of course, night life was when the truly essential lessons were learned. "The First Aid tent... was the place for the staff to gather at night and tell stories and learn about why we are here on this earth and learn about how to present ourselves to girls and important things like that."[73]

These are not simply old age recollections of cohesiveness that only existed in imagination. Perhaps the single best example of the closeness of this group was an event well documented in the newspapers. In 1953, right after camp ended that summer, eight staff members decided to take a canoe trip. Canoe trips were nothing particularly new to Boxwell or to Scouting. This trip was unique for two reasons. First, the trip would be a six day, 209 mile journey from Boxwell on the Caney Fork River, through Center Hill Lake, and then down the Cumberland River, all the way into Nashville. Second, the trip was not simply youth staff, though that was most of the group. Camp Director Richard Parker went along as well.[74]

The trip began on Monday, August 10. The staff members traveled in four canoes, two per boat. Covering about twenty-five miles a day, the group nicknamed themselves the "Caney land expedition" and even named their canoes: the *Robert E. Lee*, the *Wa-Hi-Nasa III*, the *Natchez*, and the *Shushugah*. The first day they made it to Sligo dock on Center Hill Lake and reached the Center Hill dam the second day. The lake was considered the hardest part of the trip: it was "60 miles across the dead-calm waters." There they paused and took a guided tour of the dam and hydroelectric equipment. The next morning the engineers at the dam released some water to help speed them along the next portion of their journey and they were off toward Carthage.[75]

The trip details are interesting, but the trip itself showed how this staff worked together. When the group stopped for the night, Parker and Barry Goad (the camp's kitchen director) did the cooking while the other gathered firewood and cleaned dishes. They awoke early, ate quickly, and traveled all day, usually stopping around 6 p.m. When they landed at Carthage, they all took time "for their first night of recreation." The staff that worked hard together, played hard together.[76]

Knowing a crowd of family, friends, and other professional Scouters was to meet them at Fort Nashborough, the group made a stop upon arriving in Nashville. Sulliman Evans, publisher of *The Tennessean*, made his boat *Tennessee Lady* available to the group. They had "soft drinks and snacks" as well as a shave. Rested and energized, the group loaded back up into their canoes and "tore water downstream for the last mile to Fort Nashborough and land." There the group pulled their canoes out of the water, met their friends and family, and grinned giddily the whole time. A new story to be told and retold in the years to come had just been completed.[77]

Boxwell, Race, and Camp Burton

In spite of the innovations discussed above, the new understandings about family, and even the closeness of the staff that made the camp work, the summer camp program at Boxwell remained resolutely unchanging in regard to one issue: race. While just about everything else about the Linton and Narrows camps had been jettisoned, the approach to race at summer camp remained. Just like its' predecessors, the Rock Island Boxwell was a segregated Boy Scout camp. No African American Scout or troop ever set foot on the property for summer camp during the eleven year operation of Boxwell Reservation at the site.

This is not to say African Americans were not involved in the operation of the Rock Island Boxwell. Just like at the previous two incarnations of the camp, African Americans were hired as cooks for the Rock Island camp. Walter Whittaker actually returned for one more year in 1949, making him the only staff member in all of Boxwell's history to serve at three different locations. Completing his twenty-ninth summer at Boxwell, Whittaker was joined by Ike Davis from West Virginia that summer. Davis was on his thirty-fifth year "as a faithful colored cook." For Whittaker, however, 1949 would be his last summer.[78]

Given how little remains in the record about Walter Whittaker's background and life, it is especially abhorrent to admit the record contains even less about Ike Davis. He appears once in the *Tennessean*, in the article referenced above. He is not mentioned again throughout all the years of the Rock Island Boxwell. No article on the camp ever references him again, not even when explaining the roles that Mrs. Murdock and Mrs. Pedigo would play. He may have returned to West Virginia every year or he may have found work in the mid-state area. In fact, Bob Alley and John Parish both recollect that Davis did not come from West Virginia at all, but came with Akers from Arkansas.

Rock Island cook Ike Davis (right) with two Scouts, ca. 1955. Personal collection of the author.

Regardless, this paucity of information means no birth or death dates can be provided. Very little is known for sure beyond the fact that Davis existed and cooked at the Rock Island Boxwell. [79]

What is known is that Davis served as the camp cook throughout most of the run at Rock Island. In fact, Davis generally came to camp every summer with his friend, Lovey, and the two men cooked all the meals for the camp. They lived in a tent not far from the dining area and kitchen. A surviving photo of Ike Davis from around 1955 shows him to be an older man with a grey mustache and bald head, but with a big smile. Parish described Davis as a good guy whom everybody liked and respected. Davis' pancakes were especially memorable. Ward Akers' younger son James had more pleasant memories of Davis, whom he apparently spent a fair amount of time with while at

Boxwell. Davis taught the youngest Akers how to "hambone," a type of dance made by stomping and slapping your legs and chest. Akers developed a particular affinity for Davis. "I was the boss's kid so most people tried to stay as far away from me as they could. Not Ike. He was like a grandpa." He told stories, sang, and played music in his tent at night. He was apparently the best grandpa one could hope for. Nevertheless, even with eyewitnesses still alive who remembered the man, Davis is an unknown quantity and while Lovey was mentioned as either his brother or simply his friend, no specifics on him ever made it into the record.[80]

In terms of black Scouting in the newly reorganized Middle Tennessee Council, the situation had not changed dramatically. The J. C. Napier division for African Americans Scouts still existed and still occupied its own offices separate from the main Council offices. This is important to note because Akers moved the Council office in 1947, again in 1951, and a third time in 1956, each time to accommodate a desire for more space. The J. C. Napier Division office remained in its location on Charlotte Avenue. Wilbur Creighton, Jr. stated in *Boys Will Be Men* that when his father, Wilbur Creighton, Sr., was Council President, he "started the move for integration of scouting" in 1953. This was accomplished by closing the Napier division office, putting the Napier Division Field Executive in the main Council office, and increasing black representation on the Council's interracial committee. It was not clear what the timeline was for these changes however. By 1956, the Napier division was still alive and recognized as a separate unit within the Council.[81]

For summer camp, Camp Burton was still the primary destination for African American troops. The camp followed a similar Sunday to Saturday schedule as Boxwell and included traditional camping activities, such as swimming, rifle marksmanship, boating, fishing, archery, nature study, outdoor cooking, tracking, and campfires. Not much remains in the record concerning the camp program beyond this. Whether Burton's program evolved to reflect the changing social norms of the post-war world, and especially those concerning the family displayed so well in the Boxwell changes, simply is not known.[82]

The numbers at Burton remained fairly respectable, though small. In 1950, the camp ran for three weeks and in total served approximately 145 Scouts. Burton planned for similar numbers in 1951. Running a two week program instead, the numbers that summer totaled approximately ninety-three Scouts: fifty in week one and forty-three in week two. This two week program with approximately 100 Scouts remained the pattern in 1952 and 1953 as well.[83]

But then, starting in 1954, circumstances began to change. When Boxwell opened at Rock Island, Camp Burton was still located off of Couchville Pike. The camp remained there until 1953. As the Council bought that property in 1946 and improved upon it with capital developments completed in 1948, there seemed to be little reason to relocate, but it did. In June 1954, a *Banner* article announced the move south to a new site, Camp Cove Lake in Williamson County near Leiper's Fork. The name "Camp Burton" remained, but the physical location was different. No explanation was offered, just the stated move. And then the camp moved again. In April 1955, the Council sent a letter to Scoutmasters explaining that the new camp for the summer would be at the Bethlehem Center Camp at Marrowbone Creek, about seventeen miles west from Nashville. The camp was also moved from its traditional dates at the end of June into the first of July to the second and third weeks of August. It is unclear where the camp was stationed in 1956, but by 1957 it appeared to have moved to the Narrows of the Harpeth, giving that property a second life as a Scout camp. Burton would remain at the Narrows into the early 1960s.[84]

Ascertaining Burton's situation was complicated by the other change that occurred in 1954. Newspaper articles on Burton stopped. Almost every summer since its opening, there was some acknowledgement that Burton existed. After June 1954, not another article about Burton appeared in either the *Banner* or the *Tennessean*. And yet, the camp continued. It continued to move, it continued to operate. It continued to serve Scouts.

This situation begs several questions. For instance, why hold on to segregation as a policy at the camp? Further, given that the Council owned the Couchville Pike property and had improved it, why abandon it? Finally, why not advertise the summer camp in the newspapers? Clearly, the answers there could easily be the focus of a separate work, but a quick explanation is warranted.

The year 1954 is critical to the explanations concerning Camp Burton. First, remember that *Boys Will Be Men* claimed that the integration of the J. C. Napier Division began at the end of 1953. The folding of that aspect of mid-state Scouting would have some ripple effects, even if that process was a slow one. Second, by 1954, Colonel Gilbert Dorland, district engineer of the Army Corps of Engineers, Nashville District, was elected President of the Middle Tennessee Council. Like Leslie G. Boxwell before him, this was ultimately a volunteer post, but it was a post with some influence. Indeed, Dorland's position with both the Corps and the Scouts was critical to the next Boxwell, but for now, it is important to know Dorland was aware of the changes related to the Corps work in the area. For instance, on May 20, 1954, the *Tennessean* reported that the Nashville district had submitted a report for some *big* public works projects in the area. Specifically, a dam and power plant at Stewart's Ferry. A reservoir at the Stewart's Ferry site—today known as Percy Priest Lake—would flood and submerge Camp Burton. It was time to consider a move.[85]

1954 was also important in regard to a segregated summer camp because on May 17, 1954, the Supreme Court of the United States in the case *Brown v. the Board of Education of Topeka* "unanimously outlawed racial segregation in public schools." While the implementation of the order was delayed, the message was clear: segregation was on its way out. Not all the reactions to the end of the nation's racial caste system were good. Southern Congressmen and Senators presented a document known as the Declaration of Constitutional Principles, or more colloquially "the Southern Manifesto," denouncing racial integration of public places. Half of Tennessee's Representatives signed the document, though neither Senator Albert Gore Sr. nor Senator Estes Kefauver signed. Of more immediate local concern was the situation at Clinton High School in Anderson County near Knoxville. Here twelve African American students tried to enroll in the school for the 1956-57 school year. They were met with resistance, which turned violent enough that the governor called out the National Guard to quell the violence. Three bombs blew up the school in 1959. In September 1957, another bomb partially destroyed Hattie Cotton elementary school in Nashville. While Tennessee was able to integrate more smoothly than many Southern states, it did not do so without incident or bloodshed. It is impossible to think that incidents such as these did not influence Akers and Council leadership over how to handle their segregated Scout camp, either in terms of promotion or simply integrating.[86]

Integration would come and the two-camp system would eventually end, but not yet.

The End of Camp Boxwell III

Ward Akers was never satisfied with the Rock Island location; it was always supposed to be temporary. After the 1951 campaign, Akers and the Council settled into trying to build the best camp they could with the resources they had. By any reasonable standard, they were successful. The camp developed a solid program, attendance rose to the point of building new sites, and a solid cadre of leadership, both youth and adult, was dedicated to making the camp work. The new emphasis on family and troops set the stage for training a new generation of men.

And yet, the search for a new site never entirely ended. Colonel Gilbert

143

Dorland, chair of the camping committee in 1953, explained,

> The present site of Caney Fork is recognized by experts of the National Council to be one of the best sites in the country for a scout camp, but the feeling has been growing, principally in the minds of our professional staff, that it is too far from the center of scout population to be used for year-round camping by leaders and older boys. Conditions there are very primitive; it needs an adequate water supply system and a combination recreation, dining hall and kitchen and other minor improvements.

In short, Boxwell Reservation at Rock Island was a good camp, but it was not great. The Council—Akers—wanted more. This desire was not irrational. The Rock Island site had served approximately 1100 Scouts in 1949. By 1959, over 2800 Scouts registered for summer camp. In eleven years, the numbers at camp had more than doubled. The baby boom impact had begun.[87]

Thus, 1954 turned out to be an auspicious year. Dorland, in his capacity commanding the Nashville District Corps of Engineers, was overseeing an enormous project on the Cumberland River: the Old Hickory Dam. The reservoir created by the dam would lead to a potentially ideal location for a summer camp. And, as it turned out, Dorland, who had been chair of the camping committee, was now Council President. It was Dorland who told Akers and the Council about the potential site in Wilson County, significantly closer to Nashville and much larger than the Rock Island property.[88]

The creation of Old Hickory Lake was a long running topic of conversation in the Nashville area. The Old Hickory Lock and Dam had been authorized by the Rivers and Harbors Act of 1946, but had not been given funding at that time. By 1951, Army Engineers were asking Congress for $8 million to fund the building of the dam and cover the costs of "relocations made necessary by the dam," such as moving roads, bridges, power and phone lines, and cemeteries. Construction on the dam began in 1952 and was completed in 1956. Water levels in the area came up and down as work was completed or stalled. The project in total was expected to run almost $50 million

Council Presidents Col. Gilbert Dorland (1954-1956) and Charles E. Parish (1956-1958).
Official Council Portraits.

and would provide 100,000 kilowatts of power. Like other TVA projects, the
new Old Hickory Lake was going to change the way people in the area lived.[89]

The Council wasted no time with the information provided by Dorland. In 1952, the Council purchased 113 acres of land to provide access to
the proposed site. By mid-July 1954, Akers had a map in hand of the location
that showed where the new water levels would be after the dam was completed.
He could start planning out the new camp *exactly* as it would be before the
dam was even finished. By March 1957, the Council had leased 609 acres from
the U. S. Government and purchased an additional 108 acres of adjoining
land. The dam was finished and the lake was up. The Council began promoting a reservation to be ready to go by 1960. Charles E. Parish was president of
the Council now and he announced two committees to start working on a new
year round camp. Dorland chaired the development committee and T. Cecil
Wray chaired the steering committee on finance.[90]

The plans for the new camp were grandiose, especially given the rustic nature of the Rock Island Boxwell. Parish announced that the current plans included:

> 1. Three 200-boy capacity camps on the reservation, each with a central dining hall, staff cabins and waterfront areas. One of these camps would be adapted to winter as well as summer use.
>
> 2. A family camp for unit leaders, consisting of cabins, a dining hall, waterfront area and bath house.
>
> 3. Cabins and a bath house for families of camp staff members who spend entire seasons at the camps.
>
> The vast development program will include equipment such as tents, tent floors and boats in addition to buildings, waterfront facilities, roads, waterworks and an electric system.

But more importantly than the physical development, the new site would realize a dream. Not just a dream of the better camp Akers had been looking for since 1947, but a dream of what a good Scout camp could do. The Boxwell Planning Committee, led by T. Cecil Wray, expressed the vision this way:

> A good Scout camp… should be used extensively for three major purposes: summer camping, weekend year-round camping and adult leader training. Another purposed is for picnic and day hike areas for Cub Scouts.
>
> Weekend camping on a year-round basis was called 'probably the most important single program' in the Scout movement.

The new location would have it all.[91]

There was one small hurdle: the Council did not own most of the land that would make up the reservation. In short, the Council did not have clear title to the land, creating problems for fund-raising and developing. They could not build upon land to which they did not have clear title. To remedy this problem, three separate bills were introduced to the U. S. House of Representatives to direct the U.S. Army to give 535.8 acres of the Old Hickory Lake reservoir to the Middle Tennessee Council. While an Act of Congress might seem excessive, the reality was that the U. S. Army could not give the land away without such an act. The Corps of Engineers would maintain possession of the shoreline in order to properly operate Old Hickory Dam, but 525 acres would go to the Scouts. Tennessee Congressmen J. Carlton Loser of Nashville, Joe Evins of Smithville, and Ross Bass of Pulaski were all active in pushing the bills forward; E. B. Stahlman was in the background using his influence and contacts to move the process along.[92]

After two tense months of watching the progress—or non-progress— of the bill wade its way through the halls of Congress, word came on August 31, 1957 that the bill had passed both houses of Congress and was on its way to the President. For fee simple, the transfer of 525 acres of land in the Old Hickory Lake reservoir was approved. Perhaps not surprisingly, the news made the front page of the *Nashville Banner.* According to said article, "Charles E. Parish of Tullahoma, president of the Middle Tennessee Council, was jubilant today over passage of the measure." Parish argued the new camp would not only be one of the best locations in the South, but "will greatly aid Boy Scouting in general." While Parish may have overstated the value some-what, there was no question the passage of the act was a significant victory for the Middle Tennessee Council. The act only had one caveat: "the government will take back the title if the camp is not started within three years or if it is ever used for other purposes." In other words, construction had to begin with-in the next three years and if the Council ever stopped using the location for a summer camp, it would lose title to the property. Of course, neither of these stipulations were serious concerns. With the land now secured, the Council could shift its focus to a capital funds campaign to build the new reservation. It would begin in earnest in January 1959.[93]

These developments though did leave the existing Rock Island Boxwell in an awkward situation. It was still clearly *the* summer camp; it was even called "Boxwell Reservation." However, the camp was not exactly treated with warm and loving expressions in the drive to promote the "new Boxwell." What

would soon be known as "Old Boxwell" was "somewhat too small,' Scout officials agreed, and its location is considered inconvenient for many parts of the
mid-state area." Parish, whose son John had been a staff member at the Rock
Island Boxwell since 1950, was quite blunt: "At Rock Island, camping sessions
are conducted only two months of the year. The largest council of the Boy
Scout region including parts of several states, Middle Tennessee Council has
outgrown the old camp."[94]

There it was. The Council had outgrown the Rock Island camp. The
land would continue to be used by the Council; there were even some plans for
conservation and reforestation there. But Parish's assessment was accurate. In
a single weekend at "new Boxwell," 1,500 Scouts attended an opening weekend campout in September 1957. With only eight sites holding at most forty
Scouts each, Rock Island could not compete with the new location's size.
"Within three months thereafter," Creighton and Johnson write, "more scouts
had used the Old Hickory Lake camp for day camping than had used the camp
on Caney Fork during the previous seven years." Rock Island's days as Boxwell
were numbered. 1959 would be the last summer at what was once known as
"Boxwell III."[95]

And so, Middle Tennessee Council's summer camp program moved to
a new location in 1960. At that time, the Council now had three "Boxwells":
the "new" Boxwell Reservation at Old Hickory Lake, "old" Boxwell at Rock
Island, and "old old" Boxwell as Narrows of the Harpeth. All three properties
were still owned by the Council. But while the Old Hickory Lake property
was enjoying its new life as the center of attention and the Narrows was enjoying a second life as Camp Burton, Rock Island had no such rebirth. It was
never forgotten, nor was it ever quite clear what to do with the property.

In 1972, as part of the capital campaign that year, the Rock Island
property was renamed the "Charles E. Parish Wilderness Reservation." On
November 25, 1975, about six weeks before he retired, Ward Akers signed a

Resolution recognizing Parish's efforts and expressing the Council's sorrow over Parish's passing on October 22, 1975. In addition to his work as President of Worth, Inc., Parish had been an Executive Board member since 1940, Council President from 1957-1959, and a Vice-President for many years. He was an Eagle Scout and Scoutmaster. A father and a husband as well, Parish represented the new values that the program was geared toward training its charges to become.[96]

The Charles E. Parish Wildlife Reservation remains an active property for more rustic and outpost camping in the Middle Tennessee Council to this day.

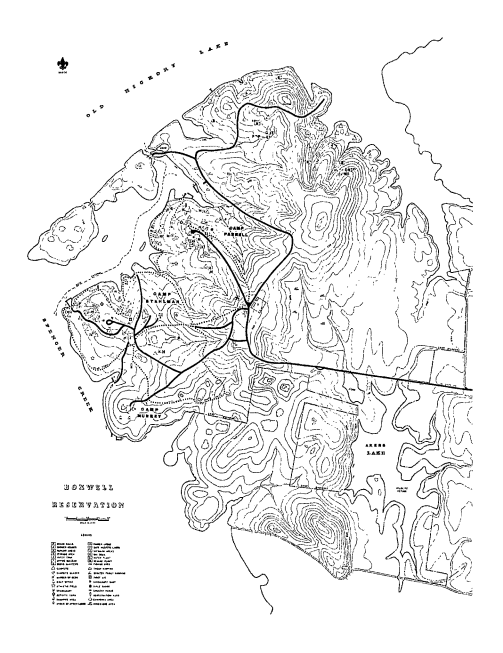

Map of Boxwell Reservation, ca. 1972. The three original camps are here with two "proposed" camps in the upper right corner. Personal Collection of Greg Tucker

Chapter 4

The Camp That Akers Built:
Boxwell Reservation at Old Hickory Lake

1960-1975

One Sunday afternoon late in the summer of 1954, Ward Akers asked his eldest son, Ward C. Akers, if he would be interested in taking a boat ride on the Cumberland River. At about twelve years of age, the younger Akers—sometimes called "Ward, Jr."—was eager for an adventure and agreed to the trip. Akers the father took several rolled up maps, including a particularly recent one from the United States Corps of Engineers, dated July 15, 1954. The two Akers men travelled from their home in Brentwood, Tennessee to the Old Hickory Lock on the north side of Nashville. The Lock had been approved for renovation into a dam, and while construction had already begun, the resulting Old Hickory reservoir would not be impounded for two more years. At the Lock, the father and son met Richard Parker, camp director of Camp Boxwell at Rock Island. Together, the three put a red aluminum boat into the Cumberland River and their adventure began.[1]

The explorers traveled east up the Cumberland River for several miles. After approximately two hours, they arrived at their destination. On the northern bank of the river was Sumner County and the southernmost tip of Gallatin, Tennessee. On the opposite bank, Spencer Creek flowed out of Wilson County into the Cumberland. Between the two was Lock Four, belonging

151

to neither county, but instead owned and maintained by the U. S. Corps of Engineers.

The Akers group turned south into Spencer Creek—a small tributary of perhaps twenty to thirty feet in width—and sailed another two or three hundred yards before putting ashore. This whole area on the Wilson County side of the river was the small, sleepy community of Laguardo, full of small land owners, tenant farmers, and clapboard churches. A good portion of this farmland would soon be flooded by the Old Hickory Dam project as it now fell under the jurisdiction of the Corps of Engineers. Even Lock Four itself would be submerged by the new reservoir. Exploring what this area would become had brought the small group to these shores. And the July 1954 map showed them exactly where the new water levels would be.

As soon as the expedition landed, the elder Akers laid his maps out on the ground and began to get his bearings. The younger Akers took stock of his surroundings. His first impressions were less than positive. The land was barren and rocky. "It looked like it hadn't rained there in 10 years. Rock everywhere. No grass, no trees, no nothing," he recalled. "Terrible looking." Meanwhile, Akers the elder had oriented himself. He rolled up his maps and the group struck out to explore the property.

Before long they came to a white farm house, undoubtedly one of the many family homesteads that had to be abandoned for the reservoir. Nearby was a large gray barn, derelict and near collapse. Father Akers again laid out his maps for a consultation. Confident of his location, he pointed out the critical information to his son and Parker: here was where the water was going to rise to when the reservoir was completed. Ward, Jr. was flabbergasted and confused. What was his father talking about? What was going on? Again, Akers the father explained that this was where the water was going to come to when Old Hickory Lake was completed. But this time, he went further in his explanation.

152

"We're going to move Boxwell down here," he said. "I'm going to a build camp here."

Incredulous, the younger Akers responded, "Daddy, you're crazy as hell. This is the most barren, rock forsaken place I've ever seen in my life."

As the exchange continued, the senior Akers explained he was going to build not one, but four Scout camps at this location. The new site would hold two thousand kids a week. And with that, Akers laid out the rest of his vision as they combed the property the rest of the day. He pointed out where a boat harbor would go. He pointed out where he wanted the base camp, what would become Camp Stahlman, to be. He pointed out where he wanted concrete slabs laid for the waterfronts, so that Scouts wouldn't have to swim in the mud—slabs that would be poured before the lake even came up. He even planned to put steel railroad rails upright in the waterfront areas to act as piers for docks.[2]

And this was not the only trip to the property. Akers also took his younger son, James, out to the property as well. James remembered visiting the site virtually every weekend. Unlike his brother though, James's recollections were more positive. That farm house? "There was a beautiful meadow there before the water came up with blackberries.... We would walk across that meadow all the way to the river and daddy would go back to where the water-front would be and showed me exactly where the water line would be." James recalled that an African American couple that lived on the Akers' farm in Brentwood were caretakers on the property during these years. Indeed, James even remembered visiting the rock quarry that would become Horseshoe Bay where the pump house and water purification center would be built.[3]

These trips were more than summer afternoon daydreams. Before the dam was completed, before the 1957 land grant from Congress, even before the 1959 Capital Development Campaign, Akers found the money to buy land, to lease land from the Corps, and to build waterfronts on what would be his new Scout camp. Specifically, "[t]he council acquired 609 acres of the reservation in 1955 under a longtime lease from the U. S. Government and purchased 108 acres of adjoining land the same year." Thus, when the waters rose, Akers was ready. The new Old Hickory Lake came up to the levels projected by the Corps, the concrete slabs submerged, and the waterfronts were ready to go. Indeed, the waterfront slabs were laid in locations where Akers wanted waterfronts to go, not necessarily where finished camps were completed. Some waterfront areas had slabs poured, but no camp ever attached to them to give them purpose. They began to enter into legend and became a source for scavenger hunts in later years, as professional staff and camp staff alike wandered the property looking for evidence of waterfronts that Akers envisioned, but never completed.[4]

A committee appointed in 1955 and headed by Cecil Wray laid out the Council's goals—Akers' goals—for a new camp. The report of the committee no longer exists, but the published record shows a vision that evolved. In 1957, there would be three 200-boy camps with central dining halls, waterfronts, and staff cabins. The reservation would include a family camp, complete with family cabins, a dining hall of its own, a waterfront, and bath house. Scouts and families alike could utilize a 100-acre lake "to be developed as a migratory bird refuge." There would also be roads, a waterworks, and an electrical system. Promotional material from Council during the 1959 campaign articulated a slightly different, grander vision for this new (legitimately named) Boxwell Reservation. There would be four camps: an adult training camp and three Scout camps, each of which would have a capacity of 200 boys a week. The scout camps would have dining halls, staff quarters, craft shelters, group sleeping shelters, rifle and archery ranges, chapels, and director cabins. There would be a central administrative area, staff living quarters, a health lodge, a central trading post, and a wildlife sanctuary. There were even plans for an OA Lodge, a reservation guest lodge, and a lookout tower. While differing in details, all accounts agreed that the new Boxwell Reservation would be a fully

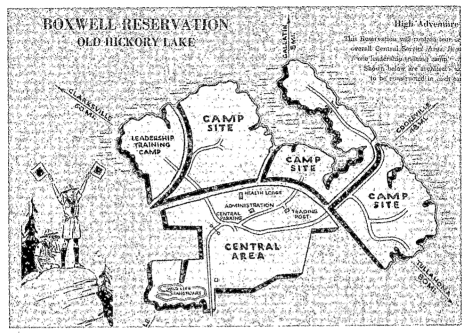

Early promotional map of the new Boxwell reservation from a pamphlet for the 1959 Capital Campaign. Personal Collection of Harry "Beany" Elam.

developed, year-round-use site.[5]

Ward Akers had a vision. The new camp—the new Reservation—was something completely different from the previous three summer camps. The facilities provided at the new site raised expectations about what a summer camp could and should offer to Scouts and leaders. The sheer size of the reservation presented new challenges to the way program was delivered and how the camp was financed. Boxwell Reservation may have been Akers' vision, but this new camp transformed the very idea of "program" in ways that neither Akers nor anyone else could have possibly imagined.

Bombs, Babies, and Boy Scouts, Part Two

As the summer of 1960 dawned, the United States was an incredible nation to behold. The fifteen years following the end of World War II saw enormous political, economic, and social changes. Clearly, unresolved issues the nation had been trying to ignore existed, but in most respects, the United States in 1960 was at the apex of its power and influence. But in another fifteen years, on the eve of the nation's bicentennial in 1976, circumstances had changed radically. Just as the United States was a very different society in 1975, so too were the Boy Scouts of America and Boxwell Reservation.

The 1960s were generally characterized by optimism, hope and promise. The vision of the young Kennedy family in the White House spurred the idea of a new "Camelot," an idea frozen in time by John F. Kennedy's assassination in November 1963. This sense of stolen promise was mobilized by Kennedy's success, Lyndon B. Johnson. Inspired by the nation's economic growth and a belief in endless possibility, Johnson launched a flotilla of legislation, collectively known as the Great Society. Included here were the new Medicare and Medicaid programs as well as the Equal Employment Opportunities Commission. "The centerpiece of the Great Society, however, was Johnson's crusade to eradicate poverty." Believing Americans had a responsibility and a legitimate opportunity both to help the poor and destroy poverty, Johnson opened a second war—completely apart from, but in addition to the war in Vietnam—this time on the domestic front. The sense of unbounded possibility was endemic to the 1960s, but was probably best exemplified in the space program when the United States put a man on the moon and brought him home again in July 1969.[6]

The Cold War continued. The fall of Cuba to communism in 1959 brought the Cold War to the nation's backyard. An attempt to oust these communists failed in 1961's Bay of Pigs Incident. But this episode paled in comparison to the nuclear stand-off in the Cuban Missile Crisis in October 1962. For almost two weeks, the world teetered on the brink of nuclear war before the crisis was resolved. The Cold War's most critical impact came as the result of an incident in the Gulf of Tonkin off the coast of North Vietnam. While the United States had been sending advisors to South Vietnam for years to protect an anti-communist government there, a reported attack by North Vietnamese communists on a American destroyer opened the door to make the Cold War hot. In 1965, American combat troops began pouring into South Vietnam. By 1968, there were over 500,000 American troops in this remote corner of southeast Asia. The Vietnam War was complex, contentious, and touched virtually every part of American society.[7]

Much of the grand hope that so typified Americans in the early and mid-1960s turned to bitterness and distrust by the late 1960s and 1970s. In November 1969, news broke of the My Lai massacre, where American soldiers killed "more than a hundred South Vietnamese civilians—women, children, and the elderly." The commanding officer was convicted of pre-meditated murder in March 1971. In April 1970, President Richard M. Nixon expanded the war into Cambodia and Laos, spurring more protests and leading to the deaths of four college students at Kent State. *The New York Times* published a collection of classified documents detailing the secret history of the war in July 1970, known as the Pentagon Paper. And, of course, the seminal example of distrust began in June 1972, when a break-in at the Democratic National Committee headquarters at the Watergate Hotel in Washington, D. C. launched an investigation that led to the resignation of President Nixon in 1974. "A long national nightmare" indeed! Needless to say, the public's faith was shaken in its institutions, its leadership, and even its own sense of purpose. This new distrust that emerged by the early 1970s expanded into all parts of American life, not just the federal government.[8]

The economic arc was very similar. The early 1960s saw the growth of the previous decade continue, fueled by both Cold War military spending and domestic consumer spending. In short, guns and butter—or bombs and babies—continued to drive the economy throughout the 1960s. There was evidence of a weakening economy as early as 1969, but it was October 1973 when the perfect storm coalesced. An oil embargo by the newly formed Organization of Petroleum Exporting Countries (OPEC) sent shockwaves through the American economy as not just gasoline, but other petroleum based products such as plastics, paint, ink, and even fertilizers were affected. Gas rationing was instituted; a national speed limit implemented. To finance both the Vietnam War and the War on Poverty, the federal government borrowed instead of raising taxes. As a result, inflation began to rise. And then in a situation that defied common economic wisdom, as inflation rose, so too did unemployment as the baby boomers entered the work force only to find there were not enough jobs for them all. While the Oil Embargo ended in 1974, the economy did not immediately bounce back as inflation, interest rates, and unemployment continued to rise, a phenomenon known as "stagflation." The great post-war economic boom—and all that went with it—was over.[9]

These political and economic issues alone would have been enough to set any society reeling, but they were compounded by social crises in race, gender, and age. The Civil Rights Movement, which had begun in the 1950s, moved into a more assertive phase in 1960. The sit-in movement, followed by the Freedom Rides (1961), the Albany Movement (1962), and the Birmingham Protests (1963) created "a moral crisis" according to President Kennedy. The March on Washington for Jobs and Freedom (1963), Freedom Summer (1964), and the Selma March (1965) moved that crisis to the next level. The resulting Civil Rights Act of 1964 and Voting Rights Act of 1965 put a legal end to segregation in the United States and changed the way discrimination was viewed in the law. The effects of integration were far reaching. As schools integrated, white parents began to remove children for private or home schooling. As busing became used a tool to force integration in the cities, white families simply moved away, a phenomenon known as "white flight." Further, "inspired in part by the conviction that racism should no longer serve as a basis of national policy, the Hart-Cellar Act [1965] abandoned the national origins quota system, substituting 'family reunification' and job skills as new, non-racial criteria for immigration." The times they were a-changing.[10]

The Civil Rights movement was successful because of a coalition of

African-Americans, youth, and women. Women were in the forefront of the movement since its beginnings and unsurprisingly began to question their own freedom. The turning point moment came with the publication of Betty Friedan's *The Feminine Mystique* in 1963, which "struck a nerve by sketching the outlines of a world that assigned women to decorative and supportive roles in a rampantly materialistic consumer culture." By the late 1960s, women were calling for "liberation," not just rights. By 1972, the movement had succeeded in getting an Equal Rights Amendment through Congress and out to the states for ratification. Though the Amendment ultimately failed, its passage through Congress demonstrated how quickly the gender expectations of many Americans changed.[11]

Youth were another part of the transforming American social fabric. The baby boom peaked in 1957, levelled through 1961, and finally ended in 1964. This generation was the proverbial "pig in a python," overwhelming every institution they came in contact with as they aged. By the mid-1960s, they were being drafted for the Vietnam War and by the early 1970s they were out trying to find jobs and get settled in life. It should be no surprise that the protests against the war and the rising unemployment rate were directly connected to the boomers. And while popular history tends to present the baby boomers as growing into pot-smoking, pre-marital sex-having hippies, the generation included a strong conservative element as well. The same generation that produced the liberal Students for a Democratic Society (SDS) also produced the conservative Young Americans for Freedom (YAF). Conservative or liberal, it was the boomers who challenged "widely held presuppositions about authority, family life, gender, race relations, sexuality, and proper behavior."[12]

Tennessee experienced the convulsions of this period as well. Youth across the nation fell in love with the musical power of Memphis's favorite son, Elvis Presley. The state's farm acreage continued to decline and urban populations continued to rise. The 1960s saw a "spectacular" growth in industry, though that growth slowed and declined in the 1970s. Nashville and Davidson County formally chartered a joint metropolitan government in 1962. Former Linton Boxwell attendee and Executive Board member of the Middle Tennessee Council Beverly Briley was the first mayor. Sit-ins in the spring of 1960 in Nashville brought pressure for civil rights change. Students from Fisk University as well as local high schools participated in boycotts and protests across the state. Indeed, one of the training grounds for civil rights activists through the 1950s was the Highlander Folk Center, found in Monteagle, Tennessee. The Center's support of civil rights activism led the more conservative state government to close the center in 1961, which would reopen in Knoxville under a new charter. One of the center's trainees was Martin Luther King, Jr., who was assassinated in Memphis in 1968 after leading a strike of and for sanitation workers in the city.[13]

Automobiles continued to matter to the Tennessee story as well. Senator Albert Gore, Sr. co-authored the 1956 Federal-Aid Highway Act, which created the Eisenhower Interstate system. The first stretch of interstate built in Tennessee was a section of I-65 in Giles County. Construction began in May 1957 and was completed eighteen months later, continuing to expand from there. I-40, one of the longest interstates in the nation, cut its way across Tennessee in the mid-1960s. It was not completed in time to aid travel to Rock Island, but would be quite useful for getting Scouts out to the Old Hickory Lake location. The state became fourteenth in the nation in terms of total interstate mileage. This was quite a change from four decades previously when Leslie G. Boxwell's Tennessee Good Roads Association began its work. Not surprisingly, this rapid transportation evolution had some ironic side effects. R. L. Parnell's Oldsmobile car dealership and car parts business had been located downtown at 1402 Broadway since 1934. It was displaced when the interstate loop cut through downtown in 1969.[14]

The Boy Scouts of America struggled to keep up with this changing landscape. The baby boom unquestionably helped the organization's overall enrollment. However, as integration and anti-discrimination became the law of the land and the population became more firmly entrenched in cities and sub-urbs (in part because of "white flight"), the program looked for ways to adapt. Scouting launched the Inner-City Rural Program in 1965 in an attempt "to show that the organization was not just a mostly white, middle-class move-ment." The goal was to bring Scouting to impoverished areas—both urban and rural—where because of poverty traditional Scouting sponsors like churches and schools were not as strong. The Scouting program also fully in-corporated integration, even in the South. In 1968, the national organization "refused to charter segregated troops." Fortunately, by this point, most local organizations had already adopted anti-discrimination policies.[15]

The big change in Scouting came with the Improved Scouting Pro-gram in 1972. The roots of this program change were simple. By 1969, Scouting suffered its first decline in enrollment in years. Clearly, this was part-ly demographic as the baby boom peak of 1957 meant boys born in that year would have been Scout age in 1968. But there was also the impact of the changing social world discussed above as baby boomers rejected traditional values and institutions. Increasingly, the Boy Scouts, which had been a symbol of wholesome Americana, were seen as out-of-touch and relics of days-gone-by. Indeed, the very idea of an organization dedicated to woodsy survival skills seemed completely antiquated in a nuclear age. The Improved Scouting Pro-gram hoped to address some of these concerns by making Scouting more mod-ern.

The revisions were far-reaching, most notably in the changes to *The Scout Handbook*. Chuck Willis explained the changes succinctly in his *Boy Scouts of America: A Centennial History*, "In the drive for relevance, especially to boys in an urban environment, the eighth edition scrapped much of the in-formation about outdoor skills [and] reminded boys to bring along change for pay toilets and advised them to consult the nearest policeman if they got lost." Scoutmaster training changed to focus more on the "personal growth" of the boy. Advancement was dramatically overhauled. Previously a Scout had to wait until First Class to earn merit badges, but no longer. Under the new program, a Scout could earn merit badges immediately. Several Eagle Scout-required merit badges, such as Camping, became optional. The new program also introduced Skill Awards for the lower ranks, painted brass loops for one's belt that focused on skill requirements. Red berets even became part of the official uniform.[16]

Enrollment remained an issue as membership continued to fall throughout the 1970s. Fortunately, revising the program was not the only option the national Boy Scouts adopted to arrest the decline in enrollment. With the nation's bicentennial on the horizon, in 1969 the BSA announced a new recruitment program: BoyPower '76. This was a long-range development plan to recruit more boys into the program over the succeeding eight years. The goal was to recruit one out of every four Scout aged boys into the program, though specific councils could set higher goals. The idea was laudable, but the pressure to reach the goals was intense. By 1974, not only was the program two years behind its goal, but some councils had been caught padding their membership rolls, causing a minor scandal.[17]

The Middle Tennessee Council grappled with these changes and pressures as well. In 1958, the Council could boast 9,703 Boy Scouts and 23,139 total Scouts, which included Cub Scouts and Explorers. By February of 1968, the Council reported 14,893 Boy Scouts, with a total Scout membership of 35,200. By 1971, the Council was serving approximately 37,000 Scouts total. Though still an increase, the rate of growth had dropped tremendously. Clearly, demographics were having an impact in Middle Tennessee. Nevertheless, when the Council launched its new capital campaign in 1972, it envisioned serving 20,000 *more* boys by 1980. Additionally, while the BoyPower '76 campaign had set goals of one in four boys, Middle Tennessee was already serving one in three. Thus, the Council set a goal of one in two boys—half of all Scout age boys available. Lofty goals remained and this was in large part due to the faith in Ward Akers and his new camp at Old Hickory Lake.[18]

Building the "New" Boxwell

"We have the boys—we have the land; the responsibility is ours." With those words, Executive Vice-President of the *Nashville Banner* and chair of the Boxwell Reservation Development Fund, Edward Bushrod (E.B.) Stahlman, Jr. launched the 1959 Capital Development Campaign. The Sunday, January 25ᵗʰ kick-off event brought over 2000 adult leaders from all over the Middle Tennessee Council's thirty-eight county service area. The *Nashville Tennessean* declared the kick-off "the largest gathering in the interest of scouting in Tennessee history." Meeting in the Air National Guard Hangar at Berry Field in Nashville, the group enjoyed a pot-luck dinner before they were regaled by a series of speakers, each making the pitch for the $891,000 campaign. A host of Council luminaries were present, including Judge Beverly Briley, Charles E. Parish, Gilbert M. Dorland, Robert D. Stanford, E. E. Murrey, and Dr. Rudolph Light. WSM radio and television announcer Dave Overton served as master of ceremonies and entertainment included music and dance by various performers, both professional and amateur. Some Council business was conducted as well with new officers elected for the coming year. Leslie G. Boxwell, 78 years old, attended—one of his last Council functions.[19]

Since Akers' arrival as Council Executive in 1947, the numbers of boys involved in middle Tennessee Scouting had almost quadrupled, from 5,421 in 1948 to 20,104 in 1958. And yet, as impressive as this growth was, the Middle Tennessee Council also had one of the lowest camp attendance rates among Scout Councils in the South. A new, improved Scout camp would address those issues and continue the growth of the Middle Tennessee Council by providing an area to train leaders, help Scouts advance, and provide a place for adventure to happen. Using colored slides of the proposed buildings, this was the argument Stahlman made at the kick-off, declaring that "scouting's biggest problem today is the lack of adequate camping facilities." Creation of such facilities would bring in more boys—Stahlman predicted 30,000 by 1967—

and retain those boys in the program. The new Boxwell Reservation was to be "the outstanding Scout Reservation in America."[20]

Actual fund-raising officially began in February 1959 and continued until June first. The campaign was well-organized and well-publicized. Each district had specific goals they were to reach. Promotional materials were sent out from the Council office on 24th Avenue in downtown Nashville, including pamphlets about what the drive was and why one should contribute. There were also larger, more involved publications, such as the full-color, sixteen-page Boxwell Reservation Development Fund booklet. Potential donor groups received personal pitches, complete with slides, in attempts to add a more personal touch by "an estimated 120 business and professional [Scout] men." Ward Akers himself, often dressed in "a dark blue suit, a neck tie, and that wavy black hair," sometimes came to a district to help move things forward. To help ease the burden, the campaign was organized as a three year pledge drive. Thus, a regular yearly contribution could be rolled into the capital contribution and paid over three years, with the idea that this would encourage one to give more. The campaign even had at least eight different divisions, including a division for major gifts, individual gifts, and special gifts. Further, E. B. Stahlman at the helm of the campaign guaranteed a steady stream of news coverage about the drive in the local news. There were even publicity stunts to keep attention on the campaign. On April 10, eight Boy Scouts set up three tents on the patio of Nashville's Chamber of Commerce building, staying overnight and cooking their meals there in order "to publicize the scouts' current drive for funds to provide facilities at Camp Boxwell on the shores of Old Hickory Lake." Clearly, Akers had learned his lesson from the 1951 campaign at Rock Island.[21]

The fund-raising itself moved quickly. The Kiwanis Club of Nashville gave $25,000 in February, specifically ear-marking the contribution for an administration building and purchasing canoes and boats. Dr. Rudolph Light, a former Vanderbilt University School of Medicine professor, was deeply in-

Dining Hall and Training Center

Proposed dining hall and training center for the Adult Leader Training Camp—Camp Murrey—in the Boxwell Reservation Development Fund booklet. Personal Collection of Archie Crane.

volved in the move to Old Hickory. He personally gave $75,000 to the campaign. Indeed, it was those who lived in Davidson County who pledged the "lion's share of the money, a whopping $621,000." There was even a little drama surrounding the end of the campaign. The *Nashville Tennessean* reported on May 29 that with the campaign ending June 1, the drive was $34,300 short of its goal. But Stahlman's *Banner*, perhaps not surprisingly, painted a much rosier picture. The *Nashville Banner* reported on June 3 that the campaign still had thirteen days to go from that point and was only $25,000 short. Indeed, "[n]umerous reports from field workers indicate that sufficient pledges have been committed to reach the desired goal," but those pledges simply had not materialized yet. On June 10, both the *Tennessean* and the *Banner* reported the end of campaign meeting would be held on Monday, June 15th and that the Council was short of its goal, though the two newspapers disagreed on how much the shortfall would be.[22]

On the night of Monday, June 15, the Council held an Executive Board meeting out at the site of the new Boxwell Reservation. While no paved roads built on the property yet, a tent had been set up for the meeting. *Banner* writer Jack Bond, who had attended the Wood Badge training at Rock Island, painted a vivid picture of the scene unfolding that night in 1959:

> Stahlman made his report at the board meeting on new Boxwell Reservation. To his left the land rolled away in a long sweep to the evening-stilled waters of Old Hickory Lake reflecting a hazy moon.
>
> As he spoke, the plaintive call of a whippoorwill sounded from nearby woods and in some distant hollow across the lake, echoes of three dogs at trail created a clamor softened only by distance.
>
> An estimated 60 shirt-sleeved men heard the report in a relaxed, informal atmosphere. Gathered under a tent, the executive board members and their guests were realizing a reality which began as an idea more than three years ago...
>
> Monday night, the idea became a reality.

Stahlman announced that the campaign had exceeded its goal. The campaign had resulted in $920,000 in pledges. "We actually had this much in pledges recorded on our books and I feel certain that contributions still to come in will cause total collections to surpass the $1 million mark," Stahlman reported to the group. He was not wrong: total pledges came in over $1 million dollars. The campaign was an unqualified success.[23]

The Executive Board meeting that night was a victory lap for all involved in the campaign. Statuettes of a Boy Scout holding his hat over his heart were given to forty-one volunteers who "achieved above-average performances." Governor Buford Ellington was in attendance that night. He spoke of spending part of the previous night with a death row inmate. The inmate had spoken to the governor about his childhood, about growing up "without guidance and without love." Ellington concluded his remarks by observing that "had [the inmate], as a boy, had an opportunity to be a Scout and have had the love and attention of men like you, he and I both would have been spared the grimness of that night. You're building something here that will pay off in the lives of many men for years and years to come. You are to be commended."[24]

This stirring anecdote aside, the highlight of the three hour event came when E. B. Stahlman was recognized. His brother, *Banner* publisher James Stahlman, had already given an emotional acknowledgement to E. B., stating, "I'm happy my own flesh and blood has participated so actively in this campaign for the youth of Middle Tennessee. I'm happy and honored to call him my brother." The adulation continued when Council President F. Murray Acker recognized E. E. Murrey, the campaign's auditor, to make a presentation. Murrey presented E. B. Stahlman with a silver serving tray. "Ornately engraved around its edges the center of the tray bears the inscription: 'To Edward B. Stahlman, Jr., In Appreciation for Distinguished Leadership. Boxwell Reservation, 1959." President Acker stated, "No man in this council has worked more unselfishly or deserves this recognition more than does our general chairman, E. B. Stahlman. I recall, too, that when I first came into scouting over 35 years ago, Jimmy Stahlman was the mainstay in this council. He fought and stood firm during those lean days... Middle Tennessee appreciated the Stahlmans and as long as there are Scouts in Middle Tennessee, the Stahlman name will stand out as the leader among Scouters." After a standing ovation for both men, three resolutions were read into the minutes. While the third honored the contribution of the Justin Potter Foundation to the campaign, the first two resolutions focused on E. B. Stahlman. The first resolution was an appreciation of his work in the Council and the 1959 campaign specifically, while the second recognized the *Banner's* dedication to Scouting.[25]

There was also a rather odd coda to the campaign. Despite the campaign's declaration of success and the start of work in July 1959, the Development Fund received one more shot in the arm at the end of the year. Pat

Boone, local celebrity, was attending the world premiere of his latest film, *Journey of the Center of the Earth*, in his hometown of Nashville. Upon Boone's arrival on December 3rd, he was greeted by "thousands of Boy Scouts [who] shouted a welcome to their idol whose world premiere will boost the treasure of the Middle Tennessee Council of the Boy Scouts. Funds are earmarked for the Camp Boxwell Reservation Development." As Boone stated at the time, "Personally, I feel that outside of the church there is no more important organization in America than the Scouts. Scouting is directly opposed to delinquency." The premiere was held at the Paramount theatre on Church Street and seats were $10 a piece at a time when the average ticket price was less than a dollar. Quite a high profile ending to the campaign![26]

Construction on the new camp began almost immediately with an in-kind contribution from the Tennessee Road Builders Association. Donating $75,000 worth of material, equipment, and labor, the Association began the road construction into the camp. Four miles of paved road and parking area would be the first act of creation. The Association was providing it all: bulldozers, scrapers, grading equipment, asphalt, and the personnel to run it all. It was the Association's donation that pushed the campaign over $1 million. Construction began on Thursday, July 2nd and the chert base was completed by mid-August. Blacktop paving would come later. In the meantime, work would continue as funds became available. "Scout officials hope that sufficient construction will have been completed by next summer to open the camp for regular summer training for more than 20,000 Boy Scouts."[27]

A Boxwell different from any of its predecessors slowly emerged. Buildings were all unique and rustic in design, using local or even on-site materials for construction. The dining halls in particular were "constructed of native limestone and redwood." When the heavy machinery came on site, Akers walked in front of the bulldozers, pointing out what trees could be knocked down and which needed to stay. Tom Willhite, who began as a District Executive in 1964, heard these stories, which lined up with his own experience

168

working for Akers. "Ward Akers was a real fanatic about trees," Willhite recalled. "When they built the camp, he would tell 'em, don't touch that tree!
Don't touch that tree! And they'd mark [the trees] and they'd run the road
there into camp." No detail was too small to create the perfect Scout camp
experience.[28]

This "new Boxwell" was a true reservation, holding four separate
camps within its boundaries. Two of the camps were Boy Scout summer
camps, one was a family camp, and the fourth was a wilderness camp. All of
these were officially named at a ceremony in May honoring E. B. Stahlman as
the "Campaign Chairman of the Year." The first Boy Scout camp (previously
known as "Camp B" on promotional materials) was Camp Stahlman, named
for Edward Bushrod Stahlman. The honor was bestowed in recognition of E.
B. Stahlman's efforts in 1957 to secure the property and his leadership in the
1959 capital campaign. The majority of the camp was laid out between two
points, the dining hall being one point and the waterfront the other. Stahlman
was truly a year-round camp, with a fully functioning kitchen and easy access
to the camp's water and waste water systems. The second Boy Scout camp
("Camp C") was Camp Parnell, which was named for R. Lanier Parnell, the
Oldsmobile car and car parts dealer. Parnell had been active for several years
and would serve as Council President in 1965. While surviving records do not
disclose the actual amount, Parnell "donated a considerable sum of money for
the construction of the camp." Like spokes on a wheel, the camp bearing his
name had sites and program areas encircling the dining hall, which sat atop a
small ridge. Camp Parnell was a satellite camp. It had a kitchen, but did not
prepare its own food. The third camp on the reservation ("Camp A") was the
family camp, known as Camp Murrey. Murrey was named for Council Treasurer Edward Ennis Murrey. The family camp was also a satellite camp with a
smaller dining hall. Scoutmasters and their wives stayed here in addition to
adult married staff. The final camp ("Camp D") was a wilderness camp, meaning it was undeveloped. It was named for Vanderbilt's Dr. Rudolph Light.

Camp Light was meant to be a developed Boy Scout camp—there was a waterfront for it--but despite Light's personal donation of $75,000, there was insufficient funding to complete it. A gravel road and (later) a chapel on a hill would be the extent of the camp's development until the 1970s.[29]

Still, as the 1960 summer camp season approached, none of these camps were ready. In early June, three weeks before the camp's opening on June 26, staff arrived at camp and got to work, preparing the camp for Scouts. While construction continued on the buildings, the adult staff handled the smaller jobs, such as building tent platforms and moving them into place, all by hand. This was no easy job as the platforms were made of oak planks, not the lighter pine boards used in later years. Still, with enough motivation, two men could each grab a side, run it into the woods, and set it down. No tree cutting involved. But even "small" jobs were not all that small. The docks at the waterfront had to be built. The rifle and archery ranges, though both open air, had to be created as well. All of this work was done in the three week window before camp began in 1960. And though still incomplete, the camp opened on time.[30]

Dedication ceremonies for the new reservation soon followed. Held on Saturday, July 9, 1960 on the 741 acre property, an "open house" began at 1:30 p.m. with official dedication ceremonies beginning at 4 p.m. The Tennessee highway patrol even provided two helicopters for the first air views of the reservation. District Executives, fully decked out in official Scout Uniforms, including knee socks, helped park cars for the incoming guests. And there were a lot of guests. Jack Bond estimated there were 1,000 Scouts, parents and visitors who stayed for the dedication ceremonies after the open house tours, which ended at Stahlman dining hall.[31]

A temporary platform had been erected in front of the dining hall for the speakers and other dignitaries. James G. Stahlman presided over the festivities, setting the tone for the afternoon. Indeed, Stahlman painted a powerful

Flag raising ceremony at Camp Stahlman at the Dedication on July 9, 1960. Personal Collection of John Cooper-Ernie Ragsdale.

picture of the importance of the new reservation:

> I express the hope that this facility from this day forward and
> for many generations of Scouts yet unborn, may become the
> cradle of character, the incubator of close fraternity and true
> sportsmanship, the haven of those who through the high ideals
> and principles inculcated by Scouting seek to become service-
> ful American citizens…
>
> And may these waters, woods and templed hills encompass a
> hallowed shrine of personal decency, human understanding,
> spiritual strength and faith without which there can be no
> hope for America, now or in the turbulent days and years
> which lie ahead.

And then, as if on cue, a light rain began to fall.[32]

Robert G. Neil of Brentwood Church of Christ continued forward
with the invocation, trying to ignore the liquid sunshine. The Scouts in attendance, standing by the platform, "stood their ground—stiff and at attention
while their uniforms wilted." The program soldiered forward. Council President F. Murray Aker gave a dedication address. E. B. Stahlman read letters
from those dignitaries who could not attend, including a telegram from Governor Buford Ellington, and messages from former governor Frank Clement,
Senator Al Gore, Sr., and Representatives Joe Evins and Ross Bass. There was
a tribute to past Council Presidents, including Wilbur F. Creighton, Gilbert
Dorland, Charles Parish, and, of course, Leslie G. Boxwell. And then, "after
about 10 minutes, with thunder booming louder than the public address system, there was a mass exodus to the shelter of the dining hall, where the Scouts
lined up around the wall and the show went on." The very first "Boxwell
Dew" had forced a change in the program.[33]

Once indoors the dedication program continued. Representative J.
Carlton Loser, one of the men responsible for the special act of Congress in
1957, attended personally. He received a standing ovation in the dining hall
when he rose to speak. Yet another part of the program was dedicated to the

Congressman J. Carlton Loser (far right) returned to Boxwell later in July. After his visit, Loser paused for this photo at Camp Stahlman with (l-r) Council President F. Murray Acker, E. B. Stahlman, Jr., and Ward Akers. Holding the flag are (l-r) Scouts Melton Abernathy, Thomas Smith, and James Seay. Photo by John Morgan, Nashville Banner, July 29, 1960.

camp's namesakes, E. B. Stahlman, R. L. Parnell, E. E. Murrey, and Rudolph Light. Dr. Light was the only one of the four not attending as he was away in England at the time. Parnell was awarded the Silver Beaver, the highest council level award given to adult volunteers. As the rain subsided, Council President Acker reminded those in the crowded dining hall that "the values imbued by the Scout program are the essence of hope in combatting 'the cancerous growth of communism.'" As the ceremony moved outside, the flag was blessed by "the Very Rev. Robert M. Shaw, dean, St. Paul's Cathedral in Buffalo" and the Rev. William E. Morgan concluded the day with a benediction.[34]

Interestingly, despite the grandeur of the dedication, nothing in the record indicates that either Leslie G. Boxwell or William J. Anderson attended. Boxwell had been ill for some time. He passed away in September of 1960 at age 79. Though he "traveled extensively" in retirement, Anderson had disappeared from the public record by this point. But he too eventually fell ill, passing away almost exactly three years after Boxwell. The torch had unquestionably passed to a new generation.[35]

Not surprisingly, the ceremonies were covered on the front page of the Stahlmans' *Nashville Banner*, but the *Nashville Tennessean* took the opportunity afforded by the event to reflect about the camp and scouting as well. But more importantly, writer Sarah Taylor waxed eloquent about the camp:

> The purpose of the camp is to give Scouts a chance to earn their merit badge and develop skills. But there are other benefits.

> 'The greatest advantages for a boy here is living with a group of clean-cut kids that give him a better outlook on life, and living the Scout oath and Scout law each day,' [Reservation Director James] Johnson said. 'When he's lived a week under those conditions, he's a better boy from then on.'

The *Banner* was not about to be outdone. Sam McPherson had the following reflections:

> The visitor received one lasting impression of Boxwell Reservation. It will, in all probability, be the same impression, made on the scores of visitors at the camp today.

> That is: Boxwell is an impressive community. Designed to help boys grow adequately into manhood, it achieves its purpose. Here on the sprawling 750 acres of nature, Scouts learn to be what a Scout should be: trustworthy, loyal, helpful, friendly, courteous, kind, obedient, cheerful, thrifty, brave, clean and reverant [sp].[36]

But it was an unsigned editorial in the *Banner* that was perhaps the most important piece written about the new Boxwell. The editorial not only captured the importance of the moment, it demonstrated how much had changed. "Camp Boxwell" had been a training school for citizens. As outlined—and emphasized—in the editorial, "Boxwell Reservation" was something wholly different:

> Those who attended the dedication exercises Saturday came away with a new comprehension of what vision can accomplish; not just in the conversion of wilderness into facilities for healthful recreation, but with that provision of opportunities of service. The ideals of Scouting here find the formulative setting. Here indeed a plant adequately equipped for such an assignment, and fitly dedicated to the glory of God, and the betterment of our youth.
>
> *As an organization and individually, the Boy Scouts of America have blessed the nation—with training and influences directed to making men out of boys. As a factor in the development of character, it is an answer to degenerate influences striving to turn this into a Beatnick, cynical, anti-social age. Its attitude is the positive one of combatting alien and atheistic philosophies with a concept of duty to Country and to God...*
>
> *For Middle Tennessee youth, the hard-won Boxwell Reservation has been created—because there was a recognition throughout the area of both the need and the opportunity...*
>
> *It is more than a shrine; more than a monument to faith and work. It is a plant facility for service; its product stalwart, God-fearing, patriotic men.*[37]

All the Camp's a Stage...

The 1959 Capital Development Campaign and the 1960 dedication ceremonies demonstrated a significant change in the way Middle Tennessee Council approached summer camp program. At the previous three Camp Boxwells, program had focused on citizenship and family. The rustic and primitive nature of the camps had not allowed for much more. Even the successful "capital campaign" at Narrows of the Harpeth had not shifted the emphasis of the summer camp program.

Boxwell Reservation was an entirely different beast. Trying to separate

175

the buildings and the equipment used to make the summer camp program happen from the program itself became impossible. Facilities *were* program now. At first, this might seem like a fairly radical concept. Program is not a physical structure or item, it is the transmission of ideals and skills, mainly through advancement, instruction, and activities. Facilities and items are simply tools to deliver program. And while there is some truth to this understanding, it is not wholly accurate.

Program is like theater, a play. Part of the play is the acting. This is the delivery of lines, emotion, and plot. But the play is more than acting. It is the stage. It is the sets and the costumes and the lighting. It is also the behind the scenes activity, which is not always attractive, but completely necessary to the delivery. Watch the credits on any film and it becomes apparent there is a great deal more going on than what the actors on screen are doing. Summer camp and the new Boxwell were the same way. There were an enormous amount of behind-the-scenes facilities and materials that made program possible. There was another level of camp "set design" and staging that was also critical to program delivery. Teaching merit badges mattered, but they were only one part of much more complicated stage show.

It is also important to understand that facilities were important to the financial well-being of the camp and the Council programs as well. Buildings and physical materials became critical to fund-raising. The Council would never have been able to raise over a million dollars to provide program to the Scouts of middle Tennessee without the promise of buildings and structures. Donors needed to be able to "see" where their contributions were going. Indeed, contributing to physical facilities helped tie donors to the Scouting cause. Facilities also became critical for recruitment of Scouts. New ranges, boats, better shower facilities, and more all made summer camp more attractive to Scouts and to leaders. Better facilities meant more people came to camp and more people supported the Council.[38]

This subtle shift in thinking about camp program was evident very early in the process of building the reservation. Remember that Cecil Wray's planning committee for the new reservation proposed dining halls, cabins, and bath houses—all physical facilities. Further, "the vast development will include equipment such as tents, tent floors and boats in addition to buildings, waterfront facilities, roads, waterworks and an electric system." These facilities would be available year-round to maximize use.[39]

The 1959 campaign had been even more explicit than the planning committee. E. B. Stahlman had declared at the kick-off event that the biggest problem facing Scouting in middle Tennessee was the "lack of adequate camping facilities—a problem which Boxwell Reservation will correct." The Council's *Boxwell Reservation Development Fund* booklet was more subtle about the goals. The 1959 campaign "provides the opportunity for each of us to demonstrate our faith in boys and their future." To show that faith, the booklet "listed the hundreds of facilities and pieces of equipment required" for the new camp. The Boy Scouts of Middle Tennessee "need a completely developed Boxwell Reservation to be even more successful." The *Tennessean*, however, pushed subtlety aside.

> The Boxwell reservation on Old Hickory lake, less than 30 miles from Nashville, is ideally situation for a Boy Scout camp. Facilities for boating, swimming, and other water sports, roving and camping out are ready-made, but the necessity for equipment and improvements should be apparent to all...
>
> Talk of juvenile delinquency is of little consequence unless shored up by the do-something-about-it philosophy which is inherent in Scouting. The council deserves the support of those who share that philosophy.

In short, better facilities were not only critical to program delivery, they would arrest juvenile delinquency! Thus, the facilities at the "new" Boxwell had to be impressive.[40]

Boxwell Reservation at Old Hickory Lake was really five camps. There were the two Boy Scout summer camps, Camps Stahlman and Parnell. There was the family camp, Murrey, and the wilderness camp, Light. But the Reservation itself was also a camp. There were buildings, facilities, and activities that took place on the property not assigned to a particular camp that were critical to functioning of the program.

The three developed camps—Stahlman, Parnell, and Murrey—all shared some basic facilities. Each had a permanent dining hall. These dining halls were not simply military tents like at Rock Island. Supported by steel skeletons, the dining halls used limestone rock and thick redwood paneling built atop concrete floors and covered with pitch roofs. Walls of windows graced the north and south sides of the buildings. Large fans embedded in these walls near the ceiling pulled air through the building to cool it. Each had working chimneys and fireplaces for use in the winter months, as well as both baseboard and radiant heaters. Attached to each dining area was a kitchen, though at Stahlman, this kitchen was significantly larger than at Parnell or Murrey. Stahlman was the base camp—all food for the entire reservation was prepared there. Murrey and Parnell were satellites. Food was literally trucked to both of these camps from Stahlman for every meal.[41]

The dining halls were a simple, yet excellent, example of the "behind-the-scenes" dimension of how facilities were critical to reservation program. Sarah Taylor reported in her *Tennessean* article on the camp's dedication that camp cook Martha Cardiff prepared meals for 660 people a week in 1960. This number would include all the Scouts, leaders, and staff at Stahlman, Parnell, and Murrey. Thus, the sheer size of the reservation made the facilities critical. The food had to be cooked, transported, and distributed. The material that the food was cooked with and distributed with had to be cleaned and returned. Garbage generated from the meals had to be disposed. Further, not everything was prepared at the base camp. Items such as toast and coffee were prepared on site at the satellites. Some refrigerated items had to be kept at the

The Parnell (top) and Murrey (bottom) dining halls. Both lacked complete working kitchens and had food trucked in to them. Photos by Michael Seay.

179

satellites as well and each camp's kitchen staff also washed their camp's dishes. And, just to make this all a little more complicated, food counts had to be adjusted for guests. The enormous complexity of meal time was beyond anything any of the three other Boxwells had encountered.[42]

Breakfast most mornings involved eggs. Eggs, like virtually everything, were fresh, not prepackaged. So, in order to make scrambled eggs for the 660 people in camp, each egg had to be cracked by hand before breakfast at 7:30 a.m. At two eggs per person, this meant the Stahlman cook staff was cracking and preparing approximately 1,320 eggs. The eggs were usually accompanied by either two strips of bacon or two sausage patties, which again meant approximately 1,320 items to be cooked in tandem with the eggs. Both the eggs and the meat were cooked using large three foot by three foot square aluminum pots, called square heads. The eggs were cooked in the pot itself, the meat in the significantly shallower top. Interestingly, the interaction between the eggs and the aluminum pots sometimes—not always, but sometimes—turned the eggs green. If a fruit was involved, it too had to be cut or prepared in order to be loaded for delivery. Of course, all of this food had to be refrigerated before use and whatever was left had to be stored for future use. Industrial grade refrigeration was necessary for this. Toast was prepared at the satellite kitchen, so it did not need to be transported, but the bread did need to be started early enough to coincide with meal arrival from Stahlman. At two pieces per person, approximately six hundred pieces of bread had to be toasted through a carousel toaster, sending three pieces through at a time. If the toast was to be buttered, a staff member stood by with a four inch paint brush which was dipped in melted butter. The toast was then stored in a squarehead where it awaited distribution and gained a rubbery texture. This was just the food preparation; there was still food transportation.[43]

Food transportation involved something called the Trivary truck. There were actually several trivary trucks over the years, but the important point is that this was the name of the camp's food truck. The name came from the large stainless steel containers called trivaries. Trivaries held the food and could be plugged into an electrical socket to keep the food inside warm. The trays were approximately sixteen by thirty by eight inches, and could be deep or shallow, so they could hold a good amount of food. The trivary truck itself—sometimes blue, sometimes yellow—was a walled truck or van. Inside the cargo area were shelves on either side with a walkway down the center. Sitting on the shelves, the trivaries could be plugged into to keep the food warm. Food that needed to be kept cool did not use a trivary.[44]

The truck had a driver and an assistant whose jobs were to load the food, transport the food, return whatever was necessary to Stahlman, and keep the truck clean. They often picked up trash from Stahlman's dining hall. Compared to food preparation, the responsibilities of the trivary driver seemed simple. However, appreciate the magnitude of this simple task. The trivary had to deliver all of the food for Murrey and Parnell not simply before the meal, but before the meal with enough time for the respective staffs to dish out the food into bowls and platters for the monitors. And as simple as this may have been, the truck was often late. And, every now and then, in a rush to not be late or because he was not paying attention, the driver took the turn down to Camp Parnell a little too fast, slinging the trivaries from the back of the truck out onto the road![45]

Lest it be forgotten, all of these things required one other truly simple item: water. Water was needed for cooking and potable water was needed for making the "bug juice." The very first structure built on the reservation came before the capital campaign and it was a water tower, built where the administrative area would be. It was, literally, at the top of the hill. It was quickly followed by a pump house and then a waste water treatment facility. The pump house would pump water out of the lake and send it approximately half a mile up the hill to be stored in the water tower. The tower could hold 62,000 gallons of water and could be replenished three times a day as water was "pumped to the individual camp areas for cooking, bathing, and cleaning."[46]

The behind-the-scenes world was complemented by a reservation maintenance area, or simply put, "the compound." Hundreds of acres required vehicles to move cots and mattresses and other program materials. Tractors were used to mow fields. Large trucks moved materials. The compound area itself stored these vehicles as well as cots and mattresses.. It had a garage to work on the vehicles when they failed. The ranger staff repaired the equipment in the dining halls. Storage areas warehoused items for the trading post and tents during the off-season. The Trading Posts' goods were now more than simply candy and cola. There were Boxwell t-shirts and camp specific belt buckles to accompany camp specific patches that all Scouts received at the end of the week. This was the world Scouts did not see, but made possible the world they did see.[47]

Of the easily observable world, tent platforms were the first step in a truly different Boxwell that Scouts and Scouters would notice immediately. Aside from the family area at Rock Island, none of the previous versions of Boxwell had used tent platforms. Greg Tucker camped at Rock Island and recalled the experience quite clearly, "I can remember up at the old camp, it rains and there's a stream of water running through your tent, and there's no way you're ever putting anything on the ground because it was ground." The difference from Rock Island at the "new" Boxwell was striking. The initial platforms were simple in design. A large square made of one inch by six inch oak planks had struts extending diagonally from each corner. The front and back struts on each side were connected by another plank that served as a cross arm. The tent was pitched directly onto the platform with the sides tied off on the crossarm. Cots with mattresses for two people fit comfortably inside the tent on the platform base. Rain water would no longer wash out the floor nor would building small frames or shelves to hold your foot locker or suitcase be necessary. Rustic and efficient, every Scout stayed under canvas in this manner. Family and even adult staff who stayed at Camp Murrey lived the same way.[48]

Showerhouse One at Camp Parnell. Scout showers on the left. Wash basin in the center. Scout toilet facilities to the right of the wash basin. The door at the far right was for the Adult/Staff area. Photo by Michael Seay, April 1972.

This experience was complemented by showerhouses, another physical facility innovation over Rock Island. The showerhouses were combination bathing, washing, and toilet facilities. These were free-standing outdoor bathrooms that followed a similar aesthetic to the dining halls: redwood exterior walls and pitch roofs. A pitch roof was very expensive, but high quality. The showerhouse roofs had a marble chip in the pitch and a gravel guard along the edge. One small portion of the building was dedicated to staff and Scoutmasters. A shower area for two, a single toilet, a urine trough, and two sinks, all complete with running water. And, the sinks had mirrors, which was a truly rare item on the reservation.[49]

The rest of the building was dedicated to Scouts and broken into three sections. The building followed a 'dog-trot' design with an open pass-through in the middle. A water trough was placed in the middle of this area. A Scout pushed a button on the end and water sprayed through holes in a pipe the length of the entire twelve foot long wash basin. Scouts could wash hands or face or brush their teeth. There were no mirrors to help with this. On one side of this washstand was the shower area. This area had wooden benches to sit

183

on to remove clothes and opened into a group shower. There were no shower stalls, but approximately eight shower heads above a sunken portion of the concrete floor. To the other side of the washstand were the restroom facilities: a urine trough on one wall and a row flush toilets—again, no stalls—opposite.

Stahlman and Parnell each had three showerhouses, serving approximately five campsites each. Camp Murrey only had one showerhouse serving all the families there. It afforded a bit more privacy and had a section of the building for an electric washer and dryer. The days of the pit toilets in the site itself were over. A Scout may have had to walk a small distance, but the facilities were far superior to anything Rock Island had provided.[50]

And yet, despite these grandiose facilities and the dedication ceremonies, the camp—or camps as was now the case—was not completed when Scouts arrived in 1960. Parnell dining hall was open and operational, but still did not have the rock façade added. Parnell's metal flag pole had not been installed yet either. Instead, Scouts met in the Athletic Field and the flag pole was actually three wooden utility poles—two on the outside, one higher in the middle. The reservation's administrative building was not built yet. When a Scout arrived a camp, they stopped at a tent before being directed to the appropriate location. This tent had the camp's switchboard in it. None of the roads were yet paved and the tents for the Handicrafts and Commissaries were a mis-matched hodge-podge of military surplus tents. Even the camp offices were simply tents and flies on platforms, though each had a toolbox for camp work.[51]

The 1959 Boxwell Development Fund Campaign had been a three year capital development campaign. Thus, 1961 was the year when the money finally ran out. While most of the camp was built by this point, the final original buildings were completed that summer. As the construction wrapped up, the firm of Brush, Hutchinson & Gwinn could congratulate themselves on a job well done. Quality buildings with unique designs peppered the property.

The Crippled Crab, ca. 1972. Photo by Michael Seay.

One of the most unique, and last built, was the Reservation Administrative office. Faulkner Hickerson, scoutmaster of Troop 99 and the reservation's chief architect was charged with designing the "entrance lodge." As Hickerson explained,

> Ward [Akers] wanted something different, built of poles, stone and other materials indigenous to the site which the Scouts could relate to as there [sp] type of construction. I went to work on sketches and then built a model, when Ward came by our office and saw the model, he called Mr "Ebee" Stahlman and requested that we come see him. We took the model over to him – he said 'let's build it" – and said it look [ed] like a "crippled crab", but I like it. This name has "stuck" and every scout, scout leader, parent, and friend of scouting has remembered the place and the name.
>
> Few people know how the name came to be, and a very few know its full nomenclature – this structure was built by Foster -Creighton Co. – I had to take the model to the site to assist the superintendent in laying out and building it. The structure was nearing completion before Mr. Wilbur Creighton Sr. saw it. On seeing it, he exclaimed "what in the devil do you call it," I told him Mr. Stahlman called it a "crippled crab" – whereby Mr. Wilbur said "yes, with an erection."

The Crab's enormous flat roof was constructed on a 45 degree angle and supported by massive telephone poles. Angled uprights created an vast overhead space between the ground and the apex of the roof. A 15 foot overhang extended beyond the central stone building. This eccentric design served a practical purpose: vehicles were to drive up under the roof to a window on the side of the office. Here Scouts would register before they entered the camp. This operation never materialized, but it was the design's intent.[52]

With the completion of the Crab in 1961, the first phase of the development of the new Boxwell Reservation was complete. The location had not *quite* lived up to the promises of the 1959 campaign. There was no reservation health lodge, no staff lodges, no lookout tower, no amphitheater, no OA Lodge, and no family cabins at Murrey. And, most importantly, there were only two Scout summer camps, not three as promoted in all the literature. While the simplest explanation is that the money just did not stretch as far as planned, Hickerson suggested Akers was "out maneuvered by some board members." Nothing in the existing record explains this idea.[53]

While another full camp would have to wait, Akers was not patient. Over the next decade building and expansion continued at the reservation. Some projects were small, but important. For instance, in 1963 the Reservation added a hanging cedar sign at the entrance to the camp. State Highway 109 was the route into camp. A turn onto Creighton Lane—named for Wilbur Creighton, Sr.—would bring a guest to camp. On all sides of the road were high dirt embankments. On the northern Creighton Lane embankment was a large entrance sign. An upright and an overhang supported four six foot cedar planks, each with a title carved into them. From top to bottom, the signs read:

> Boy Scouts of America
> Boxwell Reservation
> Camp Stahlman Camp Light
> Camp Parnell Camp Murrey[54]

186

The hanging sign at the entrance was as iconic as the Crippled Crab, but was only one of the projects completed after the Reservation was up and running. In 1962, the Council purchased another 190 acres to add to the existing property. 1963 saw a lease from the Corps for another 112 acres and yet another 75 acres purchased outright in 1965. This brought the total acreage up to 1,133 acres. In 1964, the Reservation added a chapel to the backside of Camp Light. In fact, the Don Stanford Chapel was the only permanent structure built on the "wilderness camp" of Camp Light. 1966 saw the addition of two new fifty foot rifle ranges, paid for by a $5000 unclaimed reward offered by the *Nashville Banner* in an Federal Bureau of Investigation case. As a result, the Camp Stahlman range was named for J. Edgar Hoover and the Camp Parnell range for the FBI generally. And, in 1968, the family of Henry Fitts finally got the Order of the Arrow Lodge promised back in 1949.[55]

There was one last building project worth noting that went on in these years: the creation of Ittabeena. The generally understood, but unstated assumption was that Ward Akers planned to retire at Boxwell. The original 1957 property purchase included a small cabin. Akers had originally planned to tear the building down, using the clapboard elsewhere on the reservation. But as his son James removed the boards, a log cabin emerged. This became the core of a larger building. Additional lumber came from all over. Some came from cabins torn down by the Corps of Engineers at the Land Between the Lakes; other lumber came from cabins around the mid-state area. Built primarily by the ranger staff, the renovated cabin had its own unique design, specifically with two long logs protruding out from under the metal roof that Akers refused to have cut. The site was off-limits to the camp staff and was generally considered the private residence of Akers and his family. As Hickerson stated, "as most everyone said upon seeing it—'it would have been' better if you done this or done that." From here, the name "Ittabeena" was born.[56]

What exactly happened down at the cabin is a matter of some conjecture. Ward and his second wife Elizabeth would stay there on the weekends

187

before the cabin was completed. After completion, unquestionably, the site was used for cook-outs that Akers hosted, usually for the financial contributors. In short, it was used for "promotional work." Alcohol was often present, even though such beverages were illegal on the reservation. And, in a field nearby, at least one, possibly two trailers were set: one trailer was the summer home of E. E. Murrey, the other was for E. B. Stahlman. Akers even had a boat there—the *Gladys*, a red and white motorboat donated to the Council by Elvis Presley. But beyond this, the site served no official Council functions. Akers' Cabin, or Ittabeena, was there for personal use.[57]

An operation of this size obviously cost money. A week at Linton in the 1920s had cost $4.50 a Scout. A week at Rock Island cost $19 per Scout if registration occurred after the early registration deadline. When the Reservation opened, a week of camp cost $20 and stayed that way for the better part of a decade. After a slow crawl, by 1975, this fee finally rose to $35 per boy per week. As former Finance Director Ken Connelly explained, Akers' "focus on finances was that we make the program as cheap as possible for kids and the volunteers. He didn't want to raise the camp fees until they just had to." Even with camp attendance at its high water mark, camp fees did not cover all the expenses. In fact, at this point in time, the generally accepted financial wisdom concerning summer camp was that it was a money-loser. Thus, it was critical to create other revenue streams that could be utilized to support the costs of the summer camp program.[58]

There were two visible avenues through which the reservation generated income that were not directly connected to the summer camp program. The first were the field trials. These were retriever events held on the reservation on ponds specially built for this purpose. Using guidelines set by the American Kennel Society, these field trials attracted hunters from all over the southeast. The events were held on select weekends from October to February—the camp Off-season—and breakfast was served at camp. Indeed, Boxwell became such a popular location, it was considered for national competitions.

188

Top: The "hanging sign" at the corner of Highway 109 and Creighton Lane. Personal Collection of John Cooper—Ernie Ragsdale.
Bottom: Akers' Cabin or "Ittabeena," August 1973. Personal Collection of James Akers.

Perhaps not surprisingly Akers had a dog named Tar Shed that often competed.[59]

The second revenue stream was a much more complex endeavor: a working farm. It would perhaps be more accurate to say that Boxwell had multiple aspects to its farming operation. There were cattle. Cattle roamed the property down near Akers' Cabin, all over Camp Light, and on Explorer Island as well. At any given time there were a 100 to 150 head of cattle. Occasionally, the cattle escaped, either through their own volition or through fences being cut. Cow-pies on the concrete porches of the dining halls was not an altogether uncommon occurrence. And there were pigs. The pig farm operation was in a little corner of the Reservation right off of Tyree Access Road, near Akers Lake. There were about half as many hogs, running from sixty to eighty head, who were generally fattened by slop from the dining halls.[60]

These were not random herds and the Council did not accidentally fall into this work. These were deliberate choices from the start. Charles Parish had been involved in raising both Black Angus cattle and Yorkshire pigs for years. The inception of the farm undoubtedly originated here. The idea grew and at one point went beyond simply a financial offset to include husbandry as part of the camp program. Hamilton Paine, president of the Tennessee Beef Producers, was in conversations with Akers about cattle by May 1959. As Paine explained, "The council would like to run a herd of beef cattle in conjunction with the camp. They would set up a training program for boys interested in animal husbandry and help stimulate members to become future cattle men." Paine's group had been "asked to donate a beef heifer to Camp Boxwell." Rotary Clubs across the mid-state area followed suit. The cattle were part of the Boxwell Development Plan from very early on.[61]

However, cattle and pigs were only part of the operation. The Council also grew tobacco on the reservation property. The tobacco property was near the pig farm, also close to Akers Lake. Because of the proximity to the lake, the ranger staff utilized an irrigation system to pump water out of the lake to water the tobacco. The camp staff helped with the maintenance and harvesting of the tobacco crop, generally after summer camp was over. In addition to the tobacco was a fairly healthy corn crop. Grown in the fields along the road to Akers' Cabin (or Ittabeena), corn was a reliable crop for this area, but hardly the only one. Over the years, sunflowers were grown in this same area as was beans and millet and hay.[62]

It is important to note that this agricultural production was used to offset cost, not for camp consumption. To put it more plainly, the cattle and pigs were sold to slaughterhouses, but the resulting meat was not used in camp meals. No Scout ate bacon from Boxwell pigs or a hamburger made from Boxwell beef or a vegetable from the Boxwell farm. Some cuts of meat were used for gifts for donors or staff or even for personal use by the Akers family. But none of it was used for Scout camp or found its way into the dining halls. Ken Connelly, who was Assistant Finance Director and then Finance Director from 1967 to 1973, put it quite aptly, "We were not in the farming business. We were in the summer camp business."[63]

And it was the summer camp business where there was still work to be done. Akers had a vision for Boxwell Reservation that had not been fully achieved by the 1959 campaign or by the succeeding years of piecemeal development. 1968 saw yet another record summer enrollment with over 4,300 Scouts attending the eight weeks of summer camp. This continued growth was seen as proof of the camp's success and thus, planning began for another capital development campaign. At the Executive Board meeting in September 1969, Council President Crawford Adams "reported that 1972 has been agreed on with the [United Givers Fund] for the Middle Tennessee Council to seek five million dollars in capital campaign."[64]

Thus, in November 1971, the Council announced a $4.6 million development campaign to run through the first four months of the following year. The 1972 Development Program Campaign was broader in scope than the 1959 campaign, which was focused primarily on building Boxwell, but would be a similar three year collection effort. As the 11ᵗʰ largest council in the nation with over 40,000 boys, a number of fronts were targeted. A third of the funds would pay for program needs outside of Boxwell. The "construction of a new Boy Scout Office Service Center at Woodmont Boulevard and Hillsboro Road on property purchased several years ago by the council" was one goal. Another was the development of a canoe base on the Buffalo River. Given by Mr. and Mrs. Dick Grimes of Flatwoods, this thirty-two acre property would become Grimes Canoe Base.[65]

The previous Boxwell properties were both to benefit from renovations as well. The Narrows of the Harpeth was to be updated for long-term camping, meaning it needed fencing, gates, and a full time ranger and ranger's home to secure and maintain the property. The location was primarily being used for weekend camping at the time, so the ability to upgrade the site was seen as an asset. Rock Island was to get an even more extensive upgrade. Rock Island would become an official wilderness camp ready for year round use and renamed the Charles E. Parish Wilderness Reservation. Indeed, campaign funds were utilized to purchase an additional 106 acres adjacent to the reservation with the idea of creating two separate camps on the site: Camp Walling and Camp Tubb. With two camps, Rock Island would actually be a real reservation, finally.[66]

The remaining two thirds of the campaign total—$2.8 million—was earmarked "for expansion and improvement" at Boxwell. For Akers, this meant a host of new construction projects. First and foremost would be two new camps, both cut out of Camp Light. As Light would no longer be the wilderness camp, the renovations at Rock Island were needed. Additionally, each camp would get its own permanent office building and permanent trading post buildings. Washhouses and cabins for families at Murrey would make the stay there more comfortable. And, at long last, a reservation health lodge—

replacing each camp's first aid tent—would be constructed near the Crippled Crab.[67]

All of these developments rested on one central assumption: there were going to be more boys joining Scouts and more boys coming to camp. William C. Weaver, Jr., president of National Life and Accident Insurance, would serve as chair with C. A. "Neil" Craig, II, the Vice-President of National Life and Accident Insurance, as co-chair. Weaver explained that "[w]ith expanded facilities, enlarge[d] programs, and increased capacity, this council can serve more of the boys of Middle Tennessee, and improve its services to the boys, their families, and their communities." Craig expanded on this idea, stating that the goal of the council was to use these resources to serve 44% of the eligible boys in Middle Tennessee by 1980. In order "to serve 20,000 additional boys, new and expanded camp facilities will be needed[,] a new Boy Scout Office Service Center is required, and program capabilities must be increased," explained Craig. Indeed, at the campaign launch in November 1971, Weaver spoke to 300 supporters, stating, "Our efforts will make possible the expansion of our camping facilities and improve and sustain our programs so we will reach our goal of 57,000 boys in 1980."[68]

At the kick-off dinner on January 18, 1972, the Council reported more than $1 million in cash and pledges had been already made. By May, funding was secured for a new $386,000, 200 acre Boy Scout camp at Boxwell as well as the canoe base on the Buffalo River. By July the campaign surpassed the $4 million mark. Not having quite reached it goal, the campaign pushed forward to November, when the campaign was finally declared "a great victory for Scouts and boys of Middle Tennessee." After all the pledges were accounted for, the campaign raised a total of $4,360,000. While short of its $4.6 million goal, this was hardly an embarrassment at four times the size of the 1959 campaign. In fact, like the 1959 campaign thirteen years earlier, the 1972 Capital Development Campaign achieved "the largest single amount ever raised in the nation by a local Scout council." Akers had done it again.[69]

193

The new camp at Boxwell was carved out of Camp Light on the far side of the Reservation near Don Stanford Chapel and Duck Head. The camp was named in honor of Edwin W. Craig, a Giles County native who became a Nashville icon for his work through the Grand Ole Opry, WSM radio, and National Life and Accident Insurance. Craig had died in 1969 and had never been a scout, but the Craig family hoped the new 260-boy camp would "represent a continuation of his lifetime commitment to the principles that have always undergirded the Scout movement." To that end, the camp featured a unique central facility. An enormous, two story building shaped like at arrowhead from above, Camp Craig dining hall was built into a hill. The top floor held a satellite kitchen, a dining hall, and a grand veranda overlooking the waterfront at the lake below. The lower floor had a basement storage area, but also a Trading Post, a Handicraft, an indoor rifle range, and a gathering area for Scouts. There was nothing like this anywhere else on the reservation.[70]

Not surprisingly, Akers had a very unique vision for Craig. Akers walked the site with James "Jimmy" Stevens, who was not only in the construction business, but was the Council treasurer for several years—and a former staff member at Narrows of the Harpeth. When the two men found the ideal spot for the dining hall, Akers apparently became quite specific about where the dining hall should be and how it should look. Ken Connelly explained the story this way,

> [Akers] said, "I'd like the roof of this to be fanned out from
> that tree to that tree and everything overlooking the water
> from the front of the dining hall." Jimmy Stevens takes that
> direction and goes back and, working with Faulkner Hicker-
> son, they come out there and they start. Well, once they start
> building the [dining hall], and they finally get the roof on, Mr.
> Akers comes out there and he said, "Jimmy, my God, y'all have
> overbuilt this dining hall. This is much bigger than I ever
> dreamed it was going to be." [Stevens] said, "Ward, you told
> me the roof needs to start over the on that poplar tree or
> whatever it was, and then it need to span over here to this."

194

Top: The Don Stanford Chapel, ca. 1972. Bottom: Camp Craig Dining Hall, 1975. Photos by Michael Seay.

He said, "That's [it] exactly, I can take you over
there." [Akers] said, "Well, it looked different when there was
no building here!"[71]

Camp Craig also incorporated another rather unique feature that was
specifically at Akers' insistence. When the camp was built, it had no showerhouses or toilet facilities out in the camp. There were flush toilets for men and
women in the dining hall, but nowhere else in camp. If a Scout wanted a
shower, he went for a swim. As for toilet facilities out in the camp, Akers
brought in an idea he had seen in a magazine, a Swedish outhouse system
known as a kybo. A kybo was a chemical toilet. Utilizing hay and a venting
system, human waste decomposed on the spot, meaning that pumping a septic
tank was unnecessary. Given the exceptionally rocky terrain of Camp Craig,
the kybo made a great deal of sense. Putting in septic tanks would have been
very expensive, but this was not simply cost-driven decision. The decomposed
material from the kybos could be used as fertilizer for the farming operation
and, perhaps equally important, Akers wanted to have a more rustic camp for
Scout and Scouters.

Those Scouts and Scouters were not as enthused about this approach
as Akers. Here was the newest camp on property, but with the poorest sanitation facilities. Further, the kybos apparently never worked quite as advertised.
Again, Ken Connelly explained,

> That first summer, about the middle of operation, about the
> third week in July, those things started stinking so bad and not
> working. We had more fun in kind of kidding Mr. Akers. He
> would only take the kidding so far but finally convinced him
> that [laughs] we had to put up some permanent showers and
> latrines and go to the expense of building that. It took us a
> little while before we got to that point.

Construction on the camp's single showerhouse began in 1975. Situated behind the dining hall, the building had flush toilets, hot and cold running water,
and followed a similar structural aesthetic as the rest of the reservation's show-

erhouses.[72]

When the dedication ceremonies were held at Craig dining hall on July 11, 1974, Ward Akers could take pride in all that had been accomplished. The reservation had grown from 750 acres in 1959 to 1,133 acres. The new Camp Craig opened for one week in 1973, serving Scouts from the Heart of Tennessee (Murfreesboro) district. But in 1974 and 1975, Craig joined Stahlman and Parnell as a fully operational summer camp. Stahlman, Parnell, and Craig were all beneficiaries of camp offices, small permanent cabins for the camp leadership to live in during the summer. Stahlman and Parnell both received permanent buildings to house the camps' Trading Posts and Handicrafts. Fourteen Scoutmaster family cabins were dedicated at Camp Murrey as was a health lodge for the reservation. Fifteen years of hard work had paid off. As the council proclaimed in 1975, Boxwell offered "more to Scouts and Scouters this summer than ever before. The new 200-boy Camp Edwin W. Craig, new trading posts and offices at Camps Stahlman and Parnell, the new central health lodge and new Scoutmaster family cabins at Camp Murrey are the kind of continuing improvements that have made Boxwell Reservation one of the finest Scout camping facilities in the country."[73]

It would be impossible to overstate this shift to thinking of facilities as program. As early as 1960, just two weeks after the Reservation's opening dedication, Scout executives from other councils came to tour the property to see what Middle Tennessee had accomplished. As the late 1960s turned in the early 1970s, Boxwell Reservation was a regular host to several National Camp Schools, the official BSA training program for camp staff. Certain positions, such as the camp leadership, the aquatics staff, and the shooting sports staff, required camp school certification. Camp School brought their own staffs for the training, but there were no locations finer for hosting staff from across the nation than Boxwell Reservation. Indeed, Boxwell and the campaign(s) that built it was hailed a model for other councils in *Scouting* magazine. Boxwell became a nationally recognized name, a recognition made possible because of incredible facilities.[74]

The Rise of the Program Directors

As impressive as the new reservation's facilities were, once scouts and leaders arrived, more traditional program was necessary. While the facilities may have enjoyed a phenomenal upgrade and a new emphasis, the ultimate point of camp remained the same: summer camp existed to promote and serve the Scouting program. The size and scope of the new reservation, coupled with the ever expanding array of physical amenities, changed the more traditional program in both desired and unforeseen ways.

It should come as no surprise that the plan was simply to transplant the program from the Rock Island location onto the Old Hickory Lake location. As shown above, the prevailing wisdom was that the only thing the Council was lacking were the facilities to draw the Scouts in. Once the new camp was built, then the boys would be engaged and middle Tennessee Scouting would grow.

So, when the Old Hickory Lake location opened, there were quite a few similarities to the way the Rock Island Boxwell had operated. Scouts still arrived on Sundays, usually on a week dedicated to a particular district in the Council. After unloading their luggage, a staff member would give the Scouts a tour of the camp on the way to their site. At Stahlman, many of these sites had the same names as the campsites at Rock Island; Parnell's names were created on the fly by the staff. On the way to the waterfront for a swim skills check, each Scout would undergo a medical recheck by a local physician, a process that involved twenty to thirty doctors over the course of a summer and hundreds of volunteer man-hours. At dinner time, a bugle called for monitors and shortly thereafter assembly. Scouts gathered for a flag lowering ceremony, had a meal served family style in the dining hall, and then enjoyed an opening campfire that evening.[75]

Once the week began, the daily schedule was virtually identical to life at Rock Island. After breakfast, advancement sessions ran all morning, each held in specific program areas around the camp. Stahlman and Parnell, while laid out differently physically, had the same program areas and pre-determined slate of advancement offerings. After lunch, the one hour rest time still existed and was then followed by more activity—mostly advancement related—in the afternoon. The Native American dancing and ceremonies continued at camp-fires and a water carnival still ended the week on Friday afternoons. Commissaries adorned both camps, first as tents and later as permanent buildings, encouraging Scouts to indulge in their consumer habits. On paper, the program from Rock Island that emphasized family, consumerism, and specialized training for advancement, mixed with a hint of controlled adventure and fun was simply grafted on to the Old Hickory Lake location.[76]

However, the size of the new reservation and the facilities found there meant that changes to the summer camp program were inevitable. This became evident quickly. The summer of 1960 was an unqualified success. There was a great deal of publicity and Scouts were excited. But as stated above, camp was not finished when it opened. It was certainly workable, but it was very rough. The following summer, the numbers dropped. In an effort to stave off impending disaster, a staff meeting was called. As staff member Greg Tucker explains, what happened next was a propaganda campaign launched during staff week.

> [Reservation leadership] called a meeting of the staff and they passed out paper and pencils or pens and said, "Everybody write home"—they had the addresses of your Scoutmaster— "to your Scoutmaster and tell him what a program we got up here, how nice the camp is." Here we were, literally setting up camp and they didn't have the registrations to run the camp. We all wrote letters home, more or less dictated, and they mailed them all off.

It was not enough. Camp Parnell was closed for two weeks in the middle of the summer. Filling one camp with two hundred Scouts had not been very difficult. Filling two camps with over two hundred fifty Scouts and utilizing the family camp in tandem was a different beast. Something had to change.[77]

So, in 1962, a slow transformation occurred, beginning with the Scoutmaster. The first two summers had been approached much like Rock Island in the sense that Scouts came to camp, likely as a troop. Once in the site though, it was the staff who looked after them, often staying in a centrally located, large four man tent. After the problems of 1961, Boxwell embraced what most other summer camps had been doing for some time: troops came to camp with their unit leader. This adult leadership would now be responsible for Scouts in the sites. The additional space at Camp Murrey allowed the leader to bring up his family so the trip to Scout Camp could also serve as the family vacation. More importantly, the transition to unit leaders coming with their troops led to a greater investment by the adults. Coming to camp would no longer be just sending your boys off for a week. Now coming to camp was planning advancement, what week to come, what site to stay in, how much vacation time from work was needed, and a host of other related minutiae. In short, the change to unit leaders at Boxwell meant long range—and long term—commitments.[78]

The size of the reservation also led to changes in leadership, which had long term effects on how the program was developed and delivered. Rock Island, despite the "Boxwell Reservation" moniker after 1951, was just one camp. Thus, it had a camp director who oversaw all the camp's operations, both program and facilities. As explored previously, this person could be a professional Scouter, like Richard Parker or Gene Tolley, but the job could also be executed effectively by a volunteer, like Clarence Jung or Chester La-Fever. Indeed, Chester LaFever was listed as the Camp Director at Stahlman in 1960, so clear was the effort to simply replicate the previous system. But the Old Hickory Lake location was different because it was a *real* reservation.

There were three working camps on the property when it opened and four after 1973. The Rock Island approach was too simplistic to continue here. It could be replicated to some degree, but the larger reservation required a different approach.[79]

The solution was the introduction of a Program Director in the camps. Each camp, Murrey included, hired an adult staff member with the specific responsibility of overseeing the camp's program. This person was a volunteer and often connected to one of the local school systems in these first years at Old Hickory. Unlike the Program Director position, only the Boy Scout camps had a Camp Director. This position remained from Rock Island, but now transformed somewhat into a position held exclusively by a professional Scouter. The Camp Director was the representative of the Council on site and thus was the "buck stops here" person. Overseeing the entire reservation was a Reservation Director, who was also a professional. Specifically, the Reservation Director was the professional Scouter who served as the Director of Camping and Activities for the entire Council. Running summer camp was just another part of his job.[80]

The introduction of Program Directors was a creative solution. Here was a position that was dedicated to program development and delivery. In theory, the Program Director did not have to worry about hiring and firing staff or discipline in general. Further, areas like the kitchen and the commissary that were clearly not program areas would also fall outside his jurisdiction. Indeed, in theory, the program director was trained by the camp director, who had himself been trained at a national camp school.[81]

However, the reality was not so clear cut. As a volunteer, the program director, who was often connected with the school systems, could return summer after summer; the camp director, who was a professional with a district to look after, could not. It did not take too many summers before the Program Director was more knowledgeable about how camp operated than the Camp

Director was, regardless of training involved. Further, as a leader who returned every summer, the program director built a loyalty among the returning staff and scoutmasters that a camp director who changed every summer could not compete with. The Program Director became the person who actually ran the camp. By the late 1960s, this transition was complete and fairly unquestioned. As Parnell staff member Perry Bruce succinctly explained,

> I think the Camp pretty well ran itself, a lot of the times. The program director [ran] the camp. Camp directors in those days, you probably know, they were there to back up the program director basically. They were in one year and gone the next, they didn't really know how things run.

As a result of the Camp Director being so disconnected from the day to day realities, he became a good disciplinarian.[82]

The ascension of a program director was a philosophical transformation that cannot be taken lightly. While from time to time camp directors would attempt to assert their influence and what their role was supposed to be, program directors had to do little more than just wait them out as that individual would be gone the next summer. This effectively meant that all aspects of the camp were under the supervision of the program director. This was not a bad approach ultimately as it recognized that even mundane aspects of daily life at camp, such as a lack of toilet paper in the showerhouse or a cold platter of eggs in the morning, affected a Scout's experience at camp. This was a sea change in thinking: *everything* was program.

Leadership by long-serving program directors also carried other consequences. Each camp developed its own personality, often related to the personality of its program director. For much of the 1960s, Stahlman was led by Chester LaFever and Parnell by Jimmy Joe Jackson. LaFever had experience at the "old camp," but was also a high school principal during the year and that sense of being an educator was critical to how he saw camp program. LaFever wanted his staff to learn a Scout's name as quickly as possible, because "you can never convince a child that you care until you know their name." Further, an educator, either as a teacher or a Scouter, has to give a child "a sense of self-worth. And therefore you as a Scouter have got to work with the kids to cause them to feel they're somebody. If they're not an Eagle Scout, they're gonna be because that's what they're striving for, you see." To that end, LaFever would work with his staff to build a team and impart upon them what their responsibilities were. This sometimes led, rather famously, to long and frequent staff meetings. As Stahlman Staff member Jerry Barnett recalled, "My first year as a staff member, Mr. LaFever, the program director, had a staff meeting after every meal... We had a staff meeting after breakfast. That is except for the staff members that had shower house duty... But other than those staff members, everybody else was in about a half an hour staff meeting with Mr. LaFever. And he would go over things that he wanted done." However, the best summary of LaFever's approach was his own simply put statement: "I define life as the continuous process of problem-solving."[83]

Jimmy Joe Jackson at Parnell took a slightly different approach. A high school football coach for most of his career, Jackson's team building was a different beast than LaFever's. For Jackson, one time was all he expected to tell his staff anything. As he explained,

> I would tell them, on that first week, this is the only time you'll ever hear me tell you [this]. If Billy Brown's got a job at the campfire, and his job is to just make the fire, we know who's going to make the fire and he's a good person. Say Billy Brown is the one, and I want it fixed by 6:30. Now, I'll never tell you again Billy, but if it's not fixed at 6:30, you're going to be in the kitchen for a week. And every boy for that first week got his assignment. And I told them, that you don't want to hear all this, that Mr. LaFever over at the other camp gives it to them every Sunday for this campfire and every activity, but I'm only giving it to you once and you'd better be smart enough to do it and be there. And if you're not, you're going in the kitchen.

Incredibly straight forward, it worked. So much in fact that Parnell staff member, Greg Tucker, observed that "Jimmy Joe probably influenced me more than anybody after my father." A bit more colorfully, Parnell staff Charlie Ray Smith once quipped, "Jimmy Joe, we thought he could walk on water... Jimmy Joe could make you do the most dirtiest job—shoveling cow [manure]—and when you got through, you was sad that it was through because you'd had so much damn fun doing it. He was that type of person."[84]

An excellent case study in how the two men approached camp program in a practical sense can be seen with Staff versus Scoutmaster games. Both men had the staff challenge Scoutmasters to a volleyball tournament or a baseball game. Both men saw the events as a powerful way to get Scouts fired up and excited about their time at camp by pitting their leaders against their instructors. Both men had their respective staffs stand up in the dining hall and openly cajole, harass, and taunt Scoutmasters about the game, bragging about how staff had never lost. This could periodically get out of hand, but the idea was to shame the Scoutmasters to accept the challenge. Once the game started, the two men's approaches diverged wildly. LaFever's Stahlman staff continued the boisterous claims and played a rough game with every expectation of winning. Jackson's Parnell staff played a strong game too, always keeping the score close, but as Greg Tucker recalled, "Jimmy Joe would have fired us all if we ever won a game." The game was for the Scouts, not the leaders or the staff. As a result, Parnell staff would often show up at the next meal "battered and bandaged" as part of the show. While both provoked the competition, one camp saw the result as fair combat, while the other saw the result as part of an elaborate game. Both were worthy, but different, approaches to program.[85]

The influence of program directors could also be seen in the dining halls. On the surface, the physical dining halls at any of these Scout Camps were simply permanent versions of what had existed at Rock Island. Instead of saw dust floors, now the tables and chairs squeaked as they slide across concrete floors. Family style—or the monitor-host system—was used at all the camps. While none of the buildings would have air conditioning until the 1972 Development Campaign, even the fans would be turned off during meal time to allow communications from the staff.[86]

The similarities ended there. While it is unclear when exactly it began, very quickly the new Boxwell developed something the "old" Boxwell never had: dining hall program. Dining hall program was basically the same from week to week, but it consisted of songs and communications from the staff to the Scouts. The songs could be patriotic or sing-alongs, such as "This Land Is Your Land" or "On Top of Old Smoky," or even something more contempo- rary and popular. Songs could also be interactive with motions and gestures, such as "Head, Shoulders, Knees, and Toes," "There Once Was a Chigger," or "Grand Old Duke of York." There also needed to be something humorous and if something could be done to reflect the particular district or a troop from that district, then that should be done as well. Mealtime became a whole lot more involved than just the meal and a whole lot less like a school cafete- ria.[87]

Perhaps the best known example of this new dining hall program was the introduction of the Gizmo. The Gizmo was a simple program device, lit- erally nothing more than a round piece of leather, stained and stamped with the word "Gizmo" on it. Created by Stahlman staff member Claus "Dutch" Mann in 1971, the Gizmo was a daily lunchtime program activity. "[W]e passed it out to a young Scout," Mann recalled, "and at lunch time, we'd sing a little song about the Gizmo and then who ever had it, we'd call 'em up front. We had a lot of fun with this thing." The "lot of fun" was some sort of activ- ity or prank the Scout performed or silly award the Scout received as a result of being the holder of the Gizmo. Scouts, younger Scouts in particular, clam- ored to possess the piece of leather and to be the center of attention. It spread to Parnell, then to Craig, and continued on for decades. Gizmo became a cen- terpiece of dining hall lunch program that was just pure fun, making the camp

205

experience unique and different from anything a Scout would experience else-where.[88]

On the other hand, some program remained specific to the camp. The Parnell Hootenannies were a folk music group made up of Parnell Staff. Started in 1963, the group existed in various incarnations until about 1970. The group's name was given to them by Jackson himself, so it stuck. The band consisted of acoustic guitar players and often a banjo player. The group played folk songs of the period, such as "Greenback Dollar" and "Jesse James" by the Kingston Trio. The "Theme From Beverly Hillbillies" was part of the repertoire as were a host of patriotic songs, which Jackson preferred. The Hootenannies played at Sunday Night and Friday Night Campfires as well as most lunches. They even went to Camp Murrey to perform. Every now and then, the group would try out a new song, but if said song did not meet with Jackson's approval it did not continue. Wes Frye and John Bryant, Hootenannies at different points, had similar experiences. Frye recalls working up a version of "Double Shot Of My Baby's Love" by the Swingin' Medallions; Bryant's example was "Love Potion No. 9" by the Searchers. And the reaction from Jackson? Respectively, "You're killing me, boys. You're killing me" and "Don't ever do that one again."[89]

The changes above were unintentional transformations brought on by the size and scope of the new location. However, not all changes were unforeseen; some were desired. One of the great advantages of the Old Hickory Lake location was Old Hickory Lake itself, an expanse of water unlike anything found at the previous three locations. While the Cumberland River still served as "the channel" running through the reservoir, there was now a vast area available for activities that simply had not existed at the other Boxwell locations. One opportunity to come out of this was public entertainment. The Tennessee Water Ski Club presented a ski exhibition in the waters around Boxwell that first summer in 1960. In addition to water skiing feats of daring do, the club also had a clown act![90]

Water-skiing on Old Hickory Lake. This dock rested at the point of Ski Dock peninsula, ca. 1969. Personal Collection of John Cooper-Ernie Ragsdale.

The lake also afforded advancement opportunities like motorboating, sailing, and skiing. All were new, and all were offered through the Ski Dock. The Ski Dock was a small independent program area located between Camps Stahlman and Murrey. It offered a reservation wide program available to every Scout on the reservation. The Ski Dock staff also provided recreational boat rides and skiing instruction to the families at Camp Murrey. Boating activities had been critical to a Scout's experience at both the Narrows and Rock Island, but neither camp could have held a candle to the adventures possible with the Ski Dock at Old Hickory Lake.[91]

Still other changes were deliberate, but beyond the Council's control. The most significant of these was the implementation of the Commissioner System in 1971. A directive from the National Council, the Commissioner

System was a different way of approaching the Activity Yard. It was seen as a way to decentralize that particular program area to provide more direct and hands on instruction to Scouts. The centralized Activity Yard, home of Pioneering, Cooking, First Aid, and Camping, was broken up into four smaller staffs. Each staff was headed by a Camp Commissioner, who led a staff of three others, known as Program Aides. That staff of four was responsible for several campsites. Each Commissioner's Area was centrally located for their sites and each Commissioner Staff was responsible for instruction of all the traditional Activity Yard skills to those sites.[92]

The Commissioner System was the precursor to the Improved Scouting Program that was implemented the following year. The new national program did away with rank specific skill requirements, such as camping, first aid, or swimming, for the early ranks and replaced those with the Skill Award system. For example, instead of working on first aid appropriate skills for Tenderfoot, then Second Class, and the First Class—what educators today would call "scaffolding"—a Scout would simply take First Aid Skill Award. The switch to these Skill Awards would result in some shifting in how things were taught, but not anything more serious than when a merit badge changed requirements. Indeed, Skill Awards were essentially "baby merit badges." However, Skills Awards coupled with the Commissioner System represented fairly significant imposed changes back to back.[93]

For the staff, the changes were not welcome. In addition to the instructional responsibilities, each Commissioner and his staff was responsible for site inspections and showerhouse cleaning. But it was this very duplication of effort that rubbed people the wrong way. While it was supposed to provide more personal service to the Scoutmaster and his troop, the set up did not make much sense. Parnell Program Aide Ed Mason was blunt about his experience, "You would have three commissioners' systems or three areas doing the same job. You were teaching the first aid three times at the same time. Or

Working on Handicraft projects in the Murrey dining hall, 1970. The boy on the left is a staff member. The two girls in the center are daughters of Reservation Director Ed Human. Photo by camp photographer Chris "Kit" Eckert.

cooking, you'd have three groups doing cooking merit badges at the same time. It was like a waste of manpower."[94]

Still, from a program perspective, the Commissioner system was not a total loss. When Stahlman's Commissioners—Jerry Barnett, Kerry Parker, and Dutch Mann—decided that Friday Night Campfires were getting stale, a new idea was born. The three, with the help of some program aides, developed a floating Burning Eagle. By taking some old metal cots and fashioning those into a frame with a grid lining the inside, the Stahlman commissioners put the frame on two metal fifty-five gallon drums. The drums, usually used as trash cans, became floatation devices for the frame. Using old mattress covers soaked in diesel, they secured the shape of an Eagle to the frame, which would then be set aflame at the appropriate moment in the campfire. From the Stahlman Friday Night Campfire Area, a Burning Eagle would be floating in the middle of the lake.[95]

While the Boy Scout program fired on all cylinders at Camps Stahlman, Parnell, and later Craig, there was an entirely different program going on
over at Camp Murrey, the family camp. Murrey was similar to the other
camps in that it had a program director, an assistant program director, and
some program staff, mainly a waterfront director. With the occasional exception of the waterfront director, these were all adult women. There was kitchen
staff as well—of three to four traditional staff aged boys, but in total the staff
numbered less than ten. There was no professional Scouter as Camp Director,
in part because there was no Boy Scout Program and in part because there were
no female professional Scouters. To make Murrey attractive to the Scoutmaster and his family, the Council subsidized the costs, keeping the weekly fee
low.[96]

The camp itself was considerably smaller than the Boy Scout resident
camps, but this served its purposes well as a family camp, putting everything
within easy walking distance around a centrally located dining hall, and a single
showerhouse nearby. Down the hill from the dining hall and showerhouse was
a waterfront area, an inset horseshoe off the Spencer Creek side of Old Hickory Lake, likely not far from where Ward Akers had landed back in 1954. The
waterfront had a sand beach—something the Boy Scout camps did not—as
well as a boat dock nearby. And as far as living arrangements, the camp was
basically divided into two parts: an area of tents for the volunteer families staying for a week or more and another area for staff families, who were there most
of the summer. The volunteer family tents formed a large semi-circle between
the dining hall and the waterfront area. This included a large grassy area and
most all of the camp could easily be viewed from any of the tents. The staff
area, often referred to at "the Hole" or "the Horseshoe," was off a dirt road to
the left coming into Murrey. It was a little further away from the dining hall
and showerhouse, but also afforded a bit more privacy for the staff wives and
children.[97]

Until the 1972 Capital Development Campaign brought in some family cabins, everyone who stayed at Murrey—volunteers and staff alike—stayed in a tent. Sometimes these were two-man tents pushed together, but generally they were larger four-man tents, which provided a little more living space. Tents came equipped with cots and mattresses accompanied by a small table and a chest of drawers. The cots and mattresses could be pushed together to make a more "family friendly" bed, but they did not come that way. Most tents had a light hanging from the center ridge pole. If a Scouter had children, two four-men could be pushed together to create more space. Virtually all tents had a "back yard" for hanging clothes as mildew was an issue.[98]

As program was geared toward families, and particularly children, Murrey operated on a different schedule than the Boy Scout camps. There were breakfast, lunch, and dinner meals, but no call for monitors. There was a literal dinner bell that was rung to bring the kids in from playing. Meals were mostly still family style. Lunch was often cafeteria delivery to get the children in and back out to play, but dinner was a sit-down, table set, family style meal with parents and kids monitoring themselves. There was no dining hall program as there was in the boy camps, but the dining hall was definitely utilized. In the non-meal hours, the dining hall was used for crafts and indoor activities when "the Boxwell Dew" fell. The dining hall had a record player as well to play whatever vinyl was brought to camp. There was a Sunday night campfire, held in an area to the right of the waterfront. There was cooking on a campfire and making homemade ice cream. In the evenings, one could easily spy children chasing fireflies or just rolling down the hill from the dining hall. And of course because of the presence of families—and sometimes their teenaged daughters—Boxwell staff were prohibited from visiting Murrey unless on specially approved missions.[99]

Water activities were the most popular. The Murrey waterfront had a Water Safety Director, who had to be 21 years of age, just like the Waterfront directors at the other camps. And while there was some swimming instruction here, for the most part, the Murrey waterfront was a free swim area. There was a floating dock out in the middle of the swimming area with a ladder. Jumping into the water was easy from here. The whole area was divided into beginners' and swimmers' areas. If a child could not pass a swim test, he or she could not swim in the swimmers' area. The floating dock was the back edge of the swimming area; Murrey residents were not permitted to swim in the open lake. Just north of the waterfront area along the Boxwell shoreline was a "t-dock." This dock was specifically in place for motorboats from the Ski Dock to pick up passengers. Adults and children alike could take tours of the camp shoreline or rides out on the lake. Many Murrey residents learned how to ski over the summer and this t-dock was their point of departure.[100]

In many ways, Murrey reflected the family life values that the Council was trying to promote. Wives and children stayed at Murrey, enjoying an idyllic social life while the men worked. Sometimes the Scoutmasters stayed with their troops, though the staff usually came "home" in the evenings. Staff stayed over on the weekends, socializing and enjoying each other's company, leaving a neighborhood boy to cut the ever-growing lawn back home. Adult staff would bring their families out too, allowing the children to bond. One of Reservation Director Ed Human's daughters, Lisa McCormack, spent several summers at Murrey and summed up the life quite succinctly, "It was just an idyllic life to be there in the summer."[101]

Aside from the core camps, there were other program ideas that were tested in these years, some of which proved successful and others that did not. For instance, one way that Akers thanked all the Scoutmasters in camp was by having a supper just for them. Usually on Thursday night underneath a large oak tree just below Stahlman dining hall, the meal was a nice spread. Most summers it was a filet mignon wrapped in bacon, accompanied with a tossed salad, often corn on the cob, and completed with a yellow cake with chocolate icing. While most of the meal was prepared by the cooks, Akers himself prepared the steaks. For a few years in the 1970s, the steak was replaced by barbeque chicken, which was prepared by Schleicher and her cooks. The meals served as a tool for Akers to promote whatever plans he had for camp or the Council, but also to field concerns by leaders in a one-on-one environment.[102]

Some ideas were not so long lived. The Giant Leap Leadership Development Program was developed for the 1973 camp season. The goal of the program was to "incorporate the teaching and practical application of leadership development skills." Executive Board Member Jimmy Stevens spearheaded the program, which came down from the National Council's Improved Scouting Program. The program was a Junior Leader Training program, offered during "free time" at camp. Both younger Scouts (aged 11 and 12) and older Scouts (aged 13 and up) could participate, receiving instruction in leadership skills and writing a "Leadership Growth Agreement" to take home to his troop. It was, in reality, a mini-Wood Badge and was evaluated by "Wood Badge men." The program was mandatory in 1973, but became optional in 1974. There is no evidence the program continued beyond 1975, though it was suggested that the program be made a two-hour course available as part of the regular program, just like a merit badge.[103]

Similar program that did not enjoy a long life was the FAST program. Introduced in 1969, the For All Students Today (FAST) program was an early attempt by the Council to expand Scouting principles beyond Scouts. In other words, this program would be focused on inner city youth aged 11 to 14 who were not Scouts. Specifically the program brought 300 Nashville youth to Camp Stahlman for a week-long camping experience. On the surface, the program appeared to be a win-win for everyone. The Nashville business community raised $10,000 to pay the way for the 300 to attend camp for a week, an experience they would not have had otherwise. Further, they were exposed to Scouting principles and ideals. The Council and the staff got to enjoy another full of week of paid campers. The idea was good; in practice, it had some issues. The boys did not monitor themselves in the dining hall. They threw rocks at the work trucks. They tried to break into the commissary to steal drinks and ice cream. They did not follow the camp rules. As one staff member described the experience, the nighttime eventually broke down into a small war between the staff and the campers for control of the camp. There is no official statement as to the decision making here, but FAST did not happen again.[104]

While FAST may not have had traction, the idea of offering the camp to a group of youth who were not Scouts did. In 1972, Camp Stahlman became Camp SHAPE for a week as a specially designed program for those with mental and physical disabilities. The week was masterminded by Don Endsley of Tullahoma and was part of larger federal grant known as "Project Shape." The goal of the grant and the camp was to get the charges out of the institution and into the world. The first summer the Boxwell staff was a little taken by surprise. They were told their new campers, over a hundred males and females from all over the state, were physically disabled, not mentally disabled. As a result, they were unprepared for some of the challenges, such as campers choosing to sleep in the dining hall or incessant smoking. Still, there were bright spots. One staff member recalled, "Q-Ball was there and there was a little girl...[Q-ball] spent time with Erin, her favorite song was, "You Are My Sunshine." She sang it over and over again." This program was a bit more of success. It returned in 1973 under the name "Camp Jaycee," focused more on recruits from the Clover Bottom School Development Center for mentally disabled, and continued for several summers in the 1970s.[105]

Finally, from a program perspective, it should be remembered that an essential part of the vision of New Boxwell was that it be a year round camp. And it was. While summer camp only took up nine weeks, ten weeks if National Camp School was held on site, other programs utilized the property throughout the year. Executive Board meetings were often held on the property; sometimes Akers cooked pheasant from the dog trials for Board members. OA Ordeals were held in the Spring and Fall. Weekend camping by local troops was common, sometimes with their own gear, sometimes using the tents and platforms of the Reservation. There was also a Webelos Day on site to cater to Cub Scouts, which involved bringing boys and their parents up for an afternoon "jammed with activities, an open air supper and a campfire program." Showando (pronounced "Show And Do") was another off-season program on the property. Essentially, Showando was a training weekend for adult volunteers, a mini-Wood Badge. It involved a model campsite, demonstrating Scout skills, and the patrol method. It was a weekend event, but very hands on.[106]

Of course Wood Badge itself migrated to the new camp from Rock Island. The program continued to operate on a two year rotation, so the first Wood Badge sessions on the Reservation were in 1961, MT-6. For the next several years, Wood Badge operated out of the back side of Camp Light, not far from the Chapel, utilizing one of the coves Akers had identified as a potential waterfront. Stahlman used the location during summer camp as a destination for overnight troop canoe trips. As Wood Badge did not convene until August, there was little conflict. Eventually the Wood Badge site moved away from the cove and closer to Explorer Island. In 1968, the program packed up and moved across the Reservation to an area near the compound. This site would eventually be called "Camp Beany Elam" in honor of Harry "Beany" Elam, who had been so instrumental in making the program successful.[107]

Wood Badge program itself experienced changes during these years as well. The explosion of boys in the Scouting program led to a commiserate explosion of leaders, all of whom needed training. With the space now available and the demand there, Wood Badge became a yearly program, usually as a week long program every summer in August, right after summer camp ended. Boxwell piloted a new weekend-only approach in 1973, consisting of three weekends of instruction with two or three weeks in between. As a result, for a time, Wood Badge offered a weekend course in the spring (April and May) and a week-long course in August.[108]

Boxwell Reservation was a program success.

Integration

Boxwell Reservation was a program success if you were white. If you were African American, you watched the money and effort poured into the sprawling new Boy Scout summer camp from afar. You might have even wondered to yourself, if this new reservation is so large, why is there not a place for Scouts of color? There would not be a good answer for that question. Fortunately, the world was changing, and changing in unpredictable ways.

While Boxwell Reservation was being completed, getting ready for its opening in the summer of 1960, the Civil Rights Movement was moving into its direct action phase. The Greensboro sit-ins began on February 1 and Nashville followed suit on February 13. Nashville lunch counters began to integrate on May 10. From here civil rights activists participated in the Freedom Rides and other critical protests over the next few years. On July 2, 1964, the Civil Rights Act was signed into law, banning "segregation in public accommodations of every kind through the country." This landmark legislation was followed in 1965 by the Voting Rights Act, signed on August 6, 1965. The law gave the 15th Amendment to the Constitution some backbone, "prohibit[ing] states from imposing literacy requirements, polls taxes, and other similar obstacles to the registration of black voters."[109]

For the Boy Scouts, not much changed immediately. Officially, the policy of the program was non-discrimination, but local councils were still allowed to practice what worked best in their localities. In the Middle Tennessee Council, the closure of the J. C. Napier division appears to have been completed by 1960. Nevertheless, while black Boy Scout troops may have had somewhat better representation on the Council's board and perhaps even black professional Scouters to oversee their troops, they still camped separately. Indeed, there were two summer camps that African American Scouts attended. The first was Camp Burton. After several moves, Burton seems to have finally settled at the Narrows of the Harpeth. What is not clear is how long Camp Burton remained here. Most of the evidence to support this location is thin and becomes thinner after 1960.[110]

The second location was the more common summer camp for African American Boy Scouts and this was Camp Tagatay. Tagatay was located in Clarksville, specifically at Fort Campbell as part of the posts' Scouting program. At various points in the year Tagatay was utilized by Cub Scouts, Boy Scouts, and Explorer Scouts. Brownies and Girl Scouts used the camp too. And unlike Burton, Tagatay was a full service camp. It had a dining hall and it had a lake for swimming. Further, Tagatay was a facility that was used equally by white and black Scouts. The Council provided a Camp Director, but the program was considered "very bare-bones."[111]

By the summer of 1964, it was clear that segregated facilities of this type would not be able to continue. African American civil rights lawyers and activists, such a Z. Alexander Looby and Dr. Carr Treherne, were pushing for changes. Looby had been actively fighting for integration in Nashville for some time and became well known nationally when his home was bombed by segregationists in April 1960. He had filed lawsuits in Nashville after *Brown v. Board* to integrate Nashville schools and with his law partners Avon Williams and Robert Lilliard, he defended the 1960 sit-in protestors. Following the passage of the Civil Rights Act in 1964, Looby and allies began to pressure Akers and the Council to integrate. And one of the most visible ways to demonstrate this integration was through summer camp.[112]

Thus, on December 15, 1964, the Middle Tennessee Council issued a "Policy Resolution on Discrimination." The policy was not particularly long or detailed. It began by reaffirming the long-standing policy of the BSA in regard to non-discrimination. The statement outlined how the Council was open to all citizens and would not discriminate in regard to hiring and promotions. However, it was the second resolution that was the critical change for this story: "RESOLVED, the many services of the Middle Tennessee Council in its thirty-eight counties are rendered without discrimination or segregation because of race, color, creed, or national origin." In short, summer camp and any other camping activity of the council would no longer be segregated. Integration had come at last.[113]

However, that integration came slowly. In 1965, the first African American troops were permitted to come to Boxwell, which was a significant victory in terms of access to resources, facility, and staff. All of this represented an enormous upgrade for black Scouts and improved advancement opportunities. Indeed, one Scout who attended Boxwell and Tagatay said going to Boxwell "was like being at a resort" in comparison to the Fort Campbell camp. But that said, African American troops were only allowed at Camp Parnell and only the very last week of the summer. Thus, that last week of camp in 1965 at Camp Parnell was, for all practical purposes, a segregated week at camp. There was a white staff, but all the scouts who attended that week were black. And this quasi-segregated week would continue until 1968 when white troops and black troops finally spent a week together.[114]

Howard Gentry, Nashville's Criminal Court Clerk since 2011, was among the African American Scouts who attended Boxwell in these years. According to Gentry, there were a variety of rules that governed the Scouts behavior during these years. Scouts were not allowed in Camp Stahlman, not in the dining hall or in the waterfront. "We could not get in the [Stahlman side of the] lake at the same time as the white kids," Gentry further explained. "We had our time to be in the lake. A whole lake. A fish could be in there with you, but not a black person." Aside from these barriers, which they were told came directly from E. B. Stahlman himself, the troops in camp were very competitive with each other. They participated in regular advancement and had field day activities toward the end of the week. Gentry explained that they even had a "razzle dazzle relay":

Pearl and John Schleicher. Pearl was the Reservation's head cook from 1962 to 1994. Photo by Michael Seay.

> A razzle dazzle relay is from the counselor's tent up the hill
> [from the waterfront]. Somebody takes a note, and they race
> down the hill. They give it to a canoer, and you've got to keep
> the note dry... They do a canoe, and then they do a rowboat,
> because you're doing the skills. And then you give that note to
> a swimmer, and that swimmer swims all the way back. Got to
> keep the note dry, and ring the bell. I think everybody did that.
> Of course I was a swimmer, and I won.

Gentry came back the following summer and completed his mile swim.[115]

The white staff that first week in 1965 was a little apprehensive. Staff member Pat Bray recalled that "support for desegregating Boxwell was far from universal or enthusiastic. However, potential dissenters were soon set straight by our boss, Coach Jimmy Joe Jackson, who made it clear that ALL the Parnell staff would treat black scouts and leaders with respect or be gone." The Waterfront in particular was curious about what to expect as stereotypes said that black children would be poor swimmers. Of course, as public pools around

Nashville had been closed rather than integrate, it would be easy to argue any lack of skill was because of lack of opportunity rather than lack of ability. Waterfront staff member Wes Frye remembers those first swim tests well:

> And we saw this big bulky fellow come in, one of the leaders, and he says he's going to try for swimmer. I can remember Greg [Tucker] and I looking at each other and saying, "Okay, it's going to take both of us to get him out of here if something happens." He jumped in and swam like an Olympic pro. And when he came out and Greg was registering to write down his name for his tag, it was Ed Temple. It was the track coach from TSU!

Of course, not all the Scouts were star swimmers, but the point is that integration had plenty of surprises. By 1966, the Parnell Staff had their first African American staff member—Billy Pincham. Billy Wheat, who had been a part of the Murrey and Stahlman staffs since 1962, left the behind-the-scenes support positions, like the Kitchen, and joined Stahlman's Activity Yard in 1967.[116]

Still, the transition had some hiccups. While the Council seemed committed to moving forward with integration, bringing African American troops to summer camp at Boxwell was often a challenge. While Akers wanted to keep fees low, for families just emerging from segregation and the poor wage economy that accompanied it, summer camp was still expensive. Ken Connelly recalled that during his tenure as Finance Director with the Council, 1963 to 1979,

> [W]e had a difficult time getting a lot of our predominantly black troops to come to summer camp, and that we were always trying to create some special efforts for scholarships. We did have Jack Massey, who was the founder of Kentucky Fried Chicken, would give us $10,000 a year that we could help with that issue. That paid a lot of the scholarships that they applied for.

The implementation of the Improved Scouting Program was also seen as directly connected to integration, which helps to explain some of the negativity surrounding this program as well. The idea of carrying a dime in your pocket for a public toilet not only did not seem very Scout-like; it was also not a reality that suburban white kids had to confront often.[117]

With Boxwell integrating, there was little need for the Council to hold on to Camp Burton, in any of its incarnations. The Narrows of the Harpeth returned to its weekend camping status and the occasional Cub event. It had no permanent ranger and people were all over the property. Indeed, some college students were arrested for smoking marijuana there. Thus, the need to upgrade the property as part of the 1972 Campaign was clear. The original Burton site presented a different problem. Construction of the Percy Priest Dam began in 1963, meaning the resulting new reservoir—Percy Priest Lake—would submerge the original Camp Burton property off of Couchville Pike. Thus, in March of 1965, E. E. Murrey, Jr., E. B. Stahlman, and A. J. Baird were empowered by the Executive Board to handle the "disposal" of the property with the Corps of Engineers. And just like that, the separate black summer camp programs faded into history.[118]

Of course, these troops at Parnell in 1965 through 1967 were not the first African Americans at the new Boxwell. Those honors resided with those African Americans who were behind the scenes making the camp work. In Stahlman kitchen, there were "black girls" who worked for Martha Cardiff, the first reservation cook. How many there were and how old they were is lost, but they were there. Much more is known about the Ranger Staff. While headed by a white ranger, the staff employed several African Americans in the 1960s and early 1970s. From almost the day camp opened, William "Punkin" Green and his younger brother Larry served as rangers at Boxwell, as did their uncle, "Uncle Bill" Harris, doing mechanical work on the equipment or helping with the farm. (The Green's mother was occasionally asked by Akers to prepare the pheasant from the field trials). Along with the other assistant, a white tenant farmer named Farmer Bush, these men ran the farm operation, cutting tobacco, planting whatever crop was the plan that year, and maintain-

ing the herds of pigs and cattle. They also worked on the equipment, which
included a large amount of old military vehicles that had been screened from
Fort Campbell as well as old cars that collected in the camp's compound.[119]

And then a fascinating thing happened. While all of these individuals—known and unknown—were employed on the Reservation prior to the
1964 anti-discrimination policy, they were all in support positions. In fact,
they were all in positions that would be considered "appropriate" for their skin
color—all subordinate, all in helping position, all involved in cooking or
maintenance. As integration took hold, African Americans stopped holding
these positions. Pearl Schleicher came in as camp dietitian after Martha Cardiff. Her staff included members of her family—her husband John and her
sister Estelle Lankford, known as "Mrs. B"—and other white cooks. While
she may have had African Americans on her youth kitchen staff, Schleicher did
not have black cooks in her thirty-two year run as head cook. The Ranger
staff underwent a similar transition. "Uncle Bill" Harris died in the fall of
1969. Larry Green left to join the ranks of the professional staff in August of
1971. William "Punkin" Green was gone by the end of 1974 for better opportunities. All were replaced by white men. No African American has served
on the ranger staff since the Greens left. As Boxwell integrated publically, it
self-segregated privately. There is no evidence this transition was intentional,
but it happened just the same.[120]

Perhaps the most interesting consequence of the slow move toward
integration was how the camp's traditionally African American roles were now
staffed. Since Linton, the cook at Boxwell has almost invariably been a black
man. Walter Whittaker performed this function from Linton through the
Narrows and Ike Davis filled the role for most of the years at Rock Island.
Boxwell Reservation at Old Hickory has never had a head cook other than a
white female. Women serving in this capacity should not be a surprise.
Women's Liberation only begins to gain a foothold at the end of this period
and the two women who served as cooks from 1960 to 1975 were both older

women. Further, having a woman as the cook, even as head cook, served the domestic gender agenda the Boy Scouts promoted. For the Boy Scouts in the 1960s, it was not necessary to explain that women belonged in the kitchen. It was an accepted, unquestioned assumption.

However, that assumption should not include the idea that these women did not play important roles. Just like Whittaker and Davis were not hidden characters at their Boxwells, neither was Schleicher a hidden character at Old Hickory. Indeed, most who knew her well would have considered her a powerful force to be reckoned with. She was hired in 1962 to help stretch the few dollars the Council had following the Capital Development Campaign. As explained above, her staff worked hard, making almost everything from scratch. But she pushed the youth staff too. She had a certain stern look she would give when she disapproved that would make young men shutter. And while well known to be a feisty personality, Schleicher always deferred to the male leadership, especially to Ward Akers, whom she respected deeply, and who always called her "doll."[121]

The Fall of Ward Akers

Since that first walkabout on the Old Hickory Lake property in 1954, Ward Akers and the Council had enjoyed phenomenal success. For almost 20 years, the Council had shown growth in numbers, property, and facilities. Boxwell had benefitted from not one, but two capital development campaigns. The Council had purchased and had broken ground on a new multi-purpose Scout Center on Hillsboro Road. A canoe base had been purchased and was fully operational by 1975 with over two thousand "float days." Rock Island and Narrows of the Harpeth were both going to get renovations from the 1972 Capital Campaign. And the growth in people was equally impressive. In 1958, Middle Tennessee Council could boast 20,104 total boys—Cub, Boy Scouts, and Explorers. By 1967, that number was up to 35,200. In that same period, the professional staff grew from 14 to 33. By most all metrics, the council under the leadership of Ward Akers was wildly successful.[122]

Nevertheless, the Akers Scouting juggernaut, like many other organizations, struggled with the end of the post-World War II economic boom. While the 1972 Campaign had been a success, 1973 proved more trying, as rising inflation and then the oil embargo at the end of the year complicated the Council's best efforts to move forward. Costs for construction rose. Camp costs, such as food, increased. As costs went up in the real world, disposable income decreased. Pledges made were not always pledges collected. Thus, plans began to shrink to fit the new reality. Instead of two new camps at Boxwell Reservation, just one, Camp Craig. Instead of two wilderness camps at Rock Island, just one, Camp Tubb. Instead of improved facilities at the Narrows, no improvements. Perhaps the most evident example of this collapsing of ambition was the family cabins at Murrey. Fourteen family cabins were dedicated at the July 11, 1974 ceremonies; only six were built. Indeed, the "ghost cabins" inspired a camp legend. While there were only six cabins, there were plaques for all the contributors. So, whenever a donor came to look at the cabin he or she had helped build, the plaque was simply switched out.[123]

To add to this new economic reality, the baby boomers' influx into Scouting had peaked by the early 1970s. This meant two critical things. First, an enormous number of adults began to seek work when inflation was already on the rise, leading to the stagflation phenomenon (high unemployment and high inflation), further hurting the economic realities of the Council and camp. Second, and more importantly, the end of the baby boom meant fewer Scouts coming to camp. This was also undoubtedly aided by the change to the Improved Scouting Program, which turned many long time Scouters away, as well as a wider social outlook on Scouting because of the Vietnam War and the counterculture movement. In short, Scouts were not "cool" by the early 1970s and that was reflected in attendance. All three Boy Scout camps—Stahlman, Parnell, and Craig—were open in 1974 and 1975, but some creative thinking was required to make this work. In 1975 for example, Stahlman only ran for

six weeks, instead of the long-standing nine weeks. Parnell was open all summer, but Craig was closed the first week and the last week, and its third week
was dedicated to Webelos. This was not exactly the march to 45,000 boys the
1972 Campaign had predicted, especially compared to earlier summers when
staff had to sit outside the dining hall for meals because the camp was literally
overflowing with people.[124]

These were challenges that most American businesses and organizations were faced with at the time. The real problems began when the growing
distrust of institutions turned its focus on the Boy Scouts of America. Con-
ventional wisdom, then and now, held that any question of impropriety with
the Council, or Scouting in general, had long been fended off by the Stahlman
family. In short, the *Nashville Banner* defended and protected Akers and the
Council. But the Stahlmans were gone by 1974. James G. Stahlman, the publisher of the *Banner*, retired in June 1972. E. B. Stahlman suffered a debilitat-
ing stroke in September 1968, leading to his resignation from the paper. He
died in June 1974. Pearl Schleicher remembered the moment well:

> [Akers] came in the kitchen over [at Stahlman] one morning,
> right at breakfast time, went directly into the store [room] and
> [Reservation Director] Ed [Human] went in there with him.
> And he stayed and stayed and stayed. Finally, Ed come out
> and when he did, I went in. I said, "Mr. Akers, come and eat
> some breakfast." And the tears were dropping off on the
> floor. He had lost his best friend... I said, just come on out
> here and eat. And them tears were really dropping. I couldn't
> imagine what was making him cry so. And then when he said,
> "Well doll, I've lost the best friend I've ever had. The best
> friend I've ever had." He repeated it! And I said, "Well come
> on and eat something, you'll feel better." "Doll, I don't want
> anything. I'm full." He meant he was full of grief, I reckon is
> what he meant.[125]

The first sign of this newly focused distrust came in June 1974 with
the BoyPower '76 campaign. As mentioned above, BoyPower '76 was a na-

tional recruitment program launched in 1969 with a goal of recruiting one in
every four eligible boys into Scouting by the nation's centennial. But by 1974,
the campaign was behind. The news broke that ten different councils were
padding their roles. *The Chicago Tribune* ran a two part series on the scandal
the week of June 11, leading reporters to ask the Middle Tennessee Council if
it had been doing the same. And the paper that did the investigating was not
The Tennessean, but the *Nashville Banner!* Assistant Council Executive Ken
Connelly at first denied there was any abuse, or even any need for abuse as the
Council comfortably recruited 36% of eligible boys—well above the desired
quota. Upon further pressing, Connelly conceded there had been some padding in the past, but the action had been discovered and "we took direct action." An unnamed secretary for the Council reported the padding and said it
was still going on. Nevertheless, Connelly's repudiation was enough to let the
issue die at the time. But this story showed quite clearly that the Council was
no longer safe from uncomfortable investigations.[126]

The investigation into Akers began not with the Boy Scouts, but with
Nashville's United Cerebral Palsy (UCP) chapter. Financial indiscretions were
discovered, investigated, and exposed by *Banner* reporter Larry Brinton. The
entire Nashville Board resigned in May 1975. Having met success here, Brinton was tipped off on the Boy Scouts and Ward Akers, in particular. Who
exactly tipped off Brinton remains something of a mystery, with the most logical explanation a disgruntled employee. Nevertheless, with a tip to investigate
and no Stahlmans to redirect him, Brinton began to ask questions.[127]

The story broke in an odd way on July 1, 1975. Brinton had requested information from both the Council and the Nashville Area United Way,
which at the time still partially financed Scouting. He was looking for information on the salaries of Akers and his family, the Council's budget, money
that had been earmarked for travel by the professionals, who exactly was on the
payroll, and information on the fleet of cars that the Council leased for the
professionals. Council President C. A. "Neil" Craig, II, son of Edwin W.

Craig, received the request and transmitted it to the Board on Saturday, June 28. Brinton's request "was widely discussed over the weekend." Nevertheless, it was the *Tennessean* that ran the first article on the story. As the city's morning newspaper, the *Tennessean* had received the information request about what was going, though it does not appear they understood the purpose of the investigation. Nevertheless, the *Tennessean* reported Tuesday morning, July 1, that Craig had sent a letter to the Board defending Akers' annual salary of $44,500. Further, Craig pointed out that the investigation came at a time when the Council's fundraising efforts were stalling because of the "pall that has been cast over all fund raising of this kind by the unfavorabl[e] publicity surrounding one organization." In short, the investigation into the UCP was hurting the Scouts' fundraising efforts and a new investigation into the local Council would not help. Craig was clearly trying to stop this train before it left the station.[128]

The afternoon edition of the *Banner* clarified exactly what Brinton had been fishing for in his requests and what the *Tennessean* could not quite put its finger on. Brinton charged that together with his wife, mother-in-law, and stepdaughter, the Boy Scouts were paying Akers $68,000 a year. The amount was important because the council "is finding it increasingly difficult to raise $1 million in pledges and plans to cut back on expenses for the reminder of the year." Brinton was making the case that Ward Akers, by using nepotism to hire his wife and his step-daughter, was not only taking in an unacceptably high salary, but this high salary was being paid out at a moment when the Council was having trouble reaching its fund-raising goals. Of course, broken down, Akers himself was only making $44,500 a year, but this was still double his assistant Ken Connelly. His wife made $9,500, his mother-in-law $7,600, and his stepdaughter $7000.[129]

Some of this was easily explained away. Mrs. Elizabeth Akers had been with the Council for 20 years and had only married Ward in 1967. A solid ten years before Ward married Elizabeth, the woman who was now his mother-in-law had been employed by the Council for eighteen years, first as a bookkeeper then as a data processor. Clearly, neither of these was an example of nepotism. The stepdaughter was a murkier situation as she had only been in the employ of the Council for two years. Together, the three were the highest paid office employees. As for Akers' salary, Craig was quick to defend the executive in a four page statement:

> Mr. Akers has been in scouting since 1938, and he has been with our council since 1946. That year there were 4,963 boys registered in scouting in 235 Middle Tennessee units. At the end of last year, there were 32,532 boys in 1,033 units—which means that we are serving 33 per cent of all the available boys in the Middle Tennessee area as compared with a nationwide average of just over 20 per cent. That kind of performance has made our council the 14th largest in the U.S....
>
> This is largely the result of the leadership of Ward Akers, who is recognized as one of the outstanding professional career Scout executives in the country...

Brinton explained that "Akers' salary in 1971 was $27,250 and has been increased more than 60 per cent during the past four years to the present day. Craig said Akers had asked each time that his salary not be increased, but it was done so by the council's salary committee of volunteer members." To this charge, Craig replied,

> While the salary committee wished to compensate him in line with his contributions to scouting and in harmony with comparable pay levels for other Scout executives, they were also mindful that Mr. Akers is now two and a half years away from retirement, and his retirement benefits will be based on his average annual compensation during the five years prior to his retirement.

Additionally, Akers had received offers at other Councils for more money and had even turned down an offer to work as a regional director, which also would have meant more money. Akers was serving Middle Tennessee at a cost to himself, and "Lest your questioning raise the suspicions that this is another CP (United Cerebral Palsy) situation, let me assure you that the executive board of the council maintains the strictest control over the fiscal affairs of the council, through its volunteer finance committee, and our records are audited yearly by the firm of Davis and Martin, Certified Public Accountants." Clearly, Craig was frustrated. It was inappropriate to compare the salary of the Director of the UCP, which served just Metro Nashville, and that of the Council Executive of Middle Tennessee, which served thirty-eight counties of the mid-state area.[130]

Other charges were more difficult to dismiss. There were questions about Akers' $50 a month expense check, his new fleet vehicle, and what was essentially a second personal residence at Boxwell, Ittabeena, that was clearly Council property. Further, Akers, and many other professionals, took their wives with them to meetings and conventions at the Council's expenses, suggesting that the Council was inappropriately subsidizing personal vacations in the name of work. And there were questions about who got to use the Council -leased Beaman Pontiacs, which were supposed to be exclusively for the professional staff to conduct Council business.[131]

After these initial allegations and the Council rebuttal, both the *Tennessean* and the *Banner* ran related stories, but no new information came out. The *Tennessean* reported that the United Way would not disclose salaries for any of the agency heads who received their funding. The *Banner* ran an editorial asking "Can the Boy Scouts Enjoy Extravagance?" The editorial mused that perhaps the Boy Scout bureaucracy had begun "to multiply in a fashion most often observed in governmental agencies." Coming from the conservative *Banner*, this was an insult to be taken seriously. This lull in the news cycle was short-lived. July 3rd brought a new round of attacks from Brinton. "Attack" would be the appropriate word as Brinton had no new evidence, simply frustration at the Council's reaction to his allegations. A call for a "special 'blue ribbon' panel of citizens" to investigate the charges was shot down, allegedly by

229

none other than Executive Board Member and Nashville Mayor Beverly Briley himself. Further, the Council "curtailed the flow of information to the news media in what were described as 'high hopes that recent criticism concerning financial extravagance will blow over' during the July 4 weekend..."[132]

And the issue may well have blown over too, but Brinton found more. On July 8, five days after his initial frustration, Brinton put forward new allegations, this time on a conflict of interest charge. Pointing out that the Council had "a policy against any professional staff executive holding an outside job or having another business interest," Brinton explained that Ward Akers himself was "a founder and a member of a partnership formed in 1971 in a corporation which purchased Camp Hy-Lake, a leading private camp for boys at Quebeck, near Sparta..." Hy-Lake of course was not a Boy Scout camp; it was located down the river from the Rock Island Boxwell under different management. The two camps had been friendly rivals throughout the Fifties. But now, it turned out, Akers was involved in a continuing business interest in the camp, which would be a direct conflict to his work with the Middle Tennessee Council, who of course still owned the Rock Island property. Further, Brinton pointed out, in trying to explain the salary issue away, Akers had not only cited the policy but provided the example of the Council's public relations director, Terry Mayers, who "gave up his post... because he was not permitted to hold outside 'moonlighting' jobs." Brinton was suggesting Akers was a hypocrite.[133]

For this new wave of allegations, Brinton set something of a trap for Craig and Akers. He called Craig on Monday, July 7, asking about any outside business interests Akers might have. Craig denied any knowledge, but promised to look into it. Having spoken with Akers, Craig returned Brinton's call to say Akers had "no outside interests aside from being former director of a Savings and Loan Association and a Retriever's Club." The call ended. Brinton sprung his trap, calling Craig back five minutes later to ask specifically "if Akers does not own 20 per cent of Hy-Lake Camp and Recreation Corp., a company chartered in Tennessee Oct. 26, 1971, listing his son, Ward C.

230

Ward Akers at the dedication for the Camp Parnell Program Director's Cabin, July 11, 1974.
The cabin was named for Richard M. Hawkins. Photo by Michael Seay.

231

Akers, as president." Craig now confirmed the allegation. When asked why he had not mentioned this in any of the previous calls, Craig confirmed he had just learned it... "from Akers who was seated in his office during the two calls." From here, Craig tried to hedge. He explained that he believed that being a stock-holder and "outside business interests" were different things. The first was an investment, while the other required time and money away from primary employment. Craig "saw no conflict of interest in Akers' involvement in the ownership of a private boys camp, operated to make a profit for his corporation, and Akers' role in operating the non-profit Camp Boxwell for Scouts."[134]

These additional charges provoked a different response. By Friday, July 11, Ward Akers and his wife Elizabeth "temporarily relinquished their duties pending a 'no stone unturned' full review of the council's scouting program." The review would run approximately sixty days as several committees were formed within the Council to investigate the various allegations. Indeed, Craig charged the committees to "fully review the entire scouting program in Middle Tennessee." Such an extensive and thorough review was critical to clear the Council's name and reputation. "Whether rightly or wrongly," Craig said, "statements have been made about your council that can cause irreparable harm. We have made every effort the last two weeks to answer these questions, but ladies and gentlemen, Scouting is too precious to you and me and our little friends in the community to allow any doubt to continue to exist." Further, to protect the work of the committees, Craig released the names of the committee members on July 13 and would "issue no further statements" until the investigations were completed and reported in October. Any questions about the work would simply be directed to the appropriate committees.[135]

And so the internal investigation began. None of the committees' work made its way into the newspapers, but people were busy. Craig viewed Brinton as simply out to get Akers and truly believed the "Blue Ribbon Committees" would exonerate him. Thus, the men chosen to lead the committees were "top-notch board members," as Assistant Executive Ken Connelly recalled, "their credibility could not be questioned." The committees explored the hundreds of pages of documents and conducted dozens of interviews. When the work was completed, each committee put together their own report and the findings were signed by all the members of that committee, again in hopes of adding credibility to the research. The committee reports were compiled into one large report, which was submitted to the Executive Board and put out to the press. Events moved quickly from there.[136]

The committee reports were over 200 pages in total, complete with supporting documentation. According to Craig, "some of the charges have been refuted and some have been verified." The work of the committees also found other issues that needed to be addressed and offered recommendations as to how these problems be corrected. While the committees took no issue with Aker's salary, again citing his long service and extraordinary achievements, the employment of other members of his family was recognized as nepotism, though an explicit policy against such did not exist at the time. Hy-Lake was a problem. The 20% stock ownership was not a conflict of interest, however it turned out "130 Army surplus cots and mattresses intended for Camp Boxwell" were transferred to Hy-Lake. This was "inappropriate." The committees recommended the cattle and hogs be removed, specifically because Akers and some of the professional staff sometimes kept meat for themselves. While there was some debate about the Council's service area of thirty-eight counties and therefore the maximum salary allowed, it was determined Akers' salary of $44,500 was below the $45,400 maximum. Business contracts of the council raised no flags. However, "a railroad rail 24 feet long, which had been left over from the original construction of the waterfront at Boxwell in 1957 had been used by Akers for a support at the rear of [his] house." Some numbers padding from years earlier was discovered as well. While the extent was "impossible to determine," the evidence pointed toward "isolated cases." And perhaps not surprisingly, the report found that the Executive Board, who was supposed to be running the Council, was "little more than a 'rubber stamp' to the scout executive." And while rumors swirled around Ittabeena, the committees found there were no misappropriation of funds to construct the cabin.[137]

The report did not exonerate Akers, but it was hardly damning either. The question now was what would happen moving forward. Connelly began contacting board members to see if they would ask for Akers' resignation. Overwhelmingly, "they would not ask for his resignation." But Akers had apparently already been in contact with Craig and three other—unnamed—board members. The four board members meet with Akers at his home and recommended he take an early retirement. The group promised financial incentives to make retirement easier for Akers and thus resignation a less bitter pill. When Connelly finally met with Akers, the decision had been made: Akers would retire. For the good for the program, Akers needed to step aside.[138]

And so, on October 1, 1975, Ward Akers submitted his resignation as Scout Executive for the Middle Tennessee Council, twenty-seven years after he started his work there and thirty-seven since becoming a professional. In his resignation letter to the board, he acknowledged that "[m]ost of the time it has been a happy, glorious experience working with the greatest volunteers on earth, watching young professional men grow into manhood, watching youngsters come into Scouting, grow through to Eagle and on to take their rightful place as community leaders." He recounted how when he took over the Council it was $9,000 in debt and now it had $3.5 million in assets and was running without a deficit, one of only four councils in the nation to be doing so. But most importantly, Akers took responsibility, writing,

> I will personally accept the blame of all problem areas that could have been corrected with more time given to the desk and dedication to paper work....
>
> This, my friends, is my biggest sin of commission and omission. I care little for desk work, for bookkeeping, filling out

forms, writing letters or directives. My work is with people and when you are working with people it is very hard to keep from making some mistakes and I have made my share in 37 years...

So, if it pleases the Executive Board of the Middle Tennessee Council, I shall seek retirement immediately or as soon as my successor can be found.

It has been an exhilarating experience to have had this much fun for 37 years.[139]

On Thursday evening, October 9, 1975, the Executive Board of the Middle Tennessee Council met at Stahlman Dining Hall. Akers was not present, but he was the evening's central concern. Akers' resignation letter was read to the board and a motion was made to accept this early retirement. A debate followed. A motion was made to defer a vote until the Novemeber meeting when everyone had had a chance to review all the material. The motion was initially seconded and more discussion followed. After some fairly intense debate, Jimmy Stevens rose and addressed the question before the group, "No one loves Ward Akers and the Scouting program anymore [sp] than I do. I have been in contact with Ward and I believe this request is his sincere wish." More debate followed. Ultimately, the motion to discontinue the question was seconded and approved. The original question concerning deferring was taken up again... and defeated by a vote of 83 to 7. A new motion was put forward to accept Akers' request for early retirement. With a majority of 67 Board members approving, the motion carried. The Board went on to approve Akers' becoming "Scout Executive Emeritus" when a new Executive was hired.[140]

The Board then moved on to other business. So ended the era of Ward Akers.

*1966 Stahlman Waterfront Staff. Left to right: Lynn Davis, Kerry Parker,
Charlie Ray Smith, Don Gaffin, Jim Brown, Richard Parker, and Denis Fussell.
Personal Collection of Charlie Ray Smith.*

Chapter 5

"Improvise and Adjust":
Implementing Program at Akers' Boxwell

1960-1975

"Here I go!" An elderly man's voice crackles with enthusiasm off an old cassette tape. He rustles with the recorder, the sound of microphone scratches caught on the recording.

"I don't know just what to talk to you about," he continues, a Southern drawl clearly evident now. A short giggle follows before he resumes with an almost sing-song opening, "I know one thing - this is now Thursday...oh, I don't even know what date it is. I'd have to go look. I'll find out. I'll find out about that..."

This is Floyd "Q-ball" Pearce from Clarenden, Arkansas. As he would soon discover, the tape was recorded on Thursday, June 20, 1985. A staple of the camp staff since the Rock Island days, Q-ball did not return in 1985. He had taken years off before, but this time was different and even Q-ball seemed to know it. He was 85 years old and in January had tripped on some stairs at the Clarendon Masonic Lodge. His new bifocals had confused him. He had banged his face up pretty badly and lost some teeth, finally getting a set of false ones. A few weeks later, he had some heart issues, which caused shortness of breath and gave him a second trip to the hospital in less

than a month. The recording relayed all of this in the sort of real time, play-by
-play the elderly give when discussing their ailments. Still, Q-ball wrapped up
the tape with the most important message, the real reason for the cassette that
he mailed to Boxwell: he missed camp and he hoped some of the guys would
come visit him soon.[1]

Q-ball never returned to Boxwell and passed away in 1987. Around
his bedside when he died were his wife, his brother, and three of his good
friends from the staff. These were all younger men, men who had been kids
during the heyday of Ward Akers' Boxwell. Ward himself had passed on in
September 1981, or perhaps he too would have been there, his bond with Q-
ball stretching back into the 1940s when he was Scout Executive for East Arkansas Council. The world, and Boxwell, had changed a great deal since those
years, but the camp staff friends at the bedside demonstrated that something
important about Boxwell had not changed—the bond between the staff.[2]

In the years since his death, Q-ball passed into legend. A plaque to
him hangs on the wall outside the Stahlman Handicraft, where he worked for
years. No capital campaign contribution or professional dedication placed the
plaque there; it just appeared before camp one summer. Friends of Q-ball told
stories of their friend, relishing in his eccentricities. Q-ball would always clear
his throat before he was going to say anything. "You know?" was a well-
known saying of his. When he came to camp, he brought several trunks of
personal gear and in particular his personal tools for the woodworking and
leatherworking he would do over the summer. As he did not drive to camp
from Arkansas, the trunks were shipped by freight and had to be picked up
every summer in Nashville and brought out to camp. After the OA Lodge was
built in 1968, he lived there during camp, enjoying the air conditioning and
listening to recordings of the Mormon Tabernacle Choir and Elvis Presley.
He participated in the Handicraft staff's side business, making belt buckles and
then belts for Scouts who would pay extra for them. He had a small recorder
with open reel tapes and he would talk with people, collecting their stories.

Floyd "Q-ball" Pearce, center, with several of the "all summer" kids at Camp Murrey, 1973.
Personal Collection of Lisa and Cindy Human.

And of course, Q-ball had a deep love for the Order of the Arrow. "Chief" Q-ball had an enormous headdress with feathers trailing to the ground, a peace pipe, and buckskin clothing. The stories of Q-ball Pearce are legion.[3]

But the stories are only partly about Q-ball. While a recurring character in many stories of people who worked these years, Q-ball is really a gateway to an almost golden age of Scouting in Middle Tennessee and Boxwell in particular. Talking about Q-ball is to remember when the Reservation was new, when the possibilities seemed endless, when Akers and those who worked for him seemed like an unstoppable force for good. And Q-ball was just one of many personalities in these years. He was just one example of the many people—professionals and volunteers—who graced these years and made Akers' vision a reality. People who made the program happen.

The Professionals

As mentioned previously, "new" Boxwell's size created unique challenges for leadership and running the camp. At Rock Island, the professional staff had been closely connected with the workings of the camp, demonstrating in a very real sense what Scouting was. But the enormity of the Old Hickory Boxwell made this sort of one-on-one contact much more difficult. The growth in Scouting led to both a larger camp and a larger (and growing) professional staff. More boys and men involved meant more districts and more assistance in those districts. When Richard Parker had served as Camp Director at Rock Island, he was still simply a District Executive; Boxwell was an extra responsibility he took on in addition to those other responsibilities. Those days were no more. There needed to be a professional dedicated full-time to the Reservation and the Council's camping activities and District Executives (DE) needed to keep supporting their districts as much as possible to ensure that there were boys to come to camp.

Thus, the professional hierarchy transformed. A new Council level position was created: the Camping and Activities Director (Director of Support Services in later years). This individual's job was to run the Reservation, not just for summer camp, but for all the year round activities. He would also oversee the other Council properties, such as the Narrows, Rock Island, and after 1972, Grimes Canoe Base. Eagle Banquets and Council Jamborees fell under his umbrella as well. It was a big job. The Camping and Activities Director—referred to simply as the Reservation Director at Boxwell—was assisted in each camp by District Executives who served as Camp Directors. Again, the Camp Directors, as the representatives of the Council in camp, were supposed to run the camp, though in practice, the Program Directors came to be the people in charge.[4]

Part of the Camp Directors' weakness as effective leaders within the camps was that they did not tend to stay very long. While there were exceptions, most Camp Directors stayed in the position one summer, maybe two. It so happened that two or three different Camp Directors even graced Parnell one summer! This was not a good way to build loyalty amongst the staff or a good way to develop a clear understanding of the operation. Nevertheless, the professional staff was a very dedicated group. In the 1960s, most of the men who served on Boxwell staff experienced promotion in some capacity. Indeed, the Executive Board meeting minutes read as a constantly shifting roster of promotions and departures as someone was promoted out of council and then a domino effect of others rising to fill the empty roles. Bruce Atkins, Ken Connelly, Bob Holt, Ron Oakes, and Ken Goad all served as Camp Directors and all went on to become Scout Executives in their own councils. Serving at Boxwell and on the professional staff of Ward Akers was good experience for promotion. Ralph Manus was an excellent example. He began his career as a DE and served for two summers as Camp Director in Camp Parnell. As Camp Director, he sought out the homesick Scouts and gave them chewing gum. Every morning, he was up at the dining hall with coffee to talk with Scoutmasters. His efforts were rewarded. He quickly promoted within the Council, eventually becoming Assistant Executive right behind Akers. In 1973, he became Council Executive of his own his council, the Chickasaw Council out of Memphis.[5]

Unlike Camp Directors, the Reservation Directors stayed for a number of years. In fact, throughout this period, there were only three Reservation Directors: James Johnson (1960-1965), Bruce Atkins (1966–1969), and Ed Human (1970-1975). All three men had risen through the ranks of the professional organization, all three were deeply devoted to the camp and to Scouting, and all three had trained for years under Ward Akers. This did not mean they were cookie cutter drones, simply executing Akers' wishes. Each had different personalities and brought different approaches to how the summer camp program was executed in this brave new world.

James Johnson was well-qualified as Reservation Director. He had served on the Rock Island staff not only as Camp Director in 1956, but on the Waterfront Staff there as well in 1958. When Richard Parker became Assistant Scout Executive in 1959, James Johnson became Camping and Activities Director and the first Reservation Director at the new Boxwell Reservation. Other members of the professional staff called him "Jim," but amongst themselves the Boxwell staff quickly gave him the well-earned nickname, "Foxy." Though balding, his remaining hair was a strong and flowing red and he had a wiry build with "piercing blue eyes," a slender face and long nose. He had a keen memory, recalling not only your name, but every detail you had ever told him. Of course, the real origin of "foxy" seemed to also be wrapped up in the fact that Johnson would sometimes watch his staff at work from afar, often behind cover, like a fox on a hunt.[6]

Johnson's responsibilities were immense as the Council had never run an operation of this magnitude before. Thus, Johnson established the position and how the multiple camps would operate. He hired the summer camp staff and also chose which professionals would be Camp Directors. He kept a tight budget and created the purchasing and food processes used for years to come. He did his part to keep to Akers' vision of making "the program as cheap as possible for kids and the volunteers." And he did all this with a reservation that was constantly under construction.[7]

But Johnson brought more to the program than simply good management skills. He brought two critical philosophies to camp that were critical to its early success. First, Johnson understood that the while the buildings were important, the program was what mattered. Stahlman Staff member Jerry Barnett explained the simplicity of these ideals when describing how he first became Stahlman Kitchen Director. Barnett had been hired in 1965 for the Activity Yard, a position he truly wanted. But after the original Kitchen Director left three weeks into the summer, LaFever and Johnson called Barnett to the dining hall to ask him to take up the position. After some back and forth, including protests from Barnett, "Mr. Johnson just looked at me, and he said,

The professional Scouters of Middle Tennessee Council, at the Crippled Crab, 1963. Front row, left to right: James Wright, Charles Biederman, James Johnson, Joe Gafford, Ward Akers, Richard Parker, Bill Jennings, Frank Lawrence, Bobby Chaffin, Ron Oakes. Back row, left to right: Tom Atkinson, Cal Orvetz, Ralph Manus, Al Wood, Bob Holt, Ken Young, Archie Crain, Bruce Atkins, Bob Nash, Unidentified, Don Coleman, John Scoble, Gene Hensley. Personal Collection of Archie Crain.

now Jerry, he said, this is for good for the program." And that was it. Barnett took the position even though he did not really want to take it. Sacrificing individual desires for the needs of the program became a common refrain as the years progressed.[8]

The second philosophy Johnson brought to camp was that of mentorship. He had a program to run at camp, but he had staff to train as well. He was clear about his expectations. In the Staff Manual for the new Reservation, started under Johnson and continued for years, the very first page read, "As a Staff member, this is no vacation for you." But these expectations did not just apply to executing summer camp program, but to life: hard work and loyalty mattered. At interviews to hire staff, "he would sit back in his chair with his arms crossed and just stare at you... It wasn't an intimidating thing, but you knew your place." In this situation, a staff member had to negotiate for pay. For returning staff, this meant asking for a raise. For new staff, this meant being bold enough to ask for some level of compensation as most first year staff worked for free. These were skills applicable in the world of business, after camp life. And Johnson also rewarded those who worked hard. When a group of Parnell staff members came to Johnson in 1965 asking for a vehicle so they could take a canoe trip after camp to Ely, Minnesota at the Charles L. Sommers Wilderness Canoe Base, Johnson not only provided a vehicle, but "made arrangements for [the group] to stay at scout camps and military posts all the way up there and all the way back."[9]

When Johnson took a position as a Scout Executive of his own Council in Jonesboro, Arkansas in early 1966, Bruce Atkins was promoted to Director of Camping and Activities. Atkins had been a Scout himself. After a stint in the Army, Atkins joined the Boy Scouts in 1960, serving as District Executive for two districts before becoming a Field Director in 1965. Atkins was red-headed, like Johnson, but a lighter shade. He was 6'4" and 240 pounds. In other words, he "was a big guy. He was big and sort of loud." Even more specifically, as Stahlman staff Kerry Parker explains, "Bruce was a huge fellow.

Big. Probably 6 feet, 3 , 4, or 5 or something like that... He was big, muscu-lar. He [had] big arms. I mean, he would come out there and [say,] 'Alright boys, grab the end of that wagon, or grab that, grab this. Grab it and growl.' That was one of his things, 'Grab it and growl.'" During the blitz to prepare Boxwell for its first summer, it was Bruce Atkins who led the charge. With the assistance of another able body, Atkins would grab platforms and "run back through the bushes as far as they could go and that's where a tent platform was established." In short, Atkins was "a man's man. He could outdrink anybody, outwork anybody. [He] just had this attitude that was unbelievable."[10]

Atkins also battled cancer. He was taking Wood Badge in what was not yet Camp Craig when he discovered it. A doctor who was taking the course with him noticed a mole on his back and told him to check it out. It was can-cer. As there was no chemotherapy at the time, the cancer had to be cut out. The doctors "cut Bruce all the way up from right below his ear, all the way down his neck, and down his... right arm, all down his right side and ... [s] ewed him back up." Neither the cancer nor the surgery to remove it seemed to slow him down much. As Parnell staff member Wes Frye recalls, "He had cancer, and you could see the scars, and his left arm wasn't... he used it but he couldn't pick up a lot of stuff. I can remember seeing him pick up a 50-pound bag of something up at the compound with one hand and put it on his shoul-der, start walking across there. [Y]ou saw that and said, 'Oh, I don't want to mess with him.'"[11]

As Reservation Director, Atkins refined the operation established by Johnson. He gave Pearl Schleicher more flexibility in the food decision-making, including purchasing. As a result, the food improved. The Scoutmas-ters' Steak Suppers originated under Atkins. Scoutmasters loved him. This was a man who, when he was a Camp Director, would get up early and take a volunteer a cup of coffee if there was a problem, just for the opportunity to engage with him. His wife helped too, working with Elizabeth Jackson to make Murrey the best experience possible. It was during Atkins' tenure that

245

Boxwell hit its high water mark with the greatest attendance it ever experienced.[12]

Atkins brought a different philosophy to the Reservation. He moved faster, had less patience, and wanted the work done now. For Atkins, this was *his* camp, a philosophy he very much adopted with Ward Akers. When he told his staff to do something, he expected it done. When a National Inspection team stopped a group of staff working (really riding) on the back of tractor's trailer, Atkins set the group straight. He demanded they ignore the team from National, get on the trailer, and keep working because "I run this camp." He expected his staff to take pride and ownership in their work. Kerry Parker gave this example of a salary negotiation with Atkins in the Stahlman Kitchen his second summer on staff. The episode summed up Atkins quite well:

> I just assumed I'd be making what I was making the last year -
> $25. I never went in and negotiated. Never went to any inter-
> view. And there we sit. Not sit. We was in there working. I
> was moving cereal boxes or something around this way and
> that. And Bruce, he was runnin' in and out and movin' 'em
> around. And, I mean, we were working. We were *workin'*.
> 'Cause when you was around Bruce, buddy, you worked. And,
> "When you work boys, you work hard. When we play, we
> play hard." That was one of the things he always said.
>
> Anyway, he came whizzing out of [the back of] that kitchen...
> [a]nd he says, "By the way Parker, what am I gonna have to
> pay you this summer?" And I, in my usual mild way, said,
> "Well, Mr. Atkins, just whatever you want to pay me is all
> right with me." ...And I remember this: he swirled around at
> me... He looked me right square in the eye and he took that
> finger and he shook it in my face and says, "Let me tell you
> something, young man. You don't get nothing out of the Boy
> Scouts unless you ask for it or anywhere else. So, you need to
> say what you want and stand behind what you say. So you
> understand me, mister?"
>
> And I mean, I was like God had spoke to me, and I was scared

Ed Human at the Camp Craig Dedication Ceremonies, July 11, 1974. Photo by Michael Seay.

to death. I was scared to death. But I was also just a little bit irritated. And so in my mind, I says, "I'll fix his sorry butt. I'll ask him for more than he's gonna give me." And I said, "Well Mr. Atkins. I made $25 dollars last year and I want $50 this year." Now it wasn't smart or anything, but it was solid.

He says, "Okay," and turned around and walked off. And I got $50, or in other words, double the pay I'd gotten last year, which would be like about $200. I was flabbergasted. I mean, nobody got double the money.

Intense, stern, and fair: this was Bruce Atkins. Atkins took over the West Tennessee Council in 1970 and moved up to the Great Smoky Mountains Council in 1976. Unfortunately, his cancer returned and he died at age 48 in 1982.[13]

Ed Human became the new Reservation Director a week into camp 1970. Atkins' West Tennessee Council promotion took him away in the beginning of 1970, leaving District Executive (and former Camp Director) Ralph Manus as the one temporarily in charge of camp while a permanent replacement was chosen. Tall with jet black hair, stooped shoulders, and an incessant smoker, Human brought his own Scouting-centric resume to the job. For starters, like Atkins, Human had been a Scout. In fact, Human had served on camp staff—the waterfront no less—in his youth at Camp Pellissippi in Andersonville, TN, part of the Great Smoky Mountains Council. He "loved the outdoors life and the camping life more than he did the professional scouter life." This did not mean he ever neglected his responsibilities; he was just more interested in the program side of the house than the business side.[14]

Human benefited from the fact that Boxwell was not a new operation anymore. By 1970, when he first started as Reservation Director, most operations and procedures were already well established. Human clearly benefited from a decade of effort by his predecessors and those previous staffs. Thus, when a group of staff approached him one morning while was drinking coffee with the Schleichers and asked what he wanted them to do, he could unblinkingly ask what they had been doing. After outlining all the activities they would normally be doing on this day, Human simply replied, "Just go ahead and do what you been doing" and returned to his coffee and his conversation.[15]

Human was also a very different personality in the Reservation Director position. He was more laid back, easy going, and slower to anger. Several former staff members relate tales of joining Human on excursions— walkabouts if you will—around the Council properties. Some of this was necessary preparatory work for construction related to the 1972 Capital Campaign, some of it was simply Human's love of the outdoors. Human sometimes played practical jokes on his staff. An example would be when he needed a trench dug behind the compound. Seeing an opportunity for a win-win, he made "a bet" with a staff member about what would be served at lunch. As the lunch menu rarely changed from week to week (or year to year), it was easy to predict with certainty what lunch would be. The staff member took the bet. Human of course had inside information and the staffer lost the bet, spending three days digging a trench behind the compound. Human was also well known for an activity known as "lurching." Lurching was Human, often accompanied with the Camp Director and Program Director, wandering the camp at night, looking for the staff getting into mischief. It is unclear how effective this was, but as it was well known that it took a great deal to get Human mad—unlike Atkins—some rule bending and breaking was undoubtedly happening.[16]

Of course, all three of these men worked for and were loyal to the visionary responsible for the Reservation and the management of the Council, Ward Akers. These were both wildly successful and wildly stressful years for Akers. Still dark haired and spry, he was out at Boxwell as late as 1961 working—*working*—in a torn t-shirt and shorts, helping staff to unload cots in the middle of the night. He was going to make sure camp was successful. By the time of the Larry Brinton scandal in July 1975, he was completely grey, looking a bit grizzled and tired. He had put in the time and it showed.[17]

For those at Boxwell, Akers was not an everyday presence. When the National Camp Inspection team came every summer, he was there, touring the property and explaining what was happening. When Atkins brought the Scoutmaster Steak Supper to the summer camp program, Akers often made an appearance. He was of course present at the off-season dog trial events, generally because he was hosting and often competing with Tar Shed. And he made an appearance at Staff Week, giving a speech to the staff at the end of the week, often with the reminder that the boys were the reason they were all there. "Mr. Akers" was a distant entity, known, but not common. Indeed, when he did arrive on property, the phone operator at the Crippled Crab immediately rang the other camps to let them know "the boss was coming." Otherwise, if Akers was on-site, he was likely at Ittabeena. And because Ittabeena was located near the front entrance of the Reservation, Akers could come and go without disturbing the camp program.[18]

As stated previously, Ittabeena was considered the summer home of Akers and his family, and it was off-limits to staff, with exceptions. Murrey staff families usually had an event there before the summer ended. The children in particular enjoyed this chance to explore the house with its narrow staircase to a second floor loft, which allowed one to basically spy on the people below. Staff occasionally visited upon special invitation. And, of course, the Reservation Directors often visited the locale as they had business with Akers.[19]

Despite this particular shortcoming, virtually to a person, everyone who remembered Ward Akers praised his leadership and vision. Among those who knew him best were his professional staffs. Archie Crain started as District Executive for the Council before moving on to become a Scout Executive on his own. In his estimation, "Ward Akers was a real visionary. He's a real motivator. He was great at recruiting top-notch people that had resources and were strong leaders. He was a great fundraiser and well organized." Ron Oakes came on as a professional in 1960. His first job with the Council was helping to park cars at the Boxwell dedication. He was there throughout the period, finally getting his own Council just before the investigation of Akers began. For Oakes, Akers "loved being a winner. I tell you he sure did, and he developed a winning staff of young men that dedicated themselves... Ward developed a great staff of men and we were known as being a team." Perhaps most effusive was Ken Connelly. Connelly was hired to the professional staff in 1963, worked his way up to Finance Director, was Assistant Council Executive during the investigation, and went on to lead his own Council before returning to Middle Tennessee Council as its executive in 1992. Connelly explained Akers' philosophy and what made him such a great leader:

> As far as professional scout leader, he was way ahead of his
> time in a way that he came in and ran a Boy Scout council...

He stressed basically three things. One is to try to recruit the strongest executive board available in the community. The CEOs of the corporations, the men of wealth, people of influence, as he would say, that knew the right button to push to make the bell ring. That was number one.

Secondly, to hire a very competent [professional] staff that would work with the volunteers and work with board members that would make the board members' job as easy as possible, and just use their time in the most efficient way. Handled day-to-day operations for them and take a lot of the details off the board and the volunteer teams.

Then third, is delegate responsibility to good people, and let them do their job. Those were his three manager skills.

Then the part he incorporated in all of that is a stress on recruiting the right volunteers to be your scout masters, cub masters, your district level people. Try to go after whoever is the best to do that job... Don't settle for just anybody. If they are not someone that would say, "I would like that man to be the scoutmaster of my son's troop," [then they aren't a good fit]. Use that as a kind of a dialogue when you're involved in recruiting new scoutmasters...

That's the reason that he produced more scout executives for the Boy Scouts of America than any professional ever, up to that time and since. There's been 40. I think there's been-- we're now up to 43 people that have served on the Middle Tennessee Council staff that have left this staff and become scout executives somewhere in the country.

Ward Akers set a standard and an expectation that was embraced by those who worked for him.[20]

The Volunteer Staff

Most Scouts, leaders, and staff did not have that much interaction with the professional staff at Boxwell. They were unquestionably important, providing the framework and the materials that made Boxwell possible. But in terms of giving Scouts a positive experience they would take with them, the volunteer staff breathed life into the program. The adults and the youth who made up the summer camp staff lived by Akers' philosophy on summer camp, namely "that a good scout troop had to have the summer camp experience, or they would not be a good scout troop long." Providing that troop with a powerful experience was the work of the camp staff. And while all had a part to play, there were some adults in particular who were synonymous with this period in the camp's history.[21]

Tom Parker was part of the Old Hickory Boxwell staff from the very beginning. A graduate of Florida State University, Parker dropped out of medical school to take care of his ailing parents in Sparta, Tennessee. He became a science teacher at Overton County High School, but in the summers from 1960 well into the 1970s, he was the Conservation Yard Director at Camp Stahlman. Parker was as serious about teaching Conservation as Q-ball was about craft skills. Every summer Parker brought a truckload—and sometimes an aluminum boat load—of "mason jar after mason jar filled with biology samples of birds, baby pigs, and other sundry animals all preserved in formaldehyde." Parker set a high bar for his Scouts. He expected them to read and understand the entire merit badge pamphlet before coming to his merit badge session. If Scouts wanted to take Bird Study merit badge, Parker expected those Scouts to meet him at the flagpole at 5:30 am. He was there, even if they were not. The Con Yard Director was guided by two philosophies. One was his definition of conservation, which he expected his Scouts to know: "Conservation is the wise and efficient use of our natural resources, so that they be of the greatest use for the largest amount of people for the longest amount of time." The second was that the young men he worked with were "Scouts," not "boys." One term carried understandings of active responsibilities, while the other did not. The distinction mattered.[22]

Two contributions from Parker made him legendary in his own time. The first dealt specifically with his conservation work. When the Old Hickory camp opened, there were high embankments of dirt on both sides of Creighton Lane where it met Highway 109 and opposite Creighton Lane on the other side of the two-lane highway. On the north side of Creighton Lane, the iconic hanging cedar sign would eventually be placed. However, when "new" Boxwell opened, the whole area was simply these dirt embankments. So, as a good conservationist wanting to prevent erosion, Parker took his Soil and Water Conservation merit badge Scouts out to the highway to put their skills to work. They planted kudzu all over the embankments. Parker often drove out to the highway in the evenings, checking the progress of the invasive and fast growing species. In time, the kudzu completely overtook the embankments and moved down the road.[23]

The second contribution was less permanent, but every bit as invasive in its own way. Blessed with a rich tenor voice, Tom Parker could sing. He sang at home, at church, and at Scout camp. And while Parker often sang at the Wednesday evening services held at the Don Stanford Chapel, his campfire performances left his audiences awe-struck. Stahlman's Friday night campfires were on the edge of the lake and every week, a portion of the program was dedicated to Parker. "Old Man River" and "Shadrack, Meshach, and Abnego" (sometimes just called "Shadrack") were his favorites, both twentieth century African American spirituals. Lisa McCormack, one of Reservation Director Ed Human's daughters, spent her summers at Camp Murrey, where Parker lived with his daughter, Kathy. McCormack and her sisters often attended Stahlman's Friday night campfires and those closing moments of the campfire left an imprint on her, "It was nighttime, the moon was on the water. There was a campfire glistening on the water. It was still and you had this deep barrel chested guy singing this song... all of it together, it was good. It was like, "Oh good he's going to sing 'Old Man River'! Let's be quiet." It was almost like a reverence." Tom Parker's "Old Man River" was a staple of the early Boxwell experience.[24]

Parnell's answer to Tom Parker was Luke Gaffin. Gaffin had been at

"Old Boxwell" and simply transitioned over to the new location. He too was a conservation man, and also a school teacher in the Sparta area. Gaffin was a bit more of a Renaissance man that Parker, often teaching the Handicraft skills at the old camp. Indeed, Steve Eubank, who camped at Rock Island as a Scout, remembered Gaffin quite vividly,

> One of the traditions at Rock Island was the campfire; when an Indian Chief would come out to start the campfire. It was very impressive. I don't know if it was a Sunday night or Friday night campfire, but I can remember that Indian chief and he looked like a real Indian too. He had the headdress and all. That same man ran the Handicraft at Rock Island, and his name was Mr. Luke Gaffin. I was amazed by Mr. Gaffin. He could tell stories, and he could also carve. As a matter of fact, I have an Arab and a Roman sword that he carved out of cedar. I probably only gave maybe 50 cents or a dollar for them, but I still have those swords. I wouldn't take one thing for them.

Gaffin was also the man who regularly told stories of the "hangin' tree" at Rock Island![25]

At the new Boxwell, Gaffin started with the first group of staff, but was more sporadic than Parker. In the 1960s, he spent some years in the Handicraft Craft, but he also had a solid run of years as Conservation Yard (Con-Yard) Director himself in the early 1970s. But just like at Rock Island, it was his turn as a Native American sachem that truly struck a chord. Staff member John Bryant remembered Gaffin at campfires this way:

> [W]e had the Sunday night fire, [and] we always used an Indian starting. And we had somebody dressed up like the chief. They bought all the buckskins and the headdress with the big regalia. I think Luke Gaffin did it. Luke was sort of an older guy, he looks a little like an Indian. Sort of had a round face and had a big deep voice...
>
> He would come in there, and of course, all the boys would

come in with Scout Sign [held] up. There's dead silence. We'd march them in there quietly and Gaffin would sort of appear out of the twilight, out of the woods and be dressed to the nines in all this Indian stuff. He'd walk up there and say, "The people of my village are sad tonight because the keeper of the fire has gone to sleep and has allowed the fire to go out. So we must call on the fire god to send us fire." So, he had this ritual, he'd turn around and say, "Hail to the North Star that guides our way through the forest at night." And he'd turn around and, "Hail to the south wind that warms our teepees." And he'd do the four corners of the compass. Then he'd turn around and say, "And hail to the fire god that sends us fire!"

And with those words, the campfire would then explode into flame, ignited by a simple concoction of sugar and sulfuric acid. Jimmy Joe Jackson would simply pull a thread dumping the acid in the sugar and Gaffin's calls to the fire gods were answered.[26]

Gaffin also represented both the simplicity and, perhaps the word is "chilvary," of the period. Unlike many of the adults, he stayed in camp instead of Murrey. An older man, he would often to walk to the showerhouse in nothing but a loin cloth. When he drove the tractor around the camp, he openly smoked a pipe. Indeed, at staff meetings, Gaffin would sit calmly under a cedar tree, calmly puffing away on his pipe. But nothing captures Gaffin and the period better than a story that Steve Eubank told about 1973. Eubank was not only an adult now, but Program Director at Parnell. His new wife, Judi, was Parnell's Kitchen Director. One particular morning,

> Mr. Luke, along with some other of the main staff, was in the dining hall as usual, drinking coffee. I had noticed when I entered the dining hall that there were footprints on [top of] the tables. About that time, Mr. Luke looked up, and said, "Gentlemen, there are ladies present." Well, I knew Judi was in there. But when we looked up to the very center top of the rafters of the dining hall, we saw that someone had stacked the tables during the night and had pinned a *Playboy* pin up at the

top of the ceiling of the dining hall.

With monitors already in the building, the staff scrambled to get the center-fold down. Meanwhile, Scouts outside got a little extra practice with flag rais-ing and lowering that morning. Still, it was the image of a calm, coffee-sipping Luke Gaffin nodding up at the ceiling remarking, "Gentlemen, there are ladies present" that illustrated the period so well.[27]

From a program perspective, the program directors drove the show. Amazingly, there were remarkably few during these years for either camp. However, as mentioned previously, the period was really dominated by two men: Chester LaFever and Jimmy Joe Jackson. Both men were about the same height and complexion, but easily discernible in physical appearance. Jackson was "bow legged," and he "always had sort of a dark blue baseball cap... It was one of those screen type things, hot weather cap for ventilation. He always wore that." LaFever could be described as either bald, balding, or with a severe-ly receding hairline and a paunchier build than Jackson. In terms of personali-ty though, the two were virtually night and day. Professional Scouter Ron Oakes described the two succinctly, "Jimmy Joe was quick, Quick Draw McGraw type person and he'd get things done pretty quick, and then Chester would be very thorough because he wanted everybody to understand that first of all you stick by the rules and regulations."[28]

Given these differences and the high school educator background both men shared, it was perhaps inevitable that a rivalry between two the camps emerged. It is difficult to know whether the inter-camp rivalry emerged natu-rally or if a specific incident lit the fuse. Oakes explained how it may have started with a phone call in either 1962 or 1963. At the time, there were a series of hard-wired phones on the reservation, all connected by a switchboard at the Crippled Crab. One day, someone at the Parnell Office (at this point, just a tent) called their counterpart at the Stahlman Office (again, a tent). As Camp Director, Oakes answered the phone, but instead of simply saying, "Hello," he answered with, "Greater Camp Stahlman." Each camp's sense of

Chester LaFever and Jimmy Joe Jackson in July 1983. Personal Collection of Kerry Parker.

pride was already so well established by this early date, that Parnell staff took great umbrage at this "bragging." Inter-camp pranks began. The pranks became so bad that an inter-camp pow-wow was called. Oakes apologized, LaFever and Jackson shook hands and all was well. But the rivalry did not stop. For years, inter-camp pranks continued. Mirrors disappeared from showerhouses. Staff sites were attacked with oranges in the dark of night. While pranks and inter-camp rivalries could be detrimental to program, on the whole they served to encourage each staff to be their very best, or at least better than the other camp.[29]

It should not be surprising that some suggested LaFever and Jackson—who were good friends—quietly spurred on these pranks to create an *esprit de corps*. After all, the two men did retire to Murrey every night and had ample time to laugh at the antics of their staffs. Jackson admitted as much years later. Having his staff finish earlier on Saturdays so Parnell got to go home before Stahlman was a point of pride for his staff. He told a story of trash barrels to illustrate to show how the rivalries could be used for good. At the time, metal 55-gallon drums were used as trash barrels, but before they could go into service, the barrel heads had to be cut out and the barrels painted. It was a big job. So, to ensure none of Parnell's barrels disappeared and thus new barrels had to be made, Jackson "had arrangements made" with two of his staff to arrive early, get the appropriate number of barrels and hide them. Successful the first year, this strategy continued for several summers. It was an excellent example of how "the good of the program" was served by some camp pride and rivalry.[30]

Virtually every staff member who worked for Jackson or LaFever swore loyalty to his particular program director. Not a literal swearing, but a sense of pride of being associated with the man. Even the mundane became touchstone moments. Every Stahlman staff member remembered LaFever's staff meetings, laughing at the length of the things. Parnell staff members individually and repeatedly told a story of picking up trash with Jackson. On Saturday mornings, the staff would take a tractor and trailer and would drive the road from inside the reservation out to Highway 109, picking up any trash spotted on the road along the way. The camps alternated weeks, but when it was Parnell's turn, Jackson often drove the tractor himself. Sitting atop a John Deere tractor with a wad of Cannonball chewing tobacco in his mouth, Jackson and his group of volunteers crawled down Creighton Lane. When Jackson saw a piece of trash, he'd yell out "Hawkeye," for a beer can "headache!" and even "super headache" for a whiskey bottle. Staff sat on each side of the trailer and when the call came, one would jump off, race for the trash, and then return to the wagon, deposit the trash in the barrel, and take his place then at the back of the line. On one trip, someone asked to try some of the tobacco—a decision everyone one of them regretted, but Jackson found hysterical. Even decades later, members of Jackson's staff still recalled two euphemisms of his as if no time had passed: "Improvise and Adjust" and "Make It Happen."[31]

Jackson and LaFever were not the only program directors. At Parnell, Jackson was preceded by Robert Nicholson (1960) and Harold Hitt (1961-1962). Nicholson was the first Program Director when the position was still ill-defined. For instance, his responsibilities included being the First Aid man that summer. He was called to the ministry and did not return to camp. Hitt was a high school coach and paternalistic, often referring to himself as "daddy." When offered a job in Nashville's music industry, he took it and never looked back to teaching or summer camp. The next several years were the LaFever-Jackson "Golden Age." Both men left Boxwell about the same time: LaFever did not return for 1970, Jackson for 1971. After Ted Naylor served for one summer, Stahlman's next long term program director was Garland Russell. Energetic and easy going, short and stocky Russell was a McGavock football coach. Staying on until the start of 1976, Russell's major contribution was an emphasis on sports. The time after lunch transformed from a rest period to a new activity period. Russell also borrowed at 16mm film projector from Nashville's Channel 5, rented a screen, and showed movies from Channel 5's film library outside Stahlman dining hall, often two nights a week. At Parnell, David Farrar, who had served as Kitchen Director previously, stepped up for two summers. Farrar had grown up under Jackson, but because of this, he was also a contemporary of his staff. Thus, he was often teased, though apparently he could take it. He was succeeded by a slightly older Steve Eubank in 1973. Eubank had actually just left professional Scouting after a brief run as a DE, realizing it was not for him. As Program Director, Eubank was laid back and wanted to make sure his staff had what they needed. As Ed Mason explained, Eubank had a very easy approach to getting things done: "He [would] kind of come up, put his arm around ya, you need to do this." Like Russell, Eubank left camp staff at the start of the 1976 season. Unlike Russell, Eubank returned.[33]

Of course, the camp's operation was possibly only because of the ranger staff. Over the period in question, there were three head rangers: Coleman

"Skinny" Wright (1960-1965), Bobby Smith (1965-1973), and Norman Patterson (1973-1981). While not technically volunteers as they were year round, salaried employees, they were not really professional Scouters either. Still, much as the program directors infused their camps with a personality that reflected their own, so too did the ranger staff upon the reservation as a whole. Wright, for instance, was first and foremost a farmer. His interest was in the farming operation, building the cattle herd, and even acquiring land from surrounding farmers for more farming. For the most part, Wright handled this operation alone with temporary assistance from others. For instance, Wright, along with Tom Parker, killed off the original fish in Akers Lake so that it could be restocked with bass or catfish. This focus on agriculture and wildlife was Wright's approach to the camp. While there are some conflicting stories as to why, Wright was let go in 1965.[33]

Following Wright was Bobby Smith, who, according to staff member Greg Tucker, was "probably the most popular guy" to hold the head ranger position. Smith had been a Scoutmaster for a troop at Indian Mound, TN and was working as a civilian at the Fort Campbell motor pool. This experience and these connections made Smith a very different ranger, much more interested in the mechanical operations of the camp and very capable of screening supplies from the military to help the camp run. These were undeniable assets. Smith brought together the team mentioned previously, a collection of farmers and mechanics, to make the camp work.[34]

But the balding Smith was a more gregarious and open personality as well. He got along well with everyone. His four children spent time with the children of the other staff and professional families at Murrey every summer, building extended families for all of them. He employed college-aged staff to work after camp was over and in off-seasons. As staff member Kerry Parker explained, Smith epitomized what it meant to be a good ranger. In fact, according to Parker, a good ranger could be identified by the items he kept in his truck, which was a lesson he learned from Smith:

A good ranger has several things in his truck... One, he has a good deep dash. And on that dash, he keeps everything that a ranger could possibly need... Now, I mean, you just stack 'em up on top of that dash. If you need a screwdriver, why you dig through there and you find it. If you needed a chew of tobacco, it's up there. Bobby chewed tobacco. Big time. He chewed King Edwards cigars.

But a few things a ranger keeps under his seat... There's three or four things he keeps under his seat. One, a ranger always keeps a set of binoculars under seat. Now, what would a ranger need with a set of binoculars? Well, he could use them for lots of things. Looking across [the property] and seeing who's doing this and who's doing that. You need them so you can go around to the road, Cole's Ferry Road over there, and look across to see if Mr. Akers was at the Cabin [Ittabeena]... If he wasn't there, you could go over there to work. You need them when the women come out to sun on the boats. And he always had them glasses for that.

Need a gun. You always need a gun. You never know when you're going to have to have a gun to...shoot a varmit... Shoot a varmit of some kind, a wild dog or something like that, you keep a gun. Keep a pint of whiskey under the seat. You never know when you're going to meet friends. And if you meet friends, you'll always want to share a drink of whiskey – pass the whiskey bottle around.

And the last thing that you want to keep under your seat is a good roll of toilet paper. You never want to be without your toilet paper. So, you can always tell a good ranger if you go out there and check those things out.

Obviously, this list was somewhat in jest, but it demonstrated well the kind of relationship Smith had with the camp staff. Further, the list of items he was able to secure from Fort Campbell made him a favorite of the professionals as well. Over the years, Smith was able to screen military trucks, jeeps, old furniture (which went to the staff sites), clothing such boots and field jackets, and even at least one pool table. And it was Smith and his staff, primarily Punkin

Green, who physically built Ittabeena in 1967.[35]

The Youth Staff... And Their Hijinks

When Coach Anderson introduced youth staff to his Narrows of the Harpeth Boxwell, he likely had no idea they would become the primary conduit through which Scouting skills were delivered. By the time of Old Hickory Boxwell, this was exactly what had happened. While there were a handful of bona fide adults, including the waterfront staffs who were all over eighteen and the medics and rifle range officers who were generally Fort Campbell soldiers on loan for the summer, the majority of staff were high school aged boys. Most went through an interview process with the Reservation Director and were hired for "staff," not a specific area. During Staff Week, they were then lined up and selected for their program area. Once hired and sorted, it would not take too much imagination to realize that one hundred high school boys (along with some college aged young men) left to their own devices for nine weeks in the summer were going to get into mischief, Boy Scout or not.

Youth staff was truly in an interesting position in that they were more involved with the Scouts than any other group, but they also were different and separate from the Scouts. Because most of the adults were married and staying over at Murrey in the evenings, the youth staff lived in their own world, monitored only by a "night man" and the occasional "lurching." The staff lived in tents, just like everyone else, but generally in groups. In Stahlman, just to the west of the dining hall was a large staff site known as Staff Row, where a row of mostly two-man tents housed the majority of the staff. There were smaller staff sites at the Trading Post and Handicraft tents as well as the Waterfront. Parnell had a similar situation, with a large staff site down in the woods near Site 16 and the Athletic Field. Smaller sites dotted the camp with one at the Trading Post and another site near the Dining hall, occupied by mostly older, mostly waterfront staff. By the mid-1960s, all of these sites had electricity run to them, something the Scouts did not have. This was used mostly to power fans and lights which hung from the tent ridge pole. The truly lucky had small refrigerators. The cold drinks stored there could be used for personal enjoyment or sold, like true entrepreneurs![36]

Of course, being Boy Scouts, the staff had a uniform. There was the "dress," or Class A, uniform. This uniform consisted of either the light green Boy Scout uniform shirt or the dark green Explorer Scout uniform shirt. These were accompanied by green Scouts short, green knee socks, a belt, and brown or black shoes. The knee socks were sometimes held up by hidden sock garters with the tops folded over. The Class A was worn to flag ceremonies, dinner, and campfires. During the day and on work detail, there was a work uniform, or Class B. Shorts, belt, and shoes remained, but the shirt could be either a white t-shirt or a Boxwell t-shirt. A Boxwell t-shirt was pretty simple as there was not a cornucopia of options. It was a white shirt with a large round map of Boxwell either on the chest or a smaller version over the breast. In the early 1970s, blue piping was added to the neck and sleeves of this shirt. The first staff hat did not appear until 1972. It was a cloth green hat with a small black patch with the words "Boxwell Reservation Staff 1972" embroidered in gold. The 1973 hat followed the same pattern, with different coloring: a red hat with a gray patch and blue lettering. As first year staff was not paid, getting a staff t-shirt or a staff hat was an important symbol.[37]

And in addition to delivering program, the staff kept the camp running. They ran trash, using a tractor and a small crew to transport the metal 55-gallon drums filled with garbage to a dump behind the compound. On the weekends, they cleaned the showerhouses between weeks of camp. At the start of camp every summer, they stuffed the heavy, blue ticked cotton mattresses into protective bags—nicknamed "fart sacks"—to extend the life of the mattress. They cleaned program areas, cleaned up and prepared camp sites from week to week, built campfires, cleaned the dining hall, moved luggage in and out, and just did a variety of tasks to keep the camp running. In some years, staff even assumed responsibility for the filtration of the lake water at the pump house. Tractors helped with some of this work, but so did large work trucks. There were several one-and-a-half-ton and two-ton Ford trucks on the reservation. "Truck Driver" was an assigned position and each truck had its own name, specifically the Parnell Panther, Clyde, Blue Goose, and Big Red. The trucks would be used for most of the camps' work and in the early years, cattle rails were put up on the side, and the trucks took the staff into town on staff night out. And staff did get a night out. On Tuesday night, the entire staff got the night off and went into town, usually into Lebanon to watch a movie and/or wash clothes. Eventually, two Brill buses—large passenger buses—were screened from Fort Campbell and these were used for taking staff out for several years, as well as taking people out to Don Stanford Chapel. By the mid-1970s, even the buses were retired and staff became responsible for their own destinies. Older staff took out the younger staff on Tuesday nights, and then got a night of their own on Thursdays. Those who were over 21 years of age—the 'real' adults—could leave any night of the week. A particular favorite hot spot of the older staff was "a hamburger joint, drive-in type place on [Highway] 109, just south of Gallatin," called Dave's. Adult staff often congregated here on Friday nights after campfires and without younger staff. Imbibing occurred.[38]

These are general observations, of course. There were differences within each camp. As similar as both Stahlman and Parnell were in the beginning, each developed in their own unique characteristics. Some were program differences. There was not Stahlman equivalent of the Parnell Hootennannies. Parnell may have had a fire altar out in the water for its Friday night campfire, but it did not have a floating Burning Eagle. Other differences were physical. Both camps started their existence using large military GP-Medium tents for their Trading Posts and Handicrafts. By the late 1960s and early 1970s, this had changed. Stahlman's Handicraft remained a tent, but around 1970 a staff member's father built a wire fence not just around the tent, but the entire Handicraft area. Meanwhile, at Parnell, while the Handicraft had no fence, the

Trading Post evolved into a small shack. The Parnell Trading Post also had a row of drink machines and a candy machine. Stahlman's Trading Post had a popcorn machine. Clearly, these differences were not vast. Fortunately, the 1972 Capital Development Campaign built permanent buildings that were exactly the same.[39]

With all of this in mind, the staff was ultimately responsible for the program that worked well. For instance, campfires brought over a critical element from Rock Island: Native American dancing. This dancing occurred at both camps, usually at the Sunday night campfire while Scouts entered the campfire area and segued into the campfire opening. Indeed, Native American culture in general was a critical component to setting the appropriate mood at campfires. Both Parnell and Stahlman had a water carnival. On Friday afternoons, the water carnival took up the entire period after lunch and was, in many respects, a throw-back to the events of the Narrows. The afternoon started with a volleyball game and then moved to the waterfront. There were rowboat and canoe races as well as relays for swimmers and a Scoutmasters' race. There was also the greased watermelon event, which resulted in actual watermelon delivered to the winning troop's site. And there was some program that was not only camp and year specific, but so unique it was incredibly memorable. One year, at Parnell, a troop from Estill Springs brought "a monster billy goat" to camp. To make the program that week more exciting, Jackson had a penny spray painted silver. That silver penny became a hot potato. Whatever Scoutmaster had the penny at lunchtime announcements—or who had just messed up that week—got the goat to take care for the day. This went on for several summers. It was that kind of world.[40]

These were all planned program. There was also a constantly evolving world of unplanned, spontaneous program that the youth staff was responsible for implementing. Those ideas that just emerged from a late night conversation or from a spur of the moment inspiration. Here are two quick examples, one from each camp. For Parnell, Ed Mason recalled how David Farrar—one of the Hootennannies—picked up his guitar one night, grabbed a few folks out of the staff site, and went around to campsites, singing songs. The group would pick a song, sing it, and then move on to another site. It was an inspired and fun idea and happened several more times that summer. At Stahlman, Claus "Dutch" Mann related how he and his fellow Commissioners decided to put the screened military vehicles to good use. Borrowing one of the command cars from the compound, they dressed themselves and the car up as generals and arrived at flag raising one morning all suited up. They came complete with "swagger sticks and inspected all the troops which were in formation." Everyone had a good laugh.[41]

Staff was also there when things went wrong. Before the 1972 Capital Development Campaign, the GP (General Purpose) Medium tents used for the Trading Post and Handicraft came from Fort Campbell and were returned every year. At Stahlman, the Handicraft tent was erected on one end of the Activity Yard, while the Trading Post tent was on the other, on the circle that passed the camp office. These were large tents, the size of two four-man tents. One summer, Fort Campbell did not have any tents available, so the camp rented a large circus tent for the Trading Post and Handicraft. When the GP tents became available about two weeks into camp, staff stayed over the weekend, dropped the circus tent and replaced it. A completely different episode involved the water supply. Water was pumped in from Old Hickory Lake, filtered and purified in the pump house, and then stored at the steel water tower at the top of the hill by the Crippled Crab. One summer a college aged staff member decided to test his engineering education and used charcoal in one of the pump house filters. His goal in using the charcoal was to remove the fishy taste from the water. Unfortunately, he turned the water—all the water on the reservation—black. The fire hydrants had to be opened to flush the blackened water from the water system, dumping thousands of gallons. Once the filters were replaced, the tower was refilled. Even worse, no one tasted the water to see if the fishy taste was gone! Neither of these were life-threatening events, but

both demonstrated when things did not quite work the way they were supposed to work.[42]

There were, sadly, more serious examples of when things did not go
quite right and the staff had to compensate as best they could. One summer
the unthinkable happened—a swimmer was unaccounted for. Despite the
buddy system, despite the board with buddy tags that Scouts removed when
they left the waterfront, someone had been lost. There was an unclaimed tag
on the board at Stahlman. Using the hardwire phone system, the call went out
to Parnell for assistance. The Parnell Waterfront staff grabbed their grappling
hooks (the appropriate tool of the day to drag the bottom of the lake), loaded
up in a rowboat with an outboard motor, and took off around the bay to assist. Every staff member was terrified with the thought of "please don't let me
find this boy," but executed through the protocols and procedures nonetheless.
And then, just like that, the whole search was called off. The Scout was found
asleep in his campsite. He had forgotten to take down his buddy tag. Another
equally harrowing moment came in 1973 during one of the mentally disabled
camp weeks at Stahlman. The camp was sponsored by the Jaycees this summer
and they provided some of their own staff, as had been the case with the earlier
camps. One of the male campers was insulted by a female Jaycees staffer during the course of the day. That night, he broke into the rifle range, stole a rifle, and climbed up into a tree in the nearby woods. It was two staff members,
the rifle instructor and a waterfront instructor, who talked the young man
down out of the tree. The camper was taken back to the institute in Nashville,
and the two staff members who talked him down rode with him all the way
back. These are not the things one thinks of when contemplating Boy Scout
summer camp, but they happened.[43]

And then there were the hijinks, the pranks, the shenanigans. No history can hope to capture the variety or volume of shenanigans that happened at
Boxwell over the summer by its youth staff. Indeed, some stories probably
should remain untold. Nevertheless, the stories that have been passed down

are the kinds of anecdotes that would not only make great television program-ming but one would expect from a male summer camp staff on a large lake in the 1960s and 1970s in the South. Staff members fell for and were spurned by young women staying at Camp Murrey. Staff would chase cattle out by Akers Lake in the middle of the night, in a car, with staff on either side of hood doing the herding. Staff would sometimes attack the Brill bus with water balloons as it came back from staff night out, launching their assaults from atop the dirt mounds that lined the entrance to the reservation. Upon return-ing to the staff site, staff members might find their beds up in a tree or their tent platform raised on top of 55 gallon drums. The truly unfortunate awoke in morning to find that somehow they and their bed were now standing out in the lake. Every now and then, a table from the dining hall, complete with chairs and all the accouterments for a meal, would end up on the roof of a din-ing hall. And of course there were late night, epic games of *Monopoly*.[44]

There were other stories that were more person and time specific. Af-ter integration happened at Parnell in the summer of 1965, an African Ameri-can joined the staff in 1966, Billy Pincham. There was some tension among the white staff about how he would fit in, but Pincham met the challenge. One day as the white staffers were passing around Coppertone to help protect themselves from the sun, Pincham asked for some. A tense moment passed as he took the bottle, rubbed it into his skin, and said, "I don't want to get any blacker than I am." Pincham's willingness to make fun of himself immediately ingratiated him with the staff. Around the same time, Stahlman had a truck driver named Doug Dietz. Dietz took great pride in his truck, but apparently was a bit gullible. As the story goes, he was convinced to change the air in the tires as part of the truck's maintenance. Not check the pressure, but physically remove the air and replace it with new air because the "air gets old in there. [It will] Rot your tires." Dietz let the air out. And then realized he did not know how to put new air in.[45]

Ward Akers and Ed Human at the Ski Dock, ca. 1970. Photo by Chris "Kit" Eckert.

A World Beyond

The baby boomers who worked on the staff in this period see it as a Golden Age of Scouting in Middle Tennessee. In some ways, it absolutely was. The attendance at camp was higher during these years than at any other point in the camp's history. Scouting had hit a high water mark and so had Middle Tennessee Council.

And yet, in many critical ways, camp had not changed all that much. There was still a program that was delivered to Scouts that emphasized values they would need in the real world. The hierarchy of the camp had become more complex, but the end goal remained similar in the Akers years as to the Anderson years: to provide a program to strengthen the troop and the individual Scouts. The only difference now was that the size, the resources, and the complexity of the new Boxwell Reservation meant more staff, program varied by camp, and a new leadership organization—a new bureaucracy—to deliver that fundamental goal.

As Q-ball's recordings demonstrated, there was a world beyond what Scouts saw. A world that the staff—young and old, professional and volunteer—inhabited. This world delivered the program to Scouts, but it also built bonds of friendship, created mentors, and taught its own life lessons that embodied Scouting's values and goals.

The question now was how well would the Reservation and its staff weather the forced retirement of Ward Akers?

.

.

FOREWORD

This is an attempt to put into the hands of the Staff at Boxwell
Scout Reservation, some pertinent information concerning the
objectives, the policies and procedures, and general information
that a Staff member should know and have on hand. From time
to time, this material will be added to and supplemented by other
material. This should be your guide for this summer. You should
add to it, that information and material that has to do with your
individual program at Camp.

AS A STAFF MEMBER

THIS IS NO VACATION FOR YOU

*The opening page of the staff manual during the Akers years. Note the final message: "AS A
STAFF MEMBER THIS IS NO VACATION FOR YOU." 1967 Staff Manual. Personal
Collection of John Stewart.*

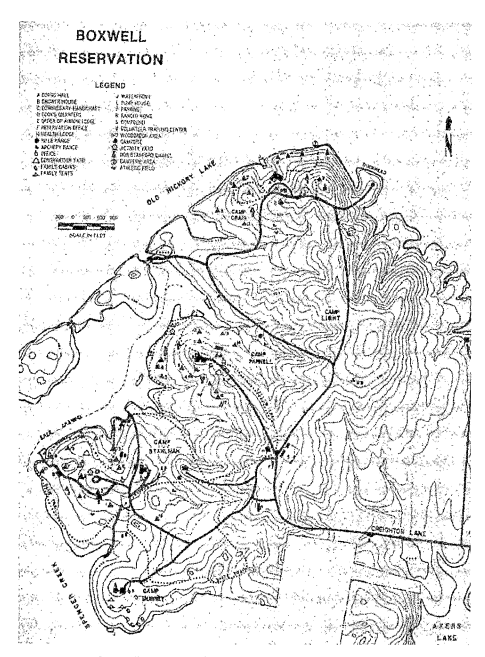

Map of Boxwell Reservation from the 1982 Summer Camp Leader's Guide.
Personal Collection of Russell Parham.

Chapter 6

The Willhite Era:
Boxwell Reservation at Old Hickory Lake

1976-1996

The Great Staff Walkout of 1976 occurred on a Sunday morning, in that little window of time between weeks of camp. Conflict had been percolating throughout Staff Week. A host of changes had come to Boxwell in the wake of the various committee reports and recommendations made during the Akers' investigations. Older staff, particularly the leadership, was not pleased with many of these changes, which included removing the hot water heaters from the showerhouses and closing the Ski Dock and its associated boating programs.

Staff Week concluded Saturday morning and the first week of Scouts, Scoutmasters, and guests would begin arriving at 1pm Sunday afternoon. On a normal weekend, most of the youth staff went home and then rushed to return to camp before troops arrived. Others—generally the older staff and all of the adults who were living in "the Hole" at Camp Murrey—stayed in camp Saturday night and enjoyed a quiet, lazy Sunday morning. Pearl Schleicher and Mrs. B often prepared special request breakfasts for those staying over, displaying their true culinary skills when cooking for those smaller groups. Normally, Sunday mornings were a virtual utopia of peace before a tumultuous week began. Normally that is, but not in 1976.

As this lazy Sunday unfolded, the adult and married staff was called to a meeting at Camp Murrey Dining Hall at 10 o'clock in the morning. The meeting turned sour quickly. This staff was told they were being charged for room, board, and food. Under different circumstances, such deductions would have been laughable, but to an already highly disgruntled group, they were enough to light the fuse. The outrage was only partly about the charge itself. Having completed an entire week of preparing camp and attended multiple meetings, the deduction had never before been discussed. The move had apparently been decided upon at the Council office to avoid some IRS issues. For a number of older staff, such as Program Directors Garland Russell and Steve Eubank, this was finally a step too far. Russell in particular was livid, arguing the staff had been doing the Council's "dirty work" since the start of the summer and to then be treated this way was unconscionable.[1]

The tense situation was undoubtedly amplified by the newness of Tom Willhite, the new reservation director. Willhite had been Reservation Director for a mere three weeks. Thus, he had no allegiances and no one wanted to give him the benefit of the doubt or trust that the situation might resolve amicably with more time. And knowing he had no leverage, Willhite ended the meeting simply by saying, "Y'all decided what you want to do. [The] ones of you that's gonna stay, meet me up at the Crab at 11:00." The line was drawn. Those who were staying were to report to the Crippled Crab at 11am to get ready to move forward; everyone else was to pack up and get out.[2]

Malvin Thomas "Tom" Willhite had joined the professional staff of the Middle Tennessee Council in March of 1964. A portly man with a bulbous nose, wavy black hair, and a knack for frugality, the thirty-four year old District Executive established himself quickly, serving as Parnell's Camp Director in 1967 and then accepting promotion to Field Director. Willhite's tenure took him through the 1972 Capital Development Campaign, where he even helped to wire Camp Craig Dining Hall, and through the scandal surrounding Ward Akers. When Ed Human left Scouting at the start of 1976, an internal

Program Director Russ Parham (standing, left) checking in a Murfreesboro troop at Camp Stahlman, July 1976. Photo by Michael Seay.

search for a new Director of Camping—the official professional position to which Reservation Director was just one part—began. Willhite, now 46, was promoted the last week of May 1976, literally just before camp began. He had not hired the staff; he had not even met them. Willhite was thrown directly into the fire and it was now his fire to manage.[3]

While Willhite waited at the Crab, many of the adult staff who lived together down in the "Hole" in Camp Murrey discussed their options. Stahlman Waterfront Director James "Jim" Barr and his new friend, the freshly hired Stahlman Field Sports Director Ernie Ragsdale, quickly decided to stay. Ragsdale had just been hired during Staff Week when he arrived on his motorcycle, a Vietnam vet gone school teacher looking for something to do with his summer. Ragsdale had no interest in going home. In fact he was trying to escape his failed marriage and recent divorce. Barr's wife was working on her Master's degree; he had no reason to be home over the summer either. For neither of the bearded late-twenties Baby Boomers did the deduction matter much.[4]

Others opted to leave. Garland Russell was among that number. Both coaches in the Metro school system, Russell and Barr had a history together, but this was a breaking point. Russell asked Barr why he was not packing; Barr said he was not going to leave. The two men "had a parting of the ways that morning." For Barr, Garland Russell was there for Garland Russell, not for the good of the Scouts, or the program. For Steve Eubank, as well, it was time to go. Eubank had been a District Executive; he had been part of the Council. Now, he was a teacher and while he respected the difficulties the Council was experiencing, to be charged for room, board, and food was just too much. Eubank packed up to return home. As it turned out, his troop was coming to camp that week anyway. So, Eubank simply stayed at Parnell as a leader with his troop.[5]

Staff began to congregate at the Crippled Crab for the 11 a.m. meeting. It was not entirely clear who had left, but there were whispers. As Barr arrived at the Crab, Willhite met him in the road, uncertain whether he was coming for the meeting or leaving the reservation. "What are you gonna do?" he asked, in the short, curt, direct way Willhite asked questions. "I'm staying," Barr replied. Barr swore a look of relief crossed Willhite's face, just knowing he was not going to have to replace a waterfront director.

"Who else is staying?" Willhite asked.

"Ragsdale," Barr replied

"Who else?" Willhite pressed.

"Nobody," laughed Barr.

"Well, go down there and get him," Willhite nodded. "Come on back up here."[6]

Russell Parham had an equally powerful recollection of those mo-

276

ments. Parham had been on staff for several years now, working his way up from youth Kitchen staff in 1970 to one of Stahlman's Commissioners by 1974. By the time of the showdown that Sunday morning, Parham was a twenty-one year old college student at Tennessee Tech. Unmarried and just barely out of the youth category, Parham had not even been invited to the Murrey meeting as he still lived in the Commissioner's site in Stahlman. Even if he had been part of the affected group, there was no reason for him to leave, so he was struck when Willhite asked him directly, "Are you leaving me too?" For Parham, the answer was unquestionably no.[7]

With two hours remaining before the first troops arrived for the 1976 summer camp season, the second meeting of adult staff began, this time at the Crippled Crab. In total, not that many individuals left, but the ones who did leave were important. Both Stahlman and Parnell lost their program directors. Two or three others joined them. Russell Parham was promoted to Program Director at Stahlman. Parnell was led by its Camp Director for a short period until Program Director Steve Eubank returned and finished the season. Thus, the actual "walk-out" did not involve that many people, but it became the stuff of legend.[8]

And the deduction that started it all? Before the summer was over, before even the next paycheck, the issue was resolved. It was never collected again. As it turned out, the deduction did not need to be done at all. As Willhite himself put it in his characteristically brusque way, "And it all ironed out. It didn't amount to anything. We didn't do [the deduction] but [it was] probably a good idea that some of them did go home because they had been there a long time and they thought they were the kingpin of the camp."[9]

And so began the era of Tom Willhite.

Making America Great Again... the First Time

Much as Akers' Boxwell reflected the early 1960s sense of optimism to achieve impossible dreams, Willhite's Boxwell reflected the changing nation of the late Seventies through mid-1990s. This two decade period was marked by a reaction against expanding liberal values, difficult economic times that gave way to an economic boom reviling the post-World War II boom, and an understanding that the old family order had passed. Not surprisingly, the baby boomers continued to dominate the landscape, though increasingly now in leadership roles as they aged to become the adults in the room.

The 1970s in the United States were dominated by crises of faith in the political system and economics. Inflation continued to rise to incredible levels due to a combination of adult baby boomers out in the economy, the end of cheap petroleum, and a changing environment for major corporations. Families continued to leave the cities for the suburbs, a process often accelerated by integration and known as white flight. Tax bases dried up, services stopped, and some cities even declared bankruptcy. Rising costs for food and gasoline amplified the situation. Even American industry, envy of the world for a century, demonstrated a slow death as the Rust Belt emerged due to falling steel and automobile production.[10]

Politically, the fallout from the Vietnam War and Watergate left Americans distrustful of the federal government in a way they had not been before. Gerald Ford's pardoning of Nixon did not help this situation nor did the Carter Presidency. Ford's "Whip Inflation Now" (WIN) campaign and Carter's "malaise speech" by a fireside in a sweater, asking Americans to change their thermostat to conserve energy did not instill Americans with the hope of what was possible. The taking of American hostages in the Iranian Revolution, the inability to save those hostages, and even the nuclear meltdown at Three Mile Island added to this sense of gloom. Instead the United States, the great superpower, appeared unable to solve its own problems. The nation's Bicentennial celebrations in 1976 presented a brief respite from a generally gloomy decade.[11]

Many Americans saw these economic and political setbacks tied to declining values and abandoned morals. From the mid-1960s forward, the Supreme Court had ruled that pornography was free and protected speech, that contraception could be purchased (and used!) by unmarried couples, that employee-led school prayer was illegal, and that abortion was legal. A host of minority groups—African Americans, Native Americans, homosexuals, even prisoners—organized and demanded better treatment. Women too were part of this push, with Women's Liberation blossoming in the early Seventies as women expected and often received better access to school athletics, college educations, and employment. But these demands for equality came with unintended consequences. School busing to bring integration in urban areas not only led to white flight but also the destruction of the neighborhood school in some areas and the rise of the giant comprehensive high school in others. Divorce and abortion rates rose. What some hailed as a Rights Revolution, others saw as the loss of the nation's moral compass.[12]

Thus a conservative backlash against the cultural changes of the Sixties and Seventies emerged and riding this wave of discontent was actor gone politician Ronald Reagan. Reagan was able to unite economic and moral conservatives in a new voting coalition. He not only promised lower taxes, but he also promoted the idea that government was the problem. Indeed, the great Reagan joke was that the nine most terrifying words in the English language were, "I'm from the government and I'm here to help." Reagan's conservative vision for America—his slogans in 1980 were "Let's Make America Great Again" and "Are You Better Off that You Were Four Years Ago?"—was presented as a back-to-basics idea: the United States had to get back to what made it great: a strong military, few regulations on businesses for a strong economy, a smaller and less intrusive federal government, and a values-driven culture. As the Boomers aged, this halcyon image of their youth was incredibly appealing, even if it had never really existed. Nevertheless this conservative vision dominated the political landscape for rest of the century and beyond, transforming local, state, and federal politics.[13]

By the 1990s, Reagan's American "revival" was underway. The fall of the Soviet Union, the end of the Cold War, and the wildly successful Desert Storm campaigns in 1991 returned the nation to undisputed superpower status. The wild inflation of the 1970s was an unpleasant memory. Indeed, a new economic boom had begun. The end of the Cold War meant new markets and the rise of the technology revolution was opening new levels of productivity and innovation as personal computers seeped into businesses and then homes. Here was a nation that could do things!

The newly confident nation now told a more inclusive story. Divorce and single-parent homes, once so abhorred, had become far more common. Married couples were barely half—53%—of American households according to the 1990 census. With 40 percent of children no longer living in two parent homes with both their biological parents, families looked different and more diverse in their configuration. The Family and Medical Leave Act of 1993 sought to protect women's employment with twelve weeks unpaid leave to new mothers who needed the time. Women's work for equality continued to show growth as more entered graduate programs and women made up just over half of college admissions. Homosexual demands for equality led to the infamous "don't ask, don't tell" policy of the US military under the Bill Clinton administration. African Americans developed a solid middle class in these years. Asian and Hispanic immigration increased as well. The American story was increasingly diverse.[14]

The Boy Scouts followed a similar path. The 1970s were the "dark ages" of Scouting. Membership fell, both for boys and adults. This was understandable given the end of the Baby Boom, but the collapse of faith in institutions and the cultural image of Scouts as out of step with the times made the organization unpopular. Rising inflation, which meant less disposable income, was also to blame. For Scouters though, it was the Improved Scouting Program that was the culprit responsible for the decline. Introduced in 1972 to reflect the changing landscape of the nation, the program was widely viewed as the wrong path for Scouting, no matter how well-intentioned it was. And it was not just Boy Scouts. Despite allowing Cubs to engage in overnight camping in this era and introducing the new Webelos program, enrollment in Cub Scouting fell too. Exploring stayed relatively strong, but this was because females, who were allowed to enter the program in 1969, "made up about one-quarter of all Explorers by the 1980s." Scouting was in crisis.[15]

Thus, a "back to basics" approach in Scouting occurred as well. In late 1970s, Scouting "now harked back to its historic roots in search of revival—by putting the "boy" back in "Boy Scouts" and putting the "outing" back in "Scouting." An emphasis on the outdoors returned, promoted and amplified by the ninth edition of the *Official Boy Scout Handbook*, written by William "Green Bar Bill" Hillcourt. Even the 1979 Annual Report of the organization echoed this return to form, arguing that outdoor skills led to "self-reliance, ability to work with others, and personal fitness… [C]itizenship, first aid, family, community living, communications, and physical fitness" were second-fiddle to the outdoors.[16]

In the 1980s, the resurgence began. Membership rose for the first time since 1972 in 1980. Indeed, 1980 was "the best growth year on record." Cub Scouts and Explorers experienced the same. In 1982, Cub Scouting expanded, adding Tiger Cubs, which allowed boys as young as seven to join Scouting. By 1984, extended camping, not just an overnight, was approved for Webelos. For Boy Scouts, the change was especially profound. In 1990, the skill award system was abandoned. Rank specific skills for Tenderfoot through First Class returned as the bedrock of the Boy Scout program.[17]

But perhaps the most profound change in Scouting was a direct response to the changing outside world: a youth protection program. In 1974 in New Orleans, a Scout troop was formed by predators to recruit boys. They were discovered in 1976 when a roll of film depicting the sexual acts was reported by the photo store employees. Police raids subsequently uncovered a pedophile ring that reached into Tennessee, Georgia, Florida, and Massachusetts. While these men were all sentenced to extremely long jail terms, the ripple effect of this failure within the organization was profound.[18]

For Nashville in particular, the dangers posed to youth out in the public became apparent in February 1975. Marcia Trimble, a 9 year old girl, disappeared when delivering Girl Scouts cookies. A month later on Easter Sunday, "Marcia's body [was] found covered with a shower curtain, on a storage shelf in a seldom-used garage behind a house one block away from her home." It was a horrific tragedy.[19]

Nashville Boy Scouts were not immune to predators either. In 1985, the case of Robert Bowden dominated the headlines much the way the Trimble case had a decade earlier. An Assistant Scoutmaster who pled guilty to abusing two Boy Scouts, Bowden was denied probation and sentenced to five years. Several years later, in 1991, Assistant Scoutmaster Ron Rice was arrested after abusing several Scouts within his troop over a twelve to thirteen year period. A plea bargain settled eleven different cases against Rice, sending him to prison for thirty years. While neither was related directly to Boxwell, the Bowden and Rice cases demonstrated locally the need for a youth protection program in the Boy Scouts of America. Indeed, the Middle Tennessee Council saw the urgency and brought on local lawyer and Eagle Scout Marshall Greene. Greene not only dealt with youth protection issues within the Council, but developed a Youth Protection Plan for the Council, which eventually became a template for the national BSA program.[20]

The National Youth Protection program started slowly, but grew to a gallop. The idea of two-deep leadership, which required that there always be two adults present in *any* dealings with a Scout, was first mentioned in the *Scoutmasters' Handbook* in 1981. The official Scout position in regard to child abuse prevention was announced in 1985. Adult leaders were no longer allowed to be unaccompanied with individual Scouts; adults could not invite individual Scouts to their home. By 1987, the BSA adopted a training program for youth and a video *A Time to Tell* was produced in 1989. By 1990, new guidelines were created and even appeared in the new *Boy Scout Handbook*. By 1994, adult background checks were required of professional Scouters; checks for adult volunteers soon followed. The program was robust. As the current Middle Tennessee Council Scout Executive Larry Brown recalled, "In the 90's I can remember going to a Scout meeting to get a physical description of a new leader who national thought might be on the [ineligible] list." The Scouts were keeping a close eye on who entered their ranks and their Youth Protection program "has since been hailed as one of the country's finest."[21]

Youth Protection was a big, outward program change, but it was not the only change Scouting was making. Increasingly, Scouting became associated more and more with "traditional values," an idea that the back-to-basics push embraced. In many ways Scouting put itself on the front line of the emerging culture wars as it entrenched itself against the "Three G's": "Gays, Girls, and the Godless." The ban on women and atheists were baked right into the name "Boy Scouts" and the organization's Law and Oath, but the ban on homosexuals was less clear cut. Scouting often conflated homosexuality and pedophilia. The advent of the child abuse prevention program actually began the work of untwisting this coupling. Nevertheless, for the Boy Scouts, homosexuals were still considered immoral and thus a homosexual could not be "morally straight." Scouting's legal battles to defend their admission standards would continue well into the twenty-first century with consequences that extended all the way into summer camp program.[22]

A Scout Is Thrifty

The Staff Walkout in 1976 was only partly about the charge for food, room and board; it was really about the new direction that Boxwell was taking. The Blue Ribbon committees which had investigated Ward Akers had made a host of suggestions about the direction of the Council and its summer camp. While Akers' resignation had turned the spotlight off of the Council, the investigations and resulting recommendations required that changes be made.

First and foremost, the Council could not afford to slack on the program it delivered to the thousands of Scouts under its tent. The first real test of the post-Ward Akers Middle Tennessee Council came the first weekend of April 1976: the Bicentennial Muster. In celebration of the nation's bicentennial, the state's "largest encampment of Boy Scouts" took place at Boxwell. Over 8,000 people participated in the celebration of Scouting and the United States. There was a fishing contest, an American Revolution Patriot costume contest, boat races, and even a re-enactment of the Battle of Ft. McHenry from the War of 1812, which spawned "The Star Spangled Banner." The muster also had musket firings, obstacle courses, flaming arrows, log rolling, a linear accelerator—a globe with the electric bolts to make a person's hair stand on end—and a fireworks display. And there were hats: coonskin hats, Smoky the Bear hats (often called campaign hats), tri-corner hats, Cub Scout beanies, and just regular old cowboy hats. As an added bonus, all the participants gathered in the field below the Crippled Crab to form the word "Liberty." By virtually every standard, the Bicentennial Muster was an enormous success. Indeed, the Executive Board meeting directly after the event described the Muster as "the greatest thing that has happened to Scouting in many a year in Middle Tennessee." Middle Tennessee Scouting had survived Ward Akers' resignation.[23]

But survival was not flourishing. As camp opened in 1976, the fall-out from the Ward Akers investigation was immediately apparent. As Russ Parham explained, "By the time the summer camp of '76 rolled around, the money flow was nil. People had taken what they heard on the news to heart and decided the Scouts were wasting their money." Indeed, the Council dipped into its trust fund for operating funds in both 1975 and 1976. With funding dry-

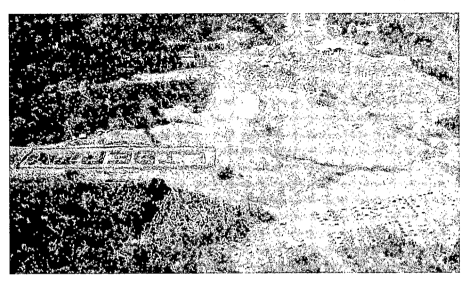

Aerial photo of the 1976 Bicentennial Muster at Boxwell Reservation, April 1976.
Photo by Michael Seay.

ing up, significant cost-cutting measures would have to be made. In fact, the
Council's Camping Committee was charged "to determine if there are areas
where we can reduce cost without affecting the program and review the needs
of increasing the camp fee. Also, investigate the condition of the permanent
structures, equipment, and machines at Boxwell as recommended by one of the
Ad Hoc Committees."[24]

Often drastic cost-saving measures, the recommendations from the
Camping Committee were immediately instituted at Boxwell for the 1976 season. And despite the charge to "reduce cost without affecting program," some
recommendations directly affected program. The Ski Dock area, which included motor-boating, sailing, and water-skiing, was shuttered entirely. The
fuel and maintenance for the boats was deemed too costly. Under the guise of
conservation, "allowing camps and campsites to rest from constant use," Camp
Craig was closed; only Parnell and Stahlman would operate. In the coming
years, a "camp rest" rotation would be implemented. In truth, the closure was
less about conservation and more about the number of Scouts coming to camp.

285

Indeed, the summer camp season itself was cut down from nine weeks to seven. Even that reduced season was not enough to prevent camp itself closing down July Fourth week because of low attendance.

Other measures were less overtly drastic, but would have long term ramifications. Electricity costs were an easy target. The electricity that had been slowly spreading into the staff sites since the mid-1960s was removed. Because the cost of replacing water heaters was deemed too high, there were no hot showers in the Scout camps at all in. Family style feeding was replaced with cafeteria style feeding. According to the Camping Committee, other camps using cafeteria style had seen a ten to twelve percent savings. The farming operation was closed at the end of 1975, with "all but two or three" of the cattle sold off. The only good news was that the Committee recommended that the fee for attending camp for the summer not be increased. For the moment, a week at camp still cost a Scout $35 a week.[25]

These changes presented only a partial picture of the immediate aftermath of the Ward Akers investigation. There was a new Council Executive—Hershel Tolbert—and the Council and its districts were reorganized. Soon after arriving, Tolbert sold off the additional 110 acres at Rock Island that had been bought to expand the camp. For the first time in approximately a decade, the Council missed its annual fund raising goal. In December 1976, the State Health Department notified the Council that the water at Boxwell was no longer up to standards. According to Wilbur Creighton III, Vice-President for Finance, the Pump House, which had been donated by the Clover Bottom Development Hospital in 1959, "had simply 'worn out'." The Council could either pay $35,000 to improve the system and possibly experience the same problems again, or pay $15,000, tie in to 'city water,' and avoid further issues with the State Health Department on the quality of the water. Thus, Boxwell joined the West Wilson Water District. Additionally, the Stahlman, Parnell, and Murrey dining halls all required some roof repair. The only unquestionable bright spots were the Council's move into new Jet Potter

286

Ken Connelly, Hershel Tolbert, and Tom Willhite outside the Jet Potter Service Center, sometime between 1976 and 1978. Personal Collection of Tom Willhite.

Center office building in August 1976 and dedication ceremonies held on November 7th.[26]

Recovery came slowly and there were still a few bumps over the next few years. The cost for going to camp was increased to $40 as "inflation and the spiraling cost of food" made operating the camp more expensive. Even the fee increase was just enough to help the camp break even. In July 1978, the Narrows of the Harpeth property was sold to the state of Tennessee for $75,000. The Long Range Planning committee had been looking at unloading the Narrows for a while—it just did not serve much purpose after Grimes Canoe base became fully operational—and the timing helped the Council. Camp itself continued to shorten. In 1977, Boxwell ran again for eight weeks, but 1978 was down to seven weeks total. 1979 saw the shrinking summer camp schedule finally stabilize at six weeks: a staff week and five weeks for Scouts. This pattern would maintain for the next forty years.[27]

For the Good of the Program

Not all of this could be attributed directly to fallout from Ward Akers, obviously. Some of these difficulties, such as the shortening of the weeks of camp, were due to the end of the Baby Boom. There just were not as many Scouts as there used to be. Inflation, rising fuel costs, and rising food costs contributed as well. And of course, it should be remembered that the Reservation was not new anymore. The original buildings were all approaching twenty years of age and not all had been updated or maintained as well as they should have.

This was the world Tom Willhite inherited when he became Director of Camping at the end of May 1976. And it was Willhite's world; no Council Executive would ever again be as engaged with the camp the way Ward Akers was. For a lesser man, such an environment would have been for overwhelming. But Tom Willhite was the living embodiment of the tenth point of the Scout Law: A Scout is Thrifty. This was a man who lived and breathed the adage, "time is money." When he was done with a phone conversation, he hung up, even if the caller was his wife. For Willhite's first ten years as Reservation Director, actual rope was almost impossible to come by. Staff had to make due with twine instead; it got the job done. During Staff Week, it was not unusual for Willhite to call on a staff member, usually someone older, and ask what he thought the reservation's water or electricity bill had been the year before. Indeed, a decade after his retirement, Willhite recalled without missing a beat that the final water bill under his management was $4000. Willhite knew how valuable material and time were and he expected others to know too.[28]

Two quick anecdotes demonstrate Willhite's approach to people and money. Jason Bradford had already worked on camp staff in 1990, hired at fourteen years old, half way through the summer by the program director. Thus, he was fifteen years old when he went to interview with Willhite in 1991 and described the process "as intimidating as you could ever imagine." After waiting around the Jet Potter Center for thirty to forty-five minutes,

288

Bradford was called into Willhite's office for the interview. "No, there was no interview involved. I went in there and sat down and he told me what I was going to make, and I said, "Thank you, Sir," and walked out of the room. I don't even think it took a full minute." Understanding that Bradford was young and inexperienced, the example still demonstrates Willhite's personality: direct, often gruff or brusque, and tightly holding onto the reins where the money was concerned.[29]

A second example provides a bit more levity. Staff members Andy Whitt and Michael Allen, having worked for Willhite for several summers, at different times both had opportunities to ask Willhite big "what is the meaning of life" questions. The Reservation Director gave essentially the same answer to both men. Willhite explained to Whitt that you should pay top dollar for three things: shoes, an easy chair, and a mattress because you'll be spending your whole life in one of those three things. To Allen, he gave a somewhat modified version. The three things one needed in life were a good pair of shoes so your feet don't ache, a good mattress for a good night's rest, and a good woman to put in that bed. The exchanges epitomized Willhite. The staff members came to him because they knew he held on tightly to money, but the answer showed he was willing to pay for things that were truly important. The stories also demonstrated a dark sense of humor.[30]

Thrifty did not mean cheap. Thrifty meant using resources wisely. Being able to make the case for the value of what you needed was the key to working with or for Tom Willhite. In short, when you had a request, you had to show Willhite that what you needed was necessary. Once he was assured the program would suffer without whatever the item was, he found a way to come up with whatever was needed. Stahlman Staff member Web Webster used an apt metaphor: "[A]nyone who worked for Tom Willhite knew that the difference between a nickel and a dime is the same difference between fifty and a hundred bucks." Fellow professional Ken Connelly concurred, "Tom was the ideal person to run Boxwell at that time because he had to make a nickel stretch or a quarter. [Connelly laughed] He wasn't bashful about asking businesses...Instead of us [the Council] buying it, [Willhite would ask,] will you give it to us? [chuckled] Then, if they won't give it to us, "Well, will you give it to us at your cost, or provide it at your cost?" Willhite was the man for the hour.[31]

In addition to the roof work that was done in 1976, Camp Craig was in need of serious improvements. The rustic camp vision had not gone over well when the camp opened. So, while the camp was closed under the new conservation approach, upgrades were made. A new metal roof (covering the original shingles) was put on the dining hall. A showerhouse had been completed in 1975, but those kybo toilets still dotted the camp. Thus, on both of the camp loops, pit toilet stands were installed. These wash stands had a small metal trough sink for washing hands or filling up water bottles, but the toilets were toilet seats over pits. The only flush toilets for Scouts were at the new showerhouse behind the dining hall. The pit toilets had to have lye poured into them every morning and periodically they were pumped out during the summer.[32]

Camp Craig was a never ending project. Though closed, the 1976 *Leaders' Guide* showed the camp with only ten sites. By 1978, the camp was up to 12 sites, along with the new showerhouse and washstands. By 1982, it had fourteen sites. Indeed, the new sites were inserted so pell-mell, all the sites had to be renumbered for 1983's camping season. Two new showerhouses were also added in the summer of 1986, one on each loop of the camp, usually near the washstands. The start of camp in 1990 saw that the rifle range had moved out of the dining hall basement into its own free standing structure. For 1991, two more sites were added out on the fringes of the camp, bringing the total up to sixteen sites. The washstands, the showerhouses, and the rifle range were all legitimate construction projects, completed by outside contractors.[33]

However, the developments at Camp Craig also presented a fascinating example of how cost-savings would now be achieved: staff labor. Most of the new sites at Craig were carved out by the staff themselves, who would clear trees for an entrance and where platforms needed to be placed. The ranger staff would take care of the platform construction, but placement and preparation were often also done by the staff. A better example involved the shower-houses in 1986. While a construction company built the actual facilities, Willhite used staff labor during staff week to save money. The builders dug trenches for the water and electric lines, but to keep from tearing up the land-scape any further, the staff would cover the lines. Because the terrain was so rocky, the trenches had be cleared and the lines padded and re-laid by hand. It was a big job, but the staff got it done. At the upper loop showerhouse, the staff ended up digging a four foot deep, six foot long trench through solid rock to complete the job. It may have saved Willhite on labor, but it cost him sixteen pick-axes, four crowbars, three pull bars, four hoes, and a pry bar.[34]

"The Willhite Method" was utilized in other ways as well. Since moving to "Camp Beany Elam" by the compound, Wood Badge had settled in and begun to develop the area. Wood Badge staff had already secured a large pond and three flag poles, but the Wood Badge Scouters wanted a building of their own, a request dating back to the Akers' years. Finally, in 1984, all the pieces came together for a building. The rangers built a retaining wall of large cross-ties and the Wood Badge volunteers themselves secured a bulldozer to grade the area down level. Willhite secured most of the building supplies—the timbers and the basic design—from Metro Parks, which dismantled Sycamore Lodge in Shelby Park in early 1984. "We're marking the logs number by number, and we're going to rebuild it exactly as it was before, except with a new roof," Willhite promised. The metal roofing was donated, so the only thing the Council paid for were the rafters and the labor to put the roof up. All the work of erecting the building was done by the Wood Badge volunteers.[35]

But before the building could be erected, the foundation had to be poured. Enter the camp staff. For Willhite, the staff labor was not a big deal. "The staff that worked at Boxwell, on their extra-curricular activities, they did some gravel spreading and so on," he explained later. "And we got the stuff laid to pour the concrete one day." Experiencing a slow week, the Parnell staff was directed to work on the foundation when they had time. Instead, the majority of the staff went over after lunch one day and did the work in an hour. While a great deal of gravel was undoubtedly slung in a haphazard fashion to get the work done quickly, the entire episode demonstrated Tom Willhite finding ways to operate on a shoestring and without a lot of fanfare.[36]

"Without fanfare" was almost a mantra for these years when it came to capital developments. One of the little known realities of Willhite's tenure was something he called "the Quasi-Campaign." Since money remained tight well into the 1980s and a true capital campaign was simply not an option, Willhite executed a covert operation to raise "a half million dollars that nobody ever knew about, except the ones that gave the money." The Quasi-Campaign replaced all the chipped marble roofs from the original construction with metal roofs. Two new large cabins at Camp Murrey were built as part of this program. Indeed, these cabins had toilets and showers in them, which the cabins from the '72 campaign never received. A tent storage building in the compound, the new outdoor rifle range at Camp Craig, new docks for the waterfronts, and a permanent skeet range in Camp Light were ultimately results of these efforts.[37]

As the Quasi-Campaign demonstrated, Willhite was able to get Scouters and local businessmen to donate materials and time to make little things happen all over the Reservation. As Willhite explained, in 1976, "we didn't have hot water at the showerhouses because they thought they didn't have enough money. But we brought it back in '77 and everybody was elated." For the rest of Willhite's tenure, the camp never bought a single water heater; every single one was donated. When the first forty foot rappelling tower was erected in 1978, Willhite used donated materials. When the C.O.P.E. program began, Willhite bought the cable, but most everything else was donated. Even the seventy-five foot tall Al Hendrickson tower that was built in 1990 on ninety foot tall telephone poles donated by Nashville Electric Service had most of the labor donated, including a concrete floor by the Navy Seabees as well as use of a bucket truck to line the walls. The roads all over the Reservation were shot and tar—layer of gravel, layer of tar—and Willhite had all of the roads shot three or four times in his tenure, all with donated material and labor. Even the concrete pad Willhite had laid around the Crippled Crab, replacing the gravel bed that the Crab staff had to rake every morning, was done with donated material and donated labor.[38]

Occasionally, there were some high profile contributions and construction projects. "High profile" in this case means they were covered in the newspapers. The first was the Grizzard Gateway—the stone obelisk with hanging signs—dedicated on July 11, 1976. The gateway was paid for by long time Scouter Western Grizzard to honor his wife Eleanor's work, which had made his work possible. In November 1980, the Nashville Scottish Rite Foundation donated three flag poles to the Reservation to be placed near the Crab at the top of the hill. Technically, the group donated the money to purchase the flagpoles and pay for their installation. Willhite being Willhite made the most of this donation. He was able to purchase the poles, get them installed, *and* have a nice rock wall built as well, in which was placed a time capsule for future generations. In 1985, an amphitheatre was built in the slope down the hill from the Crab and the flagpoles. The site had a concrete pad with an enormous fire altar on either side. The amphitheater was funded and constructed by the Order of the Arrow, Wa-Hi-Nasa Lodge and dedicated to the memory of William C. Weaver, Jr., who had chaired the 1972 Capital Campaign. The site was dedicated on October 26, 1985 and would be used for joint campfire programs between the camps every summer on July Fourth.[39]

If there was any one area where the Willhite magic did not work, it was with the hanging cedar plank entrance sign. The hanging cedar sign had been installed on a high embankment just north of Creighton Lane at the turn-off from Highway 109. Unfortunately, this embankment was private property and the Council had never been able to secure it. So, when the land's owner realized he could make some money for selling the dirt in the early 1990s, the hanging sign came down. It moved temporarily into the compound and quietly disappeared into history. It would take the 1994 Capital Campaign before a new sign was built at the Highway 109 exit onto Creighton Lane.[40]

While Willhite's thriftiness led to amazing cost savings, it did not pay the bills. Without a farming operations and the end of dog trials, other revenue had to be generated. Willhite started with the most obvious option first. Years of screening materials from Fort Campbell had led to literal piles of equipment in and around the compound. Willhite sold it off, multiple times in fact. He sold the old camp trucks, like the Parnell Panther and Stahlman's Clyde. He sold the Army surplus 1956 Chevrolets that were lined up and parked behind the compound, first for parts. Then, he sold to another individual who worked for months taking what he wanted from the cars. He sold to another individual, who also worked to strip down the cars and other vehicles. When that individual was done, Willhite had Oldham Construction use a bulldozer to dig a pit behind the compound and the remaining cars were pushed into the hole and buried. The bulldozer work was donated and Willhite made $5500 on the part sales transactions.[41]

A logical extension of this was an auction. For at least his first four years as Reservation Director, toward the end of the year, Willhite would hold an auction at Boxwell, selling anything from electric typewriters to army cots to kitchen equipment to the generic "many usable items." In fact, Willhite began using the auction as an opportunity for people in the community to make tax deductible donations to the Boy Scouts of their junk. People could get rid of their unwanted items, get a deduction on their taxes, and Willhite could make a little extra money for camp. Some years, in the same space where the auction

The Grizzard Gateway at the time of its dedication, July 11, 1976. Photo by

was advertised, Willhite also openly asked for materials he might actually need for camp, like binders twine, hammers, life jackets, and even aluminum canoes. He could then sort through these as well, keep what he needed and sell what he did not. This was the Willhite magic at work, generating income by spending virtually nothing.[42]

Camp fees were the other avenue of revenue available. Throughout the 1960s, a week of summer camp cost twenty-five dollars. It was not until the run-away recession of the 1970s that the fee began to rise. After two increases in the final years of Ward Akers, a week of camp cost thirty-five dollars. Beginning in 1977, the cost for attending camp increased every other year. By 1985, a week cost sixty-five dollars; by 1995, a hundred dollars if the troop registered before June 1, $115 after. Indeed, the "late" fee began in 1985 as a simple way to generate some income while encouraging troops to register early. Fees for staying at Camp Murrey increased as well, though not with the same frequency or value. A week at Murrey cost a family twenty-five dollars per adult and an additional fifteen dollars for every child under eleven. By 1990, just before the end of Murrey's run, the fees were seventy dollars per adult and thirty-five dollars for children under eleven. As the cost for camp continued to rise, new methods were introduced to break up the fee to make it an easier hurdle to overcome. A leaders' fee, a site reservation fee, and an early registration fee were all introduced in these years. All of these fees ultimately came back to the troop, lowering how much was actually due at Sunday registration. So while the Council did not make money off of the fees themselves, it did benefit from the steady rise in camp costs.[43]

New programs however were another avenue forward. An extra week at camp for older boys was an event that a fee could be attached to. A weekend or two of a single overnight for Cub Scouts and parents was another example. Junior Leader Training, like Brownsea, or High Adventure options, like C.O.P.E. or the "Above and Beyond" program were all ways additional revenue could be generated. These programs all had costs, primarily in staff and food, but as staff and food were already paid for or were volunteers, generally these programs all produced *some* revenue.[44]

Of course, a primary generator for summer camp was the Trading Post in each camp, overseen by the camp's Business Managers Michael Seay and later Russ Parham. Both men had been staff members who moved into the role, Seay under Ed Human and Willhite from 1974 to 1979 and Parham for Willhite and Larry Green from 1980 to 1996. As Seay explained, when he convinced Human to create the position for him, the Reservation Business Manager was responsible for "looking after the two different camps' handicrafts and trading post, making sure that they had stock when they needed it." On the weekends, he would travel to Nashville to stock up whatever handicraft supplies may have been needed. His interest in photography also led Seay to take most of the staff photos in these years as well as a variety of promotional photos for the Council, such as the construction of the Jet Potter Center, the Camp Craig dedication, and aerial photos of the Reservation. Seay was an ex-

296

*Serving Scouts from the service window at Parnell's Trading Post, early 1980s.
Photo by Russ Parham.*

cellent investment as he was not paid a staff salary and came in only in the evenings because of a cooperative educational experience through his college. All
he was "paid" was room and board.[45]

Russ Parham became Reservation Business Manager in 1980 and he
was a natural fit for the job. Parham was good friends with Seay, so he knew
what the position entailed. And after not walking out in 1976 and completing
a solid four years as Program Director, he had established his loyalty and com-
petence with Willhite as well. Parham was out of college by 1980 and had
landed a full time job, so he too worked nights as Seay had done. It was not
uncommon at all for Parham to show up after taps at either camp's Trading
Post to begin work. It was a hectic schedule and even Parham admitted, "[Y]
ou never saw me at breakfast on Saturday because I hid and then I would sleep
late and catch up on counting money, making deposits on Saturday and Sun-

day before the next round of camp started."[46]

As he continued in the position, Parham performed the same work Seay had done, but the position expanded. In addition to Boxwell, Parham ran the Trading Posts for council Jamborees and coordinated with the Council office on buying program items like tents or rope or bulk items. He handled the ordering in the spring, which included all the standard items, such as hand-icraft materials, candy, the knives, the patches, the t-shirts, and the like. On Sundays, he was either personally on hand or had his hand-picked Trading Post Directors at each camp involved in the registration process at check-in. If money changed hands during summer camp, it was likely Parham was involved.

Parham used the position to experiment with new products to generate revenue. Because of their history together, Willhite generally trusted him without a great deal of oversight. Every year, Parham came up with new patch designs, both for those troops that completed early registration and to be sold at the Trading Posts. T-shirts were an area where Parham really got to stretch his creative wings. Every summer saw a "classic" or "serious" design—something that was clearly camp related, but somber—and a more kid friendly and "funny" design. Seymour Duck was one of the most popular "funny" designs. Some ideas, like Seymour, worked well. Others, like a pen with a spring load-ed clip that could attach to a belt loop, were good ideas, but were so cheap they did not perform well. Still, a good day at a Trading Post could bring in over $2000 and just about every year the Trading Posts managed a 30% to 40% profit.[47]

Parham's responsibilities also included assisting with summer camp program. In addition to the Trading Post and Sunday registration, Parham also oversaw the annual *Leaders' Guide* updates. This meant an intimate un-derstanding of not only fees, but what program was utilized and what was hap-pening at Boxwell. All of the *Leaders' Guides* in this period included a large, two-page merit badge schedule that could be removed, placed on a bulletin board, and utilized to keep track of what merit badges Scouts were taking. Parham developed this. Further, Parham was also instrumental in getting a lot of the basic paperwork completed. He helped create the merit badge incomplete forms, attendance rosters, and in the 1990s, the "green sheets" that laid out the Rank Requirements information of the Davy Crockett program. Willhite himself once joked that had he not married his wife Marie, he would have married Parham as he was that essential to Willhite's work.[48]

It is important to note here the prevailing assumption about summer camp from a financial perspective. Summer camp was seen as a "cost center" for a council. In other words, councils had lots of ways to make money, such as the Sustaining Membership Enrollment (SME) campaigns every spring as well as a slice of United Way monies. But summer camp was not seen as a way to make money. Summer camp, for some time, was something a council expected to lose money on every year. A best case scenario was to break even. At the very least, summer camp was not expected to make money. By the 1990s, this would change and summer camp would be seen as a "profit center." In short, the use of fees for different programs and shifting costs onto the Scouts for activities—shells for shotgun, gas for motor boating—allowed summer camp to *make* money. However, this transition did not happen until late in Willhite's run.[49]

The years 1976 to 1984 were unquestionably difficult years for the Council and for Willhite at Boxwell. By the mid-1980s, the economic situation was clearly turning around. There were a couple of tell-tale signs. First, the year to year income numbers were clearly increasing. For example, in 1976, the camping revenues of the Council were $76,406. Camping Revenues were mostly derived from summer camp, but did include any of the other council wide camping activities for which there was a fee. By 1986, the camping revenue had increased to $200,670, an almost 300% increase. By way of comparison, the total support and revenue in 1978 was $1,138, 500. In 1986, the total support and revenue for the council was $1,758,879, which was approximately a 30% increase. Camp may have been viewed as a cost center, but it was doing well. The other tell-tale was far more aesthetic. The 1978 Annual Report was a straight forward document. With heavy stock paper, a few photos, and printed statistics, if the booklet was not produced in-house, it could have been. This was true for the next several years. The paper may have changed and there may have been better graphics or color photos, but the information was very simple and straight forward. By 1986, this same document, the Annual Report, was clearly produced by an outside agency. The information was less direct and forthright, the photos more aspirational. The 1986 Annual Report was clearly the point at which there was enough money coming in again that success could be explained more vaguely and between glossy, staged and often thematic photographs. By 1986, Middle Tennessee Scouting had recovered. From Akers. From the recession. The years of plenty had returned.[50]

The Barnett and Ragsdale Era

While maintaining physical facilities on a shoestring budget was solidly within Willhite's wheelhouse, program presented a different challenge for the new Reservation Director. As he said in July of 1976, "We have a new Scout Executive for the council and we are working really hard to upgrade the buildings and facilities at the camp. But more importantly perhaps, we are more concerned with the needs of the individual camper and the scout masters, where in the past the administration may have been a little arrogant towards them." Program needed to embrace a back-to-basics approach, putting the focus back on the leaders and the real reason for summer camp: the Scout.[51]

A back-to-basics program was already in development by the National Council. The idea of putting the "outing back in Scouting" and putting the "boy back in Boy Scouts" were outgrowths of the push to get back to the outdoors and basic Scouting skills. Clearly, this was going to be part of Willhite's push as well. Nevertheless, the financial stresses required a little broader thinking about what program might mean. With the end of the Ski Dock, there was no real program for older Scouts. Further, to avoid a situation like this again in the future, some thought needed to be given to Cub Scouts. If they could be exposed to the outdoors in a positive way, they might stick with the program longer. While the term was not used at the time, *retention* of both older and younger boys was clearly a driving force in the back-to-basics philosophy. Give these boys and young men a positive outdoor experience and they will come back to camp. This meant that not only was the core summer camp program going to be important, but peripheral programs—events that were not directly part of summer camp, but connected in some way—were going to matter a great deal going forward.

The problem here was that for all his strengths in terms of making ends meet with very little, Willhite was not an outstanding program person. This did not mean he was not an excellent manager or leader, because he was. Willhite recognized that if he hired good people to take care of the program, he could let those individuals set the standards and implement the program ideas that were best for their camps. He could then hold the line as established and support those individuals while making sure everything worked well behind the scenes, where his strengths were. Willhite was an administrator; he needed to hire the right set of people to implement a strong summer camp program.[52]

Until that proper combination emerged, there was still a summer camp to manage. As expressed above, much of 1976 was inherited. The staff and the program both came to Willhite from work that Ed Human and his assistant Skip Dickens had completed. The commissioner system still existed and the Boy Scouting program was still using Skill Awards for younger Scouts, and thus so too did Boxwell. Even the program changes—the shortened camp term, the end of the Ski Dock, and the move back to just two summer camps in operation—were decisions made by the Council's Camping Committee. Willhite simply had not been Reservation Director long enough to have a guiding hand in any of these decisions.

In addition to the changes mentioned above, there was one 1976 change that must be discussed in detail: the shift to cafeteria style feeding. The idea was part of the cost-saving measures discussed above and part of the package Willhite inherited. The monitor-host system had provided an indispensable component to program since Rock Island, emphasizing the family values that were so critical to Scouting in that period. Cafeteria style therefore represented a profound program shift. This approach to feeding was the same as the youth experienced in school. Scouts still entered the dining hall and said grace, but where monitor-host had Scouts immediately sit down to eat, cafeteria style utilized a line. Using a plastic tray with indented compartments, a scout went through a line where food was shoveled onto his tray. If there was milk with the meal, he picked that up too, along with his silverware. If there was "bug juice" to drink, the pitcher and cups were waiting at the table thanks to the monitor. Food in hand, the Scout returned to his table where he ate with his friends.

Program changes reverberated throughout the Willhite era from this move. Staff no longer sat at the table with the Scouts. Instead, they congregated at "staff tables," which were situated near the head table for the camp leadership. With no staff at the tables, it was more difficult to detect dissatisfaction early. A direct contact person for Scoutmasters—and a significant public relations tool—was lost. Conversely, removing staff from the Scout tables freed them to serve the food. To make this job more tolerable, staff often broke into song while serving. Staff tables also allowed staff to congregate and easily execute songs, skits, and communications from a centralized location. In short, more spontaneous dining hall program was a direct result of the shift.[53]

Unfortunately, another result of the shift was the increased time involved. Family style, or monitor-host, was inherently a quick feeding system. With food on the table when Scouts and staff sat down, it was easy to get through a complete meal with seconds served and program and communications delivered in approximately half an hour. With cafeteria style, it took thirty to forty minutes just to feed everyone, with staff being served last. This meant that by the time staff sat down to eat, the first groups were finished and ready for seconds if they were available. This time involved was a concern early on because it was such an enormous change. A lunch that started at noon might not end for an hour or more, depending on what happened that day. That was a great deal of sitting and it cut into time after the meal for other activities, like baseball or volleyball challenges. These still occurred, but the time available for them diminished significantly. Fortunately, or perhaps as a direct result, the period after lunch from Ipm to 2pm was no longer promoted as a "rest period."[54]

The transition was critical. Family style had symbolized core values of Scouting; cafeteria style placed cost efficiency over values. After all, the stated reason for the transition was that other camps saw a 10-12 per cent savings by making the move. And while this may have been true on the financial side of the house, there were other costs involved that were not monetary. One could argue that the cafeteria system began a shift toward individual responsibility that was more in fitting with the shifting cultural values of the times. But for an organization that touted the importance of family, values, and morals, the move to cafeteria was an abdication of responsibility in the name of saving some money. This one change—a system that had been so core to the values of Boxwell's program for a quarter century—demonstrated powerfully how the financial situation after Akers affected program.

But in most respects, 1976 was an anomaly and a new Boxwell began to emerge in 1977. Willhite had had a year to plan and implement his own changes. He was able to focus on the older boy problem, the younger boy problem, and trainings. The year also gave him time to make changes at camp that fit better with his vision of what a solid summer camp program should look like. Willhite's vision was expressed clearly in *Jet Trails*, the Council

303

newsletter, now named after the Jet Potter Service Center,

> Summer camp... is the climax of the troop's year-round pro-
> gram. In this Boy Scout training center, boys live Scouting's
> ideal, participate as members of a patrol, make strides in their
> personal growth, and have opportunities for advancement and
> other meaningful programs. With a trained camp staff, the
> summer camp helps the troop, the patrol, and the individual
> Boy Scout. The summer camp experience strengthens the
> troop by providing a goal toward which the troop can strive to
> prepare throughout the year.

Willhite's plan then was simple: build a strong summer camp program that
brings the scouts back every year and plug in the peripheral activities—the
adult training and the experiences for Cub Scouts and more older boys. It was
a big job and there was little money available to do. But it was nothing a
thrifty Scout could not handle.[55]

First, Willhite promoted summer camp. Beginning in January 1977, a
Camp Promotions team was put together in each district. These teams, which
often included former or current staff members, visited troops, gave slide
presentations, and "sold" summer camp. In keeping with Willhite's idea to
keep summer camp focused on the needs of the scoutmaster and his scout, the
teams went to the troops directly. Each promotions team was encouraged to
set up Family Night events that brought parents to a regular troop meeting
when the slides were shown. With all materials provided by the Council, these
promoters made the hard sell, pushing the facilities and the activities at camp
in a forty-five minute presentation that covered all the bases and answered
questions. All across the Council in February and March, these events were
happening. And they were successful enough that they continued well into the
1980s. The slideshows eventually turned into VHS video presentations when
a seven-minute promotional video was made for the 1987 season. To sweeten
the deal, early registration t-shirts, patches, or hats became part of the promotional pitch.[56]

Indeed, the Council newsletter *Jet Trails* joined in the promotion. In addition to publishing simple updates, like how many sites were still available and when fees were due for the summer, *Jet Trails* began publishing articles that sold camping to its Scouting audience. According to *Jet Trails*, camping performed a number of functions. It was "a creative, educational experience in cooperative living... [that] utilizes the resources of the natural surroundings to contribute significantly to physical, mental, spiritual, and social growth." Camping also promoted "good health... aids in spiritual development... [and] is an experience in citizenship training..." Boxwell offered everything a youth, a leader, or a parent could want.[57]

Next, camp set up transformed. Generally, the camp staff did a great deal of this work, putting up tents, moving cots and mattresses into those tents, and setting out trash barrels and all the grunt work necessary to get camp ready to go for the summer. Some evidence exists that the Order of the Arrow periodically used the Spring Ordeal to aid in this work, but the assistance was not consistent and it was not Council-wide. Willhite, working with Howard Olson, the Lodge Advisor, brought together all the local Spring Ordeals into one large Lodge Ordeal at Boxwell the weekend before Staff Week began. Willhite began hiring a "Bull Crew," or "Bull Gang" as he often called it, to come out the week before staff week to set up tents. Cots and mattresses were put out and general camp clean up was accomplished by the Ordeal the weekend before Staff Week. The Ordeal members left Sunday morning and the staff rolled in for a new summer Sunday afternoon.[58]

With the heavy lifting of camp set up complete and a staff now available to do the rest of the work, Willhite could now focus on his next innovation: a red staff hat. Ed Human had introduced the staff hat concept to Boxwell in 1972 with a green hat. He continued in 1973 with a red hat. Both had simple circular patches on them, but no designs. Human ultimately abandoned the hats though. As Russ Parham explained, "I recall Ed Human saying something to the effect that these [hats] lead to inflated egos by the staff so he

For the Good of the Program

dropped the idea in 1974." For Human, the hats promoted elitism.[59]

For Willhite, the red hat was a morale builder; it helped create his team. He had red hats donated from the Murfreesboro Co-op and had his wife Marie sew on the patch. The hat by itself was not enough; there needed to be an understanding about the terms of the hat in order for it to be special. "Every boy who worked on the staff wanted the red hat," Willhite explained. "And we had a special patch made each year... [A] boy on the front end, he understood that if he didn't live up to what we set at the starting of camp, as far as the rules and regulations, his cap would be confiscated; he could be sent home... That was the most revered thing of the camp staff." Staff Member Lance Ussery probably articulated this reverence behind the hat best. "There are guys that I could call right now that wore that red hat," Ussery explained, "and I wouldn't have to give them any information. 'I need help. Here's where I am.' And they'd come." The hats were a symbol of a bond between a band of brothers.[60]

From here, Willhite turned to program itself. Some of the changes were small; some had incredibly long-term consequences. Each week of camp dedicated to a specific district was ended; troops could come on the week most convenient for them. Doctors no long performed in-person medical rechecks. It was up to the troop leadership to make sure the paperwork was in order. The Commissioner system was jettisoned; the Activity Yard returned as a program area. Thus, instead of four small staffs scattered around the camp all teaching the same thing, the Activity Yard (AY) served as one central program area teaching all the same material, such as Camping, Cooking, Pioneering, Signaling, Orienting, and First Aid. This was arguably a cost-saving measure (one staff instead of four), but it clearly had program benefits as well by putting all these skills in one location with one director to lead. Further, with the end of electricity the year before and the end of the Commissioners, there was no longer any logic sense in keeping the staff together in one large staff area. For those who were not already near their program areas, like the Trading Post and

Handicraft, staff sites were created around the camps, breaking up the staff, but building smaller, more cohesive units closer to the areas where they worked.[61]

New programs were introduced in 1977 as well. The first was a bead program for younger Scouts. A Scout could earn a different colored bead for the completion of different tasks. The idea was not fundamentally different from the beads that Cub Scouts earned for the same type of accomplishments or even young Boy Scouts working on their Skill Awards. The skills were fairly simple as the program was geared toward first year campers. A Scout earned a bead for starting a fire with flint and steel (red bead), exploring a nature trail (green bead), tying the knots needed for Camping Skill Award (brown bead), shooting at the archery or rifle range (black bead), or completing a two hour service project (white bead). The program's goals were painfully obvious: it provided quick rewards for simple tasks. Further, it was easily expandable with different colored beads over succeeding years. Indeed, the program would continue and expand through the 1984 season.[62]

The second program, one for older boys, was less detailed, but would ultimately grow into something far more successful. The program was rappelling, and it started quite humbly. A single line in the 1977 *Leaders' Guide* denoted its arrival: "Rappelling offered to those who want it." A similar message appeared in the 1978 *Guide*, adding only "at no additional charge." The qualifier here was important because in 1978, a rappelling tower was added to the Reservation. There was no merit badge tied to this activity; it was purely recreational. In the afternoons at 4pm when all the merit badge sessions were over, a free rappel was held, first at the old water tower, then at the new rappelling tower. And the tower itself was nothing spectacular. At approximately forty feet tall, it was little more than four telephone poles with a wall of planks to rappel down and a set of stairs with which to get to the top. As unimpressive as this was, by 1982, a second shorter tower was added nearby, specifically noted as a "rock climbing tower."[63]

307

A third program re-thought how summer camp could be used. By definition, Boxwell was a Boy Scout camp and thus the summer camp program
focused on Boy Scouts. Understanding that Cub Scouts were "feeders" for Boy
Scouts and thus summer camp, Willhite developed special programs for Cub
Scouts—Bobcats, Wolfs, and Bears—and Webelos. Beginning in April 1977,
Boxwell would host a Webelo and father's weekend. The event was very
straight forward—day camping on Saturday, cooking over an open fire, an OA
led campfire program Saturday night, and then out by noon on Sunday. The
main advantage to such an event at Boxwell was the "Show and Do Trail."
The trail was a small program area with a model campsite to demonstrate the
highlights of Scout camping: a knife and ax display, a cooking demonstration,
a Native American dance team, marksmanship, fishing, and canoe demonstrations. There would even be church services Sunday morning. And while technically outside of summer camp, the timing was critical. April would be right
before Webelos crossed over into Boy Scouts in May. A good experience in
April would bring more Scouts to camp in June and July. The event proved
successful enough to continue the following year.[64]

Young Cubs got to go camping at Boxwell too. The first "Lad and
Dad" event was held at Stahlman. Unlike the Webelos event, Cubs were so
young they needed some extra help, so this excursion was held on weekend in
the middle of summer camp, the last weekend in June. This meant the Cubs
could arrive Saturday after the regular troops left, move into a site with tents
and beds, and basically get an introductory overnight camping experience. Saturday dinner and Sunday breakfast were provided in the dining hall with the
program consisting of "fishing, archery, hiking, swimming, campfire, boating,
canoeing, and rifle range." All of this was aided by the camp staff, which was
required to stay over the weekend to work this event. The cost was minimal--
$10 for a father and son—but proved very successful. 900 "Lads and Dads"
attended in 1977. Thus, the program not only continued the following summer, but by its third summer in 1979, it expanded to two weekends during

summer camp and took place at both Boy Scout camps. Eventually renamed "Cub and Partner" to reflect changing family realities, the program remained in place until the opening of CubWorld in 1996.[65]

The final significant change that Willhite made in 1977 was to the Scoutmaster's supper. There had been a special dinner during the Akers years. The meal was generally limited to just Scoutmasters and steak or barbeque chicken were the main course. The event was usually held under a large oak tree down below Stahlman Dining hall, though there were years it was held up at the Crippled Crab. Willhite, along with Tolbert, decided to move the event to Ittabeena, now known as either Akers' Cabin or the Training Center. The new location gave leaders "a chance 'to get away from it all,' and sit back to enjoy a scrumptious steak dinner." The dinner was open to any adult leader in camp, not just Scoutmasters, and held every week, at first on Thursday and later on Tuesday night. Willhite prepared and cooked the steaks personally, while Tolbert talked with the leaders and the leaders talked back. In short, the supper served as an appreciation event, an opportunity for fellowship, and a chance for leaders to voice their opinions. In true Willhite fashion, the steaks were donated by different groups, including Shoney's Inc. Willhite estimated that he cooked over 22,000 steaks during his tenure as Reservation Director.[66]

Despite what appears to be a number of changes, the core summer camp program was not significantly different from what it had been in 1960 or even in 1949. Specific program areas taught merit badges that fell within that area's theme. The slate of merit badges had not changed in any significant way. There were still campfires on Sunday and Friday night, still baseball and volleyball games in the afternoon. There was still a free swim at the Waterfront and free shoot at the Rifle Range in the afternoon. In other words, Willhite's goal was not to radically transform the program, but instead shore up the weak areas so that camp would be stronger in the future.[67]

Accomplishing these goals required a responsible staff. Unlike 1976, in 1977 Willhite got to choose his own staff, holding interviews for returning staff in February and new staff applicants in March. At the top of his leadership hierarchy were the program directors at Stahlman and, in 1977, Craig: Russ Parham and Ernie Ragsdale. For Parham, 1977 was his first truly legitimate summer as Program Director, having been thrown into the role after Garland Russell walked the previous year. Still fresh faced at 22 years old, Parham was a Tennessee Tech student who had worked his way up the Stahlman hierarchy. He started in 1970 in the Kitchen and eventually became a Commissioner under the Commissioner system. When he became Stahlman's Program Director in 1976, he was the youngest program director in the history of the camp. Parham understood camp and Scouting. Indeed, his background in computer science made him a stickler for details, though he did play the practical joke from time to time as a younger staff member. However, Parham was not a disciplinarian, a situation his age did not help.[68]

Ernie Ragsdale, however, was a very different personality. Ragsdale was thirty years old when he arrived at Boxwell in 1976 and he carried some life experience with him. He had been a Captain in the US Army during the Vietnam War and had the distinction of being the sole surviving member of a 850 man battalion that was ambushed in-country. He was awarded the Bronze Star for his service. But Ragsdale was not a solider, he was a teacher. He taught at several high schools in the mid-state area, including Carthage and Hendersonville, eventually ending up as the chemistry teacher at White House High School. He whittled and he loved practical jokes. And because he was a chemistry teacher, he was legendary at lighting campfires. In short, Ragsdale was an artist forced to be a science teacher. He had arrived at Boxwell in 1976 during Staff Week and took on the role of Field Sports Director. His loyalty in the walk out was rewarded with the leadership of Camp Craig in 1977.[69]

It should be noted that unlike Parham, who operated on his own in terms of navigating the challenges of leadership, Ragsdale was part of a team. Jim Barr, who had been Waterfront Director at Stahlman in 1976, hit it off

Ernie Ragsdale, Program Director at Camp Stahlman, 1988. Photo by Russ Parham.

with Ragsdale instantly in 1976. The two bonded and when Ragsdale moved to Craig in 1977, Barr went with him. The two men stayed in the Craig Program Director's Cabin, not at Murrey. The two loved pranks and were virtually inseparable. While the two made life for Parham difficult in 1976 with incessant teasing, given their own camp in 1977 they thrived. As Barr explained, both he and Ragsdale were "clowns," so dining hall program became a special area of entertainment. They both showed off.

A simple example of the Barr-Ragsdale chemistry could be seen with the Sunday night campfire at Camp Craig in these years. Craig's Sunday Night Campfire was in a large bowl-shaped depression. During their tenure at Craig, Ragsdale's staff would call on the fire gods to light the fire. The idea of calling on a fire god to light the campfire was not a new idea. However, wearing a monkey mask and driving into the pit on a motorcycle while wearing the mask was a new twist! Ragsdale would drive his motorcycle into the pit with Barr in a monkey mask as the fire god. Using black powder and a homemade napalm developed by Ragsdale, the fire was lit at the appropriate moment, exploding in an impressive fireball. It was loud, showy, and spectacular. It was Ragsdale and Barr.[70]

Willhite let the program directors run their own shops, but it almost seemed as if the camps themselves dictated the programs. Stahlman was the Reservation's first camp. It was established, it was known. This was Parham's camp. Parham preferred the rules and was himself a workaholic. He had also grown up in the camp staff tradition, at Stahlman no less. He had worked under Akers and Ed Human. His approach to program was to maintain these traditions. Ragsdale and Barr had no such roots and, really, neither did Camp Craig. Barr had worked in 1975 at the tail end of the Akers era, but Ragsdale started under Willhite. Neither man was bound by the "way things used to be done." Their Camp Craig was often irreverent. When Camp Director Hugh Travis showed up on Barr's Waterfront in his Class A Uniform while Barr was painting the docks during Staff Week, Barr literally kicked Travis in the backside into the lake because Travis clearly had not come down to work. Ragsdale could often be found carving something, either for staff or Scoutmasters as a gift or award. A Scoutmaster's Horseshoe Award was camp favorite. Barr put great emphasis on hand painted paddles as awards for the troop that won the Water Carnival. It was a looser, more personal experience, reflecting the work-in-progress that was Camp Craig itself.[71]

Perhaps not surprisingly, given a young program director at one camp and youthful pranksters at the other, it was during the mid to late 1970s, when Scoutmasters became concerned about camp. Specifically, they were concerned about standards. "Standards" here meant how the staff was behaving and how that behavior affected the program. Under aged staff went out regularly, not just one night a week. Hair was grown out, longer than the above the collar rule of earlier generations. Uniforming was lax. There were rumors that women sometimes stayed over in staff sites. But most importantly, quality of instruction was poor. The facilities may still have been first rate, but the rumors were that the staff and the program were lacking.[72]

These were not issues that would transform overnight, but in 1979 a chain of events unfolded that reset the board of Willhite's Boxwell. The first domino to fall was, ironically, Camp Stahlman itself. While Craig and then Parnell had both closed as part of the "camp rest" program, Stahlman had not. In 1979, it was Stahlman's turn in the rotation and thus, the camp closed. This created some interesting side effects. First and foremost, Stahlman had the only working kitchen on the Reservation. So, while the camp could be closed and most of its operations moved, the Schleichers and their kitchen staff had to stay behind and continue to prepare all the meals for the Reservation. This also meant that *all* of the Reservation's food was transported to the satellite camps. The decision proved disastrous. Only one food truck—the trivary truck—transporting all the food to three locations was a scheduling nightmare. Further, Stahlman kitchen still required a youth staff for cleaning and some basic food preparation. But without an active camp going on there, there was nothing for these youth to do in their off hours. In short, the logistics of closing Stahlman proved so burdensome, everyone realized it was mistake. It would never be done again.[73]

The second domino involved the camp staffs. Obviously, if Stahlman closed, Stahlman staff had to go somewhere else. That somewhere else was Camp Parnell, which was reopened after a two year rest. Craig remained open for a third year. Thus, Parham moved with Stahlman staff to Parnell, while Ragsdale and Barr remained at Craig. The close proximity of the two groups created some tension as the Waterfronts instigated an escalating series of pranks. The pranks culminated in the Craig waterfront sinking Parnell canoes in the lake; Parnell staff—formerly Stahlman staff—retaliated by throwing railroad ties from the Craig Friday Night Campfire area into the lake. Parnell Bay was shallow enough the swamped canoes could be retrieved. The same could not be said of crossties thrown in the lake at Camp Craig. Willhite fired

Parnell's waterfront staff and Barr picked up extra responsibilities as their new director. 1979 was not a good summer at Boxwell.[74]

Thus, the summer of 1980 presented some interesting opportunities. Parham had graduated from college and moved to a new full time job. He would not be able to return as Program Director, but he did begin a seventeen year run as Business Manager. Parham's retirement was important because had he asked for Parnell Staff to return to Stahlman, Willhite undoubtedly would have done so, leaving Craig Staff to move to Parnell. Instead, because Parham was not returning, Willhite approached Ragsdale and Barr about how they would like to proceed. There were a few factors to consider, according to Barr:

> We kicked it back and forth. We didn't like the rock. We
> didn't like the campsites. We liked the convenience of the way
> that Stahlman was laid out, where the trading post is, where
> the dining hall is, and the waterfront. You kinda had the
> whole nine yards right there. You know, field sports was still
> not out of the way too much, and so you—just the way the
> camp laid out, we liked that better than we did Parnell, too.

Additionally, Stahlman had the Schleichers, who by this point had warmed up to Ragsdale and Barr and prepared them special foods upon request. Barr also detested Parnell waterfront. Unlike Stahlman and Craig Waterfronts, which were both either close to or on the Cumberland River, Parnell Waterfront was in an enclosed bay. There was no circulation and the water become warmer and warmer as the summer continued. Barr was not interested in another summer of that environment. And so it was decided: The Craig staff became the Stahlman staff. The Great Staff Switch was complete.[75]

The summer of 1980 also brought new players to the table. With Parham now Business Manager, Parnell needed a new Program Director. Into this void stepped Perry Bruce, who had worked on Parnell staff from 1971 to 1975, serving as a Commissioner and in the Trading Post. He had even worked briefly as District Executive in 1975 for about six months. When

Jerry Barnett, Brian Wood, and Larry Green (l-r) outside the Program Director's cabin at Camp Parnell, 1981. Photo by Russ Parham.

Willhite was without a program director in the spring of 1980, Bruce was between jobs and became the natural pick. It was under Bruce that the clean-up began. A single staff night for those under eighteen was reinstituted at both camps. For Bruce, instituting some standards "was our major concern."

Bruce was not working alone to achieve these goals in Parnell. Indeed, Bruce recalled that fortunately when he returned there "were two or three areas" he did not need to worry about. His Camp Director, District Executive Buff Groth, promised to look after the Kitchen and any of the physical needs the camp may have, such as looking after the showerhouses and extra platforms a site might need from week to week. Parham of course would keep an eye on the Trading Posts. His unusual late night hours and distance from the staff in this new position gave him an authority he had lacked as Program Director.

This left the program areas and while there may have been some issues elsewhere, the Activity Yard was under control. The Activity Yard Director was a man named Jerry Barnett.[76]

Tall, thin, and lanky, Barnett's return in 1980 was actually his third tour at Boxwell. He had started in 1965 in the Activity Yard at Stahlman, only to be moved to the Kitchen because he was needed there. He spent the last part of the 1960s in Vietnam, mostly as Military Police, before returning to camp again in 1970. He was Stahlman Kitchen Director that summer—a position he detested, though it allowed him to build good relationships with the Schleichers and one of his first year staff, a young Russ Parham. He returned as Commissioner in 1971 for the program's inaugural year and then left again, spending most of the 1970s as part of the Tennessee Highway patrol. He did not leave Scouting entirely. He and Parham had a troop together and he would occasionally serve as a provisional leader at camp if he was needed. Indeed, while not a staff member, Barnett was a regular at Parnell in 1979, often visiting the camp in his Highway Patrol uniform after his shift ended. Coming back to Boxwell as the Activity Yard Director was the job Barnett had always wanted.[77]

Of course, as had happened to him and several others before, the good of the program demanded he consider another position. Toward the end of the six weeks in 1980, Bruce landed a new full time position with U. S. Corps of Engineers. He had to begin that job while camp was still in session so Barnett picked up the program director's work, pulling double duty for the rest of the summer. Even then, he and Willhite never discussed the possibility of returning in that position. According to Barnett, he attended a meeting when someone asked Willhite who the program director was going to be. Willhite looked over at Barnett and said, "There's the boss sitting right there." This makes for a great story, but Parham suggested that Willhite had some trepidation about hiring Barnett. Barnett was a bit of an unknown to Willhite and he therefore did not have confidence in Barnett at first. Nevertheless, Willhite took the chance. According to Barr, the Three Musketeers had arrived.[78]

Barnett's personality was definitely a new variable in the equation. By the early 1980s, Ragsdale had calmed some. He was, as Barr explained, "never too serious about nothing." Barnett however "still had that State Trooper mentality." While Ragsdale could live with and could even encourage a certain level of chaos for the sake of creativity, Barnett wanted order from the madness. He wanted uniforming and a clean cut appearance in addition to high standards in instruction. And while Barnett commanded respect and adherence to his high standards, his influence was mostly paternal. "We were all Jerry's kids," Ron Bailey, another Parnell-Craig staff member, explained. "Jerry was the dad out there. He was the person you most wanted to please. The person you least wanted to offend or get in trouble with. It was basically just a great, big dad- figure out there." The laconic Tom Willhite probably summed up Barnett's impact best, .

> Jerry could manage a staff. And they loved him. Sometimes they didn't like him while he was working. But on the day came for them to go home, on the day camp closed, after we got all the work done, they were all crying and hugging on each other, loving each other because they had come together as a team, hated to see the camp end.[79]

Of course, Ragsdale and Barnett were both Vietnam vets and both struggled with their experiences there. While Barnett believed Ragsdale was "probably one of the most laid back war veterans I ever met," both men struggled with Post-Traumatic Stress Disorder. Ragsdale was haunted by the surprise attack on his unit of which he was the only survivor. He rarely discussed the event, but apparently his survival was pure chance. On the day of the attack, he had been at the back of the column; the day before he had been at the front. At camp, Ragsdale and Barr stayed in the Program Director's cabin at Stahlman. In the night, when Barr would leave the cabin to make his way to Showerhouse I for the restroom, he always took a canoe paddle with him. Ragsdale had actually taken a swing at Barr upon his return one night, but had no recollection of it. Barr was going to defend himself. Ragsdale's PTSD did manifest from time to time regardless of how well he appeared to handle it most days.[80]

Barnett also struggled with PTSD. He was known to fly into a rage in a moment's notice, often over a simple incident. Whether these fits were simply theatrics to make a point or his PTSD, the behavior became known as a "BP"—a Barnett Panic. This trauma also manifested in much simpler ways. Parnell-Craig staff member John Estes recalled the ways Barnett struggled with his trauma: "In '83, when Mike [Brown] and I hired on, Jerry was going through some very hard times, dealing with some repressed memories of his experience in Vietnam... he couldn't sleep. He might get an hour's sleep a night and the rest of the time, he walked the trails at night." Barnett himself admitted that his PTSD led him to alcohol and it was 1984 before he became sober. In 1986, he did not return to camp for a summer to get therapy for his PTSD. The therapy would eventually lead him to a Master's degree in Psychology and becoming a counselor to others struggling with the disorder.[81]

But this experience led to some common threads in program as well. Both men made uniforming an issue. Flag ceremonies were important as well. As a staff member, you were not late to flag raising or flag lowering. To insure compliance, both men instituted a common clock. At Stahlman, this was "Ernie Time"; at Craig and Parnell, it was "Jerry Barnett Standard Time." Both men put great emphasis on campfires. Ragsdale was personally involved in the explosives and setting off the charges to light a campfire. He became nationally known for his work, lighting the campfires at three National Jamborees. Barnett was also interested in the closing ceremonies, particularly on Friday night, making sure the correct tone was set. For Parnell and Craig, the closing campfire generally employed staff in canoes with torches, each reciting a point of the Scout law. With the benefit of Explorer Island in the background, Parnell utilized the image of a burning eagle as the capstone to Barnett's "Scout Values" campfire.[82]

Both men brought program innovations as well. As campfires were an important program component for Ragsdale, he needed a place to showcase them correctly. So, in 1985, he and his staff built an enormous stage out of crossties at the Friday Night Campfire Area. As Activity Yard Staff member Andy Whitt recalled, these ties were "not your normal little landscaping railroad cross ties. They were probably every bit of foot and a half to two feet wide. Because they're big and no telling how long. At least 10 to 15 feet in length or so. They were big, heavy things." In this same period, Ragsdale engineered and Ranger Willie Claud welded a fencing grid for a Burning Eagle closing. Rolled up and diesel soaked canvas was rolled into stripes and laid out in the shape of an Eagle. The grid was on Explorer Island, just opposite the Friday Night Campfire area. At the appropriate moment at the end of the fire, the Eagle was lit and burned through the campfire's closing. Indeed, a similar closing was developed at Parnell, where an Eagle grid on Explorer Island could be utilized as well. With the addition of the Weaver Amphitheater, both camps began doing an elaborate joint campfire every year for July Fourth. In 1985, this new program involved not only a patriotic campfire program, but ended with an enormous Burning Flag further down the hill. Built by Barnett's Parnell staff, this closing worked on the same principles as the Burning Eagles, but it was quite a bit larger and had to be raised from the ground since a permanent frame was not an option.

Parnell and Craig staff also brought new dining hall programs. The Activity Yard in particular utilized blue milk crates to build castles and other structures in the night that would amaze Scouts when they showed up for breakfast in the morning. Both camps began incorporating more popular culture songs into their dining hall repertoire, like the "Oscar Meyer Weiner" song from the hot dog commercial or the theme songs from *Gilligan's Island.* Both staffs also began dining hall program that involved utilizing the aluminum and paper pull-off box tops to the single serve cereal boxes. According to whichever staff member started the joke that week, if enough of the box tops could be collected, they could be used to buy a boat or sending someone to college! Parnell and Craig also began executing "tree checks" at lunch, which involved the staff en masse running out of the dining hall, running in front of the windows "counting" the trees in camp before returning in for a report. By the mid-1980s, Willhite's Boxwell program was firing on all cylinders as Ragsdale and Barnett ran their camps.[83]

The best example of the two men's different approaches was seen with take-down. Putting camp together every year was roughly a two week process. A crew spent a week putting up tents, then the OA Ordeal did more set up work over the weekend, and then the staff arrived to set up program areas and finish getting the campsites and common areas ready. Take-down torn down the entire camp—program areas, tents, cots and mattresses, trash barrels, every-thing—and packed it all up and stored it in less that twenty-four hours. De-pending on the year and the camp, this might involve moving material literally across the Reservation to have it ready for the next summer. It was an intense, end of camp blitz. The actual work done in both camps was not that different. For instance, both camps started the work Friday night after campfire, usually working late into the night to hopefully make Saturday shorter.[84]

However, how Ragsdale and Barnett ended the process was telling. For Ragsdale, there was no end-of-camp meeting. The goal was to finish the work and get out. As Andy Whitt explained, "We all really enjoyed each other but after 6 (or more) weeks living together, we were ready to get out of there ASAP." This was in fitting with Ragsdale's approach. He allowed a lot of flexibility, a lot of individualism, and expected a lot of personal responsibility. He rewarded that by not belaboring this point: when you were done with take-down, you could go. Barnett's approach was completely the opposite. When an individual's work was done, he found another crew to work with. No one left until everyone was done and the work was completed. If parents showed up, they waited. And at the end, there was a big group meeting. Directors were usually given some sort of recognition—likely a hand carved plaque of by

*William "Green Bar Bill" Hillcourt and Claus "Dutch" Mann at Camp Craig, 1986.
Personal Collection of Dutch Mann.*

woodworking master Dutch Mann when he was working--and Barnett gave a version of the same speech every year. "This staff will never be together again. This group of people will never exist again," he would say. "The circle is broken. The hat is now yours." This circle idea was central to Barnett's philosophy: they were all in this together and camp only functioned when they all pulled their weight.[85]

Amusingly, much like siblings trying to be the favorite of the parent, both Barnett and Ragsdale seemed to be locked in a competition with each other for Willhite's praise. Despite solid work from both, each felt that Willhite preferred the other. Barr pulled no punches on this point. "[Ragsdale] used to think Tom [Willhite] gave Jerry [Barnett] whatever he

321

wanted to have for the Program. His favorite saying was, "Tom gives me two #10 cans and a string of binder's—a roll of binder's twine and tells me to put on a Program over here." For Barnett, the opposite was true. Ragsdale had "endeared himself [to Willhite] when they had the great walkout of senior staff members." Ragsdale's loyalty to Willhite in 1976 created a bond that Barnett felt he could never match. Willhite, of course, played the situation like any good parent. Privately, he may have had a favorite, but publicly he liked them both equally. "We had some outstanding years during the years of Ernie Ragsdale and Jerry Barnett," recalled the Reservation Director.[86]

Perhaps the greatest symbol of how far Boxwell had rebounded came in 1986, when Scouting living legend William "Green Bar Bill" Hillcourt came to Boxwell. Scout Executive Tolbert had run into Hillcourt at a meeting and Hillcourt essentially invited himself to Boxwell. So, the first week of summer camp in June 1986, Camp Craig hosted the legend. Hillcourt was fairly active during his visit. With Lance Ussery, he laid out a reservation wide Orienteering course. He signed Scout Handbooks. He encouraged pioneering projects. Indeed, for the staff, Hillcourt's arrival was a godsend. To make sure the camp looked good, Willhite finally loosened up on the purse strings. For the first time, staff actually got real rope—un-manila—to use for their pioneering projects. Some spools disappeared for later summers in case this generosity did not continue! New pioneering poles were cut as well. Hillcourt's visit also brought a new song to Boxwell: "Bananas, Coconuts, and Grapes," a simple song of four repeating lines that got louder on every delivery. To be visited by such a Scouting luminary was a seminal moment. To meet Hillcourt was to be one step removed from Baden-Powell himself.[87]

With camp program now firmly in capable hands, Willhite could focus on other program that required his attention. Several ideas from earlier had taken root and needed more room to grow. Others had not done well and needed to be trimmed and let go. Most of these program pieces were happening on the periphery of the core summer camp program, though there were some with direct connections.

The Cub Scout experiments had done well. The weekend camping for Webelos had done well enough to require an upgrade. Beginning in 1983, Boxwell hosted a Webelos Week. The "week" was actually two back-to-back sessions of completely different Webelos Scouts. The week ran in July at Camp Stahlman after the regular summer camp session was over. The sessions were packed. *Jet Trails* explained, "The Webelos will be able to take advantage of the summer camp facilities, tents, staff and programs. The programs will include canoeing, swimming, nature, Scoutcraft, rifle, archery, fishing, camp- fires and the dining hall with eight great family-style meals. There will be hikes and other opportunities to work on a number of activities badges." In later years, the week would be condensed down into one session. Nevertheless, Webelos Camp continued from at least 1983 to 1986.[88]

With an expansion of Cub Camping—both Webelos Week and the Lad and Dad Weekends—came an expansion of Cub leader training. The first outdoors training for Webelos leaders came in October 1981. The course was "designed to teach adult leaders how to plan and conduct outdoor activities for Webelos." The overnight program offered skills training in "knife and ax safe- ty, fire-building, camp site selection, field sanitation, cooking, campfire plan- ning and other basic skills used in leading Webelos boys." Another such pro- gram was held in October 1984. In 1986, "in response to the request of many Cub and Scout leaders," a Den Chief Conference was held at Boxwell over a weekend in June. Of course, all of these events had small charges attached to them.[89]

As successful as the Cub expansion was, it could not hold a candle to the continued popularity of the rappelling activities. By the early 1980s, Willhite became aware of an actual, formal program known as the Challenging Outdoor Physical Encounter, or C.O.P.E (pronounced "cope"). C.O.P.E. was a team-building program for older boys that used ropes courses, both low course obstacles and high course elements like a zipline, to get Scouts to work together to overcome the literal hurdles, while encouraging individual achievement. The program was considered "high adventure," which meant it was only open to boys over fourteen years of age. C.O.P.E. took the rappelling activities to the next level by offering a fully developed, week-long program specifically for older boys. C.O.P.E. could be a proverbial "brass ring" that would bring older boys back to camp.

In this same period, around 1983, Billy Walker, an Assistant Scoutmaster of Troop 137 in Franklin, Tennessee, had been out to Philmont with his troop. Philmont Scout Ranch had the first permanent C.O.P.E. course in the nation, known as the "Dean Challenge." The course was not a large course, but the seed was planted. The idea matured with Walker, owner of Chevrolet Oldsmobile dealership, when he attended a dealers' conference in Florida and they participated in a C.O.P.E. course there. Walker was inspired: Middle Tennessee Council needed a C.O.P.E. course of its own. Walker approached Wilhite about the idea. Along with two other interest volunteers, Carl Hyland and Al Hendrickson, the group began investigating other courses and what was needed for Middle Tennessee. Walker was the chairman and in charge of the fundraising. But as Walker admitted, "I never was too good at asking for money." After securing a $1000 donation from the Rotary Club, Walker funded the rest of the development himself.[90]

In 1985, Billy Walker's Boxwell C.O.P.E. was born. Willhite and Hyland did a great deal of the initial work on the course themselves with assistance from interested volunteers. There were over thirty obstacles to overcome for Scouts who would tackle the course in groups of ten. Even the names of the obstacles—Trio Traverse, Nitro Crossing, Meat Grinder, Giant's Ladder, Noggin Knocker—suggested a sense of adventure not found in the regular camp program. The C.O.P.E. program had seven goals: leadership, self-esteem, decision-making, problem solving, communication, teamwork, and trust. As C.O.P.E. staff member and later Director Lance Ussery explained,

On the left, Boxwell's original (abandoned) rappelling tower in 2002. On the right, the Al Hendrickson tower in 1995. Photos by Kerry Parker.

"It's still the patrol method... [N]o one person is successful. We have to be successful as a team, as a group." Sometimes this meant standing back and letting the Scouts fail in their first attempts to master an obstacle. It always meant being aware of your resources, knowing what the members of your team had to offer. As an added bonus, adults were allowed to participate as well, but they were not allowed to talk. The Scouts had to figure out the problems themselves. And though an extra fee was required for the program, it was clear where that money was going: back into C.O.P.E. and its staff. Completion of the course was considered a significant accomplishment with a certificate and an "I Survived C.O.P.E." t-shirt awarded by C.O.P.E. staff to the participants at flag lowering assembly on Friday afternoons.[91]

Once established, C.O.P.E. continued to grow. By 1987, new elements were added, again with exotic names like the Chicken Coop and Wild

Woozey. By 1990, work began on a new rappelling tower. As described above, the new tower was a major improvement and one of the few genuinely new capital improvements of the Willhite years. Completely enclosed and roofed, it could support rappelling down two walls. And with the top floor at approximately sixty-five feet up, when the tower was completed in 1991, it was the tallest building on the Reservation, even allowing for a view above the trees of Camp Light. Around this same time, Advanced C.O.P.E. was added to the program. To participate, Scouts had to have already completed C.O.P.E. the previous summer. They would learn more technical skills and assist with rappels. By 1995, a decade into existence, C.O.P.E. was indisputably the favorite program of older scouts.[92]

C.O.P.E. was not only a winning program, it was a model for a winning formula. It offered something to older Scouts to keep them coming back to back camp even after their prime advancement years were over. Because the skills of team-building and leadership were not simply Scouting specific, the program could also be utilized by outside groups, both non-profit and corporate, meaning a new revenue stream for the Council. And the program and facility had a patron saint—in this case Billy Walker—who continued to financially support the namesake program long after the initial investment. C.O.P.E. was the holy grail of a non-profit program.

Aside from C.O.P.E., the most important program geared toward older Scouts during Willhite's tenure was the arrival of Brownsea II. Pronounced "Brownsea Double Two," but generally just referred to as "Brownsea," the program was a new youth leadership training event rolled out by the National Council. As part of the late 1970s drive to pull Scouting away from its urban expansion, Brownsea was the crown jewel of the National Council's "back to basics" program. The program focused on outdoor skills and tried to rectify some of the oversights of the Skills Awards program, such as a Scout not having to take a hike before the rank of First Class. For Boxwell, Brownsea II would be held July 31—August 5, 1978 and would

> parallel as closely as possible Sir Baden Powell's first Scout camp... Each boy will wear that first Scout hat ("Smoky the Bear"), carry a stave that can be used for measuring distances and finding directions, and have the special "eye tooth" commitment symbol. He will have a distinctive scarf and wear a brown and gold segment for the rest of his Scouting career with the words "Brownsea."

At the end of the course, not only were parents and Scoutmasters invited to a concluding feast, but so too were members of the Executive Board. This was a big event.[93]

After the initial hoopla faded, Brownsea stuck around. It went through slightly different iterations—Brownsea Plus II in 1982 for instance—but at its heart it remained an outdoor skills centered, youth leadership program. In most respects, Brownsea was Wood Badge for youth. Whatever its name, the program continued through the 1980s into the 1990s, usually running for a week not long after the traditional summer camp ended. And it was often staffed by Boxwell staff members, either former staff who were returning to help out, like Steve Eubank and Perry Bruce, or active staff who just did not want to leave at the end of the summer, like Jerry Barnett, Russ Parham, Lance Ussery, and Jason Bradford. Indeed, Brownsea served as a training ground not only for troop leadership, but for future staff members as well. For example, scouts Josh Sain and Ben Whitehouse both cut their teeth on Brownsea staff before joining the Boxwell staff.[94]

While C.O.P.E. and Brownsea were both successful, other older boy centered program ideas failed. In 1979, two older boy programs were introduced. One was "Super Adventure Week." This was a special week held at Boxwell after the traditional camping sessions had ended on July 21. Open to any registered Scout over 14 years old, "Adventure Camp" included "Fishing in catfish pond, rappelling, orienteering, water sports above and beyond, pioneering projects, competition and super Scout games. Outdoor excitement and Scouting advancement are only two of the opportunities that are waiting in this action packed week at camp." To participate, a Scout had to have orienteering, cooking, pioneering, and camping merit badges. And, as the program was held after summer camp, regular camping equipment including a backpack and hiking boots were required. The program was apparently a spectacular failure as it was never mentioned again.[95]

The other 1979 innovation was an idea that happened during camp. Lacking a formal name, this idea was to hold special afternoon sessions for older Scouts "away from the regular camp." There were events planned every day, including a special Pioneering project, an Old West themed day with black powder and arrowhead making, outdoor cooking and rappelling, and even a "sweat lodge (like Indians of old)"! On Friday, the participants would demonstrate to other campers what they had been doing. The program was only open to those over 14 years of age and because it was an afternoon program, the participants could still take merit badges in the morning. And like Super Adventure Week, it did not survive.[96]

However, by 1984, elements of both of these ideas were remixed, re-branded, and re-tried as "Above and Beyond." A program for boys 14 years old and older, "Above and Beyond" was a camp away from camp. After arriving at Boxwell on Sunday, participants took a canoe trip on Monday to their campsite "away from camp." Here they prepared their camp, built their shelters, and received an orientation, not totally unlike a Wilderness Survival merit badge overnight trip, but longer. Each day had events. Tuesday kept the Native Americans theme with a sweat lodge, trap and snare methods, fire building, and fishing and gigging. Wednesday focused on wilderness tool making and orienteering work, while Thursday was pioneer themed. Scouts learned how to load and shoot black powder, stalk animals, and skin and clean small game, as well as how to cook over an open fire. Friday had rappelling—demonstrating Scouts had not gone *that* far away—before a return to their respective camps. The program was limited to twenty scouts.[97]

"Above and Beyond" enjoyed enough success a return was planned in 1985. However, some of the details changed, most notably that the program was going to be held on a specific week (June 2-7) and at a specific location, Parish Wilderness Reservation, formerly the Rock Island Boxwell. The number of participants was also increased from twenty to seventy-five. With a whole camp and a whole week to work with, the schedule of "Above and Beyond" had to change too. Sunday night added an opening campfire and Monday focused on one of the Rock Island area's wilderness strengths: caves. Tuesday had a canoeing overnight campout. The frog gigging moved to Wednesday night and rappelling moved to Thursday. Raccoon hunting was added to Thursday and the pioneer day of all things black powder moved to Friday. After all of this, the program was cancelled in 1985. Schools did not let out until June 7 that year, so there were no Scouts and no staff. The program returned in 1986, though it moved to the end of the summer (July 20-26) where it remained through 1988. "Above and Beyond" was discontinued at this point.[98]

Just as the youth were getting training to carry on the Scouting program, so too were the adults. Willhite's Boxwell offered a slew of adult leader training. And just like the youth training, the adult versions were usually on the weekend and usually for a small fee. And there was *a lot* of adult training. There was the Triple-T training, led by Dr. Carr Treherne and Gene Beck. There was the Camp Master Program in 1980, "designed to give a troop basic knowledge in campcraft skills, scouting games, and leadership corps training." There was outdoors training for Webelos leaders. There was a Den Chief Training open to adults. By 1990, there was youth protection training for every adult leader.[99]

And of course, there was Wood Badge. Wood Badge remained the premier outdoor training experience for adult leaders. It was "Back to Basics" before "Back to Basics" was cool. Thus, the program enjoyed a bit of a renaissance in these years as a new group of dedicated Scouters formed a closely knit

329

Wood Badge staff. By Willhite's time, the Wood Badge staff had settled into their new home in Camp Light with its small man-made pond stocked with catfish and Israeli carp. The new location was christened "Camp Beany Elam," after the Father of Middle Tennessee Wood Badge, Harry "Beany" Elam. But the staff wanted a permanent facility of some kind at the location, a place to store their equipment and to hold trainings in poor weather. It was from this desire that the Wood Badge shed was eventually built in 1984, as described above.[100]

But even this program had to adapt in these lean years. Historically, Wood Badge had been a week long program. In short, if a leader was going to participate, he had to take a week off of work. After taking time off for either his family or his troop to come up during the camp season, this additional week was a big ask. The Council had experimented with weekend courses in the early 1970s as a way to manage the influx of leaders. There was a weekend only course in the Spring, but still the full week course in the fall. But by the late 1970s, as the number of adult volunteers dropped, the weekend only approach looked more reasonable. By 1979, weekend courses in the fall became the new standard. Occasionally a week-long course would be offered again, but they were no longer the norm.[101]

And finally, as had been done in earlier years, Willhite used the Reservation and its facilities to provide special programs to disabled Scouts and even some non-Scouts. Much like Camp Shape in the early 1970s, Boxwell hosted Explorer Post 151, which was a post of mentally disabled scouts from the Bailey School in Nashville. The Bailey School was an institution designed to teach the students how to hold a job out in the world, mainly assembly single-action jobs. The group began coming to Boxwell in 1979 and had stayed in the Murrey cabins. In 1981, they moved to Stahlman for a week of tent-camping. As Steve Perkins, the adult leader of the post explained, "Tents will be an interesting experience. We haven't done that before. For the vast majority, that will be the first time."[102]

Along those same lines, the Dede Wallace Center also served special needs kids. Instead of Stahlman though, the Dede Wallace Center rented out whichever camp—Craig or Parnell—that was closed that summer. And the children, aged 6 to 16, were a different kind of special needs, mostly with "moderate and mild behavior problems." The Center provided its own staff and its own program, which "work[ed] to modify behavior of the children by a system of points." The program handled a little over forty kids and was an annual event. It started as a day camp, but became the overnight program around 1976 and continued into the early 1980s. For the staff, the only responsibility was setting up the tents and cleaning up the camp after the group left.[103]

Interestingly, the big hit of all three trips was not the campfire and related Native American dancing; it was Head Ranger Willie Claud. When Claud arrived in his pick-up truck and announced he was looking for volunteers, the boys clamored for a space in the back. As Claud explained, "With this bunch I don't have to worry about volunteers. They don't mind working. You tell them to do something and they do it. I enjoy working with them. They appreciate everything you do for them. I kid around with them a lot." Claud's wife Betty was equally effusive, "[The boys] just thought Willie was something because he called 'em Sergeant of you know gave 'em a title of some kind and then he assigned 'em jobs to do. They like that."[104]

Toward the end of Willhite's run, he also had to deal with one more change to program from the National Council. In 1990, the Boy Scouts of America dropped Skill Awards and went back to simply using the rank requirements for the early ranks of Tenderfoot, Second Class, and First Class. In other words, the last vestige of the Improved Scouting Program was jettisoned and the Boy Scout program went back to how it had been during its first half century of life. It was the ultimate "back to basics" move.[105]

For Boxwell, this required some rethinking and it took several years

331

before the camp really came up with an adequate solution to the transition. Simply removing the Skill Awards themselves was not an enormous problem. The difficulty came in how that removal was handled. Instead of keeping all of the pieces where they were—Conservation requirements in the Con-Yard for instance—all of the pieces (except swimming) went to the Activity Yard. This program area swelled as a result, both in terms of the number of Scouts visiting the area, but also with the number of staff needed to handle the teaching load. From 1990-1992, the requirements were simply taught like a merit badge: First Class First Aid, Second Class Camping, Tenderfoot Nature, and so on. However, Barnett and Willhite were both interested in a First Year Camper Program.

The Davy Crockett Program, Boxwell's first attempt at a First Year Camper program, was rolled out in the summer of 1993. The program attempted to teach the patrol method by taking the scouts and placing them in patrols by rank. Staff members would serve as patrol leaders. Thus, most new Scouts would end up a Tenderfoot Patrol, which would then focus on Tenderfoot requirements throughout the week. If these were completed in a timely fashion, scouts could progress to Second Class requirements. Conceived as a two hour block, scouts could then take simple merit badges in either the afternoon or morning. Leaders were unhappy about losing the "menu approach" to rank requirements and some modifications were made. The program was shifted to allow scouts to take two ranks concurrently, one on the morning and a different one in the afternoon. Thus, a Scout could enter brand new at the start of the week and leave with two ranks in hand by the end. Davy Crockett was a first attempt at program designed for young Scouts and remained intact for the next few years.

By the early 1990s though, the Barnett-Ragsdale era was already coming to a close. Jim Barr was the first to leave. A near-drowning incident on the waterfront spooked him because he did not feel that he had responded quickly enough. The boy was safe, but Barr was rattled. 1987 was his last summer.

Ragsdale stayed for two more summers. He took 1990 off for Barr. Barr was going with his son's troop to another summer camp that summer. Ragsdale went along. Upon returning, Barr's mother was diagnosed with breast cancer and had a double mastectomy. Ragsdale stayed close by. The two men were that close. And then, that fall, at 43 years old, Ragsdale suffered a heart attack in the early morning hours of October 31 and passed away. Barr was devastated.[106]

After returning from his PTSD therapy and rehab in 1987, Barnett stayed on as Program Director for several more years. By 1992, he had secured a new position as a veterans' counselor at a place called Base Camp, where he was helping other vets through their trauma. By the summer, the elderly woman from whom Barnett rented was dying. The woman had known Barnett since his state trooper days and helped finance his graduate degree in Psychology. She had no close family, so Barnett stepped in to assist. Coupled with continuing unresolved mental health issues, the woman's passing led to Barnett's decision not to return to camp. Without any explanation to anyone but his closest friends, he did not return to Boxwell in 1993 and simply disappeared from that world for many years.[107]

Willhite still had a camp to run, so new faces stepped in. At Stahlman, for most of the early 1990s, Ragsdale-trained young men who had come up through the ranks served as Program Director. The first to serve was Brent Limbaugh in 1990. Though only a one summer man, Limbaugh had the support of long time Camp Commissioner Trent Craig and Camp Director *par excellence* Larry Green. Indeed, 1990 at Stahlman was Green's fourth run as a Camp Director, the only professional to have served in that role so many times. Retired Major Ralph Walker stepped in as Program Director in 1991, but his dismissal of Ragsdale's legacy the first summer after the latter's death was not well received by the Stahlman staff. In 1992 and 1993, Andy Whitt, who had also grown up under Ragsdale took the helm as Program Director and became the last with a direct link to Ragsdale's leadership. Travis Spivey served two years as Program Director in 1994 and 1995, but his tutelage had been under Barnett, not Ragsdale. When Spivey departed, the Barr-Ragsdale years were ancient history to most of the Stahlman staff.[108]

For Parnell-Craig, the transition was somewhat different. When Barnett took his year off in 1986, long-time friend and former fellow Stahlman Commissioner Kerry Parker filled in. Parker had returned in 1985 as Field Sports Director and stayed on as Program Director in 1986, the Green Bar Bill summer. It was generally understood this was a one shot summer, so it was not surprising when Parker did not return in 1987. He came back for Barnett in 1990 as Waterfront Director at Camp Craig and from here became the most experienced person to take over when Barnett did not return in 1993.[109]

Unlike 1986 when he was mostly a placeholder, Parker immediately began making changes that would have long term consequences in his second run. The most important of these was a return to family style feeding at Parnell. The transition was difficult and had starts and stops, but by the end of summer 1996, the kinks had been worked out and Stahlman was sold on the delivery as well. Parker also tried to relax some of Barnett's uniforming he felt was overly strict, such as hair length, which could be allowed to the bottom of the collar instead of the top. Parker also brought a Beach Party program to the Waterfront as well as a camp-wide competition, called the Parnell Path or the Craig Adventure Trail, depending on the camp.[110]

Thus, when Willhite retired in 1994, camp program had not only recovered, but had moved through another period of Program Director dominance. The heirs of the Barnett-Ragsdale era were still running that camp program when Willhite stepped down and a new Reservation Director, Larry Green, stepped in.

The Three G's at Camp

As outlined above, social norms and institutions had transformed by the time Tom Willhite became Reservation Director, and continued to change throughout his tenure. Women, homosexuals, and minority groups continued their respective demands for equality. Additionally, simple demographic and economic concerns exacerbated the tension about these demands. Nevertheless, all of these changes, and many others, not only transformed society, they changed the Boy Scouts. The Scouts became increasingly concerned about the Three G's: God, Girls, and Gays. As the Scouting program shifted to address these concerns, by extension, summer camp shifted as well.

Of the three G's, the most evident change was with "girls." Women were more involved with troop level Scouting and at the Council level too. In 1990, three women joined the Executive Board for the first time. At Boxwell, women had been involved for some time, but again primarily in what could best be called "pink collar" positions. Ms. Schleicher and Mrs. Bea were still cooks at the Stahlman kitchen. A woman always ran Camp Murrey, the family camp. By the early 1980s, there were some minor shifts that reflected bigger changes. The first women began coming to camp with their troops, not as wives of Scoutmasters, but as part of the leadership. They were committee members and they were Assistant Scoutmasters. Their arrival complicated life at a resident camp with showerhouses built on the assumption men had no trouble showering and using the toilet in close proximity to each other.[III]

Indeed, demographics were changing enough that women were—cautiously—encouraged to come to camp. The Cub Weekends that had been so successful eventually changed their name from Lad and Dad to Cub and Partner. The switch from "Dad" to "Partner" recognized that fathers were not always available. Ideally, the "Partner" would be another male figure, but as the Eighties rolled into the Nineties, "Partner" could mean "Mom" if she was willing and the only parent available. Even more directly, in 1985 and again in 1986, the Council partnered with the Cumberland Valley Girl Scouts to host a "Single Parent Weekend." The event was open to "any Scout age youth living in a single-parent household, and that parent." No one involved had to be a

Scout; girls and women were included. "This is a weekend of camping in tents, swimming, canoeing, volleyball, and more," Willhite said. "Our rifle range will be opened and we have a nature hike planned... This is a weekend for single parent families. Things are flexible because we want the participants to do things at a family pace. We are simply providing the instructors, facilities, and food. After that, it is a family affair, and family is the key word in the plans we have made." The single parent weekend acknowledged an important reality: the family was changing and thus program had to adapt to fit that new reality.[112]

Women's roles expanded on the staff too... in a manner of speaking. Almost since the opening at Old Hickory, the Reservation had enjoyed the talents of the soldiers of Fort Campbell. These soldiers generally served as Rifle Range officers or camp medics, or rarely, on a kitchen staff. A female medic from Fort Campbell arrived in 1986. Unlike the female leaders, the medic was substantially younger adult. And while not exactly program staff or even in the camps, her arrival symbolized a change outside camp that affected life inside of camp. A few of the older youth staff—those who were in the late teens to early twenties range—were captivated by a young woman on the property and flirted with her incessantly. Several of the adult leadership were incensed by flirting, not at the staff for not being able to control themselves, but at the perceived disruption her presence caused. She was ultimately banned from Camp Craig before the summer was over. Looming behind this conflict was the fear that perhaps a young woman might get pregnant at Scout camp.[113]

While the presence of women expanded in some non-traditional places, it was shrinking in some traditional areas. The numbers of those attending Camp Murrey were already declining by the time Willhite became Reservation Director. However, camp attendance was not yet in free fall. Thus, the new reservation director set to work on encouraging Scoutmasters to make Murrey a vacation location... for their wives. The first approach was apparently to shame Scoutmasters to come to camp, but not stay at Murrey. As *Jet Trails*, explained, Murrey "was not built with the intention of the Scoutmaster (or leadership of the unit) taking a vacation with his family at the Reservation." Murrey was for "the wives, daughters and boys too young to attend the Troop camps."[114]

Generally, the appeals to leaders for their wives to come to Camp Murrey missed the mark because they were appeals to the leaders and not the wives. "Mr. Scoutmaster," a 1978 *Jet Trails* article began, "why not bring your wife and small children to camp Murrey this summer. They can swim, relax and have fun while you work with your Scouts." The message had not changed dramatically by 1980. "Also, Mr. Scoutmaster," *Jet Trails* gently prodded, "bring your wife to Camp Murrey and let her enjoy the fellowship, stay in a cabin and relax for a week." At least one article actually asked the leader to include his wife in his camp planning, which was a step forward. There was even some reverse psychology used in 1985: "why leave Mom behind with her envying all the fun you are having." That same article in *Jet Trails* went on to make the hard—and somewhat patronizing—sell:

> Camp Murrey, Boxwell Reservation's family camp has been
> the resort many women have raved over during its twenty-five
> year history. A week's cost is what you normally pay for a
> night anywhere else, but oh what fun you can have at a Boy
> Scout camp for a week in the summertime. No cooking, no
> washing dishes, nobody really cares if the beds aren't made, she
> can work on her tan 'til her hearts content, or she can learn a
> new knitting pattern or spin yarns with the other ladies...
> Whatever your plans, why not make them a little easier by in-
> cluding Mom in your week at Boxwell Reservation.[115]

The falling numbers were not for lack of trying. There were six new cabins built at Murrey as part of the 1972 Capital Campaign; Willhite's 1980's "quasi-campaign" built two more cabins, larger and with running water. There were still plenty of program activities. In 1976, these included "swimming, boating, skiing, canoeing, camp fires, movies, bridge, crafts," and swimming lessons. By 1983, that list had shrunk somewhat, but there was still "ping-pong, crafts, swimming, canoeing, and a nice beach for sunning." And, on top of all this, the camp enjoyed remarkably stable leadership. Gladys Roberts was Murrey's Program Director from roughly 1973 to 1982 and Willhite's daughter Christy ran the camp from 1984 to 1994. The interim year was Willhite's wife Marie accompanied by Lisa Hamilton. Overall, Murrey still had a lot to offer.[116]

In many ways, Christy Willhite was an ideal choice to run Murrey in its latter years. She had been to the camp several times as a child, either when her father was there as camp director or with his son's troop. She enjoyed the campfires and the CPR training. She even engaged in some clean teen aged shenanigans with members of the staff as she got older. This may or may not have involved taking a boat to the nearby Laguardo Swimming Area and, for some reason, needing to be dragged back to camp by the Boat Harbor staff. Happy memories in place, when her adult job as a teacher made her summers available to earn some extra money, she went to Boxwell. By that time, Murrey was a shadow of what it had been. The only tents left in camp were used by the Murrey staff; the cabins were used only by the camp's non-staff residents. Generally, families did not come to Murrey anymore. Most of the residents were the wives of the Camp Directors, a couple of the adult staff, and perhaps a visitor or two.

As a result, there was very little program for Christy Willhite to supervise. She had a staff of two youth—both male—and for the most part their responsibilities were in the dining hall. With the exception of the cafeteria style serving line, Murrey was much like a restaurant. Willhite and her staff served the food, monitored the tables, cleaned the dining hall and the trays, and took care of the kitchen. There was no longer a campfire program and the boating, skiing, and swim lessons were all gone as well. Occasionally, there was ice cream. CPR training was still held at Murrey, but it was for the whole reservation, not Murrey families. It was clear by the late Eighties the once innovative and necessary family camp idea was past its prime.[117]

As visible as "Girls" were, the other two "G's"—the "Godless" and the "Gays"—were as equally as invisible. For the atheist, there was some choice in how to stay invisible. While the idea that "A Scout Is Reverent" was constantly on display, some events could simply be avoided. Camp still began on Sunday afternoon to give families the opportunity to attend church before coming to camp. Don Stafford Chapel was still the official non-sectarian, religious hub of the Reservation, holding services regularly on Wednesday evening. Prayers were said at every meal. At campfires, closing songs from the staff on Sunday and Friday nights often involved call-outs, spirituals, and hymns including "Kum-by-Yah," "Swing Low, Sweet Chariot," and "Amazing Grace." The atheist could skip all the church services as they were not required. Scouts rarely led grace or sang the songs at a campfire. For atheist staff, these were all more difficult to avoid, but hardly impossible.[118]

For homosexuals, invisibility was more necessary. Understand that "invisible" does not however mean non-existent. There is evidence there were homosexuals on the staff at least as far back as Rock Island. By the 1990s, there was one or two known homosexuals just about every year on the staff. The "known" note is important. These individuals may not have been "known" at the time and came out later. Further, this was just the staff. There was no way to know how many were in the general camp population of older scouts and leaders. And this reality existed, of course, because of the BSA policy against homosexuals in Scouting. Should someone identify as gay, they were out of the program. Thus, invisibility was a necessity if the individual cared about the Scouting program in any way. Unlike an atheist who could deny a comment made as potential anti-religious, not anti-God, or just shrug off any question as "just having a debate," the hyper-masculinity often associated with Scouting made this same sort of "brush off" difficult for young men of "questionable" orientation.[119]

Parnell-Craig staff member Lee Hagan was one of the youths who struggled with the choice between staying in Scouting or living a lie. Hagan knew by thirteen years old that he was attracted to other males, though he denied and fought the feelings for several years, even getting baptized in hopes "that I wouldn't be gay anymore." He finally came out to his parents at seventeen years old when he was a senior in high school. The timeline is important because it was also during the same years that Hagan participated in Scouting, earned his Eagle Scout, and joined the Boxwell staff. Hagan left Scouting after his eighteenth birthday because while "I never had a problem going through as a kid, but I knew it would never fly as an adult." After leaving Scouting in 1998, Hagan accepted his orientation and began building a life in the open.

As for being gay at camp, Hagan made strategic choices about his homosexuality. For the most part, "hiding it was for life. So just because I came to Boxwell didn't make it any more difficult; I was already hiding it. I didn't know what it was like to be myself then." As time went on and he built relationships with people he trusted, he told a select few his secret, but never the leadership. Ironically, despite the explicit ban on homosexuality, Hagan wanted to come to Boxwell. Not only did he love the physical location, but camp was out of his parents' house. It was a place where he could relax somewhat in terms of his double life, but only somewhat. His fear of being discovered by the wrong people was real and discovery meant he would have to leave his haven. While Hagan was only one example, his story demonstrated the difficult choices that faced these young men.[120]

Transitioning: The 1994 Campaign and Beyond

As Willhite began his fifteenth summer as Reservation Director in 1991, the situation in the Council and at Boxwell had improved quite a bit. In 1976, total revenues generated from camping, which included Boxwell, were $76,406. But Council wide, the Trustees had turned over $59,647 by October of that same year because the Council was over expended by $47,000. 1,885 boys had attended Boxwell that year. By 1991, camping revenue was $437,435 and the total Council budget $2,667, 475. As the 1991 Annual Report stated quite clearly, "Funds from Sustaining Membership and United Way contributions have similarly increased during that period [from 1976-1991], and the operating budget has more than doubled, enabling the Council to serve young people, and the community as a whole, in new and better ways."[121]

It was on this note of unqualified success that the end of the Willhite era began, though no one knew it at the time. First, Scout Executive E. L. "Hershel" Tolbert retired. Tolbert had arrived in January 1976 in the wake of Ward Akers' early retirement. He officially retired June 20, 1991 and his run was largely without scandal. While certainly not as beloved or as polarizing as Akers, Tolbert was remarkable for not being remarkable. He was followed by Ken Connelly, who was far more personable—a "night and day" difference from Tolbert. Connelly of course had been with the Council for years, serving as District Executive, Finance Director, and even Assistant Executive before he left for his own Council in 1979. He spent four years in Gastonia, North Carolina as Scout Executive of the Piedmont Council before taking an Executive position in 1983 at the larger Louisville, Kentucky Old Kentucky Home Council (today part of the Lincoln Heritage Council). In 1991, Connelly returned to Middle Tennessee Council.[122]

In both of the councils Connelly had led, he had been instrumental in capital campaigns to develop new Scout camps. Clearly, Connelly was well associated with Boxwell and was not interested in developing a wholly new summer camp facility. But under Connelly's guidance, in 1992 the Council's Long Range Development Plan was approved by the Executive Board; it provided an opportunity to improve the existing reservation. It should be remembered there had not been a Capital Campaign—not an official one at least—in the Middle Tennessee Council since 1972. And there was cause to do a major renovation. Willhite had already begun a push to bring motorboats back to camp. A re-opened Ski Dock would be a program boon. Murrey was languishing and could be transformed if needed. Further, 1990's Americans with Disabilities Act meant that Boxwell had to upgrade facilities in some way to accommodate the physically disabled. The arrival of more women suggested upgrading showerhouse facilities would be money well spent too. And so the planning began.[123]

The 1994 Camp/Endowment Development Campaign launched at the end of 1993 with leadership named in November and the first hint of details released in December. E. W. "Bud" Wendell, president of Gaylord Entertainment, was named chairman of the campaign and his vice chairman was Dick Evans, the Executive Vice-President at Gaylord. The largest capital campaign "ever undertaken by a local Scout Council in the United States," the 1994 campaign had a goal of $7.8 million "to enhance camp facilities in three counties." Titled "Scouting. The Handbook for Life," the Campaign officially began in February 1994 and concluded with a "Victory Celebration" on October 19th at Opryland Hotel. By that point, Wendell could announce that the campaign had exceeded its goal by $768, 254, making the total raised by the campaign just over $8.5 million. By final accounting in 1995, the campaign had raised over $8.8 million.[124]

Big fund-raising goals meant big plans. Capital Improvements were made at Grimes Canoe Base and at Parish Wilderness Reservation (Rock Island), including a caretaker's residence at the latter. Some money would be spent on renovations at the Jet Potter Center, while some would go to program. A major portion, about $3 million, would "be used for endowment funds to expand programs for boys in low-income families and to further extend scouting into inner-city areas." Connelly also pointed out that "Additional endowment will help maintain the council's aging properties and further improve district and unit service. The long-range plan, unanimously approved in 1992, recommended building the council's endowment resources so they could provide 20 percent of its operating budget by the year 2000."[125]

The major transformations happened at Boxwell. Indeed, the 1994 Capital Campaign transformed the landscape of Boxwell in ways that even exceeded the 1972 Campaign. First, the campaign brought the "construction of barrier-free campsites, paved trails and new shower facilities for special-needs Scouts at Boxwell, at a cost of $140,000. Another $200,000 will be spent on asphalt paving for handicapped Scouts." In each camp, a site was selected with easy road access and was partially paved to provide smooth, even terrain for Scouts with physical disabilities. As having a special needs site only mattered if a disabled Scout could get to it, all four camps were given a series of asphalt paths, connecting the special needs campsite with other important parts of the camp.[126]

The Special Needs Access paths and campsites were only part of the renovation. All of the Activity Yard and Con Yard program areas received program shelters. The program shelters were park-like pavilions on concrete slabs with green metal roofs. Each Con-Yard received one shelter and each Activity Yard received two. Ittabeena, which the professional staff had taken to calling the Training Center and the staff called Akers' Cabin, was renovated and expanded thanks to a donation by Scouter George Fehrmann, president of the manufacturing company APCOM Inc. The site officially became the Fehrmann Training Center and became more a place for meetings than a summer home. The Ski Dock also returned. While both camps had been doing some boating work, it was clear that there was a need for trained and dedicated individuals to run a boating program and to care for the boats. Now dubbed the Boat Harbor, this area could be useful not just for motorboats, but sailboats and perhaps even jet skis, all far from the swimming activities on a waterfront. Equally importantly, with the contributions of the Pfeffer family behind the renovated Harbor, it was hoped that another C.O.P.E.-like benefactor could be established. And of course, some campaign money actually went directly to camp program, primarily the development of more High Adventure activities, "including wind surfing, white-water canoeing, rock climbing and mountain biking for older Scouts."[127]

     More than Stahlman or Parnell, Camp Craig saw a dramatic transformation as a result of the 1994 Campaign. While the camp did receive the Special Needs site and paved trails, Program Director Kerry Parker used the Campaign to push for a new waterfront. The original waterfront was in a small cove below the dining hall and had been one of the locations Akers had poured concrete pads for back before the 1959 campaign. But because this site was directly on the Cumberland River, it was exposed to harsher conditions than the other waterfronts and by the early 1990s, those concrete slabs were deteriorating. After a visit, Parker convinced Willhite and Connelly that a new waterfront was needed, but there was disagreement on location. Willhite wanted the new site on the road into camp, providing a good view of camp activity as people arrived. Utilizing Perry Bruce and his Corps of Engineers connections, Parker sounded the entire area around Craig looking for the best location, which ended up being on the opposite end of camp on the backside of the Duck Head peninsula. There was nothing on this side of Craig, so moving the waterfront would necessitate reimagining the camp layout. Parker, Willhite, and Connelly agreed that this would be the plan. A new waterfront was built at Duck Head, the two Activity Yard program shelters were built nearby, and a new road—immediately called "Parker's Highway" by the staff—was cut along the backside of the camp. Parker and his directors had a long range plan to move the Friday Night Campfire Area and sites 2 through 7 onto the new road, completely flipping Camp Craig.[128]

     The principle showcase of the 1994 Capital Campaign was the creation of a new camp just for Cub Scouts. As Willhite had shown with his Cub and Partner weekends for well over a decade, there was a strong interest in Cub Scouting. If facilities could be developed for them, then a positive experience might translate into more Boy Scouts. Further, as only one of six councils in the nation with a camp specifically for Cub Scouts, such a camp would be a wonderful feather in the Middle Tennessee cap. Beaumont Scout Reserva-

Cub-A-Lot Castle, December 1995. Note the special needs access trail.
Photo by Russ Parham.

tion's Camp Grizzly Cub World in the Greater St. Louis Area Council was particularly inspirational. The plan for Boxwell's CubWorld would include several similar elements found at Camp Grizzly Cub World including an Old West Fort, pirate ships, and a rock castle. With a plan now formulated, the original idea was to build an entirely new camp for Cubs, utilizing some of the old farm property on the front end of the property around Akers' Lake. However, long time Executive Board member C. A. "Neil" Craig suggested that since Murrey was not getting the use it once did, it could be renovated. As there were no longer any Murrey heirs or family alive to protest the decision, Camp Murrey became the chosen location. The old farm property at Akers Lake became the Percy Dempsey Camporee Area instead and the family camping concept came to an end.[129]

CubWorld was not a small undertaking. First, it was costly. In December 1993, the first reports on the new camp, which included additional elements such as a treehouse campsite, estimated the camp would cost approximately $780,000. By the time the campaign was over in October 1994, before construction had begun, the cost was estimated at $1 million. The camp ultimately was given the name Gaylord CubWorld because Gaylord Entertainment donated half of this sticker price for the construction of the camp. Gaylord CubWorld began with its own unique gateway of Cub Scout symbols. The old showerhouse—the only one on the reservation with a washer and dryer—was torn down. Two new male/female, all weather, all-purpose showerhouses were built, as were four latrine stations, which were similar to the washstands Craig used, though with no pit toilets. There were eight campsites, a program shelter, a fitness course, BB and archery ranges, and a campfire area, all in addition to the major attractions listed above. (It should be noted though that when CubWorld opened, there was only one Pirate Ship, it actually floated, and it had a slide into the swimming area). The Murrey dining hall was also renovated, made larger to accommodate its new purpose. All the cabins remained, with a Special Needs Trail connecting them all. And while just about everything that was "Murrey" disappeared, the large dinner bell behind the back dock remained.[130]

The new camp was dedicated on October 26, 1995, just a little over a year after the Victory Dinner. In addition to the Council dignitaries who attended, the dedication was attended by Cub Scouts, who climbed all over everything, as designed. *The Tennessean* quoted 10 year old Chris Irwin's reaction. "It's awesome, totally cool. You can climb, walk, and jump on it. Everything about it is cool." Aubrey Harwell, Jr., Council President, commented on the larger goal: "The objective of Gaylord CubWorld is to combine physical activity with historical learning experiences." The camp certainly embraced physical activity—just straight play—in a way that nothing else on the Reservation or any other Council property did.[131]

In many ways, the return of Connelly was the return of the Akers' philosophy of facilities as program. All of the Council's properties enjoyed benefits from the 1994 Capital Campaign. And while some of the changes were necessary in some form—the ranger's residence at Parish or the Special Needs changes—clearly many of the changes were program delivery related. The upgrades to the waterfronts, the program shelters, the Boat Harbor, and the Training Center were all related to delivering camp program, but doing so with facilities that aided that delivery. CubWorld was truly the epitome of this philosophy at work. A solid Cub Scout program had been going on with Cub and Partner and Cub Day camps for some time, but CubWorld took a good program idea and took it to a new level. While Murrey was sacrificed in the process, CubWorld was the best example of a program being exceptional because of the physical facilities the campaign made possible.

Perhaps it was not surprising then that in February 1995, Tom Willhite retired. It would be easy to say that as the financial circumstances had turned around, Willhite's special brand of thriftiness was no longer required. By the mid-1990s, with the post-Cold War, technology driven economy taking off, the money certainly appeared to be flowing again. But the fact was that the 65-year-old Willhite had been involved in Scouting for thirty years. The Council hired him as Development Director to oversee the actual construction projects at Boxwell. Given that he had experience with this type of work because of his construction experience before Scouting and his work with Camp Craig during the 1972 campaign, Willhite's knack for thriftiness still had a role—making sure the Council got the best use out of its $8.8 million campaign.[132]

1995 had other important personnel changes. With Willhite retired from the Director of Support Services position, which included Reservation Director at Boxwell, a new man was needed. That new man was Larry Green. Green had been with the Council as a professional since 1971, but he had been working on the reservation as part of the ranger staff as far back as 1966. Green's experience with the Council was quite unique. He served as Camp Director five separate times, and at all three camps. As one of the few African

Americans associated with the Council, Green's rise to Field Director and then Director of Support Services demonstrated that much had changed. And so, in the summer of 1995, Boxwell had a new Reservation Director.[133]

By and large, Green was an extension of the Willhite era. Green and Willhite were good friends, traveling and rooming together for Council business, and counseling each other over a variety of Scouting issues. Both had been with the Council for a long time and understood how the other worked. Green recognized the large shadow Willhite cast, especially as the predecessor was still on the grounds as Development Director. Still, Green was his own man. He was more approachable and laid back. He was also more visible in the camps, often visiting at meal times and laughing with leaders and staff. He could also often be found in the compound tinkering with an engine or on a tractor mowing. Green had a clear affinity for Boxwell.[134]

Unfortunately, Green's arrival to the position of Reservation Director—a job he had specifically asked for—turned out to be ill-timed in many ways. In 1994, the elderly Pearl Schleicher had fallen in the freezer at Stahlman and broken her leg and hurt her back. Green was filling in for Willhite at the time and actually called an ambulance for Schleicher. She had recovered, but the accident raised questions about her age and ability to do the job. Soon after taking the new position, Connelly suggested it was time to make a change in regard to Pearl Schleicher and Green had to let go of a Boxwell institution. He made a personal visit to her home to give both her and John the news, and "she handled it like a lady." Schleicher told Green, "I appreciate you coming over to talk with me. If there's anything I can do, just let us know." The job was done, but Green was crushed.[135]

The personnel changes continued. Connelly accepted an offer to move up in BSA leadership. He became the Regional Director of the Northeast Region and then later moved up to become Chief Financial Officer/Assistant Chief Scout Executive over the entire Boy Scouting program. It was an incredible move for someone who had no background in Scouting as a boy and had initially only planned to work for the Boy Scouts for three years when he first started in 1963 for $4200 a year.[136]

Connelly's departure before the summer of 1995 meant a new Executive was in order. The new man was Joe Long, the National Personnel Director for the BSA. Long had actually applied for the Council Executive position in 1991 and even been interviewed then before the Selection Committee went with Connelly. Long was a very different Executive than Connelly. Connelly "wanted to get to know the staff members he had working for him. And he would listen [and] give you opportunities." Long was considerably more hands on. He "didn't want to be surprised by anything, or anybody asking him any question he couldn't answer." Long was a man who wanted to know what was going on. To that end, he actually visited Camp Craig in July 1995, shortly after being hired. He toured the camp, saw the new Waterfront, and stayed for a meal and the Friday Night Campfire, a level of engagement not utilized by either of his predecessors. Still, most of 1995 could best be characterized as "a year of observation" by Long.[137]

However, Long's need for constant updates did not work well with Green's more laid back and personal approach. In the year between Long's hiring and summer camp 1996, the working relationship quickly soured. As Director of Support Services, others in the Council Office came to Green for help, asking why Long was handling things the way he was. Green could not answer these questions. He was personally coming into the office early and leaving late, often waking up in the middle of the night because of the stress. By April Green wrote up a letter of resignation. Confident he could do the job, Green was equally confident he could not do the job to Long's satisfaction. The two discussed the issue and Long convinced the Reservation Director to stay on through the summer. They would reassess when camp was over.[138]

Thus, when the summer of 1996 came around, Green was anxious to get out to Boxwell. Much like Willhite in 1976, Green had inherited the 1995 staff. The 1996 staff was made of his hires. He even put his stamp on the staff hat. He kept the red hat, but instead of having patch sewed on the front of the camp, he had a design embroidered directly onto the hat. 1996 was the first summer of CubWorld. After all the fanfare the previous October, Cub-World was open for two weeks in 1996 and as Green admitted, "we didn't have a camping program, not really." The facility had been built, but no one had given much thought about what to do with that facility. Otherwise, camp program in 1996 was not significantly differently than it had been in the previous few years. A minor tweak that Green added was a Staff of the Day program. Essentially, if a Scout or Scouter thought a staff member had done an exceptionally good job, he could fill out a small card nominating the staff member as Staff of the Day. It was an appreciation call-out for the staff, but not a significant program transformation.[139]

Long, however, did not stay away. He visited during Staff Week and gave a talk about customer service, which seemed inappropriate at a Scout camp where personal responsibility and self-control were core values. The talk set a very different tone for many of the old timers. Once camp began, Green was beleaguered by Long. Russ Parham continued as Business Manager for Green and recalled that Green "would come in just gung-ho every morning, and [then] he'd get a phone call [from Long], about ten o'clock every day. And I'd see his spirit just sink." Long was checking in, asking what had and had not been done. As Green admitted, "I had a cell phone. And at that time, over on Duck Head, there was very poor service. So I spent a lot of my time over there. [laughs] I'm serious. So that Joe could not reach me."[140]

A prime example of the stress Long could cause came when the Executive came out to visit again. He arrived at Camp Parnell at lunch time and instead of sitting with the directors as he had the year before, he sat at Scout table to enjoy the meal. Family style feeding had been reintroduced by Program

Director by Kerry Parker several years before, but not all leaders had been happy about the change, which was no longer new by 1996. With the Scout Executive in their midst, the leaders expressed their concerns. They felt the portions were smaller and the boys were not getting enough food. At a post-visit meeting, Long told Parker to feed the boys more food. Parker explained Parnell was a satellite camp. The food was prepared at Stahlman based on a head count and then shipped to Parnell. Further, the amount was the same as it had always been as the head count system had not changed. In short, Parker could not feed the Scouts more as he did not have more food to feed them. The next morning, the count was doubled. As a result, boys got sick because they were gorging themselves. Even then, enormous amounts of food were being thrown away—multiple garbage cans full—all completely wasted. Green took some of the extra to a local church. By the start of the next week, things had returned to normal. For Parker though, "Joe Long Day" represented the definitive end of the Willhite era.[141]

By the time camp ended, Green was worn out. Of course, there had been other issues at camp that summer. Parker and Green, long-time friends, had at least two serious shouting matches over personnel issues. For Green though, it was the constant management by Long that defined the summer. As agreed, the two met again after camp ended. As Green recalled,

> We got together in August. He said, "Well how do you feel?"
> I said, "Joe, I haven't—my feelings haven't changed at all."
> And he said, "Well, you know, I think you're right. Maybe
> this job isn't for you." He said, "Dan Beard District is open.
> Would you consider going back in the district?" I said,
> "Yeah." Because I was gonna [quit], you know, I was leaving.

And so, after only two summers as Reservation Director, Larry Green stepped down and returned to a district level position. The Tom Willhite era had ended; the modern era had begun.[142]

Tom Willhite, at the Crippled Crab. Personal collection of Tom Willhite

Chapter 7

"Good Enough for Government Work":
Staff Life in the Age of Willhite

1976-1996

Dinnertime at Stahlman Dining Hall during Staff Week in the mid-1980s followed a familiar pattern every day, every year. Shortly before six o'clock in the evening, staff from all over the Reservation would congregate at the dining hall. Stahlman staff was closest and would generally walk up, though those in faraway places would arrive in a car or two, parking in the small lot by the dining hall. All three Murrey staff—the director and her two staff—would arrive by car as well.

The Parnell-Craig staff was often a bit less predictable. Because this group was coming from either Camp Craig or Camp Parnell, depending on the year, they all arrived in separate vehicles as well. The question became the formation in which those cars arrived. They could trickle in one at a time. A large blue rebuilt 1950s era Ford one-and-a-half ton truck could come instead, carrying an unseemly amount of people in the cab and the rest of the staff in the bed enclosed by cattle rails. More often than not though, Parnell-Craig staff arrived at most meals in a convoy of vehicles, hazard lights flashing, swerving from one side of the road to the other and back again like giant vehicular serpent. The swerving usually subsided as the caravan pulled into Camp Stahlman, but the hazard lights flashed all the way up to dining hall parking lot.

Aside from these initial shenanigans, there was little else to distinguish between the camp staffs. All members of the staff lined up in front of the dining hall for flag lowering, mixing into one big group. They all dressed similarly in various work clothes. Umbro soccer shorts. Cut-off jeans or camouflage pants. T-shirts with the sleeves cut off. T-shirts with the sleeves still on. Some staff members were dirtier than others, but everyone got their hands dirty during Staff Week. Those older staff members who had been around for a few years were likely wearing a battered and dirty red hat, a symbol of their service.

An impromptu color guard assembled to lower the flag. An older staff member gave the calls to the staff as they practiced the evening process. The program directors were inside the dining hall, waiting. The entire staff stood at attention as the color guard approached the post. The staff saluted, hand over heart, hat removed, as was appropriate for their dress. Next week, staff would salute with three fingers to the edge of their hat as they stood at attention in either Class A or Class B uniform. Flag lowered and folded, a quick prayer was said before the staff dismissed to enter the building.

The Stahlman Dining Hall was now approximately a quarter century old. A metal roof replaced the building's original marble chip roof. The exterior red cedar walls, exposed to the elements, looked worn. The steel uprights and window frames were both painted a brown so light in tone, they were almost cream. Just inside the doors were two sets of curtains. Large, navy blue curtains were found on either side of the doors, to be pulled closed to block the sun. Smaller, golden curtains hung over the top windows like kitchen drapes, never moving, always blocking the light. The ceiling was covered with alternating rows of state flags and sound-dampening tiles. A large wooden cut of the Middle Tennessee Council shoulder patch hung over the fire place. A single enormous plaque hung on the west facing wall—a commemorative for the contributors of the 1959 Capital Campaign.

As staff entered the building, they removed their hats. No hats were to be worn inside. Friends found each other and gathered around square wooden tables. A long time tradition held that when someone hit the top of one of these tables, the staff would yell out, *"Don't beat on the tables! These tables have been here for [insert number] years and they're going to be here for an-other [insert number] years when you're children are here! So don't beat on the tables!"* While this object lesson in conservation of materials would continue for decades to come, at this point in the Old Hickory Boxwell's history, the chant was true. These were in fact the same tables that had been used for family style feeding when the camp opened in 1960. However, by the 1980s, the meal service had moved to cafeteria style.

A short non-sectarian prayer was given and the staffs lined up to be fed. There was no one to call tables during Staff Week; the staff simply got in line when they were ready. Some got in line early, passing sea green colored plastic trays back to the people behind them. Others sat and waited at their table for the line to get shorter or to be the last served. During a week of camp, the staff themselves would be the ones serving the food in the serving line to the Scouts. They would often break into song, showing how the world of camp was different from the world of school. During Staff Week, however, the Kitchen staffs of each camp got that honor of serving.

Staff Week was warm-up week for everyone, including the kitchen and cook staffs. Pearl Schleicher and her sister Mrs. B were usually floating around nearby in their white cook suits, preparing the same meals during this week that will be prepared during the summer. Depending on the particular day, the meal at dinner would be ham or spaghetti or chicken and dumplings or perhaps even a mystery meat. Desert was some kind of baked goodie. The Schleichers' tasty rolls were likely in the mix somewhere as well. There was no salad bar, no carbonated drinks. There was government issued peanut butter for those who needed to do something different. These were the options that would exist all summer, every summer, every dinner during the Willhite years.

Of course, once camp started, a good deal of the program the staff presented was trial by fire. Marching in on Sunday and Friday nights was done for the first time Sunday night of Week One. The same was true of the Camp Spirit song, which was generally sung for the first time that same first Sunday of Week One. The same would be true of campfire programs and teaching sessions. Very little of this was practiced during Staff Week during the Willhite years, though that began to change in the 1990s. Staff Week in the Willhite era was focused on putting camp together; it was almost all physical labor.

In front of the chimney were two square tables pushed together to make a long directors' table. Here was where Willhite, Barnett, Ragsdale, and the Camp Directors for the summer usually sat. Parham had a regular day job and often joined this group in the evening for dinner and whatever group training was offered. Barnett and Ragsdale were ever present, camp versions of Laurel and Hardy. Barnett was tall and lanky. His hair was thin to balding, but still jet black. A few summers he had a beard, but was generally clean shaven. He was rarely without a cigarette in hand. Ragsdale was shorter and stouter. He was almost always bearded and his hair still thick and full. He always had a pocket knife handy, as connected to him as a lit cigarette was to Barnett, constantly whittling on something. And then there was Willhite. Older than the other men, Willhite's build fell somewhere in between the two program directors. Wiry black hair, bulbous nose, and dark, piercing eyes, Willhite carried himself like the man in charge and he soon led the evening meetings in his terse, direct manner.

"Signs up!" Willhite began quickly, directly, holding the three fingered Scout sign in the air. The goal was to get the staff to quiet and pay attention to what was now going to be imparted. As such, the sign was not usually announced.

If the room did not quiet quickly, "This is serious business, boys!

Time is money, money is time. If you're wasting my time, then you're wasting my money!" The phrases were clichés. It was almost as if Willhite knew there was a character he was supposed to play, so he played to type.

With the room finally quiet, staff members from either camp became targets for the coming inquisition. Here, newer staff members tended to fare better. As Willhite did not know them yet, he was unable to call them out by name. The older staff, though more likely to be singled out, generally were not bothered. This call and response exercise was entertainment for them.

"Webster," barked Willhite. "What's the policy on illegal drug use at Boxwell Reservation?"

"109, sir."

"We're settin' examples up here," Willhite nodded. "If you're doing dope or pot or pills or needles, I'll kick you off this reservation so fast your momma will have to pack your bags."

Uncomfortable and muffled snickers would follow at the poorly made "your momma" joke. The respite was short as the next question soon followed.

"John Estes, of the AY Yard," Willhite called out, voice dripping with a sarcastic pride at having recalled the staff member's program area, a smirk crossing his face.

"Yes, sir," came the reply with no hint of a correction that "AY" already stood for "Activity Yard" making "AY Yard" superfluous and foolish.

"What's the speed limit on the reservation, Estes?"

"24.9 miles per hour, sir."

"24.9. 25 is speedin'," the reservation director would nod. And then, without skipping a beat, "Trent Craig. How much was electricity last year?"

And so it went. There was the question on the water bill. The admonition on lights left on at a showerhouse the night before. The not-so-thinly-veiled reference to staff trying to pirate electricity for their staff sites. Willhite knew and he was letting those staff know he knew. There were the half-hearted reminders to Barnett and Ragsdale that there was a budget.

Staff Week in the Age of Willhite was an object lesson in frugality. And this was incentive to use one's resources in the most creative ways possible.[1]

Staff Life

The staff experience during the Willhite years differed both from what came before and what came after. From the moment when the electricity was pulled out of the staff sites in 1976, a new camp staff was born.

The staff life of the Willhite staffs was born in part out of the Commissioner system. The Commissioner system had built little Activity Yard staff sites all around Stahlman, Parnell, and Craig. When the electricity came out in 1976, there was no incentive to move the staff back into (mostly) centralized staff areas. Instead, modifying the Commissioner system sites, program area staff sites emerged. Each defined staff received its own living area. Thus, the Activity Yard had its own site near the Activity Yard, the youth Kitchen Staff had a site near the kitchen, and so on. These sites were different from Scout campsites in two significant ways. First, they often included large four-man tents, whereas every Scout campsite only had two-man tents. Second, staff sites were often clustered together with "living platforms" connecting the tent platforms. Living platforms were basically just tent platforms without the arms. In short, they were large square decks. Once placed between tent platforms and covered with tarps, a staff site became a hidden and guarded oasis. They were close to where the staff taught sessions, but absolutely off limits to Scouts.

Program area staff sites produced mixed results in terms of benefits.

There were advantages certainly. Staff was closer to their program areas, which allowed them to watch over their program materials. Program area staff also became tight units as they lived together in close quarters for extended periods. This proved to be a double-edged sword. A close program area staff might function well as a unit, but it also promoted that unit over the larger staff. In short, intra-staff rivalries between program areas were not uncommon. Further, program area staff sites left areas traditionally staffed by first year staff, like the Kitchen and the Trading Post, at a disadvantage. Not only were these groups not steeped in camp tradition and had very few people to guide them forward, simple necessities like how to best hang a tarp had to be relearned every summer with each new group.[2]

Program area staff sites were only one of the significant differences between the Willhite staffs and the Akers years. The fact that these sites did not have electricity was another. Nighttime for these staffs was not dramatically different than the camper experience. There were lanterns, running on either propane or white gas, which burned late into the night. Despite the obvious danger, candles on footlockers were not at all uncommon.

There were also repeated attempts to re-acquire electricity, even after having electricity had passed into the mists of time. For some staff, acquiring electricity was simple. The Trading Post and Handicraft Staff Site at Stahlman was directly behind the Trading Post and Handicraft building, which had been part of the 1972 Capital Development Campaign. Thus, running a few extensions cords for fans or lights or whatever was desired was not difficult. Proximity to a showerhouse often had the same result as those buildings also had electricity tied to them. A simple extension cord or the more creative light socket adaptor would get the job done. Some sites, such as Craig's Activity Yard, required more creative solutions, such as digging a small trench and trying to tie directly into the fuse box at the Program Director's Cabin.[3]

The program area staff sites and the lack of electricity combined to form a perfect storm for staff extra-curricular activity. As has already been seen, the staff had always engaged in late night "devilment." Without electricity and housed in close quarters with other young men, the staff found a variety of ways to entertain themselves in the evening hours. None of these activities had malicious intent, but many did push the envelope of what could be considered "Scout-like" behavior.

Living quarters were not the only way that staff life in this period was different; staff night out was a different experience as well. When Boxwell at Old Hickory Lake opened in 1960, there were not many places to go for a Staff Night out. Gallatin was closest, but did not have much to offer. Lebanon was a better choice with laundry mats and a movie theater. There was one staff night out and staff travelled together. This might mean traveling on a cattle truck or on a bus. Either way, the end result was the same. All the staff travelled together to one location for the one night on the town.[4]

Staff Night Out in the Willhite years was different in some profound ways. First, Old Hickory Lake was changing the region. The attraction of the lake brought an increased population to the north Nashville area, including Madison and Hendersonville. Increased population led to new businesses and new infrastructure. Rivergate Mall—a nod to Old Hickory Dam—opened in 1971 and was the state's largest mall for several years. Increasing population in nearby Hendersonville led to construction of a new state highway, Highway 386, in 1981, which would connect Gallatin and Hendersonville with Interstate 65. The new by-pass, known locally as Vietnam Veterans Boulevard, passed directly north of Rivergate Mall. Old Hickory Lake had transformed the area north of Nashville and, by extension, Staff Night Out at the mall and the area surrounding it became a new popular destination for Boxwell staff.[5]

Second, the basic mechanics of going out also changed. While there was still only one staff night out for all of the staff, it was no longer a joint activity. The staff bus and the large truck with cattle railings were gone. To go out, staff took their own personal vehicles. This obviously involved several more vehicles and, by extension, more destinations. This method also shifted responsibility from the Council, which before had provided the truck or the bus, to the staff, who now took their personal vehicles. As only those over eighteen years old and above were allowed to drive, the insurance responsibility shifted to this group as well. In other words, if an accident occurred on staff night out, the Council had no accountability in that process.[6]

All of this meant that Staff Night Out became a very fractured affair. The range of where staff went on Staff Night Out expanded. Rivergate Mall and the surrounding opportunities—pool halls, movie theaters, go karts, book stores—were popular destinations. When Highway 386 was completed, Nashville also became a more reasonable destination, though midnight curfews still limited these trips. Still, personal vehicles and the mall meant that the staff did not all have to go to the same place. It also meant that eighteen and over drivers could take a group of younger staff and drop them off somewhere to return later for pick up. Staff Night Out became a much more individualistic event than it had been in years past.[7]

The Willhite staffs were also steeped in popular culture. While popular music had been influential to staff life at least as far back as Rock Island, the Willhite staffs had grown up on television and reruns. As children, many in this group had grown up on PBS and *Sesame Street*. By the end of the period, MTV had exploded and transformed into reality television. All of these things seeped into the very program the Willhite staffs presented. The Muppet song "Mahna Mahna" became a staple when staff served meals, not simply because it was so catchy, but because its jazz foundation allowed individual staff to have their own improvised solos. Televisions theme songs, such as "Gilligan's Island" and "The Brady Bunch," became regular songs sung by the staff. Even the song from the Oscar Meyer Weiner commercials "I Wish I Were An Oscar Meyer Weiner..." was adapted. Popular comedy programs like *Saturday Night Live!* and *The State* served as inspiration for campfire skits.[8]

While popular culture played a role in shaping these staffs, so too did the conservative movement that emerged in the late 1970s and early 1980s. A distrust of professionals and the professional organization permeated the staff culture. There were exceptions, of course, such as Willhite himself and Larry Green, but the higher up the Council chain of command a professional was situated, the less like the staff would be to view that individual with respect. This conservative line of thinking was demonstrated well by two well-worn staff phrases. The first—"What are they going to do? Fire me?"—was one such casual and flippant phrase, underscoring the idea that the staff as individuals were unconcerned with what "the establishment" thought or required. This was primarily because staff increasingly viewed professionals as simply money men, who did not understand what the staff understood: how to make a Scout program work. The second phrase—"It's good enough for government work"—dealt primarily with labor. Staff knew they were being used for cheap labor by Willhite to complete grunt tasks. As a result, the idea that the effort was "good enough for government work" implied that the result could be better, but would get the job done. The idea was almost self-aware: Staff understood they were "government workers" at camp and they were doing just enough to complete the task, especially when it was labor they were compelled to complete. While all staff in this period may not have defined themselves as "conservative thinkers," they all grew up in this world seeped in "tradition" and "values."

Staff Stuff Stays Staff Stuff... Mostly

When Russ Parham interviewed Tom Willhite in 2002, almost a decade after his run as Reservation Director, the two men discussed a variety of topics covering Willhite's tenure. The now white haired Morrison, TN resident did not wax eloquent over anything in particular, but mostly ran through a list of achievements. Nevertheless, he did pause to mention one of the highlights of his Scouting career: the staff.

> We would have 65-70% return for Boxwell staff each year.
> We kept a lot of key people for 7 and 8 year... And we built a
> staff that was second to none in the whole country, as far as
> Boxwell Reservation. [Council Executive] Ken Connelly one
> night said he had never seen a staff like he'd saw that night at
> Boxwell... He could not believe how many older people we
> kept and what we built it into it. I think that's one of the
> highlights of my time at Boxwell.

And along with Barnett and Ragsdale, the staff deeply respected Willhite,
though sometimes this respect was expressed by focusing on his peccadillos.[9]

And truly, Willhite's peccadillos were many. He constantly drove in
reverse, so that he would "never put any miles on his car." He knew that the
Sysco toilet paper rolls had 156 sheets to a role. While everyone else called the
Activity Yard the "AY" for short, Willhite called it "the AY Yard." When he
filled up a vehicle with gas at the compound, he shook the nozzle to get every
last drop. When you checked out material from the compound, you had to
record every item, every nut, every bolt, every link of chain, no matter how
small. For at least a few years, even saying the name "Willhite" triggered the
"Willhite Salute"—removing the staff hat and covering the wallet.[10]

This incomplete list should not be misread. Behind this chuckling at
Willhite's expense, every staff member was quick to note their admiration.
"I'm one of those people," Stahlman staff member Andy Verble explained,
"and I will say it unabashedly, I just worship the ground that Tom Willhite
walk[ed] on." Web Webster, another Stahlman staff member, related a simple
anecdote of working for Willhite. The one summer that Ragsdale was gone in
1986, Webster as a senior staff member was giving the replacement Program
Director Harold Tracy a difficult time, constantly challenging his leadership.
Willhite drove into camp one day, pulled up to Webster, rolled the window
down, and simply said, "Let's take a ride." Driving back up toward the Crab at
a crawl, Willhite got directly to the business at hand, "You and Harold have a

problem... You have a decision to make... You can either work for Harold or you don't have to work here anymore. We clear?" And just as abruptly, Willhite spotted some trash on the side of the road, stopped the car, and told Webster to grab it. As the young man got out of the car to get the cup in the woods, Willhite drove off, leaving Webster to walk back to camp and reflect:

> He's driven me up to the top of the hill and he's left me. It's not that long a walk, it's no big deal, but it was the underline. It was the period at the end of the sentence. What I learned from Tom in that particular instance and what has really sort of stuck with me as a leader since... is I don't much care why we're having this conversation... Why we're having this conversation is immaterial. The fact is a problem exists and... "I trust you've got the brains to know how to fix this and I expect you to fix it." And that is a leadership quality that doesn't get a whole lot of play anymore.

That was the kind of leader Willhite was.[11]

And while there were similar stories about Ragsdale and Barnett, most tales from staff members in these years were about what they could—or could not—get away with. Some of the staff shenanigans were harmless stories, tales that became legendary to succeeding generations of staff as the stories were told and retold. For example, who participated in which events was openly discussed amongst the youth staff. If adults were present, the standing rule was that names were changed or excluded "to protect the guilty." Exploits with the camp tractors often loomed large. Staff routinely "surfed" on tractor flatbed trailers as they moved from work project to the next. Every Staff Week saw an older staff member regale a tale of "that time" when picnic tables were stacked too high on the trailer. Sometimes the story ended in successfully dropping off the wooden picnic tables to the appropriate site; sometimes the story ended with a table or two crashing to the pavement and its remains moved into the woods, out of site. Both stories existed. Trash runs became one of those staff jobs that everyone should have hated, but did not. The dining hall became

Parnell staff working on a tractor and trailer in the 1980s. Photo by Russ Parham.

home to amazing program, such as moving a car into the building. Some years even saw fan clubs, like the Mr. Mushroom Fan Club at Stahlman in the mid-1980s or CARP at Parnell in 1993.[12]

Other stories related episodes which were far more dangerous. Riding and surfing on the tractor trailers was always good fun, but there were a number of tractor accidents over the years. Jack-knifing a trailer and throwing off all the staff who were riding happened more than once. Bottle rocket wars started in this period, with staff shooting bottle rockets or Roman candles at each other in the dead of night. Multiple locations have been reported including Explorer Island, a field near the Assistant Rangers' residence, and even below the amphitheater in the field between Stahlman and Parnell. A well-known secret was the cargo net that the Craig staff hung in the trees *above* the staff site. Called the "Thunderdome," wrestling matches were held in the net and the loser was the one who was thrown out.[13]

These individual camp stories were often part of a larger mosaic of inter-camp rivalry stories. Each staff tried to somehow embarrass or prank the other. Barr and Ragsdale lit one of Barnett's campfires early. A group of Parnell-Craig staff took a truck with a dump bed over to Stahlman during lunch and dropped a full load of driftwood in their assembly area. Stahlman staff collected cereal box tops to "buy a boat" for Barnett after a comment he had made during Staff Week. They formed the letters "Here's Your Boat Jerry" from the box tops and hung them on the windows in Craig Dining hall. It had taken so long to collect the box tops, several weeks had passed. No one at Craig got the joke. And so it went, back and forth.[14]

In interviews years later, staff on both sides reflected on the seriousness of the rivalry. Some still believed it mattered, others simply brushed it off to tribalism and loyalties of youth. Of all the comments, Web Webster of Stahlman best articulated the differences between the two staffs:

> I always perceived Parnell-Craig were always much more
> rough and ready. The trouble they got into was deeper and
> more profound, but the stuff they pulled off was always much
> better... [They] lived in a camp that was overrun by weeds
> and was not nearly what we perceived as... [They] lived in the
> sticks. [They] lived in the boonies and we, on the other hand,
> we were living in the front yard of *Tara,* because of the fact
> that it was the older camp. I really sort of always believed and
> felt that, as Stahlman, it wasn't so much that we were better it
> was just that we sort of took the genteel approach to being up
> at camp than the Parnell guys. [They] were crazy, [they] did
> crazy stuff, [they] sang these songs that didn't make any
> sense... If we did stuff with *esprit d'corps,* [they] did it with a
> mania that was a little bit scary to watch and [they] were al-
> ways talking about somebody's butt.

Webster's perception was only reinforced by Staff Night Out stories. When Michael Allen and the other Stahlman Waterfront staff went out on staff night out, they went to the nearest Books-A-Million by the mall in Rivergate on the north side of Nashville. There they started a book club that would last several years. A similarly sized group of Craig AY staff was meanwhile at a Pizza Hut in Gallatin, the small town up the road from the Reservation. Instead of reading books, this group was using a paper napkin to sketch plans for a treehouse or how to run electrical wire from the program director's cabin to the staff site.[15]

Perhaps the best known staff story from this period is the famous SPAM Hunt from 1989. Given Webster's description above, it should not be surprising this event involved the Parnell staff on a night out. This particular trip saw most of the Parnell staff congregate at the local Kroger grocery store in Gallatin. For reasons that remain lost to history, the group formed a single file line and marched through the aisles of the grocery story chanting, "SPAM, SPAM, SPAM." Having found the item in question, the ensemble marched to the check-out, still chanting. The canned meat product was rung up and upon hearing the cost, the chant changed to "Too Damn Much! Too Damn Much!" and the staff marched out without paying. Needless to say, the spectacle upset the store's management. As it turned out, one of the marchers was wearing a Boxwell t-shirt, which prompted a call to Willhite, who was waiting for the staff when they returned to camp. Lined up in the compound in the middle of the night, the whole group was dressed down and given work detail—known as SL, or Special High Intensity Training List—for the next week. Ultimately, the episode was completely inconsequential in the grand scheme of the staff or the camp, but it became a touchstone story, passed down for years and a badge of honor for those who had participated.[16]

While "getting away" with something under the watchful eye of Barnett, Ragsdale, or Willhite was part of the bonding experience, the staff experience was more than late night devilment and shenanigans. Youth staff had unique opportunities for growth as they had front row seats to see how older men dealt with life. Q-ball received regular letters from his wife Tillie and allowed no one else to see them; they were private. The message to others was that a good marriage could last and be intimate in ways a teenager might not understand. Ragsdale often had his young son, David, at camp with him, modeling how a father behaved even in an age of divorce. Barnett had to fire

his mentor, a man he had brought back to staff and looked up to as a youth.
When the mentor struck a young staff, Barnett had to fire him. Later that
evening, the Program Director cried over firing his mentor, but it had to be
done. These personal stories mattered as much as the glorious adventures.[17]

Perhaps it should not be surprising then that staff itself became something of an institution. It was not simply a group of Boy Scouts together for a
few weeks every summer. The red hats demonstrated that they were a unique
group, different from other scouts or scout organizations. Staff had traditions
and "institutional memory" and by the mid-1980s both camps began passing
that memory on in more formal ways. After the closing songs of a campfire,
the staff was together, but the crowds had dispersed, creating a perfect opportunity to pass on this shared history. At Stahlman, "Swing Low, Sweet Chariot" became the favored song for this activity after the Sunday Night Campfire.
During the song, which already had a call and response dimension to it, individuals would pay tribute to former staff members. Perhaps nothing more than
calling out a name, it was an opportunity to pass on a shared history, to teach
the next generation about the "heroes" in the camp's legacy. Parnell-Craig did
something very similar. At the Friday night campfire, after communications or
reminders were given, someone would give the camp mantra, "Every Week Is
the First Week," meaning that the next week's group of Scouts deserved the
same level of enthusiasm as the first week did. The introduction to the mantra
always began "In the immortal words of...." and a former staff members' name
was usually inserted, allowing this staff to pass on their own heroes.[18]

This idea of honoring "staff" saw a more formal iteration in 1983
when the first Staff Reunion took place at Boxwell. Spearheaded by a group
former 1960s and early 1970s staff, most of whom had been District Executives, the reunion was completely organic. It did not come from the council or
because of any particular anniversary. At the group's annual Memorial Day
campout, the idea emerged and they decided to do more than simply talk
about it. This group built a staff list of everyone who had worked (the council

Reunion staff of the first Boxwell Staff Reunion, July 1983. Personal Collection of Kerry Parker.

had kept no such lists), tracked down the individuals, and invited them to re-live a day at camp on July 4th weekend, 1983. Before the internet or even personal computers, this was quite an undertaking. After a day of camp activities and a reception in Craig's dining hall, there was a dinner with awards at Stahlman dining hall. The day ended with a campfire, complete with songs and "words of wisdom" from Q-ball. The group bankrolled the event themselves and reimbursed themselves from a small charge from the attendees. They made enough to sponsor a second reunion, which followed a similar pattern and program in 1989.[19]

      Perhaps part of what transformed camp staff in these years into an institution of their own were Ragsdale and Barnett. Where most of the previous program directors had been teachers, Ragsdale and Barnett had both been powerfully shaped by their experience in the military. While each cultivated an *esprit de corps* differently for their particular camp, there is no denying that institutionalizing how camp worked, what staff meant, and how important traditions could be were all part of the package of working for these men.

Ranger Staff

When Willhite became Reservation Director in 1976, Norman Patterson was in his second year as the Reservation's Head Ranger. Bobby Smith had moved on to greener pastures with Gallatin Steam Plant in 1974. Succeeding Smith was Patterson, a "kind of a thin fellow" who had previously worked at the Arnold Engineering Development Center in Tullahoma as a machinist. Because of this experience, he was very handy around the Reservation. He understood how things worked and using his skills and training, he could make improvements to those things.[20]

Patterson had the misfortune of serving as ranger after Bobby Smith, who was so well liked. It would have been difficult for any new man to fill those shoes, but Patterson had a difficult time, though it was not always clear why. As Business Manager Michael Seay explained, "I feel he was really a little bit misunderstood. I don't know whether or not he just rubbed people the wrong way, or they rubbed him the wrong way, and then it got worse." For Jim Barr, Patterson's "problem" was pretty simple: "Norman was...a good guy. Introverted personality. He took care of the reservation... So, you know, all the grass is cut, all the stuff, whatever, the...physical job of being a Ranger at Boxwell, but he stayed to himself. He wasn't a Program person at all."[21]

Generally speaking, Patterson was less gregarious and open than Smith and untrusting of people he did not know. Once he became familiar with an individual, then he was far more trusting and friendly, though he still had a quick and hot temper. He was nicknamed "Stormin' Norman" by the staff. Parham recalled an incident from when he was a Program Commissioner in 1975 that demonstrated how apropos the nickname was. Parham's commissioner site was right next to Stahlman's Showerhouse Three, so Parham had tied into the electrical box there to run power to his staff site. Patterson was not having it. He "roared down there one day, went in there and cut my wire and didn't say a word to me and zoomed off." This was apparently fairly typical behavior.[22]

While working as ranger, Patterson learned how to fly a plane. He earned his pilot's license and owned a plane. Some of the earliest known aerial photos of the reservation were taken on two separate trips in Patterson's plane. It was Patterson's interest in planes that eventually led to his end as Ranger. He started doing work at the Gallatin airport, using those machinist skills on planes. It was extra work, and it was extra work that began to demand more of his time. From Patterson's perspective, the extra work made it possible for him to continue working at Boxwell. When the moonlighting was discovered, an impasse was reached. Patterson did not want to quit his work at the airport and Willhite was not going to pay him more. Norman Patterson's tenure came to an end.[23]

Dean Claud took up the mantle as Head Ranger in 1982 following Patterson's departure. Like Smith and Patterson before him, Claud came from a military background. From 1947 until 1972, Claud worked for the government, either in the Army or as part of the civil service. When he retired, he went directly to work for the Middle Tennessee Council at the newly acquired Grimes Canoe Base. Up to this point in his life, Claud had gone by "Dean." It was Ralph Manus, long-time Boy Scout professional, who began calling Claud by his first name "Willie" and it stuck.

"Ranger Willie" was the first ranger at the new Grimes Canoe Base. Indeed for approximately two years, while the base itself was being built, Claud ran Grimes out of his home. Every week he would haul canoes over to the base on Friday and bring them back to storage at his home on Sunday. Once the house was finished, Claud and his family—a wife, a son, and a daughter—

moved to the property. The Canoe Base experience was a good one. Claud would carry troops up river into Lewis County to put them in the water and check on them every night of their week-long float. Once they arrived at Grimes, if their clothes and sleeping bags were wet, Claud's wife Betty would dry them. It was a good life and so when Claud was offered the ranger position after Bobby Smith left, he turned it down.

When the Clauds finally did move to Boxwell after Patterson left, it was a shock. Grimes Canoe Base was approximately thirty-three acres of property. While there was activity outside the base itself, Claud only had to maintain the limited thirty-three acres of Grimes itself. Boxwell was significant larger, both in terms of acreage and program. There was more land, more people, and just more things going on. Boxwell was a bigger job than Grimes had been.[24]

But the rewards were larger as well, particularly in terms of the people. Betty Claud and the children made good friends with the other families who were still attending Murrey. The Wood Badge volunteers were also "a fine group of people." Percy Dempsey in particular was held in high regard. Dempsey traced his roots back to MT-2 at Rock Island and by the 1990s was a regular member of the Wood Badge staff, even serving as Scoutmaster for MT-30. Also held in high regard by Claud were Ernie Ragsdale and Jim Barr and that feeling was reciprocated. Ragsdale picked up almost immediately that while Claud had a gruff exterior, really "he was just a big old teddy bear." Claud was willing to do just about any program related task the two men could come up with and his connections to Fort Campbell gave them access to pyrotechnics they had never dreamed of before. Indeed, the metal frame used for Stahlman's Burning Eagle closing for the Friday Night Campfire was welded by Claud.[25]

For most of the youth staff, Claud was more distant. The older youth who were entrusted with the weighty responsibility of tractor driving had the closest interaction with Claud through "tractor driving school." Every staff member who drove one of the camp's work tractor's was required to attend this "school" Monday morning of staff week directly after breakfast. Stahlman's Web Webster described the entire process in wonderful detail:

> The green John Deere used gas, but the Massey [Ferguson] used diesel... Willie Claud, Willie Claud had a cigarette going all the time. He smoked Kents. Kents were the ones with the plastic trifold filter in the middle. He had a real grizzled up face and he had this thing dangling and an ash about an inch long.
>
> He'd go "Alright, ya'll come over here. John Estes. What runs in the Massey?"
>
> And John, in his John Estes voice, which I won't even try to imitate, [said,] "Diesel, Willie Claud."
>
> "What do we put in the Deere?"
>
> "Gasoline, Willie Claud."
>
> "What happens if you run the diesel dry?"
>
> "Pump, pump, pump, Willie Claud."
>
> "That's right, there was one boy who ran the Massey till it was dry and ran out of diesel over there on Duck Head. I had to go down there, I had to pump, pump, pump, cause I had to clear all them lines out if the diesel runs out. Pump, pump, pump, pump, pump, pump. Webster what is the first thing you going to do when you get to Massey?"
>
> "Check the diesel, sir."
>
> And so it was, it was a liturgy as much as it was anything else...

The "School" did not change dramatically over the entire time that Claud was ranger. Parnell-Craig staff member Jason Bradford—who came along after both Webster and Estes were gone—remembered a school that was much the same as Webster's description. No actual lessons on how to drive the tractor,

373

but an incredible stress on not running out of diesel or oil. The driving was generally trial and error or older staff passing on the necessary skills to the new recruits.[26]

Much as the camp leadership shifted and then stabilized in this period, so too did the ranger staff. The Greens—Uncle Bill and Punkin—were gone by the time Patterson took over. There were some fluctuations in this period, as people like Frank Arias joined on as assistants briefly and then left. By the mid-1980s, the ranger staff stabilized. Claud's son Brian became an assistant and was joined by Cecil Pitts. Pitts stayed at the Assistant Ranger's house coming into the residence and Brian Claud took up residence in one of the cook's cabins. This team would continue until Claud's retirement in 1995.

See Rock City

Summarizing the camp staff experience in the Willhite years is difficult. But perhaps nothing better encapsulates the ability of the staff to use limited resources in creative ways than the story of "See Rock City."

Rock City, of course, was a popular Georgia tourist destination in the northwestern corner of the state, just south of Chattanooga, Tennessee. In addition to breathtaking vistas and some amazing rock formations, the tourist destination was very kitschy. Garden gnomes peppered the property. There were also bird houses there, red buildings with black roofs that look like little barns. This was part of the hook. All across the South as one sped down an interstate or state highway—especially in Tennessee—one saw barns with "See Rock City" painted on the roof. In an article by former camp staff member Greg Tucker, *The Tennessean* reported in 2009 that over 900 roofs in nineteen states had been painted by 1969. In other words, this little bit of Georgia kitsch was part of the popular culture and burned into the brain of just about every youth growing up in the period.[27]

And so it was, early in the summer of 1988, the Tennessee Department of Transportation donated several gallons of paint to the Middle Tennessee Council. The paint was significant not simply because there were several gallons of it, but because it was so unusual in tint. The paint was purple. It was identified as an Occupational Safety and Health Administration (OSHA) tint, specifically "safety purple." Four or five gallons of the paint made its way down to Camp Parnell under the auspices of completing a Con-Yard project.

Summer camp ended on Saturday, July 23, 1988. In the early morning hours of the last day, shortly after midnight in fact, several Parnell Staff members executed a legendary camp prank. While specifics on something like this are difficult to nail down, at least five different individuals were involved. Of those confirmed five, several were not planning to return to camp staff the following year. This activity would be a crowning achievement, a bar by which all other staff pranks might be measured.

A prank by which none involved could be punished because most were leaving later that afternoon never to return.

Working in the dark of night, this "elite" group of Parnell staff climbed atop the dining hall with the acquired—or to use the parlance of the time, "commissioned" or "re-appropriated"—paint. As two campsites were located nearby, they tried to be as quiet as possible, which was no small feat on the metal roof. The group painted enormous letters on to the roof of the Parnell Dining Hall. The message was on the north side of the building, making it invisible to anyone on the ground as the trees surrounding the building prohibited the view. However, because the letters stretched eight to ten feet in height, the message was easily visible from the air.

And the safety purple message that adorned the metal roof of Parnell Dining Hall? "See Rock City."

While all those involved were sworn to secrecy ("staff stuff stays staff stuff"), by the Staff Reunion the following year, the word was out. "See Rock

A collection of patches from staff hats during the Willhite era. Clockwise from top: 1979 hat, 1982 hat, 1988 hat, 1990 hat, 1986 hat. Collection of Russ Parham.

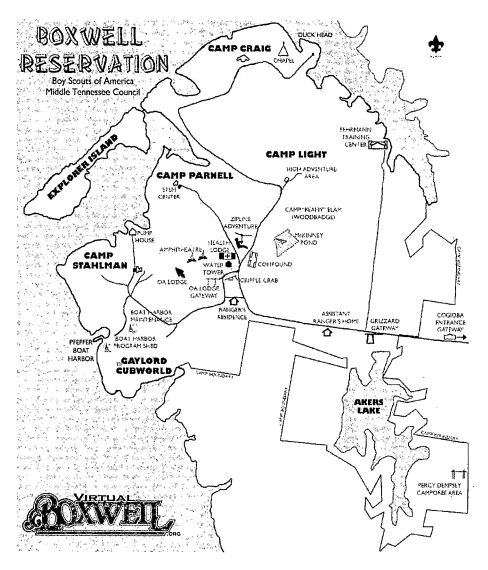

Digital Map of Boxwell Reservation from VirtualBoxwell.org.

Chapter 8

The Modern Era:

Boxwell Reservation at Old Hickory Lake

1997-2021

In the summer of 2007, Cubmaster Rob Ward came back to Boxwell after an absence of thirty years. The twenty boys he was taking to Boxwell were a mixture of both Webelos Scouts and traditional Cub Scouts. The entourage was on its way to CubWorld for the Cub Scout summer resident camp. This was not day camp, but a multi-day, overnight experience. As Ward approached the Reservation with his carload of boys, he quickly realized Boxwell had changed a great deal since his last visit to the property.

Ward's first experience with Boxwell had been as an 11 year old youth. He lived in Mississippi at the time, but came to middle Tennessee in the summer to stay with his grandparents in Lebanon. His grandmother gave him the opportunity to go to Boxwell. Ward was part of a troop back in Mississippi, but he did not have a troop to camp with at Boxwell. So, he spent the week as a provisional Scout. Provisionals were individual scouts who attended camp without a troop, but were grouped into a "provisional troop" to ensure they had adult leadership. Ward's faux troop camped at Stahlman, allowing the Mississippi transplant to spend his free time hanging around the kitchen and chatting with "Miss B," Pearl Schleicher's sister and one of the camp cooks. And why would an 11 year old boy spend his free time hanging out at the Stahlman Kitchen? "I was always hungry. Always hungry. Today, I'm still hungry." Estelle Langford—Miss B's real name—told the young Ward she would put him to work if he came back the following year. He did and she did. Ward joined the camp staff for a week in 1976 at twelve years old. He followed the same pattern in 1977, except this time he worked for two weeks. And then Ward moved on with his life.

At 43 years old, Rob Ward returned to Boxwell as a Cubmaster. No longer a blonde, scrawny pre-teen, the black haired and bearded Ward immediately recognized he was not the only one to have changed. As he and his Cubs came up Highway 109 to the entrance of the Reservation, the landscape was very different. The half-circle "Boxwell Reservation" sign—which warned "Caution Camp Open" during June and July—that had been the first warning the camp was approaching, was missing. Kudzu still graced the hill opposite the entrance, but the cedar plank hanging sign—even the hill that the sign had hung upon—was now gone. Ward and group were instead greeted with a ground level sign made of stone and wood. This sign, just completed that spring, was itself a replacement for a sign that looked similar, but had been destroyed in a storm the year before.[1]

The drive down Creighton Lane into the Reservation held more changes. Once nothing but hills and farmland, the southern side of the road was now adorned with homes, all less than fifteen years old. The community was growing; even Highway 109 itself was under construction to be widened. As the crew continued toward the main entrance of the camp property, a sign pointed to the Percy Dempsey Camporee area. In Ward's youth years, this Camporee Area had been part of the farming operation. One could find tobacco, corn and the pig farm on this part of the Reservation.[2]

After crossing into the Reservation itself, the changes continued. A cedar sign with the words "Fehrmann Training Center" pointed to a long, gravel side road. There was no need for Ward's group to travel this lonely gravel highway. However, if they had, what they would have found at the end

The stone entrance sign to Boxwell Reservation on Highway 109, which replaced the cedar hanging sign, June 2016. Photo by the author.

of the road was the once secret, now renovated, Akers Cabin, also known as the legendary Ittabeena.

Continuing on Creighton Lane, just beyond the caretaker's cabin, a series of vertical cedar signs on four by four posts now lined the right hand side of the road. Each sign was emblazoned with one of the twelve points from the Scout Law. The canopy of trees had grown up as well, completely covering the road and killing off the low level brush that had at one time made it difficult to see very deeply into the woods. In a small clearing opposite the line of Scout Law posts was a canvas sign, advertising an Order of the Arrow event—Winter Camp—that would be held after Christmas.[3]

Of course for Rob Ward, the most jarring detail came once his crew left the woods and came to the top of the hill. The Cripple Crab—the name shortened over the course of time from Crippled Crab—stood where it had since the earliest days of the Reservation, a familiar sight amidst so much change. The familiarity was short-lived. "I remember pulling up to the stop sign, looking over at the Crab," Ward recalled. "The pay phones were gone. *The pay phones were gone.*" The long standing link to the outside world, the place where staff, Scouts, and leaders alike stood waiting their turn to call home or touch base with the office, was no more. The nearly ubiquitous personal cell phone had replaced the pay phone. Ward and his group continued to Gaylord CubWorld for their camping experience. For Ward this same camp had been Camp Murrey, though he had never visited it as a camper.

The program at CubWorld showed Ward not everything had changed. It was an incredible, positive experience for Ward and his Scouts. As he explained,

> CubWorld was exciting. Again, that Cub World staff impressed me so much... I was so impressed by the way those kids work[ed] together. It's like they'd been working together the whole time, their whole lives. The team spirit... They wouldn't tell you no for nothing. If you came to them with a question, they had an answer... I went home, told the wife after that week, "I want to go work there. I want to go work with these kids, because I'm so impressed by them."

And so, for the second time, Rob Ward joined the Boxwell staff. He came back in 2008 as part of the CubWorld shooting staff, where he quickly adopted the persona of the Australian Archer to entertain the kids. He kept coming back too, as a director, then CubWorld Commissioner, and then joined the Ranger Staff in 2012. He stayed on a full time employee at Boxwell Reservation until the end of 2020.[4]

Rob Ward had moved through Scouting to the adult side of the program. Like so many others, his kids brought him back into Scouting. But it was his experience at Boxwell, at the Cub camp, just barely ten years old, that motivated him for the following decade. Physically, the Reservation was a different place. But the emphasis on program remained Boxwell's most important feature as the camp entered the new millennium.

Revolutions

In June of 2007, about the same time that Rob Ward was bringing his Cubs and Webelos to CubWorld, the computer company Apple released the very first iPhone. The device was a technological wonder. It combined a cellular phone with a handheld internet capable computer, using a touch screen interface. It was the sort of invention that transformed not just markets, but the way people lived and interacted with each other. And as amazing as the iPhone was, it was simply the culmination of several revolutionary technological changes that had been unfolding over the preceding decades.[5]

As the United States entered a new millennium, a technological revolution was reshaping every aspect of American life. Computers had their roots in the Second World War, but the rapid change did not really occur until the introduction of the microchip by International Business Machines (IBM) in 1971. By 1980, Microsoft's Disk Operating System, otherwise known as MS-DOS, allowed for the creation of easy-to-use Personal Computers (PCs). Graphical interfaces were eventually added to these operating systems, allowing point and click operation with the aid of a mouse. The PC was then combined with a new international system of communication, the Internet. Once the electronic infrastructure was built, documents, sites, and content could be located using a specific address—a Uniform Resource Locator, or URL. The World Wide Web was born.[6]

Despite this wildly simplified explanation, this technological revolution was profound. The arrival of microchips, computers, and the internet touched every aspect of American life. Television screens became wider and thinner. Telephones moved from dials to buttons with each producing a specific electronic tone. Information was transferred to a digital state and sent to others over wired networks around the world. Internet businesses sold goods with a fraction of the overhead of a brick and mortar store. White collar work could be produced through a variety of software; blue collar could be replaced by robots. More accurate weather reporting and sharing of scientific research expanded. Developments that had only been possible in science fiction—the ability to call up digital music and video for instance—became real life. The impact of this "new economy" was enormous, leading to increased globalization as post-Cold War markets opened.[7]

With the 21st century and the arrival of new inventions such as the iPhone, technology became personalized and portable in a way it never had been before. With a smartphone, not only could an individual call someone else without a hard line to connect them, but he or she could also shop online from wherever they happened to be standing. To put this revolution in perspective, consider the Apollo missions through which the United States landed man on the moon in 1969. This had been possible because expensive and powerful mainframe computers did the mathematical computations to guide the spacecraft, monitor the astronauts, and maintain communication. The iPhone 6—not even the most powerful such device at this writing—was "32,600 times faster than the best Apollo era computers and could perform instructions 120,000,000 times faster." Americans quite literally had more power and more information at their fingertips than any other generation in all of human history.[8]

The technological revolution was only part of the transformation sweeping the nation. Social changes unleashed during the Civil Rights Era continued to reweave the nation's social fabric. Women, African Americans, homosexuals, and immigrants all demanded equal access and treatment. With a legal code in place to protect against discrimination, the work of these groups now focused on defining what exactly equality meant. For African Americans and Hispanics, many achieved middle class and professional status, while others found a criminal justice system that treated them differently than other groups. Homosexuals struggled to enjoy the same rights and privileges as heterosexuals. As homosexuality was still illegal in many states, homosexuals were unable to join certain organizations, get legally married, or bequeath assets to a partner at death as would be the case with a spouse. This situation changed slowly through a series of Supreme Court rulings. *Lawrence v. Texas* (2003) overturned a Texas law, which essentially made homosexuality illegal, and reaffirmed an individual's "right to privacy." The decisions in *United States v. Windsor* (2013) and *Obergefell v. Hodges* (2015) ruled key provisions of the 1996 Defense of Marriage Act (DOMA) unconstitutional under the Fourteenth Amendment's equal protection clause. Nevertheless, questions about how this ruling might conflict with First Amendment religious freedoms remained to be solved.[9]

Overall demographics were changing too. In 2000, there were approximately 300 million Americans; by 2014, 320 million, an enormous increase. Over 80% of these 320 million lived in the cities and suburbs. Population analysts predicted that by 2040 the four major minority groups—African Americans, Hispanics, Asians, and Native Americans—would together make up the majority of the nation's population. Still, since native born birth rates (regardless of race) had been declining in the final years of the 20th century as both parents worked outside the home, a good portion of this growth was due to immigration. The end to immigration quotas in 1965 had led to steady immigration increases every decade, with most families coming from Asia, Africa, and Latin America. Not surprisingly, immigration became a political hot button in the 21st century.[10]

These economic and social transformations led to increasing partisanship in politics. Each presidential election in the period—Bill Clinton (1996), George W. Bush (2000, 2004), Barack Obama (2008, 2012), Donald Trump (2016), and Joe Biden (2020)—seemed to be more bitterly contested than the one before it. The rise of social media—itself a result of the technological revolution—transformed campaigns, administrations, and how information (as well as disinformation and misinformation) was transmitted to the public. Finding common ground solutions seemed less possible as both sides retreated into 'echo chambers' created and reinforced by the algorithms of their social media or their preferred internet news outlet.

Americans also faced terrorism, both foreign and domestic, in this period. The attacks on New York City and Washington, D. C. on September 11, 2001 shocked the nation and the world, as Islamist terrorists used hijacked airplanes as weapons. Nearly 3,000 people died in the attacks. The resulting "War on Terror" led to the invasion of Afghanistan in October 2001 to root out the terrorist leadership and those who harbored them. Executed with NATO allies, this became the longest war in United States history. Using the doctrine of preemptive war—attack enemies abroad before they attack the home front—the United States also invaded Iraq in March 2003. Considerably more contentious than Afghanistan at the time, the second Persian Gulf War removed Iraqi leader Saddam Hussein from power, but failed to create a beacon of democracy out of the Middle Eastern state. The U. S. officially withdrew in December 2011. The war on terror also led to a dramatic reorganization of the federal government as well as drone warfare and the rise of an enormous surveillance state, both made possible by the technological revolution.[11]

Unfortunately, some terrorism was homegrown. This quarter century period was peppered with a variety of mass shootings, often in schools. The first and perhaps most infamous was Colorado's Columbine High School shootings in April 1999, when two high school students attacked their classmates and forever changed school security practices. Other school shootings involved outside attackers, such as the Sandy Hook Elementary School shooting in December 2012. But schools were not the only scene of domestic terrorism. The bombing of the Alfred P. Murrah federal building by Timothy McVeigh and Terry Nichols in 1995 was the deadliest such attack, but not the only example. White nationalism resurged in the early 21st century, often leading to violence such as the Charleston church murders in June 2015 or the Unite the Right white nationalist rally in Charlottesville, Virginia in August 2017. The political climate mentioned above —again, aided by social media—made it difficult to reasonably address these issues.[12]

Just as the industrial revolution over a hundred years earlier had ultimately led to the creation of the Boy Scouts of America, the new world unleashed by the technological innovations and social transformations of the period led the organization to do some soul searching. Could an organization
rooted in outdoor activities and wilderness skills compete with video games
and the addictive influences of social media? In an increasingly polarized political climate, what did it mean to be a good citizen? As both homosexuals and
women became more integrated participants in American society, were the organization's positions on these populations outdated or were they timeless
moral imperatives? How should the organization with its own 100 years of
history navigate the politicized environment to maintain enrollment? And perhaps the most critical question in this new world: how does Scouting provide a
quality outdoor program and still keep the children safe?

Scouting struggled with answers to these questions. To meet the challenges of immigration and demographic change, the old Inter-Racial Service
and Inner City-Rural Program again evolved, becoming Scoutreach. Scoutreach
was a Scouting outreach program "aimed to foster Scouting in underserved
areas." Like its predecessors, Scoutreach focused on bringing minority groups
into Scouting. Some populations, like the Asian American community, saw
strong growth in the 21st century. These efforts were somewhat counterbal-
anced by lackluster growth in Scouting's overall membership. 1980 had been
hailed as pivotal year for the movement as membership began to rise again with
4,326,082 youth and adults active in the program. In 2005, with its centennial on the horizon, the organization boasted approximately the same numbers,
despite a nationwide population increase of over thirty million in the same period. The nation was growing, but Scouting was not growing with it.[13]

While Scoutreach was a clear path forward, other issues were not handled as deftly. In the 1990s, Scouting took a hard line position on homosexu-

ality. Homosexuals—adult or youth—were not allowed in the program. If a Scout or a volunteer was discovered as such, he was expelled from the program. This led to the highly publicized Supreme Court verdict in *Boy Scouts of America et al v. James Dale* in April 2000. Dale had been a Cub and Boy Scout, earning his Eagle in 1988. The award was presented to him by the grandson of Baden-Powell himself. At 19 years old, Dale admitted his homosexuality in an interview when discussing his work for the Lesbian, Gay, and Bisexual Alliance at Rutgers University. An Assistant Scoutmaster at that time, Dale was immediately expelled from Scouting. The Court ruled that as a private organization, the BSA set its own rules for membership and could legally bar homosexuals. The First Amendment's right of association allowed the Scouts to assert "that homosexual conduct is inconsistent with the values it seeks to instill." The Court's ruling validated the position the Scouts had held since 1980.[14]

By the time of the verdict, the social acceptance of homosexuality was already shifting. A position that had seemed reasonable to the majority of Americans in 1980 was increasingly seen as discriminatory in the 21st century. Indeed, new lawsuits erupted, arguing that if the BSA were to hold this position of exclusion, then the organization should be barred from using government facilities, which guaranteed equal access under the law. Eventually, such lawsuits even led to the Scouts being barred from using Fort A. P. Hill in Virginia for national jamborees. These lawsuits had a chilling effect on state governments as well, leading to the Scouts being banned from state government facilities, such as schools. School districts feared that if they allowed in the Scouts, which openly barred homosexuals, females, and atheists, they could not turn away groups like the Ku Klux Klan who wanted to recruit as well. In short, winning *Dale* came at an enormous cost. By winning in the courts, the BSA lost the public support and, without the schools available for recruitment, already stagnant membership began a steady decline.[15]

It was obvious by the organization's centennial in 2010 that membership was suffering and changes would be necessary if the Boy Scouts were going to see another hundred years. As late as July 2012, the ban of homosexuals was still publicly supported as "the best policy" of the BSA. And then, within a year, an abrupt about-face occurred. In May 2013, the 1,400 member Executive Council voted to remove the ban. Beginning January 1, 2014, the Boy Scouts would allow gay youth, but not adults, to participate in the program. Then, in July 2015, the Executive Council rescinded its ban on adult leaders as well. While an exemption was made for troops whose charter organizations were religious organizations, the die was cast. After decades of overt exclusion, homosexual youth and adults were welcomed in the organization.[16]

Women presented another membership challenge. Families had been changing. Not only were there more single parent families by the early 21st century, but even when the parents were together, both worked. Excluding women therefore meant keeping youth from participating. Adult women had been encouraged as Den Mothers in Cub Scouts, but by the 1990s, women were commonly part of a Troop Committee and were increasingly serving as Assistant Scoutmasters and even Scoutmasters. The youth side of the program was a little different. No female youth were allowed in Cub Scouts or Boy Scouts, but were allowed in Venturing and Exploring. However, in October 2017, the BSA announced that female youth would be allowed to participate in the program, first as Cubs in 2018 and then older youth in 2019. Formerly known as the Boy Scouts of America, the older youth program would now be called Scouts BSA. In both Cubs and Scouts BSA, the packs and troops would be gender segregated.

The policy change concerning females presented challenges. The BSA's national organization argued that allowing female youth was a logical extension of the program as the values expressed in the Scout Oath and Scout Law were universal. Further, the change would benefit families by allowing consolidation of the extracurricular activities of their children. Critics were more skeptical. The most common argument was that the move was designed to bolster still falling membership numbers. In 2012, the BSA had dropped to 2.8 million youth members and continued to fall to 2.3 million youth members by 2016. Other arguments posited that having girls in the program, even in gender segregated units, would undermine the benefits of a single-gender program. The Girls Scouts of America took this position, arguing, "The benefit of the single gender environment has been well-documented by educators, scholars, other girl- and youth-serving organizations, and Girl Scouts and their families. Girl Scouts offers a one-of-a-kind experience for girls with a program tailored specifically to their unique developmental needs." Clearly, this same position was staked out by those within Boy Scouts as well, except focusing on the boys instead of the girls. Boys could not learn how to be men from or with women was the crux of this position.[17]

These changes alone would have been significant for the Scouting program, but they were only part of the institution's story as it began its second century. Because of the policy changes above—as well as allowing transgender boys—the Mormon Church and its 400,000 youth left Scouting. The Latter Day Saints had been using the Boy Scouts as their primary youth program, but the shifts in Scouting policy led them to leave the program. Other Christian based organizations began to emerge to provide a home for those unhappy with the policy changes. Additionally, years of hiding sexual abusers came to the surface. Multiple lawsuits from multiple states came forward as states changed their statute of limitation laws regarding child abuse. The national organization, not the local councils, carried the burden of these lawsuits because it was national policy that was at issue. As the pressure mounted, an internal review of the organization revealed more than 12,000 children had been assaulted. To survive the legal onslaught, the Boy Scouts of America filed for Chapter 11 bankruptcy in 2020. The actual claims that surfaced as a result of the bankruptcy litigation surpassed 85,000, more than the Catholic Church's sex abuse scandal. The long term effects of the bankruptcy remain to be seen.[18]

These changes played out in the Middle Tennessee Council. After a rebound in membership in the late 1990s, Middle Tennessee membership began to fall as well. In 2003, the Council reported its 28th year of consecutive growth, serving approximately 47,000 youth. By 2015, the total youth served was just over 15,000, an enormous loss in membership. Some of this loss was clearly due to the larger battles Scouting was engaged in, but most was due the fallout over the 1984 Equal Access Act, the interpretation of which prevented the Scouts from entering public schools for recruitment. By 2016, the Tennessee State Legislature circumvented these prohibitions by essentially carving out an exemption. The legislature passed a bill sponsored by Senator Bill Ketron—a former Boxwell staff member—that allowed for a "patriotic society... that is intended to serve young people under 21 years of age, such as Boy Scouts of America..." to enter public schools and recruit. By the end of the year, with the bill signed into law, Middle Tennessee Council could boast it had the fastest growing Cub Scout program in the nation and its overall Scout program was the third largest nationwide.[19]

Other aspects of the BSA's membership challenges played out at the local level as well. The Council and the Church of Jesus Christ of Latter Day Saints (LDS) had a strong working relationship. There was a Mormon Week at summer camp for many years and an LDS committee was part of the Council's organizational structure. Both ended after the policy changes on admitting homosexual leaders. Women served in a variety of capacities in troops and in the Council. By 2018, Karen Bengston began a long tenure as Council Commissioner, one of the top volunteer positions. The Council's first all-female Scout troop—Troop 2019—formed in Murfreesboro in February 2019. By December of 2020, four young women from the troop had earned the rank of Eagle.[20]

The quarter century from 1996 to 2021 was period of enormous transformation, not just for the nation, but for Scouting as well. At the very least, Scouting had an identity crisis as it struggled to define what it was, what it was going to be, and how it would survive. Publically, the rhetoric seemed similar: Scouting was a values-based program for character building. Internally though, the policy shifts raised questions of whose values were being served. Was the program doing whatever it could simply to save itself or did the program understand that values had changed for the majority of Americans and it needed to catch up? Those questions cannot be answered here, but they are relevant as they could easily be applied to camp program. Faced with these transformations, the summer camp program that emerged in these years pivoted and evolved to keep Scouts in Scouting. A new modern Boxwell emerged.

Rebooting Boxwell

Larry Green officially moved down to the Senior District Executive position of the Dan Beard District on August 15, 1996. His departure opened the door for a new Director of Support Services, the man who would be Reservation Director. There were a number of Middle Tennessee professionals who had moved on, but who could return to the Council to fill the position. There were also internal possibilities. But Council Executive Joe Long decided someone from outside the Council was needed. A new person who had not been groomed extensively under Akers or Willhite would bring a different perspective to the Council and to Boxwell. Ron Turpin, a Council Executive from the Westark Area Council at Fort Smith, Arkansas, started as the new Director of Support Services on September 15, just a month after Green's departure.[21]

Turpin came to the job with excellent professional credentials. He was an Eagle Scout himself, having been part of a troop in Oliver Springs in Eastern Tennessee. He had moved to Nashville in 1974 to attend David Lipscomb and when he graduated in May 1978, he started as a District Executive with the Middle Tennessee Council in those first years under Hershel Tolbert. He stayed with the Council for a few years, left professional Scouting, but then returned to Scouting in the Great Smoky Mountains Council. Turpin moved up the ranks in the Knoxville, Tennessee area council before becoming a Council Executive himself in West Arkansas in the early 1990s. These moves gave

Ron Turpin at the Jet Potter Center, August 2015. Photo by the author.

him not only immense professional experience, but powerful first-hand summer camp experience as well. Both of these other councils had not one, but two different summer camps: Camp Buck Toms and Camp Pellissippi in the Great Smoky Mountains Council and Camp Orr and Rogers Reservation in the Westark Area Council. Turpin had experience with all these camps and had personally run both of the Westark Area camps, even as Council Executive. When he returned to the Middle Tennessee Council, he came with a wealth of experience.[22]

   Turpin also brought with him a philosophy about Scouting and summer camp different from his immediate predecessors. First, Turpin wanted to make summer camp more attractive for staff. This meant, in part, better pay. Whereas a first year staff member for Willhite made $10 a week, for Turpin that weekly pay rose, eventually settling at $75 a week. He saw camp staff as a ten hour a day job and to ask a fifteen year old to take home so little was unreasonable. Turpin also had a similar view of program developments. Camp had to work for the Scouts and the leaders. If that meant changing the way something had been done for years and years, so be it. Building a program that ran smoothly and served those who were paying for that program was central. This program approach applied to capital developments as well. If something needed to be built or fixed, then his job was to find a way to make that happen.

While this philosophy had benefits, the reality was it required funding. The Council had just come off of a successful capital development campaign, but that money was allotted already. New monies were needed. And this is where Turpin's philosophy represented a distinct break from the Willhite years. As Turpin explained,

> My training as I advanced as a professional was, you know what, we got a great program, we got a great facility, and don't be embarrassed to go ask somebody for money. And if they tell you no, OK, fine, go ask someone else. And don't be afraid to ask them for what you would think would be the sky, because they are going to be honored and humbled that you felt that they were capable of giving that amount.

And with these philosophies in place, Turpin got to work.[23]

Beginning in January 1997, Turpin launched a Camp Promotion Kick -off meeting. The kick-off meeting centralized camp promotion into a single, large event. Changes to summer camp could be discussed and questions answered all in one evening. Dinner was served to encourage leaders to attend the week night event. Hard copies of summer camp leader's guides and promotional materials could be distributed on site and if a promotional video was handy, it could be projected onto a screen as part of the presentation.[24]

The changes announced at the Kick-Off event outlined a number of new approaches to camp operations. A new Sunday check-in procedure would be implemented. Troops would be assigned a specific time to arrive at camp instead of simply showing up when they wanted. Set staggered times would ease congestion on Sundays in terms of camp check-in, moving in to sites, and performing swim checks. Pre-registration for courses was introduced. Previously, when Scouts wanted to take a merit badge, they simply showed up at a designated time and place. This could lead to very large sessions or very small. Pre-registration allowed the Council to use some simple office software to create schedules for Scouts that would keep the sizes manageable and still allow Scouts to get the advancement they needed. The class reservation forms and the check-in times would be part of another new innovation: the Ten Day Out Meeting. On the Thursday evening ten days before a troop was to arrive at camp, the leaders of the troops attending summer camp that week met at the Jet Potter Center. Here they would pay final fees (again, making their Sunday check-in smoother), turn in their reservation forms, receive their arrival time, and get any updates on last minute changes to the camp program. In short, check in, registration, and class scheduling—all issues that had plagued the camp before but were just seen as part of how things were—were reorganized into an efficient machine. All of these ideas came from Turpin's time at Camp Buck Toms.[25]

Summer camp 1997 arrived in June and several more program changes were instituted. The Davy Crockett Program, the First Year Camper program for the starting ranks, was broken off into its own program area Reservation wide. Formerly part of the program offered by the Activity Yard, Davy Crockett now had its own dedicated program space as well as staff. Further, the program was shifted from an all-day patrol approach to two hour sessions, one in the afternoon and one in the morning, each covering the same material. The changes indicated the importance the First Year Camper program had gained. Metalworking Merit Badge was added to the roster of Handicraft merit badges. A High Adventure Week focused on Whitewater and Rappelling was added after regular summer camp ended. A Cycling program was piloted the fifth week of camp. To demonstrate the idea that all of Boxwell was one camp, not Camp Stahlman and Camp Parnell, Friday Night Campfires were moved out of the individual camps to the Weaver Amphitheatre. A joint campfire ended each week of camp.[26]

New safety protocols were implemented. Every staff member over 18 years old had a background check performed to meet youth protection guidelines. Further, every staff member, youth and adult, had to wear an identification badge to demonstrate they were supposed to be on site. Visitors to camp had to sign in and out and wear a visitor's identification badge when on property. Critical personnel on the Reservation—Turpin, the Program Directors, the Waterfront Directors, the Kitchen Directors, the Range Officers, the Medic, and the Rangers—were all issued handheld radios. The CB radios were removed from the kitchen and an antenna was placed atop the long abandoned water tower.[27]

For the staff, there were two other changes of note. First, Turpin hired Diane Gregory as the Reservation Shooting Sports Director. "Mama Bear," as was her self-styled nickname, became the first female on the program staff. While women had worked on Boxwell staff for years, none had served on the program staff for the resident camps. Turpin himself was initially skeptical of the hire, offering her that particular position with the idea it would dissuade her from joining the staff. But as he explained, "Well how in the world was I to know that she was an Army brat, and she had won the high school marksmanship in Guam when her father was stationed there? Duh! I didn't know it until we started talking about it. It was a perfect fit, really." The second change involved the staff hat. Instead of the solid red hat with some sort of patch on the front, the 1997 staff hat was a two tone hat: a white hat with a red bill. In a blue and red ying-yang type oval were the words "Boxwell Reservation" on the front and on the back of the hat in red lettering was the word "Staff."[28]

The final and most significant change dealt with food service. Citing the increasing attendance at camp, meals moved to a split shift, cafeteria style approach. Originating from Camp Orr, the approach meant that, instead of the entire camp eating together for each meal, each meal would have two shifts—an A meal and a B meal—with half the camp attending one meal and half the camp the other meal. Flag ceremonies would be held in between shifts at breakfast and dinner. This was a particularly dramatic about-face for the Reservation. Parnell-Craig had been using family style for the previous four years. By the end of 1996, Stahlman saw the time benefits and the family focus and planned to move to family style the following summer. This did not come to pass. Regardless, the transition to shifts was a dramatic program change, creating real challenges for mealtime program and increasing the overall time dedicated to meals.[29]

Reactions to the changes were mixed. As Parnell's Waterfront Director Jason Bradford explained, "We had been raised all these years about the importance in the symbolism of you being able to wear this [red hat]. When you were going to get fired or if you were in trouble, you handed your hat to your program director. It was always just this big thing. Ron [Turpin] didn't understand that. To him, it was just a hat." Parnell Trading Post Director Lee Hagan was equally direct: "The traditions of Boxwell were just ingrained in me and he [Turpin] just seemed so flippant about it. [H]e didn't try to teach you anything; he just barked orders." Others were more circumspect about the changes. Stahlman's Program Director Ron Ramsey recalled that "the changes were different, but not drastic or impactful to the way we were conducting camp." C.O.P.E. Director Lance Ussery quipped, "A new sheriff had come to town," and grousing about the changes did not serve the Scouts, the leaders, or the program.[30]

The leadership at Camp Parnell, led by Program Director Grady Eades, did not handle the transition well at all. Constant complaining about the changes and trying to find ways to resist them affected the camp's program. As Ussery explained, "I got more complaints and more Scoutmasters [complaining] every day that year. Every day. About what was going on in that camp..." By mid-summer, Parnell staff was almost in open revolt, leading to a confrontation one Sunday night after campfire at the Crippled Crab. Turpin called a meeting to address a string of pranks that had been happening on the Reservation and the Parnell staff arrived by marching in as a show of solidarity—or outright insubordination.[31]

> Ramsey watched the whole event unfold from the sidelines.

> I remember it as an us or you moment that I wish had not ever occurred. I understand that it was a summer in the making and not simply about that event. I understand that it was about change and that "outsider" feeling with [Turpin's] arrival and change/improvement approach. I remember it as a lesson in how to lead, be responsible to the folks we lead, but that that type of outward defiance should always be done in private and not with the ones we lead. It was one of the most painful experiences of my time at Boxwell.

Turpin could not afford to fire Parnell's leadership with two weeks to go in the summer, but all understood a line had been drawn. As a result, most of Parnell's leadership was not asked to return the following summer. However, as time passed, even Turpin recognized a lot had happened, reflecting, "It was so much change that was taking place. And it was—it was almost like this bulldozer came and tore up our playground."[32]

Despite the unfavorable depiction of Turpin by Parnell's older staff, most who worked with the new Reservation Director had a very different impression. Balding with stooped shoulders and carrying a little weight around the middle, Turpin had a wicked sense of humor and a fierce sense of loyalty. Stahlman Program Director Andy Verble remembered Turpin as "a lot of fun to be around. Management style was completely different than Willhite. Willhite had a separation from the staff that maybe Turpin didn't." Cub-World Program Director Dominick Azzara defined Turpin this way: "Turpin was good to work for. He played when it was play time and he worked when it was work time." Danny Waltman, who worked all over the Reservation in various capacities, summed up Turpin with the following anecdote:

Ron had a sense of humor. I'll never forget, there was one time where I think, Ron needed some help with something, moving something.. But we're driving around in his pickup truck and he's got the FM radio was on and he's got his [handheld] radio.

I'm sitting there... I'm on cloud nine because I'm like, man, this is the boss. I better be good. Here's my chance. Ron has The Rock 105.9 on. He turns it up and he keys up the mic and he starts playing the [truck] radio over the Reservation [handheld] radio for 30 seconds, which is an eternity on the radio. Then he turns the FM radio off and he unkeys the mic and he gets back on, "I don't know who's messing around with this radio, but this is for camp communications only in an emergency, blah, blah." He was really tearing into it. Then he does it again. He turns on the radio and I'm over here just trying not to lose it because I don't want to give it away. "We are triangulating your position right now!"

Man, and I just thought, "That is Ron Turpin." He was going to have fun. I think camp ran pretty well from my eyes at the time but that was him. He was going to have a good time. I think that's the biggest takeaway from his leadership style was he is going to put in people that he trusts and he's going to trust them to do the things.[33]

With the initial growing pains of 1997 behind him, the rest of Turpin's run as Reservation Director was considerably smoother. And for the next five years, Turpin's Boxwell was constantly changing as he focused on fine tuning existing programs, adding new programs, repairing aging infrastructure, and even launching a "small" capital development campaign. Indeed, immediately after camp in 1997, Turpin asked the Camping Committee to form a task force "to evaluate and recommend improvements for the 1998 camp season." With recommendations pertaining to everything from food service to staff recruitment to camp program, the Task Force, led by former staff member John Stewart, laid out a roadmap for the next several years.[34]

Food and food service became one of the top priorities to address.

Cafeteria style was endorsed as was the split shift approach. The committee report justified the shifts on the *1991 Standard Building Code* occupancy limits. But the recommendations went further, requesting a salad bar as well as a peanut butter and jelly bar if a Scout just did not care for what was served. A Food Service Director with experience in large scale distribution, preparation, and management should be hired as well. Even the need for mealtime program during shifts was addressed. These changes were all implemented by the 1998 season. In fact, Turpin was able to secure new cooks from the Sumner County Board of Education as well as equipment from the recently closed Opryland theme park, including a gas grill and stove, convection ovens, and steamers. The weekly menu was even published in the *Leaders' Guide*.[35]

Specific program recommendations were put forth as well. There were minor suggestions like troops serving as color guards for flag ceremonies and a Senior Patrol Leader meeting with staff at the start of week. Further, merit badges were ranked by difficulty and Scout experience. Some merit badges were best taken by first year campers, others by older boys. The list organized every merit badge offered. And while never strictly enforced, camp-wide quotas were also established "on the number of Scouts in attendance each week at camp to assist in the overcrowding we have experienced." Ten Day Out Meetings were "universally acclaimed," but the weekly joint campfires required review and the Davy Crockett program was taken to task as needing "serious improvement." The program needed a course syllabus for staff to follow and "signoffs have to be real (not automatic) and given only when the boys learn the material."[36]

Most of these program recommendations were simple changes, but clearly the Davy Crockett program required an overhaul. The focus of continuous improvement over the next several summers, Davy Crockett emerged in 1998 as a skills driven program. A Scout could pursue a particular skill set instead of a specific requirement, working on several ranks at once, just like with his troop. For instance, a Scout would come to camp and focus on First

Aid, which meant exposure to all the First Aid skills in the early ranks. Patrols of ten Scouts were still modelled and patrol leader elections were held at random. The program would be concentrated into four days, leaving Friday for review and Skills Challenge activities.[37]

In 1999 and 2000, Davy Crockett moved to a menu based approach. No more patrols or patrol elections. Called the "smorgasbord approach" by staff member Danny Waltman because of the patchwork quality of the offerings, under this version of Davy Crockett a Scout could take precisely the requirements he needed. The instructors were still skills based—one staff member taught all the First Aid requirements for instance—but the Scouts took just what they needed and could spend the rest of their time doing other activities. Indeed, this version of Davy Crockett was also syllabus driven, meaning each instructor worked from a specific script developed by the Camping Committee. The Staff were "instructed on what to teach, how to instruct, on what day, at what time frame, and with what materials will be necessary." The program would continue this way with minor modifications until 2005.[38]

Following Food Service and Program, Staff and Facilities were the last major areas of recommendations made by Stewart's Task Force. The group recommended mostly broad suggestions, such as "resolve excessive turnover of senior staff and find ways to retain" and "Better maintenance of facilities." There were some concrete suggestions for both staff and facilities though, such as a picture board for staff and their responsibilities, cabins for staff, a staff area with electricity, raising salaries, and providing a bonus for Eagle Scouts. In terms of facilities, the group suggested adding PA systems to the dining halls and converting existing gang showers and toilets into individual stalls. Of course, these recommendations could not just be changed. These recommendations meant new budgets and new money to build things. These would not be as simple to accomplish as the other recommendations.[39]

Capital improvements and maintenance were definitely on Turpin's radar by this point. For the expansion in camp attendance that he envisioned, Parnell was simply too small. The camp may have been laid out well, but there really was not anywhere else to go. Further, the size of the dining hall limited any serious expansion of the camp under the new code requirements. Moving to Craig permanently made more sense. It was larger geographically, meaning it had plenty of room for new sites to be built to accommodate increases in attendance, and it had the largest dining hall on the Reservation. With single shifts, it could hold larger numbers than either Parnell or Stahlman. With split shifts, it could hold even more. But there were concerns about Craig. The uprights that supported the overhanging roof and provided the skeleton for the veranda were deteriorating. "I had this horrible nightmare," Turpin explained, "that we would have a bunch of people standing out there [on the veranda] getting ready to go in to eat, and the thing would fall off." Craig needed help. As a result, Parnell stayed open one more year beyond its typical two year rotation so that Craig could be repaired.[40]

These facility needs—both for Craig and from the Task Force recommendations—resulted in two developments. The first was quite small. Starting in 1998, Turpin started a new program called "Beaver Days." Beaver Days were volunteer work days at camp. It was a simple way to get leaders and Scouts invested in the property themselves by putting in a little labor to help maintain the property. There were generally two days in the spring, both all day affairs with lunch provided. Work included tree trimming, repairing cots, clearing brush, painting, plumbing, carpentry, and just general cleaning. It was a simple way to give the rangers an extra hand, get a lot of work done quickly, and provide some much needed basic maintenance.[41]

The second development was a capital campaign. While the Scoutmaster's Task Force had been at work, so too had the Council's Long Range Planning Committee. Almost exactly a year after the Task Force's Report, the *1998-2003 Long Range Plan* was published and it reinforced the capital development plans of the Task Force. In fact, it recommended even larger im-

The Boxwell Pool from mid-level of the Al Hendrickson COPE Tower, June 2017.
Photo by the author.

provements. In addition to repairing Craig's uprights, the Long Range Plan recommended new showerhouses for Stahlman and Craig, a centralized High Adventure Area, which would include upgraded shooting sports, improvements to C.O.P.E., and a High Adventure Building to be used for instruction, staff housing, and equipment storage. It also recommended centralized staff areas and a "Year Round Aquatic Complex," otherwise known as a swimming pool. The report had broader goals, of course, evaluating membership and finances of the Council, but in regard to the Council's properties, the report was quite clear. The Council's properties should be profit-centers, or put another way, the Council should "continue to increase utilization of Boxwell Reservation, Parish Reservation and Grimes Canoe Base to further programs that will make these facilities self-supporting."[42]

To achieve these goals, the Council launched another capital campaign.

Compared to the recently completed 1994 Campaign, the "millennium campaign" was small. John Finch, the President and co-owner of Powell Building Group, chaired the $2.5 million dollar campaign and coordinated with the Council's Development Director Don McKinney and new Finance Director Carl Adkins. The campaign began in July 1999 and ran through December 2000, though the construction resulting from the campaign would continue into 2003. "We've taken a low-key approach on this and feel it is paying off," explained McKinney at the time. By the Victory Celebration on December 12, 2000, the council reported $2,433,850 in pledges already made with another $100,000 in pledges projected.[43]

By the time the campaign celebrated victory, a great deal of work had already been done. Before summer camp started in 1999, the uprights on Craig Dining Hall had been replaced and redesigned to protect them into the future. New showerhouses were built at Stahlman and Craig. Gone were the gang showers, the row of toilets, and urine troughs. Craig's pit toilets began to fade into memory, much like the kybos. The new facilities included individual rooms for showers and rooms for toilets, but not complete bathrooms. Sinks and mirrors were outside and for public, group use. The Trading Posts at both Stahlman and Craig were also renovated. The service window approach was abandoned. Both Trading Posts became walk-in, browse, and shop facilities: a camp store. The new stores even started taking credit cards. Stahlman also had a new Staff Center built. What had originally been Site 16 at Stahlman became a group staff site. The site included slightly larger tents on a pipe frame, instead of just wooden uprights and a ridge pole. Each tent had an electrical outlet for simple summer tools, such as fans and alarm clocks. The new Staff Center was adjacent to this site. It included showers and bathroom facilities just for the staff as well as a washer and dryer. There was also a commons area, complete with a pool table. And this was all before the Victory Celebration.[44]

Work continued over the next three years. That period saw a central staff site built at Craig in a wooded area between the parking lot and the Athletic Field. Just like with Stahlman, the site included a Staff Center, framed tents, and electricity. Construction began on a new waste water treatment plant for Craig. This was a much needed development for a camp where open sewage during the summer had been a common occurrence. C.O.P.E. received needed maintenance as well as two new elements. More new showerhouses were built at Stahlman and Craig, eventually replacing all six of the older buildings. The shotgun range was renovated as well, complete with new traphouses. A new High Adventure Center was constructed at Camp Light, adjacent to C.O.P.E. and the Shotgun Range. It housed sixty-four people, had a kitchen, and separate gender bathrooms. Named for former Rock Island staff member and Executive Board member John Parish, the building served as a storage and training center and opened the door for non-camping groups to stay the night and take advantage of C.O.P.E.'s team building activities. With the completion of a new swimming pool nearby in May 2003, a true High Adventure Area emerged out of Camp Light.[45]

Conspicuously absent from these developments was Camp Parnell. While even CubWorld received a new parking lot, Parnell had no renovations or upgrades of any kind made to it. When Parnell closed at the end of the summer in 1998, it had been open for three summers. Conversely, by the time the "millennium campaign" concluded in 2003, Craig had been open and running for four summers. There was no indication it would close anytime as parts of the camp were renovated for long term use. The former waterfront staff site below the dining hall became a new camp site as did the old Friday Night Campfire Area. Craig was going to remain open and house more Scouts. Meanwhile, Parnell saw some activity as the site for Webelos Camp and a Venturing Camp in 2001 and 2002. Additionally, Turpin had some long range plans to possibly use Parnell as a church camp and thus generate some revenue for the Reservation, but these plans never materialized. But with no renovations from the campaign, the expectation for Parnell was that it would remain closed as a Boy Scout resident camp. After the summer of 2002, Parnell was abandoned and left to decay.[46]

All of these changes were just the Boy Scout program aspect of the camp; CubWorld now existed and had program that needed attention as well. Given the physical newness of the camp, CubWorld did not need the renovations and improvements that the other camps needed. During Turpin's years, a parking lot was added. Additionally, a small shed was built to serve as the camp's (inexplicably absent) Trading Post. Thus, from a facilities perspective, CubWorld was still new and generally in good shape.[47]

From a program perspective though, CubWorld had to be built from the ground up. A group of volunteers was assembled to start piecing together a program. In the initial efforts, the only real requirement was that the activity areas—the castle, the pirate ship, the fort—be utilized as part of the program, not simply as play areas. So, the original plans involved activities, such as skits and games, at the activity areas. The goal was less to teach the campers skills and more to engage and entertain them. The early themes reflected these attempts to utilize the activity areas. "Folklore Adventure" (1996) and "The World Around Us" (1997) basically followed the same format: "In this adventure, you will meet and participate with historic people of our American heritage, including pirates, frontiersmen, Native Americans and others." Both adhered to the same philosophy as well, designed to "Encourage the development of character, citizenship and fitness in the Scouts through participation in outdoor activities." Advancement was not the top priority.[48]

But leaders and parents wanted advancement, not just a weekend of outdoor play. From here, two programs emerged. There was one resident camp for Cub Scouts—the earliest ranks, such as Tiger, Wolf and Bear—and there was another resident camp for Webelos—the program that transitioned into Boy Scouts. The Cub Scouts program had to be shorter in duration and geared to children in first, second, and third grades. These would be short weekend sessions. Cubs and parents would arrive at 1pm on Friday and leave by 5pm on Sunday. The Webelos program could be longer and was focused on older boys in fourth and fifth grades. Webelos and parents arrived on Monday at 1pm and left Thursday morning around 10am. Indeed, at first, because the program was deemed so different, the Webelos program resided at Camp Parnell after the Boy Scout Resident Camp had moved to Camp Craig. By 2003, both programs ran out of CubWorld.[49]

Even once the dual program approach was settled, there was still a fair amount of finding the right combination and tone for Cub Scouts. Many activities and approaches mimicked the Boy Scout camps. There were songs at meals, site commissioners to help Scouts to their sites and get them started, flag ceremonies in the morning and evening, and activity sessions. There were differences too. After attempting opening and closing campfires, it was clear this was too much, especially for the weekend Cub Program. Opening campfires were jettisoned and closing campfires became a CubWorld specialty. Indeed, CubWorld staff was the first on the Reservation to regularly retire flags at campfires, a practice that spread to the Boy Scout camps. Swimming started in Pirates' Cove, with the floating pirate ship as a centerpiece. After the pool arrived, this ended and Cubs swam exclusively in the pool. The CubWorld staff even adopted a cross-over program developed by the Key Three leadership at Stahlman. "Follow Me Boys" gave the second-year Webelos a tour of Stahlman, introducing them to what adventures awaited them in Boy Scouts.

Of course, Cubs had plenty of adventures of their own. While earning activity badges was certainly part of the experience, there was no directive to master a skill. The goal was to expose Cubs to Scouting and give them a good experience, not only so they would come back to camp, but would stay in the Scouting program. Thus, CubWorld had a lot of fun activities. There were BB gun and Archery ranges. There were water balloon fights with the staff at the Fort. There was dodgeball. There were ice cream socials. In many ways, CubWorld was still the home of the kid-centered family fun that Murrey had been in its heyday.[50]

Experiments with week-long High Adventure programs began in this period as well. The 1994 Capital Campaign had raised funds specifically to expand the High Adventure programs at Boxwell and some of this was now being put to work. Starting in 1997, the summer camp calendar added a High Adventure Week—a week after normal summer camp program dedicated to High Adventure. The first summer a Whitewater/Rappelling program started at the Reservation with two days of training before traveling to whitewater and rock climbing areas in the mid-state. Scaled back to just whitewater, this program continued for several summers. 1999 saw the introduction of the Mountain Man program. Mountain Man followed a different approach. Scouts came to camp with their troop, stayed Sunday night, and then Monday morning left to do rock climbing, spelunking, whitewater canoeing, and outdoor cooking before returning to Boxwell on Friday. Thus, the Mountain Man program did not run just during a special "High Adventure Week," it ran all summer. The momentum continued in 2001, with the addition of a Venturing Camp. Two sessions were held over long weekends at Parnell in July 2001 and 2002, both following two Webelos sessions that occupied the first part of the week. All of these programs were geared toward older Scouts, had limited availability, and included their own costs.[51]

While the above were the major program renovations, there were a host of smaller changes and innovations. "A Day of Scouting" began in 1997 and continued for approximately ten (10) years. Here a private business, such as Averitt Express, O'Charley's, or Sumner Regional Medical Center, covered "the operating revenue for one day's worth of the program" which included training, Camp and Day Camp Programs and more. In return, each company received positive publicity. Field Sports as a program area ceased to exist; its non-shooting merit badges moved to the short-lived Recreation area and then to the Activity Yard. New merit badges were added, including Astronomy, Cycling, Climbing, Whitewater, and Hiking, while old standbys were discon-

tinued, namely Sports and Athletics. As the leaders were already present, adding adult trainings to the camp schedule made sense as a good way to help keep
them busy. Topics such as "Advancement Policy and Procedure," "High Adventure in Your Troop," "Why Knot—Teaching values," and Unit Safety
were offered in the morning and afternoon. To keep track of these changes,
the *Leaders' Guides* slowly began to grow, including more handouts, permission slips, and forms. A thirty-three (33) page booklet in 1997 had grown to
seventy-five (75) pages by 2002. If this was too difficult to flip through, a
CD-ROM version using HTML pages was available as well.[52]

And, of course, the Boxwell property continued to host programs outside of summer camp. A special week of camp just for Latter Day Saints
(LDS) troops began in 2001. Brownsea, the youth version of Wood Badge,
continued, but moved to Parish Reservation (Rock Island) in 1999. Wood
Badge continued as well, but the adult leadership program that had first come
to the Rock Island Boxwell in the 1950s was discontinued and replaced by
Wood Badge for the 21st century. This was a new national program that focused on leadership rather than outdoor skills. The program utilized more traditional classroom learning with a single outdoor weekend component. The
last traditional Wood Badge course was held at Boxwell in the spring of 2001.
Learning for Life was another program outside of summer camp. This BSA-
run program offered values-based instruction with no advancement or merit
badges and held a camp event at Boxwell in the spring for several years. Finally, there were "Hooked on Scouting" days, which were recruitment events. The
Reservation was open to whomever was interested--ideally a Scout bringing a
non-Scout and his parents--to participate in a day of activities. These activities
included fishing, shooting sports, hiking, games and sometimes even horseback
riding demos. It was a big day, sometimes bringing in over 600 boys and families.[53]

Unfortunately, interwoven with these achievements were three tragedies: the first deaths on Boxwell property since 1925. In 1998, the launched

rocket of a Scout participating in Space Exploration merit badge at Stahlman became entangled in power lines near the dining hall on its descent. The boy's father, Bryant Laroy Rogers, returned the following week to retrieve the rocket. Climbing on top of his mini-van, he "tried to free the rocket with a metal rod" and was electrocuted. The following summer tragedy struck the staff itself when Aaron Rook, Craig staff member, died at camp. Along with other staff, Rook was riding on a car from the waterfront to the dining hall. The car was never speeding, but as it approached the dining hall the staff saw some Scouts and slowed further. Knowing they were setting a poor example, Rook and another staff member jumped off the back of the car where they were sitting. Rook slipped on the gravel and fell, hitting his head on the pavement. The fifteen year old was life-flighted to Vanderbilt Medical Center, but did not survive. A tree was planted at Duck Head, just across from the Craig Waterfront, in his memory. The third fatality occurred in 2001. A female Scoutmaster with a Conway, Arkansas troop suffered a heart attack at Camp Craig. The woman had a heart condition she never reported to the Scouts or her family. In all three cases, staff was on hand to provide immediate aid and assistance, often providing CPR for some time before paramedics arrived.[54]

On July 1, 2002, Ron Turpin was promoted to Director of Field Services. The announcement was made at Boxwell at an Executive Board meeting by Council Executive Joe Long. As *Jet Trails* reported, during Turpin's tenure as Director of Support Services, he "greatly improved Scout and Scoutmaster satisfaction with our camping program working with volunteer task forces. The camp's food quality, quantity, facilities, program and staff have improved dramatically these past six years. Boxwell Camping Facilities have been upgraded with outstanding development as well." In 2007, Turpin was promoted again to Assistant Scout Executive. In this position, he began to oversee the new High Adventure property that became known as Latimer Reservation.[55]

Turpin's run as Reservation Director rewrote the book on how Boxwell would operate in a modern world. While the summer of 1997 saw the most program changes, it was hardly the only summer that experienced change. The restructuring that took place in these six years became the basis for modern Boxwell. Virtually all of the efforts at modernization begun under Turpin continued to be used twenty-five years later. The program had been transformed.

The Interregnum

Pat Scales joined the Middle Tennessee Council Staff as Director of Support Services on September 1, 2002. Scales came from the Circle Ten Council out of Dallas, Texas. He came to the position of Reservation Director with little experience in camp operations. Over his decade in professional Scouting, he had served as Field Director, Director of Exploring, and of course as a District Executive. He had most recently spent time as the Circle Ten's Learning For Life Director. Before Scouting he had graduated from Liberty University and worked in the health care industry. Council Executive Joe Long proclaimed Scales had "a wealth of knowledge that will enhance The Middle Tennessee Council programs for our youth and volunteers."[56]

Scales brought some new changes to the summer camp program. Indeed, at the kick-off meeting in January, "the watch words were 'this is what's new at Boxwell.'" For the 2003 season, he introduced Photography Merit Badge, Black Powder Shooting on the Reservation, the BSA Kayaking program, weekly themes, a new High Adventure program, and inflatables at the waterfronts. These changes for Scouts were clearly to get the youth invested in the program. Photography Merit Badge brought with it an additional fee to get the film processed (digital cameras existed, but were still not affordable to most), but it also brought a camp-wide photo contest. The winners of the contest would have their photos mounted, framed and hung in a prominent location at camp and the overall winner would have his photo made into a postcard and used in Boxwell promotional materials. The inflatables were large floating inflated objects at the waterfronts. Craig received the first inflatable object, known as "The Blob." A striped, multi-colored, thirty-five foot long tube, The Blob was quite popular. Ideally, a Scout climbed atop and crawled out to one end. Another Scout jumped on to the other end from an elevated platform, sending the first Scout soaring into the air. "The dads loved it," Jason Flannery, waterfront staff, explained. "Man, watching their kid go 20 feet in the air and watching them smack [on the water]. It was great." The new High Adventure Program, known as the Boxwell Extreme Outdoor Adventure Experience, was really a combination of previous programs under one roof. Backpacking, rock climbing, rappelling, whitewater canoeing, horseback riding and outdoor meal preparation were all part of the new program. Open to older Scouts, especially Venture and Explorers, the program took Scouts to Big South Fork National Scenic Area for a week. At $250 for the week, it was a pricey program, but also a clear attempt to keep older boys coming to camp.[57]

Nevertheless, the consensus was that the new Reservation Director did not fare well his first year. A "this is how we did it in Texas" attitude was not well received by the staff. Rumor has it he also did not get along well with some major donors, particularly Boat Harbor patron Phil Pfeffer. But more importantly, depending on which camp you were at, he was either around too much or not at all. Andy Verble was Program Director at Stahlman in 2003. As he explained, "[Scales] camped out at Stahlman that year that he was there. *Camped out.* He never went over to Craig. Absolutely was on us 24/7." Danny Waltman worked Craig staff and completely concurred. "We always assumed that he was at Stahlman, and that he loved Stahlman more than Craig." According to Waltman, the only time the Craig staff saw Scales that summer was when he came out to check on the work being done on the waste water treatment plant. "He would just sit [on the fence] and watch them work," Waltman recalled. As a result, the plant received a nickname. "It was the Pat Scales Memorial Sewage Treatment Plant," explained Waltman.[58]

Despite this dubious honor, a significant new program did arise during Scales' first year, though the program came not from Scales, but the Wa-Hi-

Nasa Lodge, the Council's chapter of the Order of the Arrow. The Lodge had been developing a very simple concept: have camp at Boxwell in the winter. Building on that concept, the execution was more complex. The Lodge envisioned Winter Camp as something wholly different from the summer camp program. It would offer a different set of merit badges, a different style of camping, and a different program structure. Winter Camp would be offered for only one week, December 27 to December 31, and would be run by an unpaid, volunteer staff. Further, Winter Camp was an enormous service project of the Order of the Arrow for the benefit of the council from start to finish. Ian Romaine was the first adult coordinator and Tyler Belew the first youth leader.

The Winter Camp idea was modeled on the program used in the Circle Ten Council. Romaine and Belew visited the Winter Camp at Circle Ten, exploring what worked, what could work better, and what could make the best program for Middle Tennessee. Thus, much as CubWorld was a modified concept from another Council, the version of Winter Camp that was emerging for Boxwell did not look much like what existed in Texas. To ensure the program was built and promoted properly, the first Winter Camp spent over a year in development, launching in December 2003.[59]

The extra year of preparation paid off and a unique program emerged, one very different from summer camp. Winter Camp offered merit badges not offered at summer camp, a total of twenty-five total, which was only ten less than during the summer. Merit badge sessions were taught by approved counselors, who people in those particular fields, teaching what they did every day. The program itself was run by volunteers mostly from the Lodge. It was a themed program, much like CubWorld, so it appealed to younger Scouts. It also offered workshops to expose older boys to Junior Leader Training as well as the possibility of Summer Camp staff. Thus, it served as a recruitment tool as well as advancement experience. The camping was "Jamboree style," meaning that troops brought their own tents and camped on the ground. About the only thing that looked the same as summer camp was that meals were in the dining hall.[60]

The structure of the program was where the difference from summer camp was most evident. Despite the ambitious advancement offerings for only four days, instruction was only in the mornings. Afternoons were activity driven and there was a whole separate set of challenges in the evening. Many events were tied to the yearly theme. These generally emphasized Scout Skills through troop and patrol competition as well as team building and problem solving. Romaine provided the following example,

> [W]e had a large circular puzzle where groups could earn 2 different puzzle pieces by being the best at a predetermined undisclosed activity conducted that day. Part of the final campfire [involved] those groups competing against each other to win the piece that linked all of the puzzle pieces together.

Other activities fit a more generic "winter camping" theme. The first Winter Camp had a Polar Bear Dash, where leaders took a running leap from the docks into Old Hickory Lake. Even Scales participated that first year, quipping as he exited the lake, "Am I purple? That was a little more refreshing that I thought it would be." In many ways, Winter Camp was full circle for Boxwell as the basic approaches to program and camping for Winter Camp were very similar to the way Linton and the Narrows of the Harpeth camps had run under Coach Anderson.[61]

Held at Camp Stahlman that first December, Winter Camp was a clear success, boasting approximately 300 participants. From here, the program continued to grow and mature. By 2011, Winter Camp was hosting over 1000 participants. Indeed, participation had to be capped to ensure the quality of the program. The program moved beyond Stahlman to locations in Cub-World. By 2012, the Winter Camp concept had become so popular Latimer Reservation developed a High Adventure version of Winter Camp. By 2017, in coordination with summer camp, Boxwell offered every Eagle required merit

Patch for the first Winter Camp at Boxwell, December 2003. Featured in the 2004 Leaders' Guide CD-Rom. Personal Collection of Russ Parham.

badge because of Winter Camp. It was unquestionably a game changing program.[62]

Winter Camp was also important because it demonstrated the growth and influence of the Wa-Hi-Nasa Lodge within the Council. Clearly, the OA had a long history with both the Council and Boxwell in particular, as detailed above. But from the mid-1980s forward, the Lodge began to play an increasingly important role at Boxwell, leaving its mark in very substantive ways. The Weaver Campfire Area in 1985 was a camp addition for the whole Reservation. Spring and Fall Ordeals took on larger roles, setting up more of the camp before staff arrived and completing larger projects after. One example of this was the mundane task in the 1990s of removing the old springs from the cots and bolting a cut plywood sheet to the metal frame. This project involved enormous man-hours and saved even more man-hours in future maintenance. It was not flashy, but it was beneficial and it was all the OA. The Lodge also took on more of camp promotions as well, making promotional videos, visiting troops, and partially paying for the Leaders' Guides. Having the Lodge execute a yearly event like Winter Camp demonstrated both the trust in the group and how influential the Wa-Hi-Nasa #III Lodge had become.

Scales, however, did not stay long. Realizing the job just was not the right fit for him, he stepped down. He helped transition the new Reservation Director during staff week the following year, but in 2004, Scales was done. He became a Senior District Executive for the Hermitage District that summer and left Scouting entirely before the end of the year.[63]

Here We Are, Now Entertain Us

Much like Ed Human and Tom Willhite before him, Carl Adkins began as Reservation Director at the last minute. He started as Director of Support Services on June I, 2004 and Staff Week began June 6. Summer Camp began in days and was nowhere near ready. No Boat Harbor staff had been hired, necessary items had not been ordered. Adkins was on the phone every day recruiting people. His wife came up to camp to help in the kitchen. The new Reservation Director was overwhelmed. With every intention of re-signing, Adkins called Joe Long and asked the Council Executive to meet at Boxwell to walk through the problems. Long encouraged the new Director: Adkins would have Long's support if he would just stick with it. And Adkins did stick with it... for the next fourteen years, making him the second longest Reservation Director after Tom Willhite, one of his mentors.[64]

Adkins had been with the Middle Tennessee Council his entire professional career. After graduating from Middle Tennessee State University, he used the university's placement office to find employment. There he found an offering to join the Boy Scouts of America as a District Executive (DE). The pay was low, but there was a car included. Adkins began as the Elk River District Executive serving Coffee and Franklin counties in 1986. In 1989, he moved back to Murfreesboro as a Senior DE for the Trail of Tears District. He continued his rise through the professional ranks, becoming Finance Director in 1998. In this position, Adkins ran the Council's Friends of Scouting campaign, the annual fundraising drive that accounted for 42% of the Coun-

Carl Adkins, Staff ID photo, 2006. Photo by Carl Head.

cil's revenue. He also oversaw Public Relations for the Council. And finally, after two unsuccessful attempts in 1994 and 1996, Adkins secured the Director of Support Services position.[65]

Adkins brought some personal Boxwell experience to the position of Reservation Director that neither of his immediate predecessors had: he had been Camp Director at Stahlman under Ernie Ragsdale in 1989. This experience allowed Adkins to work closely with Tom Willhite, one of his mentors, from whom he learned to plan for the future and look for future staff leaders. Adkins also learned from Ragsdale. The two were regular volleyball partners that summer and they worked together on staff problems. Andy Whitt was Activity Yard Director in 1989 and remembered Adkins as having a good sense of humor. Specifically, Whitt recalled that "Carlsbad" was Adkins nickname among some of the staff. Murrey's Program Director Christy Willhite and Stahlman Waterfront Director Michael Allen recalled a slightly more amusing story. After a summer of mild practical jokes back and forth between Adkins and the staff, Ragsdale orchestrated a final send-off. Taking up contributions from willing staff after the last Friday Night Campfire, Ragsdale went out and bought a thousand crickets and left them in Adkins' cabin at Murrey. As soon as the Camp Director turned his lights off, crickets were everywhere. In his underwear. His contact lens case. His Coke can. Ranger Willie Claud even claimed crickets were coming out of that cabin for two years.[66]

When he returned in 2004, Adkins was in charge of the entire Reservation, not just one camp on that reservation. Not only were his responsibilities greater, but how he was perceived and treated by the staff was different as well. A fair skinned man with light hair and an athletic build, Adkins was a details person. First thing in the morning, he was out and about checking on the morning meal, checking on the pool, preparing deposits, and monitoring a constant barrage of calls coming in through thirty-five different hand-held radios across the staff. Following the details meant Adkins generally was "wound up. He worried about things. And worried about things the other [Reservation Directors] didn't." Adkins' approach to management was "inspect what you expect" and he had high expectations. Indeed, as Stahlman Staff member Danny Waltman recalled, "we all felt bad for him. We were like, man, this guy's going to have a heart attack. Dude, just calm down." Cub-World staff member Rachel Paris reinforced both the attention to detail and the stress-level. According to Paris, Adkins "cared a lot about uniform and always wearing your name tag and hat and looking your best." And yet, despite having known Adkins for years, "Carl scared me... whenever he was set on something, he was a tough guy." As for Adkins, he was aware of all this. "You don't want people to shake when they see you coming. That would bother me greatly... I'm going to treat you the way I'd want to be treated. As a Christian, I felt like that that's important to me and I want to treat people fair." High expectations brought high intensity. But as Ranger Rob Ward also pointed out, "Carl was big on second chances."[67]

Adkins had no interest in re-inventing the wheel. But he did want to improve that wheel and get people to keep using it. "Just from my experience working with Carl," remarked Ward, "he's about program. He wanted to give the Scouts all he could give the Scout." Adkins realized that both leaders and Scouts wanted "to see new programs..." and to that end, "I wanted to constantly add new things each year." New merit badges, new activities, or new programs would all keep Scouts and leaders coming back. New programs were prominently listed in the *Leaders' Guides* and showcased at the Kick-off meetings. Adkins understood that camp was not simply competing with other jobs or the already over-packed and over-planned summers of teenagers, but with technology. From video games and television to smart phones and then social media, Scouts had a lot of distractions and the exact same program every summer was not going to keep people coming back to camp.[68]

All that said, it is important to remember that Adkins had two distinct hurdles to overcome. First, he was managing a larger program than any previous Reservation Director. The changes made in the previous ten years had expanded Boxwell a step at a time, but taken as collective whole, the program at Boxwell had a multitude of moving parts. It could easily be overwhelming for someone who came on the job days before the program began. With Cub-World, Winter Camp, and a brand new pool, there was more that had to be juggled than ever before.

Second, Adkins came into the position at the exact moment that Scouting's and Middle Tennessee Council's membership numbers plummeted. In 1998, the Council reported it served 45,000 youth and 8,800 volunteer adults. In 2003, the year before Adkins came aboard as Director of Support Services, the Council served 47,000 youth. In 2005, the year after Adkins had accepted the position, total youth served had dropped to 29,744. By 2015, right at the end of Adkins' run, membership had dropped to 15,027 total youth. But what is remarkable about these numbers is that the summer camp attendance numbers remained fairly stable. At the high water mark in 2003, "more than 3,000 Scouts attend[ed] camp," according to the 2003 Annual Report. In 2009, 2,844 Boy Scouts attended camp. Once Cubs and Webelos were added, attendance rose to 3,905. In 2010, 3,230 Boy Scouts attended camp with a total of 4,027. In 2015, 4,062 total participated in a resident summer camp. In the face of dropping membership, Adkins kept fairly stable numbers at camp. His approach to "constantly add new things each year" paid off.[69]

The addition of the pool in 2004 immediately shook up traditional program. Swimming Merit Badge moved to the pool as did the Instructional Swim sessions, elements of the BSA Lifeguard program, and recreational swim. Stahlman had two days for free swim as did Craig. The water clarity of the pool allowed Snorkeling to be introduced as well. All of these programs at the pool presented some new challenges. With activities at the Boat Harbor, the High Adventure Area, and at the resident camps, there were literally things to do all over the Reservation. A Scout from Stahlman could easily walk to the Boat Harbor, but could not get to the pool on time for the next session or back to Stahlman in time for the last pre-lunch session. Transportation was needed. Paneled vans were used at first, but these were eventually replaced by literal school buses on loan for the summer.[70]

The pool created other ripples. Previously, a Scout needed a buddy tag for the Waterfront and another buddy tag for the Boat Harbor. The pool required a third buddy tag. To simplify this system and cut down confusion, Scouts began wearing color coded wrist-bands. These could not only be used for Youth Protection purposes, showing the wearer was supposed to be in camp that particular week, but the color indicated the status as a swimmer or learner. Buddy tags were still needed to know who was in the water and who was not, but the wristbands clarified the status of the Scout and made replacing a tag easier.[77]

The pool also transformed the waterfronts. The loss of Swimming merit badge was a blow, but free swim became a completely different endeavor. Instead of a hundred Scouts crowding the area, perhaps two dozen came to the waterfronts for free swim in the afternoons. The inflatables thus became a very important draw for Scouts. After the success of the Blob at Craig, Stahlman received the Iceberg in 2005. Both waterfronts retained inflatables from that point forward, though what the inflatable itself was often changed. Wholly new programs were introduced as well. Kayaking merit badge was added as was a Paddle Boarding activity and a Scoutmaster Belly Flop. These were the first significant changes to waterfront program in decades.[72]

High Adventure continued to be a central focus. C.O.P.E. and the Boat Harbor both saw new programs and program elements added, including the Flying Squirrel at C.O.P.E., and Wake Boarding and Jet Skiing at the Harbor. Indeed, the Boat Harbor enjoyed a renaissance in the later part of the Adkins years. Just as Billy Walker was C.O.P.E.'s benefactor, Phil Pfeffer had emerged as the Boat Harbor's godfather. Pfeffer was a Sea Scout when he was a youth and made a name for himself through Ingram Publishing, before moving into investment with Tremont Enterprises. He became a contributor to variety of organizations, including several different Scout councils and Lipscomb University. When Adkins approached Pfeffer with a five-year plan for the Boat Harbor, including a teaching pavilion, a boat maintenance area (basically a second compound), and maintenance and upgrades to the existing harbor, Pfeffer was on board. To accompany this, Boxwell even ran a Pfeffer Regatta out of the Harbor for two years, featuring eight different teams running eight races. For Adkins, the relationship with Pfeffer and the Harbor was the crown jewel for Boxwell. "We have storage, we have tools, we have lifts, we have everything you can imagine down there," he explained. "I had a guy tell me, 'You guys have a better set up in aquatics than National Council.'" I like hearing stuff like that."[73]

The Extreme Outdoor Adventure continued and was joined by two new High Adventure programs: High Adventure Fishing and High Adventure Caving. Unlike previous summers, these were not offered all summer long. Every two weeks, the program changed. In theory, this would encourage a troop with older boys to switch weeks—potentially spreading troops out of the highly congested Weeks 1 and 2—or simply getting older boys to come back to the program later in the summer. By 2008, the three High Adventure programs ended. The specialized weekly Adventure program at Boxwell disappeared into the mists of time, though Grimes Canoe Base picked up a dedicated High Adventure Canoe Week about this same period. However, a new High Adventure element was added to property in 2013 with the installation of a third of a mile long zipline course. Built by former staff member Lance Ussery's Upper Edge Adventures, the treetop course saw Scouts glide from platform to platform through the woods by the Crippled Crab down to the entrance of the High Adventure Area at Camp Light. It was not a program, but it was an adventure only available to older boys, with over 300 using the course its first summer.[74]

The most significant, and easily the most successful, of the new High Adventure programs were a new series of National Rifle Association (NRA) shooting sports activities. The first was the NRA Light Rifle or Marksmanship Qualification program. Utilizing the rifle range at Camp Parnell because of its easy access to camp roads, the NRA program was point based. The more proficient and more skilled a Scout was, the higher ranking a Scout could achieve within the program. Each level had a patch associated with it and Scouts could shoot as much as they wanted. Overseen by a retired Army veteran with over twenty-three years of service, "Old Soldier" Pat Deugaw was an unlikely folk hero. Gruff but with a wily attitude, Deugaw became the face of the program. The rifle program was so successful, the NRA shotgun program was added in 2008. It used a similar ranking system, but while the rifle program was open to all Scouts, the shotgun program required a Scout to be enrolled in Shotgun Merit Badge.[75]

Perhaps the most dramatically new innovation was an idea that was wildly outside the box for summer camp: a STEM Program. Science Technology Engineering and Math (STEM) Programs were sweeping the public schools by the 2010s. Simply given the nature of the material, these were not outdoor programs. Indeed, with a focus on skills like chemistry, robotics, and computers, STEM was in many ways the antithesis of summer camp. Nevertheless, at the insistence of Council Executive Larry Brown, a STEM program was developed for Boxwell. Parnell Dining Hall, which had become a storage room since its abandonment in 2002, was renovated to become the new STEM Center. As Adkins explained with some deadpan humor in November 2017,

> If you had gone over there two years ago and looked at Parnell
> dining hall, mattresses stacked to the ceiling, it was a huge
> mess. [Larry Brown] said, 'let's do this', and so we did it. The
> building is nice now. The renovations that have taken place
> there... All the plumbing works, the building's been painted
> inside and out, it's got heating and cooling, it's got nice parti-
> tions, and we've kept some old school stuff in there with the
> old tables. It's got chairs in there. The supply area in there
> [has] drones, 3-D printers, flat screens. It might even have
> some uranium in the supply room, I'm not sure.

With office style partitions dividing the main hall into classrooms, conferences area, and computer work stations, Parnell dining hall found new life as the Boxwell STEM Center.[76]

The STEM program began in 2016. Boasting the best wi-fi on the Reservation, the program added nine new merit badges to the summer camp program, including Chemistry, Digital Technology, Electricity, Electronics, Engineering, Nuclear Science, Programming, Robotics, and Animation. Indeed, Scouts actually built little robots, wrote their own programs, and literally blew things up with science. The program was a success from the start with 600 participants the first summer. Adkins was shocked.

> I didn't think it would work. I thought, I'm going to do this
> because I've been told to do it, but I could not have been more
> wrong. It was unbelievable. We filled up every class in the first
> year. I never would have imagined wanting to go to camp to

do these things. It just didn't make sense, but that shows you what thinking out of the box creates.

Realizing that Parnell could be an untapped resource for further expansion, a Music Department was added in 2017, using the abandoned Trading Post shed as its home base. Scouts utilized an Artiphon—a digital instrument similar to guitar in shape but like an advanced keyboard in function—to earn the merit badge. The Computer and Technology Revolution had firmly ensconced itself at Boxwell.[77]

These were the significant new programs; there were a host of smaller programs and activities. Sometimes these programs lasted for several years. The Boxwell Triathlon, which involved swimming, biking, and running, began Adkins' first summer and extended beyond his tenure. The Frisbee golf course, the Dolphin Society (an award for completing multiple aquatics merit badges and skills across multiple areas), the Scoutmaster Merit Badge (a checklist of activities for leaders during the week), and Boxwell Boot Camp (an *early* morning history class on Boxwell) were all similar programs that lasted for several years. Others were more short-lived. Theme weeks for Boy Scout Camp, Knockerballs (inflatable balls you climbed inside with your lower legs still exposed for running), and Mountain Boarding (all-terrain, downhill skateboarding) lasted one or two summers and disappeared. There was even one summer with high wheel bicycle riding.[78]

Of course, the simplest "new" program was just to add new merit badges to the teaching roster. As Adkins served as Reservation Director for fourteen years, there were a plethora of new merit badges. Some were literally new—new to Scouting or new to the Reservation—and others were "recycles"—merit badges that had been taught in the past, were discontinued for whatever reason, and then returned. While some of these choices were simply to add something new to the roster, there was also a plan involving offerings. Between the summer camp program and winter camp program, every Eagle required merit badge was offered to Scouts.[79]

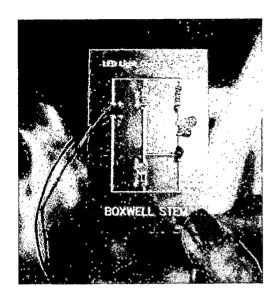

STEM Director Lisa Boyce holds an LED Light Control Circuit board branded with "Boxwell STEM," July 2018. Personal Collection of the author.

Adkins' years were not simply about creating new programs. Some programs, particularly those serving younger Scouts, were critical to providing a positive experience so those Scouts would not only return to camp, but would stay in Scouting. The Davy Crockett program, for instance, was replaced by the Green Bar Program in 2005. Green Bar abandoned the menu driven program and returned to a patrol method based approach. Scouts formed patrols the first day and worked with that group all week. Certainly skills were a focus as advancement mattered, but the patrol approach also emphasized "team work, patrol competition and getting a taste of some of the camp activities available." The program was still syllabus driven, meaning specific guides were provided to staff "on what to teach, how to instruct, on what day, at what time frame, and with what materials that will be necessary." The breakdown of what was taught at what time changed some over the years, and at Stahlman the physical program area itself moved around quite a bit, but once this first change was made in 2005, the program did not shift significantly again.[80]

CubWorld presented a larger challenge. CubWorld had a program, but prior to Adkins had largely run independently of the Boy Scout resident camps. Part of this was due to the abbreviated schedules the Webelos and

Cub programs ran. But some of this independence was also because no one other than CubWorld staff seemed to quite understand what was happening at CubWorld. For instance, during a standard week, the food truck brought food to CubWorld dining hall just like it brought food to Camp Craig's dining hall. But on the weekend, Stahlman and Craig staff went home, which meant the food truck driver went home too. Unlike the Boy Scout programs, CubWorld still had a program to run over the weekend. They had to go get their food themselves. Some summers the CubWorld staff had to bring their own tents to stay in. Finally, every summer at the end of camp, a steak dinner was held for the staff as a thank you for their work. CubWorld staff was not even invited.[81]

All of this changed with Adkins. He included the CubWorld Staff in Staff Week, bringing them to meetings and participating—to varying degrees—in the training. Indeed, he brought a whole new attitude regarding CubWorld. Not only did he come to meals there and attend their campfires, he had a philosophy specifically for CubWorld program: Give the Scouts the Disney World Experience. In other words, focus on having fun, focus on the experience. At CubWorld, having Cub Scouts advance was never as important as the experience that they had while at camp.[82]

The most significant program changes came to the Webelos program. First year Webelos could come to Webelos camp—still Monday through Thursday at CubWorld—and take two or three activity badges. Approximately ten activity badges were offered, giving incoming Webelos a fairly wide selection to get started with. Second year Webelos had the opportunity to take either more activity badges or to participate in a "Boy Scout Skills Round Robin program." The Round Robin focused on Scout skills, like knots and lashing, orienteering, and first aid, instead of advancement. The goal with this approach was to better prepare and to excite Webelos for their move into Boy Scouts.[83]

Indeed, much of what appeared at CubWorld throughout this period was an attempt to give Cubs a better taste of what awaited them. A portable climbing wall was brought out one summer. Webelos got their own winter camp in January 2016. It was a weekend event instead of a week, but many of the same "advancement coupled with activity" principles applied. CubWorld also received its own aquatics area in 2017. Cubs swimming in the lake basically stopped with the arrival of the pool, but Camp Director Jason Flannery had an idea in 2016 to introduce boating to Cubs. The following summer the Pfeffer CubWorld Aquatics Center was born. A dock, a storage center, canoes, kayaks, lifejackets, and a pontoon boat added a new level of adventure for the Cubs... and whetted their whistles for what could be done as Boy Scouts.[84]

A final piece to the summer program was the expansion of regular adult leader training. Leaders could learn how to plan high adventure trips, how to teach Scouts effectively, and about advancement policies. There were also trainings on the more fundamental aspects of Scouting, such as "The Patrol Method—Why?" Perhaps not surprisingly, some of the expanded sessions were on safety, such as Climb On Safely, as well as more basic Scout tenets, like sessions on Leave No Trace camping. By 2012, the Army Corps of Engineers was even offering a water safety training for adults. There was more camp program for everyone.[85]

The aforementioned programs—new and improved—were just the tip of the iceberg. Some changes were communicated at the Ten Day Out meeting and others at camp. There were a host of events that were created on the fly and were never part of an official record. That creative spark is part of the camp experience. This constant newness and activity was one of the primary ways the modern camp program was different from the program of the past. Perry Bruce had worked on Parnell staff in the 1970s and returned as Camp Commissioner at Craig in 2012. He was shocked by the changes, primarily in the sense that the staff was so busy. As he explained, "Nowadays, the staff, they're busy a lot of nights except their night off. They're working, doing different things at night, teaching even. That's the first thing I noticed when I went back was how many hours these guys had to put in."[86]

There was one final, significant program change of note during the Adkins years. Camp Directors became volunteers. Since the arrival of Boxwell at Old Hickory Lake, the Camp Director had been a professional Scouter. The Camp Director had changed every year and generally been of little consequence. This lack of impact was due mainly to three causes. First, the Reservation Director was a long-standing professional who did the work a Camp Director would do at a one camp property. Second, each of the resident camps had program directors who were long-standing volunteers, building loyalty with the staff, acting as father figures in many cases, and keeping the emphasis on program. Finally, a camp director had generally stayed for one summer and left. While they handed out the checks and some were great people to work with, the camps ran smoothly without them because of the Reservation Director and the Program Director. Generally speaking, the Program Director ran the camps, as was detailed previously.

This changed in 2008. Council Executive Hugh Travis, who had been a Camp Director at Camp Craig in 1978, suggested the change to a non-professional Scouter. Having a volunteer do the job meant professionals were free to continue to work in their districts. It was also a bit of a cost savings as a volunteer could be sent to National Camp School to be trained as a Camp Director and could then be kept on in that position for as long as his certification was valid, as opposed to sending two new District Executives every summer. This particular detail was important because it indicated a subtle shift: Camp Directors became the long-standing volunteer leaders at camp. Only at Cub-World did the Camp Director remain a professional. At the Boy Scout camps, Tony Turner became the first non-professional Scouter to serve as Camp Director since the move to Old Hickory Lake.[87]

Turner was a logical choice in many ways. He was retired, so he could he return year after year. He had a longer experience with the Council than most professionals (approximately thirty years) and had served as a troop leader. Turner also had a long history on the old Wood Badge staffs, even serving as Scoutmaster in the old program. Perhaps most importantly, Turner had an "old school Scouting philosophy," meaning he was a good rutter for the ship. Turner worked out so well in the position that in 2009 Stahlman made the same transition, this time with Steve Eubank. Eubank was also retired, had been a Wood Badge Scoutmaster, and had a longer history with the Council than anyone on the professional staff. Eubank also had the benefit of having been a Program Director himself from 1973-1976 and a Camp Commissioner in the modern period from 2003 to 2008.[88]

This change had ripples. Hand in hand with the change to older, long serving Camp Directors came a shift to younger Program Directors, who only stayed for a few years. This change was already underway naturally. Ron Ramsey (1996-1999) and Andy Verble (2000-2003) at Stahlman and Michael Salazar (1998-2000) at Parnell-Craig were the last of the "old school" program directors and even they were younger than most of their predecessors. After Verble, no program director retained the position for more than three years. Usually the program director came up through the ranks, underwent a specific interview for the position while still at camp, and Adkins announced the hire at the Staff Appreciation dinner, part of his plan to have the key people in place for the next summer as early as possible. For Adkins, having the program director be a younger man was important because he was closer to the Scouts and would present the new ideas needed to keep the program fresh.[89]

The Camp Commissioner positions also flipped. Traditionally an older youth leadership position, Commissioner became an adult position. The Commissioner was not expected to stay as long as the Camp Director, maybe only three years, and was responsible for "doing all the grunt work." If there was a toilet that was broken or a tree that was down, the Commissioner was responsible to handle the issue. The person who drove around camp picking up the bagged trash from each site was the Commissioner. The Commissioner was in most respects a mini-ranger in each camp.[90]

The shift of the "Key Three" leadership was significant. It inverted what had been the power structure for fifty years. Before the change, the Program Director ran the camp. If he needed to fire someone, he may consult with the Camp Director, but he was the one who made the decision. After the change, the Camp Director ran the camp. The Program Director still oversaw program, but program was no longer defined as everything. If there were personnel issues, paperwork, timesheets, issues with Scoutmasters, or even meetings with leaders, the Camp Director took the lead. As the Program Director was now just older youth staff, the Camp Director handled conflicts and issues with leaders, essentially providing cover for the Program Director. And the Camp Director retained the stability the Program Director had in the past. Turner served as Camp Director until 2017, while Eubank as of this writing is still in the position, having "retired" in 2018 only to return the next year. This was the same stability seen in the LeFever-Jackson years or the Ragsdale-Barnett years. The difference was that this arrangement favored Adkins' emphasis on new ideas to keep the program fresh by changing out Program Directors every two or three years.[91]

Of course, as Reservation director, Adkins dealt not just with program, but oversaw a variety of capital developments, in addition to the projects listed previously such as the Boat Harbor maintenance area and the zipline. As volleyball, and especially baseball, fell out of favor, dodgeball—and dodgeball's cousin Gaga ball at CubWorld—ws the game of choice among youth. Adkins added lighted dodgeball courts at both Stahlman and Craig to allow nighttime tournaments. There was also a new waste water treatment facility constructed to replace the original system at Stahlman that had been running since 1959. Property in Nashville had to be sold to pay for the system, but it was a necessary upgrade as pressure from the state to do so had been building.

The Order of the Arrow built a gateway entrance to the High Adventure Area dedicated to former staff member and National Lodge Chief Josh Sain. Sain had been killed in a car accident in 1997 and his parents—as well as the Lodge—had been looking for an adequate way to memorialize the nineteen year old. Built with mostly donated material and volunteer Lodge labor, the Gateway was dedicated December 3, 2005.[92]

Weather issues also created their own set of difficulties. A wind storm destroyed the entrance sign in the winter of 2006-2007. A new sign of similar design, though one that could be moved should Highway 109 construction ever reach Boxwell, was installed in the summer of 2007. In 2011, a tornado caused damage to Stahlman and Parnell Dining Halls as well as the Fehrmann Training Center. The best known weather event though was the 500 year flood in May 2010. As Steve Belew explained, the Corps of Engineers markers all along the coast line were accurate. The waters never breached Old Hickory Dam, but it was close and the water level of the reservoir reached the markers all around the property. Platforms began floating away. Ranger Steve Belew and future ranger Rob Ward rushed around tying platforms to trees before they floated away. A contingent of Scouts and leaders preparing for the National Jamboree later that summer, barely escaped being trapped on the Reservation as even Akers Lake rose and crossed over Creighton Lane. The greatest casualty of the day was the Lancaster Pirate ship at Cubworld. As the water levels rose and the boats moorings strained, the tension finally "broke the back" of the ship. She never floated again. She was moved to the shoreline and permanently fixed to the banks atop a concrete pad. A counterpart ship was built on the opposite bank and the modern "Pirates Cove" emerged. Indeed, severe weather had become so common that weather alerts were added to the camp's emergency plans and a lightning detection system was installed at the Crippled Crab.[93]

Adkins also worked to have the Reservation utilized more during the off-season. These efforts led to an annual Cub and Family month in October.

Every weekend in October Cubs and parents came out for a weekend of activities and advancement. Wood Badge for the 21st century continued to use the Reservation, usually meeting weekends in September. Brownsea proved not quite as permanent, remaining at Parish through 2005. The following year Brownsea was retired and a new national youth leadership training program was developed, aptly (if uncreatively) titled National Youth Leadership Training (NYLT). Held in July, NYLT's first summer was held at Parish Reservation, where it stayed through 2007. Then the program bounced back to Boxwell in 2008 and stayed put until 2012, after which it again left for another property. The Reservation also exploded with various kinds of training. Outdoor Leadership Skills (OLS), Webelos Leaders Outdoor Experience (WLOE), and of course a Trainer Development Conference—training to train the trainers—all dotted the calendar. Scoutreach, Scouting's outreach program, experimented with a fun run event in 2013 and 2014. This list does not even take note of the Order of the Arrow events that occurred on site year-round as well.[94]

External groups were another way to utilize the property and generate some revenue. Learning For Life (LFL) continued to hold an event in the spring, either a Leadership Day or simply a Fun Day, where teens came to the Reservation for outdoor activities. Junior Reserve Officer Training Corps (JROTC) programs began using the camp in 2004. Boxwell eventually became host to the Commando Challenge, where JRTOC programs from multiple high schools and states came to camp to participate in a series of events. The program was popular enough that college ROTC programs began to use the Reservation as well and even built an obstacle course in Camp Light to be utilized by all the programs. Along these same lines, the National Guard began renting out the Reservation for a week after camp was over in July and running their own youth program. The National Guard weeks were particularly beneficial as they brought in substantial revenue, but also often in-kind payment. Most of the Reservation's roads were repaved in the 2010s by the

Renovations to the Howard Olson OA Lodge took place in Spring 2012, bringing the almost forty-five year old building into the modern era. Photo by the author.

Guard. Even Pope John Paul II High School in Hendersonville had a freshman retreat at Boxwell for several years at the start of the fall term. One of the school's guidance counselors was a former Boxwell staff member, Mike Brown.[95]

A renewed emphasis on the Venturing program began in 2007. A Venturing Leadership Skills Course (VLS) was offered in February 2008 and by the end of the year a new weekend event, Venturing Rendezvous, brought Venture Crews out to Boxwell for networking, games, and workshops. The Rendezvous was a successful event. It moved to April and continued for several years and even expanded into another Venturing Day in November.[96]

And then a unique twist occurred. In 2007, as part of a long range plan developed in 2002-2003, the Council secured a 1,587 acre property on the Cumberland Plateau in Van Buren and White Counties. With "limestone rock bluffs, unique caves and waterfalls" and access to the Caney Fork River and the Fall Creek Falls and Bledsoe Forest State Parks the site was a high adventure wonderland. Development of the site led to a capital campaign with a goal of $7 million. The site benefited immensely from a $4 million gift—the largest single gift in the Council's history—from William H. Latimer, III of Union City. Latimer supported the High Adventure vision for the property and his support allowed the site to develop in remarkable ways including not only lodging, trails, a chapel, and campsites, but a manmade lake and an observatory. Grand Opening celebrations were held on May 3, 2014.[97]

Latimer Reservation was never intended to compete with Boxwell. Though an immense facility, it was designed as a High Adventure base and not a Scout resident camp. Thus, non-Scout groups could use the facility, though Scout groups always received priority in scheduling. With that in mind though, Latimer increasingly became home to several activities and groups. NYLT moved to Latimer in 2013. Venturing began moving to Latimer too. A Venturing event called Kodiak, an event that taught leadership skills while on a high adventure hike, was the first official event held at the site in 2008. Former Stahlman Program Director Andy Verble was the Course Director for the first Kodiak, which has continued since that first year. Venturing even began having a Winter Camp at the site. Events for Cub Packs, Venture Crews, and Scout Troops, as well as training, quickly filled the Latimer calendar.[98]

While Latimer demonstrated the importance that High Adventure programs had gained within the Scouting movement, Boxwell's program and offerings were still the touchstone for most Middle Tennessee scouts. No other event demonstrated this better than The Great Eclipse Campout in August 2017, the final big event under Adkins' watch. Boxwell was uniquely situated to be ground zero for a solar eclipse on August 21 and the Council took advantage of the opportunity to show off Scouting. Planned events included educational activities related to the eclipse but also "games, campfires, competitions, movies and merit badge opportunities. Archery, BB guns, maybe even some drones will be part of the camp out as well." About 3,000 people from ten states were expected; over 4,200 showed up. After the Bicentennial Muster in 1976, it was easily the largest event on the property, demonstrating the full-service operation of the modern Boxwell.[99]

Staff

A modern Boxwell required a modern staff. Just as the other aspects of Boxwell had changed to meet new understandings of how program should operate, so too did the staff. The composition of the staff, staff traditions, staff life, and even staff reunions all went through very visible "modernizations."

Like many of the other changes detailed above, changes to staff composition were a combination of both organic evolution and deliberate decisions. The transformation with Program Directors was one example of this. Program Directors were already trending younger at the start of the modern period. Ron Ramsey and Andy Verble at Stahlman were adults, but neither were the mid-thirties or older of an Ernie Ragsdale. When Michael Salazar took over at Parnell and Craig, he too was in his mid-twenties. When Adkins moved to volunteers as long-term Camp Directors and older youth as Program Directors who served for no more than three years, he was, in part, formalizing a system with Program Directors that had already emerged. CubWorld added an entirely new understanding to the mix. CubWorld's first Program Director was an adult woman, Savantha Tesar, whose son Alex served on Parnell-Craig staff. From there the ages fluctuated wildly from an older youth Griffin Bridgers to an adult male older than Tesar, Dominick Azzara. By 2009, CubWorld introduced Co-Program Directors. One was usually twenty-one or older, while the other was over eighteen and often being trained to take over.[100]

Below what came to be called the Key Three Leadership—Camp Director, Program Director, and Camp Commissioner—there were other subtle changes. Waterfront staff were no longer all over eighteen years of age, though the Director remained over twenty-one, per national standards. Counselors-in-Training, or CITs, were used much more extensively. CITs were youth staff who were right on the bottom edge of being eligible to work at fourteen years old. They were brought on as "volunteer" staff. In short, they did all the work of a regular staff member, but did not get paid and only stayed for a week or two. Serving as a CIT was an excellent opportunity for a youth to get some staff experience and freedom from home. For the existing staff leadership, using CITs not only provided needed personnel for camp operation, but hopefully provided an experience to entice the CIT to return the following summer as a full-fledged, paid staff member. And of course, a CIT could go on to do great things at camp. Jason Flannery began his Boxwell career as a CIT on the Parnell waterfront in 1997. He went on to become Craig's Program Director in 2007 before becoming a professional Scouter himself.[101]

Interviews changed as well. While there may still be an interview to be hired, though not always, the assumption by the Adkins years was, if you were on the staff, you were *on the staff.* As J. J. Norman put it, "As far as Carl Adkins was concerned, you had signed in blood." While clearly an exaggeration, the idea was exemplified in the fact that returning staff did not go through yearly interviews. Each year returning staff filled out an application indicating the top three choices for position the following summer and that was it. In the fall, they received a letter with position and pay on it and then chose to either accept or decline the offer. There were generally no negotiations over salary. Commitments for area directors were generally settled first, returning staff came next, and the new staff interviews would be held by the end of the year, within six months of the summer that had just concluded.[102]

Aside from new hires, the only positions that were really interviewed positions were those Key Three positions; everything else was by application or casual conversation. And of course, since Camp Directors and Camp Commissioners generally were returning people, the Program Director ended up being one of the few interviewed positions. About week four, if a staff member were interested, that individual signed up to be interviewed. The interviews were held at the OA Lodge and conducted by Adkins and his Camp Directors. There were some generic questions and then some that were more personal. Again, Norman explained, "Steve [Eubank] loved the analogy of the duck where it's smooth sailing on the top, but under the water, under the surface, the feet are just going a mile a minute. He used that in all three of my program director interviews." Norman missed the lesson at the time, but after his first summer as Program Director, he understood the metaphor.[103]

The most dramatic change to the composition of the staff was the introduction of women. Women had long been part of the camp staff, but the introduction of women to deliver camp program was new. Diane Gregory had been first in 1997. Lisa Ballew came next, joining the Craig staff as a Co-Director for the Con-Yard with her husband Hank in 2002. After these two episodes of testing the waters, the turning point came with the introduction of Amanda Monroe as Craig's Waterfront Director in 2003. Monroe was a college student working on her Recreation degree at Middle Tennessee State University. Working with a non-profit recreation program was a requirement of that degree. These facts were less important than the idea that Monroe was a single, college-aged female in a bathing suit on the Waterfront. Monroe presented a "danger" in a way Gregory and Ballew had not because she represented the ideal that young men in the woods by themselves were not supposed to be able to resist. Aware "that there were a lot of people watching," Monroe excelled as director. While Monroe herself did not return, she had paved the way. Several women joined the program staff in 2004. Ironically, most of the new female staff members were in aquatics, either on the waterfront or at the pool. But this too would change as time went on.[104]

The CubWorld staff integrated women into the staff exceptionally well. As Jonathan Azzara pointed out, "For the kids, they like boys or girls teaching. It's something they can identify with that's still within ten years of their age." In short, mixed gender worked well at CubWorld because the Cubs were more interested in the age than the gender. Further, the fraternization concerns that accompanied the introduction of females on the staff was not prevalent at CubWorld because of the closeness of the staff. Instead of seeing the women as distractions or potential conquests as earlier generations had, CubWorld accepted the females as family. Thus, even dating was not a significant issue among the Cub Staff because the staff viewed each other more as brother and sister. As CubWorld Staff member Rachel Paris stated quite succinctly, "We really are like one family."[105]

The argument against women on the staff—or in Scouting for that matter—tended to revolve around two points. First, women would change the dynamic. Boys behave differently around other boys than they do around girls. That freedom "to be boys" would be lost with females present. Second, young women in the program would lead to "distractions," in other words, sex, pregnancy, and a general inability to perform one's job. So the question has to be asked, how did these concerns play out with women on the staff?

Once the younger women joined the staff, clearly the dynamic did change somewhat. The women both played along when appropriate and drew lines when stories or behavior were not appropriate. "The girls would really put us in our place," J. J. Norman explained. They would laugh along with the boys' tall tales, until it involved them, then they set the record straight quickly. And the males did self-police what they said somewhat. Not every joke was told, not every explicit story related. Danny Waltman assessed the situation most equitably though,

> Overall we were really glad to have females that were willing to be around guys in that type of setting. I think it was valuable for those teenagers and young men to be around females and see them doing the same work we were doing, seeing these females pitching in the same way we did. And so, having that kind of equality, I think was important for a lot of people that wouldn't necessarily see that otherwise. I would say it was worth any kind of risk of late night shenanigans.[106]

It was these "late night shenanigans" that most worried the adults and those fears of sex and pregnancy were addressed both overtly and covertly. Part of Staff Week now included the admonition from Adkins: "We're not a dating service." Both men and women were hired because "they can do the best job for that position" and were expected to treat each other professionally, just as if they were in the outside world. Thus, if staff wanted to date, they needed to do so on their time and not let it interfere with work. Nevertheless, precautions were still taken. Females did not stay in the staff sites. Indeed, they did not even stay in tents; they stayed in cabins. Nor were women allowed into male staff sites; men were not allowed in the female cabins. Clearly there was a fear here of what unchaperoned teens at night might do. But as Ranger Rob Ward pointed out, "We haven't had the serious issues that were projected. One of the big things is teenage pregnancy. That hasn't happened."[107]

While the men were worried about the potential for pregnancy, the women who actually worked on staff worried about issues that were often much more basic. One young woman was asked—told—during her hiring interview, "You know you can't just come here to flirt?" Upon arriving at camp, women often discovered that the showerhouses were not entirely female-friendly. One had to carry her "used menstrual product out of the stall to the trash can that was propping open the door." Some problems were more person or job specific. Women in aquatics were often leered at by "hormonal boys and bored dads." Changing clothes for waterfront staff was challenging as well since the women were not always housed in camp with the men. When in her working uniform of swim shorts and t-shirt at breakfast and lunch, Craig Waterfront Director Emily Fish often ate her meals on the back dock rather than put up with conversations about her "inappropriate attire," which was the same as what the boys wore. She then had to find a simple way to change into her Class A uniform for dinner as she lived not at Craig but in the Cooks' Cabins on the other side of the Reservation. Almost to a person, all the women interviewed said they worked harder than the boys to prove they were capable and worthy of respect. And to be exceptionally blunt, the stories they related proved one great truth: if there was a problem for the women, it was rarely the scouts, but almost always the adult men.[108]

By and large, the women were good sports and were included in camp life. They laughed at most of the gender bending skits or jokes that were part of program. They often participated in late night "devilment" with the guys and sometimes against the guys. The separate housing situations did complicate this sort of bonding, but it happened. From sinking cinder blocks into the pool at night to pranks involving cling wrap and shaving cream, the women—particularly the younger women—were involved. The inclusion of females on the staff also could be inspirational to a new generation. CubWorld staffer Audrey Creighton related this story:

> The little girls who were tagalongs but couldn't be campers
> had a huge impact on me. A girl who was 7 or 8 was sitting in
> on one of my classes and tried to start a fire with the boys.
> Her mom pulled her away and told her that fires were for
> boys and she should go play on the castle. The girl walked
> right up to me, looked at her mom and said, "Well if fires are
> for boys then why can she be here?" From that day on it felt
> like everything I did was so a little girl could see me and know
> that she could do it too.

Apparently, Scouting's values and skills transcended gender.[109]

The addition of women also had an interesting and unpredicted side effect: marriage. Since the introduction of young women to the staff, there have been several staff members who met a camp, began dating, and later married. Danny Waltman married Brooke Aldridge of CubWorld staff. On Stahlman staff, Brandon Aldridge married Megan Kasper, April Messer married Alex Mangrum, and Eric Hersh and Anna Hartzhiem married as well. More followed. Weddings on the Reservation involving a staff member were not new, dating all the way back to 1970 and David McWilliams' nuptials. But staff marrying staff was a new thing entirely. Perhaps though, it should

Stahlman Waterfront Staff April Messer (left) and Megan Kasper (right) performing the highly popular song "Zumba!" at lunchtime, 2004. Personal Collection of Chase Standifer.

not have been too surprising. As Waltman pointed out with only partial sarcasm, "It's a target rich environment. If you are a young lady, there's a lot of upstanding gentlemen of particular character and class. Makes sense." He laughed and then explained that not only did he marry a member of the camp staff, his in-laws were camp staff too. Boxwell staff became a literal family.

The other major compositional change was the arrival of homosexuals on the staff. Of course, "change" and "arrival" are incorrect as homosexuals had been part of the staff for decades. What was different in the modern period was a more general acceptance in society at large and the acceptance within Scouting after the removal of the youth ban (2013) and the adult ban (2015). Homosexuals had the advantage of not looking different, which was a problem that clearly haunted the women. Boat Harbor Director Ed Mason was almost flippant about this particular issue,

> The homosexual issue. Scoutmaster comes in, it's not broad-cast. Staff members that have come out of the closet. Having done [staff] up here, normally they have done it [come out] after they left. We had one last year come out of the closet

> and everybody could have probably walked around and went,
> "Yeah, so? It's not like we didn't know." It's not broadcast
> and it's not, to my knowledge, ever created a problem.

Michael Allen, another Boat Harbor Director, was even more direct concerning homosexuals in the Scouting program, "They have been in it all along. They've been in it all along." In short, for the straight men, the policy change allowing homosexuals into the program did not appear to be a problem.[110]

For the homosexuals who were on the staff, life was a bit more complicated. J. J. Norman was Craig Program Director in 2014 and 2015, just as the policy bans were lifted. He explained, "I made a conscious decision not to fully come out due to work at Camp. Regardless of the policy, the Scouting movement meant, and continues to mean so much to me. I wasn't about to do ANYTHING to potentially damage my future in Scouting." As a result, Norman waited until his last night on camp staff to finally come out to his closest camp friends. All accepted him without hesitation, putting a nice bookend on his time at Boxwell. But even as Norman explained his experience, he still maintained a blanket of protection for others. "There were about 10 guys over the years that I either knew about at the time or learned were gay later on," Norman explained. "In an effort to not out anyone, I'll say that I was in good company of fellow Program Directors, Aquatics staff and directors, C.O.P.E. staff and directors, shooting sports staff and directors, etc." Even after the bans were lifted and none of these individuals worked on camp staff anymore, secrets still needed to preserved.[111]

As an interesting side note, Carl Adkins was Reservation Director when the homosexual bans were lifted and was responsible for more women on the staff than any of his predecessors. But neither of these changes were issues that appeared to concern Adkins. For the man who built the staff every year, the biggest struggle was not whether you were a man or woman, gay or straight, but how technology might have impacted you. The advent of the smartphone "ruined a lot of communication skills with young people... Kids can't stand in front of you and talk." Even if in the same room together, youth would rather text an adult than come speak face to face. Adkins was ultimately quite direct on this point, "Technology's great, but it has ruined the social skills of young people." For an organization that had leadership and character building as its reason for being, this sort of failure of communication potentially presented a long term problem.[112]

Compositional changes went hand in hand with changes to tradition and staff life. Everything from staff sites to staff night out to how basic work was accomplished transformed in these years. As with most of the other changes detailed above, some of this was organic, but some of it was also quite intentional. Some of these changes were quite small. For instance, during the Willhite years the red staff hat was adorned with a new patch design virtually every year. In the modern era, the entire hat changed every year.

The centralized staff sites led to significant staff life changes. Generally, the new arrangement was well received. Even if some staff still grouped together by program area, the closeness of living in a single staff site meant staff still got to know people beyond their immediate area colleagues. There were some bumps though. The first summer the staff center at Craig was opened, staff had pay to use the washer and dryer. This feature was later disabled, but it was an odd way to start the process. Further, the electricity to the staff sites was not designed for heavy usage. The idea was that staff would power a few fans and alarm clocks, just things to make life at camp a little more comfortable. Instead, staff began to bring televisions, DVD players, game systems, and even small refrigerators. When asked what you would hear if you went down in the staff site at night, Program Director Aaron Patten replied, "You would hear [the video game] *Halo* going on everywhere." Video games ruled the night... until the circuit blew. Conversely, this amenity allowed for movie nights and socialization. And, generally, kept much of the staff out of trouble at night. "Devilment" declined, though it never disappeared.[113]

The Stahlman staff site had its own issues. The site—formerly Site 16—evolved to be arranged by age. Thus, the Stahlman staff was arranged less by program area and more by seniority. Those closest to the Staff center were the youngest. Staff experience rose as you moved away from the Center. But new and experienced alike were beleaguered by shade. "Everything just stayed wet and so everyone was sick all the time. You'd get the funk. It was an upper respiratory thing. If your pillow is wet and you're sleeping on it, it's not good." Washing machines and dryers helped, but in a constantly wet environment, a staff of people washing and drying clothes simply did not work very well.[114]

Staff nights out changed too. For decades staff night out had been on Tuesday nights. With a few exceptions, the whole staff went out. In the early days, this involved everyone crowding onto a cattle truck or a bus and in the Willhite years, this had meant taking personal vehicles with those over eighteen loading up those under eighteen. In the summer of 2004 though, just after the staff had left the Reservation, "the sky turned purple. In the next 30 min[utes] we had a storm of 100 mile an hour straight winds." The emergency plan went into effect and the horn was blown, telling everyone to report to their dining halls. Stahlman staff member Danny Waltman was with the Stahlman group that had just made it in to Gallatin when they heard news of the storm. "I'll never forget," Waltman recalled, "Joe [Toplon, Con-Yard Director] reaches out of his van—he drove a minivan—reaches his arm out of the minivan with index finger up, and just makes a turnaround sign. We don't even stop. We literally just snake right back to camp." Trees had already fallen over, so the group stopped to clear those from the road, but made it back to Stahlman dining hall and delivered program. With no one in camp (save of course the actual Scout leaders) when a crisis hit, "that was pretty much the end of one staff night out." From that point forward, different areas went out on different nights to make sure a complement was left behind in the event of an emergency.[115]

Staff traditions evolved too. The Parnell Swerve—the long, snake-like caravan of vehicles with hazard lights flashing from Parnell-Craig to Stahl-man—disappeared. Working off of the trucks and flatbeds ended. Particular-ly after Aaron Rook's death, this activity was a non-starter. Indeed, even the tractors and flatbeds themselves were retired and replaced by pickup trucks to do most of the camp's work. Each camp developed its own non-denominational prayer for meals. Some songs were retired and others were brought in, some even written for the camp, such as "The Stahlman Anthem." And while staff hazing died down considerably, there were still inter-camp pranks. Sometimes waterfront inflatables ended up on the Crab roof or in the pool. One staff would still wreak some mayhem on the others. Indeed, the most interesting evolution here was CubWorld. Craig and Stahlman were so consumed with their long-standing rivalry, each assumed the other staff was guilty when a prank transpired. Neither thought to blame the real culprits: the CubWorld staff.[116]

There were also the personalities, the individuals without whom camp would not have been the same. There was muscular rugby player Joe Toplon at Stahlman who adopted a fawn and named it Dr. Fizzy Num Num. There was Ed Walker at CubWorld, the retired customs agent who was the Shooting Sports director and drove a Ford Fiesta. Walker wrecked that Fiesta one night on the way into camp, leading the CubWorld staff to erect an "Ed-Man's Curve" sign on the tree that jumped out at him. There was Randy Coats at Craig, never a director, but a program juggernaut who for a time was "the heartbeat and spine" of Camp Craig. There were the Drs. Mueller at the Health Lodge, a husband and wife team overseeing injuries and health care. There was the return of former staff, both camp staff and Wood Badge staff. And there was Larry Green, finally retired from professional Scouting, working as Camp Commissioner—a volunteer—at CubWorld with a new generation under his new alias, "Mr. Larry." And in good camp staff fashion, staff mem-bers still signed their names to the areas where they worked in whatever way they could.[117]

Of course no camp could run without its Ranger staff. The modern period was blessed with Bill Freeman (1996-2006), Steve Belew (2007-2014), and Rob Ward (2014-2020). Modern rangers struggled with their own unique set of problems. The Reservation had more activity during the summer and year round than it had at any other point in its history, but the Ranger staff actually shrunk. For most of the modern period, there were only two full-time year round rangers. A third seasonal ranger was often enlisted to help with the work load. Each of the head rangers brought skills and connections to the position. A tall man with enormous hands, Freeman brought with him electrical experience and supply connections from Nashville Electric Service. Belew had been considered by Willhite before Claud's retirement, but military life called him away. When Belew finally became available, he started as ranger at Parish Reservation before coming to Boxwell. That same military connection paid dividends with the National Guard programs at the property as well as the in-kind paving work they did. For his part, Ward not only had experience on the staff, but also experience with large construction companies. All developed unique relationships with staff and leaders and made the Reservation a welcoming place.[118]

And there were more staff reunions, three in fact. Reunions held in 1999, 2009, and 2014 varied in attendance and program. The 1999 Reunion was the last to be helmed by the XDE group. For the most part, these volunteers handed over responsibility to Greg Tucker, former staff member and Reunion Chairman. The format followed the first two reunions, but the attendance was smaller. For the first time, there was some discussion about transforming the Pump House into a museum for Boxwell historical memorabilia, but this never quite panned out. The 2009 Reunion was a 50th Anniversary celebration of Old Hickory Boxwell. Unlike the other reunions, this one was held off season, so camp was not set up. Thus, while the Reservation was open to explore, no program areas were active or able to be used. A quick program at the Stahlman dining hall capped the event; there was no dinner or campfire.[119]

The 2014 Reunion was the first to take advantage of the computer and technology revolution. Since 1998, the XDE group had been working on actively capturing camp history. This had evolved into a website in 2002, known as VirtualBoxwell.org. By 2012, VirtualBoxwell.org had established a strong e-mail mailing list as well as a digital presence through its website but social media as well. Regular postings built a following and allowed Virtual-Boxwell to become a de facto conduit for staff news. Utilizing these resources, the 2014 Reunion became the best attended reunion to date. The program did not differ significantly from the first two reunions, but the ability to disseminate the information through the World Wide Web made the task of finding wayward staff and communicating with them considerably easier.[120]

Centennials

When Carl Adkins retired in December 2017, he had the longest tenure of anyone in the position save Tom Willhite. In an effort to not overwhelm a new person, the Director of Support Services position was split into two new positions: Director of Program and Director of Camping. Boxwell and the Reservation Director's job became the responsibility of the Director of Camping, and the new Director of Camping was Jason Flannery.[121]

Flannery had joined the Boxwell staff as a Counselor in Training in 1997, serving on Parnell's waterfront. He returned as an honest-to-goodness staff member the following summer at age 15 and stuck around for a decade. Barrel chested with dark curly hair, Flannery had aspirations to be Craig Waterfront Director, but his fortunes changed in 2007. The man slated to be Craig's Program Director, Caleb "Cookie" Campbell, was a "no show," leaving the Craig staff on their own throughout Staff Week. At 23 years old, Flannery jumped head first into the deep end to become Program Director. In his first week—Week I of camp that summer—construction outside the Reservation hit the water line and Boxwell was without water. The National Guard brought in water and Budweiser brought canned water. It was a baptism by fire and after week I, the rest of the summer was fairly easy. Flannery did not return to Boxwell the next summer, but instead went to college and eventually out into the world. By August 2014, his path brought him to professional Scouting, where he started as DE for the Walton Trail District. By 2015, he was bearded and back at camp as CubWorld's Camp Director and DE for the Trail of Tears District. Flannery not only brought boating to CubWorld, he also brought his dog bowl for his meals, which had been his program hook from when he was on Craig staff. He completed a second summer at Cub-World and began pitching ideas for a skilled trade center to advance Scouting. While young, his experience and success made him a sensible choice for Director of Camping.[122]

Flannery had started on staff under Turpin and worked professionally under Adkins, so not surprisingly his vision for the camp contained elements of both of their approaches, but with his own twist. There was a strong desire to make things work in a sensible way. Tradition was important, but if there was a smarter way to do something, then it should be explored. Further, new programs were needed to keep Scouts coming back. Flannery wanted to put a strong emphasis on Cubs and older boys. For Cubs, the goal was to give them a taste of what older Scouting could do to keep them engaged and coming back. The Pfeffer Cub Aquatics Area was a prime example of this. For older Scouts, Flannery's philosophy was to give them programs that would bring them back after their third or fourth year. In essence, this was the same High Adventure approach that had floated throughout the Modern Boxwell years.

While all of these goals sound similar to the Reservation Directors before him, Flannery differed because of his personal camp staff experience. For him, Boxwell was home in a way that it could not have been for his predecessors. Because he saw it as home, he wanted camp to look a certain way and have a certain feel. Boxwell should not only be well known like the big national High Adventure sites of Philmont and the Florida Sea Base, but should be well maintained. Most importantly, Flannery wanted Scouts and Scouters to

Jason Flannery at the Parish High Adventure Center in Camp Light, December 2020. Photo by the author.

feel an ownership for the camp the way he did. "If they feel like it's theirs," he explained, "they're not going to break a picnic table or leave a rake outside. They're going to take care of it. If it's your home, you're going to take care of it." The watch phrase for Flannery's first summers was "Leave a Legacy." Take care of your home, pass on what you have learned, be the leader that inspired you.[123]

Flannery soon jumped in to make his stamp on Boxwell. CubWorld was first. In terms of physical arrangements, the BB gun and archery ranges were moved from their original locations to near the Pfeffer Aquatics area. The original sites were popular with Cubs, but were a half mile walk. Placing the popular program areas closer together and closer to the heart of camp made sense for a camp that served seven, eight, and nine year olds. Next, Flannery introduced an idea called Family Scouting. For most of its existence, Cub-World had run two separate programs: one for Cubs on the weekends and one for Webelos Monday through Thursday. While this made some sense for the Scouts, it created hardships for parents, particularly those with two children at different levels of Cub Scouting. Family Scouting turned the old program on its head. Each session was only three days long and Cub Scouting and Webelos skills were all taught concurrently. In short, a family could bring all their kids—Cubs and Webelos alike—at one time and they would all enjoy a summer camp program. This approach did not break up families or packs or make either have to make arrangements for two separate sessions. The theme approaches still worked well for all ages, and as Flannery pointed out, the age differences did not matter much. For kids, "A fart joke is still a fart joke. You'll still laugh."[124]

It was critical for the new CubWorld approach to succeed. The total number of Scouts had been dropping, but Cubs were strong. The change in the Tennessee Code allowing patriotic groups into schools helped enormously, but that momentum had to be maintained. Cub Scouts had more youth enrolled every year than Boy Scouts, sometimes twice as many. But in terms of camp attendance, only a fraction of Cubs attended camp. 2014 was a perfect example of the problem Flannery was trying to turn around. There were 10,025 Cubs registered that year as opposed to 5,316 Boy Scouts. But in terms of camp attendance, the numbers flipped. 726 Cubs attended camp in 2014 versus 3103 Boy Scouts. For the health of Boxwell and Middle Tennessee Scouting, those Cub numbers needed to turn around.[125]

Flannery also had to face the national policy change regarding women almost immediately. Boy Scout summer camp ceased to exist in 2019 as the Boy Scout program became Scouts BSA, a mixed gender program. While the troops themselves remained gender segregated, unlike Explorer posts and Venture crews, both genders could attend camp at the same time. The arrival of all female troops at Boxwell brought some complaints and grumbling by adults, but the youth got along fine. The biggest issue with having female youth attend Boxwell was found at the showerhouses. Because the showerhouses had group sinks at the end of the building, teeth brushing, hair brushing, and the like happened in a community space—and here is where the older boys and girls fraternized. Otherwise, female youth at camp was unremarkable.[126]

New programs were added to the Scout BSA program as well. For older Scouts, the Cowboy Action program was added for the summer of 2019. Cowboy Action was a High Adventure Program that allowed Scouts to "play 'good guys' who prove their accuracy by shooting at things like spinning metal targets" using either a .22 revolver, a lever action .22 rifle, and a 20 gauge side by side shotgun. The Cowboy Action program was the "only program [where] Scouts BSA can shoot a pistol." The program not only provided valuable gun safety training, but it utilized the long abandoned Parnell Archery Range. Winter camp saw a change as well with a Green Bar program was added to provide an advancement opportunity for the newest recruits to Scouting.[127]

While these changes were unfolding, the Council was gearing up for a new capital campaign. The Council's centennial arrived in 2020 with Boxwell's following the next year in 2021. There was an opportunity to make some significant upgrades to Boxwell to both better accommodate the women in Scouts BSA and improve the facilities for years to come. In January of 2019, the Council "began the silent phase of a $12 million Capital Campaign to support renovations and upgrades to Boxwell Reservation." Officially titled "The Building for a New Century: A Campaign for Boxwell Reservation" and chaired by Harris Haston, co-founder of Carter Haston Real Estate Service, the quiet phase of this Centennial Campaign was expected to raise $8 million by December 2019 before going public for the public phase in 2020.[128]

Several priority projects were associated with the campaign. The Craig family contributed $500,000 for major renovations at Craig Dining Hall. The roof was completely replaced, including new steel braces inside and metal sheeting outside. Completed in Spring 2019, the project also included new tinted glass windows and upgraded bathroom facilities. The Reservation shotgun range received a pavilion and new launchers. For the first time, shooters could shoot from beneath something other than canvas. With an eye toward the new gender inclusiveness of Scouts BSA, new showerhouses were also on the priority list. The new year-round facilities would have complete individual bathrooms, including toilets, shower, and mirror all in one spot. Flannery's Skilled Trade Center made the priority projects list as well. Essentially, a building with multiple bays to work on automobiles and do "shop" work, the Skilled Trade Center would continue the transformation of Camp Parnell. A new "100-Year Anniversary" gateway would be added as well at the entrance of the Reservation. With a parking lot and lighting, the entrance of camp would become a photo opportunity. Finally, the last major renovation (and there were a host of smaller ones) was the demolition of Stahlman Dining Hall and replacement with a new facility with "a larger kitchen and dining hall, a new conference room, restrooms, a safety shelter and space for expansion of meeting rooms." The new Leadership Center at Camp Stahlman—to be named after long time Scouter Aubrey Harwell, the campaign's Honorary Chair—was slated to begin construction in the fall of 2020.[129]

As the Council's centennial year began in 2020, Flannery had big plans, too. CubWorld was not only going to build on the Family Scouting idea, but Flannery was contemplating a climbing wall to introduce Cubs to the basics of C.O.P.E. On the Scouts BSA side, work began on an ATV Program, which would teach ATV safety skills with ten separate and distinct lessons. The program was ready to fly: ATVs were donated and a course was developed and built. Flannery also had plans for an advanced fishing program as well as a muzzleloader shooting program. With the NRA program, Cowboy Action, and the muzzleloader program, Flannery envisioned a special Boxwell shooter award if a Scout participated in all three. Finally, there were plans for an advanced sailing program, focusing on the two large sailboats the camp had secured. Both boats could hold eight person crews. Advanced sailing would require Sailing Merit Badge and was trying to utilize some of the Reservation's less frequently used equipment.[130]

All of this though—the program ideas, the capital campaign—came to a screeching halt with the coronavirus epidemic. Stay-at-home lockdowns began in March 2020 with Boxwell, the Council office, and other council properties all shut down. 2020 was the Council's centennial, but the COVID-19 pandemic forced the Council to postpone a host of celebratory activities in the spring and then later in the fall as well. The Capital Campaign lowered its goal down to $10.6 million and slowed considerably. Initially, the campaign was going to move to the public phase at $8 million in January 2020. By summer 2020, the campaign had raised just over $6.1 million. Important components, such as the demolition of Stahlman Dining Hall and construction of the Aubrey Harwell Leadership Center were put on hold. As schools were cancelled through the end of the academic year, questions began to arise about summer camp programs. On May 6, the Council officially announced summer camp was cancelled. No other crisis in the nation's history over the previous hundred years had resulted in such an outcome. For the first time ever, there was no summer camp.[131]

Until the official cancellation, Flannery planned to move forward, but with numerous precautions and safety measures in place. Temperatures would be checked as Scouts and leaders entered the Reservation. There would be three meal shifts—A, B, and C—and people would sit four to a table instead of eight. Hand-washing stations would grace every entrance to every dining hall. There was even some talk of approaching food service completely differently with troops staying in their sites and meals brought to them. The size of instructional sessions were discussed as well. Perhaps instead of twenty scouts, only ten could take a merit badge together. Boxwell's size, for so long one of its greatest assets, became a detriment. A smaller camp could take its three hundred scouts a week and half those for something manageable. If Boxwell cut its numbers in half, with three camps, the result would still be hundreds of people on site. To drive the point home, the Council was told by a consultant from national that if they had camp, they would have COVID. Flannery laid out the reality very clearly, "Now, we could have done it. It would have been very hard. Very, very hard. And a lot of steps… [But what] if a kid comes to Scout Camp and gets it? [What if he's] just a carrier and goes home to grandma? Grandma gets it from kid? It's [on] us."

The end of summer camp forced some creativity. "Scouting wasn't happening," Flannery explained. "You could see that from February. Nothing was going on. Your pack probably didn't meet, and kids wasn't getting the program, so what did we want to do? We wanted kids to have a program." Flannery's solution was something called Merit Badge Days. Merit Badge Days were single day events held on a Saturday. Scouts came to camp, went through a temperature check, and then went to a specific instructor. The Scouts stayed together in groups of ten and never wandered around. They stayed outdoors the whole time. Food was brought to them. In short, Flannery could keep the numbers smaller and control it. The first weekend was so successful, several more followed with plans to make the event a regular opportunity after the pandemic ended.[132]

As 2020 closed, the regrouping had begun. The Council's cancelled Centennial events were rescheduled for the Spring and Fall of 2021. Boxwell's Centennial approached as well with a Staff Reunion in the works. Looming over all of these plans like a dark cloud was the question of whether summer camp would even move forward. Coronavirus vaccine distribution began the year at a snail's pace as the pandemic continued. Would there be a summer camp 2021?

For Flannery, there was only one answer to this question. "Are we going to have camp next year? Yes."

Closing Campfire

Lost Boxwells

The first three Boxwells are a bit of a mystery today. After each concluded their time as "Boxwell," they slipped into history, some to a greater degree than others. This is not so with Boxwell Reservation at Old Hickory Lake. This is the Boxwell most well-known, and for good reason. The camp has a long history at this current location and has been a staple of the Gallatin-Lebanon-LaGuardo community for decades. Opening in 1960, people who first walked the trails of the Old Hickory Lake Boxwell, who remember its first years, and who can point out how it has changed, are still around to tell their stories.

The early Boxwells—Linton, Narrows of the Harpeth, and Rock Island—are different. The Scouts who attended and the staff who ran them are almost completely gone now. Not all are gone, of course, but they are fewer and fewer in number. Another piece of this story disappears with the passing of every individual. Fundamental facts about these locations are already lost.

The Linton Boxwell, for instance, suffers from the most basic of problems: most people today have no idea where it was. The name "Linton" itself is part of the problem. When someone says Linton, do they mean Linton or Linden? Linden is a small town in West Tennessee, in Perry County. As recently as the 2012 *Leaders' Guide*, the Middle Tennessee Council itself identified Linden as the site of the first Boxwell. Though part of the Council's service area today, Linden would have been much too far away to be the first summer camp for what was then the Nashville Council. Wilbur Creighton, Jr. and Leland Johnson's 1983 work, *Boys Will Be Men,* only compounds this problem. On page 49, right at the bottom, Creighton and Johnson write, "[Scout Executive William J.] Anderson and the Council chose instead a site on the S. S. Morton property at Linton about seventeen miles from Nashville on the Memphis to Bristol Highway, later numbered Highway 100." This seems quite straight forward. The problem is that the Memphis to Bristol Highway is Highway 70, not Highway 100. Indeed, just outside Kingston Springs there's a lovely roadside sign on Highway 70 identifying the road as the former Memphis to Bristol Highway. So was the Linton Boxwell off of Highway 70, which would put it near Pegram and Kingston Springs, or was it off of Highway 100, which would put it between Bellevue and Fairview?[1]

With no clear references in the published literature, one would logically turn to a map. After all, is that not what Boy Scouts do? A 1929 Nashville map published by the U.S. Geological Survey put Linton on the old Harding Road—Highway 100—just outside of Belle Meade before Bellevue, not far outside Percy Warner Park. Most modern maps do not even the list town at all, but when it does show up, it is listed as between Pasquo and Fairview—quite a few miles further down the road. This location situation is further complicated by the merger of Nashville and Davidson County in 1963 to create the Metropolitan government. Many small communities were swallowed up in the merger. No modern map—in other words, if you go look at a Google map—even lists Linton as a town at all.[2]

Contemporary sources do not make identifying the location much easier. The two primary local newspapers of the time, the *Nashville Banner* and the *Nashville Tennessean* (later just the *Tennessean*), give conflicting reports on the location of the camp. The reports don't simply conflict with each other, but with themselves. For instance, on July 1, 1928, *The Banner* reports that the camp is located on the Little Harpeth River; just five days later, on the 6th, *the Banner* reports that the camp is located on the South Harpeth River. Within a week, *the Banner* has put the first Boxwell on two different rivers! In a wonderfully detailed article on the Linton Boxwell from 1927, Helen Dahnke for the *Nashville Tennessean* states that the camp was on the Little Harpeth, but constantly uses "Little Harpeth" and "Harpeth" interchangeably in the same article, as if the two are the same river. They are not.[3]

All the sources agree that the first Boxwell was located on the S. S. Morton property. The Nashville Council never owned this property; it stayed in the hands of the Mortons. As it turns out, Samuel Spragins "S. S." Morton (1871-1948) married Tabitha Allison "Allie" Newsom (1871-1964) in 1898. Morton had married well. Allie was the grand-daughter of Thomas J. Allison, Sr., a long-time resident of the community along with the Linton family, and Tabitha Newsom, whose family founded Newsom Station outside Bellevue. The newlyweds moved in with her grandparents and "Sam" ran the farm. Allie inherited "the Allison farm" when her grandparents died and thus was born the "Morton-Allison farm" sometimes referred to in the newspapers, or the "S. S. Morton farm" as identified in *Boys Will Be Men*. The couple had two children, Sallie and Maude. Samuel Morton died in 1948. Daughter Maude died of cancer at 59 years old in 1960. Allie herself finally passed away at the ripe old age of 93 in December of 1964.[4]

All of this is set up for the fact that the farm that was home to the first Boxwell was inherited by the eldest daughter of Samuel and Allison Morton, Sallie (1906-1994). With the death of her mother, most of the Morton-Allison farm passed into Sallie's hand. Just two years after her mother's death, Sallie sold off the first parcel of the farm. She consolidated some property in 1969 and in 1971 sold off more of the farm. Somewhere between 1971 and 1975, Sallie, now well into her late 60s, married Murray King and over the next four years, she and her husband sold off the remaining pieces of the family farm, breaking it up into the various tracts that exist today. In most cases, using property records and starting with the present owner, it was not much of a leap to connect Sallie Morton to modern owners and thus the old "S. S. Morton farm."[5]

Thus, it seemed Boxwell at Linton was down Highway 100—the Old Harding Road—just about the place where Highway 100 crosses the South Harpeth River. Find where Highway 96 connects to Highway 100 and drive northeast toward Nashville. When you cross the Corporal Jessie W. Gammons Memorial Bridge, you've found the Linton Boxwell, or, at least the old Morton farm where the first Boxwell was located. There are no markers; there are no structures or remains of structures. After all, Linton was basically an encampment more than a camp. But this was the farm property where the encampment was held.

This is a lot of digging for what is very basic question: where was the camp? Something important has been lost.

Camp Boxwell at the Narrows of the Harpeth is easier to identify, mostly. The camp closed in 1948, the year after "Coach" William Anderson retired. Ward Akers spent the summer of '48 at the camp before moving Boxwell to Rock Island. The Narrows were briefly used for a segregated camp in the late 1950s and early 1960s. With the integration of Boxwell in 1965, the Middle Tennessee Council continued to own the Narrows property, but did not develop it further before selling it to the state in 1978. The property that was the Narrows of the Harpeth Boxwell is the Narrows of the Harpeth portion of the Harpeth River State Park. Where the camp was on the 112 acres and how it was set up is the mystery.

If you know where to look, you can still find pieces of the Narrows of the Harpeth Boxwell. Old Cedar Hill Road is a little one lane country road, an off shoot of the more modern two lane Cedar Hill Road. Old Cedar Hill Road is the original road in the area, winding off of Highway 70 through the hills down to the Harpeth River. It is easy to imagine the trips for Scouts in the 1930s and 1940s. Open bed trucks, rattling and rumbling down a dirt version of this road carried the boys from Nashville to camp. Bouncing with their gear in the back of the trucks, Scouts peered at the summertime green of the river through the cloud of dust emanating from the truck. They knew they were minutes from canoeing and swimming in that water and the older boys would know both of those activities would be one of the very first things they would do after arriving at camp early on a Monday afternoon.

Looking at Old Cedar Hill Road on a map, the road climbed away from the river, made a hairpin turn, and then began racing back toward the river. On the ground, the turn is marked by the lone building on the road, a small farmhouse. White-walled with a tin roof covered in burgundy rust, the house has a wrap-around porch and a small yard. It was not exactly a farm house, but it was larger than anything a tenant farmer would own. When Camp Boxwell existed in the area across the street, the building was still serving it's original purpose: it was an old school house, straight out of the late nineteenth century. When the Scouts attending the Narrows made their afternoon hikes around the property, the schoolhouse was one of the places they often visited. With a hand-pump for getting water, it was an ideal stop either on the way out or on the way back in to camp.

But the adventure really begins across the street from the old schoolhouse. About fifty yards further down Old Cedar Hill Road on the opposite side from the schoolhouse is an old, abandoned dirt road. It is difficult to find from Old Cedar Hill Road. You have to get out and wander a little bit. Look for a large cedar tree wrapped with rusted wire and hinges for a gate that no longer exists. From here the road is easy to identify. There is a clear level path, vehicle width, disappearing down into the forest, probably made by machines from Leslie G. Boxwell's culvert company. A line of older trees adorn the right hand side of the road and a ravine descends on the left. This is what used to be called "Boy Scout Road" and it will take you right to the heart of Camp Boxwell at Narrows of the Harpeth.

Of course, there's nothing there anymore. Indeed, the area is so overgrown it is difficult to imagine the large clear assembly area Scouts used for
flag ceremonies and morning calisthenics. In some years, tents were arranged
in a semi-circle in the clearing and in other years, tents were arranged up and
down the hill Boy Scout Road traversed. If you continue to wander around
the area, you'll likely find debris that has been left in the woods from decades
of campers—Scouts and non-Scouts. You may run across the rusted frame of
a wood burning stove at the bottom of the hill below the Ranger Station. If
so, feel free to imagine this is the same stove that Walter Whittaker used to
cook his famous rolls and pancakes. It might be.

Up that hill to the ranger station are the only really permanent remains
of the Narrows Boxwell. Near the Ranger Station are two items of importance. The most critical is the rangers' garage. The garage itself is not important, but the foundation was clearly built long ago. It is the foundation for
the second dining hall, the one built in 1941. Nearby is a pile of debris, mostly rocks and concrete chunks. This pile of debris is all that remains of the dining hall's chimney, which until about fifteen years ago, was still attached to the
foundation. These are the physical remains of Camp Boxwell at the Narrows
of the Harpeth.

There is no evidence of the rest of the camp. The original dining hall,
which became the Lotto Fun Lodge and was featured in James Kilgore's *A Day
at Camp Boxwell* film from 1940, was located between the second dining hall
and the river. There's no indication of the structure anywhere. The waterfront
was directly down the hill from the second dining hall on the river, just downstream from the Harris Street Bridge. Again, no evidence. No docks or evidence of docks. With the exception of the overgrown road and the foundation
to the long abandoned dining hall, all other physical evidence of the camp is
now lost to time.

Still, it is an impressive site for a Scout camp. There are at least two caves in the area. There are acres of woods to explore. The Montgomery Bell Tunnel, though partly collapsed now, is still an engineering wonder. The climb up the bluffs over the Tunnel is itself an adventure, steep and narrow. But the adventure is rewarded at the top by Table Rock and the incredible panoramic view from here is awe-inspiring. There is the river and canoe friendly Narrows bend itself. Native American mounds are nearby as well. It is easy to understand why Boxwell stayed at this site for almost twenty years. It is an Adventureland, even today.

But again, much of what was Boxwell is lost. The Harpeth River State Park Association is working to retrieve this lost history. Kiosks are being constructed around the site and one of these will detail the history of the Narrows Boxwell.

The Rock Island Boxwell presents a still different situation from the other Boxwells. Known today as Camp Tubb at the Charles Parish Wildlife Reservation, the third Boxwell is still owned by the Council. It is used primarily for more rustic camping, what some troops call "outpost" camping. The roads are not paved. Much like a state park, there are no platforms in the campsites, just a campfire ring, a picnic table, and blue fifty gallon drums serving as trash barrels. There are some improvements that have been made over the years, such as a latrine stations, an all season, mixed-gender showerhouse, two Willhite era showerhouses with pit toilets and gang showers, and a large pavilion similar in size and design to the Wood Badge shed. There is also a fairly new maintenance area—a compound near where the Yost lodge was located. Modern Boxwell, even 1960s Boxwell, would be like staying at a resort compared to Rock Island.

Generally speaking, if you want to know what the Rock Island Boxwell looked like, go to Camp Tubb at Parish Reservation. Largely, the camp is today what it was from 1949-1959. Most of the sites still exist exactly where they were then. The Assembly area is in the same place and the locations of the Activity Yard and the Con Yard are fairly easy to identify mainly because campsites inhabit those locations now. Showerhouse I—a small red building with gang showers like Old Hickory Boxwell used to have—marks where the Handicraft was. The large pavilion sits right where the dining hall tents were located.

And of course the Old Kentucky Road has not moved at all.

Some things are completely gone. The waterfront with its famous swimming cribs is gone. In fact there is nothing even at the location, nor has another swimming area replaced it. If you did not know the waterfront was across from the campsite named Winnebago—named Cherokee Village during the Boxwell years—then you would have very little idea where the spot was. The modern boating area now is a small floating dock on the point of the peninsula, in a completely different location. The water tower is gone too, replaced by actual water lines into the camp. The trading post and the first aid station are also distant memories with nothing to denote their location. The Yost Lodge where Akers and his family stayed is gone, only spring time buttercups now bloom around the remains of a rock foundation.

If you do happen to understand where everything originally was, it will be clear how well designed this camp was. From the Waterfront to the dining hall was basically one long straight shot. A Scout could go to the waterfront, come up the hill and immediately make his way to Scoutcraft skills like First Aid and Wilderness Survival, then move over a few yards for Conservation and Ecology, then a few more yards for the Handicraft tent. Once all of this was completed, it was a quick jaunt—hardly even as long as a "jaunt"—up the hill to what would have been the camp's showers and the dining hall. Virtually all of the camp's major program components were in a straight line from the waterfront to the dining hall. The Old Kentucky Trail bisected this route to form the axis on which the campsites revolved. A simple, brilliant, and easy to follow design.

Thus, the Rock Island Boxwell is not "lost" in the way the first two camps are. It is clear where it is and it's layout as a camp is largely unchanged. But the Rock Island Boxwell is "lost" in other ways. Generally referred to as "old Boxwell" now, the assumption is that Rock Island worked just like "new Boxwell," but in a different location. Clearly, this is not entirely accurate. Rock Island had its own unique flavor and style.

But Rock Island was, first and foremost, a Boy Scout resident camp. When the program and the staff left, Rock Island remained, but it was a shell, empty of the life that had animated it for eleven years. The site lacks the clear purpose it once had. Today it has virtually none of the facilities or glamor of the "new" Boxwell and it lacks the High Adventure magnetism of the Latimer Reservation, which is just down the road. Thus, it is neither a resident camp nor a High Adventure camp; it just is. Perhaps that's the way it should be. If you want to camp—really *camp* the way Boy Scouts of yore used to do—Rock Island is the place to go.

Rock Island was never supposed to be more than a temporary holding site until "new Boxwell" was finished. It has, however, ended up being part of the Council longer than any other property, facility, or professional around today. There's some irony in that fact.

The Old Hickory Boxwell has been in the same location for over sixty years now. Program areas have moved, staff sites have come and gone, and new buildings are constantly appearing. The Old Hickory Boxwell is constantly building on top of itself, reinventing itself, repurposing itself.

But it has its forgotten charms too, if you know where to look for them. There are old, pre-Boxwell house foundations hidden along rarely travelled trails. There are Order of the Arrow ceremony sites—at least seven of them—peppered in the woods all over the Reservation. There is the obstacle course built in the little corner of the Reservation between Camp Light and Camp Craig used by the JROTC programs. There is all-but-forgotten fitness

*A collection of standard Boxwell patches given every year to Scouts. Each fleur-de-lis repre-
sents a camp on the reservation. The Camp Murrey patch (upper left) is from before the
building of Camp Craig. The Camp Stahlman, Camp Parnell, and Camp Craig patches are all
after 1973. There is no Camp Light patch. Collection of the author.*

trail in CubWorld and the hiking trail completed in 2014 that connects Cub-
World to Percy Dempsey. There are cross tie bridges over creeks scattered
here and there. Both Stahlman and Craig have remnants of treehouses built by
different staffs. There are electrical insulators in trees where electricity was run
in the early days. There are rusting cots hiding in the woods, usually broken
and abandoned by staff. There's an abandoned pig barn still standing and in
remarkably good shape, paying homage to the old farming operation. The dog
trial ponds from Akers' day still exist as well. There are steel uprights rising

out of the lake denoting where docks were planned in the original 1960 vision for the camp. Boxwell at Old Hickory Lake is full of hidden treasures like these.

What Does Boxwell Mean?

And yet, as interesting as these items are, as exciting as it is to visit all of these locations, Boxwell has always been more than the physical facilities. As Reservation Director Jason Flannery put it so eloquently in December 2020, "I feel like Boxwell is Boxwell, alive, when staff are here. So right now [in December] it's just a shell. You put the staff in there, you got working parts again. It's running and going... [T]he heartbeat of the camp should be the program we offer to our youth. The staff should help embellish it..." Boxwell is the program. Boxwell is the staff. Boxwell is the Scouts and leaders. Boxwell is more than the buildings and the property.[6]

For Scouts, Boxwell is an adventure. From the Narrows to Old Hickory Lake, catching and wearing snakes is part of the fun. One Scout explained in 2000, "We caught him [a four foot long ray rat snake] right here outside the mess hall, under the deck. He's got a lot of scratches and cuts on him, so I guess he's had a rough life... We did feed him once. A field mouse. He gobbled it right down... He's a great snake." E. D. Thompson said much the same about his experience with snakes at the Narrows. Scouts get wrapped in bandages, make floatation devices out of their clothes, make things from leather, design and build robots, swamp canoes and rowboats, and fly through the trees in safety harnesses. There may be instruction, but this is not school.[7]

For staff, Boxwell is often about family, a chosen family. Lance Ussery explained this concept clearly in 2019: "There are guys that I could call right now that wore that red hat and I wouldn't have to give them any information. "I need help. Here's where I am.'" And that was all the information needed. Ussery trusted they would come. He was not the only one to express such an idea. And that bond for some is almost mystical. "My wife doesn't understand," John Estes explains when talking about his Boxwell staff friends. "She doesn't have to, and she will admit this to you if you ask her, she doesn't have the type of friends that it's unconditional. It's 'I need you.' 'I'm coming.' She doesn't understand that. None of her friends have ever been like that."[8]

Providing a program, a quality program for the Scouts, was also high on many staff members' list of why camp mattered. How the staff envisioned that program varied wildly, but it was a theme. For some, it was no more complicated than making sure the Scouts had a good time. For others, it was more complex. Summer camp was to provide role models for Scouts and staff alike. To take what had been learned and pass it on to the next generation. Others expressed how camp was an opportunity to grow and to learn how to take responsibility for themselves. In reflecting on his camp staff experience, former Stahlman Program Director Andy Verble quipped,

> I'm so glad I did it, you know? I really feel sorry for kids that go flip burgers for the summer... Don't get me wrong I'm sure there's memories of getting burned or picking a cockroach off the floor or whatever, but it's just if you weren't there you just don't understand. And there's just so many awesome stories and different memories and victories. Victories for Scouting, where you've got some kid some badge.

Helping units, helping Scouts *is* the program.[9]

Flannery, the current Reservation Director, has had the opportunity to see Boxwell from several different perspectives. He was a camper. He was a Counselor in Training. He was a full-fledged staff member at a Boy Scout Resident Camp. He was a program director. He was a Scoutmaster and volunteer. He was Camp Director as a Professional Scouters at a Cub Resident Camp. He's seen camp wearing a variety of different hats, both metaphorical and literal. When asked about the goal of Scouting and camp, Flannery passionately explained,

> Scouting is here to teach our young men and women leader-

ship skills. I don't know of another program that does that, that you get to do it outside and learn and have the opportunity to fail and learn from that. In society, now, if you fail, you're done. You get an F, it's over. You start over. Here, if you mess up, there's an opportunity to learn and grow from that. There's not many programs that have that... Camp is a tool to help young men explore new opportunities and learn skills, and make everlasting memories. I mean, that's what it is... That's from the heart.[10]

Boxwell is all of these things. It is a physical location and a place of memories. It has both a past and a future. It is a place that is both terrifying for the Scout who away from home for the first time and a place that can become a new home. Boxwell is the home to public and personal histories. There are the events published in the newspaper or the newsletters or even the promotional videos out in the world for everyone to see. These are the incontrovertible. But Boxwell is also full of personal histories. Sometimes these personal histories are wrapped up in the public histories. For example, Ron Oakes recalled his first task after being hired as District Executive was to help park cars at Boxwell's 1960 dedication. His personal story made the larger known story possible. Other personal histories are more independent of the public history, such as the Scout who could not swim, but learns how. There is the Scout who is homesick his or her first week at camp, but soldiers through the week anyway. There is the staff member whose significant other breaks up with him or her while away at camp, but manages to get up and keep going, even though it feels like the end of the world. It is a walkabout with a friend to unknown parts of camp. Personal histories are a thousand moments, just like these. These are defining moments.[11]

And these moment are history, which is, after all, just a story of people living their lives.

The Closing Campfire

467

For the Good of the Program

A closing campfire generally ends the same way every time. After giving awards, Scouts are challenged to take what they've learned, go out into the world, and use that knowledge. This could mean taking their Boxwell experience and using it for further advancement—the Arrow of Light or Eagle Scout. This could mean trying to make the world a better place in which to live. At the very end, the staff circles up, places arms on shoulders, and begins to sing. The first song is often "Scout Vespers," but others follow, such as "Kumbaya" or "Swing Low, Sweet Chariot," setting an appropriately somber tone as Scouts are asked to leave the campfire area. Camp—at least the official program aspect of camp—is over.

But camp is more than the official program. It is also the traditions passed down from one staff to the next. Stahlman, Craig, and CubWorld staffs all have their own post-campfire traditions. Whether it be a song, or a mantra, or a ritual, each camp staff concludes their program with a tradition only practiced in that camp. Regardless of camp, regardless of time period, regardless of internal staff traditions, the closing campfire ends camp.

Boxwell began its life as a tiny Boy Scout camp on a mere four acres of land. Over the last hundred years, Boxwell has become more than a Boy Scout camp. It is also a Cub Scout camp. It is also the home of the Order of the Arrow and Wood Badge. It is an adventure for some and a family for others. It is just a camp and it is also so much more.

Boxwell—Camp Boxwell and Boxwell Reservation—served the interests of the Scouting program for the past century. As Scouting and the values that Scouting purports to represent change, so too must the program at Boxwell change as well. From creating citizens to training future fathers to stressing individualism and entertainment, camp program has shifted and changed numerous times over the last one hundred years. Every change, every transition, whether it was at a Boy Scout Resident Camp, a Cub Resident Camp, or a High Adventure area, have all been guided by one simple maxim. Every change was "for the good of the program."

Boxwell Leadership

Camp Boxwell at Linton

1921-1929

Year	Camp Director
1921	C. W. Abele
1922	Hugh Nixon
1923	William J. Anderson
1924	William J. Anderson
1925	William J. Anderson
1926	William J. Anderson
1927	William J. Anderson
1928	William J. Anderson and L. H. Smith
1929	William J. Anderson

Boxwell Leadership

Camp Boxwell at the Narrows of the Harpeth

1930-1948

Year   **Camp Director**

1930   William J. Anderson

1931   William J. Anderson, Jr.

1932   Robert W. DuBose

1933   Talmadge Miller

1934   William J. Anderson

1935   William J. Anderson and J. L. Alderson

1936   William J. Anderson

1937   William J. Anderson

1938   James Gribble

1939   James Gribble

1940   James Gribble

1941   James Gribble

1942   Melvin Williams

1943   Talmadge Miller

1944   William J. Anderson

1945   William J. Anderson

1946   James Gribble

1947   James Gribble

1948   Ward Akers

Boxwell Leadership

Boxwell at Rock Island

1949-1959

Year **Camp Director**

1949   Ward Akers

1950   Reeves Little

1951   Clarence Jung

1952   Clarence Jung

1953   Gene Tolley

1954   Richard Parker & Gene Tolley

1955   Richard Parker & Gene Tolley

1956   Richard Parker & James Johnson

1957   Richard Parker & Don Starin

1958   Richard Parker

1959   Chester LaFever

Boxwell Reservation Leadership

Boxwell Reservation at Old Hickory Lake

1960-2021

Year	Council Executive	Reservation Director	Head Ranger
1960	Ward Akers	James Johnson	Bill Cyrils/ Coleman Wright
1961	Ward Akers	James Johnson	Coleman Wright
1962	Ward Akers	James Johnson	Coleman Wright
1963	Ward Akers	James Johnson	Coleman Wright
1964	Ward Akers	James Johnson	Coleman Wright
1965	Ward Akers	Bruce Atkins	Coleman Wright
1966	Ward Akers	Bruce Atkins	Bobby Smith
1967	Ward Akers	Bruce Atkins	Bobby Smith
1968	Ward Akers	Bruce Atkins	Bobby Smith
1969	Ward Akers	Bruce Atkins	Bobby Smith
1970	Ward Akers	Ed Human	Bobby Smith
1971	Ward Akers	Ed Human	Bobby Smith
1972	Ward Akers	Ed Human	Bobby Smith
1973	Ward Akers	Ed Human	Bobby Smith
1974	Ward Akers	Ed Human	Norman Patterson
1975	Ward Akers	Ed Human	Norman Patterson
1976	Hershel Tolbert	Tom Willhite	Norman Patterson

Year	Council Executive	Reservation Director	Head Ranger
1977	Hershel Tolbert	Tom Willhite	Norman Patterson
1978	Hershel Tolbert	Tom Willhite	Willie Claud
1979	Hershel Tolbert	Tom Willhite	Willie Claud
1980	Hershel Tolbert	Tom Willhite	Willie Claud
1981	Hershel Tolbert	Tom Willhite	Willie Claud
1982	Hershel Tolbert	Tom Willhite	Willie Claud
1983	Hershel Tolbert	Tom Willhite	Willie Claud
1984	Hershel Tolbert	Tom Willhite	Willie Claud
1985	Hershel Tolbert	Tom Willhite	Willie Claud
1986	Hershel Tolbert	Tom Willhite	Willie Claud
1987	Hershel Tolbert	Tom Willhite	Willie Claud
1988	Hershel Tolbert	Tom Willhite	Willie Claud
1989	Hershel Tolbert	Tom Willhite	Willie Claud
1990	Hershel Tolbert	Tom Willhite	Willie Claud
1991	Hershel Tolbert/ Ken Connelly	Tom Willhite	Willie Claud
1992	Ken Connelly	Tom Willhite	Willie Claud
1993	Ken Connelly	Tom Willhite	Willie Claud
1994	Ken Connelly	Tom Willhite	Willie Claud
1995	Joe Long	Larry Green	Willie Claud
1996	Joe Long	Larry Green	Bill Freeman
1997	Joe Long	Ron Turpin	Bill Freeman
1998	Joe Long	Ron Turpin	Bill Freeman
1999	Joe Long	Ron Turpin	Bill Freeman
2000	Joe Long	Ron Turpin	Bill Freeman
2001	Joe Long	Ron Turpin	Bill Freeman
2002	Joe Long	Ron Turpin	Bill Freeman
2003	Joe Long	Pat Scales	Bill Freeman
2004	Joe Long	Carl Adkins	Bill Freeman

Year	Council Executive	Reservation Director	Head Ranger
2005	Joe Long	Carl Adkins	Bill Freeman
2006	Joe Long	Carl Adkins	Bill Freeman
2007	Joe Long	Carl Adkins	Steve Belew
2008	Hugh Travis	Carl Adkins	Steve Belew
2009	Hugh Travis	Carl Adkins	Steve Belew
2010	Hugh Travis	Carl Adkins	Steve Belew
2011	Hugh Travis	Carl Adkins	Steve Belew
2012	Hugh Travis	Carl Adkins	Steve Belew
2013	Hugh Travis	Carl Adkins	Steve Belew
2014	Hugh Travis	Carl Adkins	Steve Belew
2015	Larry Brown	Carl Adkins	Rob Ward
2016	Larry Brown	Carl Adkins	Rob Ward
2017	Larry Brown	Carl Adkins	Rob Ward
2018	Larry Brown	Jason Flannery	Rob Ward
2019	Larry Brown	Jason Flannery	Rob Ward
2020	Larry Brown	Jason Flannery	Rob Ward
2021	Larry Brown	Jason Flannery	Dave Bauer

Camp Stahlman Leadership

Boxwell Reservation at Old Hickory Lake

1960-2021

Year	Program Director	Camp Director
1960	A.D. Hancock	Chester LaFever
1961	Chester LaFever	Robert Holt
1962	Chester LaFever	Robert Holt
1963	Chester LaFever	Charlie Biederman
1964	Chester LaFever	Ron Oakes
1965	Chester LaFever	Ron Oakes
1966	Richard Graves	Bob Whitaker & Ken Goad
1967	Chester LaFever, Tom Parker	Ken Goad & Chad Gaffin
1968	Richard Graves, Tom Parker	Ken Goad
1969	Chester LaFever	Ken Goad
1970	Ted Naylor	Joe Keathley & Bill Cherry
1971	Tom Parker	Fred Blair
1972	Garland Russell	Andy Russell
1973	Garland Russell	Andy Russell
1974	Garland Russell	Troy Feltner
1975	Garland Russell	Eddie Knox
1976	Russ Parham	Jerry Campbell & Bill Hargis

1977	Russ Parham	Allen Jones
1978	Russ Parham	Ambler Brown
1979	[closed]	[closed]
1980	Ernie Ragsdale	Doug Clevinger
1981	Ernie Ragsdale	Andy Hindman
1982	Ernie Ragsdale	Unknown
1983	Ernie Ragsdale	Unknown
1984	Ernie Ragsdale	David Collins
1985	Ernie Ragsdale	Bob Shaw
1986	Harold G. Tracy	Micheal Morgan
1987	Ernie Ragsdale	Unknown
1988	Ernie Ragsdale	George McGovern
1989	Ernie Ragsdale	Carl Atkins
1990	Brent Limbaugh	Larry Green
1991	Ralph Walker	Tony Reynolds
1992	Andy Whitt	Larry Green
1993	Andy Whitt	Dale Turner
1994	Travis Spivey	Moses Caballero
1995	Travis Spivey	John Hinds
1996	Ron Ramsey	Moses Caballero
1997	Ron Ramsey	Shane Gladden
1998	Ron Ramsey	Brad Perry
1999	Ron Ramsey	Brad Perry
2000	Andy Verble	David Williams
2001	Andy Verble	Chris Doughtrey
2002	Andy Verble	Larry Green
2003	Andy Verble	Larry Green
2004	Ian Romaine	Ben Parker
2005	Randy Coats	Josh McClure
2006	Randy Coats	Josh McClure

2007	Randy Coats	John Mitchell
2008	Nate Hudson	Justin Caruthers
2009	Nate Hudson	Steve Eubank
2010	Danny Waltman	Steve Eubank
2011	Danny Waltman	Steve Eubank
2012	Lee Craft	Steve Eubank
2013	Lee Craft	Steve Eubank
2014	Lee Craft	Steve Eubank
2015	Max Briscoe	Steve Eubank
2016	Max Briscoe	Steve Eubank
2017	Craig Carpenter	Steve Eubank
2018	Craig Carpenter/ Thomas Stroud	Max Briscoe
2019	David Peterman	Steve Eubank
2020	[No Camp:: COVID]	[No Camp::COVID]
2021	Andrew Berta	Steve Eubank

Camp Parnell Leadership

Boxwell Reservation at Old Hickory Lake

1960-1998

Year	Program Director	Camp Director
1960	Robert Nicholson	Bob Chaffin
1961	Harold Hitt	Bob Chaffin
1962	Harold Hitt	Ralph Manus
1963	Jimmy Joe Jackson	Ralph Manus
1964	Jimmy Joe Jackson	Bruce Atkins
1965	Jimmy Joe Jackson	Bruce Atkins
1966	Jimmy Joe Jackson	Ken Connelly
1967	Jimmy Joe Jackson	Tom Willhite, Earl Tatum
1968	Jimmy Joe Jackson	Earl Tatum
1969	Jimmy Joe Jackson	Unknown
1970	Jimmy Joe Jackson	Buddy Chatterfield
1971	David Farrar	Dean Lollar
1972	David Farrar	Vester Parsley, Jr.
1973	Steve Eubank	Charlie Ray Smith
1974	Steve Eubank	Larry Green
1975	Steve Eubank	Tom Young
1976	Steve Eubank	Robert Salser
1977	[closed]	[closed]
1978	[closed]	[closed]

Year	Program Director	Camp Director
1979	Russ Parham	Sam Yokely
1980	Perry Bruce	Buff Groth
1981	Jerry Barnett	Larry Green
1982	[closed]	[closed]
1983	[closed]	[closed]
1984	Jerry Barnett	Bill Evatt
1985	Jerry Barnett	Lenord Cathey
1986	[closed]	[closed]
1987	[closed]	[closed]
1988	Jerry Barnett	Chris Cox
1989	Jerry Barnett	Spencer Page
1990	[closed]	[closed]
1991	[closed]	[closed]
1992	Jerry Barnett	Andy Swallow
1993	Kerry Parker	Russ Doyle
1994	[closed]	[closed]
1995	[closed]	[closed]
1996	Kerry Parker	Kevin Beirne
1997	Grady Eades	[no Camp Director]
1998	Michael Salazar	Russ Doyle/Tony Reynolds

Camp Craig Leadership

Boxwell Reservation at Old Hickory Lake

1973-2021

Year	Program Director	Camp Director
1973	Steve Eubank	Gordon Gill
1974	Tom Young	Terrell Bain
1975	Joe Tomasso	David Larkin
1976	[closed]	[closed]
1977	Ernie Ragsdale	Don McKinney
1978	Ernie Ragsdale	Hugh Travis
1979	Ernie Ragsdale	David Larkin
1980	[closed]	[closed]
1981	[closed]	[closed]
1982	Jerry Barnett	Larry Green
1983	Jerry Barnett	Tim Cooper
1984	[closed]	[closed]
1985	[closed]	[closed]
1986	Kerry Parker	Chuck Simmons
1987	Jerry Barnett	Bruce Van Cleve
1988	[closed]	[closed]
1989	[closed]	[closed]
1990	Jerry Barnett	Greg King
1991	Jerry Barnett	Mike Kaufman

Year	Program Director	Camp Director
1992	[closed]	[closed]
1993	[closed]	[closed]
1994	Kerry Parker	Jeff Hawkins
1995	Kerry Parker	Andy Swallow
1996	[closed]	[closed]
1997	[closed]	[closed]
1998	[closed]	[closed]
1999	Michael Salazar	Phil Nixon
2000	Michael Salazar	Carl Denton
2001	Mac Barnes	Carl Denton
2002	Jonathan Nation	Greg Brown
2003	Ian Romaine	Greg Brown
2004	Griffin Bridgers	Allen Crawford
2005	Jon Elliot	Allen Crawford
2006	Caleb Campbell	Jeremy Belk
2007	Jason Flannery	Jeremy Belk
2008	Aaron Patten	Tony Turner
2009	Aaron Patten	Tony Turner
2010	Ian Weir	Tony Turner
2011	Ian Weir	Tony Turner
2012	Ian Weir	Tony Turner
2013	Nate Danielson	Tony Turner
2014	John "JJ" Norman	Tony Turner
2015	John "JJ" Norman	Tony Turner
2016	Sean Patten	Tony Turner
2017	Max Briscoe	Tony Turner
2018	Thomas Stroud	Perry Bruce
2019	Thomas Stroud	Perry Bruce
2020	[No Camp::COVID]	[No Camp::COVID]
2021	Gavin Nixon	Perry Bruce

Camp Murry Leadership

Boxwell Reservation at Old Hickory Lake

1960-1994

Year	Program Director	Year	Program Director
1960	Elizabeth Nicholson	1978	Gladys Roberts
1961	Joan Hitt	1979	Gladys Roberts
1962	Joan Hitt	1980	Gladys Roberts
1963	Elizabeth Jackson	1981	Gladys Roberts
1964	Elizabeth Jackson	1982	Gladys Roberts
1965	Elizabeth Jackson	1983	Lisa Hamilton;
1966	Vivian Connelly		Marie Willhite
1967	Marie Willhite	1984	Christy Willhite
1968	Elizabeth Jackson	1985	Christy Willhite
1969	Elizabeth Jackson	1986	Christy Willhite
1970	Elizabeth Jackson	1987	Christy Willhite
1971	Unknown	1988	Christy Willhite
1972	Unknown	1989	Christy Willhite
1973	Gladys Roberts	1990	Christy Willhite
1974	Gladys Roberts	1991	Christy Willhite
1975	Gladys Roberts	1992	Christy Willhite
1976	Gladys Roberts	1993	Christy Willhite
1977	Gladys Roberts	1994	Christy Willhite

Cub World Leadership

Boxwell Reservation at Old Hickory Lake

1996-2021

Year	Program Director	Camp Director
1996	Savantha Tesar	Alan Hamlin & Shane Gladden
1997	Savantha Tesar	Alan Hamlin & Tobie Raines
1998	Unknown	Unknown
1999	Jenny Forsythe	David Williams
2000	Jenny Forsythe	Lamar Perry
2001	Jenny Forsythe	Ben Parker
2002	Jenny Forsythe	Ben Parker
2003	Rita Media	John Mitchel, Dave Grimes, Tim Grant
2004	Dominick Azzara	Greg Brown, David Grimes
2005	Dominick Azzara	Greg Brown, Chris Beck
2006	Dominick Azzara	Meribeth Hughes
2007	Dominick Azzara	Meribeth Hughes, David Zimmerle
2008	Dominick Azzara	Mike Cowel, Kim Brisson
2009	Jody Looper, Jonathan Azzara	Danny Sutherland, Michael Martin
2010	Jakes Jones, Jody Looper, Jonathan Azzara	David Edwards, Lindsey Sublett

2011	Jonathan Azzara, Jake Jones	Brian Wolfensberger
2012	Jakes Jones	Bradford Shoemaker
2013	Jakes Jones, Nick Klomfas	Scott McCray
2014	Melissa Paris, Gaylon Greer	Ryan Vaden
2015	Amerlia Berle, Melissa Paris	Jason Flannery
2016	Amerlia Berle, Melissa Paris	Jason Flannery
2017	Amelia Berle, Kevin DeHoff	Mary Jared
2018	Mike Andrews Kevin DeHoff	Rob Wright
2019	Garrett Ladd	Max Briscoe
2020	[No Camp::COVID]	[No Camp::COVID]
2021	Hunter Garrett	Derek Maness

Chapter I Endnotes

Citizens in Training: Camp Boxwell at Linton

1921-1929

1. "News of Our Boy Scouts," *Nashville Tennessean*, January 23, 1921, pg. 27; Wilbur F. Creighton, Jr. and Leland Johnson, *Boys Will be Men: Middle Tennessee Scouting Since 1910*, Middle Tennessee Council, Nashville, TN, 1983, pg. 40; W. H. Fitzgerald, "Scouting with Scouts," *Nashville Tennessean*, September 6, 1920, pg. 3; "Boy Scouts," *Nashville Tennessean*, June 20, 1921, pg. 8.
2. "Asks Boy Scout Suggestions," *Nashville Tennessean*, March 11, 1921, pg. 3; "Scout News," *Nashville Tennessean*, April 24, 1921, pg. 31; "Boy Scouts to Hold Summer Camp," *Nashville Tennessean*, May 20, 1921, pg. 2; Serving as a cook at Vanderbilt's Kissam Hall was Whittaker's primary job when not at Camp Boxwell, "Boy Scout," *Nashville Tennessean*, June 13, 1921, pg. 5.
3. "Scout News," *Nashville Tennessean*, April 24, 1921, pg. 31.
4. Creighton and Johnson, *Boys Will be Men*, pg. 23; "Scout News," *Nashville Tennessean*, April 24, 1921, pg. 31.
5. "Boy Scouts," *Nashville Tennessean*, June 20, 1921, pg. 8.
6. "Boy Scouts Camp Site Changed—Water Bad," *Nashville Tennessean*, June 24, 1921, pg. 20.
7. "Boy Scouts," *Nashville Tennessean*, June 27, 1921, pg. 2.
8. Ibid.
9. Today, the Harding Road is Old Harding Road. The site in question can be found off of Highway 100 at the Corporal Jessie W. Gammons Memorial Bridge. "Boy Scouts Camp Site is Chosen," *Nashville Tennessean*, June 29, 1921, pg. 10.
10. Interestingly, variants of the same article ran in the *Nashville Banner* twice as well as once in the *Nashville Tennessean*. All three citations are provided here, in order of appearance. It is also worth noting that for the three weeks Boxwell was open in 1921, the papers often referred to the site as "Camp Linton" or "the Boy Scout camp at Linton." It would be 1922 before the Camp Boxwell name caught on, despite the Executive Board's naming. "With the Boy Scouts," *Nashville Banner*, July 2, 1921, pg 8; "Boy Scouts," *Nashville Banner*, July 3, 1921, pg. 9; "Boy Scouts," *Nashville Tennessean*, July 3, 1921, pg. 9.

was a camp for the YMCA. There was a camp for the Sunday School Association.
There was a camp for the Forrest Scouts as well as small camps for individual Boy Scout
troops. There was even a camp for the Corn, Pig, Calf, Canning, and Poultry Club. The
newspapers are littered with camp announcements. And if there wasn't an organization
holding a camp, individuals were camping as well. "Boys' Summer Camp Formally Dedicated," *Nashville Banner,* July 5, 1921, pg. 2; "Boy Scouts Are Enjoying Life at Linton
Beach," *Nashville Tennessean,* June 19, 1921, pg. 30.

11. Eric Foner, *The Story of American Freedom,* W. W. Norton & Company: New York
and London, 1998, pg. 116; David Shi and George Tindall, *America: The Essential
Learning Edition,* first edition, W. W. Norton & Company, New York and London,
2015, pg. 620; Robert V. Remini, *A Short History of the United States: From the Arrival of Native American Tribes to the Obama Presidency,* Harper Perennial, paperback
edition, New York, 2009, pg. 205.

12. Chuck Wills, *Boy Scouts of America: A Centennial History,* DK Publishing, New York,
2009, pgs. 16-19.

13. There is some evidence to suggest this story is a bit embellished. See more in Edward L.
Rowan, *To Do My Best: James E. West and the History of the Boy Scouts of America,*
self-published, 2005. The official story is from Chuck Wills, *Boy Scouts of America: A
Centennial History,* DK Publishing, New York, 2009, pg. 9.

14. Wills, *Boy Scouts of America: A Centennial History,* pgs. 18-34.

15. Originally published in 1911, the work cited here is a modern reprint. Boy Scouts of
America, *The Official Handbook for Boys,* Doubleday, Page & Co., New York 1911,
Applewood press Reprint, Bedford Massachusetts, n.d, pgs. v, 3.

16. Historian Benjamin Rene' Jordan, building upon a cartoon in an early Scouting publication, describes this situation as dueling archetypes of manhood: the ax-man and the bu-
reaucrat. Benjamin Rene' Jordan, *Modern Manhood and the Boy Scouts of America:
Citizenship, Race, and the Environment, 1910-1930,* University of North Carolina Press,
Chapel Hill, North Carolina, 2016.

17. Boy Scouts of America, *The Official Handbook for Boys,* pg. 16; Boy Scouts of America,
Handbook for Boys, Boy Scouts of America, first edition, 33rd printing, 1940, pgs. 408-
410.

18. "He Started Scouting in Nashville," *The Tennessean Magazine,* April 4, 1937, pg. 13.
For a more detailed discussion of Haley and Nashville Scouting's early years, see the first
two chapters of Creighton and Johnson's *Boys Will Be Men,* 1983.

19. The Scoutmasters "commanding" the camp were D. E. Hinkle, W. H. Fitzgerald, Dr.
Guy T. Denton, and Carl Hinkle. They were assisted by the following women who were
"exercising a motherly supervision": Mrs. D. E. Hinkle, Mrs. Fitzgerald, Mrs. Carl Hin-
kle, and Misses Ethel Worsham and Joella Skiles. W. H. Fitzgerald, "Nashville Boy
Scouts in Camp," *Nashville Tennessean,* July 13, 1923, pg. 3; Creighton and Johnson,
Boys Will Be Men, pgs. 23-24.

20. Creighton and Johnson, *Boys Will Be Men,* pgs. 37-38.

21. "Nashville, Tennessee," *Wikipedia,* last modified July 6, 2019, https://

en.wikipedia.org/wiki/Nashville,_Tennessee; "Springfield, Tennessee," *Wikipedia*, last modified February 7, 2019,https://en.wikipedia.org/wiki/Springfield,_Tennessee; "Murfreesboro, Tennessee," *Wikipedia*, last modified June 18, 2019,https://en.wikipedia.org/wiki/Murfreesboro,_Tennessee ; "Dickson, Tennessee," *Wikipedia*, last modified May 29, 2019, https://en.wikipedia.org/wiki/Dickson,_Tennessee ; "Lebanon, Tennessee," *Wikipedia*, last modified June 26, 2019, https://en.wikipedia.org/wiki/Lebanon,_Tennessee; "Why Every Nashville Citizen Should Support the Boy Scouts," *Nashville Tennessean*, March 5, 1920, pg. 2.

22. "Big Campaign for Boy Scouts," *Nashville Banner*, March 2, 1920, pg. 13; Creighton and Johnson state the final tally was $18,600.   They also claim the campaign was two weeks long. The record is unequivocal: the campaign was one day, Wednesday, March 10, 1920. Spreading the word to local businessmen—the target of the campaign—went on for over a week, but the campaign itself was one day, for approximately two hours. Creighton and Johnson, *Boys Will Be Men*, p.g 40; "Why Every Nashville Citizen Should Support the Boy Scouts," *Nashville Tennessean*, March 5, 1920, pg. 2; "Plan Program for Boy Scouts," *Nashville Tennessean*, March 6, 1920, pg. 9; "Goal Passed in Boy Scout Drive," *Nashville Tennessean*, March 11, 1920, pg. 5; "Scout Campaign Passes Its Mark," *Nashville Banner*, March 10, 1920, pg. 4.

23. J. G. Stahlman would become president and publisher of *The Banner* in 1930; his brother, E. B. Stahlman, Jr., would be highly involved in middle Tennessee Scouting in the decades to come. "Stahlman, 42 Years *Banner* Guide, Dies," *The Tennessean*, May 2, 1976, pg. A-1, A-8; other members of the Board were Vernon Tupper, VP of Administration; Lee J. Loventhal, VP training; C. M. Nininger, VP court of honor, an advancement review board; V. J. Alexander, treasurer; Tillman Cavert, finance; R. C. Derivaux, civic service; W. H. Fitzgerald, leadership and training, T. Graham Hall, representative to national; and Curtis B. Haley, board of instructors and examiners, "Goal Passed in Boy Scout Drive," *Nashville Tennessean*, March 11, 1920, pg. 5; It is worth noting for future reference that Daniel Earle McGugin played football for Michigan football coach Fielding Yost. Yost's summer retreat in Walling, TN becomes the Rock Island Boxwell in 1949, Ann Toplovich, "Daniel Earle MgGugin," *Tennessee Encyclopedia*, last modified March 1, 2018, https://tennesseeencyclopedia.net/entries/daniel-earle-mcgugin/ .

24. "Beloved Coach Anderson Retires as Scout Executive," *Nashville Banner*, July 30, 1947, pg. 10; "Anderson Announced Boy Scout Executive," *Nashville Tennessean*, June 20, 1920, pg. 16.

25. "Anderson Announced Boy Scout Executive," *Nashville Tennessean*, June 20, 1920, pg. 16; Creighton and Johnson, *Boys Will Be Men*, pg. 41; Anderson lived from 1882-1963, "W. J. Anderson Dies; Scout Leader, VU Coach," *Nashville Banner*, September 14, 1963, pg. 1, 2.

26. Among Boxwell's other associations were the Nashville Manufacturers Association, the Nashville Made Goods Club, the Engineering Association of Nashville, the Nashville Rotary Club, Belle Meade Country Club, Ohio State Alumni Association, and of course, the Nashville Area Council Boy Scouts of America. In 1925, he would start the Louisiana Metal Culvert Company, with which he would remain partnered until his death in 1960. Anderson and Boxwell were also very much contemporaries in age. Boxwell lived from 1881-1960. "L. G. Boxwell Dies at Home," *Nashville Banner*, September 24, 1960, pg. 1; "Sanapan Co. Incorporates," *Nashville Tennessean*, August 24, 1911, pg. 7; "L G.

Botwell Married to Miss Nettie Stacey Wednesday Night," *Nashville Tennessean*, November 5, 1911, pg. B3; "Four-Minute Speakers Assigned for Today," *Nashville Tennessean*, November 2, 1918, pg. 4; "Fit-to-Fight League Organized," *Nashville Tennessean*, November 6, 1917, pg. 4; "Duplex" advertisement, *Nashville Tennessean*, June 30, 1928, pg. 50.

27. "Beloved Coach Anderson Retires as Scout Executive," *Nashville Banner*, July 30, 1947, pg. 10; "W. J. Anderson to Retire Soon," *Nashville Tennessean*, August 1, 1947, pg. 30; "Scout Council Has Grown Rapidly Since 1920," *Nashville Tennessean*, October 9, 1938, pg. 31.

28. A truck would definitely be needed for the trip as Scouts were encouraged to bring quite a bit with them. The 1923 list included "two heavy blankets, two sheets, pillow, two extra shirts, two extra pairs of pants (old clothes), extra suit of underwear, pajamas, handkerchiefs, stockings, swimming suit, two or more towels, raincoat or poncho or overcoat, one yard cloth (for cup towel, table use, etc.), bar of Ivory soap, comb, toothbrush, tooth paste, knife, fork, brush, spoon, plate or pan, and cup." "Boy Scout Camp To Open Tuesday," *Nashville Banner*, June 15, 1923, pg. 12; The list for 1924 was only slightly better: "Scouts should bring old clothing, extra underwear and stockings, night clothes, heavy shoes, bathing suit, raincoat, toothbrush and paste, floating soap, comb and towels, two or more blankets or quilts, a plate, cup, knife and fork and spoon, preferably packed in a wooden box. A notebook and pencil, pins, scout handbook, etc., are serviceable, as are athletic equipment, musical instruments, etc.," "Scouts to Have Dinner Thursday," *Nashville Banner*, June 6, 1924, pg. 1.

29. "Boy Scouts Leave for Linton Camp," *Nashville Banner*, July 5, 1921, pg. 2; "Trucks Leave for Boy Scout Linton Camp," *Nashville Banner*, July 5, 1921, pg. 3.

30. L. G. Boxwell, "With the Boy Scouts," *Nashville Banner*, July 2, 1922, pg. 4 ;"Old TN 100 Bridge," *Bridgehunter.com*, last modified May 28, 2010, https://bridgehunter.com/tn/davidson/bh36462/; "Hey, Skinnay, C'mon Out to the Boy Scout Camp!" *Nashville Banner*, July 9, 1922, pg. 5; "Nashville's Boy Scouts in Camp At Linton," *Nashville Banner*, August 28, 1921, Weekly Gravure Pictorial pages; "Boy Scouts," *Nashville Tennessean*, July 17, 1921, pg. 18; "With The Boy Scouts," Nashville Banner, June 19, 1927, pg. 11; It is worth nothing that by 1928, the dining room and kitchen had electricity, "Prizes Awarded at Camp Boxwell," *Nashville Banner*, June 23, 1928, pg. 5.

31. "Boy Scouts," *Nashville Banner*, July 3, 1921, pg. 9.

32. The date on this paper is a misprint. The date was actually July 5. "Boy Scouts' Camping Season Opens Today," *Nashville Banner*, July 4, 1921, pg. 7; Creighton and Johnson, *Boys Will Be Men*, pgs. 51-52; "Scouts Having Great Time at Camp Boxwell," *Nashville Banner*, July 8, 1921, pg. 6; "Boy Scouts Having Big Time At Camp," *Nashville Banner*, July 11, 1921, pg. 2; "Boy Scout Camp is Highly Praised," *Nashville Tennessean*, July 30, 1921, pg. 2.

33. "Boy Scouts," *Nashville Tennessean*, July 17, 1921, pg. 18; "With the Boy Scouts," *Nashville Banner*, July 17, 1921, pg. 4; "News of the Boy Scouts," *Nashville Tennessean*, July 12, 1921, pg. 5.

34. "Boy Scouts Want Permanent Camp," *Nashville Tennessean*, July 17, 1921, pg. 9.

35. "With the Boy Scouts," *Nashville Banner*, June 25, 1922, pg. 10; Creighton and Johnson quote from this same article, but they credit William Anderson as the author. This may

well be the case, but Anderson is not given a by-line in the *Banner*. Creighton and Johnson, *Boys Will Be Men*, pg. 49.

36. "Boy Scouts Have Big Time at Camp," *Nashville Banner*, July 11, 1922, pg. 15; L. G.
Boxwell, "With the Boy Scouts," *Nashville Banner*, July 2, 1922, pg. 4; the camp would
also be used by the Lions Club in later years, "Lions to Operate Boy Scout Camp," *Nashville Banner*, June 19, 1924, pg. 18.

37. L. G. Boxwell, "With the Boy Scouts," *Nashville Banner*, July 2, 1922, pg. 4; "Who's
Who At Camp Boxwell," *Nashville Banner*, July 30, 1922, pg. 7; "Hey, Skinnay, C'mon
Out to the Boy Scout Camp!" *Nashville Banner*, July 9, 1922, pg. 5; "With the Boy
Scouts" *Nashville Banner*, July 16, 1922, pg. 7; "Another Letter from Scout Camp"
Nashville Banner, July 19, 1922, pg. 6; "Who's Who At Camp Boxwell," *Nashville Ban-
ner*, July 30, 1922, pg. 7.

38. "Camp Scribe Tells of Fun at Boxwell," *Nashville Banner*, July 22, 1922, pg. 3; "Another
Letter from Scout Camp," *Nashville Banner*, July 19, 1922, pg. 6; "With the Boy
Scouts," *Nashville Banner*, July 16, 1922, pg. 7.

39. "Have Good Times At Boy Scout Camp," *Nashville Banner*, July 16, 1922, pg. 12.

40. This particular article was a full page story in the *Tennessean*, laying out all the particulars of the program in great detail. It was not only a fascinating piece for what it contained, it was fascinating because of what it was. Feature pieces of this kind were extremely rare in 1927. Helen Dahnke, "Scouts Rule Own Kingdom on Harpeth," *Nashville
Tennessean*, July 10, 1927, pg. 32.

41. Ibid.

42. Ibid.

43. "Scouts Hold Election at Camp Boxwell," *Nashville Banner*, July 26, 1927, pg. 3; "Boy
Scout camp Scene of Contests," *Nashville Banner*, July 14, 1927, pg. 20; "Camp Boxwell
Boys Explore Cavern," *Nashville Banner*, July 10, 1927, pg. 7; "Boy Scout Camp Elects
Officers," *Nashville Banner*, July 13, 1927, pg. 18; "Honors Awarded Scouts at Boxwell,"
Nashville Banner, July 18, 1927, pg. 3; In the case of the big fish, Coach Anderson's son
Charles caught a five-pound catfish, which almost pulled him overboard. He needed
"two or three" other scouts to pull the beast ashore, "Camp Boxwell Again Has Complete
Quota," *Nashville Banner*, July 26, 1927, pg. 10.

44. Helen Dahnke, "Scouts Rule Own Kingdom on Harpeth," *Nashville Tennessean*, July
10, 1927, pg. 32; "Scout Camp Letter," *Nashville Banner*, July 11, 1924, pg. 20.

45. Helen Dahnke, "Scouts Rule Own Kingdom on Harpeth," *Nashville Tennessean*, July
10, 1927, pg. 32; Cotton West, "Scouts Enjoy Big Camp Fire Feature," *Nashville Banner*,
June 22, 1923, pg. 19; When the position of "inspector" or "inspector general" is used,
he would attend these inspections as well, "Masonic Home Boys Join Camp Boxwell,"
Nashville Banner, July 9, 1925, pg. 9.

46. "Self-Government at Boy Scout Camp," *Nashville Banner*, June 24, 1926, pg. 20; this
sources lists four beech trees, where several others identify five trees, "Boy Scouts Gather
at Camp Boxwell," *Nashville Banner*, June 23, 1925, pg. 9; "Scout Court of Honor Will
Meet Tuesday," *Nashville Banner*, June 13, 1927, pg. 17;"Scouts Rule Own Kingdom on
Harpeth," *Nashville Tennessean*, July 10, 1927, pg. 32.

47. The record is never clear about where the initial rules originated. There were clearly rules
that were told to Scouts the first night, but if the tent representatives are elected the first
night, then who made up the rules? Initially, rules only applied to one week at a time. As

time goes on, clearly rules made early in the summer are enforced throughout the follow-ing weeks, but where that first set comes from is simply not clear. Does the first week create the basic ground rules that other build upon? Are some rules carried over from previous summers? The record simply isn't clear on these particulars. "Camp Boxwell Activities Open," *Nashville Banner,* June 19, 1928, pg. 16; "Scouts Rule Own Kingdom on Harpeth," *Nashville Tennessean,* July 10, 1927, pg. 32; "Scout Camp Letter," *Nashville Banner,* June 20, 1924, pg. 18; "Scouts at Camp Study Bird Lore," *Nashville Banner,* June 20, 1928, pg. 7; "Scout Camp Letter," *Nashville Banner,* June 26, 1924, pg. 17; "Election held at Camp Boxwell," *Nashville Banner,* August 3, 1928, pg. 17; "Scout Saves Man From Drowning," *Nashville Tennessean,* June 29, 1927, pg. 12; "With The Boy Scouts," *Nashville Banner,* June 19, 1927, pg. 11.

48. "Scouts at Camp Study Bird Lore," *Nashville Banner,* June 20, 1928, pg. 7; "Scouts Rule Own Kingdom on Harpeth," *Nashville Tennessean,* July 10, 1927, pg. 32.
49. "Boy Scouts," *Nashville Tennessean,* July 17, 1921, pg. 18; "Scout Camp Letter," *Nashville Banner,* June 26, 1924, pg. 17; "Camp Boxwell Boys on Hike to Cave," *Nashville Banner,* June 26, 1926, pg. 3; "Boy Scout Saves Man From Drowning," *Nashville* Banner, June 28, 1927, pg. 1.
50. "Scout Camp Flag is at Half Mast," *Nashville Banner,* July 15, 1925, pg. 6; "Scouts En-joy Hikes at Camp Boxwell," *Nashville Tennessean,* August 10, 1925, pg. 8; "Camp Boxwell is Closed for Season," *Nashville Banner,* August 3, 1926, pg. 2; "First Boy Scout Camp Week Ends," *Nashville Tennessean,* June 28, 1927, pg. 5; "Boy Scout camp Scene of Contests," *Nashville Banner,* July 14, 1927, pg. 20.
51. "Calls Scout Camp Training School," *Nashville Banner,* June 8, 1924, pg. 10.
52. "Edgar M. Foster," *Nashville Banner,* June 21, 1926, pg. 10.
53. "Boy Scout Camp To Open Tuesday," *Nashville Banner,* June 15, 1923, pg. 12; L. G. Boxwell, "With the Boy Scouts," *Nashville Banner,* July 2, 1922, pg. 4.
54. "Boy Scout Camp To Open Tuesday," *Nashville Banner,* June 15, 1923, pg. 12; "Scouts to Have Dinner Thursday," *Nashville Banner,* June 6, 1924, pg. 1.
55. The Rotary Club sponsored several troops at the Tennessee Industrial School. Scouts from TIS were identified at Camp Boxwell as early as 1925. "Rotary to Have Boy Scout Guests," *Nashville Banner,* June 22, 1925, pg. 14; "Reform school" is a bit of a misno-mer as this institution was used to incarcerate boys and developed quite a reputation for how children were punished, "Tennessee State Training School," *Asylum Projects,* last modified on January 3, 2015, http://www.asylumprojects.org/index.php/ Tennessee_State_Training_School; "Last Camping Period Opens at Boxwell," *Nashville Banner,* August 2, 1927, pg. 3; William J. Anderson, "Letter to the Editor: Scouts," *Nashville Tennessean,* September 10, 1939, pg. 6-D.
56. Cotton West, "Scouts Enjoy Big Camp Fire Feature," *Nashville Banner,* June 22, 1923, pg. 19; "Boy Scouts have Complete Chute," *Nashville Banner,* July 24, 1922, pg. 3; "Boy Scouts Win Merits on Tests," *Nashville Banner,* June 27, 1923, pg. 6; "Scout Camp Letter," *Nashville Banner,* July 4, 1924, pg. 2; The Scout mentioned here, Ed Fitzwater, would go on to be the medic at the Narrows Boxwell, "Merit Badges Are Presented Scouts," *Nashville Banner,* July 1, 1929, pg. 11.
57. "Have Good Times At Boy Scout Camp," *Nashville Banner,* July 16, 1922, pg. 12; "Phis Are Beaten in Final Round of Vandy League," *Nashville Tennessean,* February 19, 1926, pg. 11; Russ Melvin, "Time Out for Midstate Preps," *Nashville Tennessean,* January 26,

1950, pg. 23; Lallie Richter also often served a Athletic director at camp, being team leader in organized sports versus Coach Anderson, "Boy Scouts Gather at Camp Boxwell," *Nashville Banner*, June 23, 1925, pg. 9; "Eighty-Six Boys At Scout Camp," *Nashville Banner*, June 24, 1925, pg. 9; "Rain Interferes with Scout Camp's Plans," *Nashville Banner*, July 17, 1927, pg. (Society Section) 5; "Election held at Camp Boxwell," *Nashville Banner*, August 3, 1928, pg. 17.

58. Edwin Franklin, "Scouts Enjoy Moving Picture," *Nashville Banner*, July 3, 1923, pg. 3; Edwin Franklin, "New Scouts go to Camp Boxwell," *Nashville Banner*, July 5, 1923, pg. 17; "Nashville Boy Scouts have Time of Their Lives," *Nashville Banner*, July 17, 1927, pg. (Gravure)1.

59. "'Buddy System' Employed by Camp Boxwell Scouts," *Nashville Tennessean*, July 10, 1928, pg. 4; "Elections Held at Camp Boxwell," *Nashville Banner*, July 10, 1928, pg. 7.

60. "Boy Scouts have Complete Chute," *Nashville Banner*, July 24, 1922, pg. 3; Cotton West, "Scouts Enjoy Big Camp Fire Feature," *Nashville Banner*, June 22, 1923, pg. 19.

61. "Boy Scouts Have Big Time at Camp," *Nashville Banner*, July 11, 1922, pg. 15; Wilbur Creighton, Jr, "Another Letter from Scout Camp," *Nashville Banner*, July 19, 1922, pg. 6.

62. "Scout Camp at Linton One of Best Ever Held," *Nashville Banner*, August 11, 1925, pg. 5; "Prizes Awarded at Camp Boxwell," *Nashville Banner*, June 23, 1928, pg. 5; "Boy Scouts have Complete Chute," *Nashville Banner*, July 24, 1922, pg. 3; Ben Coffey, "Boy Scouts Break Camp Tuesday," *Nashville Banner*, July 16, 1923, pg. 11; "Boy Scouts of America," *Nashville Tennessean*, July 16, 1922, pg. 24; Edwin Franklin, "Scouts at Camp Go Snipe-Hunting," *Nashville Banner*, June 28, 1923, pg. 13.

63. For more on the trial, see Edward John Larson, *Summer for the Gods: the Scopes Trial and America's Continuing Debate Over Science and Religion,* New York: Basic Books, 1997.

64. Boxwell had actually been on the front page of the *Banner* on several occasions, though for considerably more mundane reasons. "Boy Scout Killed, Another Injured in Camp Boxwell," *Nashville Tennessean*, July 14, 1925, pg. 1; "Eighty Boy Scouts Enjoying Camp Life," *Nashville Banner*, July 18, 1925, pg. 3.

65. "Boy Scout Killed, Another Injured in Camp Boxwell," *Nashville Tennessean*, July 14, 1925, pg. 1; "Second Boy Scout Dies of Injuries," *Nashville Banner*, July 15, 1925, pg. 1.

66. There is some question over the ages. *The Tennessean* initially reported that Thomas was 17 and Lackey was 18. *The Banner* reported this initially as well, but as it continued to follow the story, amended the ages to 15. "Boy Scout Killed in Storm at Camp," *Nashville Banner*, July 14, 1925, pg. 5; "Boy Scout Killed, Another Injured in Camp Boxwell," *Nashville Tennessean*, July 14, 1925, pg. 1; "Gallatin Shocked," *Nashville Banner*, July 14, 1925, pg. 5; "Second Boy Scout Dies of Injuries," *Nashville Banner*, July 15, 1925, pg. 1.

67. "Scout Camp Flag is at Half Mast," *Nashville Banner*, July 15, 1925, pg. 6.

68. The segregated division was named for Nashville lawyer and banker, James Carroll Napier, a well-known African American leader. The J. C. Napier Division would exist for approximately twenty years. Creighton and Johnson, *Boys Will Be Men*, pg. 85; James Loewen, *Lies My Teacher Told Me: Everything Your American History Textbook Got Wrong*, Touchstone Edition, Touchstone, division of Simon & Schuster: New York,

2007, pg. 161; Foner, *The Story of American Freedom*, pg. 188; Southern Poverty Law Center, *Whose Heritage? A Report on Public Symbols of the Confederacy*, 2016.

69. Wills, *Boy Scouts of America: A Centennial History*, pg. 79; Jordan, *Modern Manhood and the Boy Scouts of America*, pg. 201.

70. Whittaker had a twin brother, Willie, who sometimes filled in for him on Sundays, "Walter, Whose Rolls Scouts Like, Is Booked Again as Boxwell Cook," *Nashville Tennessean*, June 6, 1937, pg. *Tennessean Magazine* 16; "Boy Scout," *Nashville Tennessean*, June 13, 1921, pg. 5; Cotton West, "Scouts Enjoy Big Camp Fire Feature," *Nashville Banner*, June 22, 1923, pg. 19; "Scout Camp Letter," *Nashville Banner*, June 19, 1924, pg. 18; "Scouts Rule Own Kingdom on Harpeth," *Nashville Tennessean*, July 10, 1927, pg. 32; the berries for the pies were picked by Scouts and sometimes bought by Whittaker, "Election held at Camp Boxwell," *Nashville Banner*, August 3, 1928, pg. 17; "Eighty Scouts at Camp Boxwell," *Nashville Banner*, July 16, 1929, pg. 4; "Boy Scouts Learn to Be On Their Own at Camp Boxwell," *Nashville Tennessean*, July 7, 1929, pg. Rotogravure section 1. The obituary here may or may not Whittaker. The age would be about correct, but there is virtually no evidence from the existing record to confirm that Whittaker was married, had children, or even lived in Monterey, Tennessee, "Whittaker (obituary)," *Nashville Tennessean*, April 27, 1963, pg. 18.

71. "Team Competition Close at Boxwell," *Nashville Banner*, July 9, 1927, pg. 3; "Tigers Winners at Boy Scout Camp," *Nashville Banner*, July 18, 1929, pg. 12; "Elect Councilmen at Camp Boxwell," *Nashville Banner*, July 11, 1928, pg. 13.

72. "Court of Honor Meets at Boxwell," *Nashville Banner*, June 30, 1928, pg. 3; Helen Dahnke, "Scouts Rule Own Kingdom on Harpeth," *Nashville Tennessean*, July 10, 1927, pg. 32; "Boy Scouts," *Nashville Tennessean*, July 17, 1921, pg. 18.

73. Edwin Bowden, "Prizes Awarded at Camp Boxwell," *Nashville Banner*, June 23, 1928, pg. 5; A second incident occurred in 1922 when "Mr. Charles Barham, president of the Rotary Club" spoke to the Scouts at a campfire. As we have seen, local men often came to camp to regale the boys with stories and help them build contacts. Barham regaled the Scouts with "amazing fish stories." The Scouts "enjoyed his experiences on this fishing trip and were sorry when he stopped." So pleased were the Scouts with the stories that Barham won the camp mascot. What the mascot was exactly was not clear. What was clear was the camp mascot's name: "Nigger." Whittaker, who "is a singer as well as a cook," followed this moment with song until the end of the campfire. "Boy Scouts have Complete Chute," *Nashville Banner*, July 24, 1922, pg. 3.

74. "Boy Scout Camp to Open Monday," *Nashville Tennessean*, June 12, 1929, pg. 13; "Boy Scouts Break Camp at Boxwell," *Nashville Banner*, July 30, 1929, pg. 6.

75. "Boy Scouts Break Camp at Boxwell," *Nashville Banner*, July 30, 1929, pg. 6.

Chapter 2 Endnotes

Anderson's Boxwell: Camp Boxwell at the

Narrows of the Harpeth

1930-1948

1. "Site for Boy Scout Camp to be Moved," *Nashville Tennessean,* June 5, 1930, pg. 9; "Site of Scout Camp Changed," *Nashville Banner,* June 4, 1930, pg. 14.
2. "Boy Scouts Break Camp at Boxwell," *Nashville Banner,* July 30, 1929, pg. 6.
3. "A History of Tennessee," *Tennessee Blue Book, 2015-2016,* Tennessee Department of State: Nashville, 2015, pg. 541; Paul H. Bergeron, Stephen V. Ash, and Jeanette Keith, *Tennesseans and Their History,* The University of Tennessee Press: Knoxville, 1999, pg. 237-238; Peay's administration also saw conservation expansion with the creation of the Reelfoot Lake State Park in 1925 and purchasing the land that would become the Great Smoky Mountains National Park in 1927. The Great Smoky Mountains National Park would join the National Park system in 1930, after Peay's death. Both would be beneficial to Scouting in years to come. Robert E. Corlew, *Tennessee: A Short History,* Second Edition, The University of Tennessee Press: Knoxville, 1981, pgs. 457-458.
4. Bergeron, *et al., Tennesseans and Their History,* pgs. 240-253.
5. Clara Hieronymus, "Edwin Craig Had an Idea Back in '25...," *Nashville Tennessean,* Souvenir Edition, October 15, 1967, Opry Birthday Section, pg. 7; Lauren Batte, "WSM," *Tennessee Encyclopedia,* last modified March 1, 2018, https:// tennesseeencyclopedia.net/entries/wsm/.
6. "Boy Scouts Stay Clear of Juvenile Court," *Nashville Tennessean,* Main Edition, October 6, 1925, pg. 3; "W. J. Anderson To Retire Soon," *Nashville Tennessean,* August 1, 1947, pg. 30.
7. The five counties served included Rutherford, Warren, Franklin, Coffee, and Bedford. "Mid State Council for Scout Work Organized," *Nashville Tennessean,* June 19, 1927, pg. 7.
8. Robert V. Remini, *A Short History of the United States: From the Arrival of Native American Tribes to the Obama Presidency,* paperback edition, Harper Perennial: New York and London, 2009, pg. 215; Lawrence Levin, *The Unpredictable Past: Explorations in American Cultural History,* Oxford University Press: New York & Oxford, 1993, pg. 207; Eric Foner, *The Story of American Freedom,* paperback edition, W. W. Norton & Company: New York & London, 1998, pg. 197.
9. "A History of Tennessee," *Tennessee Blue Book, 2015-2016,* Tennessee Department of State: Nashville, 2015, pg. 541-542.
10. "A History of Tennessee," *Tennessee Blue Book, 2015-2016,* pg. 542; Robert E. Corlew, *Tennessee: A Short History,* Second Edition, The University of Tennessee Press: Knoxville, 1981, pgs. 461-467.

11. Wills, *Boy Scouts of America: A Centennial History*, pg. 107; "Twenty-Second Annual Report of the Boy Scouts of America," *Boy Scouts of America*, Government Printing Office: Washington, D. C., 1931, pg. 6, Hathitrust Digital Library, last modified January 24, 2017, https://hdl.handle.net/2027/mdp.39015067041882.

12. "Boy Scouts of America," *Nashville* Tennessean, March 27, 1932, pg. 13 Magazine section; William J. Anderson, "McGugins, Boxwells Make Community a Better Place," *Nashville Tennessean*, January 11, 1948, pg. 23; "Sell Material to Build Dam," *Nashville Tennessean*, December 9, 1935, pg. 6; Creighton and Johnson, *Boys Will Be Men*, pg. 63; No birthdate was given in Murrey's obituary, "Edward Ennis Murrey," *Nashville Tennessean*, May 18, 1967, pg. 61; Edwin Hughes, "Nashville Scouts' Own Page," *Nashville Tennessean*, July 23, 1933, pg. 13 Magazine Section; "T.I.S. Girl Reserves at Camp Boxwell," *Nashville Tennessean* July 21, 1932, pg. 7.

13. "Highway 100 South Harpeth River Bridge," *Bridgehunter.com*, last modified March 1, 2014, https://bridgehunter.com/tn/davidson/19SRI000001/.

14. "9 Towns Would Merge With Nashville Scouts," *Nashville Tennessean*, May 29, 1930, pg. 5. It should be noted that not all of the towns in these Councils joined Nashville at this point. Clarksville would form the Cogioba Council in 1934 and would join the (second) Middle Tennessee Council in 1950: "Scout Council is Considered," *The Leaf-Chronicle* (Clarksville, TN), February 5, 1934, pg. 1; "Executive Group of Scout Council O.K.'s Petition," *The Leaf-Chronicle* (Clarksville, TN), April 20, 1950, pg. 1. Murfreesboro would also form its own council in 1938 and would also join the second Middle Tennessee Council later: Creighton and Johnson, *Boys Will Be Men*, pg. 70; "Scout Council To Be Extended," *Nashville Banner*, November 5, 1930, pgs. 1, 7.

15. "More Scouts Go To Camp Lupton," *The Leaf-Chronicle* (Clarksville, TN), August 16, 1928, pg. 1; "75 Mid-State Scouts at Camp Fisher," *Nashville Tennessean*, June 24, 1931, pg. 7; "Boy Scout Camps," *Nashville Tennessean*, Sunday, April 10, 1932, pg. 17.

16. Potter was also an opponent of the TVA, opposed the election campaign of Sen. Albert Gore in 1958, but supported the election bids of Senator Joseph McCarthy in 1952 and President Dwight Eisenhower in 1956. While he did some charitable giving during his life, much more seems to have been done by his wife Valerie Blair, and his daughter Pat Wilson through the Potter Trust. When Potter died in 1961 (b. 1898), Anderson, who was himself older than Potter, was a pallbearer, "Justin Potter, Financier, Dies," *Nashville Tennessean*, December 10, 1961, pg. 1A, 16A ; Albert Cason, "Potter Thrived on Controversy," *Nashville Tennessean*, December 10, 1961, pg. 16A; Potter arranged the deal to rent the property in conjunction with John W. Blair and W. L. Lucas. The specific connections to the property here are unclear, though if he didn't in 1930, Potter owned the property by 1944, "Site for Boy Scout Camp to be Moved," *Nashville Tennessean*, June 5, 1930, pg. 9; "100 Acres Deeded to Scout Council," *Nashville Tennessean*, March 19, 1944, pg. C6.

17. "New Camp Boxwell," *The Bugle* [Nashville Council Newsletter], Vol. 1, No. 6, December 1940, pg. 3; "Montgomery Bell's Tunnel," *ASCE American Society of Civil Engineers*, last modified unknown, retrieved September 14, 2019, https://www.asce.org/project/montgomery-bell-s-tunnel/ ; Cheatham County Fact Book, 1994; "The Nashville Scouts' Own Page," *Nashville Tennessean*, July 26, 1936, pg. Magazine 13. Former staff member O. E. Brandon estimated that the core of the camp itself—the dining hall,

the assembly area, and tents—only utilized about five and a half acres. O. E. Brandon to Grady Eades, July 8, 2004.

18. "The Nashville Scouts' Own Page," *Nashville Tennessean*, August 4, 1935, pg. Magazine 15; "Camp Boxwell," *Nashville Tennessean*, June 25, 1930, pg. 16.

19. Creighton and Johnson, *Boys Will Be Men*, pgs. 77-78; O. E. Brandon to Grady Eades, July 8, 2004. Olpha E. Brandon, excerpts from unpublished memoirs, unknown date, pg. 18. In 1940, James Kilgore produced an 8mm film of the Narrows Boxwell. The dining hall can be seen here and the visuals concur with Brandon's description. James Kilgore, *A Day At Camp Boxwell*, 8mm, 1940; The newer dining hall would be larger than the first building, but similar design with screened windows and attached kitchen, James Wharton, "Nashville Boy Scouts Open Camping Season Monday at Boxwell to Lead Several Youth Agencies in Summer Outdoor Recreational Programs," *Nashville Tennessean*, June 8, 1941, pg. 13; "The Nashville Scouts' Own Page," *Tennessean Magazine*, June 30, 1935, pg. 13. While no official obituary for Brandon (b. 1922) could be located, this site confirmed his death in 2005, "Olpha E Brandon," *Sysoon.com*, date last modified unknown, https://www.sysoon.com/deceased/olpha-e-brandon-37.

20. "Tent No. 10 Wins Inspection Test," *Nashville Tennessean*, June 27, 1931, pg. 2; "Tent No. 8 Wins Inspection Seven Consecutive Days at Boxwell," *Nashville Tennessean*, November 1, 1931, pg. Magazine 14; the morning exercise routine and the style of tent are also showcased briefly in Kilgore's *A Day at Camp Boxwell*, 1940; James Wharton, "Nashville Boy Scouts Open Camping Season Monday at Boxwell to Lead Several Youth Agencies in Summer Outdoor Recreational Programs," *Nashville Tennessean*, June 8, 1941, pg. 13; "Boy Scouts," *Nashville Tennessean*, July 11, 1939, pg. 11; Thompson remembers the tents in pairs going up the hill from the assembly area, Ellis D. Thompson (retired music instructor), interviewer Grady Eades, March 8, 2017, Bellevue, TN.

21. Tom Neal (retired), interviewer Grady Eades, December 7, 2016, Gallatin, TN.

22. "Camp Boxwell Scouts 'Having Lots of Fun'," *Nashville Tennessean*, July 4, 1943, pg. 14; "Long Hikes Are Taken by Scouts," *Nashville Tennessean*, July 12, 1931, pg. 2; "Mound Bottom State Archaeological Area," *Tennessee Department of Environment and Conservation*, found on July 30, 2019, no page update date, https://www.tn.gov/ environment/program-areas/arch-archaeology/state-archaeological-parks---areas/mound -bottom-state-archaeological-area.html; The cemetery in question is the Scott Cemetery, right along New Cedar Hill Road; "The Nashville Scouts' Own Page," *Nashville Tennessean*, July 26, 1936, pg. Magazine 13; Thompson was born in 1925 and was still alive at this writing, Ellis D. Thompson interview; Thompson has also written on his Narrows experience himself in a series of recollections titled, *Nashville Nostalgia*, E. D. Thompson, *Nashville Nostalgia*, Nashville: Westview Publishing, Inc., 2003.

23. "Camp Boxwell Opens Monday," *Nashville Tennessean*, June 21, 1931, pg. 3;"The Nashville Scouts' Own Page, *Nashville Tennessean*, July 7, 1935, pg. *Tennessean Magazine* 13; Billy Walker (owner, Walker Chevrolet), interviewer Kerry Parker, November 19, 2003, Franklin, TN; Edwin Bowden, "Camp Boxwell," *Nashville Tennessean*, June 25, 1930, pg. 16; Sadly, Billy passed before the publication of this work, 1928-2018, "William "Billy" Helm Walker," *Tennessean*, July 14, 2018, pg. A12.

24. William Anderson, "Self-Guidance An Essential in Scout Training," *Nashville Tennessean*, February 23, 1941, pg. 11C; William Anderson, "Scout Code is Appeal to High Ideals," *Nashville Tennessean*, October 31, 1943, pg. 4C. I made this point in "Building

Citizens, Having Fun: The Boy Scouts and Camp Boxwell at the Narrows of the Harpeth, 1930-1948," *Tennessee Historical Quarterly*, Vol. LXXVII: No. 4 (Winter 2018), pg. 283.

25. "Nashville Scouts' Own Page," *Nashville Tennessean*, July 8, 1934, pg. *Tennessean Magazine* 13; "$4.50 Will Give Boy Scout A Happy Week At Camp," *Nashville Tennessean*, June, 11, 1933, pg. *Tennessean Magazine 13*; The awards are mentioned in several places, but this one is provided to show the longevity of the trio of awards, "New Plan for Camp Boxwell," *Nashville Tennessean*, April 30, 1939, pg. 6D.

26. William Anderson, "Self-Guidance An Essential in Scout Training," *Nashville Tennessean*, February 23, 1941, pg. 11C.

27. "Nashville Scouts' Own Page," *Nashville Tennessean*, July 1, 1934, pg. *Tennessean Magazine* 13; "Nashville Scouts' Own Page," *Nashville Tennessean*, July 1, 1934, pg. *Tennessean Magazine* 13; "Camp Boxwell," *Nashville Tennessean*, August 13, 1930, pg. 2; "The Nashville Scouts' Own Page," *Nashville Tennessean*, August 18, 1935, pg *Tennessean Magazine* 13; "Nashville Scouts' Own Page," *Nashville Tennessean*, July 26, 1936, pg. *Tennessean Magazine* 13.

28. William Anderson, "Divinity's Immutable Laws Guide Destiny of Mankind," *Nashville Tennessean*, March 28, 1948, pg. 16A; William Anderson, "Scout Code Is Appeal to High Ideals," *Nashville Tennessean*, October 31, 1943, pg. 4C; William Anderson, "Boy Scout Daily Good Turn Important in Indoctrination," *Nashville Tennessean*, February 23, 1947, pg. 6A; William Anderson, "Boy Scouts Traveling Way of Christ, Executive Says," *Nashville Tennessean*, November 30, 1947, pg. 22A; William Anderson, "Boxwell's Sunday Service," *Nashville Tennessean*, July 28, 1940, pg. 21.

29. William Anderson, "Camp Boxwell Includes Fun, High Ideals," *Nashville Tennessean*, June 22, 1941, pg. 8B.

30. "Scouts Take Hike at Camp Boxwell," *Nashville Tennessean*, July 7, 1931, pg. 14; "Long Hikes Are Taken by Scouts," *Nashville Tennessean* July 12, 1931, pg. 2; "Scouts Elect Camp Officers," *Nashville Tennessean*, July 25, 1931, pg. 2.

31. "Nashville Scouts' Own Page," *Nashville Tennessean*, June 17, 1934, pg. *Tennessean Magazine* 13; "Nashville Scouts' Own Page," *Nashville Tennessean*, August 1, 1937, pg. *Tennessean Magazine* 15; "Nashville Scouts' Own Page," *Nashville Tennessean*, July 25, 1937, pg. *Tennessean Magazine* 16; "Boy Scouts," *Nashville Tennessean*, July 11, 1939, pg. 11; "Camp Boxwell," *Nashville Tennessean*, August 13, 1930, pg. 2; "Busy Week at Boxwell," *Nashville Tennessean*, August 2, 1931, pg. 3; "Camp Boxwell," *Nashville Tennessean*, June 25, 1930, pg. 16.

32. "The Nashville Scouts' Own Page," *Nashville Tennessean*, July 19, 1936, pg. *Tennessean Magazine* 13; "Canoe Regatta at Scout Camp," *Nashville Tennessean*, August 11, 1931, pg. 11; "Canoeing," *The Bugle* [Nashville Council Newsletter], Vol. I, No. 4: May 1939, pg 4; James Kilgore, *A Day At Camp Boxwell*, 8mm, 1940; "Camp Boxwell Notes," *Nashville Tennessean*, June 28, 1934, pg. 7.

33. "The Nashville Scouts' Own Page," *Nashville Tennessean*, June 30, 1935, pg. *Tennessean Magazine* 13; "'Buddy System' Employed by Camp Boxwell Scouts," *Nashville Tennessean*, July 10, 1928, pg. 4; Billy Walker interview; "Precautions at Scout Camp," The Nashville Tennessean, June 18, 1939, pg. 6D.

34. Frank Sutton, "Troop 34," *Nashville Tennessean*, July 25, 1937, pg. *Tennessean Magazine* 16; Ellis D. Thompson interview; Tom Neal interview.

35. Adamz has his name alternately spelled "Adams" and was referred to as "Father," "Reverend," and "Rector." At least in 1935, he was a member of the Episcopal church, "The Nashville Scouts' Own Page," *Nashville Tennessean*, May 26, 1935, pg. *Tennessean Magazine* 13; Adamz also taught at Camp Fisher in 1932, "80 Boy Scouts Attend Camp Manchester, *Nashville Tennessean*, June 26, 1932, pg. 5; "Bare-handed Catch of Rattlesnakes Will Feature Camp Program," *Nashville Tennessean*, June 9, 1938, pg. 12; "Scouts Take Course in Reptile Study," *Nashville Tennessean* July 19, 1931, pg. 11; Ellis D. Thompson interview. Alfonso Constantine Adamz died at 57 years of age (ca. 1895-1952). "Death was attributed to a heart condition." "Mountain Priest Dies in Hospital," *Nashville Tennessean*, December 29, 1952, pg. 13.

36. "Camp Boxwell Closes," *The Bugle* [Nashville Council newsletter], Vol.I, No. I: October 1938, pg. I.

37. Elmer Hinton, "Down to Earth with Elmer Hinton: Simple Goodness," *Nashville Tennessean*, July 8, 1956, pg. *The Nashville Tennessean Magazine* 4; Creighton and Johnson claim that Elam was generally responsible for nature study, but I could not find any specific mention of Elam teaching that merit badge. However, these were all contemporaries, so this may be first hand knowledge, *Boys Will Be Men*, pg. 77; Elam did, however, serve as an assistant camp director in at least one summer, 1937, "80 Scouts Start Week At Camp," *Nashville Tennessean*, June 19, 1937, pg. 2; "Camp Boxwell Again Elects Honor Scouts," *Nashville Tennessean*, July 3, 1945, pg. 12. Elam (1902-1975) will continue to be active in Middle Tennessee Scouting for some time, "William H. Elam, Springfield, Dies," *Nashville Tennessean,* November 25, 1975, pg. 29.

38. "The Nashville Scouts' Own Page," *Nashville Tennessean*, August 11, 1935, *Tennessean Magazine* 13; Ellis D. Thompson interview; Among the "athletic directors" were Doak Campbell and Carlisle Phelps, while medics included Eugene Ellison and Hartwell Weaver. "Boy Scouts of America," *Nashville Tennessean*, June 19, 1932, Magazine Section pg. 8; O. E. Brandon points out that while Weaver was mentioned as a doctor in *Boys Will Be Men*, he was "actually a medical student at Vanderbilt." Olpha E. Brandon, excerpts from unpublished memoirs, unknown date, pg. 18; "Nashville Scouts' Own Page," *Nashville Tennessean*, June 14, 1936, pg. *Tennessean Magazine* 13; "Nashville Scouts' Own Page," *Nashville Tennessean*, June 17, 1934, Magazine section pg. 13.

39. No obituary could be found for Miller. "Nashville Scouts' Own Page," *Nashville Tennessean*, June 17, 1934, Magazine section pg. 13; Miller was principal for Fehr School, an elementary school on the north side of Nashville, "Precautions at Scout Camp," *Nashville Tennessean*, June 18, 1939, pg. 6D; "Miss Martha Elizabeth Smith Weds Lallie Richter at Home Ceremony," *Nashville Tennessean*, January 9, 1930, pg. 7; "Nashville Scouts' Own Page," *Nashville Tennessean*, August 4, 1935, pg. *Tennessean Magazine* 15; "Group of Boy Scouts Leaves for Camp today," *Nashville Tennessean*, July 7, 1947, pg. 3; "Talmadge M. Miller Named to Scout Post," *Nashville Tennessean*, September 2, 1943, pg. 21.

40. "Nashville Scouts' Own Page," *Nashville Tennessean*, July 11, 1937, pg. *Tennessean Magazine* 16; "Nashville Scouts' Own Page," *Nashville Tennessean*, July 16, 1933, pg. *Tennessean Magazine* 13; "Boy Scouts Win Swimming Honors," *Nashville Tennessean*, August 17, 1938, pg. 14; James Hughes, "80 Scouts Finish Camp Trek Livened by Snakes, Skunks," *Nashville Tennessean*, July 2, 1946, pg. 10.

41. The last formal speaker appears to be a happy accident when Regional Scout Executive Harold W. Lewman visited the camp for inspection in August 1931, "Canoe Regatta at Scout Camp," *Nashville Tennessean*, August 11, 1931, pg. 11; "The Nashville Scouts' Own Page," *Nashville Tennessean*, August 11, 1935, pg. *Tennessean Magazine* 13.

42. "With the Boy Scouts," *Nashville Banner*, July 16, 1922, pg. 7; "Elections Held at Camp Boxwell," *Nashville Banner*, July 10, 1928, pg. 7; "Scouts Observe Fourth," *Nashville Tennessean*, July 7, 1932, pg. 2; "New Plan for Camp Boxwell," *Nashville Tennessean*, April 30, 1930, pg. 6D.

43. "Scouts Take a Hike at Camp Boxwell," *Nashville Tennessean*, July 7, 1931, pg. 14; "Newcomers at Scout Camp Must Be Shown," *Nashville Tennessean*, July 16, 1931, pg. 6; "All Play and No Medicine Would Make Scouts Dull Boys," *Nashville Tennessean*, June 30, 1938, pg. 3.

44. "Officers Are Elected at Camp Boxwell," *Nashville Tennessean*, August 13, 1931, pg. 11; Ed Fitzwater, "Camp Boxwell Has 90 Boys For First Week of 13th Year," *Nashville Tennessean*, June 25, 1933, pg. *Tennessean Magazine* 13; "All Play and No Medicine Would Make Scouts Dull Boys," *Nashville Tennessean*, June 30, 1938, pg. 3.

45. It should also be noted that the State Training and Agricultural School as well as Tennessee Industrial School continued to have weeks at camp after the low years; "Camp Boxwell Reservation List Crowded," *Nashville Tennessean*, June 29, 1938, pg. 16; This article points out than 42 new Scouts arrived on Monday. Knowing that the camp ran about 80 scouts a week, that means approximately 38 scouts—almost half—stayed over from the week before, "Newcomers at Scout Camp Must Be Shown," *Nashville Tennessean*, July 16, 1931, pg. 6; "New Plan for Camp Boxwell," *Nashville Tennessean*, April 30, 1939, pg. 6D; "Camp Boxwell Scout Quota Increased," *Nashville Tennessean*, May 24, 1945, pg. 18.

46. "New Plan for Camp Boxwell," *Nashville Tennessean*, April 30, 1939, pg. 6D; "Camp Answers Call of Wild," *Nashville Tennessean*, June 11, 1939, pg. 8D; "Camp Boxwell Scout Quota Increased," *Nashville Tennessean*, May 24, 1945, pg. 18.

47. "Boy Scouts of America," *Nashville Tennessean*, June 19, 1932, pg. 8 Magazine Section; "Personnel of Camp Boxwell is Completed," *Nashville Tennessean*, June 19, 1933, pg. 3; Ed Fitzwater, "Camp Boxwell Has 90 Boys for First Week of 13th Year," *Nashville Tennessean*, June 25, 1933, pg. *Tennessean Magazine* 13; "Nashville Scouts' Own Page," *Nashville Tennessean*, June 17, 1934, pg. *Tennessean Magazine* 13; "Nashville Scouts' Own Page, *Nashville Tennessean*, July 21, 1935, pg. *Tennessean Magazine* 13. There is some evidence Junior Leaders were experimented with in 1931, but the first official announcement of the program along with names listed as to who would participate was in 1932.

48. Remember that Weaver was a Vanderbilt medical student, likely making him less than ten years older than the others involved in this story, Olpha E. Brandon, excerpts from unpublished memoirs, unknown date, pg. 18-20.

49. "Camp Boxwell," *Nashville Tennessean*, June 25, 1930, pg. 16; "Camp Boxwell Officers are Elected," *Nashville Tennessean*, July 18, 1931, pg. 13; "Boy Scouts of America," *Nashville Tennessean*, June 19, 1932, pg. 8 Magazine Section; Here is another example of the gray zone that existed the first year or two of this program, "Boy Scout Elect at Camp Boxwell Monday," *Nashville Tennessean*, July 5, 1932, pg. 4; "'Best Scout' Hon-

ored," *Nashville Tennessean,* July 12, 1932, pg. 5; "First Aid," *Nashville Tennessean,* July 16, 1932, pg. 12.

50. "Keeping Dry in Rain, Scouts Show Selves Good Campers," *Nashville Tennessean,* July 2, 1933, pg. 13 Magazine Section; "Nashville Scouts' Own Page," *Nashville Tennessean,* June 17, 1934, pg. *Tennessean Magazine* 13; "Nashville Scouts' Own Page, *Nashville Tennessean,* July 21, 1935, pg. *Tennessean Magazine* 13; "Walter, Whose Rolls Scouts Like, Is Booked Again as Boxwell Cook," *Nashville Tennessean,* June 6, 1937, pg. *Tennessean Magazine* 16; "Nashville Scouts' Own Page," *Nashville Tennessean,* July 18, 1937, pg. *Tennessean Magazine 16;* "Camp Boxwell," *Nashville Banner,* June 14, 1936, pg. *Banner Magazine* 15.

51. There is some confusion over Gribble's start date. The December 10 1937 article says he was elected to the position by the Executive Board, having just completed some national training. His official start date is listed as January 1, 1938. The 1946 article suggests he started in November 1937. Likely both are true. Gribble probably was hired by Anderson in November 1937 and completed the required training at that time, but was not approved by the Executive Board until December 1937. Therefore, his official start date would be January 1, 1938, even though he had already been doing the job prior to this point. "Gribble Made Scout Aide," *Nashville Tennessean,* December 10, 1937, pg. 34; "Gribble Returns to Scout Post," *Nashville Tennessean,* February 27, 1946, pg. 16. There is also confusion about when Gribble left his official duties. He was still Assistant Executive when Anderson retired in August 1947, but by January 1948, he was listed as a "deputy Scout commissioner," a volunteer position. Sometime between September 1, 1947 and January 1, 1948, Gribble left professional Scouting. There is no explanation as to why. "L.B. Stevens Heads Boy Scout Council," *Nashville Tennessean,* January 9, 1948, pg. 15.

52. James Gribble (ca. 1918?-ca. 1962?) remains a bit of a mystery. While everything written above is true, if one continues to follow the name some disturbing information comes to light. Specifically, a James Gribble is arrested in April 1953 for lewdness. Gribble and another man were caught in a police sting operation involving a fifteen year old boy. In short, Gribble and this other man brought a 15 year old boy in their car out to Percy Warner Park at night when they were arrested. Both eventually pled guilty and then disappear from the record. If this is the same Gribble, and it is not absolutely conclusive it is, then this incident raises serious questions about Anderson's judgement concerning Gribble's activities while he worked he worked for the Scouts. It is worth noting that despite the fact that the two men were clearly very close, when Anderson dies in 1963, Talmadge Miller is a pallbearer, but Gribble is not. The reasonable explanation is the 1962 death notice of a James Gribble, 46, of New York City, "a former Nashville resident." This Gribble had lived in NYC for "the past 9 years." 9 years prior would be 1953, the time of the arrest. Both the 1962 article and the 1953 article say Gribble was from Woodbury, TN. This IS the same man, but is it the Camp Boxwell Gribble? Did Gribble flee Nashville after the arrest and try to start over? "Two Charged with Lewdness," *Nashville Banner,* April 15, 1953, pg. 15; "Two In Lewdness Case Fined $50; Await Grand Jury," *Nashville Banner,* April 16, 1953, pg. 6; "Two Men Fined in Court Here on Lewdness Cases," *Nashville Banner,* April 18, 1953, pg. 12; "Anderson" (Obituary), *Nashville Tennessean,* September 16, 1963, pg. 19; "James Gribble," *Nashville Tennessean,* July 19, 1962, pg. 48.

53. Willis, *Boy Scouts: A Centennial*, pg. 92; Ian Romaine (ed.), *Wa-Hi-Nasa III: A Brotherhood of Cheerful Service in Middle Tennessee*, self-published, 2015, pg. 8.

54. Romaine, *Wa-Hi-Nasa*, pg. 8; Brandon writes that twelve scouts were inducted at these initial ceremonies as Arrowmen and were then immediately inducted again up to the level of Brotherhood. Brandon, excerpts from unpublished memoirs, pg. 16; Brandon's recollection is challenged somewhat by *The Bugle*, the Nashville Council newsletter of which he was an Associate Editor. The March 1940 issue clearly listed Brandon—one of the original inductees—as having recently received the Brotherhood honor. Leslie G. Boxwell and Jet Potter were also nominated for induction at this time; "Arrow News," *The Bugle* [Nashville Council newsletter], Vol. I, Iss. 5: March 1940, pg. 2; "Scouts Pick Leaders at Camp Boxwell," *Nashville Tennessean*, June 28, 1945, pg. 5.

55. "Scouts Pick Leaders at Camp Boxwell," *Nashville Tennessean*, June 28, 1945, pg. 5; Romaine, *Wa-Hi-Nasa*, pg. 8.

56. The Mansion was destroyed by fire in 1929, before the Scouts moved in, Cheatham County Fact Book, 1994. "Indian Pow Wow Great Event at Camp Boxwell Each Week," *Nashville Tennessean*, July 9, 1939, pg. 8D; "Campire," *The Bugle* [Nashville Council newsletter], Vol. I, No. 4: May 1939, pg. 5.

57. "Camp Movies are Now Ready," *The Bugle* [Nashville Council newsletter], Vol. I, No. 5: March 1940, pg. 1.

58. "Gains in 1939," *The Bugle* [Nashville Council newsletter], Vol. I, No. 5: March 1940, pg. 1.

59. James Wharton, "Nashville Boy Scouts Open Camping Season Monday at Boxwell to Lead Several Agencies in Summer Outdoor Recreational Programs," *Nashville Tennessean*, June 8, 1941, pg. 13; "New Camp Boxwell," *The Bugle* [Nashville Council newsletter], Vol. I, No. 6: December 1940, pg. 3. The current ranger's station sits on the same ridge as this new dining hall. Specifically, the garage sits on the foundation of this building.

60. The Delco lighting system is an interesting side story, though mostly in terms of speculation. Delco Lighting was a private company offering small plants to homes. There were twenty-five models, but the most popular was a hybrid plant that utilized a battery and a diesel generator. The generator would kick in when the battery was fully discharged and stop when it was charged. Such a system cost approximately $500. The speculation here is over why this was used. The Rural Electrification Act (REA) of 1935 sought to bring electric power to rural areas, especially those that did not benefit from the Tennessee Valley Authority. However, Justin Potter was a fierce and vocal opponent of the New Deal. So, did Boxwell adopt the Delco system because Potter favored a private enterprise solution or had the REA simply not made it the area yet? Was it a combination of both? The record does not clarify. "Rural Electrification Administration," *Windcharger.org*, found March 12, 2018, no page update, http://www.windcharger.org/Wind_Charger/Rural_Electrification.html; "Delco-Light Farm Electric Plant," *Doctordelco.com*, found March 12, 2018, no page update, http://www.doctordelco.com/Dr._Delco/Delco-Light/Delco-Light.html.

61. James Wharton, "Nashville Boy Scouts Open Camping Season Monday at Boxwell to Lead Several Agencies in Summer Outdoor Recreational Programs," *Nashville Tennessean*, June 8, 1941, pg. 13; "New Camp Boxwell," *The Bugle* [Nashville Council newsletter], Vol. I, No. 6: December 1940, pg. 3.

62. Robert V. Remini, *A Short History of the United States: Form the Arrival of Native American Tribes to the Obama Presidency,* paperback edition, Harper Perennial: New York, 2009, pg. 239; Eric Foner, *The Story of American Freedom,* W. W. Norton & Co.: New York and London, 1998, pg. 219.

63. W. J. Anderson, "Anderson Says Trucks Needed by Boy Scouts," *Nashville Tennessean,* March 15, 1942, pg. 16-A; "Montgomery Navy Quota Beats Schedule," *Nashville Tennessean,* December 4, 1942, pg. 22; "Talmadge M. Miller Named to Scout Post," *Nashville Tennessean,* September 2, 1943, pg. 21; "Scout Leaders Urged to Recruit Members," *Nashville Tennessean,* September 12, 1945, pg. 14; "Camp Boxwell Scout Quota Increased," *Nashville Tennessean,* May 2, 1945, pg. 18; John Walker, "Re: Write up on Billy," message to Grady Eades, August 17, 2021.

64. The assistants ranged from one to three any given time. There is no evidence that anyone other than African American cooks were used at Boxwell. "Nashville Scouts' Own Page," *Nashville Tennessean,* August 1, 1937, pg. *Tennessean Magazine* 15; "Wanted," *Nashville Tennessean,* June 29, 1943, pg. 16; "Tent No. 10 Wins Inspection Test," *Nashville Tennessean,* June 27, 1931, pg. 2; "Best Troops in Scouting Those Which Use Camps," *Nashville Tennessean,* April 16, 1939, pg. 4D; "Scout School," *The Bugle* [Nashville Council newsletter], Vol. I, No. 4: May 1939, pg. 5; "Camp Movies Are Now Ready," *The Bugle* [Nashville Council newsletter], Vol. I, No. 5: March 1940, pg. 1; "Nashville Scouts' Own Page," *Nashville Tennessean,* July 26, 1936, pg. *Tennessean Magazine* 13; "Nashville Scouts' Own Page," *Nashville Tennessean,* July 16, 1933, pg. Magazine Section 13. It is interesting to note that Whittaker was inducted immediately before Anderson announced his retirement. A skeptical person might think these events were connected. "Scout Society Adds 12 to Rolls," *Nashville Tennessean,* July 12, 1947, pg. 13.

65. "Every Bed Taken At Camp Boxwell," *Nashville Tennessean,* June 20, 1935, pg. 10; Tom Neal (retired), interviewer Grady Eades, December 7, 2016, Gallatin, TN; "Scout Society Adds 12 to Rolls," *Nashville Tennessean,* July 12, 1947, pg. 13; Whittaker's assistant cook is actually mentioned here by name, John Taylor, "Camp Boxwell Opens for Month Next Sunday," *Nashville Banner,* June 16, 1948, pg. 4.

66. W. J. Anderson, "Negro Scouting Proves Worth of Experiment," *Nashville Tennessean,* December 25, 1938, pg. 9B; Luther Carmichael, "News of Colored People," *Nashville Tennessean,* September 5, 1938, pg. 12.

67. "C. M. Cooper Heads Negro Boy Scouts," *Nashville Tennessean,* June 27, 1943, pg. 10C; W. H. Shackleford, "Happenings Among Colored People," *Nashville Tennessean,* June 18, 1944, pg. 19B; W. H. Shackleford, "Happenings Among Colored People," *Nashville Tennessean,* July 8, 1945, pg. 14B; "Scouts Buy Land for Negro Park," *Nashville Tennessean,* April 2, 1946, pg. 8; W. H. Shackleford, "Happenings Among Colored People," *Nashville Tennessean,* June 1, 1947, pg. 27A; W. H. Shackleford, "Happenings Among Colored People," *Nashville Tennessean,* May 30, 1948, pg. 5E.

68. Jordan, *Modern Manhood and the Boy Scouts of America,* pg. 201, 203.

69. Wills, *Boy Scouts of America: A Centennial History,* pg. 79; This is basically a simple summation of a much more detailed argument that Jordan lays out in *Modern Manhood,* pgs. 203-211.

70. "W. J. Anderson to Retire Soon," *Nashville Tennessean,* August 1, 1947, Pg. 30; "Boy Scouts Pick Sparta Camp Date," *Nashville Tennessean,* March 20, 1946, pg. 10. According to John Parish, it was he and his father Charles Parish, who had been part of the

Executive Board since 1940, who found the location for Camp Arrowhead, John L. Parish (retired, president, Worth, Inc.), interviewer Grady Eades, April 25, 2018, Tullahoma, TN.

71. Danny Bingham, "Beloved 'Coach' Anderson Retires as Scout Executive," *Nashville Banner*, July 30, 1947, pgs. 1, 10; "Nashville Scouts Report Achievements at Camp Boxwell," *Nashville Tennessean*, July 11, 1937, pg. *Tennessean Magazine* 16; "W. J. Anderson to Retire Soon," *Nashville Tennessean*, August 1, 1947, Pg. 30; "Scout Council Wins Acorn Award," *Nashville Tennessean*, August 22, 1947, pg. 40; Creighton and Johnson, *Boys Will Be Men*, pg. 116, 118; James G. Stahlman, "Truly Beloved," *Nashville Banner*, September 1, 1947, pg. 4.

72. "W. J. Anderson to Retire Soon," *Nashville* Tennessean, August 1, 1947, pg. 30; Danny Bingham, "Beloved 'Coach' Anderson Retires as Scout Executive," *Nashville Banner*, July 30, 1947, pgs. 1, 10; "Mrs. J. S. Boxwell Dies at Home," *Nashville Tennessean*, May 15, 1947, pg. 5; "L. B. Stevens Heads Boy Scout Council," *Nashville Tennessean*, January 9, 1948, pg. 15.

73. "New Executive Takes Over Duties," *Nashville Banner*, September 16, 1947, pg. 8; Creighton and Johnson, *Boys Will Be Men*, pgs. 118-119; Danny Bingham, "Beloved 'Coach' Anderson Retires as Scout Executive," *Nashville Banner*, July 30, 1947, pgs. 1, 10; No official article documents Gribble's exit. He was at the "hand-off" meeting with Akers on September 15, 1947 in his capacity as Assistant Scout Executive, but at the January 1948 Board meeting which elevated Lem Stevens to Council President, Gribble was listed as a deputy scout commissioner, a volunteer position. What happened is unknown, but this article is Gribble's last mention in connection with Scouting: "L. B. Stevens Heads Boy Scout Council," *Nashville Tennessean*, January 9, 1948, pg. 15.

74. Merl R. Eppse, "Activities of Colored People," *Nashville Banner*, June 25, 1948, pg. 42; W. H. Shackleford, "Happenings Among Colored People," *Nashville Tennessean*, August 10, 1947, pg. 17B; "Boy Scout Officials to Discuss Camporee," *Nashville Tennessean*, May 12, 1948, pg. 26.

75. "Camp Boxwell Opens for Month Next Sunday," *Nashville Banner*, June 16, 1948, pg. 4; "Scouts' Camp Boxwell to Open Sunday," *Nashville Tennessean*, June 17, 1948, pg. 10; "Boys and Girls Packing up to Cavort in Swim Suits," *Nashville Tennessean*, June 27, 1948, pg. 1E. Whittaker's assistant cook is actually mentioned here by name, John Taylor.

76. "Camp Boxwell Opens for Month Next Sunday," *Nashville Banner*, June 16, 1948, pg. 4; "Scouts' Camp Boxwell to Open Sunday," *Nashville Tennessean*, June 17, 1948, pg. 10; "Boys and Girls Packing up to Cavort in Swim Suits," *Nashville Tennessean*, June 27, 1948, pg. 1E.

77. Creighton and Johnson, *Boys Will Be Men*, pg. 117, 121.

78. Middle Tennessee Council, "Scouting: America's Future Leaders [Funding campaign newsletter]," *Middle Tennessee* Council, 1957, pg. 3; Ron Oakes (retired Mississippi Council Executive), interviewer Grady Eades, July 18, 2019, phone interview; The property was deeded to the Council by the Justin Potter, Jr. Foundation in 1944, making it theirs to sell; "100 Acres Deeded to Scout Council," *Nashville Tennessean*, March 19, 1944, pg. C6; "Harpeth Narrows Added to State Site," *Tennessean*, July 14, 1978, pg. 1; Cheatham County, TN, Deed Book 75, pg. 273; Cheatham County, TN, Deed Book

196, pg. 380; "Scout Committee Report Excerpted," *Tennessean*, October 5, 1975, pg.
6A.

79. W. J. Anderson, "Camp Boxwell Includes Fun, High Ideals," *Nashville Tennessean*, June
22, 1941, pg. 18; "Best Troops in Scouting Those Which Use Camps," *Nashville Tennessean*, April 16, 1939, pg. 38.

80. "W. J. Anderson to Retire Soon," *Nashville Tennessean*, August 1, 1947, Pg. 30;
"Nashville Scouts' Own Page," *Nashville Tennessean*, July 14, 1935, pg. *Tennessean
Magazine* 13; Emily Towe, "Camp Boxwell Called 'Boy Scouts' Heaven on Earth';
Coach Anderson Directs Activity in Record Year," *Nashville Tennessean*, Jun 30, 1940,
pg. 11; "Nashville Scouts' Own Page," *Nashville Tennessean*, July 16, 1933, pg. *Tennessean Magazine* 13; "Nashville Youths Acquire Sun Tans," *Nashville Tennessean*, June
30, 1946, pg. 14B; "Nashville Scouts' Own Page," *Nashville Tennessean*, July 16, 1933,
pg. Magazine Section 13.

81. Emily Towe, "Camp Boxwell Called 'Boy Scouts' Heaven on Earth;' Anderson Directs
Activity in Record Year," *Nashville Tennessean*, June 30, 1940, pg. 1B.

Chapter 3 Endnotes

The Temporary Camp: Boxwell at Rock Island

1949-1959

1. Wilbur F. Creighton and Leland Johnson, *Boys Will Be Men: Middle Tennessee Scouting Since 1910*, Middle Tennessee Council: Nashville, 1983, pg. 119; "Scout Recruitment Program Urged for Midstate Area," *Nashville Tennessean*, January 29, 1949, pg. 2.

2. There is some question over who was responsible for purchasing the property. Creighton
and Johnson claimed Leslie G. Boxwell, Will Manier, Jr., and E. B. Stahlman, Jr. secured
the location for $12,000. Tom Willhite claimed it was Charles Parish, also for $12,000.
Creighton and Johnson, *Boys Will Be Men*, pg. 122; Tom Willhite (retired, Boy Scouts
of America, Middle Tennessee Council, Reservation Director), interview by Russ Parham,
September 20, 2002, Sparta, TN. "Boy Scout Committee Discusses New Camp Site,"
Nashville Banner, April 11, 1949, pg. 6; "Scout Leaders Choose New Camping Site,"
Nashville Tennessean, April 12, 1949, pg. 6; "Camp Boxwell Put in Shape For Arrival of
Boy Scouts," *Nashville Tennessean*, June 12, 1949, pg. 8B.

3. "200 Acres Near Rock Island Soon to Start Humming," *Nashville Tennessean*, June 12,
1949, pg. 8B.

4. "Boy Scout Committee Discusses New Camp Site," *Nashville Banner*, April 11, 1949, pg.
6.

5. The two nations tested each other's resolve with a series of escalating tests: the Berlin
blockade, the Berlin Airlift, the Truman Doctrine, the Marshall Plan, the formation of
East Germany, the formation of West Germany, the creation of NATO, the creation of

the Warsaw Pact. Looming in the background of each escalation was the atomic bomb. The United States had introduced atomic weapons at the end of World War II; by 1949, the Soviet Union had developed its own atomic bomb. To prepare for a possible nuclear holocaust, schools began holding "Duck and Cover" drills and families bought fallout shelters with names like "Kidde Kokoon" for their backyards. These fears became even more pronounced when, in 1957, the Soviet Union launched *Sputnik*, the first man-made satellite, into orbit. A radar system could detect an attack by planes coming to drop an atomic bomb; a missile with an atomic warhead—the future presented by Sputnik—was a very different beast. The American response led to the creation of the National Aeronautics and Space Administration (NASA) as well as a new emphasis in public education on math and science. The Alger Hiss-Whittaker Chambers case in 1948 exemplified the fears, both real and imagined, in this period. For an easy to follow discussion of this and the larger Red Scare, see Allen Weinstein and David Rubel, *The Story of America: Freedom and Crisis from Settlement to Superpower*, DK: London, New York,Munich, Melbourne, and Delhi, 2002, pgs. 537-555; Even the Boy Scouts were not free of the fear! G. Milton Kelly, "Communist Scheme to Infiltrate Boy Scouts Revealed," *Nashville Banner*, August 13, 1952, pg. 2; "Duck and Cover," *Archive.org*, last modified December 31, 2014, https://archive.org/details/gov.ntis.ava11109vnb1; "Nuclear Fallout Shelters Were Never Going to Work," *History.com*, last modified September 1, 2018, https://www.history.com/news/nuclear-fallout-shelters-were-never-going-to-work ; Remini, *A Short History*, 265; Alvin Powell, "How Sputnik Changed U.S. Education," *The Harvard Gazette*, October 11, 2007, https://news.harvard.edu/gazette/story/2007/10/how-sputnik-changed-u-s-education/.

6. Foner, *The Story of American Freedom*, 265; Eric Foner, *Give Me Liberty! An American History, Volume 2: From 1865*, Seagull Fourth Edition, W. W. Norton & Company: New York and London, 2014, pg. 930. The best discussion on the rise of Consumer culture in the early twentieth century has to be Lawrence Levine's chapter "American Culture and the Great Depression" in Lawrence Levine, *The Unpredictable Past: Explorations in American Cultural History*, Oxford University Press, New York and London, 1993; Steven Mintz, *Huck's Raft: A History of American Childhood*, The Belknap Press of Harvard University Press: Cambridge, Massachusetts and London, England, 2004, pg. 276; Foner, *The Story of American Freedom*, 264.

7. Mintz, *Huck's Raft*, 276. Accompanying the baby boom was the rise of youth culture. The idea of the youth or the slightly older teenager as being a distinct group was not new to the 1950s. The roots were clear in the 1930s with the rise of comic books and teen movie stars such as Judy Garland and Mickey Rooney. But as with consumer culture, the post-war world accelerated these changes and youth culture came to be seen as something wholly unique and separate from the world of adults. From toys specifically marketed to children to television shows like *Howdy Doody* geared toward a youth audience to television shows and toys marketed together like *Davy Crockett*, a new emphasis on entertaining youth at the youth level emerged. As the boomers (and their slightly older siblings) grew up, so too did their tastes and the materials they consumed, such as rock 'n' roll music, like Elvis Presley and Chuck Berry, and even "rebellious" movies, such as *Rebel Without A Cause*. Mintz's chapter "In Pursuit of the Perfect Childhood" gives a detailed discussion of this entire phenomenon, Mintz, *Huck's Raft*, 251, 255. Paul Boyer, *Ameri-*

can *History: A Very Short Introduction*, Oxford University Press: Oxford, 2012, pg. 112.

8. Remini, *A Short History of the United States*, 261; "Brown v. Board of Education of Topeka, 347 U.S. 483 (1954)", *Justia: US Supreme Court*, last modified date unknown, https://supreme.justia.com/cases/federal/us/347/483/#tab-opinion-1940809; Foner, *The Story of American Freedom*, 258-259.

9. The first sales tax was set at two percent and raised to three percent in 1955. Part of the reforms of this period was the end of the state's poll tax. Also, the TVA actively engaged in strip mining, was sued multiple times for air pollution, and displaced thousands when homes were impounded for the creation of lakes. Paul H. Bergeron, Stephen V. Ash, and Jeanette Keith, *Tennesseans and their History*, The University of Tennessee Press: Knoxville, TN, 1999, pg.290; "A History of Tennessee," *Tennessee Blue Book, 2015-2016*, Tennessee Department of State: Nashville, 2015, pg. 544-546, 551; Corlew, *Tennessee, A Short History*, 472-473, 493.

10. The age of admission into both programs was lowered in 1949: eight for Cubs and 11 for Boy Scouts. Chuck Wills, *Boy Scouts of America: A Centennial History*, DK Publishing, New York, 2009, pg. 122.

11. Ibid., 125-127.

12. Mintz, *Huck's Raft*, 280-281.

13. Ibid., 281-282.

14. Ibid., 282.

15. "Retired Boy Scouts Exec, Ward Akers, Services Set," *Nashville Tennessean*, September 19, 1981, pg. 22; Floyd "Q-Ball" Pearce (1900-1987) interview, interviewed by Russ Parham, August 31, 1985, Clarenden, Arkansas; Ward C. Akers (1942-2008) interview, interviewed by Kerry Parker, July 26, 2001, Nashville, TN; Creighton and Johnson, *Boys Will Be Men*, 117.

16. "Scout Recruitment Program Urged for Midstate Area," *Nashville Tennessean*, January 29, 1949, pg. 2.

17. Rock Island State Park did not become a state park until 1969, "Rock Island State Park," *Tennessee State Parks*, last modified date unknown, https://tnstateparks.com/parks/rock-island ; "Great Falls," *Tennessee Valley Authority*, last modified date unknown, https://www.tva.com/Energy/Our-Power-System/Hydroelectric/Great-Falls-Reservoir; All four dams were owned by Tennessee Electric Power Company, "Odd Dam Out," *Tennessee Valley Authority*, last modified date unknown, https://www.tva.com/About-TVA/Our-History/Built-for-the-People/Odd-Dam-Out.

18. Creighton conducted a great many interviews for his work, but none of those interviews have survived. The existing newspaper record has no details supporting this account, so there is little choice but to accept this as the most accurate account as it is the only account. The discrepancy in acreage is likely due to the fact that some of the Yost property was on the other side of the river, across from the waterfront. An undated leader's guide identifies the camp proper as 127 acres with additional acreage on the other side of the river. This property was sold off during Tom Willhite's tenure as Camping and Activities director, 1976-1994. The Council purchased the site for $12,000. Creighton and Johnson, *Boys Will Be Men*, 121-122; Dan Brown, "Camp Boxwell, III, On Caney Fork River, To Be Opened Sunday for Midstate Scouts," *Nashville Banner*, June 25, 1949, pg.

3; "Historic Scout Camp Site Approved by Council," *Nashville Banner,* May 12, 1951, pg. 16.

19. Dan Brown, "Camp Boxwell, III, On Caney Fork River, To Be Opened Sunday for Mid-state Scouts," *Nashville Banner,* June 25, 1949, pg. 3; "Camp Boxwell Put in Shape For Arrival of Boy Scouts," *Nashville Tennessean,* June 12, 1949, pg. 8B; The photos that remain were taken after Boxwell had moved to Old Hickory Lake and show the buildings as derelict. Lodge Photos from Personal Collection of Michael Seay.

20. The Lodge also performed a similar function to what Ittabeena would do later—served as a home for Ward Akers to court important people with influence or money. Chester LaFever remembers Beverly Briley coming to Rock Island and staying at the Lodge. Briley and Akers would shoot turtles in the Collins River. Chester LaFever (1926-2011) (retired, Metro Nashville Public School principal), interviewed by Kerry Parker, October 24, 2001, Nashville, TN; James Akers (1945-2019), "RE: The Passing of Al Hendrickson," e-mail to Grady Eades, August 1, 2014, "Memories of a Camper and Staff Member" attachment; E. Robert "Bob" Alley (retired, president, E. Robert Alley & Associates), interviewer Grady Eades, March 9, 2017, Brentwood, TN.

21. Ward C. Akers interview, 2001.

22. Louis Hines, "Swimming Tops Scouting Activities at Popular Boxwell Reservation," *Nashville Banner,* July 19, 1951, pg. 32; E. Robert "Bob" Alley (retired, president, E. Robert Alley & Associates), written interview by Grady Eades, December 23, 2015, Nashville, TN.

23. James Akers (real estate agent, Jim Akers & Associates), second written interview by Grady Eades, November 18, 2017, Jacksonville, FL; "200 Acres Near Rock Island Soon to Start Humming," *Nashville Tennessean,* June 12, 1949, pg. 8B; E. Robert "Bob" Alley (retired, president, E. Robert Alley & Associates), interviewer Grady Eades, March 9, 2017, Brentwood, TN.

24. "'Buddy System' Employed by Camp Boxwell Scouts," *Nashville Tennessean,* July 10, 1928, pg. 4.

25. E. Robert Alley, "Staff Reunion," e-mail to Grady Eades, June 29, 2014, "Old Camp Boxwell at Rock Island" attachment; James Akers (real estate agent, Jim Akers & Associates), first written interview by Grady Eades, December 13, 2015, Jacksonville, FL; Ward C. Akers interview, 2001.

26. E. Robert "Bob" Alley (retired, president, E. Robert Alley & Associates), "Rock Island Walkabout, April 2018," interviewers Grady Eades and Russ Parham, April 7, 2018, Rock Island, TN.

27. E. Robert "Bob" Alley (retired, president, E. Robert Alley & Associates), written interview by Grady Eades, December 23, 2015, Nashville, TN.

28. "Camp Boxwell Put in Shape For Arrival of Boy Scouts," *Nashville Tennessean,* June 12, 1949, pg. 8B; Bob Alley, written interview, 2015; John L. Parish (retired, president, Worth, Inc.), interviewer Grady Eades, April 25, 2018, Tullahoma, TN; James Akers, first written, 2015; Ward C. Akers interview, 2001.

29. Bob Alley, "Rock Island Walkabout, April 2018," 2018.

30. James Akers (real estate agent, Jim Akers & Associates), second written interview by Grady Eades, November 18, 2017, Jacksonville, FL; James Akers, "RE: The Passing of Al Hendrickson," e-mail to Grady Eades, August 1, 2014, "Memories of a Camper and Staff Member" attachment; Bob Alley, written interview, 2015; Louis Hines, "100 Boy Scouts

Enjoy Activities At Scenic Boxwell Reservation," *Nashville Banner*, June 28, 1951, pg. 15.

31. "Another Summer's History for Area's Scout Campers," *Nashville Tennessean*, August 13, 1950, pg. 6A; "Neighborhood Notes," *Nashville Tennessean*, July 8, 1949, pg. 12; "Historic Scout Camp Site Approved by Council," *Nashville Banner*, May 12, 1951, pg. 16; Bob Alley, "Rock Island Walkabout, April 2018," 2018; James Akers, second written interview, 2017. As is often the case with legends, it is difficult to know how many of these legends are true. Certainly, Nashville newspapers from 1861 were discovered in a nearby cave, giving some validity to the Confederate treasure story, at least to the Civil War connection. Highway 136 into Walling, TN, before the highway turns southwest to Rock Island, is named the Old Kentucky Road, so that legend is larger than just the Rock Island community. Jackson's visit is harder to verify and without a name or more specifics, the "last Indian battle" is also a bit vague. "Campers Open Closed Room in Bone Cave," *Nashville Banner*, August 2, 1956, pg. 12; "Maps – Trail of Tears," *National Park Service,* last modified May 17, 2019, https://www.nps.gov/trte/planyourvisit/maps.htm.

32. "County Accidents Injure 4 Persons," *Nashville Tennessean*, July 17, 1949, pg. 6; "Fitts Rites Set for Wednesday," *Nashville Tennessean*, July 19, 1949, pg. 19; "Henry A. Fitts' Funeral Rites Slated Wednesday," *Nashville Banner*, July 19, 1949, pg. 15; "Memorial To Henry Fitts Being Planned," *Nashville Banner*, August 5, 1949, pg. 16. In August of 1985, Floyd "Q-Ball" Pearce added some personal details to the story, noting that the motorcycle was not Fitts'. Pearce implies that Fitts was not an accomplished or even a seasoned rider. Further, Pearce relates the anecdote of how Fitts took his raincoat for the ride to Nashville because there was a little rain, "just a nice stroddle time." Floyd "Q-ball" Pearce, interviewed by Russ Parham, August 31, 1985, Clarenden, Arkansas.

33. "Boy Scout Committee Discusses New Camp Site," *Nashville Banner*, April 11, 1949, pg. 6.

34. "Historic Scout Camp Site Approved by Council," *Nashville Banner*, May 12, 1951, pg. 16.

35. Louis Hines, "Improvements Suggested at Scout Camp," *Nashville Banner*, August 9, 1951, pg. 16.

36. An alternate theory was that the campaign was not truly a failure, but Akers just let it drop. By 1951, the news of Old Hickory Dam was in the papers and Akers may have simply realized he had a much closer alternative. Land was purchased at the Old Hickory location in 1952 for this purpose. It is unknown what the exact timeline here was or what Akers' thoughts were. It is entirely possible that the funds from the campaign, however large or small, were dedicated to purchasing this land instead. "Camp Boxwell Opens; Enrolls Record 200," *Nashville Banner*, July 5, 1952, pg. 14. Light was far more comfortable as chair of the Health and Safety Committee, which was in his wheelhouse, Jack Bond, "Dr. Light Among First Men of Scouting MidState," *Nashville Banner*, June 1, 1959, pg. 26.

37. Middle Tennessee Council, *Bulletin for Unit Leaders*, Middle Tennessee Council, Nashville, 1955, personal collection of Boyd Williams. In 1955, the schedule was as follows: Week 1 was Coffee, Bedford, and White Counties; Week 2 was Cordell Hull, Highland Rim, Walton Trail, Black Patch, and Upper Cumberland Districts; Week 3 was West, Cogioba, and Heart of Tennessee Districts; Week 4 was Central District and Warren

County; Week 5 was Buffalo River District and Williamson and Maury Counties; Week 6 David Crockett and Hermitage Districts; Week 7 was Explorer Week; Week 8 was for the State Training School at Jordonia, the reform school.

38. Louis Hines, "Boxwell's First Day Exciting," *Nashville Banner*, July 11, 1951, pg. 10.

39. Dan Brown, "Camp Boxwell, III, On Caney Fork River, To Be Opened Sunday for Midstate Scouts," *Nashville Banner*, June 25, 1949, pg. 3; "200 Acres Near Rock Island Soon to Start Humming," *Nashville Tennessean*, June 12, 1949, pg. 8B.

40. Much of this military material was often referred to as "surplus" by the staff. Cots and other materials were "surplus" in the sense that the local military base was willing to part with it. Generally it was screened and given to the Scouts for free. Further, Bob Alley clarifies that the pit latrines were quite large, measuring 8' wide, 6' deep, and 3' wide. They could go years without being filled. E. Robert "Bob" Alley (retired, president, E. Robert Alley & Associates), first interview by Danny Waltman, July 5, 2014, Lebanon, TN; Bob Alley, written interview, 2015; James Akers, first written interview, 2015; Bob Alley, "Rock Island Walkabout, April 2018," 2018; Ward C. Akers interview, 2001; Wolf Goethert, "Rock Island Draft," e-mail to Grady Eades, November 15, 2019, "Boxwell review comments-goethert" attachment; Bob Alley, "Re: Rock Island Project Help," e-mail to Grady Eades, May 13, 2021.

41. Wolf Goethert (retired), written interview, interviewer Grady Eades, October 30, 2018, Shrewsbury, MA.

42. Wolf Goethert, written interview, 2018; James Akers, second written interview, 2017; Bob Alley interview, 2017.

43. Middle Tennessee Council, *Bulletin for Unit Leaders*, Middle Tennessee Council, Nashville, 1955, personal collection of Boyd Williams.

44. Bob Alley interview, 2017.

45. Middle Tennessee Council, *Bulletin for Unit Leaders*, Middle Tennessee Council, Nashville, unknown date, page 7, personal collection of Barry Goad; "Midstate Boy Scouts Work, Play, Learn During Stay at Camp Boxwell," *Nashville Tennessean*, August 13, 1950, pg. 6A; Ward C. Akers (1942-2008), interview by Kerry Parker, July 26, 2001, Nashville, TN.

46. Middle Tennessee Council, *Bulletin for Unit Leaders*, Middle Tennessee Council, Nashville, unknown date, page 7, personal collection of Barry Goad. Adults who stayed at the family campsite were welcome to eat in the dining hall if they so desired, but were charged a fee depending on their age. Wives and children over 11 paid $9, children 7 to 11 $6, and $3 for those under 7 years old.

47. Bob Alley interview, 2017.

48. "Camp Boxwell Opens; Enrolls Record 200," *Nashville Banner*, July 5, 1952, pg. 14; James Akers, second written interview, 2017.

49. Middle Tennessee Council, *Bulletin for Unit Leaders*, Middle Tennessee Council, Nashville, 1955, personal collection of Boyd Williams. The list of merit badges included Camping, Pioneering, Cooking, Hiking, Fishing, Archery, Marksmanship, Athletics, Swimming, rowing, Canoeing, Life Saving, Nature, Soil & Water Conservation, Forestry, Wildlife Management, Personal fitness, First Aid, Bugling, Signaling, Indian Lore, and Leatherwork.

50. Middle Tennessee Council, *Bulletin for Unit Leaders*, Middle Tennessee Council, Nashville, 1955, personal collection of Boyd Williams; Louis Hines, "Great Variety of Scout-

ing Activities Offered Midstate Scouts at Boxwell," *Nashville Banner*, August 2, 1951, pg. 8.

51. Middle Tennessee Council, *Bulletin for Unit Leaders*, Middle Tennessee Council, Nashville, unknown date, page 7, personal collection of Barry Goad; Louis Hines, "Great Variety of Scouting Activities Offered Midstate Scouts at Boxwell," *Nashville Banner*, August 2, 1951, pg. 8.

52. James Akers to Grady Eades, "Brief Report for Grady," e-mail attachment, November 18, 2017.

53. Bob Alley interview, 2017; Wolf Goethert, written interview, 2018; Ward C. Akers interview, 2001; E. Robert Alley, "Staff Reunion," e-mail to Grady Eades, June 29, 2014, "Old Camp Boxwell at Rock Island" attachment. James Akers, first written interview, 2015; Wolf Goethert started his fires by using a vile of acid tipped into a can of soda ash, while Ward C. Akers recalled chlorine and brake fluid being used to start the fires.

54. E. Robert Alley (retired, president, E. Robert Alley & Associates), second interview by Danny Waltman, July 5, 2014, Lebanon, TN.

55. Wolf Goethert, written interview, 2018; James Akers, first written interview, 2015; John Parish interview, 2018.

56. "Camp Boxwell Put in Shape For Arrival of Boy Scouts," *Nashville Tennessean*, June 12, 1949, pg. 8B; Dan Brown, "Camp Boxwell, III, On Caney Fork River, To Be Opened Sunday for Midstate Scouts," *Nashville Banner*, June 25, 1949, pg. 3; "Neighborhood Notes," *Nashville Tennessean*, July 8, 1949, pg. 12; Bob Alley interview, 2017.

57. John Parish interview, 2018; "126 Scouts Enjoying Big Time at Boxwell," *Nashville Tennessean*, August 9, 1953, pg. 8A; Gene Tolley, Gene Tolley to Bob Alley, May 22, 1953, Personal Collection of Bob Alley; Richard Parker, Richard Parker and Gene Tolley to Bob Alley, April 29, 1954, Personal Collection of Bob Alley; Richard Parker, Richard Parker and Gene Tolley to Bob Alley, May 20, 1955, Personal Collection of Bob Alley; Richard Parker, Richard Parker and James Johnson to Bob Alley, May 16, 1956, Personal Collection of Bob Alley; Richard Parker, Richard Parker and Don Starin to Bob Alley, February 1, 1957, Personal Collection of Bob Alley; Richard Parker, Richard Parker to Bob Alley, February 10, 1958, Personal Collection of Bob Alley; "Expect Record Attendance at Boxwell," *Nashville Banner*, City Edition, June 10, 1959, pg. 14.

58. Note that the staff had grown from 34 to 37 in a short span of time. Parker lived 1928-2016. "Richard E. Parker," *Robertson County Times*, March 16, 2016, pg. A4; Johnny Havlicek, "Scouts in Canoes Conquer River," *Nashville Tennessean*, August 20, 1953, pg. 21; Ward C. Akers interview, 2001; John Parish interview, 2018; Weldon Payne, "1,850 Scheduled for Summertime Experience," *Nashville Banner*, June 22, 1957, pg. 14; James Akers, first written interview, 2015.

59. LaFever claimed he owed his position to "Dead Fish Commission." In terms of his staff tenure, in the interview, he claims 1956 as Conservation Director, then Program Director in 1957. Newspaper records put LaFever as Conservation Director in 1957. Chester LaFever interview, 2001; "G-F Appoints Counselors at 15 Camps," *Nashville Tennessean*, June 9, 1957, pg. 4C; Weldon Payne, "1,850 Scheduled for Summertime Experience," *Nashville Banner*, June 22, 1957, pg. 14; Steve Eubank (retired, high school teacher), self-interview, 2001, Pulaski, TN.

60. Pearce lived from 1900-1987 and Gaffin from 1912-1993. Louis Hines, "100 Boy Scouts Enjoy Activities At Scenic Boxwell Reservation," *Nashville Banner*, June 28, 1951,

pg. 15; "Water, Woods Share Stage at Boy Scout Camp Boxwell," *Nashville Banner,* July 7, 1955, pg. 13; "Luke Morris Gaffin," *Nashville Tennessean,* September 16, 1993, pg. 5B; James Akers, "RE: The Passing of Al Hendrickson," e-mail to Grady Eades, August 1, 2014, "Memories of a Camper and Staff Member" attachment; Bob Alley interview, 2017.

61. "Historic Scout Camp Site Approved by Council," *Nashville Banner,* May 12, 1951, pg. 16.

62. Ian Romaine (ed.), *Wa-Hi-Nasa III: A Brotherhood of Cheerful Service in Middle Tennessee,* self-published, 2015, pg. 10; Bob Alley, "Rock Island Walkabout, April 2018," 2018; John Parish interview, 2018.

63. James Akers (real estate agent, Jim Akers & Associates), first written interview by Grady Eades, December 13, 2015, Jacksonville, FL; "Memorial To Henry Fitts Being Planned," *Nashville Banner,* August 5, 1949, pg. 16. Q-ball pointed out that the new OA Lodge was supposed to be built by the money raised for Fitts, but when the time came there was not enough money to build the kind of building that was desired. Floyd "Q-ball" Pearce, interviewed by Russ Parham, August 31, 1985, Clarenden, Arkansas.

64. Bryan Wendell, "Book goes 'Back to Gilwell' to uncover 'The History of Wood Badge in the United States', Bryon on Scouting: A Blog for the BSA's Adult Leaders," Boy Scouts of America, February 28, 2019, https://blog.scoutingmagazine.org/2019/02/28/book-goes-back-to-gilwell-to-uncover-the-history-of-wood-badge-in-the-united-states/ ; Creighton and Johnson, *Boys Will Be Men,* 142; Personal collection of Harry "Beany" Elam.

65. Jack Bond, "32 Adult Scouters in Training," *Nashville Banner,* Midstate Edition, August 3, 1959, pg. 1, 2; Jack Bond, "Wood Badge Trainees After Ph.D. of Scouting," *Nashville Banner,* Midstate Edition, August 4, 1959, pg. 12.

66. Jack Bond, "Bond Biased, Doesn't give Chiggers' Side," *Nashville Banner,* Midstate Edition, August 4, 1959, pg. 12; Jack Bond, "'Have Fun' Means Work for Scouters," *Nashville Banner,* Midstate Edition, August 3, 1959, pg. 2.

67. John Parish to Grady Eades, "Re: old Boxwell pictures," e-mail to Grady Eades, September 17, 2018.

68. Louis Hines, "100 Boy Scouts Enjoy Activities At Scenic Boxwell Reservation," *Nashville Banner,* June 28, 1951, pg. 15; *The Banner* reported in 1950 on Mrs. Novella Halteman, a local Rock Island woman who operated a café close to Boxwell. She was presented a "summer mother" for the Scouts. As her shop had one of the only phones in the area at the time, her Great Falls Café was "a message center" for parents and Scouts alike. Thus, women did play a role at this Boxwell, but it was the wives of Burton and Pedigo who became the first female staff members at Boxwell.

69. "Scouts Start Drive to End Sissy City Life in Camps," *Nashville Tennessean,* July 14, 1958, pg. 5A.

70. Milner Ball, "Midstate Scouts Pooh Sissy Camp," *Nashville Tennessean,* July 15, 1958, pg. 1A; Milner Ball, "Midstate Scouts Pooh Sissy Camp," *Nashville Tennessean,* July 15, 1958, pg. 4A.

71. Milner Ball, "Midstate Scouts Pooh Sissy Camp," *Nashville Tennessean,* July 15, 1958, pg. 4A.

72. John Parish interview, 2018.

73. Additionally, Chester LaFever recalled that poisonous snakes, such as copperheads, were real work at the "old camp." Not that there were actually that many bites, but there was a real fear of the bites. Chester LaFever interview, 2001; Bob Alley, written interview, 2015; Bob Alley, first interview by Danny Waltman, 2014.

74. "126 Scouts Enjoying Big Time at Boxwell," *Nashville Tennessean*, August 9, 1953, pg. 8A.

75. Sam Neal, "Boxwell Scout Staffers Paddle on River Cruise," *Nashville Tennessean*, August 16, 1953, pg. 3B; Johnny Havlicek, "Scouts in Canoes Conquer River," *Nashville Tennessean*, August 20, 1953, pg. 21.

76. Sam Neal, "Boxwell Scout Staffers Paddle on River Cruise," *Nashville Tennessean*, August 16, 1953, pg. 3B.

77. Johnny Havlicek, "Scouts in Canoes Conquer River," *Nashville Tennessean*, August 20, 1953, pg. 21.

78. "Neighborhood Notes," *Nashville Tennessean*, July 8, 1949, pg. 12.

79. Bob Alley interview, 2017; John Parish interview, 2018.

80. John Parish interview, 2018; James Akers, second written interview, 2017. Akers claimed that Davis died at some point during the Rock Island run, but an exact date is unknown. None of the interviewees knew Lovey's last name.

81. Creighton and Johnson, *Boys Will Be Men*, 118, 129-130; "Camp Burton Ready for Scouts," *Nashville Banner*, June 2, 1950, pg. 10; "Scoutmaster Bentley to Attend National Parley," *Nashville Banner*, July 21, 1956, pg. 6.

82. "Camp Burton Ready for Scouts," *Nashville Banner*, June 2, 1950, pg. 10; "Boy Scouts Will Hold Field Day," *Nashville Banner*, July 15, 1951, pg. 9; "145 Attend Scout Camp," *Nashville Banner*, July 14, 1950, pg. 12.

83. "Camp Burton Ready for Scouts," *Nashville Banner*, June 2, 1950, pg. 10; "145 Attend Scout Camp," *Nashville Banner*, July 14, 1950, pg. 12; "Napier Division of Boy Scouts Opens Camp," *Nashville Banner*, July 17, 1951, pg. 10; "43 Boy Scouts Named in Group to Attend Camp," *Nashville Banner*, July 26, 1951, pg. 10; "100 Midstate Boys Attend Scout Camp," *Nashville Banner*, July 15, 1952, pg. 18.

84. Interestingly the only newspaper article on Burton in 1955 was in the *Leaf-Chronicle*, which announced Burton was in Cheatham County. Where exactly and dates of camp were not included, "Negro Scouts Enjoy Camp in Cheatham," *Leaf Chronicle*, August 11, 1955, pg. 5; "Scouts Buy Land for Negro Park," *Nashville Tennessean*, April 2, 1946, pg. 8; W. H. Shackleford, "Happenings Among Colored People," *Nashville Tennessean*, June 1, 1947, pg. 27A; W. H. Shackleford, "Happenings Among Colored People," *Nashville Tennessean*, May 30, 1948, pg. 5E; Burton--"Napier Scout Division Set Camp Dates," The Nashville Banner, June 15, 1954, pg. 5; Camp Burton Promotional Materials, 1955, Personal Collection of Boyd Williams; *Scouting: "America's Future Leaders"* [Council newsletter], Middle Tennessee Council, 1957, Personal Collection of Boyd Williams; Ron Oakes (retired, Boy Scout Council Executive), interviewer Grady Eades, July 19, 2019, phone interview, Hendersonville, TN.

85. Ted Solinksi, "River Program Called 'Shot-in-Arm' to State," *Nashville Tennessean*, May 30, 1954, 9B.

86. "Segregation Order Delayed," *Nashville Tennessean*, May 18, 1954, pg. 1; Tony Badger, "Southerners Who Refused to Sign the Southern Manifesto," *The Historical Journal*, Vol. 42, No.2 (June 1999), pgs. 517-534, retrieved from JSTOR September 14, 2019,

https://www.jstor.org/stable/3020998; "A History of Tennessee," *Tennessee Blue Book*, 548-549.

87. Creighton and Johnson, *Boys Will Be Men,* 144; "Neighborhood Notes," *Nashville Tennessean,* July 8, 1949, pg. 12; "Expect Record Attendance at Boxwell," *Nashville Banner,* City Edition, June 10, 1959, pg. 14. The quote from Dorland is somewhat problematic. While there is clearly truth to the statement, there is no reference point for the quote. Creighton and Johnson did not note at what event the quote was made, when exactly Dorland made the quote, or where they found the quote. The author has not been able to confirm the quote through newspaper sources.

88. Creighton and Johnson, *Boys Will Be Men,* 145.

89. "Low-Dam Fund for Cumberland Passes Senate," *Nashville Tennessean,* July 6, 1946, pg. 1, 2; "Old Hickory Dam Fund Speed Urged," *Nashville Banner,* June 7, 1951, pg. 1-2; "Old Hickory Lock to Close July 11 for 45 Day Span," *Nashville Banner,* July 6, 1956, pg. 7.

90. Middle Tennessee Council, *1968 Boxwell Staff Manual,* 1968, Nashville, TN, pg.11, Personal Collection of Ed Mason. Leaders' Guides and Staff Guides would reprint this "Location and History of Boxwell Reservation" material well into the 1990s. "Old Hickory Boxwell Reservation (Proposed) Topography," *Middle Tennessee Council,* July 15, 1954, topographic map, personal collection of Russell Parham; Tom Flake, "Scouts Given 718-Acre Campsite Boarding on Old Hickory Lake," *Nashville Banner,* March 26, 1957, pg. 10. Dorland's Camp Development Committee consisted of himself as chair, Walter E. Richardson Jr., County Judge Beverly Briley, John D. Owen Jr. , J. C. Langford, C. Vernon Hines, T. Cecil Wray, Charles Hawkins, Faulkner Hickerson, F. Murray Acker, Vincent Flaherty, C. m. Everhart, Hank Bowes and H. M. Byars. A committee for the development fund consisted of W. C. Weaver, Jr. (chairman), E. E. Murrey Sr., L. D. Stevens, W. B. Dunlop Jr., David K.Wilson, Julian Ragland, E. E. Murrey Jr., Dr. J. T. Jackson, Graydon Robsinson, Moris Moughon, Dr. Rudolph Light, John Herbet, G. A. Puryear, R. L. Parnell, and Robert Moody. "Year-Around Camp Planned," *Nashville Tennessean,* June 2, 1957, pg. 19D.

91. Tom Flake, "Scouts Given 718-Acre Campsite Boarding on Old Hickory Lake," *Nashville Banner,* March 26, 1957, pg. 10.

92. "Bills Offered To Give Reservoir Camp Sites to Midstate Scouts," *Nashville Banner,* July 8, 1957, pg. 1; Ken Morrell, "Lake Site Scouts' Dream Come True," *Nashville Banner,* August 31, 1957, pg. 1; Creighton and Johnson note that Akers, Wilbur Creighton, Sr., Dorland, and Stahlman all initially approached Congressman Loser about the land grant. Congressman Joe Evins and Clifford Davis supported the bill in the House, as did Al Gore, Sr., in the Senate, Creighton and Johnson, *Boys Will Be Men,* 145.

93. There is some conflict in the record on when the bill was signed. One article claims September 7, another September 8. Ken Morrell, "Lake Site Scouts' Dream Come True," *Nashville Banner,* August 31, 1957, pg. 1; "Midstate Scouts Jubilant Over Expanded Camp Site," *Nashville Banner,* September 9, 1957, pg. 1; "Boy Scouts Open New Camp Boxwell," *Nashville Banner,* September 30, 1957, pg. 8.

94. Tom Flake, "Scouts Given 718-Acre Campsite Boarding on Old Hickory Lake," *Nashville Banner,* March 26, 1957, pg. 10; Ken Morrell, "Lake Site Scouts' Dream Come True," *Nashville Banner,* August 31, 1957, pg. 1.

95. "Boy Scouts Open New Boxwell," *Nashville Banner*, September 30, 1957, pg. 8; Creighton and Johnson, *Boys Will Be Men*, pgs. 146-147; Tom Flake, "Scouts Given 718-Acre Campsite Boarding on Old Hickory Lake," *Nashville Banner*, March 26, 1957, pg. 10.
96. "Resolution," *Middle Tennessee Council, Executive Board*, November 25, 1975, personal collection of John L. Parish.

Chapter 4 Endnotes

The Camp That Akers Built:

Boxwell Reservation at Old Hickory Lake

1960-1975

1. Ward C. Akers interview (retired, former owner of Camp Hy-Lake), interviewed by Kerry Parker, July 26, 2001, Nashville, Tennessee; "Old Hickory Lock to Close July 11 for 45 Day Span," *Nashville Banner*, July 6, 1956, pg. 7; Gene Tolley was the other Camp Director at Rock Island that summer. Gene Tolley and Richard Parker, letter to Bob Alley, May 20, 1955.
2. Ward C. Akers interview, 2001.
3. James Akers (real estate agent, Jim Akers & Associates), second written interview by Grady Eades, November 18, 2017, Jacksonville, FL.
4. Tom Flake, "Scouts Given 718-Acre Campsite Boarding on Old Hickory Lake," *Nashville Banner*, March 26, 1957, pg. 10; Michael Seay (NASA Network and Security Engineer), interview by Russ Parham, December 22, 2009, Gallatin, TN. There is some question over the acreage in all these purchases. In the 1972 Capital Campaign Dedication book, the council claimed 528 acres in the 1957 fee simple transaction to accompany 113 acres bought in 1952 to gain access to the site and a 50 year lease on 115 acres from the Corps: the 7 miles of shoreline. Middle Tennessee Council, Boy Scouts of America, "Development Program Facilities Dedication Ceremonies" (booklet), July 11, 1974, Nashville, TN.
5. Tom Flake, "Scouts Given 718-Acre Campsite Boarding on Old Hickory Lake," *Nashville Banner*, March 26, 1957, pg. 10; Middle Tennessee Council, "You'll Want to Know About the Boxwell Reservation Development Fund" [brochure], 1959, Nashville, TN, Collection of Barry Goad; Middle Tennessee Council, "Boxwell Reservation, Old Hickory Lake" [mailing], 1959, Nashville, Tennessee, Collection of James E. Stevens; Middle Tennessee Council, "High Adventure for Middle Tennessee Boys: Boxwell Reservation Development Fund" [promotional booklet], 1959, Nashville, Tennessee, Collection of Archie Crain. The Committee in question was appointed by Council President

Dorland and consisted of Neil H. Cargile, Charles W. Hawkins, Dr. Rudolph Light, Albert W. Hutchinson, and T. Cecil Wray, chair. Creighton, Jr. reports the committee worked for two years and visited council camps in Mississippi and Missouri for ideas; Creighton, Jr. and Johnson, *Boys Will Be Men*, 146.

6.   Eric Foner, *The Story of American Freedom*, W. W. Norton & Co.: New York and London, 1998, pgs. 284-285.

7.   Robert V. Remini, *A Short History of the United States: From the Arrival of Native American Tribes to the Obama Presidency*, paperback edition, Harper Perennial: New York, 2009, pgs. 265-266, 274-276.

8.   Remini, *A Short History*, pgs. 282-284; Gerald R. Ford, "Gerald R. Ford's Remarks Upon Taking the Oath of Office as President," *Gerald R. Ford Presidential Library & Museum*, last modified date unknown, https://www.fordlibrarymuseum.gov/library/speeches/740001.asp.

9.   Kenneth C. Davis, *Don't Know Much About History: Everything You Need to Know about American History but Never Learned*, first edition, Avon Books: New York, 1990, pgs. 407-408; Foner, *Story of American Freedom*, pg. 316; James T. Patterson, *Restless Giant: The United States from Watergate to Bush v. Gore*, Oxford University Press: Oxford and New York, 2005, pgs. 6-9.

10.   Foner, *Story of American Freedom*, 280-282.

11.   James T. Patterson, *Grand Expectations: The United States, 1945-1974*, Oxford University Press: Oxford and New York, 1996, pgs. 361, 642-648; Patterson, *Restless Giant*, 52.

12.   U.S. Census Bureau, (2014, May), "The Baby Boom Cohort in the United States: 2012 to 2060" (Report No. P25-1141), Retrieved from https://www.census.gov/library/publications/2014/demo/p25-1141.html; Foner, *Story of American Freedom*, 287-313; Steven Mintz, *Huck's Raft: A History of American Childhood*, The Belknap Press of Harvard University Press: Cambridge, Massachusetts and London, England, 2004, pg. 312.

13.   "A History of Tennessee," *Tennessee Blue Book, 2015-2016*, Tennessee Department of State: Nashville, 2015, pg. 550-552; Paul H. Bergeron, Stephen V. Ash, and Jeanette Keith, *Tennesseans and their History*, The University of Tennessee Press: Knoxville, TN, 1999, pg. 303-306, 319; Robert E. Corlew, *Tennessee, A Short History*, Second Edition, University of Knoxville Press: Knoxville, 1981, 501; "History of Metro," *Nashville.gov*, last date modified unknown, found January 31, 2020, https://www.nashville.gov/Government/History-of-Metro.aspx.

14.   Tammy Sellers, *Tennessee Encyclopedia*, "Interstate Highway System, Tennessee," last update March 1, 2018, found on February 4, 2020, https://tennesseeencyclopedia.net/entries/interstate-highway-system-tennessee/ ; "Parnell Company in New Building," *Nashville Tennessean*, December 17, 1969, pg. 46.

15.   Chuck Wills, *Boy Scouts of America: A Centennial History*, DK Publishing, New York, 2009, pgs. 154-156, 161.

16.   Ibid., 161-171.

17.   "Top Scout Official Addresses Midstate Council Sunday," *Nashville Banner*, April 17, 1969, pg. 6; Lawayne Satterfield, "Scout Council Here Termed 'A Winner,'" *Nashville Banner*, April 21, 1969, pg. 1; Frances Meeker, "Local Scouting Executive Says No Scandal Here," *Nashville Banner*, June 11, 1974, pg. 13.

18. Middle Tennessee Council, Boy Scouts of America, *40th Annual Report*, "Organization and Extension Committee Report," 1961, Nashville, Tennessee, pg. 4; Middle Tennessee Council, Boy Scouts of America, *47th Annual Report*, "Organization and Extension Committee Report," February 8, 1968, Nashville, Tennessee, pg. 5; Middle Tennessee Council, *Smoke Signals* (Council newsletter), Vol 16, No. 8: Dec. 1971, pg. 1; Lawayne Satterfield, "Scout Council Here Termed 'A Winner,'" *Nashville Banner*, April 21, 1969, pg. 1.

19. "Scout Leaders Open Fund Appeal to Develop Boxwell," *Nashville Banner*, January 26, 1959, pg. 3; "2000 Here Help Kick off Boy Scout Fund Campaign," *Nashville Tennessean*, January 26, 1959, pg. 2A; "A Challenge behind New Camp Boxwell," *Nashville Tennessean*, January 28, 1959, pg. 8A.

20. Middle Tennessee Council, Boy Scouts of America, "You'll Want to Know About the Boxwell Reservation Development Fund" [brochure], 1959, Nashville, Tennessee, Collection of Barry Goad; Middle Tennessee Council, Boy Scouts of America, "High Adventure for Middle Tennessee Boys: Boxwell Reservation Development Fund" [promotional booklet], 1959, Nashville, TN, Collection of Archie Crain; Archie Crain (retired, Atlanta Area Council Scout Executive), phone interview by Grady Eades, August 23, 2018, Hendersonville, Tennessee; "Scout Leaders Open Fund Appeal to Develop Boxwell," *Nashville Banner*, January 26, 1959, pg. 3; "2000 Here Help Kick off Boy Scout Fund Campaign," *Nashville Tennessean*, January 26, 1959, pg. 2A.

21. Middle Tennessee Council, Boy Scouts of America, "You'll Want to Know About the Boxwell Reservation Development Fund" [brochure], 1959; Middle Tennessee Council, Boy Scouts of America, "Boxwell Reservation, Old Hickory Lake" [mailing], 1959; Middle Tennessee Council, Boy Scouts of America, "High Adventure for Middle Tennessee Boys: Boxwell Reservation Development Fund" [promotional booklet], 1959; Ron Oakes (retired, Council Executive), phone interview by Grady Eades, July 18, 2019, Hendersonville, TN; "Kiwanis Scout Gift Usage Decided," *Nashville Tennessean*, February 22, 1959, pg. 6B; "8 Scouts to Camp on Chamber's Patio," *Nashville Tennessean*, April 10, 1959, Second Edition, pg. 37; "Boxwell Fund short by $24,900," *Nashville Banner*, City Edition, June 10, 1959, pg. 3.

22. "Kiwanis Scout Gift Usage Decided," *Nashville Tennessean*, February 22, 1959, pg. 6B; Jack Bond, "Dr. Light Among First Men of Scouting in Midstate," *Nashville Banner*, City Edition, June 1, 1959, pg. 26; "Boxwell Still short as Pledgeline Nears," *Nashville Tennessean*, May 29, 1959, pg. 31; "Boxwell Fund short by $24,900," *Nashville Banner*, City Edition, June 3, 1959, pg. 3; "Boxwell Fund only $10,487 From Goal," *Nashville Banner*, City Edition, June 10, 1959, pg. 14; "Boxwell Fund Drive Success Expected," *Nashville Tennessean*, June 10, 1959, pg. 16.

23. Jack Bond, "Camp Boxwell Fund Tops Goal," *Nashville Banner*, City Edition, June 16, 1959, pg. 1; Middle Tennessee Council, Boy Scouts of America, *40th Annual Report*, "Boxwell Reservation Development Fund, Statement of Condition of Pledges, January 1, 1959—December 31, 1960," 1961, Nashville, Tennessee.

24. Jack Bond, "Camp Boxwell Fund Tops Goal," *Nashville Banner*, City Edition, June 16, 1959, pg. 1.

25. Jack Bond, "Camp Boxwell Fund Tops Goal," *Nashville Banner*, City Edition, June 16, 1959, pg. 1; "Scouts Turn Tables, Honor Stahlmans, The Banner," *Nashville Banner*, City Edition, June 16, 1959, pg. 2.

26. Jack Setters, "Boone Kept Busy Until Premiere," *Nashville Banner*, City Edition, December 4, 1959, pg. 12; No final accounting of the amount raised can be found. "Red Carpet Trip Given Pat Boone," *Nashville Tennessean*, December 5, 1959, pg. 3.

27. Jack Bond, "Road Builders Association Donating Boxwell Paving," *Nashville Banner*, City Edition, July 1, 1959, pg. 1; "Boxwell Grading in Final Stage," *Nashville Banner*, City Edition, July 28, 1959, pg. 13.

28. Tom Willhite (retired, Director of Support Services, 1976-1995), interview by Russ Parham, September 10, 2002, Morrison, TN; "Scouts to Test Dining Hall," *Nashville Banner*, July 6, 1960, pg. 33.

29. Creighton and Johnson claim Camp Stahlman was named for both E. B. Stahlman, Jr. and his brother James G. Stahlman. Certainly James Stahlman had been highly active in Scouting for decades, but here Creighton is incorrect. The portrait and dedication plaque in the Stahlman dining hall as well as the *Banner's* reporting on the naming ceremonies in May 1960 clearly indicate the camp was named for E. B. Stahlman, Jr. Creighton and Johnson, *Boys Will Be Men*, 148-151; Jack Bond, "E. B. Stahlman, Jr., Named 'Campaign Chairman of Year,'" *Nashville Banner*, May 26, 1960, pgs. 1, 2; Greg Tucker (retired attorney), interview by Grady Eades, June 14, 2017, Murfreesboro, TN.

30. Jimmy Joe Jackson (retired, Metro Nashville Public School principal), interview by Kerry Parker, July 16, 2002, Nashville, TN; Professionals Bruce Atkins and Bob Hensley were the men at the heart of this story. Parker remembered Atkins would say, "Grab it and growl" and then rush the platform into the woods. Kerry Parker (retired, president, Construction Management Corporation), self-interview, November 5, 1998, Gallatin, TN; James Akers, second written interview, 2017.

31. Ron Oakes interview, 2019; Jack Bond, "1,000 Attend Boxwell Dedication," *Nashville Banner*, July 11, 1960, pg. 1; Sarah Taylor, "Boxwell Dedication Takes Place in Rain," *Nashville Tennessean*, Third Edition, July 10, 1960, pg. 12C.

32. Jack Bond, "Boxwell Dedication Follows Tour," *Nashville Banner*, July 9, 1960, pg. 1; Jack Bond, "1,000 Attend Boxwell Dedication," *Nashville Banner*, July 11, 1960, pg. 1.

33. Jack Bond, "1,000 Attend Boxwell Dedication," *Nashville Banner*, July 11, 1960, pg. 1; Jack Bond, "Dedication of Boxwell Saturday," *Nashville Banner*, July 8, 1960, pg. 1; Sarah Taylor, "Boxwell Dedication Takes Place in Rain," *Nashville Tennessean*, Third Edition, July 10, 1960, pg. 12C

34. Jack Bond, "1,000 Attend Boxwell Dedication," *Nashville Banner*, July 11, 1960, pg. 1; Jack Bond, "Dedication of Boxwell Saturday," *Nashville Banner*, July 8, 1960, pg. 1;

35. "L. G. Boxwell Dies at Home; Scout Leader," *Nashville Banner*, September 24, 1960, pg. 1; "W. J. Anderson Dies; Scout Leader, VU Coach," *Nashville Banner*, September 14, 1963, pgs. 1 and 2.

36. Taylor's article also outlined a standard week for a Scout at the new location, explained the composition of the staff, and awed the readership with a simple statistic: camp dietician Martha Cardiff and her staff, living on the reservation, prepared meals for 660 people a week. Also note that Taylor, though a woman herself, follows the conventions of the period. Thus, Martha Cardiff is only identified as "Mrs. Nolan Cardiff." Nolan was Martha's husband. Sarah Taylor, "Boxwell Dedication Takes Place in Rain," *Nashville Tennessean*, Third Edition, July 10, 1960, pg. 12C; Sam McPherson, "Boxwell Reservation Polishes for Official Dedication," *Nashville Banner*, July 9, 1960, pg. 3.

37. "Boxwell—Dream Come True (editorial)," *Nashville Banner*, July 11, 1960, pg. 8.

38. It is hard to not stop and think about Assistant Camping Director David Dunbar's 1958 statement about modern camps "babying" Scouts at this point. Surely Dunbar understood that these modern conveniences were necessary to keeping a Council program healthy. Archie Crain interview, 2018.
39. Tom Flake, "Scouts Given 718-Acre Campsite Boarding on Old Hickory Lake," *Nashville Banner*, March 26, 1957, pg. 10; "Year-Around Camp Planned," *Nashville Tennessean*, June 2, 1957, pg. 19D.
40. "Scout Leaders Open Fund Appeal to Develop Boxwell," *Nashville Banner*, January 26, 1959, pg. 3; Middle Tennessee Council, Boy Scouts of America, "High Adventure for Middle Tennessee Boys: Boxwell Reservation Development Fund," 1959; "A Challenge behind New Camp Boxwell," *Nashville Tennessean*, January 28, 1959, pg. 8A.
41. Russ Parham, "RE: Old Hickory Chapter?", Message to Grady Eades, March 31, 2020, e-mail.
42. Sarah Taylor, "Boxwell Dedication Takes Place in Rain," *Nashville Tennessean*, Third Edition, July 10, 1960, pg. 12C; Kerry Parker (retired, president, Construction Management Corporation), "The Rangers," self-interview, February 16, 2000, Gallatin, TN; Perry Bruce (retired, U.S. Corps of Engineers), interview by Grady Eades, December 19, 2017, Charolette, TN; Pearl Schleicher (retired, Camp cooks), interview by Russ Parham, April 21, 1996, Mount Juliet, TN; Pearl and John Schleicher (camp cooks), interview by Kerry Parker and Russ Parham, February 10, 2001, Mount Juliet, TN; Russ Parham (former Business Manager), interview by Grady Eades, July 29, 2017, Hendersonville, TN.
43. It should be noted that Camp Stahlman operated with a youth kitchen staff and an adult cook staff. The adult cook staff prepared and cooked the meal. Youth staff cleaned the kitchen, pots and pans, dishes, and dining hall. They were responsible for simple food preparation like making toast and coffee. Pearl Schleicher interview, 1996; Pearl and John Schleicher interview, 2001; Russ Parham interview, 2017.
44. David McWilliams (retired school teacher), interview by Grady Eades, February 10, 2018, Mount Juliet, TN; Russ Parham, "Re: Trivaries," Message to Grady Eades, October 29, 2015, e-mail; Ed Mason (retired police office), interview by Grady Eades, July 18, 2018, Boxwell Reservation, Lebanon, TN. Several trucks or vans served as Trivary Truck, including a 1957 International Harvester van and a Purity Milk Truck. Russ Parham, "RE: Old Hickory Chapter?", Message to Grady Eades, March 31, 2020, e-mail.
45. David McWilliams interview, 2018; Ed Mason interview, 2018.
46. Greg Tucker interview, 2017; Russ Parham interview, 2017; Kerry Parker (retired, president, Construction Management Corporation), "The Boat Harbor," self-interview, January 1, 2001, Gallatin, TN; Jack Bond, "Boxwell Dedication Follows Tour," *Nashville Banner*, July 9, 1960, pg. 1.
47. Kerry Parker (retired, president, Construction Management Corporation), "Ford Trucks at Boxwell," self-interview, April 20, 1999, Gallatin, TN; Kerry Parker (retired, president, Construction Management Corporation), "Bruce Atkins and Ed Human," self-interview, February 12, 2000, Gallatin, TN; Kerry Parker (retired, president, Construction Management Corporation), "The Rangers," self-interview February 16, 2000, Gallatin, TN. Cots and mattresses were not always stored in the bays at the compound, but it was certainly one of the areas where these would be stored.

48. Greg Tucker interview, 2017; Kathy Howard (Retired White County teacher), interviewed by Grady Eades, June 6, 2019, Sparta, Tennessee; Vivian Connelly (former public school teacher), interview by Grady Eades, December 14, 2018, Hendersonville, TN; Ron Oakes interview, 2019.

49. Kerry Parker (retired, president, Construction Management Corporation), "1968—Roof Cement," self-interview, March 17, 2002, Gallatin, TN.

50. Kerry Parker (retired, president, Construction Management Corporation), "1960—Showerhouses," self-interview, March 27, 2002, Gallatin, TN.

51. The mis-matched, hodge podge of tents would not last much beyond the first year. The Commissary tents were usually GP-Medium tents, Russ Parham, "RE: Old Hickory Chapter?," Message to Grady Eades, March 31, 2020, e-mail. Kerry Parker (retired, president, Construction Management Corporation), "1960—Being a Scout at Camp," self-interview, February 7, 2002, Gallatin, TN; Greg Tucker interview, 2017; Jimmy Joe Jackson (retired, Metro Nashville Public School principal), interview by Kerry Parker, July 16, 2002, Nashville, TN.

52. Creighton and Johnson, *Boys Will Be Men*, 149; Faulkner Hickerson, "My Small Part in the Development of the Present Camp Boxwell at Old Hickory Lake," letter to Wilbur F. Creighton, Jr., June 19, 1982; Jack Bond, "New Building Given Boxwell by Nashville Kiwanis Club," *Nashville Banner*, July 29, 1961, pg. 4.

53. Middle Tennessee Council, Boy Scouts of America, "High Adventure for Middle Tennessee Boys: Boxwell Reservation Development Fund", 1959; Faulkner Hickerson, "My Small Part in the Development of the Present Camp Boxwell at Old Hickory Lake, letter to Wilbur F. Creighton, Jr., June 19, 1982.

54. Burkhalter-Hickerson & Associates, "Sign for Boxwell Reservation, Boy Scouts of America," artist's sketch, March 22, 1963, collection of Garry Shores.

55. Middle Tennessee Council, Boy Scouts of America, "Development Program Facilities Dedication Ceremonies" (booklet), July 11, 1974, Nashville, TN, collection of Ken Connelly; Middle Tennessee Council, Boy Scouts of America, "Executive Board Meeting Minutes," May 27, 1964; James Stahlman had offered the reward money "for the arrest and trial of any person charged with having misrepresented himself as a reporter for the *Nashville Banner* in connection with jury tampering efforts in the first trial of James R. Hoffa, head of the Teamsters Union." The men were arrested by the FBI, but because no one on the federal payroll could accept the money, Stahlman gave the reward to the Council, Elmer Stewart, "Scout Rifle Ranges Dedication Monday," *Nashville Banner*, June 30, 1966, pg. 1; Elmer Stewart, "2 Rifle Ranges Dedicated at Boxwell Reservation," *Nashville Banner*, July 5, 1966, pg. 1; Middle Tennessee Council, Boy Scouts of America, "Executive Board Meeting," May 14, 1968.

56. James Akers (real estate agent, Jim Akers & Associates), first written interview by Grady Eades, December 13, 2015, Jacksonville, FL; Kerry Parker (retired, president, Construction Management Corporation), interview by Grady Eades, September 1, 2017, Gallatin, TN; Kerry Parker (retired, president, Construction Management Corporation), "Ward Akers," self-interview, December 23, 1999, Gallatin, TN. Former Staff member Skip Dow specifically noted that he helped move lumber from a cabin in Hartsville. Skip Dow, letter to Greg Tucker, November 25, 2018; Faulkner Hickerson, "My Small Part in the Development of the Present Camp Boxwell at Old Hickory Lake, letter to Wilbur F. Creighton, Jr., June 19, 1982.

57. Kerry Parker, "Ward Akers," self-interview, 1999; Skip Dow, letter to Greg Tucker, November 25, 2018. Though the specifics are unclear, The Gladys eventually found its way back to Graceland.

58. Middle Tennessee Council, Boy Scouts of America, "Boxwell Reservation, Walling, Tennessee (Leaders' Guide)," Nashville, Tennessee, 1955, collection of Wes Oakley; Middle Tennessee Council, Boy Scouts of America, "Executive Board Meeting," September 17, 1968; Middle Tennessee Council, Boy Scouts of America, "Executive Board Meeting," March 4, 1975; Russ Parham (former Business Manager), interview by Grady Eades, July 29, 2017, Hendersonville, TN; Ken Connelly (Retired Boy Scout Professional), interview by Grady Eades, December 11, 2017, Nashville, TN.

59. Bob Steber, "Retriever Trials Draw 96 Entrants to Boxwell," *Nashville Tennessean*, October 21, 1965, pg. 34; Bob Steber, "Boxwell Eyed as Site For National Trials," *Nashville Tennessean*, February 27, 1968, pg. 18; There are no articles about the trials at Boxwell before 1963. That year C. A. "Neil" Craig, II was president of the Middle Tennessee chapter of the AKC. Craig will later become president of the Council and will be instrumental in having the third Boy Scout camp named after his father, Edwin W. Craig. The link here is intriguing. "Retriever Club Plans Show for Weekend," *Nashville Tennessean*, November 22, 1963, pg. 46.

60. Larry Green (Retired Boy Scout Professional), interviewed by Grady Eades and Russ Parham, October 13, 2015, Nashville, TN; Kerry Parker, "The Rangers," self-interview, 2000; Steve Eubank (retired, Giles County Public School teacher), self-interview, 2001, Pulaski, TN. Eubank explains how when the lake was low, cattle would wander over from Explorer Island to Camp Parnell. Larry Green suggests that a Scoutmaster regularly cut fencing at Camp Light to let cattle out as a form of protest. Scout camp should be for Scouts.

61. Middle Tennessee Council, Boy Scouts of America, "Charles E. Parish Dies," *Smoke Signals* (Council newsletter), Vol 19, No. 14: December 1975, pg. 1; Ken Connelly interview, 2017; Hal Herd, "Farm Accidents Take High Toll in Tennessee," *Nashville Tennessee*, May 24, 1959, pg. 6E; "Pulaski Rotary Starts Endowment for Scouts," *Nashville Banner*, December 14, 1960, pg. 23; "Rotarians Give Calf to Boxwell Scout Herd," *Nashville Banner*, June 29, 1961, pg. 40.

62. Larry Green interview, 2015; Kerry Parker, "The Rangers," self-interview, 2000; Steve Eubank self-interview, 2001. These ideas of extra income through farming were not limited to Boxwell. R. L. Parnell had a similar plan for walnuts at his home property. Troy and Elaine Feltner (retired Boy Scout professionals), interviewed by Grady Eades, September 23, 2016, Mount Juliet, Tennessee.

63. Larry Green interview, 2015; Kerry Parker, "The Rangers," self-interview, 2000; Ken Connelly interview, 2017.

64. Middle Tennessee Council, Boy Scouts of America, "Executive Board Meeting," September 17, 1968; Middle Tennessee Council, Boy Scouts of America, "Executive Board Meeting," September 25, 1969.

65. "Midstate Scout Unit Sets $4.6 Million Goal," *Nashville Tennessean*, November 25, 1971, pg. 63; "Midstate Scouts Report $4.3 Million Donations," *Nashville Banner*, November 9, 1972, pg. 25; Middle Tennessee Council, Boy Scouts of America, *Smoke Signals* (Council newsletter), Vol 17, No. 5: May 1972, pg. 1; Ken Connelly explained that the Buffalo River was chosen for the canoe base because Akers believed the Buffalo River

offered a better canoeing experience and that additional property could be purchased around the site, which was not true of the Narrows location. Further, Connelly stated that the Council bought the property for the new Council office for $90,000. Ken Connelly interview, 2017. The property was purchased in January 1967; Davidson County, TN, Deed Book 4093, pg. 416.

66. Camp Arrowhead in the eastern part of the Council would get some renovations as a short-term camping site as well. Middle Tennessee Council, Boy Scouts of America, "Executive Board Meeting," March 5, 1974; Ken Connelly interview, 2017; Middle Tennessee Council, Boy Scouts of America, "Executive Board Meeting," March 4, 1975.

67. "Midstate Scout Unit Sets $4.6 Million Goal," *Nashville Tennessean*, November 25, 1971, pg. 63; Middle Tennessee Council, Boy Scouts of America, *Smoke Signals* (Council newsletter), Vol 16, No. 8: Dec. 1971, pg. 8.

68. Middle Tennessee Council, Boy Scouts of America, *Smoke Signals* (Council newsletter), Vol 16, No. 8: Dec. 1971, pg. 8; "Midstate Scouts Report $4.3 Million Donations," *Nashville Banner*, November 9, 1972, pg. 25.

69. Middle Tennessee Council, Boy Scouts of America, "Middle Tennessee Council Scouts To Benefit from Recent Gifts," *Smoke Signals* (Council newsletter), Vol 17, No. 5: May 1972, pg. 1; "Midstate Boy Scouts Council Fund Campaign Passes $4 Million Mark," *Nashville Banner*, July 12, 1972, pg. 29; "Midstate Scouts Report $4.3 Million Donations," *Nashville Banner*, November 9, 1972, pg. 25; Middle Tennessee Council, *1973 Annual Report*, "Development Program Report," 1973, Nashville, Tennessee, pg. 4; Middle Tennessee Council, Boy Scouts of America, "Tribute to William C. Weaver, Jr.," *Jet Trails* (Council newsletter), Vol. 2, No. 9: May 1, 1979, pg. 1.

70. Middle Tennessee Council, Boy Scouts of America, *Smoke Signals* (Council newsletter), Vol 17, No. 5: May 1972, pg. 1; "Midstate Scout Fund Pledges Top $1 Million," *Nashville Tennessean*, January 19, 1972, pg. 23; "Boy Scout Camp Planned As E. W. Craig Memorial," *Nashville Tennessean*, March 9, 1972, pg. 43; Clara Hieronymus, "Edwin Craig had an Idea Back in '25...", *Nashville Tennessean*, October 15, 1967, Special Section "Opry Birthday," pg. 7; "Craig, Giant of Industry, Dies," *Nashville Tennessean*, June 27, 1969, pg. 1.

71. James Wharton, "Nashville Boy Scouts Open Camping Season Monday at Boxwell to Lead Several Youth Agencies in Summer Outdoor Recreational Programs," *Nashville Tennessean*, June 8, 1941, pg 13; Ken Connelly interview, 2017.

72. Kerry Parker interview, 2017; Ken Connelly interview, 2017.

73. The Craig office was dedicated in memory of William H. Wemyss and Parnell's for Richard M. Hawkins. Stahlman's office was not dedicated to anyone specific. Parnell's Trading Post was dedicated in memory of Samuel Knox Harwell, Jr.. Craig indoor rifle range was dedicated in honor of Dr. John M. Tudor. The twelve cabins at Murrey were dedicated to Dr. and Mrs. E. K. Bratton, Robert Stanley Cheek (four cabins), Dr. Walter R. Courtenay, Dr. J. T. Derryberry, Harvey and Marie Freeman, Maremont Corporation, Mr. and Mrs. William Mittlesteadt, Frank Murrey, Hugh W. Stallworth, James H. Stilz, Jr., and the Owens Family. The Health Lodge was made possible by the Hospital Corporation of America. Middle Tennessee Council, Boy Scouts of America, "Dedication Ceremonies, July 11, 1974" (program book), July 1974, Nashville, TN, Collection of Ken Connelly; Craig Dining hall was not completed for summer camp 1973 because of unusually heavy rains. Thus, the Heart of Tennessee week was in Camp Craig's basement as the

dining hall was not yet complete; Middle Tennessee Council, Boy Scouts of America, "Executive Board Meeting," March 5, 1974; Middle Tennessee Council, Boy Scouts of America, *Smoke Signals* (Council newsletter), Vol 18, No. 3: May 1973, pg.; Middle Tennessee Council, Boy Scouts of America, "Summer Camp Registrations," *Smoke Signals* (Council newsletter), Vol. 19, No. 11: May 1975, pg. 8; Middle Tennessee Council, Boy Scouts of America, "Boxwell Reservation, A Summer Camp Adventure," *Smoke Signals* (Council newsletter), Vol 19, No. 8: February 1975, pg. 1.

74. "Atlanta Scout Leaders Tour Boxwell," *Nashville Banner*, July 22, 1960, pg. 8; Jack Bond, "Florida Scouters Inspect Boxwell," *Nashville Banner*, November 11, 1963, pg. 10; The Red Cross also used Boxwell's facilities—but not its staff—for aquatics training, Jack Bond, "Water Safety Experts Heard Aquatic School," *Nashville Banner*, May 15, 1962, pg..2; Kerry Parker (retired, president, Construction Management Corporation), "First Camp School," self-interviewed, February 7, 2002, Gallatin, TN; Greg Tucker interview, 2017; John Bryant (retired, federal magistrate judge), interview by Grady Eades, July 17, 2019, Nashville, TN; Russ Parham interview, 2017; "Midstate Scout Council Model for Article," *Nashville Banner*, November 11, 1960, pg. 6.

75. "Boy Scouts Can Win Camp Prize," *Nashville Banner*, April 8, 1961, pg. 8; This basic check-in system would continue for years to come, Robert Ponder, "Chapter Five: Learning How To Ponder, Boxwell Boy Scout Reservation," excerpt from unpublished memoirs, ca. 2006; Middle Tennessee Council, Boy Scouts of America, "Executive Board Meeting," February 9, 1967; Middle Tennessee Council, Boy Scouts of America, "Executive Board Meeting," September 17, 1968; Middle Tennessee Council, Boy Scouts of America, "Executive Board Meeting," September 25, 1969; Middle Tennessee Council, Boy Scouts of America, "Executive Board Meeting," March 4, 1975.

76. Middle Tennessee Council, Boy Scouts of America, "Boxwell Reservation, Staff Manual," 1968, Nashville, TN, collection of Ed Mason; Kerry Parker (retired, president, Construction Management Corporation), "1966—Water Carnival," self-interview, June 29, 2002, Gallatin, TN; Wes Frye (retired, engineer, Metro Nashville Water), interview by Grady Eades, December 10, 2018, Springfield, TN.

77. Greg Tucker interview, 2017.

78. Jerry Barnett (retired), interview by Grady Eades and Russ Parham, November 5, 2016, Dickson, TN.

79. Middle Tennessee Council, Boy Scouts of America, *Boxwell Reservation: Bulletin for Unit Leaders*, March 22, 1960, pg. 1, collection of Robert Nicholson.

80. Chester LaFever (retired, Metro Nashville Public School principal), interview by Kerry Parker, October 24, 2001, Nashville, TN; John Bryant interview, 2009; Ken Connelly interview, 2017.

81. Ron Oakes interview, 2019. The first Program Director was actually at Rock Island in 1959 (A. D. Hancock), but it was at Old Hickory Lake that the position really took root.

82. Jimmy Joe Jackson interview, 2002; Chester LaFever interview, 2001; Perry Bruce interview, 2017.

83. Chester LaFever interview, 2001.

84. Jimmy Joe Jackson interview, 2002; Greg Tucker interview, 2017; Jerry Barnett, Russ Parham, Kerry Parker, and Charlie Ray Smith, recorded conversation by Kerry Parker, February 19, 2000, Franklin, TN.

85. Greg Tucker interview, 2017; Kerry Parker (retired, president, Construction Management Corporation), "1967—Dining Hall Program," self-interview, February 8, 2002, Gallatin, TN.
86. Steve Eubank self-interview, 2001; David McWilliams interview, 2018; Greg Tucker interview, 2017; Russ Parham interview, 2017.
87. Jimmy Joe Jackson interview, 2002; Wes Frye interview, 2018; Steve and Judi Eubank (retired, Giles County Public School teachers), "Camp Songs," self-interview, 2001, Pulaski, TN.
88. Dutch Mann (retired, high school principal, US Army), interviewed by Kerry Parker, July 18, 1996, Gallatin, TN; Dutch Mann, "Message of some importance," Message to Grady Eades, November 9, 1998, e-mail. Dutch gave slightly different years for the creation of the Gizmo, claiming either 1968 or 1971. Given that the details line up best with the Commissioner System years, 1971 seems the most reasonable.
89. Pat Bray, "Re: CD," Message to Grady Eades, October 6, 2003, e-mail; Ed Mason (retired police office), interviewed by Grady Eades, July 18, 2018, Boxwell Reservation, Lebanon, TN; John Bryant, "RE: hooten-nannies tape," Message to Grady Eades, September 17, 2003, e-mail; John Bryant interview, 2009; Wes Frye interview, 2018.
90. "Scouts to See Club on Skis," *Nashville Tennessean*, July 14, 1960, pg. 46.
91. Kerry Parker (retired, president, Construction Management Corporation), "The Boat Harbor," self-interviewed, January 1, 2001, Gallatin, TN; Ken Connelly interview, 2017; Lisa McCormack, Cindy Human, LeAnn Hillard (daughters of Ed Human), interview by Grady Eades, September 30, 2016, Mount Juliet, TN; Kathy Howard interview, 2019.
92. Russ Parham interview, 2017; Perry Bruce interview, 2017; Jerry Barnett interview, 2016.
93. Russ Parham interview, 2017; Jerry Barnett interview, 2016.
94. Ed Mason interview, 2018.
95. Dutch Mann interview, 1996.
96. Russ Parham interview, 2017; Ken Connelly interview, 2017.
97. Kathy Howard interview, 2019; Lisa McCormack, Cindy Human, LeAnn Hillard interview, 2016; Kerry Parker (retired, president, Construction Management Corporation), self-interview, "1991—Bandito is Coming," June 17, 2002, Gallatin, TN.
98. Kathy Howard interview, 2019; Vivian Connelly (former public school teacher), interview by Grady Eades, December 14, 2018, Hendersonville, TN.
99. Kathy Howard interview, 2019; Lisa McCormack, Cindy Human, LeAnn Hillard interview, 2016; Vivian Connelly interview, 2018.
100. Kathy Howard interview, 2019; Lisa McCormack, Cindy Human, LeAnn Hillard interview, 2016;
101. Ibid.
102. Occasionally, the suppers were held at the Crippled Crab. David McWilliams interview, 2018; Jimmy Joe Jackson interview, 2002; Pearl Schleicher interview, 1996.
103. Middle Tennessee Council, Boy Scouts of America, "Executive Board Meeting," April 18, 1974; Middle Tennessee Council, Boy Scouts of America, "Executive Board Meeting," October 24, 1974; Middle Tennessee Council, Boy Scouts of America, "Executive Board Meeting," March 4, 1975; Middle Tennessee Council, Boy Scouts of America, "Troop Leadership Development This Summer," *Smoke Signals* (Council newsletter), Vol 19, No. 8: February 1975, pg. 1.

104. Dick Battle, "Inner City Camping Program Set," *Nashville Banner*, July 4, 1969, pg. 42; "Camping Fun Ahead for 300," *Nashville Tennessean*, July 5, 1969, pg. 13; Kerry Parker (retired, president, Construction Management Corporation), "Inner City Boys," self-interview, March 19, 2002, Gallatin, TN.

105. John R. Mott III, "Camp Offers Retarded Week of Fun," *Tennessean*, August 7, 1972, pg. 13; John R. Mott III, "Goo Makes for Excitement," *Tennessean*, August 7, 1972, pg. 13; Russ Parham interview, 2017; Carter Eskew, "'Where Retarded Can Function'," *Tennessean*, August 19, 1973, pg. 18A.

106. Middle Tennessee Council, Boy Scouts of America, "Executive Board Meeting," April 12, 1966; "Parents, Scouts 1ˢᵗ to Weekend at Boxwell Site," *Nashville Banner*, August 30, 1960, pg. 10; "Webelos Day Offers Full Program," *Nashville Banner*, May 3, 1961, pg. 29; "SHOWANDO" Enthusiasm Grips 400 Adult Scouters," *Nashville Banner*, April 17, 1961, pg. 10.

107. The first location for Wood Badge was where the modern Craig dining hall stands today. The second location is what was the modern Site Six on Craig's lower loop. The third site—Camp Beany Elam—is in the modern location, but no pond had been built yet. The site can be seen on the map opening the chapter by the four Wood Badge emblems near the compound. "'No Greater Challenge,' Scout Leader Group Told At Boxwell," *Nashville Banner*, May 31, 1960, pg. 8; "Midtstate Wood Badge Class Now Under Way," *Nashville Banner*, August 1, 1961, pg. 4; David McWilliams interview, 2018; Wood Badge used the site primarily, but so too did Junior Leadership Development events and later Brownsea, Russ Parham, "Re: Old Hickory Chapter?" message to Grady Eades, e-mail attachment; Linda Case, "Wood Badge Course SR 726," unpublished Wood Badge history booklet, September 2005.

108. "3,000 Boy Scouts Register for Camp," *Nashville Tennessean*, June 22, 1962, pg. 7; Middle Tennessee Council, Boy Scouts of America, "Wood Badge Past Present Future," *Smoke Signals* (Council newsletter), Vol. 20, No. 2: February 1976, pg. 1; Middle Tennessee Council, Boy Scouts of America, "Executive Board Meeting," May 17, 1973.

109. Vincent Harding, Robin D. G. Kelley, and Earl Lewis, "We Changed the World, 1945-1970," in Kelly & Lewis (eds.), *To Make Our World Anew: A History of African Americans from 1880, Volume II*, paperback edition, Oxford University Press: Oxford and New York, 2005, pg. 202, 236, 239; "A History of Tennessee," *Tennessee Blue Book, 2015-2016*, Tennessee Department of State: Nashville, 2015, pg. 550.

110. Creighton and Johnson, *Boys Will Be Men*, 118, 129-130; Larry Green interview, 2015; Ron Oakes interview, 2019; "Negro Scouts Enjoy Camp in Cheatham," *Leaf-Chronicle* (Clarksville), August 11, 1955, pg. 5.

111. Kathy Dennis, "Boy Scouts Have Full Program," *Leaf-Chronicle* (Clarksville), September 20, 1957, pg. 2D; "Kathy Dennis, "Ten Troops In Girl Scout Organization," *Leaf-Chronicle* (Clarksville), September 20, 1957, pg. 42; Howard Gentry (Davidson County Criminal Court clerk), interviewed by Grady Eades, November 20, 2017, Nashville, TN; Larry Green interview, 2015; Ken Connelly interview, 2017.

112. Howard Gentry interview, 2017; Larry Green interview, 2015; Greg Tucker (retired attorney), self-interview, December 25, 2000, Murfreesboro, TN; Greg Tucker interview, 2017; "Z. Alexander Looby," *Wikipedia.org*, last updated February 26, 2020, https://en.wikipedia.org/wiki/Z._Alexander_Looby. Both Treherne and Looby will be part of the steering committee that creates the FAST Program in 1969, mentioned in the previ-

ous section. Dick Battle, "Inner City Camping Program Set," *Nashville Banner*, July 4, 1969, pg. 42.

113. Middle Tennessee Council, Boy Scouts of America, "Policy Resolution on Discrimination," December 15, 1964.

114. Howard Gentry interview, 2017; Greg Tucker self-interview, 2000; Greg Tucker interview, 2017; John Bryant interview, 2009.

115. "Howard Gentry," *Howard Gentry: Criminal Court Clerk, Metropolitan Nashville & Davidson County*, retrieved on March 12, 2020, https://ccc.nashville.gov/howard-gentry/; Joey Garrison, "Gentry: Race Looking better than last one," *Tennessean*, June 8, 2015, pgs. A1, A11; It is unclear if E. B. Stahlman really had these restrictions on his camp. It was well-known that the *Nashville Banner* was not a supporter of the civil rights protests, but no clear evidence on this particular point exists. Further, according to Greg Tucker, a Scout who was "mulatto at best" had been allowed to camp at Stahlman earlier in the year. However, he had been adopted by white parents and was, therefore, classified as white.

116. Pat Bray, "Re: Boxwell News 05-22-200," Message to Grady Eades, May 27, 2000, e-mail; Leland R. Johnson, *The Parks of Nashville: A History of the Board of Parks and Recreation*, Metropolitan Nashville and Davidson County Board of Parks and Recreation: Nashville, TN, 1986, pg. 158; Wes Frye interview, 2018.

117. Ken Connelly interview, 2017; Jerry Barnett, Russ Parham, Kerry Parker, and Charlie Ray Smith, recorded conversation by Kerry Parker, February 19, 2000, Franklin, TN.

118. "J. Percy Priest Lake: History," *US Army Corps of Engineers Nashville District website*, retrieved on March 13, 2020, https://www.lrn.usace.army.mil/Locations/Lakes/J-Percy-Priest-Lake/History/; Ken Connelly interview, 2017; Middle Tennessee Council, Boy Scouts of America, "Executive Board Meeting," March 18, 1965.

119. Greg Tucker interview, 2017; Larry Green interview, 2015.

120. Pearl Schleicher interview, 1996; Larry Green interview, 2015; Kerry Parker, "The Rangers," self-interview, 2000. "Mrs. B'"s name has created some confusion. Her name was Estelle Brewington, which was where the "B" came from originally. She later married to become Estelle Lankford, but the "Mrs. B" stuck, in part because she "always wore an old white plastic name tag, with red embossed tape, that read 'Mrs B'", Russ Parham, "Re: Old Hickory Chapter?" Message to Grady Eades, March 31, 2020, e-mail; Russ Parham interview, 2017.

121. Ken Connelly interview, 2017.

122. Middle Tennessee Council, Boy Scouts of America, "Organization and Extension Committee Report," *47th Annual Report*, February 8, 1968, Nashville, Tennessee, pg. 5.

123. The Executive Board reported that in-kind donations helped with construction costs, but costs still spiraled. Middle Tennessee Council, Boy Scouts of America, "Executive Board Meeting," March 5, 1974; Middle Tennessee Council, Boy Scouts of America, "Executive Board Meeting," October 24, 1974; Middle Tennessee Council, *Smoke Signals* (Council newsletter), Vol 16, No. 8: Dec. 1971, pg. 8; Kerry Parker (retired, president, Construction Management Corporation), "On the '72 Capital Development Campaign," interview by Grady Eades, September 1, 2017, Gallatin, TN; Middle Tennessee Council, Boy Scouts of America, "Dedication Ceremonies, July 11, 1974" (program book), July 1974, Nashville, TN, Collection of Ken Connelly; Middle Tennessee Council, Leader's Guide [booklet], 1977, Nashville, TN, Collection of Russ Parham.

124. In 1968, the Executive Board reported 4300 Scouts had attended Boxwell; in 1973, the Board reported 4,029 had participated in "long term camping." Middle Tennessee Council, Boy Scouts of America, "Executive Board Meeting," September 17, 1968; Middle Tennessee Council, Boy Scouts of America, "Executive Board Meeting," March 5, 1974; Middle Tennessee Council, Boy Scouts of America, "Summer Camp Registrations," *Smoke Signals* (Council newsletter), Vol. 19, No. 11: May 1975, pg. 8; Kerry Parker interview, 2017.

125. "Stahlman, 42 Years *Banner* Guide, Dies," *Tennessean*, May 2, 1976, pg. 1A, 8A; "E. B. Stahlman Dies at Home," *Tennessean*, June 13, 1974, pg. 1A; Pearl and John Schleicher interview, 2001.

126. Frances Meeker, "Local Scouting Executive Says No Scandal Here," *Nashville Banner*, June 11, 1974, pg. 13; Harold Lynch and Bruce Honick, "Scouts Rolls 'Padded in Past'," *Nashville Banner*, June 12, 1974, pg. 23. Years later, several District Executives admitted padding the rolls was a fairly common practice. Troy and Elaine Feltner (retired Boy Scout professionals), interviewed by Grady Eades, September 23, 2016, Mount Juliet, TN; Kerry Parker (retired, president, Construction Management Corporation), "Scout Executives," self-interviewed, February 3, 2001, Gallatin, TN; Larry Green interview, 2015.

127. "UCP Board of Directors Resigning Under Pressure," *Tennessean*, May 10, 1975, pg. 13; Larry Green interview, 2015; Ken Connelly interview, 2017.

128. Craven Crowell, "Letter Defends $44,500 Salary of Scout Exec," *Tennessean*, July 1, 1975, pgs. 1, 11; Larry Brinton, "Boy Scouts Pay Akers Family $68,000; Action is Defended," *Nashville Banner*, July 1, 1975, pgs. 1, 8. It is possible that *The Tennessean* was able to partially break the story first because both *The Tennessean* and *The Banner* were by this point owned by the same company, Gannett, and jointly shared many resources such as printing and advertising. While news and editorials were supposed to be separate, it would not be surprising if a story like this leaked from one operation to the other.

129. Larry Brinton, "Boy Scouts Pay Akers Family $68,000; Action is Defended," *Nashville Banner*, July 1, 1975, pgs. 1, 8.

130. Ibid. It is worth noting that the situation between the UCP and the MTC were not entirely comparable. The UCP was serving Nashville, while the MTC was serving a 38 county area. The Council's service area was thus considerably larger, making a larger salary more reasonable.

131. Ibid.

132. "United Way Refuses Salary Disclosures," *Tennessean*, July 2, 1975, pg. 1; "Can The Boy Scouts Enjoy Extravagance? (editorial)," *Nashville Banner*, July 2, 1975, pg. 6; Larry Brinton, "Scouts Nix Panel Look; Hope Publicity To Pass," *Nashville Banner*, July 3, 1975, pg. 1.

133. Larry Brinton, "Despite Boy Scout Policy, Akers is Partner in Top Private Camp," *Nashville Banner*, July 8, 1975, pgs. 1, 4.

134. Ibid. The Hy-Lake camp and Recreation Corp. charter listed Ward C. Akers (son) as president, Ralph Manus, (Memphis Scout executive and former Middle Tennessee professional) as Vice-president, and James V. Hunt, secretary-treasurer. Members of the board of directors included Ward E. Akers and Charles A Chalkey, Ward C. Akers' father-in-law.

135. Larry Brinton, "Akers Steps Aside During Full Review of Scout Program," *Nashville Banner*, July 11, 1975, pg. 1, 18; "Thorough Scout Probe Promised," *Tennessean*, July 13, 1975, pg. 18-A. The six committees and their chairs were Administration, John Parish, Exec. VP of Lannom manufacturing; Salary and Personnel, Webb Follin, Chairman, Synercon Corp.; Ethics, Robert C. H. Mathews, Jr., president of R. C. Mathews Contractors Inc.; Audit, William P. Gray, retired special agent of IRS intelligence division; Program, Allen M. Steele, president of Life and Casualty Insurance, Co.; and, Budget Review, Ronald S. Ligon, Executive Committee chairman of Harpeth National Bank of Franklin.
136. Ken Connelly interview, 2017; Kerry Parker, a former staff member and District Executive who had also assisted on the ranger staff, was interviewed by one of the committees at the Metro Center. Parker was asked about transporting cots to Hy-Lake, which he confirmed, as he had been involved. According to Parker, a truckload of mattresses and probably some cots had been taken to Hy-Lake. Because he had served as a professional briefly from 1972 into 1973, Parker was also asked about number padding. While he himself had not done so, he confirmed it happened. Parker was an "Akers Man," and as a result, the committee "were nice with me, appreciated it, and everybody was just nice and cordial and that was about the end of it." Kerry Parker, "Scout Executives," self-interview, 2001.
137. C. A. Craig, II, "Left 'No Stone Unturned': Scout Council President," *Tennessean*, October 5, 1975, pg. 6A; "Scout Committee Report Excerpted, Summarized," *Tennessean*, October 5, 1975, pg. 6A; Ken Connelly interview, 2017; Kathleen Gallagher, "United Way Defers Scout Report Action," *Tennessean*, October 6, 1975, pgs. 1A, 16A; Middle Tennessee Council, Boy Scouts of America, "Report of the Ethics Committee," October 1975, Nashville, TN, pg. 21, collection of Charlie Ray Smith.
138. Ken Connelly interview, 2017.
139. Ward Akers, Letter of Resignation, Executive Board Meeting, October 1, 1975.
140. Alan Carmichael, "Scout Panel Accepts Akers' Retirement," *Tennessean*, October 10, 1975, pg. 28; Ginger Kaderabek, "Scout Unit Accepts Akers' Retirement," *Nashville Banner*, State Edition, October 10, 1975, pg. 21; Middle Tennessee Council, Boy Scouts of America, "Executive Board Meeting," October 9, 1975.

Chapter 5 Endnotes

"Improvise and Adjust":

Implementing Program at Akers' Boxwell

1960-1975

1. Floyd "Q-ball" Pearce, audio recording, June 10, 1985, collection of Russ Parham.
2. Kerry Parker (retired, president, Construction Management Corporation), "Q-ball," self-interview, February 11, 2000, Gallatin, TN; "Retired Boy Scouts Exec, Ward Akers, Services Set," *Tennessean,* first edition, September 12, 1981, pg. 22; "Former Boy Scout Exec, Ward Akers, Is Dead," *Nashville Banner,* September 11, 1981, pg. CI; Floyd "Q-ball" Pearce (retired, self-employed), interview by Russ Parham, August 31, 1985, collection of Russ Parham.
3. Kerry Parker, "Q-ball"; Michael Seay (NASA Network and Security Engineer), interview by Russ Parham, December 22, 2009, Gallatin, TN.
4. The origins of the Camping and Activities Director position are a little shady. Connelly suggests the position was created as a direct result of the 1959 Capital Campaign and the enormity of the new operation. However, Richard Parker was signing letters to his Rock Island staff with a similar title in 1958. Ken Connelly (Retired Boy Scout Professional), interview by Grady Eades, December 11, 2017, Nashville, TN; Ron Oakes (retired, Council Executive), phone interview by Grady Eades, July 18, 2019, Hendersonville, TN; Richard Parker, Letter to Bob Alley, September 5, 1958, Collection of Bob Alley.
5. Every person who mentioned Manus, mentioned him as a prime example of a wonderful Scout and professional. Sadly, Manus' life was cut short, killed in a head on car accident on I-40 "on his way to Nashville for weekend exercises of the Tennessee National Guard." He was a colonel in the Guard and 48 years old. Troy and Elaine Feltner (retired Boy Scout professionals), interview by Grady Eades, September 23, 2016, Mount Juliet, Tennessee; Jimmy Joe Jackson (retired, Metro Nashville Public School principal), interview by Kerry Parker, July 16, 2002, Nashville, TN; "Service Today for Ralph Manus, Scout Executive," Tennessean, August 6, 1979, pg. 24.
6. According to John Bryant, the best way to describe Johnson was to think of *The Simpsons* character Mr. Burns and add red hair. James Johnson and Richard Parker, Letter to camp Staff ("Bulletin"), May 16, 1956, Collection of Bob Alley; Ron Oakes interview, 2019; John Bryant (retired, federal magistrate judge), interview by Grady Eades, July 17, 2019, Nashville, TN; Kerry Parker (retired, president, Construction Management Corporation), "Bruce Atkins and Ed Human," self-interview, February 12, 2000, Gallatin, TN.
7. Ken Connelly interview, 2017.
8. Jerry Barnett (retired), interview by Grady Eades and Russell Parham, November 5, 2016, Dickson, TN.
9. Bryant received $25 a week, one of the few staff members to actually receive pay his first year because he was bold enough to ask for it. Also, most of the group that went to Ely,

Minnesota got together for a "50th" Reunion trip back to Ely in 2014. John Bryant interview, 2019; Wes Frye (retired, engineer, Metro Nashville Water), interview by Grady Eades, December 10, 2018, Springfield, TN.

10. "Bruce Atkins, Scout Executive, Rites Set," *Tennessean*, December 17, 1982, pg. 44; Ken Connelly interview, 2017; John Bryant interview, 2019; James Akers, "James Akers Interview Questions," message to Grady Eades, November 18, 2017, e-mail attachment; Kerry Parker (retired, president, Construction Management Corporation), "Getting Hired," self-interview, November 5, 1998, Gallatin, TN.

11. Kerry Parker, "Getting Hired," 1998; Wes Frye interview, 2018.

12. Ken Connelly interview, 2017.

13. Kerry Parker, "Getting Hired," 1998; Kerry Parker (retired, president, Construction Management Corporation), "Riding on Wagons," self-interview, February 8, 2002, Gallatin, TN; "Bruce Atkins, Scout Executive, Rites Set," *Tennessean*, December 17, 1982, pg. 44.

14. Russ Parham (former Business Manager), interview by Grady Eades, July 29, 2017, Hendersonville, TN; Lisa McCormack, Cindy Human, LeAnn Hillard (daughters of Ed Human), interview by Grady Eades, September 30, 2016, Mount Juliet, TN; "Camp Pellissippi," *Great Smoky Mountains Council, BSA*, last update unknown, found May 25, 2020. https://www.easttnscouts.org/about/camps/pellissippi/; Ron Oakes interview, 2019.

15. Kerry Parker, "Bruce Atkins and Ed Human," 2000.

16. Steve Eubank (retired, Giles County Public School teacher), self-interview, 2001, Pulaski, TN; Michael Seay interview, 2009; Perry Bruce (retired, U.S. Corps of Engineers), interview by Grady Eades, December 19, 2017, Charolette, TN; Kerry Parker, "Bruce Atkins and Ed Human," 2000. Human was in many ways a casualty of the Akers investigation. While not directly involved in any way, Human's taste for Scouting was soured by the whole affair. At the start of 1976, he was either fired or quit. Ken Connelly says fired, while Human's daughters say quit. Perry Bruce argues there was some sort of falling out between Human and Tolbert, but never understood what the issue was. All agree that Human never returned to Scouting and never again spoke about his years with the Council. "Edwin L. Human (obituary)," *Tennessean*, May 8, 2012, pg. B7.

17. Greg Tucker (retired lawyer), interview by Grady Eades, June 14, 2017, Murfreesboro, TN; Larry Brinton, "Akers Steps Aside During Full Review of Scout Program," staff photo by Vic Cooley, *Nashville Banner*, July 11, 1975, pg. 1.

18. Kerry Parker (retired, president, Construction Management Corporation), "Crippled Crab and the Switchboard," self-interview, July 25, 2002, Gallatin, TN; Ken Connelly interview, 2017; Bob Steber, "Retriever Trials Draw 96 Entrants to Boxwell," *Nashville Tennessean*, October 21, 1965, pg. 34; Kerry Parker (retired, president, Construction Management Corporation), "Ward Akers," self-interview, December 23, 1999, Gallatin, TN.

19. Human Sisters Interview, 2016; Kerry Parker, "Ward Akers," 1999; Kerry Parker, "Bruce Atkins and Ed Human," 2000.

20. Archie Crain (retired, Atlanta Area Council Executive), interview by Grady Eades, August 23, 2018, Hendersonville, TN; Ken Connelly interview, 2017.

21. Ken Connelly interview, 2017.

22. Kathy Howard (Retired White County teacher), interview by Grady Eades, June 6, 2019, Sparta, Tennessee; Russ Parham, "Camp Stories", Message to Grady Eades, July 15, 2001, e-mail attachment; Russ Parham interview, 2017.
23. Russ Parham interview, 2017; Steve Eubank interview, 2001.
24. Chester LaFever (retired, Metro Nashville Public School principal), interview by Kerry Parker, October 24, 2001, Nashville, TN. It would be a tragic oversight to not mention the greatest Tom Parker story every told. At some point in the 1970s—no one can pinpoint it exactly—Parker was cutting tree limbs with a chain saw. For whatever reason, the chainsaw popped back and cut his throat. Parker had the presence of mind to take a handkerchief, hold it to the gash in his neck, and drive himself to the hospital. Upon arrival, he refused to remove the handkerchief until a surgical team was ready. Remarkably, he was able to sing again! Kathy Howard interview, 2019; Russ Parham, "Camp Stories", Message to Grady Eades, July 15, 2001, e-mail attachment.
25. "Luke Morris Gaffin" (obituary), *Tennessean*, September 16, 1993, pg. 5B; Steve Eubank interview, 2001; James Akers, "RE: The Passing of Al Hendrickson," e-mail to Grady Eades, August 1, 2014, "Memories of a Camper and Staff Member" attachment.
26. Jimmy Joe Jackson interview, 2002; John Bryant interview, 2019; Greg Tucker interview, 2017.
27. Perry Bruce interview, 2017; Kerry Parker, "Getting Hired," 1998; Steve Eubank interview, 2001.
28. John Bryant interview, 2019; Ron Oakes interview, 2019.
29. John Bryant interview, 2019; Ron Oakes interview, 2019; Jimmy Joe Jackson interview, 2002; Chester LaFever interview, 2001.
30. Jimmy Joe Jackson interview, 2002.
31. Jerry Barnett (retired), interview by Grady Eades and Russell Parham, November 5, 2016, Dickson, Tennessee; John Bryant interview, 2019; Wes Frye interview, 2018.
32. It is worth nothing that the wives of Nicholson, Hitt, and Jackson all served as Program Directors of Camp Murrey the same years these men were Program Directors at Parnell. Robert Nicholson, "Rev. Dr. Robert Nicholson Questionnaire," message to Grady Eades, August 4, 2018, e-mail attachment; Greg Tucker interview, 2017; LaFever left because of a change in his school contract to 12 months. Jackson's story was more personal. His son, Larry, had gotten a job working the door at a bar in Knoxville. After an altercation with a patron, he was shot and killed. His father never recovered and did not return to Boxwell. David Farrar had issues as well. He was replaced as Program Director by Eubank, but took on the Waterfront Director. He was fired that summer by Camp Director Larry Green, essentially for insubordination, and also never returned to camp. Chester LaFever interview, 2001; Troy and Elaine Feltner interview, 2016; Russ Parham interview, 2017; Larry Green (Retired Boy Scout Professional), interview by Grady Eades and Russell Parham, October 13, 2015, Nashville, TN; Ed Mason (retired police office), interview by Grady Eades, July 18, 2018, Boxwell Reservation, Lebanon, TN.
33. Bill Cyrils was actually the property's first ranger, though every indication is that he was gone by the time the camp was in operation in 1960. Archie Crain makes the assertion that in these early years, Wright operated by himself. Wright's dismissal has been attributed to several causes, including not prioritizing work requests from Akers, a disagreement with Akers over the herd of cattle and hogs, and just not a good personality match. In terms of the herds, Wright and Akers had apparently worked out some sort of share-

cropping type agreement where Wright got a cut of the profits. The details are not known, but it is suspected this was one of the sources of conflict. Kerry Parker (retired, president, Construction Management Corporation), self-interview, "The Rangers," February 16, 2000, Gallatin, TN; Archie Crain interview, 2018; Greg Tucker (retired lawyer), self-interview, December 25, 2000, Murfreesboro, Tennessee; Kerry Parker (retired, president, Construction Management Corporation), "On Coleman Wright," self-interview, September 1, 2001, Gallatin, TN.

34. Tucker says that Smith was an assistant Scoutmaster for a troop at Fort Campbell, while Parker makes the point about being a Scoutmaster at Indian Mound. Neither man was specific on dates, so both could be acrruate. Greg Tucker self-interview, 2000; Kerry Parker, "The Rangers," 2000.

35. Michael Seay interview, 2009; Human Sisters Interview, 2016; Greg Tucker interview, 2017; Wes Frye interview, 2018; Kerry Parker, "The Rangers," 2000; Steve Eubank interview, 2001.

36. The bottles were also glass, so they could be collected and recycled. The cola man came every week to pick up the used bottles from the Trading Post every week. When the Commissioner system began, Stahlman, Parnell, and Craig all also received four commissioner sites around the camp, normally fairly close to a showerhouse. Jimmy Joe Jackson interview, 2002; Russ Parham interview, 2017; Michael Seay interview, 2009; John Bryant interview, 2019; Greg Tucker interview, 2017; Kerry Parker, "Bruce Atkins and Ed Human," 2000; Jerry Barnett, Russ Parham, Kerry Parker, and Charlie Ray Smith, "Roundtable," self-interview, February 19, 2000, Franklin, TN.

37. Kerry Parker (retired, president, Construction Management Corporation), "Staff Activities," self-interview, June 18, 2002, Gallatin, TN; Michael Seay interview, 2009; John Cyril Stewart, "Report and Staff Cap," message to Grady Eades, August 20, 2015, e-mail; Russ Parham, "RE: The Staff Hat Project," message to Grady Eades, August 13, 2015, e-mail.

38. Russ Parham interview, 2017; Kerry Parker (retired, president, Construction Management Corporation), "The Boat Harbor," self-interview, January 1, 2001, Gallatin, TN; Kerry Parker (retired, president, Construction Management Corporation), "Ford Trucks at Boxwell," self-interview, April 20, 1999, Gallatin, TN; Wes Frye interview, 2018; Kerry Parker (retired, president, Construction Management Corporation), "The Brill Bus and Going into Town," self-interview, January 3, 2001, Gallatin, TN; Steve Eubank interview, 2001.

39. Michael Seay interview, 2009; Perry Bruce interview, 2017; Kerry Parker (retired, president, Construction Management Corporation), "Q-ball," self-interview, February 11, 2000, Gallatin, TN.

40. Wes Frye interview, 2018; Kerry Parker (retired, president, Construction Management Corporation), "Q-ball," self-interview, February 11, 2000, Gallatin, TN; John Bryant interview, 2019; Wes Frye, "Re: Water Carnival," message to Grady Eades, May 30, 2020, e-mail; John Bryant, "Re: Water Carnival," message to Grady Eades, May 30, 2020, e-mail; Kerry Parker (retired, president, Construction Management Corporation), self-interview, June 29, 2002, Gallatin, TN; Jerry Barnett (retired), interview by Grady Eades and Russell Parham, November 5, 2016, Dickson, TN; Jimmy Joe Jackson interview, 2002.

41. Ed Mason interview, 2018; Claus "Dutch" Mann, "Untitled," message to Grady Eades, October 18, 1998, e-mail.
42. Michael Seay interview, 2009; Kerry Parker (retired, president, Construction Management Corporation), "The Boat Harbor," self-interview, January 1, 2001, Gallatin, TN.
43. Wes Frye interview, 2018; Milton "Mac" McKinney, "Camp Story Possibility," message to Grady Eades, February 19, 2002, e-mail. The two staff in question were Milton "Mac" McKinney and Milton Clark. McKinney also points out that Norman Patterson was, unbeknownst to either Milton, in the woods ready to shoot the young man if they were unable to talk him down.
44. Russ Parham, "Camp Murrey," message to Grady Eades, April 27, 2001, e-mail attachment; Robert Ponder, "Chapter Five: Learning How To Ponder, F-Troop, Guilty By Association," excerpt from unpublished memoirs, ca. 2006. Terry recalls Kerry Parker and Charlie Ray Smith on the right and left bumper, respectively, of his 1955 Chevrolet, Terry Rodgers, "Re: Fw: Boxwell News Attachments," message to Grady Eades, February 11, 2000; Steve Eubank interview, 2001; John Bryant interview, 2019; Wes Frye interview, 2018; George Beaver, "Re: Your Bio," message to Grady Eades, May 8, 2000, e-mail; Terry Rodgers, "Re: Fw: Boxwell News Attachments," message to Grady Eades, February 9, 2000; Jerry Barnett, Russ Parham, Kerry Parker, and Charlie Ray Smith, "Roundtable," self-interview, February 19, 2000, Franklin, TN.
45. Greg Tucker interview, 2017; Kerry Parker (retired, president, Construction Management Corporation), "Ford Trucks at Boxwell," self-interview, April 20, 1999, Gallatin, TN.

Chapter 6 Endnotes

The Willhite Era:

Boxwell Reservation at Old Hickory Lake

1976-1996

1. Russ Parham suggests that Willhite may not even have known the deductions were coming himself. The call to go home and follow with a meeting on Sunday may have been to give him time to find out what exactly was happening. Russ Parham (former Business Manager), interview by Grady Eades, July 29, 2017, Hendersonville, TN; Jim Barr (retired, Metro Public Schools), first interview by Grady Eades, June 13, 2016, Fairview, TN; Perry Bruce (retired, U.S. Corps of Engineers), interview by Grady Eades, December 19, 2017, Charlotte, TN.
2. Jim Barr, first interview, 2016; Russ Parham interview, 2017. According to Tom Willhite, it was Jim Mauldin and Jerry Keathley who opted for the deduction in the

checks. Tom Willhite (retired, Boy Scouts of America, Middle Tennessee Council, Reservation Director), interview by Russ Parham, September 20, 2002, Morrison, TN.

3. The position in question has gone through several iterations. It was Director of Camping when Human left the post. It later became Director of Camping and Activities before arriving at Director of Support Services. Tom Willhite interview, 2002.

4. Jim Barr, first interview, 2016.

5. Eubank did not stay gone long. Council President Jimmy Stevens specifically came to Eubank and asked him to attend a meeting after the Scoutmasters Supper with Council Executive Hershel Tolbert. Tolbert and Eubank had an "intense" exchange as Tolbert questioned Eubank's loyalty to Scouting and the Council. For Tolbert, the fact that Eubank had left the ranks of the professionals and then quit here showed he was not reliable. Fortunately, with Stevens and Davy Crockett District Commissioner Steve Curry, the differences were ironed out and Eubank completed the summer as Program Director. Eventually, all would be forgiven as Eubank moved into the Wood Badge staff and eventually became Scoutmaster. Jim Barr, first interview, 2016. Steve Eubank (retired, Giles County Public Schools), (unrecorded) phone interview by Grady Eades, September 28, 2020, Pulaski, TN.

6. Jim Barr, first interview, 2016.

7. Russ Parham interview, 2017.

8. Claus "Dutch" Mann was one of the older staff who walked that day, but even Mann admitted, he was only out "for four or five days" before he too returned. Dutch Mann (retired school principal), interview by Kerry Parker, July 18, 1996, Gallatin, TN.

9. This interview from Willhite is a story in itself. On Saturday, September 21, 2013 four former staff members—Kerry Parker, Charlie Ray Smith, Michael Seay, and Russ Parham—visited Willhite at his home in Morrison, TN, near Sparta. The four were on an annual fall trip they had been taking for many years. They chose to visit Willhite as part of their tour. The group sat down at Willhite's home, chatting and laughing while Parham and Seay tinkered with recording Willhite on a video camera. They captured several stories that night and the recording itself saw Willhite smirking during most of the recording. He found the whole process bemusing, but he was entertaining Russell's desire to make the recording, so tight was the bond between the two men. The group left the house that night with good memories and a recording. The next morning, not twelve hours later, Willhite suffered a heart attack and died while getting ready for church. Tom Willhite interview, 2013.

10. James Patterson, *Restless Giant: The United States from Watergate to* Bush v. Gore, Oxford University Press: New York, 2005, pgs. 1-12.

11. Patterson, *Restless Giant*, 96-97; Robert V. Remini, *A Short History of the United States: From the Arrival of Native American Tribes to the Obama Presidency*, Harper Perennial: New York, 2008, pgs. 288-289.

12. Paul S. Boyer, *American History: A Very Short Introduction*, Oxford University Press: New York, 2012, pg. 130; Eric Foner, *The Story of American Freedom*, W.W. Norton & Company: New York, 1998, pgs. 317-319; Patterson, *Restless Giant*, pg. 96-97.

13. Patterson, *Restless Giant*, 148; Foner, *Story of American Freedom*, 320-322.

14. Fathers were also protected under the Family Medical Leave Act as well. Patterson, *Restless Giant*, 269-270; Robin D. G. Kelley & Earl Lewis (eds)., *To Make Our World Anew, Volume II: A History of African Americans from 1880*, Oxford University Press:

New York, 2000, pgs. 287-297; Boyer, *American History: A Very Short Introduction*, 123.

15. Wills, *Boy Scouts of America*, pgs. 172, 174, 178

16. Ibid., pgs. 196.

17. Ibid., pgs. 199, 204, 208.

18. This *Rolling* Stone article is a deep dive into the BSA's policy toward gay Scouts and Leaders and how homosexuality and pedophilia have often been linked together. As the two have been tied together for so long, the article includes a detailed discussion on youth protection. Journalist Patrick Boyle's 1994 book *Scout's Honor* takes "a comprehensive look at sexual abuse in the Boy Scouts in the 1970s and 1980s." Chuck Sudetic, "The Struggle for the Soul of the Boy Scouts," *Rolling Stone*, Iss. 844/845, July 6-20, 2000, pgs. 110, 152.

19. Further investigation showed that Trimble was not only strangled, but there were semen traces on her body. "Time Trial in Trimble Case," *The Tennessean*, February 25, 1996, pg. 43.

20. Jim Henry, "Ex-Scoutmaster admits fondling 2 Boy Scouts," *The Tennessean*, Second edition, April 25, 1985, Pg. A1; Jim Henry, "Ex-Scout aide handed 5 years in fondling case," *The Tennessean*, Second edition, May 24, 1985, Pg. C1; John Dempsey, "Police hope to ID photos from sex abuse case," *The Tennessean*, March 20, 1992, pg. B5; John Dempsey, "Rape suspect's computer seized; porn link found," *The Tennessean*, March 21, 1992, pg. B1; Jim East, "Rice gets 30 years for raping Scout," *The Tennessean*, April 21, 1992, pg. B1; Aubrey Harwell, "Re: Youth Protection History," message to Grady Eades, August 11, 2021, e-mail attachment.

21. Ethan Draddy, "BSA Youth Protection Timeline," last modified October 30, 2012, https://www.slideshare.net/EthanDraddy/bsa-youth-protectiontimeline; Boy Scouts of America, "100 Years of Youth Protection," last modified January 31, 2014, https://www.scoutingnewsroom.org/youth-protection/100-years-of-enhancing-efforts-to-protect-youth/; Larry Brown, "[no subject]," message to Grady Eades, August 3, 2021, e-mail; Sudetic, "The Struggle for the Soul of the Boy Scouts," 152.

22. Sudetic, "The Struggle for the Soul of the Boy Scouts," 106, 152.

23. "Fishing Pros To Give Scouts Instructions," *Tennessean*, April 3, 1976, pg. 25; Kathleen Gallagher, "Midstate Boy Scouts Muster Amid Drum Roll, Musket Fire," *Tennessean*, April 4, 1976, pg. 1 and 3; "Scouts 'Fight Battle' In Bicentennial Fete," *Nashville Banner*, City Edition, April 5, 1976, pg. 16; Middle Tennessee Council, Boy Scouts of America, "Executive Board Meeting," April 8, 1976.

24. Russ Parham interview, 2017; Middle Tennessee Council, Boy Scouts of America, "Executive Board Meeting," December 19, 1975; Middle Tennessee Council, Boy Scouts of America, "Executive Board Meeting," October 13, 1976; Middle Tennessee Council, Boy Scouts of America, "Executive Board Meeting," June 2, 1976.

25. Fortunately, Camp Murrey was allowed to keep its hot water heaters. Further, Parham confirms the mid-summer closure with only three or four people remaining on the reservation during the July 4th week. Camp resumed for two more weeks to finish the summer. Middle Tennessee Council, Boy Scouts of America, "Executive Board Meeting," December 19, 1975; Middle Tennessee Council, Boy Scouts of America, "Executive Board Meeting," June 2, 1976; Russ Parham, "Re: July 4th Confirmation," message to Grady Eades, July 29, 2021, e-mail.

26. Middle Tennessee Council, "E. L. Hershel Tolbert Named New Scout Executive," *Smoke Signals* (Council newsletter), Vol 20, No. I: January 1976, pg. I; Tom Willhite interview, 2002; Phil West, "Funds Ok'd for Scout Camp Water," *Nashville Banner,* ·City edition, December 1976, pg. 8; Middle Tennessee Council, Boy Scouts of America, "Executive Board Meeting," December 2, 1976; Middle Tennessee Council, Boy Scouts of America, "Executive Board Meeting," September 14, 1976; Middle Tennessee Council, "Open House, Dedication To Be Held," *Jet Trails (Council newsletter),* Vol. I, No. 2: November 1976, pg. I.

27. Middle Tennessee Council, Boy Scouts of America, "Executive Board Meeting," December 2, 1976; Nat Caldwell, "Harpeth Narrows Added to State Site," *Tennessean,* July 14, 29; Ken Connelly (Retired Boy Scout Professional), interviewed by Grady Eades, December 11, 2017, Nashville, Tennessee; Middle Tennessee Council, *Leader's Guide,* 1977; Middle Tennessee Council, *Leader's Guide,* 1978; Middle Tennessee Council, *Leader's Guide,* 1979.

28. Russ Parham interview, 2017; Kerry Parker (retired, president, Construction Management Corporation), self-interviewed, "1986—Green Bar Bill," June 18, 2002, Gallatin, TN; Jason Bradford (construction), interview by Grady Eades, April 2, 2018, Lebanon, TN; Tom Willhite (retired, Boy Scouts of America, Middle Tennessee Council, Reservation Director), interview by Russ Parham, September 20, 2002, Morrison, TN.

29. Jason Bradford (construction), interview by Grady Eades, April 2, 2018, Lebanon, TN. In terms of staff pay, there was an old camp story that was passed down through the years. When Willhite started, young first year staff literally worked for nothing. Willhite raised that first year pay to Slush Puppy tokens one summer and eventually to $10 a week. First year staff was part of the "$18.74 Club," so named for the two week check of $10 a week after taxes were taken out. The $18.74 is made up amount for illustration purposes.

30. Andy Whitt (Brown-Forman Controller) interview by Grady Eades, March 3, 2018, Tullahoma, TN; Michael Allen (Math Professor, Tennessee Tech University), interview by Grady Eades, July 12, 2018, Lebanon, TN.

31. Lance Ussery (Owner, Upper Edge Adventures), interview by Grady Eades, February 12, 2019, Lebanon, TN; James "Web" Webster (self-employed), interview by Grady Eades, June 7, 2003, Gallatin, TN; Ken Connelly (Retired Boy Scout Professional), interviewed by Grady Eades, December 11, 2017, Nashville, Tennessee. Willhite's Business Manager Russ Parham used this approach to get Willhite to raise staff pay for young first year staff from literally nothing their first year to Slush Puppy tokens to eventually $10 a week.

32. Tom Willhite interview, 2002; Kerry Parker (retired, president, Construction Management Corporation), self-interviewed, "1977—Making the Fortune," March 24, 2002, Gallatin, TN.

33. Tom Willhite interview, 2002; A company managed by former staff member Kerry Parker was responsible for the main showerhouse at Craig while former staff member Joe Harper's company Custom Building Services built the loop showerhouses. It is unknown who was responsible for the washstands and the rifle range. Kerry Parker, self-interviewed, "1977—Making the Fortune," 2002; Middle Tennessee Council, *Leader's Guide,* 1976, Nashville, Tennessee; Middle Tennessee Council, *Leader's Guide,* 1978, Nashville, Tennessee; Middle Tennessee Council, *1982 Summer Camp Leader's Guide,* 1982, Nashville, Tennessee; Middle Tennessee Council, *1983 Summer Camp Leader's Guide,* 1983,

Nashville, Tennessee; Middle Tennessee Council, *1990 Summer Camp Leader's Guide*, 1990, Nashville, Tennessee.

34. Kerry Parker (retired, president, Construction Management Corporation), self-interviewed, "1985—Covering Ditches," June 18, 2002, Gallatin, TN; Roundtable:: Mike Brown, David Dotson, John Estes, and John Walker, interview by Grady Eades, June 22, 2002, Nashville, TN.

35. Middle Tennessee Council, *1981 Summer Camp Leader's Guide*; Middle Tennessee Council, Boy Scouts of America, "Executive Board Meeting," March 11, 1976; Tom Willhite interview, 2002; Bruce Dobie, "Shelby Park lodge to get new home," *Nashville Banner*, January 4, 1984, pgs. A1, A6.

36. Legend has it that the staff made a plaque that read "Courtesy of Slave Labor" and placed said plaque in the ground at the site. It was later removed. Tom Willhite interview, 2002; Roundtable:: Mike Brown, David Dotson, John Estes, and John Walker, 2002.

37. The first new large cabin at Murrey was dedicated in honor of Jim Gray. The second was paid for by long-time volunteer Webb Follin, who specifically requested the cabin be named for Willhite. The Tent Shed was made possible by John Bouchard III and both the Craig Rifle Range and the Shotgun range were made possible by the Maddox Family for Tom and Margaret Maddox. The Quasi-Campaign also ultimately built a shelter like the Wood Badge Shed at Rock Island as well. Tom Willhite interview, 2002.

38. Raking gravel may sound remarkably anal, but consider that the Reservation's pay phones were located at the Crab. In the days before cell phones, both Scouts and Staff used these phones to call loved ones. Large groups could congregate and large groups of boys can easily make a mess of gravel. Tom Willhite interview, 2002.

39. Two side notes. First, the Nashville Scottish Rite Foundation also donated the flag poles at the Jet Potter Center in 1977. Second, in 1980 the "Soveriegn Grand Inspector General for the Scottish Rite Bodies for the State of Tennessee" was Andrew Benedict, Jr., who was also the President of the Middle Tennessee Council at the time. "Eleanor Grizzard Gateway," *Clarksville Leaf-Chronicle*, July 11, 1976, pg. 4-A; "Boxwell Reservation to Fly Three Flags," *Tennessean*, November 11, 1980, pg. 4A; Middle Tennessee Council, "William C. Weaver, Jr. Memorial Amphitheater Dedication Held," *Jet Trails (Council newsletter)*, November/December 1985, pg. 1; Joanne Wiklund, "1,200 campers attend Scout weekend," *Nashville Banner*, second edition, November 8, 1985, pg. Neighborhood 5.

40. Tom Willhite interview, 2002.

41. Tom Willhite interview, 2002; John Hickman (EMT Tristar Skyline Medical Center), interview by Grady Eades, Date, Gallatin, TN, November 15, 2018; Lance Ussery interview, 2019.

42. "Auction (want Ad)," *Tennessean*, first edition, December 8, 1978, pg 61; Middle Tennessee Council, "Want List: Camp Needs," *Jet Trails (Council newsletter)*, Vol. 2, No. 17: November-December, 1980, pg. 1; Middle Tennessee Council, "Camp Auction Items Needed," *Jet Trails (Council newsletter)*, Vol. 2, No. 17: November-December, 1980, pg. 1.

43. Middle Tennessee Council, Boy Scouts of America, "Executive Board Meeting," December 2, 1976; Middle Tennessee Council, *1983 Summer Camp Leader's Guide*; Middle Tennessee Council, *1995 Summer Camp Leader's Guide*; Middle Tennessee Council, *Leader's Guide*, 1976; Middle Tennessee Council, *1990 Summer Camp Leader's Guide*.

44. Middle Tennessee Council, *1984 Summer Camp Leader's Guide*; Middle Tennessee Council, *1985 Summer Camp Leader's Guide*; Middle Tennessee Council, "Lad and Dad Overnight Camp," *Jet Trails (Council newsletter)*, Vol. I, No. 3: March-April, 1977, pg. 3; Cub weekends during summer would continue all the way up until the creation of Cub-World. 1995 was the last summer of Cub overnight weekends during summer camp.
45. Michael Seay (NASA Network and Security Engineer), interview by Russ Parham, December 22, 2009, Gallatin, TN.
46. Russ Parham interview, 2017.
47. 1991 and 1992 were the only years that Parham did not see an increase, an anamoly he attributed to the Gulf War. *Ibid.*
48. Russ Parham interview, 2017; Kerry Parker (retired, president, Construction Management Corporation), self-interviewed, "1995—Merit Badge Paperwork," July 5, 2002, Gallatin, TN; Carl Adkins (retired, Director of Support Services, Middle Tennessee Council, Boy Scouts of America), interviewed by Grady Eades, November 15, 2017, Lebanon, TN.
49. Russ Parham interview, 2017; Larry Green (Retired Boy Scout Professional), interview by Grady Eades and Russell Parham, October 13, 2015, Nashville, TN; As the *Jet Trails* explained in 1983, the council had a 1.6 million dollar budget. 60% of that number came from the United Way and "activity income," while the remaining 40% came from SME. Middle Tennessee Council, "SME Goal to Raise $735,000," *Jet Trails (Council newsletter)*, January-February 1983, pg. I.
50. Nashville graphic artist Chuck Creasy was responsible for most of the Annual Reports in these years. He was able to get the reports donated, costing the Council nothing. In return, he was given free reign with the reports and allowed to create his own designs. The "Boxwell" logo used by Virtual Boxwell in later years was a modification of a Creasy design. Middle Tennessee Council, *1978 Annual Report*, 1978, Nashville, Tennessee; Middle Tennessee Council, *1986 Annual Report*, 1986, Nashville, Tennessee.
51. Adell Crowe, "Things Changing to Good For Scouts at Boxwell," *Tennessean*, July 30, 1976, pg. 17.
52. Jerry Barnett (retired), interviewed by Grady Eades and Russell Parham, November 5, 2016, Dickson, TN; Russ Parham interview, 2017.
53. Jason Bradford interview, 2018.
54. Kerry Parker (retired, president, Construction Management Corporation), self-interviewed, "1993—Dining Hall Program," July 27, 2002, Gallatin, TN; Jim Barr (retired, Metro Public Schools), second interview by Grady Eades, July 13, 2016, Fairview, TN; The first summer after instituting cafeteria style, the "rest period" disappeared from the leaders' guide, Middle Tennessee Council, *Leader's Guide*, 1977.
55. Middle Tennessee Council, "Why Boy Scouts Need Summer Camp," *Jet Trails (Council newsletter)*, July-August 1983, pg. 2.
56. Middle Tennessee Council, "Boxwell Sites Available," *Jet Trails (Council newsletter)*, Vol. I, No. 2: January-February 1977, pg. 3; Trent Craig, "Re: Camp Promotions," Message to Grady Eades, June 22, 2020, e-mail; Middle Tennessee Council, *Boxwell Reservation* (promotional video), 1987. It is worth noting that promotional media were not new. There was a promotional film made in 1966/1967 titled "Invitation to Adventure," which served a similar purpose, though it is unclear how it was used.
57. Middle Tennessee Council, "Camp," *Jet Trails (Council newsletter)*, Vol. I, No. 5: November-December, 1977, pg. 8.

58. Middle Tennessee Council, "Council order of the Arrow Ordeal," *Jet Trails (Council newsletter)*, Vol. I, No. 4: May-June, 1977, pg. II; Willhite also used a bull crew at the end of camp for clean-up, or perhaps taking down tents if take-down was rained out. Each crew was only four or five staff member. Willhite paid a reduced fee—not regular salary—for the week and treated the crew to pizza at the end of the week. Tom Willhite interview, 2002.

59. George Beaver, "RE: The Staff Hat Project," message to Grady Eades, August 14, 2015, e-mail; Russ Parham, "RE: The Staff Hat Project," message to Grady Eades, August 13, 2015, e-mail; Russ Parham interview, 2017.

60. Tom Willhite interview, 2002; Lance Ussery interview, 2019.

61. Middle Tennessee Council, "Boxwell Reservation—Summer 1977," *Jet Trails (Council newsletter)*, Vol. I, No. 2: November 1976, pg. 3; "Boy Scout Camp Offers New Sports," *Nashville Banner*, City Edition, May 20, 1977, pg. 10.

62. Middle Tennessee Council, *Leader's Guide*, 1977; Middle Tennessee Council, *Leader's Guide*, 1978; Middle Tennessee Council, *Leader's Guide*, 1979; Middle Tennessee Council, *1980 Summer Camp Leader's Guide*; Middle Tennessee Council, *1981 Summer Camp Leader's Guide*; Middle Tennessee Council, *1982 Summer Camp Leader's Guide*; Middle Tennessee Council, *1983 Summer Camp Leader's Guide*; Middle Tennessee Council, *1984 Summer Camp Leader's Guide*.

63. Middle Tennessee Council, *Leader's Guide*, 1977; Middle Tennessee Council, *Leader's Guide*, 1978; Lance Ussery interview, 2019; Middle Tennessee Council, *1982 Summer Camp Leader's Guide*; John Hickman interview, 2018.

64. Middle Tennessee Council, "Calling Webelos and Fathers to Boxwell Webelos Weekend," *Jet Trails (Council newsletter)*, Vol. I, No. 3: March-April, 1977, pg. I; Middle Tennessee Council, "Webelos Weekend 1978," *Jet Trails (Council newsletter)*, Vol. 2, No. 3: May-June, 1978, pg. 3.

65. Middle Tennessee Council, "Lad and Dad Overnight Camp," *Jet Trails (Council newsletter)*, Vol. I, No. 3: March-April, 1977, pg. 3; For the program staff, this made for a long Saturday, though some areas did not have much to do as Cubs did not do much pioneering and conservation work. For the non-program staff, such as the Trading Post and kitchen, this meant weeks of back to back work with no time-off and no extra pay. Business Manager Russ Parham tried to get these staffs into Gallatin to wash clothes and even provided them with an appreciation dinner as there was no extra compensation for those who did the long weekends, Russ Parham interview, 2017; Middle Tennessee Council, *1978 Annual Report*, 1978, Nashville, Tennessee; Middle Tennessee Council, "Lad and Dad Overnight Camp," *Jet Trails (Council newsletter)*, Vol. I, No. 3: March-April, 1977, pg. 3; Middle Tennessee Council, "Dad and Lad Overnight 1979," *Jet Trails (Council newsletter)*, Vol. 2, No. 8: March-April, 1979, pg. 2.

66. Part of the rationale for the move to Tuesday night was because Willhite realized there were fewer complaints if the dinner were held earlier in the week. Tommy George, "Scoutmasters Share Meal, Ideas," *Nashville Banner*, July 9, 1980, pg. 64; Tom Willhite interview, 2002; Middle Tennessee Council, *Leader's Guide*, 1977; Middle Tennessee Council, *Leader's Guide*, 1979.

67. Leaders' Guides are the best way to see how stable the merit badges offerings were. Generally, the slate was: Archery, Basketry, Bugling, Camping, Canoeing, Cooking, Emergency Preparedness, Environmental Science, First Aid, Fish and Wildlife Management, Fishing,

Forestry, Hiking, Indian Lore, Insect Life, Lifesaving, Leatherwork, Mammals, Motor-boating, Nature, Orienteering, Personal Fitness, Pioneering, Reptile Study, Rifle and Shotgun Shooting, Reptile Study, Rowing, Safety, Signalling, Soil and Water, Swimming, Weather, Wilderness Survival, Woodcarving. Nine Skill Awards were taught at camp: Citizenship, First Aid, Hiking, Camping, Cooking, Swimming, Environment, Conservation, Physical Fitness. Safety is cut in 1978 and re-added in the early 1990s; Athletics is added in 1978. Space Exploration is added in 1983. Hiking and Cooking are dropped and Backpacking added in 1985. Signalling as a merit badge was discontinued in 1991. Middle Tennessee Council, *Leader's Guide*, 1977; Middle Tennessee Council, *Leader's Guide*, 1978; Middle Tennessee Council, *1983 Summer Camp Leader's Guide*; Middle Tennessee Council, *1985 Boxwell Reservation Leader's Guide*; US Scouting Service Project, "Signaling," last updated August 24, 2018, http://www.usscouts.org/mb/Old/mb141.asp.

68. Middle Tennessee Council, "Boxwell Camp Staff," *Jet Trails (Council newsletter)*, Vol. 2, No. 1: January-February, 1978, pg. 4; Middle Tennessee Council, "Council Up-Coming Events," *Jet Trails (Council newsletter)*, January-February 1983, pg. 8; Middle Tennessee Council, "Camp Staff for Boxwell," *Jet Trails (Council newsletter)*, November/December 1985, pg. 3; Russ Parham interview, 2017.

69. There are conflicting stories about Ragsdale's arrival at Boxwell. While both Barr and Parham agree that Ragsdale showed up completely unannounced once camp had started, few of their details match up from there. Barr tells the story that Ragsdale was in the midst of his divorce, simply looking for a place to stay, which brought him to Boxwell. Parham recalls Ragsdale showing up in a jeep with a rag in the gas tank, both his wife and his infant son in the vehicle with him. Russ Parham interview, 2017; Jim Barr, first interview, 2016; Tom Willhite interview, 2002.

70. Jim Barr, first interview, 2016.

71. Russ Parham interview, 2017; Jim Barr, first interview, 2016; Tom Willhite interview, 2002; Tom Roussin (former Texas School Teacher), interview by Grady Eades, July 18, 2003, Gallatin, TN.

72. Russ Parham interview, 2017; Tom Roussin interview, 2003; Jerry Barnett interview, 2016.

73. Middle Tennessee Council, "Summer Camp," *Jet Trails (Council newsletter)*, Vol. 2, No. 5: September-October, 1978, pg. 4; Jim Barr, first interview, 2016; Russ Parham interview, 2017.

74. Russ Parham interview, 2017.

75. Jim Barr, first interview, 2016.

76. Perry Bruce interview, 2017.

77. Jerry Barnett interview, 2016.

78. Amusingly, it was difficult to know for certain who the Three Musketeers were here. It was potentially Barr, Ragsdale, and Barnett. It could also have been Barnett, Ragsdale, and Willhite. Perry Bruce interview, 2017; Jerry Barnett interview, 2016; Russ Parham interview, 2017; Jim Barr, first interview, 2016.

79. Jim Barr, first interview, 2016; Russ Parham interview, 2017; Jason Bradford interview, 2018; Ron Bailey interview, 2009; Tom Willhite interview, 2002.

80. Andy Whitt relayed that Ragsdale would often come down to the campfire area when Whitt and others were building the campfire. He would sit and chat while the staff

worked and occasionally he would relate stories of Vietnam experience. Jerry Barnett interview, 2016; Andy Whitt (Brown-Forman Controller) interview by Grady Eades, March 3, 2018, Tullahoma, TN.

81. Jason Bradford interview, 2018; Roundtable:: Mike Brown, David Dotson, John Estes, and John Walker, interview, 2002; Jerry Barnett interview, 2016.

82. Russ Parham interview, 2017; Michael Allen interview, 2018; Jim Barr, first interview, 2016; Kerry Parker (retired, president, Construction Management Corporation), self-interviewed, "1985–12Point Closing," June 18, 2002, Gallatin, TN.

83. Andy Whitt interview, 2018; Jim Barr, first interview, 2016; Michael Allen interview, 2018; Web Webster interview, 2003; Kerry Parker (retired, president, Construction Management Corporation), self-interviewed, "1985—Burning Flag Closing," March 27, 2002, Gallatin, TN; Ron Bailey interview, 2009.

84. Mike Brown (former guidance counselor Pope John Paul II High School), (unrecorded) phone interview with Grady Eades, October 2020, Hendersonville, TN; Web Webster, "RE: Ragsdale and Closing Camp Stahlman," message to Grady Eades, October 12, 2020, e-mail.

85. Web Webster, "RE: Ragsdale and Closing Camp Stahlman," message to Grady Eades, October 12, 2020, e-mail; Andy Whitt, "RE: Ragsdale and Closing Camp Stahlman," message to Grady Eades, October 12, 2020, e-mail; Mike Brown interview, 2020; John Estes, "RE: Barnett and Closing Camp," message to Grady Eades, October 13, 2020, e-mail; John Walker, "RE: Barnett and Closing Camp," message to Grady Eades, October 13, 2020, e-mail.

86. Jim Barr, first interview, 2016; Jerry Barnett interview, 2016; Tom Willhite interview, 2002.

87. Tom Willhite interview, 2002; Lance Ussery interview, 2019; Middle Tennessee Council, "Green Bar at Boxwell June 15- June 21," *Jet Trails* (Council newsletter), May/June, 1986, pg. 1; Roundtable:: Mike Brown, David Dotson, John Estes, and John Walker, interview, 2002.

88. Middle Tennessee Council, "Webelos Camp at Boxwell '84," *Jet Trails (Council newsletter)*, March-April1984, pg. 2; Middle Tennessee Council, "Cub Scout Fun at Camp," *Jet Trails (Council newsletter)*, May-June1984, pg. 7; Middle Tennessee Council, "John Parish to Chair Council Strategic Planning Effort," *Jet Trails (Council newsletter)*, May - June 1985, pg. 1; Middle Tennessee Council, "Webelos Camp July 20-23," *Jet Trails (Council newsletter)*, May/June, 1986, pg. 2

89. Middle Tennessee Council, "Council Offers First Outdoors Training for Webelos Leaders," *Jet Trails (Council newsletter)*, Vol. 2, No. 20: September-October, 1981, pg. 2; Middle Tennessee Council, "1984 Webelos Outdoor Experience," *Jet Trails (Council newsletter)*, July-August 1984, pg. 2

90. Tom Willhite interview, 2002, Morrison, TN; Lance Ussery interview, 2019; Billy Walker (owner, Walker Chevrolet), interview by Kerry Parker, November 18, 2003, Franklin, TN; John Walker, "Re: Write up on Billy," message to Grady Eades, August 17, 2021, e-mail.

91. Future ranger Bill Freeman of Nashville Electric Service provided a bucket truck to put up much of the high course elements. Tom Willhite interview, 2002; Lance Ussery interview, 2019; Middle Tennessee Council, *1985 Boxwell Reservation Leader's Guide*; Middle Tennessee Council, *1986 Boxwell Reservation Leader's Guide*; John Hickman inter-

view, 2018. Future ranger Bill Freeman of Nashville Electric Service provided a bucket truck to put up much of the high course elements.

92. The tower was named for long time C.O.P.E. staff member and early director Al Hendrickson in September 1994. Hendrickson had been load master with the Air Guard at Nashville Airport. He was retired by this point, but his organizational skills and strong will were assets in C.O.P.E.'s early years. For many years, the claim was that the tower was the tallest structure in Wilson County. Lance Ussery interview, 2019; John Hickman interview, 2018; Middle Tennessee Council, *1990 Annual Report,* 1990, Nashville, Tennessee; Middle Tennessee Council, *1995 Boxwell Reservation Leader's Guide.*

93. Brownsea was part of much larger push in the Middle Tennessee Council, known as the "All Out for Scouting" program. All Out for Scouting was a national program written in 1969 by William "Green Bar Bill" Hillcourt. Brownsea II was a part of that program, but only a part. The program was designed to be an eighteen month "action packed, fun filled, outdoor Scouting program." As Russ Parham explained, "The National BSA introduced the 'All Out For Scouting' and returned Scouting to a Scout Skills emphasis. But by this time most adults had to be re-taught this approach." Thus, while All Out For Scouting kicked off with "Operation Launch" in November 1977--a big publicity event at the National Life Building in Nashville—training was going to be critical part of the whole endeavor. In March 1978 at Boxwell an event known as Triple-T: Train The Trainer was held. Wood Badge participants were encouraged to come to the event that would lay out the whole program in detail. With the trainers trained, the outdoor emphasis was taken back to the districts. Brownsea II was held that summer and Senior Patrol Leaders who attended came back to Boxwell in October for "Operation Flying Start," which was "a program designed to train all junior leaders of your troop to use effectively the new approach Scouting will take." The true culminating event was a Council Wide Jamboree in May 1979. For a program dedicated to the outdoors, the concluding event was not only Star Wars themed event, but held indoors at the MetroCenter in Nashville. Wikipedia, "Leadership Training (Boy Scouts of America)," last modified August 2, 2020, https://en.wikipedia.org/wiki/Leadership_training_(Boy_Scouts_of_America) #Brownsea_II_focuses_on_Scoutcraft; Middle Tennessee Council, "Brownsea II—A Remarkable Experience," *Jet Trails (Council newsletter),* Vol. 2, No. 4: July-August, 1978, pg. 3; Middle Tennessee Council, "Brown Sea Double Two," *Jet Trails (Council newsletter),* Vol. 2, No. 5: September-October, 1978, pg. 2; Russ Parham, "Re: Brownsea?," Message to Grady Eades, October 2, 2017, e-mail; Middle Tennessee Council, "President's Report," *Jet Trails (Council newsletter),* Vol. 1, No. 5: July-August, 1977, pg. 2; Middle Tennessee Council, "All Out for Scouting: Operation Triple-T (Train the Trainer)," *Jet Trails (Council newsletter),* Vol. 2, No. 1: January-February, 1978, pg. 2; Middle Tennessee Council, "All Out for Scouting—Operation Triple-T," *Jet Trails (Council newsletter),* Vol. 2, No. 3: May-June, 1978, pg. 2; Middle Tennessee Council, "All Out for Scouting—Operation Flying Start," *Jet Trails (Council newsletter),* Vol. 2, No. 5: September-October, 1978, pg. 2; Middle Tennessee Council, "Jamboree May 18-19," *Jet Trails (Council newsletter),* Vol. 2, No. 9: May 1, 1979, pg. 5.

94. Middle Tennessee Council, "Brownsea Plus II," *Jet Trails (Council newsletter),* Vol. 3, No. 1: February-March, 1982, pg. 1; Middle Tennessee Council, "Brownsea '84," *Jet Trails (Council newsletter),* March-April 1984, pg. 3; Middle Tennessee Council, "Brownsea '85," *Jet Trails (Council newsletter),* March-April 1985, pg. 2; Lance Ussery

interview, 2019; Jason Bradford interview, 2018; Russ Parham, "Re: Brownsea?," Message to Grady Eades, October 2, 2017, e-mail.

95. Middle Tennessee Council, "Super Scout Adventure Camp, July 22-28," *Jet Trails (Council newsletter)*, Vol. 2, No. 9: May 1, 1979, pg. 4

96. Middle Tennessee Council, "Special Program Each Week for Old Scouts at Boxwell Reservation," *Jet Trails (Council newsletter)*, Vol. 2, No. 7: January-February, 1979, pg. 3.

97. Middle Tennessee Council, *1984 Summer Camp Leader's Guide*.

98. Middle Tennessee Council, *1985 Summer Camp Leader's Guide*; Middle Tennessee Council, "Above and Beyond Cancelled for 1985," *Jet Trails (Council newsletter)*, May - June 1985, pg. 2; Middle Tennessee Council, *1986 Summer Camp Leader's Guide*; Middle Tennessee Council, *1987 Summer Camp Leader's Guide*; Middle Tennessee Council, *1988 Summer Camp Leader's Guide*.

99. Middle Tennessee Council, "All Out for Scouting—Operation Triple-T," *Jet Trails (Council newsletter)*, Vol. 2, No. 3: May-June, 1978, pg. 2; Middle Tennessee Council, "All Out for Scouting—Operation Triple-T," *Jet Trails (Council newsletter)*, Vol. 2, No. 3: May-June, 1978, pg. 2 ; Middle Tennessee Council, "Campmasters Slate Summer Schedule," *Jet Trails (Council newsletter)*, Vol. 2, No. 16: July-August, 1980, pg. 4; Middle Tennessee Council, "Council Offers First Outdoors Training for Webelos Leaders," *Jet Trails (Council newsletter)*, Vol. 2, No. 20: September-October, 1981, pg. 2; Middle Tennessee Council, "Den Chief Conference—June 14-15," *Jet Trails (Council newsletter)*, May/June, 1986, pg. 3; Middle Tennessee Council, "Council Programs," *1990 Annual Report*, 1990, Nashville, Tennessee, pg. 12

100. Elam himself would pass away on November 24, 1975. "William H. Elam, Springfield, Dies," Tennessean, November 25, 1975, pg. 29; Middle Tennessee Council, *1981 Summer Camp Leader's Guide*; Pearl Schleicher (camp dietician), interviewed by Russ Parham, April 21, 1996, Mt. Juliet, TN; The carp were put in the pond by Ward Akers to control the algae, Betty Claud (ranger's wife), interviewed by Russ Parham, January 19, 2006, Centerville, TN. Over time, the Wood Badge staff, made up of a dedicated set of volunteers, would develop Camp Beany Elam to include not only the Wood Badge shed, but a pole barn to house pioneering poles, a set of three flag poles at the end of "Gilwell Field," and a small, hidden in the wilderness chapel. The area would also be used by various Junior Leader training courses over the years, including Brownsea II.

101. Middle Tennessee Council, "Wood Badge and Troop Leader Development invitation in the Mail," *Jet Trails (Council newsletter)*, Vol. 1, No. 3: March-April, 1977, pg. 4; Middle Tennessee Council, "Calendar of Meetings and Activities," *Jet Trails (Council newsletter)*, Vol. 2, No. 6: November-December, 1978, pgs. 3-4

102. Max York, "Special Explorers Earn High Marks on First Campout," *Tennessean*, first edition, July 5, 1981, pg. F1, F2.

103. Vickie Kilgore East, "Breakfast in Bed Just One Benefit of Camp Parnell," Tennessean, first edition, July 11, 1982, pg. E1, E11; John Hickman interview, 2018.

104. Max York, "Special Explorers Earn High Marks on First Campout," *Tennessean*, first edition, July 5, 1981, pg. F1, F2; Betty Claud interview, 2006.

105. Wills, *Boy Scouts of America*, pgs. 199, 204, 208.

106. Jim Barr, first interview, 2016; Michael Allen interview, 2018.

107. Jerry Barnett interview, 2016.

108. Andy Whitt interview, 2018; Larry Green interview, 2015.

109. Kerry Parker (retired, president, Construction Management Corporation), self-interviewed, "1985—Going Back," March 24, 2002, Gallatin, TN; Kerry Parker (retired, president, Construction Management Corporation), self-interviewed, "1985—Being Recruited as Program Director," June 18, 2002, Gallatin, TN; Kerry Parker (retired, president, Construction Management Corporation), self-interviewed, "1990—On the Waterfront," June 18, 2002, Gallatin, TN; Kerry Parker (retired, president, Construction Management Corporation), self-interviewed, "1993—Third Camp School 1993," February 7, 2002, Gallatin, TN.

110. Kerry Parker (retired, president, Construction Management Corporation), self-interviewed, "1993—Dining Hall Program," July 27, 2002, Gallatin, TN; Kerry Parker (retired, president, Construction Management Corporation), self-interviewed, "1991—Craig Beach Party," June 29, 2002, Gallatin, TN; Kerry Parker (retired, president, Construction Management Corporation), self-interviewed, "1992—Todd's Revolt," June 29, 2002, Gallatin, TN; Kerry Parker (retired, president, Construction Management Corporation), self-interviewed, "1993—Parnell Path," June 29, 2002, Gallatin, TN.

111. Jan Reed, "Women on Boy Scout Council for first time," *Nashville Banner*, second edition, December 1, 1990, pg. 5B.

112. Russ Parham interview, 2017; Middle Tennessee Council, "Single Parent Weekend Planned," *Jet Trails* (Council newsletter), November-December 1984, pg. 3; Middle Tennessee Council, "Single Parent Family Weekend," *Jet Trails* (Council newsletter), May/June, 1986, pg. 8. The existing record does not denote exactly when the transition to "Cub And Partner" appeared. However, the patch collection at Middle Tennessee Council Patches give some indication. The name change had occurred by at least 1990. Middle Tennessee Council Patches, "Cub Scouts," found October 13, 2020, http://www.mtcpatches.com/cub-scouts.html.

113. The medic's name is not identified here because no one could agree on what her name was. Her last name was completely unknown, but her first name was either Charlene or Charmaine and she went by "Charlie." All estimated she was between 18 and 20 years old. Russ Parham, "Re: Tom Roussin," Message to Grady Eades, August 28, 2020, e-mail; Ron Bailey interview, 2009; Kerry Parker (retired, president, Construction Management Corporation), self-interviewed, "1986—Female Medic," June 18, 2002, Gallatin, TN.

114. Middle Tennessee Council, *Leader's Guide*, 1976.

115. Middle Tennessee Council, "Boxwell Reservation," *Jet Trails* (Council newsletter), Vol. 2, No. 3: May-June, 1978, pg. 2; Middle Tennessee Council, "Boxwell Reservation," *Jet Trails* (Council newsletter), Vol. 2, No. 13: February, 1980, pg. 3; Middle Tennessee Council, "Adventure '80," *Jet Trails* (Council newsletter), Vol. 2, No. 14: March-April, 1980, pg. 2; Middle Tennessee Council, "Mom Deserves a Vacation Too!," Jet Trails (Council newsletter), May - June 1985, pg. 6.

116. Middle Tennessee Council, *Leader's Guide*, 1977; Tom Willhite interview, 2002, Morrison, TN; Middle Tennessee Council, *Leader's Guide*, 1976; Middle Tennessee Council, "Camp Murrey Scouter's Family Camp," *Jet Trails* (Council newsletter), November-December 1983, pg. 2; Christy Willhite Bryan (co-owner Murfreesboro Funeral Home), interview by Grady Eades, October 9, 2015, Murfreesboro, TN.

117. Christy Willhite Bryan interview, 2015.

118. Middle Tennessee Council, *Leader's Guide*, 1977; Middle Tennessee Council, *1995 Summer Camp Leader's Guide*.
119. John L. Parish (retired, president, Worth, Inc.), interview by Grady Eades, April 25, 2018, Tullahoma, TN; Lee Hagan (Pharmacist), phone interview by Grady Eades, September 2, 2018, Hendersonville, TN; Chuck Sudetic, "The Struggle for the Soul of the Boy Scouts," *Rolling Stone*, Iss. 844/845, July 6-20, 2000, pgs. 106, 152.
120. Lee Hagan interview, 2018.
121. Middle Tennessee Council, *1978 Annual Report*, 1978, Nashville, Tennessee; Middle Tennessee Council, Boy Scouts of America, "Executive Board Meeting," October 13, 1976; Middle Tennessee Council, Boy Scouts of America, "Executive Board Meeting," December 2, 1976; Middle Tennessee Council, *1991 Annual Report*, 1991, Nashville, Tennessee.
122. Bob Battle, "Scout exec's legacy is achievement," *Nashville Banner*, June 5, 1991, pg. 1B, 5B; Larry Green interview, 2015; Ken Connelly interview, 2017; Wikipedia, "Lincoln Heritage Council," last updated October 2, 2020, https://en.wikipedia.org/wiki/Lincoln_Heritage_Council; "Scout Executive," *Nashville Banner*, second edition, August 21, 1991, pg. 4G.
123. Ken Connelly interview, 2017; "Wanted Ski Boats Needed," *Tennessean*, December 11, 1991, pg 5G; Middle Tennessee Council, *Dedication Ceremonies Program*, "Scouting. The Handbook for Life. Development Program," October 26, 1995, pg. 1.
124. Others involved in the campaign included Harice Page, Council President, Aubrey Harwell, Jr., Sam O. Franklin, III, David K. Wilson (son-in-law of the late Justin "Jet" Potter), Richard M. Miller of Willis Corroon Corp, John Bouchard III, and Joe Lancaster, "Boy Scouts name leaders of fund drive," *Nashville Banner*, November 16, 1993, pg. 4B; Linda A. Moore, "Local Boy Scouts plan large fund-raiser," *Tennessean*, December 4, 1993, pg. 3B; Bob Battle, "Boy Scouts launch $7.8M drive for camp, program funding," Nashville Banner, December 3, 1993, pg. 1B; Middle Tennessee Council, *Scouting. The Handbook for Life: Development Program Update*, "Scouting. The Handbook for Life."--A SUCCESS!", January-February 1995, pg. 1; Middle Tennessee Council, *Scouting. The Handbook for Life: Development Program Update*, "Campaign Success Continues to Grow", May-June 1995, pg. 2; Middle Tennessee Council, *Dedication Ceremonies Program*, "Scouting. The Handbook for Life. Development Program," October 26, 1995, pg. 1.
125. The program money was earmarked specifically for the expansion of the Career Awareness Explorer Program, which was co-ed Exploring dedicated to career opportunities. In regard to the endowment dimension, this move was the Council providing itself with a safety net. Because of the national policy on homosexuals, United Way funding was becoming less reliable for local councils. Thus, a permanent endowment for funding was viewed as way to alleviate any financial pressure should United Way funding completely disappear. The ultimate breakdown was pretty straight forward: About $2.5million for capital improvements and expansions, $3 million for endowment, and another $2 million for SME contributions over three years, as had been done in 1972. Larry Green interview, 2015; Linda A. Moore, "Local Boy Scouts plan large fund-raiser," *Tennessean*, December 4, 1993, pg. 3B; Bob Battle, "Boy Scouts launch $7.8M drive for camp, program funding," Nashville Banner, December 3, 1993, pg. 1B.

The Willhite Era

126. Bob Battle, "Boy Scouts launch $7.8M drive for camp, program funding," Nashville Banner, December 3, 1993, pg. 1B; "14 local organizations given grants by Gannett," *Tennessean*, first edition, December 30, 1994, pg. 2B; Ken Connelly interview, 2017; Tom Willhite interview, 2002; Larry Green interview, 2015.

127. Other smaller capital improvements included a sound booth and lights at the Weaver Amphitheater, repaved roads across the reservation, construction of the tent shed at the compound, and renovations for the Stahlman kitchen. Bob Battle, "Boy Scouts launch $7.8M drive for camp, program funding," *Nashville Banner*, December 3, 1993, pg. 1B; Linda A. Moore, "Local Boy Scouts plan large fund-raiser," *Tennessean*, December 4, 1993, pg. 3B; "George Fehrmann," *Tennessean*, May 13, 2002, pg. 5W; Ken Connelly interview, 2017; Tom Willhite interview, 2002; Kerry Parker (retired, president, Construction Management Corporation), self-interviewed, "1991—Metcalf Crashes a Boat," June 6, 2002, Gallatin, TN; Middle Tennessee Council, *Scouting. The Handbook for Life: Development Program Update*, "Campaign Success Continues to Grow", May-June 1995, pg. 2.

128. As a side note, the Stahlman, Parnell, and Murrey waterfronts all received mild upgrades as well, primarily in the form of yellow debris bumpers to prevent lake debris from entering the area and sand beaches for the first time. Parker also noted that he was promised a showerhouse on the new road to accompany the camp flip plan; it never materialized. Kerry Parker (retired, president, Construction Management Corporation), self-interviewed, February 3, 2001, Gallatin, TN; Tom Willhite interview, 2002; Middle Tennessee Council, *Scouting. The Handbook for Life: Development Program Update*, "Campaign Success Continues to Grow", May-June 1995, pg. 2.

129. Two interesting side notes here. First, when the decision was made to make the old farm land a camporee area, the last of the tobacco base had to be sold off. This was land that that could be used for tobacco cultivation, but was rented out to area farmers. Never more than a few acres, this was the last remnant of the Boxwell farm. Second, the original construction blueprints for CubWorld note that the family camp concept was not completely abandoned. There was to be a part of CubWorld dedicated to RV Camping, so families could still enjoy staying at camp during the summer. Further, the Percy Dempsey Area was developed with a gateway, water, and road improvements. Ken Connelly interview, 2017; Tom Willhite interview, 2002; Larry Green interview, 2015; Jim East, "Cub World Plan Now Under Way," *Tennessean*, first edition, October 16, 1994, pg. 1B; Middle Tennessee Council, *Scouting. The Handbook for Life: Development Program Update*, "Campaign Success Continues to Grow", May-June 1995, pg. 2.

130. Bob Battle, "Boy Scouts launch $7.8M drive for camp, program funding," *Nashville Banner*, December 3, 1993, pg. 1B; Jim East, "Cub World Plan Now Under Way," *Tennessean*, first edition, October 16, 1994, pg. 1B; Warren Duzak, "Young Scouts give Merit to Cubworld," *Tennessean*, October 27, 1995, pg. 1B; The design work was done by Gresham, Smith, and Partners, while the actual construction was completed by Ray Bell Construction Company. Middle Tennessee Council, *Scouting. The Handbook for Life: Development Program Update*, "Scouting. The Handbook for Life."--A SUCCESS!", January-February 1995, pg. 2. For a few years, the name "Murrey" remained on the plaque in the dining hall, but it too was eventually replaced, erasing Camp Murrey from the Boxwell map.

131. "Camp Dedicated," *Tennessean*, second edition, October 26, 1995, pg. 2B; Warren Duzak, "Young Scouts give Merit to Cubworld," *Tennessean*, October 27, 1995, pg. 1B; Warren Duzak, "Camp Offers fantasy, fitness," *Tennessean*, first edition, November 1, 1995, pg. 2G.
132. Larry Green interview, 2015; Tom Willhite interview, 2002.
133. Green's experience with the Council was unique. During his time as a professional, he met and spoke with Dr. Carter Treherne, who had been instrumental in integrating the council. It was from Treherne that Green learned about Camp Tagatay. His own work in the office led him to stumble across records of the J. C. Napier Division. And while much of this was ancient history, Green did have at least one issue with race he was willing to share. Whenever Scout Executive Tolbert needed a ride to the airport, he called Green. Indeed, Green described himself as a "personal chauffeur" for Tolbert. It is possible this was simply personal, but there were hints it was more than that. Larry Green interview, 2015.
134. Jason Bradford interview, 2018; Andy Verble interview, 2009.
135. The Schleichers recalled their dismissal somewhat differently. They remembered that Green had arrived not alone, but in tandem with Willhite and that it was Willhite who did the firing while Green sat in shock, side swiped himself by the news. Larry Green interview, 2015; Pearl Schleicher interview, 1996; John and Pearl Schleicher (camp dietitian), interview by Russ Parham and Kerry Parker, February 10, 2001, Mount Juliet, Tennessee.
136. Ken Connelly interview, 2017.
137. Ken Connelly interview, 2017; Larry Green interview, 2015; Ron Turpin (Assistant Scout Executive, Middle Tennessee Council), interviewed by Grady Eades, August 5, 2015, Nashville, TN; Kerry Parker (retired, president, Construction Management Corporation), self-interviewed, "Scout Executives," February 3, 2001, Gallatin, TN; Russ Parham interview, 2017.
138. Larry Green interview, 2015.
139. Larry Green interview, 2015; Jason Bradford interview, 2018; "Staff of the Day" cards, completed by Larry Green for Grady Eades, Personal Collection of Grady Eades.
140. Russ Parham interview, 2017; Larry Green interview, 2015.
141. Kerry Parker, self-interviewed, "Scout Executives," 2001.
142. Kerry Parker (retired, president, Construction Management Corporation), self-interviewed, "1996—Keith Belcher Bargains for Pay," June 30, 2002, Gallatin, TN; Jason Bradford interview, 2018.

Chapter 7 Endnotes

"Good Enough for Government Work":

Staff Life in the Age of Willhite

1976-1996

1. All of the sayings from Tom Willhite here come from an e-mail staff newsletter the author put out from 1999-2002. A number of staff members were solicited to contribute to a "100 Things About Willhite" list. The details were the published in the July 8, 2002 issue of *The Boxwell News*, which was a special Tom Willhite Issue. Grady Eades, "100 Things About Tom Willhite," *The Boxwell News*, July 8, 2002, e-newsletter.
2. Many staff discussed their living accommodations with great affection. Jason Bradford (construction), interview by Grady Eades, April 2, 2018, Lebanon, TN; Andy Whitt (Brown-Forman Controller), interview by Grady Eades, March 3, 2018, Tullahoma, TN; Ron Bailey (Gallatin City Engineer), interview by Grady Eades, October 9, 2009, Gallatin, TN.
3. Roundtable: Mike Brown, David Dotson, John Estes, and John Walker, interview by Grady Eades, June 22, 2002, Nashville, TN; James "Web" Webster (self-employed), interview by Grady Eades, June 7, 2003.
4. Kerry Parker (retired, president, Construction Management Corporation), self-interview, "The Brill Bus and Going to Town," January 3, 2001, Gallatin, TN.
5. Wikipedia, "Rivergate Mall," last modified May 29, 2021, https://en.wikipedia.org/wiki/Rivergate_Mall; Wikipedia, "Tennessee State Route 386," last modified February 14, 2021, https://en.wikipedia.org/wiki/Tennessee_State_Route_386.
6. Kerry Parker (retired, president, Construction Management Corporation), self-interview, "The Brill Bus and Going to Town," January 3, 2001, Gallatin, TN.
7. Jason Bradford interview, 2018; Eric Cole self-interview, 1998; Michael Allen (Math Professor, Tennessee Tech University), interview by Grady Eades, July 12, 2018, Lebanon, TN.
8. Background on all this program could be listed, but the point is to keep in mind that all of this entertainment existed or was created during the years in question. The consumerism of the baby boomer generation led to a wider consumer entertainment landscape for their children. Wikipedia, "Sesame Street," Last modified May 21, 2021, https://en.wikipedia.org/wiki/Sesame_Street; Wikipedia, "MTV," last modified May 23, 2021, https://en.wikipedia.org/wiki/MTV.
9. Tom Willhite (retired, Boy Scouts of America, Middle Tennessee Council, Reservation Director), interview by Russ Parham, September 20, 2002, Morrison, TN; Eric Cole (Engineer, Missile Defense Agency), self-interview, November 14, 1998, Huntsville, AL.
10. Michael Allen interview, 2018; Andy Whitt interview, 2018; Ron Bailey interview, 2009.
11. Andy Verble (Beech High School History Teacher), interview by Grady Eades, September 23, 2009, Gallatin, TN; Web Webster interview, 2003.

12. Roundtable: Mike Brown, David Dotson, John Estes, and John Walker, 2002; Tom Roussin (former Texas School Teacher), interview by Grady Eades, July 18, 2003, Gallatin, TN; Andy Whitt interview, 2018; Kerry Parker (retired, president, Construction Management Corporation), self-interviewed, "1992—Mark of the Carp," June 29, 2002, Gallatin, TN; Kerry Parker (retired, president, Construction Management Corporation), self-interview, "1993—Intense Program," July 27, 2002, Gallatin, TN.
13. Roundtable: Mike Brown, David Dotson, John Estes, and John Walker, interview, 2002; Web Webster interview, 2003; Andy Whitt interview, 2018; Michael Allen interview, 2018; Ron Bailey interview, 2009; John Hickman (EMT, Tristar Skyline Medical Center), interview by Grady Eades, November 15, 2018, Gallatin, TN; Lance Ussery (Owner, Upper Edge Adventures), interview by Grady Eades, February 12, 2019, Lebanon, TN.
14. Jim Barr (retired, Metro Public Schools), first interview by Grady Eades, June 13, 2016, Fairview, TN; Web Webster interview, 2003; Kerry Parker (retired, president, Construction Management Corporation), self-interview, "Ford Trucks at Boxwell," April 20, 1999, Gallatin, TN.
15. Roundtable: Mike Brown, David Dotson, John Estes, and John Walker, interview, 2002; Web Webster interview, 2003.
16. Eric Cole self-interview, 1998.
17. Roundtable: Mike Brown, David Dotson, John Estes, and John Walker, interview, 2002; Web Webster interview, 2003.
18. Andy Whitt interview, 2018.
19. Kerry Parker (retired, president, Construction Management Corporation), self-interview, "1983—The First Reunion," March 28, 2002, Gallatin, TN; Kerry Parker (retired, president, Construction Management Corporation), self-interview, "1989—The Second Reunion," March 28, 2002, Gallatin, TN; Russ Parham (former Business Manager), interview by Grady Eades, July 29, 2017, Hendersonville, TN..
20. Kerry Parker (retired, president, Construction Management Corporation), self-interview, "The Rangers," February 16, 2000, Gallatin, TN.
21. Michael Seay (NASA Network and Security Engineer), interview by Russ Parham, December 22, 2009, Gallatin, TN; Jim Barr (retired, Metro Public Schools), first interview by Grady Eades, June 13, 2016, Fairview, TN.
22. Kerry Parker, "The Rangers," 2000; Michael Seay interview, 2009; Russ Parham interview, 2017.
23. Kerry Parker, "The Rangers," 2000.
24. Willie Claude (Boxwell Ranger, retired), interview by Kerry Parker, January 19, 2006, Centerville, TN; Betty Claud (Boxwell Ranger wife, retired), interview by Russell Parham, January 19, 2006, Centerville, TN.
25. Betty Claud interview, 2006; Linda Case, "Wood Badge Course SR 726," unpublished Wood Badge history booklet, September 2005; Jim Barr, first interview, 2016.
26. Web Webster interview, 2003; Jason Bradford interview, 2018; Andy Whitt interview, 2018.
27. Gregory Tucker, "Rock City painter left mark on South," *Tennessean*, September 7, 2009, pg. 6B.
28. Roundtable: Mike Brown, David Dotson, John Estes, and John Walker, interview, 2002.

Chapter 8 Endnotes

The Modern Era:

Boxwell Reservation at Old Hickory Lake

1997-2021

1. Rob Ward (Boxwell Property Manager), interviewed by Grady Eades, September 28, 2018, Lebanon, TN; The original sign was erected in 1996 by the Cogioba district and was destroyed in the winter of 2006-2007. . The new sign (pictured) was erected in 2007 by Troop 406 of the Cherokee district (Hendersonville), recognizing the original sign. Middle Tennessee Council, "Have You Seen the new entrance sign at Boxwell?" *Jet Trails* (Council newsletter), Vol. 17, No. 3: July/August/September 2007, pg. 15.
2. Larry Green (Retired Boy Scout Professional), interviewed by Grady Eades and Russell Parham, October 13, 2015, Nashville, TN.
3. J. J. Norman (Executive Director at Maryland Music Educators Association), interviewed by Grady Eades, April 10, 2018, Lebanon, TN.
4. Rob Ward (Boxwell Property Manager), interviewed by Grady Eades, September 28, 2018, Lebanon, TN.
5. The "smartphone" had been announced in January, but was not released until June as it required approval from the Federal Communications Commission (FCC). Ken Mingis and Yuval Kossovksy, "Update: Jobs touts iPhone,'AppleTV," last modified January 9, 2007, https://www.computerworld.com/article/2549128/update--jobs-touts-iphone---appletv-.html; April Montgomery and Ken Mingis, "The evolution of Apple's iPhone," last modified October 15, 2020, https://www.computerworld.com/article/2604020/the-evolution-of-apples-iphone.html.
6. Paul S. Boyer, *American History: A Very Short* Introduction, Oxford University Press: New York, 2012, pg. 104; Robert V. Remini, *A Short History of the United States: From the Arrival of Native American Tribes to the Obama Presidency*, Harper Perennial: New York, 2008, pgs. 315-317; Wikipedia, "Microsoft," last modified January 11, 2021, https://en.wikipedia.org/wiki/Microsoft#1972–1985: Founding.
7. David Shi and George Tindall, *America: The Essential Learning Edition*, W. W. Norton & Company, Inc.: New York and London, 2015, pgs. 1135-1136.
8. Tibi Puiu, "Your smartphone is millions of times more powerful than the Apollo 11 guidance computers," published February 11, 2020, http://www.zmescience.com/science/news-science/smartphone-power-compared-to-apollo-432/.
9. Boyer, *American History*, 124; Remini, *A Short History of the United States*, pgs. 315-318. For a detailed discussion of the problems of the criminal justice system, see Michelle Alexander, *The New Jim Crow: Mass Incarceration in the Age of Colorblindness*, New Press: New York, 2012; Wikipedia, "*Lawrence v. Texas*," last updated July , 2021,

https://en.wikipedia.org/wiki/Lawrence_v._Texas; Wikipedia, "*Obergefell v. Hodges*," last updated January 5, 2021, https://en.wikipedia.org/wiki/Obergefell_v._Hodges; Shi and Tindall, *America: The Essential Learning Edition*, pgs. 1159-1160.

10. Jennifer D. Keene, Saul Cornell, and Edward T. O'Donnell, *Visions of America: A History of the United States*, Second Edition, Pearson: Boston, 2013, pg. 890; Shi and Tindall, *America: The Essential Learning Edition*, pg. 1130.

11. Shi and Tindall, *America: The Essential Learning Edition*, pg. 1142-1145; Keene, Cornell, and O'Donnell, *Visions of America*, pgs. 896-900; Britannica, "Afghanistan War, 2001-2014," last update October 31, 2020, https://www.britannica.com/event/Afghanistan-War; Britannica, "Iraq, 2003-2011," last update November 4, 2020, https://www.britannica.com/event/Iraq-War.

12. Britannica, "Columbine High School Shootings," last updated April 13, 2020, https://www.britannica.com/event/Columbine-High-School-shootings; Britannica, "Sandy Hook Elementary School Shooting," last updated December 7, 2020, https://www.britannica.com/event/Newtown-shootings-of-2012; Britannica, "School Shootings," last updated September 19, 2019, https://www.britannica.com/topic/school-shooting; Alan Blinder and Kevin Sack, "Dylann Roof is Sentenced to Death," *New York Times*, January 10, 2017, https://www.nytimes.com/2017/01/10/us/dylann-roof-trial-charleston.html; Vanessa Romo, "Charlottesville Jury Recommends 419 Years Plus Life for Neo-Nazi Who Killed Protestor," *NPR*, December 11, 2018, https://www.npr.org/2018/12/11/675682912/charlottesville-jury-recommends-419-years-plus-life-for-neo-nazi-who-killed-prot.

13. Chuck Wills, *Boy Scouts of America: A Centennial History*, DK Publishing: New York, 2009, pgs. 199, 239-240, 259.

14. Oyez, "*Boy Scouts of America v. Dale*," Accessed January 23, 2021. https://www.oyez.org/cases/1999/99-699; Wikipedia, "Boy Scouts of America v. Dale," last updated January 12, 2021, https://en.wikipedia.org/wiki/Boy_Scouts_of_America_v._Dale; Wikipedia, "Boy Scouts of America membership controversies," last updated January 21, 2021, https://en.wikipedia.org/wiki/Boy_Scouts_of_America_membership_controversies.

15. Another result of the lawsuits was that the U. S. military would no longer sponsor Scout troops. Further, in terms of the schools, the lawsuits prompted a re-interpretation of the 1984 Equal Access Act. Fearing lawsuits themselves, school districts simply banned Round-Ups, recruitments, and prevented schools from being charter organizations or meeting places. Mike Madden, "Frist Moves to protect Boy Scouts' Access," *The Tennessean*, March 17, 2005, pg. A1; Wikipedia, "*Winkler v. Rumsfeld*," last updated January 21, 2021, https://en.wikipedia.org/wiki/Winkler_v._Rumsfeld; Eugene Paik, "Scouting: It isn't what it used to be. Troops fight changes affecting recruitment, image problem among peers to keep the fires burning," *Cecil Whig (Elkton, MD)*, sec. News, 29 Dec. 2006. *NewsBank: Access World News*.

16. Wikipedia, "Boy Scouts of America membership controversies"; BBC, "Boy Scouts of America votes to ease ban on gay members," last updated May 24, 2013, https://www.bbc.com/news/world-us-canada-22650143; Ashby Jones, "Boy Scouts Vote to End Ban on Gay Leaders," *Wall Street Journal*, July 28, 2015, https://www.wsj.com/articles/boy-scouts-to-vote-on-ending-ban-on-gay-adults-1438016457 ; Laurie Goodstein and Christine Hauser, "Mormon Church Ends Century-Old Partnership with Boy

Scouts of America," *New York Times*, May 9, 2018, https://www.nytimes.com/2018/05/09/us/boy-scouts-mormon-church.html .
17. Boy Scouts of America, "The BSA Expands Programs to Welcome Girls from Cub Scouts to Highest Rank of Eagle Scout," last updated October 11, 2017, https://www.scoutingnewsroom.org/press-releases/bsa-expands-programs-welcome-girls-cub-scouts-highest-rank-eagle-scout/; Holly Uan and AJ Willingham, "Boy Scouts to Allow Girls to Join," CNN, October 12, 2017, www.cnn.com/2017/10/11/us/boy-scouts-will-allow-girls-to-join/; David Crary, Associated Press, "With girls joining the ranks, Boy Scouts plan a name change," PBS, May 2, 2018, https://www.pbs.org/newshour/nation/with-girls-joining-the-ranks-boy-scouts-plan-a-name-change.
18. Brady McCombs and David Crary, "Mormons pulling 400,000 youths out of struggling Boy Scouts," Associated Press, December 17, 2009, https://apnews.com/article/4415256925664852096cb7d57abe1df8; Kathy Lohr, "Trail Life USA, The 'Other' Boy Scouts of America," NPR, September 13, 2013, https://www.npr.org/2013/09/09/220499562/trail-life-usa-the-other-boy-scouts-of-america; David Crary, "Boy Scouts could be hit with more sex abuse claims," Associated Press, April 24, 2019, https://apnews.com/article/e1ccae7cfce749169db80adf83a267cb; Wade Goodwyn, "Abuse By Boy Scout Leaders More Widespread Than Earlier Thought," NPR, April 26, 2019, https://www.npr.org/2019/04/26/717201092/abuse-by-boy-scout-leaders-more-widespread-than-earlier-thought; Laurel Wamsley and Wade Goodwyn, "Boy Scouts of America Files for Bankruptcy As It Faces Hundreds of Sex Abuse Claims," NPR, February 18, 2020, https://www.npr.org/2020/02/18/806721827/boy-scouts-of-america-files-for-bankruptcy-as-it-faces-hundreds-of-sex-abuse-cla; Kim Christensen, "Boy Scouts Propose more than $300 million, Norman Rockwell paintings to settle sex abuse claims," *Los Angeles Times*, March 1, 2021, https://www.latimes.com/california/story/2021-03-01/boy-scouts-reorganization-plan-sex-abuse-claims.
19. Middle Tennessee Council, "Scouting Strengthens America," *Annual Report 2003*, 2003, Nashville, Tennessee, pg. 3; Middle Tennessee Council, "Dear Scouts and Scouters," *2009 Annual Report*, 2009, Nashville, Tennessee, pg. 3; TrackBill, "Tennessee SB2098," found February 11, 2021, https://trackbill.com/bill/tennessee-senate-bill-2098-education-as-enacted-requires-the-principal-of-a-school-to-allow-a-patriotic-society-the-opportunity-to-speak-with-students-during-school-hours-amends-tca-title-49-chapter-6-part-3/1239060/; Jason Flannery (District Executive, Middle Tennessee Council, Boy Scouts of America), interviewed by Grady Eades, March 18, 2017, Lebanon, Tennessee.
20. Middle Tennessee Council, Boy Scouts of America (Tran Tran), "Update from Middle Tennessee Council Leadership on Recent BSA Changes," message to volunteers, May 9, 2018, e-mail; Nancy DeGennaro, "It's Official" Rutherford County welcomes all-girl Boy Scouts of America troop," *Daily News Journal* (Murfreesboro), February 3, 2019, https://www.dnj.com/story/news/2019/02/03/girls-join-boy-scouts-bsa-troop-2019-murfreesboro-tn-mtsu/2728501002/; Nancy DeGennaro, "Murfreesboro teens among first to earn Eagle Scout rank in all-female Boy Scouts troop," *Daily News Journal* (Murfreesboro), December 25, 2020, https://www.dnj.com/story/news/2020/12/26/boy-scouts-troop-2019-eagle-all-female-scouts-bsa-murfreesboro-tn/6549406002/.
21. Carl Adkins "made a play" for the position both in 1994 when Willhite announced his retirement and again in 1996 when Green stepped down. Carl Adkins (retired, Director

of Support Services, Middle Tennessee Council, Boy Scouts of America), interviewed by Grady Eades, November 15, 2017, Lebanon, Tennessee; Ron Turpin (Assistant Scout Executive, Middle Tennessee Council), interviewed by Grady Eades, August 5, 2015, Nashville, TN; Middle Tennessee Council, "Staff Changes Announced," *Jet Trails* (Council newsletter), Vol. 8, No. 6: November/December 1996, pg. 4.

22. Ron Turpin interview, 2015; Middle Tennessee Council, "Staff Changes Announced," *Jet Trails* (Council newsletter), Vol. 8, No. 6: November/December 1996, pg. 4.

23. Ron Turpin interview, 2015.

24. Middle Tennessee Council, "Camp Promotion Kick-off to be Held January 16, 1997," *Jet Trails* (Council newsletter), Vol. 9, No. 1: January/February, pg. 8.

25. Middle Tennessee Council, "Camp Promotion Kick-off to be Held January 16, 1997," *Jet Trails* (Council newsletter), Vol. 9, No. 1: January/February, pg. 8; Middle Tennessee Council, *1997 Summer Camp Leaders' Guide*, 1997, Nashville, TN; Ron Turpin interview, 2015.

26. Middle Tennessee Council, *1997 Summer Camp Leaders' Guide*; Metalworking Merit Badge was a failure. It was put in the Leaders' Guide, but ample materials were not secured. The merit badge was cancelled before the summer was over. Russ Parham, "Ten Day Out Meeting Notes," June 1997. Davy Crockett had split into its own area at Stahlman in 1995 under Ron Ramsey. Ron Ramsey (Department Chair, Science Outdoor Program Director Dean of Campus Life, Christ School), written interview responses to Grady Eades, August 26, 2018, e-mail attachment.

27. Russ Parham, "Ten Day Out Meeting Notes," June 1997; Jason BradfordMiddle Tennessee Council, *Pride in the Past Footsteps to the Future: 2002 Summer Camp Leader's Guide*; Middle Tennessee Council, *2008 Summer Camp Leader's Guide*; Middle Tennessee Council, *2012 Cub Resident Camp Leader's Guide*. interview, 2018; Ron Turpin interview, 2015.

28. Jason Bradford interview, 2018; Ron Turpin interview, 2015. It should also be noted here that Turpin did not want to run a separate Business Manager position, leading to the resignation of long-time Business Manager Russ Parham. Russ Parham (former Business Manager), interview by Grady Eades, July 29, 2017, Hendersonville, TN.

29. Jason Bradford interview, 2018; Ron Turpin interview, 2015; Kerry Parker (retired, president, Construction Management Corporation), self-interview, "1993—Dining Hall Program," July 27, 2002, Gallatin, TN; Ron Ramsey interview, 2018.

30. Jason Bradford interview, 2018; Lee Hagan (Director Operations: Mid-Atlantic, PET-NET Solutions), phone interview by Grady Eades, September 2, 2018, Hendersonville, TN; Ron Ramsey interview, 2018; Lance Ussery (Owner, Upper Edge Adventures), interview by Grady Eades, February 12, 2019, Lebanon, TN.

31. Jason Bradford interview, 2018; Lee Hagan interview, 2018; Lance Ussery interview, 2019.

32. Ron Ramsey interview, 2018; Ron Turpin interview, 2015.

33. Andy Verble (Beech High School History Teacher), interview by Grady Eades, September 23, 2009, Gallatin, TN; Dominick and Jonathan Azzara, interview by Grady Eades, November 9, 2019, Clarksville, TN; Danny Waltman (Sycamore High School, Cheatham County Public Schools Teacher), interview by Grady Eades, July 16, 2018, Hendersonville, TN.

34. John Cyril Stewart (chair), "Scoutmaster's Report and Recommendations on Needed Boxwell Improvements to Council Camping Committee," Middle Tennessee Council, December 2, 1997.

35. John Cyril Stewart (chair), "Scoutmaster's Report and Recommendations on Needed Boxwell Improvements to Council Camping Committee," 1997; Middle Tennessee Council, "Equipment from Opryland and New Cooks from Sumner County Board of Education Improve Quality of Food at Camp," *Jet Trails* (Council newsletter), Vol. 10, No. 4: August/September/October 1998, pg. 9; Ron Turpin interview, 2015; Middle Tennessee Council, *1998 Summer Camp Leaders' Guide*, 1998, Nashville, TN.

36. John Cyril Stewart (chair), "Scoutmaster's Report and Recommendations on Needed Boxwell Improvements to Council Camping Committee," 1997; The quotas were a bit of a failure. Week 2 remained unwieldy and the quotas were not successful in moving troops around enough to create equity weeks of camp. Middle Tennessee Council, "Great Summer Experience at Boxwell," *Jet Trails* (Council newsletter), Vol. 10, No. 4: August/September/October 1998, pg. 9.

37. Middle Tennessee Council, *1998 Summer Camp Leaders' Guide*.

38. Danny Waltman interview, 2018; Middle Tennessee Council, *1999 Summer Camp Leaders' Guide*, 1999, Nashville, TN; Middle Tennessee Council, *2000 Summer Camp Leaders' Guide*, 2000, Nashville, TN. Ironically, with the exception of the syllabus, the menu approach was very similar to the way Rank Requirements were first taught at Boxwell in the years before Davy Crockett, 1990-1992.

39. John Cyril Stewart (chair), "Scoutmaster's Report and Recommendations on Needed Boxwell Improvements to Council Camping Committee," 1997.

40. Ron Turpin interview, 2015.

41. Middle Tennessee Council, "Beaver Days at Boxwell," *Jet Trails* (Council newsletter), Vol. 10, No. 2: March/April 1999, pg. 7; Middle Tennessee Council, "Beaver Days at Boxwell," *Jet Trails* (Council newsletter), Vol. 10, No. 1: January/February 2000, pg. 6.

42. Middle Tennessee Council, Boy Scouts of America, *1998-2003 Long Range Plan*, Nashville, TN, 1998, pgs. 7, 15.

43. *Jet* Trails reported a $2.5 million goal in 1999, but by the Victory Celebration, the goal had risen to $2,698,000. Middle Tennessee Council, "John Finch to Chair Capital Campaign," *Jet Trails* (Council newsletter), Vol. 10, No. 5: September/October 1999, pg. 4; "Boy Scouts start capital campaign," *Tennessean*, first edition, September 3, 2000, pg. B1. Fifty-two different companies, foundations, and individuals made commitments to campaign, Middle Tennessee Council, "Capital Campaign reports $2,433,850 at Victory Celebration," *Jet Trails* (Council newsletter), Vol. 12, No. 1: January/February 2001, pg. 10.

44. The work on Craig dining hall was rolled into the goal of the campaign. Ron Turpin interview, 2015; Middle Tennessee Council, "Boxwell 2000," *Jet Trails* (Council newsletter), Vol. 10, No. 2: May/June 2000, pg. 8; Middle Tennessee Council, "Capital Campaign reports $2,433,850 at Victory Celebration," *Jet Trails* (Council newsletter), Vol. 12, No. 1: January/February 2001, pg. 10.

45. Middle Tennessee Council, "Capital Campaign reports $2,433,850 at Victory Celebration," *Jet Trails* (Council newsletter), Vol. 12, No. 1: January/February 2001, pg. 10; Middle Tennessee Council, "Boxwell Construction Continues," *Jet Trails* (Council newsletter), Vol. 12, No. 1: January/February 2002, pg. 5; Middle Tennessee Council,

"Capital Campaign Update," *Jet Trails* (Council newsletter), Vol. 13, No. 1: January/February 2003, pg. 4; Middle Tennessee Council, "Nine New Facilities Dedicated at Boxwell," *Jet Trails* (Council newsletter), Vol. 13, No. 5: September/October 2003, pg. 5.

46. Middle Tennessee Council, *2001 Webelos Resident Camp Leader's Guide*, 2001, Nashville, TN; Middle Tennessee Council, *Looking for Adventure: 2002 Cub Resident Camp Leader's Guide*, 2002, Nashville, TN; Ron Turpin (Assistant Scout Executive, Middle Tennessee Council), interview by Grady Eades, August 5, 2015, Nashville, TN.

47. Middle Tennessee Council, Boy Scouts of America, *1998-2003 Long Range Plan*, Nashville, TN, 1998, pgs. 7; Middle Tennessee Council, "Camping," *Annual Report 1999*, 1998, Nashville, TN, pg. 5.

48. Dominick and Jonathan Azzara, interview by Grady Eades, November 9, 2019, Clarksville, Tennessee; Middle Tennessee Council, "Camping News," *Jet Trails* (Council newsletter), Vol. 8, No. 3: May/June 1996, pg. 5; Middle Tennessee Council, "Gaylord Resident Camp," *Jet Trails* (Council newsletter), Vol. 9, No. 3: May/June 1997, pg. 2.

49. Middle Tennessee Council, "Cub Scout Resident Camp," *Jet Trails* (Council newsletter), Vol. 10, No. 2: March/April 2000, pg. 7; Middle Tennessee Council, "Webelos Resident Camp," *Jet Trails* (Council newsletter), Vol. 10, No. 2: March/April 2000, pg. 7; Middle Tennessee Council, *Cub Resident Camp 2001 Leader's Guide*, 2001, Nashville, TN; Middle Tennessee Council, *2001 Webelos Resident Camp Leader's Guide*; Middle Tennessee Council, *2003 Webelos Resident Camp Leader's Guide*, 2003, Nashville, TN.

50. Dominick and Jonathan Azzara interview, 2019.

51. "Super Adventure Week" and "Above and Beyond" in the Willhite years were technically High Adventure programs, but were not billed that way at the time. In terms of the new programs, without whitewater, the Rappelling program became several days shorter. Middle Tennessee Council, *1997 Summer Camp Leaders' Guide*; Middle Tennessee Council, *1999 Summer Camp Leaders' Guide*, 1999; Middle Tennessee Council, *Summer Camp Leader's Guide: Looing for Adventure*, 2001, Nashville, TN; Middle Tennessee Council, *Pride in the Past Footsteps to the Future: 2002 Summer Camp Leader's Guide*, 2002, Nashville, TN.

52. After 1997, the Business Manager position returned, now occupied by Bill Schwartz. Jared Lazarus, "Scouting Skills," *Tennessean*, July 8, 1998, pg. 8B; Middle Tennessee Council, "Day of Scouting," *Jet Trails* (Council newsletter), Vol. 9, No. 6: November/December 1997, pg. 5; Middle Tennessee Council, "District Patron Luncheons," *Jet Trails* (Council newsletter), Vol. 17, No. 2: April/May/June 2007, pg. 18; Middle Tennessee Council, *1997 Summer Camp Leaders' Guide*; Middle Tennessee Council, *1998 Summer Camp Leaders' Guide*; Middle Tennessee Council, *1999 Summer Camp Leaders' Guide*; Middle Tennessee Council, *2000 Summer Camp Leaders' Guide*; Middle Tennessee Council, *Summer Camp Leader's Guide: Looing for Adventure*; Middle Tennessee Council, *Pride in the Past Footsteps to the Future: 2002 Summer Camp Leader's Guide*; Danny Waltman interview, 2018.

53. Jack Bond undoubtedly would have been disappointed by the new approach to Wood Badge, as were many old time Scouters. Most of the old Wood Badge staff did not transition to the new program. Bonnie Burch, "Scouts out and about doing deeds," *Tennessean*, first edition, May 1, 2001, pg. W1; Middle Tennessee Council, "Brownsea 1999," *Jet Trails* (Council newsletter), Vol. 10, No. 2: March/April 1999, pg. 6; John Bryant

(retired, federal magistrate judge), interview by Grady Eades, July 17, 2009, Nashville, TN; Middle Tennessee Council, "Friends of Scouting Campaign 2001," *Jet Trails* (Council newsletter), Vol. 12, No. 1: January/February 2001, pg. 4; Middle Tennessee Council, "LFL Character Camp Day Success," *Jet Trails* (Council newsletter), Vol. 10, No. 2: July/August 2000, pg. 6; Middle Tennessee Council, "Get Hooked On Scouting," *Jet Trails* (Council newsletter), Vol. 12, No. 2: March/April 2002, pg. 6; Middle Tennessee Council, "'Get Hooked on Scouting' Day Offers Fun For All," *Jet Trails* (Council newsletter), Vol. 12, No. 4: July/August 2002, pg. 4.

54. The death of the female Scouter was never reported to the news or in the *Jet Trails*. Neither Turpin, nor Patten or Ratliff could remember her name. And while Rook was the only staff member to perish on camp property, there are memorials to 2 other staff members. Tyler Cates, a Parnell-Craig staff member, was a Marine who died in Anbar Province in 2004. His family had a stone erected to him at the Craig Waterfront. John Sain was an OA Lodge Chief who served on Brownsea staff as well as the OA Representative and as Stahlman's Camp Commissioner in the 1990s. Sain was killed in a car accident in 1997. Initially three small trees were planted at the Crippled Crab in his memory, the trees placed in a triangle reflecting the Vigil Honor in the OA. Only one tree survives at this writing. In 2005, the Wa-Hi-Nasa Lodge erected a large gateway for the High Adventure Area to serve as a more prominent and permanent memorial for Sain. Cole Corbin, "Power-line accident kills man," *Tennessean*, June 28, 1998, pg. B2; Ron Ramsey interview, 2018; Ron Turpin interview, 2015; Warren Duzak, "Boy Scout jumps from moving car, dies from severe head injuries," *Tennessean*, second edition, July 23, 1999, pg. B1; Jason Flannery interview, 2017; Tim Ratliff and Aaron Patten, interview by Grady Eades, July 8, 2009, Lebanon, TN; Natalia Mielczarek, "Mt. Juliet Marine killed Iraq remembered for his smile, loyalty," *Tennessean*, main edition, September 23, 2004, pg. B1; "Josh R. Sain (obituary)," *Tennessean*, October 26, 1997, pg. B13; Wa-Hi-Nasa Lodge No. 111, "The Josh Sain Memorial Gateway," *The Flying Eagle* (Lodge newsletter), Vol. 141 No. 2: June 2005, pg. 5; Wa-Hi-Nasa Lodge No. 111, "The Josh Sain Memorial Gateway," *The Flying Eagle* (Lodge newsletter), Vol. 142 No. 1: March 2006, pg. 2.

55. Turpin retired in August 2021. Middle Tennessee Council, "Ron Turpin Promotion Director of Field Service," *Jet Trails* (Council newsletter), Vol. 12, No. 5: September/October 2002, pg. 4; Middle Tennessee Council, "Staff News," *Jet Trails* (Council newsletter), Vol. 17, No. 1: January/February/March 2007, pg. 21.

56. Middle Tennessee Council, "Pat Scales – New Director of Support Services," *Jet Trails* (Council newsletter), Vol. 13, No. 6: November/December 2002, pg. 4

57. The Business Manager position was also dropped again, but this time the Trading Posts were put under the management of the Jet Potter Center Scout Shop. The Trading Post staff moved under this management umbrella as well. Trading Post staffs were no longer directly beholden to the Reservation Director. Middle Tennessee Council, "Summer Camp Promotion Kick Off Big Second Time around," *Jet Trails* (Council newsletter), Vol. 13, No. 2: March/April 2003, pg. 6; Middle Tennessee Council, "Attention Boxwell Campers," *Jet Trails* (Council newsletter), Vol. 13, No. 3: May/June 2003, pg. 4; Middle Tennessee Council, 2003 Summer Camp Leader's Guide, 2003, Nashville, TN; Jason Flannery interview, 2017; Middle Tennessee Council, "Are You An Extremist?," *Jet Trails* (Council newsletter), Vol. 13, No. 3: May/June 2003, pg. 4.

58. Verble opined that perhaps the reason Scales never left Stahlman was because of a person-
    ality dispute of some kind over at Craig. C.O.P.E. Director Lance Ussery outlined just
    such a conflict between himself and Scales that occurred during Staff Week. Tim Ratliff
    and Aaron Patten interview, 2009; Andy Verble (Beech High School History Teacher),
    interview by Grady Eades, September 23, 2009, Gallatin, TN; Danny Waltman interview,
    2018; Lance Ussery interview, 2019.
59. The first Winter Camp only cost $70 for the week, which was half the cost of summer
    camp. Middle Tennessee Council, "Summer Camp Promotion Kick Off Big Second Time
    around," *Jet Trails* (Council newsletter), Vol. 13, No. 2: March/April 2003, pg. 6; Dan-
    ny Waltman interview, 2018; Carl Adkins interview, 2017; Ian Romaine, "Re: Boxwell
    Book," message to Grady Eades, June 1, 2021, e-mail; Middle Tennessee Council, 2003
    Summer Camp Leader's Guide, 2003, Nashville, TN; Middle Tennessee Council, "Boy
    Scout Winter Camp," *Jet Trails (Council Newsletter)*, Vol. 13, No. 4: July-August 2003,
    pg. 6.
60. Middle Tennessee Council, "Boy Scout Winter Camp," *Jet Trails* (Council newsletter),
    Vol. 13, No. 4: July-August 2003, pg. 6; Ian Romaine, "Re: Boxwell Book," message to
    Grady Eades, June 1, 2021, e-mail.
61. The Polar Bear Dash was something of a contentious event. The Dash was rejected out-
    right by Romaine as directly violating BSA Safe Swim Defense policies. Nevertheless, on
    the day of the event, Scales contacted the media and told them to come out. He informed
    Romaine an hour before the event the media were on their way, so he needed to make it
    happen. There was little choice but to move forward, though the event was limited to
    adults only. The Polar Bear Dash did not happen again. Holly Edwards, "Scout Leaders
    take a dip fit for polar bears," *Tennessean*, main edition, December 31, 2003, pg. B1;
    Middle Tennessee Council, "Boy Scout Winter Camp," *Jet Trails* (Council newsletter),
    Vol. 13, No. 4: July-August 2003, pg. 6; Middle Tennessee Council, "Winter Camp is
    Coming!!," *Jet Trails* (Council newsletter), Vol. 13, No. 6: November-December 2003,
    pg. 9; Danny Waltman interview, 2018; Carl Adkins interview, 2017; Ian Romaine, "Re:
    Boxwell Book," message to Grady Eades, June 1, 2021, e-mail.
62. Ian Romaine , *Wa-Hi-Nasa III: A Brotherhood of Cheerful Service in Middle Tennes-
    see*, Middle Tennessee Council: Nashville, TN, 2015, pgs. 33-34; Carl Adkins interview,
    2017.
63. Middle Tennessee Council, "Middle TN Council Staff News," *Jet Trails* (Council news-
    letter), Vol. 14, No. 4: July - August 2004, pg. 9; Tim Ratliff and Aaron Patten inter-
    view, 2009.
64. Middle Tennessee Council, "Middle TN Council Staff News," *Jet Trails* (Council news-
    letter), Vol. 14, No. 4: July - August 2004, pg. 9; Middle Tennessee Council, *2004 Sum-
    mer Camp Leader's Guide*, 2004, Nashville, TN; Carl Adkins interview, 2017.
65. Middle Tennessee Council, "Middle TN Council Staff News," *Jet Trails* (Council news-
    letter), Vol. 14, No. 4: July - August 2004, pg. 4; Carl Adkins interview, 2017; Middle
    Tennessee Council, *Annual Report 1998*, 1998, Nashville, Tennessee.
66. Carl Adkins interview, 2017; Andy Whitt (Brown-Forman Controller) interview by
    Grady Eades, March 3, 2018, Tullahoma, TN; Michael Allen (Math Professor, Tennes-
    see Tech University), interview by Grady Eades, June 9, 2006, Lebanon, TN; Christy
    Willhite Bryan (co-owner Mufreesboro Funeral Home), interview by Grady Eades, Octo-
    ber 9, 2015, Murfreesboro, TN.

67. Carl Adkins interview, 2017; Andy Whitt interview, 2018; Michael Allen interview, 2006; Christy Willhite Bryan interview, 2015; Danny Waltman interview, 2018; Lance Ussery interview, 2019; Rachel Paris (college student), interview by Grady Eades, July 12, 2018, Lebanon, TN; Rob Ward interview 2018.
68. Rob Ward interview, 2018; Carl Adkins interview, 2017.
69. Cub Scout numbers were an important part of this success; Boy Scout numbers were more erratic. Some summers saw the last week being cancelled at one camp or the other and occasionally staff was laid off to stay within budget as the numbers were so low. Carl Adkins interview, 2017; Middle Tennessee Council, *Annual Report 1998*, 1998, Nashville, Tennessee; Middle Tennessee Council, *Annual Report 2003*, 2003, Nashville, Tennessee; Middle Tennessee Council, *2005 Annual Report*, 2005, Nashville, Tennessee; Middle Tennessee Council, *2009 Annual Report*, 2009, Nashville, Tennessee; Middle Tennessee Council, *2010 Annual Report*, 2010, Nashville, Tennessee; Middle Tennessee Council, *2015 Annual Report "This Is What We Do Best,"* 2015, Nashville, Tennessee. These numbers are even more impressive when put in context. 1968 was the highwater mark overall for Boxwell attendance at just over 4300 Scouts that summer. The Council also had a Scout membership of over 35,000 youth. Middle Tennessee Council, Boy Scouts of America, "Executive Board Meeting," Setpember 17, 1968.
70. Tim Ratliff and Aaron Patten interview, 2009.
71. Tim Ratliff and Aaron Patten interview, 2009; Jason Flannery interview, 2017.
72. Middle Tennessee Council, *2004 Summer Camp Leader's Guide*, 2004, Nashville, TN; Middle Tennessee Council, *2005 Summer Camp: A Great Outdoor Experience*, 2005, Nashville, TN; Middle Tennessee Council, *2008 Summer Camp Leader's Guide*, 2008, Nashville, TN; Middle Tennessee Council, *2009 Summer Camp Leader's Guide*, 2009, Nashville, TN; Middle Tennessee Council, *2011 Summer Camp Leader's Guide*, 2011, CD-ROM, Nashville, TN; Middle Tennessee Council, *2012 Summer Camp Leader's Guide*, 2012, Nashville, TN; Middle Tennessee Council, *2013 Summer Programs*, DVD, 2013, Nashville, TN; Middle Tennessee Council, *2014 Summer Programs*, DVD, 2014, Nashville, TN.
73. Middle Tennessee Council, *2011 Summer Camp Leader's Guide*,; Middle Tennessee Council, *2008 Summer Camp Leader's Guide*, 2008, Nashville, TN; Middle Tennessee Council, *2013 Summer Programs*; Kim Chaudoin, "Graduate School of business named in honor of Nashville's Pam and Phil Pfeffer," published February 6, 2019, https://www.lipscomb.edu/news/graduate-school-business-named-honor-nashvilles-pam-and-phil-pfeffer; Carl Adkins interview, 2017; Middle Tennessee Council, "First Annual Pfeffer Regatta," *Jet Trails* (Council newsletter), Vol. 23, No. 2: April/May/June 2013, pg. 14; Middle Tennessee Council, "Pfeffer Regatta," *Jet Trails* (Council newsletter), Vol. 24, No. 3: July/August/September 2014, pg. 13.
74. Middle Tennessee Council, *2012 Cub Resident Camp Leader's Guide*, 2012, Nashville, TN; Middle Tennessee Council, *2013 Summer Programs*; Middle Tennessee Council, *2004 Summer Camp Leader's Guide*; Middle Tennessee Council, *2005 Summer Camp: A Great Outdoor Experience*,; Middle Tennessee Council, *2008 Summer Camp Leader's Guide*; Middle Tennessee Council, "About the Cover," Jet Trails (Council newsletter), Vol. 23, No. 4: October/November/December 2013, pg. 2; Carl Adkins interview, 2017; Lance Ussery interview, 2019.

75. Interestingly, "Old Soldier" was Deugaw's second spin as a folk hero. He had been part of the Parnell-Craig staff since the 1980s. In those first years, he had driven a yellow Datsun pick-up truck with a camper top on the back. During Staff Week, he brought Kool Aid to the youth staff as a break, earning him the name "Kool Aid Man." Middle Tennessee Council, "Summer Camp 2004," *Jet Trails* (Council newsletter), Vol. 14, No. 5: September-October 2004, pg. 4; Don Montjoy, "Veteran scouter Pat Deugaw will be sorely missed," *The Leaf-Chronicle* (Clarksville), July 1, 2011, pg. C-1; Middle Tennessee Council, *2008 Summer Camp Leader's Guide*.

76. Middle Tennessee Council, "Letter from the Big Three," *Jet Trails* (Council newsletter), Vol. 26, No. 1: Spring 2016, pg. 2; Carl Adkins interview, 2017.

77. Animation was not part of the original offerings. It was added in 2017. Middle Tennessee Council, "Letter from the Big Three," *Jet Trails* (Council newsletter), Vol. 26, No. 1: Spring 2016, pg. 2; Middle Tennessee Council, "Boy Scout Summer Camp 2016," *Jet Trails* (Council newsletter), Vol. 26, No. 1: Spring 2016, pg. 9; Middle Tennessee Council, "2017 Boy Scout Summer Camp," *Jet Trails* (Council newsletter), Vol. 27, No. 2: Fall 2017, pg. 6; Carl Adkins interview, 2017.

78. Middle Tennessee Council, *2005 Summer Camp: A Great Outdoor Experience*; Middle Tennessee Council, *2009 Summer Camp Leader's Guide*, 2009, Nashville, TN; Middle Tennessee Council, "Scoutmaster Comments on Summer Camp," *Jet Trails* (Council newsletter), Vol. 15, No. 4: August-September-October 2005, pg. 13; Middle Tennessee Council, "2013 Boy Scout Summer Camp," *Jet Trails* (Council newsletter), Vol. 23, No. 1: January/February/March 2013, pg. 7; Middle Tennessee Council, "Boy Scout Summer Camp 2011," *Jet Trails* (Council newsletter), Vol. 21, No. 1: January/February/March 2011, pg. 5; Middle Tennessee Council, "Boy Scout Summer Camp 2016," *Jet Trails* (Council newsletter), Vol. 26, No. 1: Spring 2016, pg. 9; Middle Tennessee Council, "Summer Camp 2004," *Jet Trails* (Council newsletter), Vol. 14, No. 5: September-October 2004, pg. 4; Middle Tennessee Council, *2013 Summer Programs*.

79. Among the "new" merit badges were Whitewater, Astronomy, Radio, Archeology, Cinematography, Energy, Sculpture, Chess, Golf, Kayaking, Search and Rescue, Dog Care, Game Design, Inventing, Salesmanship, and Public Speaking. The recycled included Soil and Water, Sports, Athletics, and Cooking merit badges. Middle Tennessee Council, *2005 Summer Camp: A Great Outdoor Experience*; Middle Tennessee Council, *2009 Summer Camp Leader's Guide*; Middle Tennessee Council, *2010 Annual Report*, 2010, Nashville, Tennessee; Middle Tennessee Council, "Boy Scout Summer Camp 2011," *Jet Trails* (Council newsletter), Vol. 21, No. 1: January/February/March 2011, pg. 5; Middle Tennessee Council, "Help Send Scouts to Camp Through Camp Card Sales," *Jet Trails* (Council newsletter), Vol. 22, No. 1: January/February/March 2012, pg. 16 & 17; Middle Tennessee Council, "2013 Boy Scout Summer Camp," *Jet Trails* (Council newsletter), Vol. 23, No. 1: January/February/March 2013, pg. 7; Middle Tennessee Council, "Boy Scout Summer Camp 2014," *Jet Trails* (Council newsletter), Vol. 24, No. 1: January/February/March 2014, pg. 5; Carl Adkins interview, 2017.

80. Middle Tennessee Council, *2005 Summer Camp: A Great Outdoor Experience*; Middle Tennessee Council, *2012 Summer Camp Leader's Guide*.

81. As CubWorld Camp Commissioner and later Program Director Dominick Azzara stated, only partly tongue in cheek, the CubWorld staff "were the bastard children, not even the stepchildren." Dominick and Jonathan Azzara interview, 2019.

The Modern Era

82. Dominick and Jonathan Azzara interview, 2019; Rachel Paris interview, 2018.

83. Middle Tennessee Council, *2004 Webelos Resident Camp Leader's Guide*, 2004, Nashville, TN; Dominick and Jonathan Azzara interview, 2019.

84. Middle Tennessee Council, *Scouting: A Great Outdoor Experience, 2005 Cub Resident Camp Leader's Guide*, 2005, Nashville, TN; Middle Tennessee Council, "2016 Fall & Winter Activities," *Jet Trails* (Council newsletter), Vol. 26, No. 2: Fall 2016, pgs. 8 & 9; Middle Tennessee Council, "Cub & Webelos Resident Camp," *Jet Trails* (Council newsletter), Vol. 27, No. 2: Fall 2017, pg. 5.

85. Middle Tennessee Council, *Pride in the Past Footsteps to the Future: 2002 Summer Camp Leader's Guide*; Middle Tennessee Council, *2008 Summer Camp Leader's Guide*; Middle Tennessee Council, *2012 Cub Resident Camp Leader's Guide*.

86. Perry Bruce (retired, U.S. Corps of Engineers), interview by Grady Eades, December 19, 2017, Charolette, TN.

87. Carl Adkins interview, 2017.

88. Middle Tennessee Council, "Latimer Society Recipients," *Jet Trails* (Council newsletter), Vol. 29, No. 2: Fall 2019, pg. 15; J. J. Norman interview, 2018; Steve Eubank (retired, Giles County Public School teacher), self-interview, 2001, Pulaski, TN.

89. Ron Ramsey interview, 2018; Andy Verble interview, 2009; Carl Adkins interview, 2017.

90. Carl Adkins interview, 2017; J. J. Norman interview, 2018; Steve Eubank, self-interview, 2001.

91. Carl Adkins interview, 2017; J. J. Norman interview, 2018; Danny Waltman interview, 2018.

92. Middle Tennessee Council, "Summer Excitement at Boxwell Reservation," *Jet Trails* (Council newsletter), Vol. 20, No. 4: October/November/December 2010, pg. 4; Carl Adkins interview, 2017; Interestingly, dodgeball was banned by National policy in 2018, Boy Scouts of America, "Activity Planning and Risk Assessment," found September 15, 2019, https://www.scouting.org/health-and-safety/gss/gss07/. Sain had served in multiple positions at Boxwell. He was a Senior Patrol Leader in Brownsea in 1994, the OA Representative in 1995, and Stahlman's Camp Commissioner in 1996. Wa-Hi-Nasa Lodge No. 111, "The Josh Sain Memorial Gateway," *The Flying Eagle* (Lodge newsletter), Vol. 141 No. 2: June 2005, pg. 5; Wa-Hi-Nasa Lodge No. 111, "The Josh Sain Memorial Gateway," *The Flying Eagle* (Lodge newsletter), Vol. 142 No. 1: March 2006, pg. 2;.

93. Middle Tennessee Council, "Have You Seen the new entrance sign at Boxwell?," *Jet Trails* (Council newsletter), Vol. 17, No. 3: July/August/September 2007, pg. 15; Steve Belew (former Boxwell ranger), written interview responses to Grady Eades, May 29, 2019, e-mail attachment; Middle Tennessee Council, "2011 Cub and Family," *Jet Trails* (Council newsletter), Vol. 22, No. 1: January/February/March 2012, pg. 11; Middle Tennessee Council, *2008 Summer Camp Leader's Guide*, 2008, Nashville, TN.

94. Middle Tennessee Council, "Cub and Family Weekends," *Jet Trails* (Council newsletter), Vol. 18, No. 1: January/February/March 2008, pg. 10; Middle Tennessee Council, "Woodbadge for the 21st Century," *Jet Trails* (Council newsletter), Vol. 15, No. 3: May/June/July 2005, pg. 10; Middle Tennessee Council, "Spend a Week at Brownsea," *Jet Trails* (Council newsletter), Vol. 15, No. 3: May/June/July 2005, pg. 4; Middle Tennessee Council, "National Youth Leadership Training," *Jet Trails* (Council newslet-

ter), Vol. 16, No. 2: April/May/June 2006, pg. 11; Middle Tennessee Council, "National Youth Leadership Training," *Jet Trails* (Council newsletter), Vol. 18, No. 2: April/May/June 2008, pg. 13; Middle Tennessee Council, "2012 NYLT," *Jet Trails* (Council newsletter), Vol. 22, No. 4: October/November/December 2012, pg. 11; Middle Tennessee Council, "Every Boy Deserves a Good Leader," *Jet Trails* (Council newsletter), Vol. 13, No. 6: November-December 2003, pg. 8; Middle Tennessee Council, "Webelos Leaders Outdoor Experience," *Jet Trails* (Council newsletter), Vol. 14, No. 5: September-October 2004, pg. 6; Middle Tennessee Council, "Trainer Development Conference," *Jet Trails* (Council newsletter), Vol. 15, No. 4: August-September-October 2005, pg. 10; Middle Tennessee Council, "Scouting on the Run," *Jet Trails* (Council newsletter), Vol. 24, No. 1: January/February/March 2014, pg. 6.

95. The LFL programs ended about 2008 in the Council, though LFL still exists. Middle Tennessee Council, "2005 Learning For Life Fun Days," *Jet Trails* (Council newsletter), Vol. 15, No. 4: August-September-October 2005, pg. 11; "Every School Every Day: Franklin High," *Tennessean*, other editions, October 4, 2004, Pg. W4;"Franklin High," *Tennessean*, other editions, October 15, 2008, pg. U4; Steve Belew interview, 2019; J. J. Norman interview, 2018; Rob Ward interview, 2018.

96. Middle Tennessee Council, "Council Secures Property for New Wilderness/High Adventure Reservation," *Jet Trails* (Council newsletter), Vol. 17, No. 3: July/August/September 2007, pg. 4; Middle Tennessee Council, "Venturing Training," *Jet Trails* (Council newsletter), Vol. 18, No. 1: January/February/March 2008, pg. 5; Middle Tennessee Council, "Venturing Rendezvous," *Jet Trails* (Council newsletter), Vol. 18, No. 3: July/August/September 2008, pg. 8; Middle Tennessee Council, "2013 Venturing Day at Boxwell," *Jet Trails* (Council newsletter), Vol. 24, No. 1: January/February/March 2014, pg. 5.

97. From 1999 through 2008, the Council ran basically back to back Capital Campaigns of which Latimer was the third and final. The first had been the Millennium Campaign for Boxwell renovations of approximately $2.5 million. The second kicked off in 2004 with a goal of $2 million for renovations and expansion of the Jet Potter Center. It completed in 2005. Middle Tennessee Council, "Capital Campaign Kickoff Yields 67% or Two Million Dollar Goal," *Jet Trails* (Council newsletter), Vol. 14, No. 4: July - August 2004, pg. 4; Middle Tennessee Council, "Council Secures Property for New Wilderness/High Adventure Reservation," *Jet Trails* (Council newsletter), Vol. 17, No. 3: July/August/September 2007, pg. 4; Middle Tennessee Council, "Venturing Training," *Jet Trails* (Council newsletter), Vol. 18, No. 1: January/February/March 2008, pg. 5; Middle Tennessee Council, "Venturing Rendezvous," *Jet Trails* (Council newsletter), Vol. 18, No. 3: July/August/September 2008, pg. 8; Middle Tennessee Council, "2013 Venturing Day at Boxwell," *Jet Trails* (Council newsletter), Vol. 24, No. 1: January/February/March 2014, pg. 5; Middle Tennessee Council, "Council Undertakes Capital Campaign to Fund Wilderness Reservation," *Jet Trails* (Council newsletter), Vol. 17, No. 3: July/August/September 2007, pg. 4; Middle Tennessee Council, "Latimer Grand Opening," *Jet Trails* (Council newsletter), Vol. 24, No. 2: April/May/June 2014, pg. 14; Ron Turpin interview, 2015.

98. Middle Tennessee Council, "National Youth Leadership Training," *Jet Trails* (Council newsletter), Vol. 23, No. 2: April/May/June 2013, pg. 8; Middle Tennessee Council, "Kodiak," *Jet Trails* (Council newsletter), Vol. 18, No. 1: January/February/March

2008, pg. 5; Middle Tennessee Council, "Venture Leadership Award Winners," *Jet Trails* (Council newsletter), Vol. 19, No. 4: October/November/December 2009, pg. 12; Middle Tennessee Council, "Latimer Update," *Jet Trails* (Council newsletter), Vol. 24, No. 4: October/November/December 2014, pg. 2; Middle Tennessee Council, "Latimer Reservation Update," *Jet Trails* (Council newsletter), Vol. 27, No. 2: Fall 2017, pg. 17; Ron Turpin interview, 2015.

99. Andy Humbles, "Boy Scouts expect 3,000 for eclipse campout," *Tennessean*, August 14, 2017, pg. A4; Rob Ward interview, 2018; Middle Tennessee Council, Boy Scouts of America, "Executive Board Meeting," April 8, 1976.

100. Ron Ramsey interview, 2018; Andy Verble interview, 2009; Tim Ratliff and Aaron Patten interview, 2009; Middle Tennessee Council, "Gaylord Cub Camp Opens," *Jet Trails* (Council newsletter), Vol. 8, No. 4: July/August 1996, pg. 1,3; Dominick and Jonathan Azzara interview, 2019; Carl Adkins interview, 2017.

101. Danny Waltman interview, 2018; Jason Flannery interview, 2017.

102. Danny Waltman interview, 2018; Jason Flannery interview, 2017; J. J. Norman interview, 2018.

103. J. J. Norman interview, 2018.

104. Ron Turpin interview, 2015; Tim Ratliff and Aaron Patten interview, 2009; Danny Waltman (Sycamore High School, Cheatham County Public Schools Teacher), self interview, August 2, 2018, Pleasant View, TN.

105. Dominick and Jonathan Azzara interview, 2019; Rachel Paris interview, 2018.

106. J .J. Norman interview, 2018; Jason Flannery interview, 2017; Danny Waltman, self interview, 2018.

107. Ward did point out that nationally, there were approximately 28,000 Venturers and the pregnancy rate was only 2%. Carl Adkins interview, 2017; Emily Fish, written interview responses to Grady Eades, July 25, 2018, e-mail attachment; Rob Ward interview, 2018.

108. Audrey Creighton, written interview responses to Grady Eades, July 8, 2018, e-mail attachment; Candace Boyce, written interview responses to Grady Eades, August 11, 2018, e-mail attachment; Meredith MaGuirk, written interview responses to Grady Eades, July 30, 2018, e-mail attachment; Emily Fish, written interview responses to Grady Eades, July 25, 2018, e-mail attachment.

109. At least early in the transition to young females on the staff, there is also some evidence of hazing, though hazing of the worst kind. One young woman on CubWorld staff explained "there were certain areas of camp girls were warned not go without a guy." Specifically, the road between the Crippled Crab and Camp Craig around Parnell was unsafe because the site was so far away from anywhere else. The young woman was told girls had been assaulted and raped there. This individual was part of the first cohort of younger females on the staff, so there were no other women this could have happened to and there is no reported evidence it did happen. Nevertheless, this young woman was traumatized by young men who wanted to keep her on their side of camp. Megan Barnett Cook, "Re Boxwell Reserach Help," message to Grady Eades, July 25, 2018, e-mail; Candace Boyce interview, 2018; Emmie Donaldson interview, 2018; Rachel Paris interview, 2018; Meredith MaGuirk interview, 2018.

110. Ed Mason (retired police office), interview by Grady Eades, July 18, 2018, Boxwell Reservation, Lebanon, Tennessee; Michael Allen (Math Professor, Tennessee Tech University), interview by Grady Eades, July 12, 2018, Lebanon, TN.

111.J. J. Norman, "Re Questionnaire," message to Grady Eades, March 3, 2018, e-mail.

112.Carl Adkins interview, 2017.

113.Tim Ratliff and Aaron Patten interview, 2009; Jason Flannery interview, 2017; Danny Waltman interview, 2018.

114.Danny Waltman interview, 2018.

115.Waltman also points out that as he understood it, Craig staff did not return that night, adding to the crisis of the event. Danny Waltman interview, 2018; Ian Romaine, submission to Grady Eades (VirtualBoxwell), February 15, 2018, web form.

116.Tim Ratliff and Aaron Patten interview, 2009; Jason Flannery interview, 2017; J. J. Norman interview, 2018; Danny Waltman interview, 2018; Dominick and Jonathan Azzara interview, 2019.

117.Danny Waltman, self interview, 2018; Dominick and Jonathan Azzara interview, 2019; Danny Waltman interview, 2018; Jason Flannery interview, 2017; J. J. Norman interview, 2018; Tim Ratliff and Aaron Patten interview, 2009; Rachel Paris interview, 2018; Larry Green interview, 2015.

118.Ron Turpin interview, 2015; Steve Belew interview, 2019; Rob Ward interview, 2018.

119.Kerry Parker (retired, president, Construction Management Corporation), self-interview, "1999—Third Reunion," March 28, 2002, Gallatin, TN; Carl Adkins interview, 2017.

120.VirtualBoxwell.org, "Virtual Boxwell: A History of a History," last updated July 1, 2012, http://www.virtualboxwell.org/history.php; VirtualBoxwell.org, "Staff Reunions," last updated December 9, 2017, http://www.virtualboxwell.org/staff_reunions.php.

121.Carl Adkins interview, 2017; Jason Flannery (Director of Camping, Middle Tennessee Council, Boy Scouts of America), interview by Grady Eades, December 5, 2020, Lebanon, TN.

122.Middle Tennessee Council, "Staff News," *Jet Trails* (Council newsletter), Vol. 24, No. 3: July/August/September 2014, pg. 21; Jason Flannery interview, 2017.

123.Jason Flannery interview, 2020; Rachel Paris interview, 2018.

124.Middle Tennessee Council, "Family Scouting at CubWorld," *Jet Trails* (Council newsletter), Vol. 29, No. 2: Fall 2019, pg. 5; Jason Flannery interview, 2020.

125.Middle Tennessee Council, *2014 Annual Report*, 2014, Nashville, Tennessee.

126.Initially, the female troops were going to get a gender segregated week, much as African American toops had in the mid-1960s. However, once camp arrived, the female troops camped with the male troops in fully integrated weeks. Middle Tennessee Council, "2019 Scouts BSA Summer Camp," *Jet Trails* (Council newsletter), Vol. 29, No. 2: Fall 2019, pg. 6; Jason Flannery interview, 2020.

127.Middle Tennessee Council, "Summer Camp a Success," Building for the New Century: A Campaign for Boxwell Reservation (quarterly newsletter), Fall 2019, pg. 3; Jason Flannery interview, 2020.

128.Middle Tennessee Council, "Boxwell Capital Campaign," *Jet Trails* (Council newsletter), Vol. 29, No. 2: Fall 2019, pg. 21; Middle Tennessee Council, "A Note from the Campaign Chair," *Building for the New Century: A Campaign for Boxwell Reservation* (quarterly newsletter), Summer 2019, pg. 2.

129.Other campaign goals included a new Family and Staff Lodge (funding secured by summer 2019, but no construction) and renovation of the rangers' houses. Middle Tennessee Council, "Craig Family Generosity Continues a History in Scouting," *Building for the New Century: A Campaign for Boxwell Reservation* (quarterly newsletter), Summer

2019, pg. 1, 3; Middle Tennessee Council, "Priority Campaign Projects," *Building for the New Century: A Campaign for Boxwell Reservation* (quarterly newsletter), Summer 2019, pg. 4.

130. Jason Flannery interview, 2020.

131. Middle Tennessee Council, "A Newsletter for 100th Anniversary of Middle TN Council," message to Russ Parham, February 5, 2020, e-mail; Middle Tennessee Council, "MTC,BSA COVID 19/Coronavirus Update - Communication #3," message to Russ Parham, March 18, 2020, e-mail; Middle Tennessee Council, "MTC,BSA COVID 19/Coronavirus Update - Communication #4," message to Russ Parham, March 24, 2020, e-mail; Middle Tennessee Council, *Building for the New Century: A Campaign for Boxwell Reservation* (quarterly newsletter), Summer 2020, pg. 1; Middle Tennessee Council, "MTC,BSA COVID 19/Coronavirus Update - Communication #6," message to Russ Parham, May 28, 2020, e-mail; Middle Tennessee Council, "Scout Shorts May Ediciton," message to Russ Parham, May 14, 2020, e-mail; Middle Tennessee Council, "MTC Summertime Activities: Day Camp at your Doorstep and Merit Badge Days," message to Russ Parham, May 30, 2020, e-mail.

132. Jason Flannery interview, 2020.

Endnotes

Closing Campfire

1976-1996

1. Middle Tennessee Council, Boy Scouts of America, *2012 Boy Scout Summer Camp Leader's Guide*, Nashville, TN, 2012, pg. 4; Leland Johnson and Wilbur F. Creighton, *Boys Will Be Men: Middle Tennessee Scouting Since 1910*, Middle Tennessee Council: Nashville, TN, 1983, pg. 49.

2. The University of Texas at Austin, University of Texas Libraries, Perry-Castaneda Library Map Collection, "Nashville 1929," found October 7, 2019, http://legacy.lib.utexas.edu/maps/topo/tennessee/; Ironically, the first mayor of Metro Nashville was Beverly Briley, who attended the Linton Boxwell in 1927, the week of July 18 through 25. "New Scouts Register at Camp Boxwell," *Nashville Banner*, July 19, 1927, pg. 9.

3. "New Notes from Camp Boxwell," *Nashville Banner*, July 1, 1928, pg. (sports)6; "Boy Scout Rescues Girl From River," Nashville Banner, July 6, 1928, pg. 20; Helen Dahnke, "Scouts Rule Own Kingdom on Harpeth," *Nashville Tennessean*, July 10, 1927, pg. 32.

4. "Samuel S Morton," *The Nashville Tennessean*, May 19, 1948, pg. 5; Gordon H. Turner, "Linton Family Finds Superlative in Living," *The Tennessean*, October 21, 1951, pg 21; "Miss Maude Morton," *The Tennessean*, August 11, 1960, pg. 80; "Mrs. Allie Morton," *The Tennessean*, December 1, 1964, pg. 25.

5. The Metro Planning Commission provides an excellent website to explore all of the deeds. Through the site, you can explore back several generations of scanned documents. Metro Planning Department, "Parcel Viewer," found November 6, 2017, https://maps.nashville.gov/ParcelViewer/.
6. Jason Flannery (Director of Camping, Middle Tennessee Council, Boy Scouts of America), interviewed by Grady Eades, December 5, 2020, Lebanon, Tennessee.
7. Leon Alligood, "Scouts add fun to being prepared," *Tennessean*, second edition, June 27, 2000, pg. 1A, 5A; E. D. Thompson (retired music instructor), interview by Grady Eades, March 8, 2017, Bellevue, TN.
8. Lance Ussery (Owner, Upper Edge Adventures), interview by Grady Eades, February 12, 2019, Lebanon, TN; Roundtable:: Mike Brown, David Dotson, John Estes, and John Walker, interview by Grady Eades, June 22, 2002, Nashville, TN.
9. Lance Ussery (Owner, Upper Edge Adventures), interview by Grady Eades, February 12, 2019, Lebanon, TN; Danny Waltman (Sycamore High School, Cheatham County Public Schools Teacher), interviewed by Grady Eades, July 16, 2018, Hendersonville, Tennessee; John Hickman (EMT Tristar Skyline Medical Center), interview by Grady Eades, November 15, 2018, Gallatin, TN.
10. Jason Flannery (District Executive, Middle Tennessee Council, Boy Scouts of America), interviewed by Grady Eades, March 18, 2017, Lebanon, Tennessee.
11. Ron Oakes (retired, Council Executive), interview by Grady Eades, July 18, 2019, Hendersonville, TN; James "Web" Webster (self-employed), interview by Grady Eades, June 7, 2003, Gallatin, TN.

Closing Campfire

For the Good of the Program

564